Edexcel GCSE

Mathematics A Linear Foundation

Teacher Guide

Series director: Keith Pledger

Series editor: Graham Cumming

Authors:
Chris Baston
Julie Bolter
Gareth Cole
Gill Dyer
Andrew Edmondson
Michael Flowers
Karen Hughes
Peter Jolly
Joan Knott
Jean Linsky
Graham Newman
Rob Pepper
Joe Petran
Keith Pledger
Rob Summerson
Kevin Tanner
Brian Western

A PEARSON COMPANY

Published by Pearson Education Limited, a company incorporated in England and Wales, having its registered office at Edinburgh Gate, Harlow, Essex, CM20 2JE. Registered company number: 872828

Edexcel is a registered trademark of Edexcel Limited

First published 2010
13 12 11 10
10 9 8 7 6 5 4 3 2 1

British Library Cataloguing in Publication Data
A catalogue record for this book is available from the British Library
ISBN 978 1 84690 087 7

Typeset by Pantek Arts Ltd

Printed in Great Britain at Ashford Colour

Acknowledgements

The publisher would like to thank the following for their kind permission to reproduce their photographs:
We are grateful to the following for permission to reproduce copyright material:
Every effort has been made to trace the copyright holders and we apologise in advance for any unintentional omissions. We would be pleased to insert the appropriate acknowledgement in any subsequent edition of this publication.

Disclaimer

This material has been published on behalf of Edexcel and offers high-quality support for the delivery of Edexcel qualifications. This does not mean that the material is essential to achieve any Edexcel qualification, nor does it mean that it is the only suitable material available to support any Edexcel qualification. Edexcel material will not be used verbatim in setting any Edexcel examination or assessment. Any resource lists produced by Edexcel shall include this and other appropriate resources. Copies of official specifications for all Edexcel qualifications may be found on the Edexcel website: www.edexcel.com

Contents

11 Measure

12 Processing, representing and interpreting data

13 Sequences

14 Perimeter and area of 2D shapes

15 Graphs 1

16 Averages and range

17 Circles

18 Constructions and loci

19 Percentages

20 Three-dimensional shapes

21 Equations and inequalities

22 Graphs 2

23 Transformations

24 Ratio and proportion

25 Line diagrams and scatter graphs

26 Probability

27 Pythagoras' Theorem

28 Formulae

Functional Skills

Answers

Introduction

Edexcel's GCSE Mathematics materials

This GCSE Mathematics course has been developed by Edexcel to support you in teaching our new GCSE Mathematics specifications. All the materials have been fully referenced to the specifications. The course offers the following components for each of the Foundation and Higher Tiers:

- **Student Book** with graded questions, lots of support for the new Assessment Objectives and our unique Examiner insight from Results Plus.
- **ActiveTeach** CD-ROM to support you in your use of ICT for whole-class teaching, and in your lesson planning and management.
- **Teacher's Guide**, providing lesson objectives, topic grades, ideas for activities including the use of ICT in ActiveTeach and resource sheets to support students completing exercises in the Student Book. Word and Pdf files of all material available on the CD-ROM which is included and which will integrate with the ActiveTeach.
- **Practice Books**: with one-to-one matching of Student book exercises. Pdfs of the material for upload to the school VLE or network are available separately and will integrate with ActiveTeach.
- **Targeted Practice Books:** providing support for G to F students; extension material for A to A* students and Booster C material for those all important borderline D/C students. Pdfs of the material for upload to the school VLE or network are available separately and will integrate with ActiveTeach.
- **Assessment Pack** containing End of chapter tests; extra A02 and A03 practice questions; and a set of Exam Practice Papers with mark schemes. Word and Pdf files of all material are available on the accompanying CD-ROM which will integrate with ActiveTeach.
- **ResultsPlus Booster C**, designed to boost the grades of your D/C borderline students. It provides web-delivered homeworks and tests for individual formative assessment with detailed teacher and pupil feedback.
- **ResultsPlus Progress tests** provide web-delivered individual summative assessment matched to the new specification.
- **SupportPlus website** contains information about the specifications, training events, support and sample materials. An Edexcel Maths-users-only area gives further detailed support for teaching the specification.

Support for teaching the new Assessment Objectives

Assessment Objective	What it is	What this means	Approx % of marks in the exam
A01	Recall and use knowledge of the prescribed content.	Questions testing your knowledge of each topic.	45-55
A02	Select and apply mathematical methods in a range of contexts.	Questions asking you to decide what method you need to use to get to the correct answer.	25-35
A03	Interpret and analyse problems and generate strategies to solve them.	Problem solving: Deciding how and explaining why	15-25

The new assessment objectives means that question styles within the exam are changing, with more problem-solving, open-style questions being set. These new question types are clearly marked in the Student books and also have dedicated spreads for further practice. Yet more questions are available in the Practice Books and in the Assessment Pack. Further interactive support is offered in the ActiveTeach with interactive examples and in the Assessment pack

The examination and the course

Written by examiners who thoroughly understand the new specification, all the material you need to prepare students for the examination is available from this course and has been carefully developed and reviewed.

- All questions show targeted grades.
- ResultsPlus examiner tips help students to gain those extra few marks in the examination.
- Past exam questions and exam style questions can be found in the Chapter Review at the end of each chapter. These have been chosen or specifically written to ensure they are a true reflection of the style of questions that might appear in the examination.

- Written by examiners. the Assessment Pack contains:
  - editable end-of-chapter tests for you to use or adapt for student assessment. All answers are provided.
  - a bank of A02 and A03 questions for extra practice of these assessment objectives
  - examination practice papers, to help your students become familiar with the types of questions they will be asked in the exam.
- Formative and summative electronic tests are available through our online ResultsPlus Booster C and Results Plus Progress tests.
- References to the specification are given in student friendly language in the Student books and in full in the Teacher's Guide.
- The Teacher Guide CD contains electronic copies of the scheme of work and the specification both of which contain references to the relevant sections of the Student book, Practice books and Teacher Guide.
- A blank self-assessment sheet is available on the Teacher Guide CD to enable students to reflect on a topic. Cross referencing on the self-assessment sheet points students back to the book if they need to revise.

A topic from Edexcel's GCSE Mathematics course

As well as the concise Starters, Main teaching and learning points and Plenary, the lesson notes also contain:

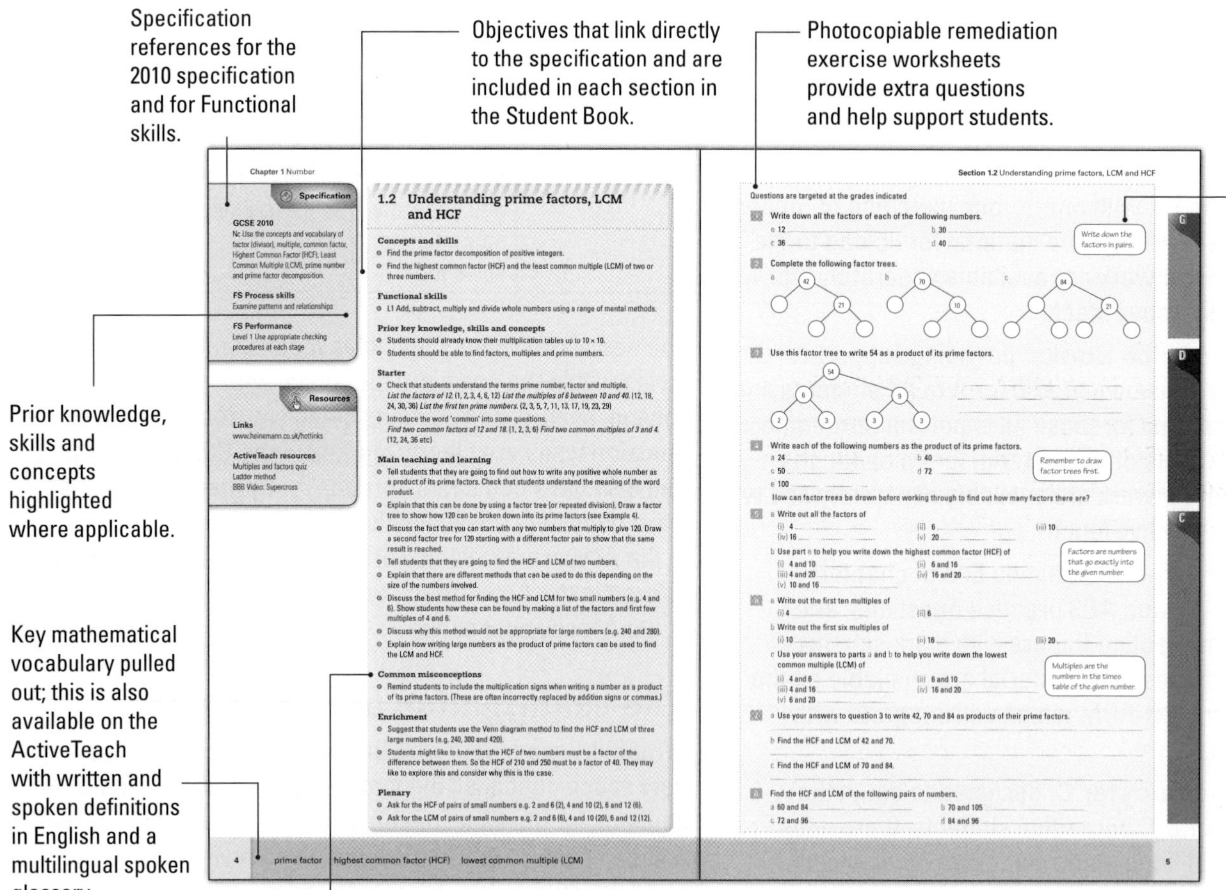

Teaching and Learning

Saving you time and guiding you through the new specification, the Teacher's guide contains concise, easy-to-read Lesson plans and extra Guided Practice Worksheets which are available as editable Word files and pdfs on the CD-ROM.

- At a glance specification references and detail.
- Starter ideas to check that students have the required prior knowledge.
- Main teaching and learning points to help you teach the topic itself.
- Plenary questions to test understanding and application of the mathematics.

- Common misconceptions, and possible enrichment activities are also included where appropriate.
- Editable scheme of work available on the CD-ROM.
- Guided practice worksheets with remediation questions. As these are support worksheets, some of the questions may fall below grade levels.
- Integrates fully with ActiveTeach if installed.

Digital products

ActiveTeach

ICT is seamlessly incorporated into mathematics lessons by using the unique, networkable, VLE compatible ActiveTeach.

ActiveTeach is a front-of-class teaching tool allowing you to display the Student Books on your whiteboard or through your VLE, while giving access to a wealth of activities, video clips, quizzes and other activities.

- BBC Active clips bring maths to life. Accompanying each clip are teacher mediated questions, and a worksheet for students to complete.
- ResultsPlus interactive problem-solving activities provide whole class practice of the new AO2 and AO3 style questions with our unique three-part tool.
- ResultsPlus knowledge checkers test AO1 recall with a multiple choice test at the end of each chapter.
- High-quality interactive content integrates seamlessly with the Student Book.
- Multi-lingual glossary gives audio translations for common maths terms in five languages.
- My lessons area allows you to personalise content by adding your own links, interacting directly with the text and saving your annotations, enabling you to reapply your thinking the next time you deliver the lesson.

ResultsPlus Booster C

Easy to adopt, set up and administer, ResultsPlus Booster C is an online service that takes borderline D/C students through highly targeted practice to boost their performance and help them get that all-important C grade.

- Dynamically generated guided practice questions, labelled by grade, give students a variety of practice to meet their needs exactly.
- Edexcel exam-style questions onscreen, give the benefits of instant examiner feedback, and familiarity with the new GCSE question types and requirements.
- Online delivery ensures total currency of questions for the new specification.
- Links to other course components, give students and teachers a clear, consistent learning experience.
- Advanced reporting tools give unmatched insight into student performance, enabling teachers to pinpoint exactly where individuals are going wrong.
- Works alongside ResultsPlus Progress to allow you to address the weak areas that ResultsPlus Progress diagnoses.

ResultsPlus Progress tests

Our online diagnostic assessment service helps you improve your students' performance before it's too late. Great for embedding Assessment for Learning into your course, it gives you access to exactly the information you need, to help tackle areas of weakness for each student.

- Ten topic-based tests, all with 25 questions that are perfect for both linear and modular courses.
- Each topic test can be taken individually or linked with others to create more comprehensive unit, termly or mock-style assessments.

SupportPlus website

www.edexcelmaths.com/supportplus

Our dedicated website with information about the specifications, training events, support and sample materials. An Edexcel Maths users-only area gives detailed support including

- Interactive Schemes of Work
- Teaching Resources – Lesson Plans and Practice Worksheets
- Exam Question Editor
- Updates from Subject Leader Graham Cumming
- ICT Blog
- Community Area
- Answers to questions in printed materials not included with the book

Icons used in the Student books

- AO2 AO3 **Assessment objective** questions are classified as AO2 and/or 3. These questions follow the more open structure demanded by QCDA for the new specification and are not available in earlier GCSE publishing schemes.
- FS **Functional skills** indicates questions that cover functional elements of GCSE maths.
- * **Quality of Written Communication** (QWC) identifies questions that follow the style of QWC questions in the exam.
- **Non-calculator** indicates questions where students must not use a calculator to find the answer. It does NOT indicate that the subject area covered by the question will only appear in the non-calculator paper of the exam.

Specification

GCSE 2010

N a Add, subtract, multiply and divide any number
N b Order rational numbers

FS Process skills

Select the mathematical information to use

FS Performance

Level 1 Understand practical problems in familiar and unfamiliar contexts and situations, some of which are non-routine

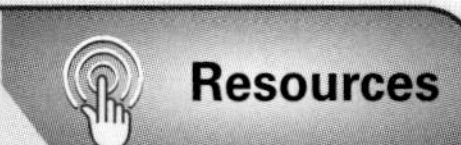

Resources

Resources

Number lines

ActiveTeach resources

Word numbers quiz
Place value animation
Number line addition interactive

1.1 Understanding digits and place value
1.2 Reading, writing and ordering whole numbers
1.3 The number line

Concepts and skills

- Understand and use positive numbers… both as positions and translations on a number line.
- Writing numbers in words.
- Writing numbers from words.
- Order integers….

Functional skills

- L1 Understand and use whole numbers … in practical contexts.

Prior key knowledge, skills and concepts

- Students should already know addition number bonds to 9 + 9 and times tables to 10 × 10.

Starter

- *Would you rather have 5p or £5? Why?* (Both have the same face value but the place value is different.)

Main teaching and learning

- Teach students to equate place value with column value.
- Write the column headings shown on p.2 of the Student Book on the board. Include Ten Thousands, Hundred Thousands and Millions if you wish.
- Write 3429 on the board. Point to one of the figures in 3429 and ask *What is the **value** of this figure?*
- Ask students to place each figure under the appropriate column heading.
- Write 'five hundred and seven' on the board (in words) and ask students to place each figure under the appropriate column heading.
- Write the numbers 327, 40, 635, 9003, 500 on the board. Ask students to place the numbers under the column headings and using this, order the numbers from smallest to largest.
- Revise the number line for positive integers
- Ask students for three numbers between 20 and 40. Write the numbers on the board and then, together, construct an appropriate number line (appropriate length and scale divisions) to show these three numbers. Use the numbers to check students can pinpoint their position on the line and ask students to explain how the number line can help them order these three numbers.
- Ask students for 6 pairs of numbers less than 20, write these on the board, numbering the pairs 1 to 6. For even pairs ask students to mentally add the numbers, for odd pairs they should mentally subtract the smaller number from the larger. Ask students to explain their mental strategies for doing this and compare different strategies.

Common misconceptions

- Some students will write 428 for four thousand and twenty-eight. Remind students that if 'hundreds' (for example) is not mentioned it still has a place value and needs a place holder of zero.

Enrichment

- Include ten thousands, hundred thousands and millions.

Plenary

- Discuss moves on a number line (see Exercise 1C) in preparation for the next lesson.

digits value place value

Guided practice worksheet

G

1 Write down the place value of each digit in the number 2376.

....

....

2 Write in words, the numbers:

a 326 ....

b 4152 ....

c 15 370 ....

d 2006 ....

Hint Start with the biggest place value number on the left.

3 Write as numbers:

a eight hundred and thirty seven ....

b nine thousand three hundred and twenty-five ....

c twenty-two thousand and fifty-three ....

Hint There are no hundreds so put 0 in the hundreds column.

d three thousand six hundred and five. ....

4 Put these numbers in order of size. Start with the smallest.

9781 15 361 6542 6452 6524

....

5 Put these numbers in order of size. Start with the biggest.

2371 8711 2731 2317 20 317

....

6 Write down the biggest and the smallest number you can make using each of the digits 8, 1, 9, 3, 4 once only.

....

Specification

GCSE 2010

N a (part) Add, subtract… any number

FS Process skills

Recognise that a situation has aspects that can be represented using mathematics

Use appropriate mathematical procedures

FS Performance

Level 1 Understand practical problems in familiar and unfamiliar contexts and situations, some of which are non-routine

Resources

Links

http://nlvm.usu.edu/en/nav/frames-asid_188_g_4_t_l/html?open=instructions&from=category_g_4_t_l.html

1.4 Adding and subtracting

Concepts and skills

- Add, subtract… whole numbers….

Functional skills

- L1 Add, subtract… whole numbers using a range of strategies.

Prior key knowledge, skills and concepts

- Number bonds to 9 + 9
- Place value
- Number differences to 19 – 1

Starter

- Practise instant recall of number bonds.
- Extend to 70 + 50 etc.

Main teaching and learning

- Teach formal column addition that has no carrying.
- Move on to addition that has carrying.
- Teach subtraction with decomposition from tens column.
- Teach fully general column subtraction.

Common misconceptions

- Giving the answer 254 when asked to subtract 89 from 235.
- Reinforce decomposition of 1 from previous column into 10 for the column being considered.

Enrichment

- Write four consecutive numbers into the boxes at the bottom.
- Get the number for the box above by adding the two numbers in the boxes below.
- Continue doing this until you get the top number.
- *Can you see any link between the top number and the numbers at the bottom?* (The top number is twice the sum of the bottom numbers.)
- You might need to do several before you see the pattern.
- *Does your rule work if the bottom numbers are all the same?* (Yes.)
- *Does it work for consecutive odd numbers?* (Yes.)
- *Does it work for consecutive even numbers?* (Yes.)

Plenary

- Use the darts match context from Exercise 1E question 6. Change the scores to James 423, Sunita 402 and Nadine 364. Repeat the questions using these scores. Discuss methods.

Guided practice worksheet

1 Work out:

a
```
  23
+ 41
```
....

b
```
  274
+ 142
```
....

c
```
  97
+ 24
```
....

Hint Keep digits in correct column.

d
```
  107
   89
+  22
```
....

e 37 + 15 + 48

....

f 129 + 207 + 96

....

2 Work out:

a
```
  57
− 32
```
....

b
```
  307
−  95
```
....

c
```
  121
−  89
```
....

d
```
  403
−  76
```
....

e
```
  5000
−  187
```
....

3 Sharon drives a van.

On Monday she drove from York to Leeds, then from Leeds to Doncaster and finally back to York.

How far did she drive?

Hint Check distances are in the same units.

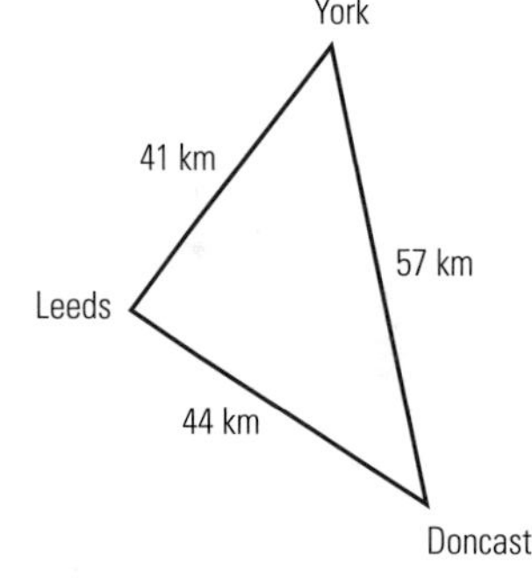

....

4 When Peter goes from A to B he either goes through P or Q.

Which is the shorter route and by how much?

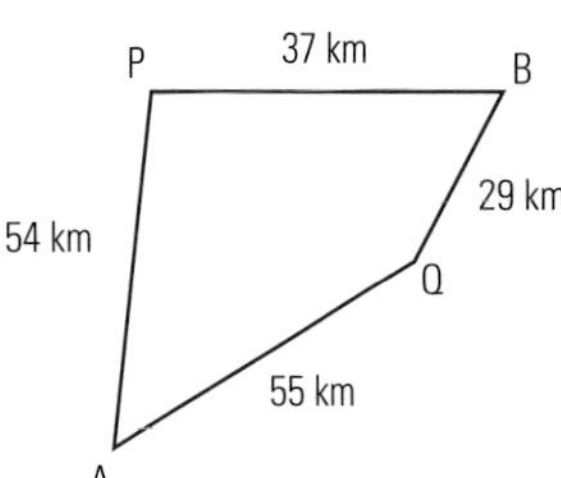

....

5 There were 23 people on a bus.

At the first stop, 19 people got on and 6 people got off. At the second stop 12 people got off and just 6 people got on.

How many people are now on the bus?

....

G

Specification

GCSE 2010

N a (part) … multiply and divide any number

N q Understand and use number operations and the relationships between them, including inverse operations and hierarchy of operations

FS Process skills

Recognise that a situation has aspects that can be represented using mathematics

Use appropriate mathematical procedures

FS Performance

Level 1 Understand practical problems in familiar and unfamiliar contexts and stituations, some of which are non-routine

Resources

CD Resources

Resource sheet 1.5

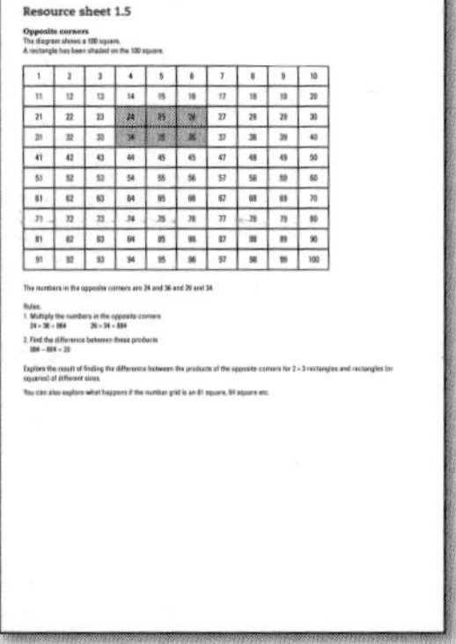

Links

http://www.bbc.co.uk/schools/gcsebitesize/maths/number/multiplicationdivisionact.shtml

ActiveTeach resources

All the rides video

Binding video

1.5 Multiplying and dividing

Concepts and skills

- … multiply and divide whole numbers….
- Multiply and divide numbers using the commutative, associative, and distributive laws and factorisation where possible, or place value adjustments.

Functional skills

- L1 … multiply and divide whole numbers using a range of strategies.

Prior key knowledge, skills and concepts

- Tables to 10 × 10
- Number bonds to 9 + 9

Starter

- Practise instant recall of products.

Main teaching and learning

- Teach students to **multiply** a 3-digit number by a 1-digit number.
- Ask students to explain two or more different methods for multiplication, for example 157 × 3.
- Extend to 3-digit by 2-digit.
- Teach general multiplication using formal column procedures.
- Teach students to **divide** a 3-digit number by a 1-digit number.
- Ask students to explain two or more different methods for division, for example 352 ÷ 8.
- Teach long division by a 2-digit number.

Common misconceptions

- Not appreciating column importance, which is seen as ×20 becoming ×2, etc. Stress that although you are only multiplying by a single digit, that digit has place value.
- Mistakes are commonly made with: 7×9, 7×8, 8×9, 6×9. Write 7×9 as 7×10. As this is 10 sevens which is 7 too many, $7 \times 9 = 70 - 7 = 63$. This is a useful check if you are not sure and works for any product with 9. $7 \times 8 = 7 \times 2 \times 2 \times 2 = 14 \times 2 \times 2 = 28 \times 2 = 56$.

Plenary

- Write questions based on Exercise 1F questions 7 and 8, using your students' names and the local football club.

G

Guided practice worksheet

1 Work out:

a $\begin{array}{r}23\\ \times 2\\ \hline\end{array}$ b $\begin{array}{r}37\\ \times 3\\ \hline\end{array}$ c $\begin{array}{r}182\\ \times 5\\ \hline\end{array}$ d $\begin{array}{r}279\\ \times 8\\ \hline\end{array}$ e $\begin{array}{r}153\\ \times 10\\ \hline\end{array}$

2 Work out:

a 73 × 10 b 73 × 20 c 73 × 100 d 73 × 2000

3 Work out:

a 91 × 20 b 83 × 50 c 41 × 40 d 82 × 70 e 143 × 300

4 Work out: (these are exam-type questions)

a 27 × 21 b 59 × 18 c 28 × 32 d 15 × 97 e 38 × 23

5 Work out:

a 2)142 b 3)189 c 4)384 d 5)875

6 Work out:

a 846 ÷ 2 b 546 ÷ 3 c 195 ÷ 5 d 176 ÷ 8 e 2370 ÷ 10

F

Guided practice worksheet

7 Work out:

a 245 divided by 5 b 245 divided by 7 c 245 divided by 35

8 Work out:

a 3200 ÷ 20 b 7320 ÷ 30 c 48 400 ÷ 400 d 6400 ÷ 50

9 A football club hires twelve 61-seater coaches to take supporters to an away match.
How many supporters can they take?

10 Work out (these are exam-type questions):

a 294 ÷ 14 b 3679 ÷13 c 1875 ÷ 25 d 7776 ÷ 24 e 1095 ÷ 15

11 Burgers are packed in boxes of 24.
How many boxes of burgers are needed to provide 504 burgers at a barbeque?

12 A prize of £34 560 is shared equally between five winners.
How much does each winner get?

Specification

GCSE 2010
N u (part) Approximate to specified or appropriate degrees of accuracy including a given power of ten....

FS Process skills
Select the mathematical information to use

FS Performance
Level 1 Identify and obtain necessary information to tackle the problem

Resources

Resources
Jar of beads

Links
http://www.bbc.co.uk/schools/gcsebitesize/maths/number/roundestimateact.shtml

ActiveTeach resources
Reading scales quiz
Rounding interactive

Follow up
Chapter 5 Decimals and Rounding

1.6 Rounding

Concepts and skills

- Round numbers to a given power of 10.

Functional skills

- L1 Understand and use whole numbers ... in practical contexts.

Prior key knowledge, skills and concepts

- Place value

Starter

- Ask for estimates of the number of beads in a jar (or similar). The important thing is to get an estimate.
- Discuss whether or not exact suggestions make sense.
- Discuss whether nearest 10 or nearest 100 is most sensible.

Main teaching and learning

- Give students an exact value, and ask them to tell you the nearest 10. (Students' own answers.)
- Extend to nearest 100, 1000, million.
- Use some or all of the following questions and ask students to say whether numbers should be left as they are, or rounded up, or down, to the nearest 10, 100, 1000 or other degree of accuracy:
  (a) 43 people lift a train!
  (b) 6845 people attended a football match.
  (c) 24 572 people live in Hightown.
  (d) 285 people turned up to a public meeting.
  (e) 2348 people attended a pop concert.
  (f) 405 people were watching the game.
  (g) The distance is 2014 km.
  (h) He walked for 10 206 m.
  (i) The weight of the van was 3803 kg.

Common misconceptions

- Students often truncate numbers instead of rounding.

Enrichment

- Ask what is the smallest number which, when rounded to the nearest 100, gives 700? (650).
- Repeat using other numbers if necessary.

Plenary

- Use Exercise 1B question 5 and ask students to round the figures to the nearest 1000, 10 000, 100 000.

Guided practice worksheet

When you give your age, you give it to the nearest year because this is sensible.
The editor of a magazine might ask for articles of 300 words.
Anything more accurate would not be sensible.

Note If the number ends in 5 it is usual to round up.

G

1 Round these numbers to the nearest 10.

a 58 .... b 22 .... c 79 .... d 35 ....

e 7 .... f 234 .... g 359 .... h 762 ....

i 293 .... j 307 .... k 1003 .... l 3204 ....

m 2995 .... n 555 ....

2 Round these numbers to the nearest 100.

a 204 .... b 390 .... c 83 .... d 5430 ....

e 445 .... f 649 .... g 12 381 .... h 53 807 ....

i 100 093 .... j 230 988 .... k 45 ....

Hint Make sure number keeps same order of magnitude.

3 Round these numbers to the nearest 1000.

a 5500 .... b 842 .... c 3200 ....

d 6455 .... e 9786 .... f 24 488 ....

4 Write the number 4117 to the nearest hundred.

....

Specification

GCSE 2010
N a Add, subtract, multiply and divide any number
N b Order rational numbers

FS Process skills
Recognise that a situation has aspects that can be represented using mathematics
Find results and solutions

FS Performance
Level 2 Apply a range of mathematics to find solutions

Resources

Resources
Thermometers with negative values

Links
Substitution in expressions and formulae
http://www.bbc.co.uk/schools/gcsebitesize/maths/number/negativenumbersact.shtml

ActiveTeach resources
Scales 2 interactive
Directed numbers (addition and subtraction) quiz
Number lines interactive

Follow up
21.6 Solving equations with negative coefficients

1.7 Negative numbers
1.8 Working with negative numbers
1.9 Calculating with negative numbers

Concepts and skills
- Understand and use positive and negative integers both as positions and as translations on a number line.
- Add, subtract, multiply and divide … negative numbers….

Functional skills
- L2 Understand and use positive and negative numbers … in practical contexts.

Prior key knowledge, skills and concepts
- The number line.
- All number bonds.

Starter
- Establish the need for negative numbers through temperature, height above sea level, etc.

Main teaching and learning
- Extend the number line to include **negative** integers.
- Teach students how to add with negative and positive numbers.
- It may help some students to work out the difference between two numbers starting with positive numbers. This naturally leads on to the difference between a positive and a negative number as adding the sizes of the two numbers together. Another way is to consider subtraction as the inverse operation to addition; otherwise the answer always seems to be positive.
- Teach students how to find the difference when negative numbers are involved (this is best done within the context of temperature using a thermometer as the number line).
- Teach students the rules for multiplying and dividing negative numbers.

Common misconceptions
- The difference between a negative number and subtracting a positive number is sometimes misunderstood.
- Emphasise the distinction between a minus sign that belongs to a number and the minus sign that signals 'do a subtraction'.

Plenary
- Ask students to explain the rules for multiplying and dividing negative numbers.

negative number positive number

F

Guided practice worksheet

1 Write these numbers in order of size. Start with the smallest.

3 −4 −2 5 −7 −12

....

2

City	Temperature
Cardiff	−2°C
Edinburgh	−4°C
Leeds	2°C
London	−1°C
Plymouth	5°C

The table gives information about the temperature at midnight in five cities.

a Write down the lowest temperature. ....

b Work out the difference in temperature between Cardiff and Plymouth.

....

c Work out the temperature which is half way between −1°C and 5°C.

....

3 At midnight, the temperature was −5°C.

By 9 am the next morning, the temperature had increased by 3°C.

a Work out the temperature at 9 am the next morning.

....

At midday, the temperature was 7°C.

b Work out the difference between the temperature at midday and the temperature at midnight.

....

4 Work out:

a −3 + 2 .... b 3 + −1 .... c −7 + −3 ....

d −11 + (+4) .... e (+3) + (−5) ....

5 Work out:

a (−4) − (+2) .... b (+5) − (−2) .... c (−3) − (−5) ....

d 8 − −3 .... e −6 − 2 ....

6 Work out:

a (−2) × (6) .... b (+3) × (+5) .... c (−4) × (−3) ....

d (+3) × (−7) ....

7 Work out:

a −15 divided by 3 b 16 ÷ (−4) c −80 ÷ −5 d 40 divided by −8

....

8 Simplify:

a $\frac{-12}{3}$ .... b $\frac{14}{-7}$ .... c $\frac{-24}{-8}$ ....

d $\frac{+24}{+3}$ .... e $\frac{-48}{6}$ .... f $\frac{35}{-7}$ ....

Specification

GCSE 2010
N c (part) Use the concepts and vocabulary of factor (divisor), multiple, common factor,... prime number and prime factor decomposition

FS Process skills
Select the mathematical information to use
Examine patterns and relationships

FS Performance
Level 1 Select mathematics in an organised way to find solutions

Resources

CD Resources
Resource sheet 1.10

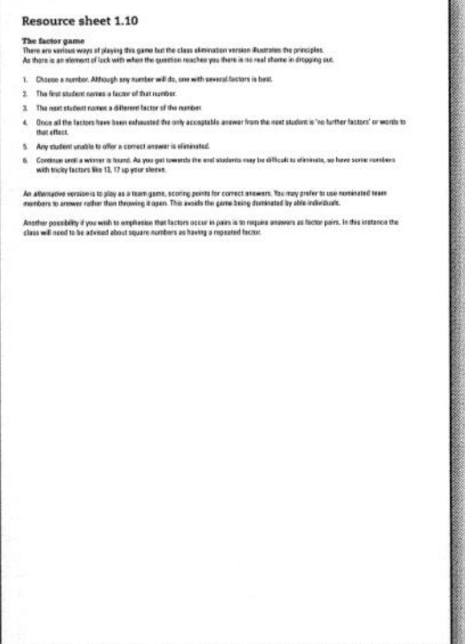

Links
http://nrich.maths.org/public/search.php?search=factors
http://www.bbc.co.uk/schools/gcsebitesize/maths/number/primefactorsact.shtml

ActiveTeach resources
Qualifying heats 1 video
Word problems quiz 2
HCF and LCM interactive
Ladder method interactive

Follow up
8.2 Equivalent fractions

1.10 Factors, multiples and prime numbers

Concepts and skills

- Recognise even and odd numbers.
- Identify factors, multiples and prime numbers.
- Find the prime factor decomposition of positive integers.
- Find common factors and common multiples of two numbers.

Functional skills

- L1 ... multiply and divide whole numbers using a range of strategies.

Prior key knowledge, skills and concepts

- Tables up to 10×10

Starter

- Counting aloud in 2s starting from, say, 30. Then from, say, 250. *Would it be any more difficult from, say, 2310? What is the pattern?*
- Continue similarly from an odd number start. *What is the pattern?*
- Although this is the introduction to odd and even numbers, it can also be used for multiples.

Main teaching and learning

- Even numbers always end in 2, 4, 6, 8 or 0.
- Odd numbers always end in 1, 3, 5, 7 or 9.
- Multiples are obtained by multiplying the number by a positive whole number.
- The factors of a number are whole numbers that divide exactly into the number, including 1 and the number itself.
- Prime numbers only have 1 and the number itself as factors.
- Numbers can be written as products of prime numbers.
- Explain the tree method of decomposition.

Common misconceptions

- Students sometimes confuse factors and multiples. (Tell them that multiples come from multiplying.)
- Thinking that 1 is a prime number.

Enrichment

- Most numbers have an even number of factors. There are some numbers that have an odd number of factors. *Find some of these and say what is special about them.*
- Factors – Packing and tiling problems.
- Multiples – *How many biros costing 19p can I buy with £5?* (Multiples of 19 are not easy, but using multiples of 20 you can buy 25 biros and get 25p change. Enough to buy another biro. Answer: 21 biros.)

Plenary

- Ask students to give examples of: prime numbers, factors of a given number (say 72 (1, 2, 3, 4, 6, 8, 9, 12, 18, 24, 36), multiples of, say, 4 (e.g. 8, 12, 16, 20), and to write a number such as 144 as a product of its prime factors. ($144 = 2 \times 2 \times 2 \times 2 \times 3 \times 3$ or $144 = 2^4 \times 3^2$)

factor multiple prime common factor common multiple prime factor prime number

Guided practice worksheet

F

1 Using only the numbers 1, 4, 7, 2 write down as many even numbers as possible.

....

....

> **Hint** There are 12 possible numbers and they must end in 2 or 4.

2 A postwoman is going to walk up the side of a street with the even numbered houses and come back down the side with odd numbers. She has letters for houses 34, 17, 3, 20, 14, 9, 31, 22, 20, 3, 28, 6.
Put the house numbers in the order in which she will deliver the letters.

....

3 List all the factors of:

> **Hint** Try 1×, then 2×, then 3×, then 5× and 7×.

a 32 ....

b 54 ....

c 27 ....

d 36 ....

4 Write down three multiples of:

a 12 ....

b 6 ....

c 20 ....

d 29 ....

5 From the numbers in the cloud write down:

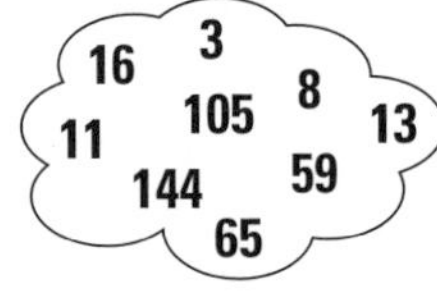

a two numbers that are factors of 72 ....

b a number that is a multiple of 15 ....

c all the prime numbers. ....

6 Why is it not possible to make an odd number from the digits 4, 2, 0, 8?

....

7 Write down a prime number that is greater than 20.

....

Specification

GCSE 2010

N c (part) Use the concepts and vocabulary of … Highest Common Factor (HCF), Least Common Multiple (LCM)….

FS Process skills

Select the mathematical information to use

Examine patterns and relationships

FS Performance

Level 1 Select mathematics in an organised way to find solutions

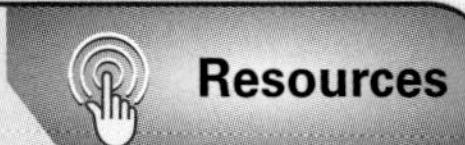

Resources

Links

http://www.bbc.co.uk/education/mathsfile/shockwave/games/gridgame.html

ActiveTeach resources

Multiples and factors quiz

Follow up

8.7 Adding and subtracting fractions

1.11 Finding lowest common multiple (LCM) and highest common factor (HCF)

Concepts and skills

- Find common factors and common multiples of two numbers.
- Find the LCM and HCF of two numbers.

Functional skills

- L1 … multiply and divide whole numbers using a range of strategies.

Prior key knowledge, skills and concepts

- Mental division by 2, 3, 5 and 7.

Starter

- *A stamp measures 6 cm by 3 cm. There are to be 60 stamps to a sheet, which has to be rectangular. Work out possible sizes for the sheet.* (3 cm by 360 cm, 6 cm by 180 cm, 12 cm by 90 cm, 9 cm by 120 cm, 18 cm by 60 cm, 24 cm by 45 cm, 15 cm by 72 cm, 30 cm by 36 cm.)

Main teaching and learning

- Explain how to find the LCM by listing families of multiples. The product of the numbers is always a common multiple but not necessarily the least. (List the first few multiples of the numbers. Pick out the smallest that is in all lists. This is the LCM.)
- Ask students to write out lists of up to twenty multiples of each of the following numbers: (a) 2 and 3 (b) 5 and 7 (c) 6 and 4 (d) 12 and 8 (e) 9 and 6.
- For each pair of numbers, circle the smallest number that appears in *both* lists of multiples. *Is the circled number always the product of the two original numbers?* For (d) and (e) ask *What are the factors? What are the common factors?*
- Explain how to find the HCF. (List all the factors of the numbers. Pick out the smallest that is in all lists. This is the HCF.)
- Some students might benefit from knowing that the HCF of any two numbers must be a factor of the difference between the two numbers.

Common misconceptions

- Confusing HCF with LCM.

Enrichment

- Question 2 of the guided practice worksheet may be used here.

Plenary

- Discuss question 5 on the guided practice worksheet.
- Discuss question 32 of the Review exercise. Explore the possibilities if the cartons contain 144 bottles.

Guided practice worksheet

F

1 a Workout all the factors common to 18 and 20.

....

b Which is the highest of these common factors?

....

2 a Write down all the common factors of:

i 18 and 30 ....

ii 42 and 60 ....

iii 84 and 108 ....

b Examine the link between these factors and the number you get by subtracting the two numbers.

....

....

C

3 Alan goes up some stairs two at a time. Peter goes up the same stairs three at a time.
They start together with their right foot and go up at the same speed.

a How often do they tread on the same stair?

....

....

b How often do they tread on the same stair each with the right foot?

....

....

4 On a long main road lamp posts are placed at 56-metre intervals. On the same road the drains are spaced at 84-metre intervals. At a point on the road there is a lamp post and a drain together.
How far down the road is it to the next point where drain and lamp post are together?

....

....

....

5 Three lemons are showing on a fruit machine.
The lemon symbol in the first position appears every 4th turn. The lemon symbol in the second position appears every 5th turn. The lemon symbol in the third position appears every 6th turn.

a Explain why all the lemon symbols will show on the 120th turn.

....

....

b Do all three lemons appear together before this? If so, when?

....

....

Specification

GCSE 2010

N d Use the terms square, positive and negative square root, cube and cube root

FS Process skills

Use appropriate mathematical procedures

FS Performance

Level 1 Use appropriate checking procedures at each stage

Resources

CD Resources

Resource sheet 1.12

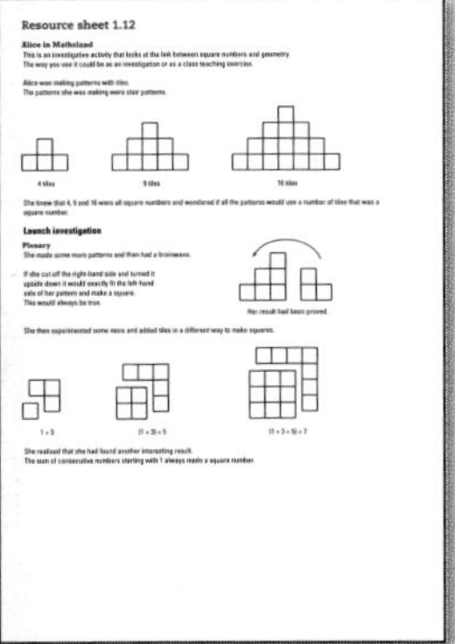

ActiveTeach resources

RP KC Number knowledge check
RP PS Number Travel problem solving

Follow up

10.4 Using a calculator – working out powers and roots

1.12 Finding square numbers and cube numbers

Concepts and skills

- Recall integer squares up to 15 × 15 and the corresponding square roots.
- Recall the cubes of 2, 3, 4, 5 and 10.
- Find squares and cubes.

Functional skills

- L1 … multiply … whole numbers using a range of strategies.

Prior key knowledge, skills and concepts

- Long multiplication

Starter

- Use the Alice in Mathsland resource sheet as a class activity.

Main teaching

- Teach students about square numbers.
- Show the number 9 represented by nine dots in a square. Ask students to say what other numbers, represented by dots, would form a square. *Without drawing squares, how can we work out the first 10* ***square numbers****?* (2 × 2; 3 × 3 etc).
- Teach students about squaring.
- Teach students about cube numbers.
- *If we calculate square numbers by multiplying a number by itself, how would we calculate a* ***cube number****?* (Write the number down three times then multiply.) Ask students to calculate the first 5 cube numbers.
- Teach students about cubing.

Common misconceptions

- Students sometimes double numbers instead of squaring them.
- Students sometimes multiply by 3 instead of cubing.

Enrichment

- 1 000 000 = 1000^2 = 100^3 1 million is a square number and a cube number. *Can you find another number which is both a cube number and a square number?* There are nine of them less than 1 million. (1, 64, 729, 4096, 15 625, 46 656, 117 649, 262 144, 531 441)

Plenary

- Devise a quiz based on the chapter review. For example, ask students to define a factor.

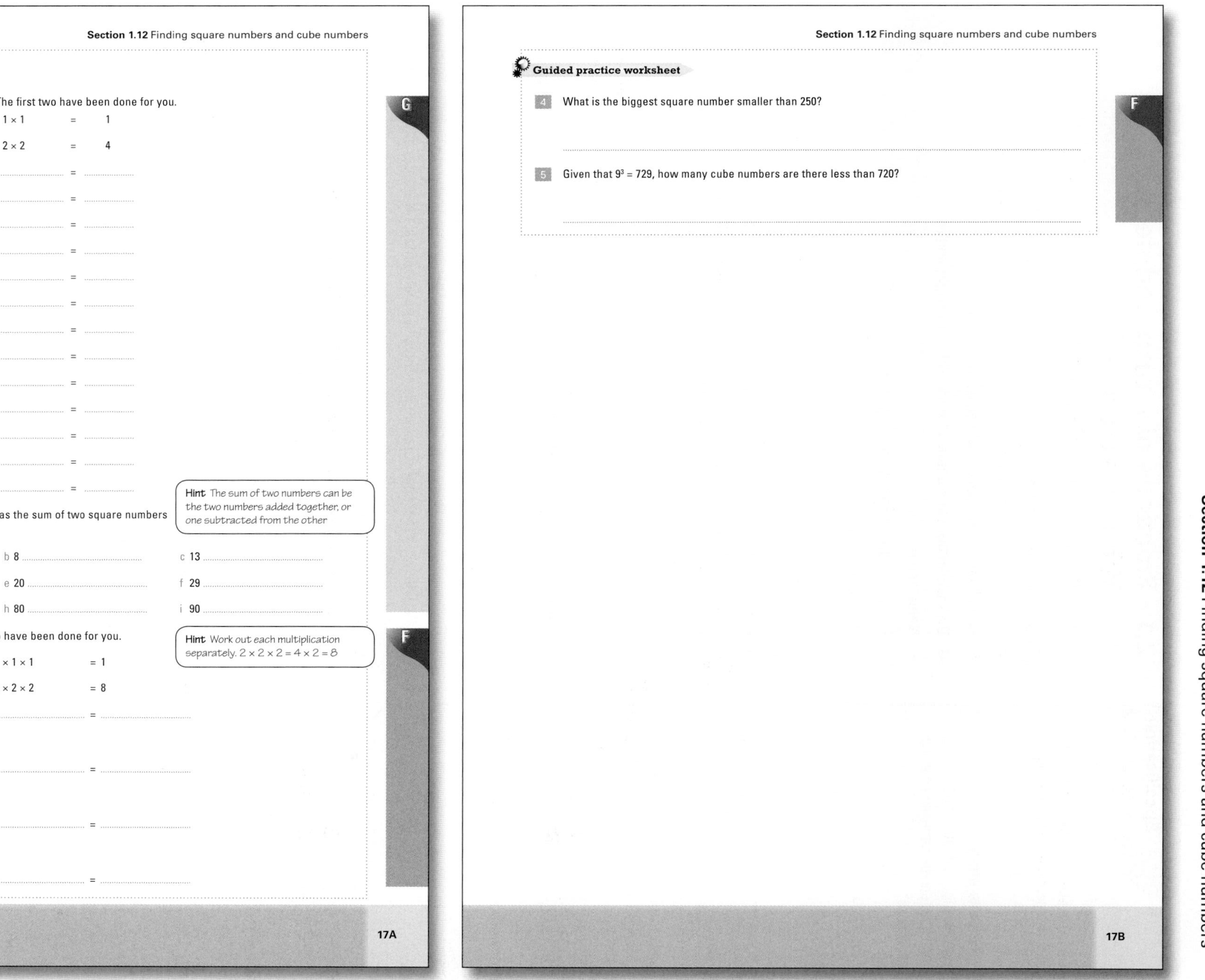

G

Guided practice worksheet

1 Find the first 15 square numbers. The first two have been done for you.

1 squared = 1^2 = 1 × 1 = 1

2 squared = 2^2 = 2 × 2 = 4

3 squared = 3^2 = ... = ...

4 squared = 4^2 = ... = ...

5 squared = 5^2 = ... = ...

6 squared = 6^2 = ... = ...

7 squared = 7^2 = ... = ...

8 squared = 8^2 = ... = ...

9 squared = 9^2 = ... = ...

10 squared = 10^2 = ... = ...

11 squared = ... = ... = ...

12 squared = ... = ... = ...

13 squared = ... = ... = ...

14 squared = ... = ... = ...

15 squared = ... = ... = ...

2 Write each of the numbers below as the sum of two square numbers taken from question 1.

Hint The sum of two numbers can be the two numbers added together, or one subtracted from the other

a 5 .... b 8 .... c 13 ....

d 58 .... e 20 .... f 29 ....

g 61 .... h 80 .... i 90 ....

F

3 Find the first 6 cube numbers. Two have been done for you.

Hint Work out each multiplication separately. 2 × 2 × 2 = 4 × 2 = 8

1 cubed = 1^3 = 1 × 1 × 1 = 1

2 cubed = 2^3 = 2 × 2 × 2 = 8

3 cubed = 3^3 = ... = ...

4 cubed = ... = ... = ...

5 cubed = ... = ... = ...

6 cubed = ... = ... = ...

17A

F

Guided practice worksheet

4 What is the biggest square number smaller than 250?

....

5 Given that 9^3 = 729, how many cube numbers are there less than 720?

....

17B

Specification

GCSE 2010

GM a (part) Recall and use properties of angles at a point, angles on a straight line (including right angles)....

FS Process skills

Recognise that a situation has aspects that can be represented using mathematics

FS Performance

Entry 3 Select mathematics to obtain answers to simple given practical problems that are clear and routine

Resources

Links

http://nrich.maths.org/public/search.php?search=angles
http://nrich.maths.org/5656

ActiveTeach resources

Fractions of circles quiz
Angles interactive
Extreme 1 video
Asymmetric bars 1 video

2.1 Fractions of a turn and degrees
2.2 What is an angle?
2.3 Naming sides and angles

Concepts and skills

- Recall and use properties of angles at a point.
- Distinguish between acute, obtuse, reflex and right angles.
- Name angles.
- Use geometric language appropriately.
- Use letters to identify points, lines and angles.
- Use two-letter notation for a line and three-letter notation for an angle.

Functional skills

- EL3 Recognise and name simple 2D ... shapes and their properties.

Prior key knowledge, skills and concepts

- Students should already know how to add and subtract numbers to 360.

Starter

- Talk about turning; maybe get students to turn through $\frac{1}{4}, \frac{1}{2}, \frac{3}{4}$ and full turns.

Main teaching and learning

- Tell students they are going to learn about measuring turns.
- Explain that turns are called angles and are measured in degrees.
- Explain that a full turn is 360 degrees.
- Get the students to work out the number of degrees in $\frac{1}{4}, \frac{1}{2}, \frac{3}{4}$ turns. (90°, 180°, 270°)
- Talk about the fact that some angles have special names, i.e. acute, obtuse, reflex and right angles.
- Ask students to draw examples of acute, obtuse, reflex and right angles. (By inspection.)
- Demonstrate how angles are named using letters.

Enrichment

- This work could be linked to geography by talking about the 4, 8 or 16 points of the compass and the number of degrees turned between them.
- Students could be asked to identify acute, obtuse, reflex and right angles in the classroom.

Plenary

- Draw a variety of angles and ask students to identify those that are acute, obtuse, reflex and right angles.

degree angle acute obtuse reflex right angle

Guided practice worksheet

G

A B C

H G I

L K J

D E F

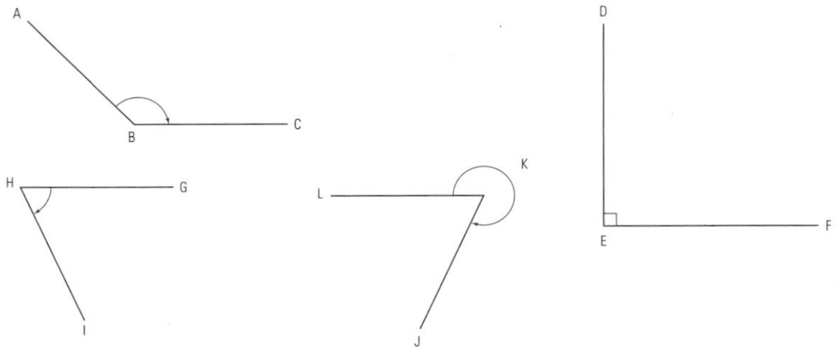

1 Write down the special names of each of the angles above.

....

....

....

....

2 Draw a an acute angle

b a reflex angle

c a right angle

d an obtuse angle

Section 2.1–2.3 Degrees and angles

Guided practice worksheet

G

3 Use letters to write down the name of the angles drawn above.

....

....

....

....

4

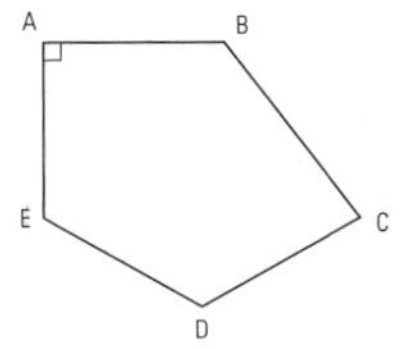

A B C D E

a EAB is a .... angle

b ABC is a .... angle

c .... is an acute angle.

Specification

GCSE 2010

GM a (part) Recall and use properties of angles at a point, angles on a straight line (including right angles)....
GM t Measure and draw lines and angles.

FS Process skills

Recognise that a situation has aspects that can be represented using mathematics
Find results and solutions

FS Performance

Level 1 Identify and obtain necessary information to tackle the problem

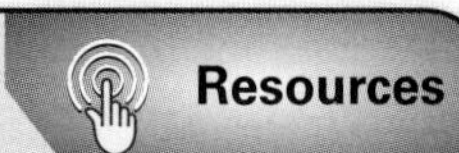

Resources

Resources

Ruler and protractor

Links

http://nrich.maths.org/1235

ActiveTeach resources

Estimating angles quiz
Measure angles interactive

2.4 Estimating angles
2.5 Measuring angles

Concepts and skills

- Estimate sizes of angles.
- Measure and draw angles, to the nearest degree.

Functional skills

- L1 Construct geometric diagrams, models and shapes.

Prior key knowledge, skills and concepts

- Students should know that a full turn is 360 degrees, a right angle is 90 degrees and a half turn is 180 degrees.
- Students should be able to name angles.

Starter

- Ask students to name some angles using three-letter notation. (Student's own answers.)
- Ask students to state the number of degrees in $\frac{1}{4}$, $\frac{1}{2}$ and full turns. (90°, 180°, 360°)

Main teaching and learning

- Tell students that they are going to learn to measure angles and that estimating the size of angles first will help them ensure that they will get sensible answers.
- Ask the students to look at some angles and decide if they are more or less than a right angle.
- Discuss with students that an angle that is less than a right angle will be in the range of 0–90 degrees and an angle that is more than a right angle will be in the range of 90–180 degrees.
- Refine the process by using half of a right angle.
- Introduce students to a protractor.
- Ask students to look at a protractor and identify key features (scales, baseline, and the point at which 90 crosses the baseline).
- Take the students through the process of measuring acute and obtuse angles, asking them to estimate the size of the angle first.
- Tell students that angles must be drawn to the nearest 2 degrees in the examination.

Common misconceptions

- Students sometimes use the bottom of the protractor rather than the baseline.
- Sometimes students use the wrong scale.

Enrichment

- Discuss how a protractor could be used to measure a reflex angle by measuring the smaller angle and subtracting from 360.

Plenary

- Ask students to give an estimation of the size of some angles and, if possible, measure them.

Guided practice worksheet

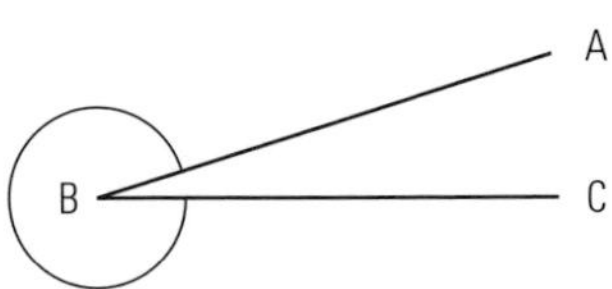

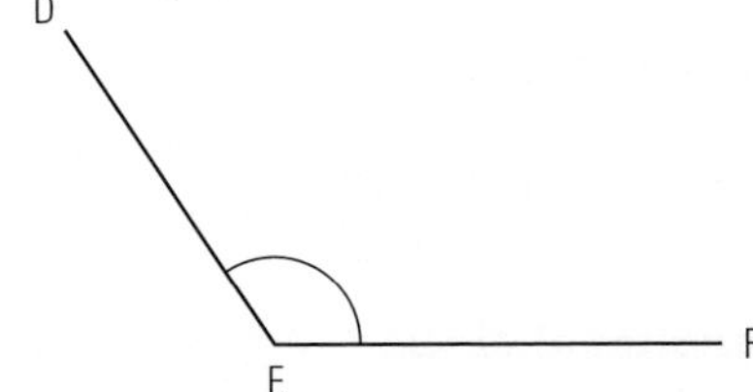

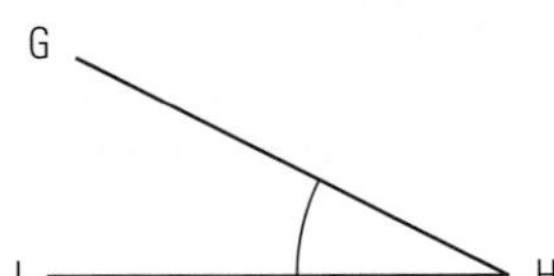

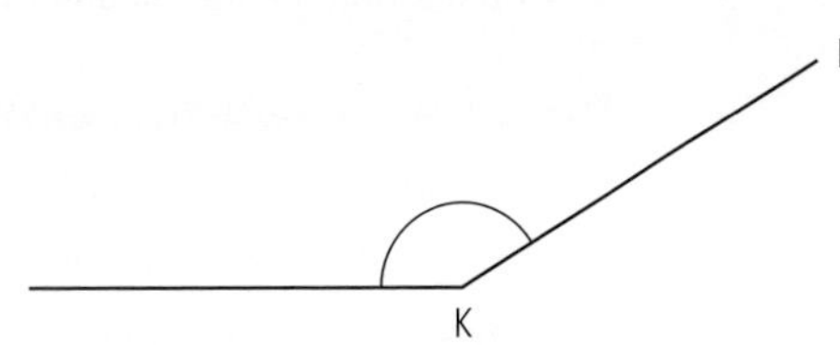

1 Which of the above angles are:

a more than a right angle ....

b less than a right angle. ....

2 Estimate the size of each angle.

....

....

....

....

3 Measure each of the above angles accurately.

....

....

....

....

4 Measure the size of the reflex angle MNO.

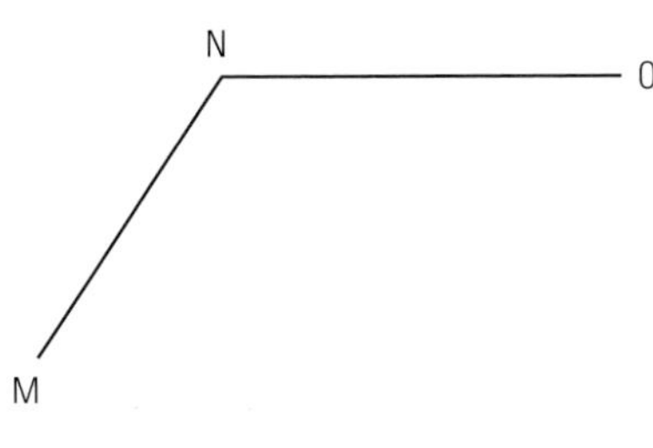

....

G

F

Specification

GCSE 2010
GM t Measure and draw lines and angles

FS Process skills
Recognise that a situation has aspects that can be represented using mathematics

FS Performance
Level 1 Identify and obtain necessary information to tackle the problem

Resources

Resources
Ruler and protractor

2.6 Drawing angles

Concepts and skills

- Measure and draw lines to the nearest mm.
- Measure and draw angles, to the nearest degree.

Functional skills

- L1 Construct geometric diagrams, models and shapes.

Prior key knowledge, skills and concepts

- Students should already be able to name lines and angles using letter notation.
- They should be able to draw a line to the nearest 2 mm.
- They should also be able to use a protractor to measure angles.

Starter

- Draw a shape and ask students how they would make an accurate copy of it, drawing out that they would need to draw lines and angles accurately.

Main teaching and learning

- Take students through the process of drawing a specified acute angle:
  - draw an estimate of the angle
  - draw the baseline
  - place the 'cross' on one end of the line
  - discuss which scale needs to be used
  - mark the angle
  - join the marked point to the baseline.
- Tell students that angles must be drawn to the nearest 2 degrees in the examination.
- Repeat for an obtuse angle.
- Take the students through the process of drawing a specified shape accurately, emphasising the need to draw lines that are accurate to the nearest 2 mm.
- Discuss the order in which sides and angles should be drawn.

Common misconceptions

- Students sometimes use the wrong scale.
- Sometimes students use the bottom of the protractor, instead of the baseline.
- Students might join the wrong end of the line to the marked point when drawing an angle.

Enrichment

- Discuss how to draw a reflex angle using a protractor.

Plenary

- Discuss the common errors in drawing angles.

Guided practice worksheet

F

1 Without a protractor, draw a sketch of

a 45°

b 110°

c 75°

d 165°

2 Use a protractor to measure your estimates.

....

....

....

....

3 Use a protractor to draw the following angles:

ABC=30°

DEF=105°

Section 2.6 Drawing angles

Guided practice worksheet

F

GHI=77°

JKL=142°

4 Use a ruler and a protractor to make an accurate drawing of this shape.

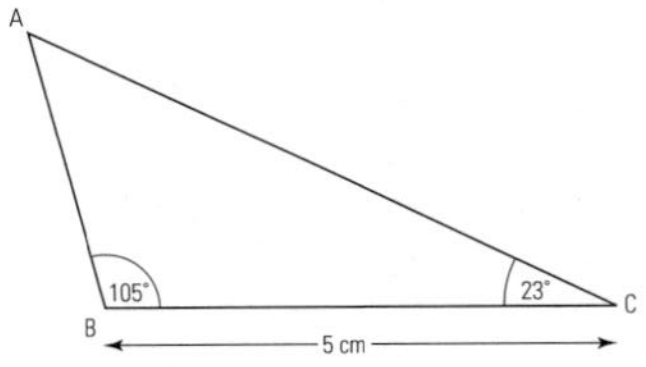

A

105°

B

23°

C

5 cm

a Measure AC ....

b Measure BAC ....

Specification

GCSE 2010

GM b Understand and use the angle properties of parallel and intersecting lines, triangles and quadrilaterals

FS Process skills

Select the mathematical information to use

Find results and solutions

FS Performance

Level 1 Select mathematics in an organised way to find solutions

Resources

Resources

Protractor and ruler

Links

http://nrich.maths.org/2844

ActiveTeach resources

Triangles interactive

2.7 Special triangles

Concepts and skills

- Distinguish between scalene, equilateral, isosceles and right-angled triangles.
- Understand and use the angle properties of triangles.
- Find a missing angle in a triangle, using the angle sum of a triangle is 180°.
- Use the side/angle properties of isosceles and equilateral triangles.

Functional skills

- L1 Use simple formulae ... for one- or two-step operations.

Prior key knowledge, skills and concepts

- Students should already know how to measure and draw angles.
- They should be aware that the angle sum of a triangle is 180°.

Starter

- Ask students to draw a triangle, measure the angles and add them up.
- Establish that, for all triangles, the angle sum is 180°.

Main teaching and learning

- Using students' triangles, demonstrate that the angle sum of a triangle = 180° by tearing the corners and placing them along a straight line.
- Demonstrate how, if you know two angles of any triangle, you can find the third.
- Give the students examples of equilateral, isosceles and right-angled triangles. Ask them to measure the sides and angles to establish each triangle's properties (see resource sheet).
- Demonstrate that, given one angle, you can find all the angles in an isosceles triangle.

Common misconceptions

- Students fail to recognise that a triangle can have the properties of more than one special triangle, e.g. a right-angled triangle could also be an isosceles.

Enrichment

- Investigate different types of triangle to establish some 'truth' statements about the different types. For example, an equilateral triangle is also an isosceles triangle but an isosceles triangle, may or may not be an equilateral triangle.

Plenary

- Review the properties of different types of triangle.

interior angle

Guided practice worksheet

Equilateral triangles

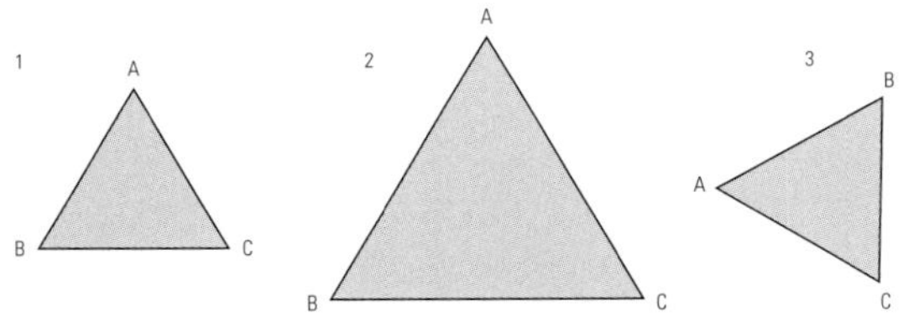

	Sides			Angles		
	AB	BC	CA	A	B	C
1						
2						
3						

Equilateral triangles have .... sides and .... angles.

Isosceles triangles

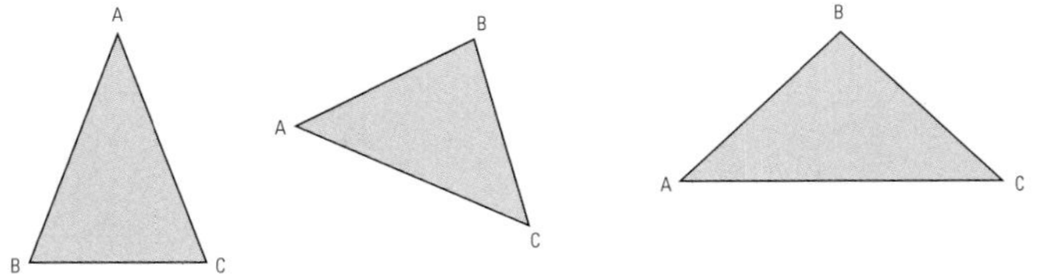

	Sides			Angles		
	AB	BC	CA	A	B	C
1						
2						
3						

Isosceles triangles have .... sides and .... angles.

Guided practice worksheet

Right-angled triangles

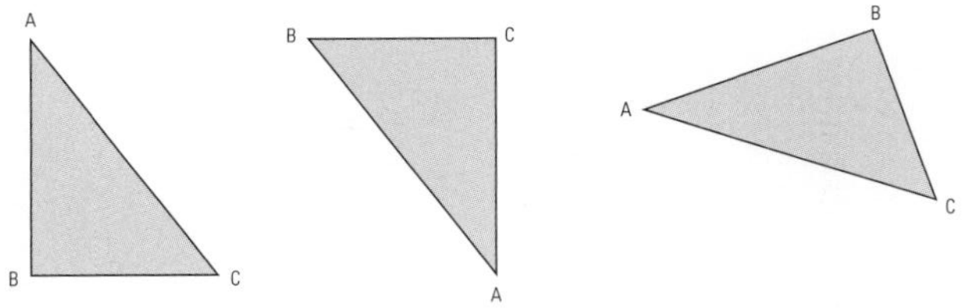

	Sides			Angles		
	AB	BC	CA	A	B	C
1						
2						
3						

All right-angled triangles have .... sides and .... angle.

Specification

GCSE 2010

GM a Recall and use properties of angles at a point, angles on a straight line (including right angles), perpendicular lines, and opposite angles at a vertex
GM b (part) Understand and use the angle properties of parallel and intersecting lines...

FS Process skills

Select the mathematical information to use
Find results and solutions

FS Performance

Level 1 Select mathematics in an organised way to find solutions

Resources

ActiveTeach resources

RP KC Angles 1 knowledge check
RP PS Angles 1 problem solving

2.8 Angle facts

Concepts and skills

- Recall and use properties of:
  - angles at a point
  - angles on a straight line, including right angles
  - vertically opposite angles.
- Find the size of missing angles at a point or at a point on a straight line.
- Give reasons for angle calculations.
- Understand and use the angle properties of intersecting lines.

Functional skills

- L1 Use simple formulae ... for one- or two-step operations.

Prior key knowledge, skills and concepts

- Students should know that a full turn is 360° and a half turn is 180°.

Starter

- Ask students to recall the fact that a full turn is 360° and a half turn is 180°.
- Ask students a series of questions of the type: *If I turn 50°, how much more do I have to turn for a full/half turn?*

Main teaching and learning

- Give students the 'formal' statements of angles at a point and on a straight line.
- Represent examples from the starter visually as diagrams; discuss methods for finding solutions.
- Highlight that in the examination students might be asked to state the angle fact that they use to solve problems and that 'give reasons' is a common cue.
- Using some examples of pairs of crossed straight lines with one marked angle, ask students to deduce the remaining three angles.
- Establish that in all cases the opposite angles are equal.
- Introduce the term 'vertically opposite' and the formal statement of 'vertically opposite angles are equal'.
- Work through some examples using vertically opposite angle facts.
- Work through some mixed examples asking students to state which angle facts they are employing.

Common misconceptions

- 'Vertically' is used regardless of the position of angles.
- Vertically opposite angles do not appear in all problems involving four angles around a point, just where two straight lines cross.

Plenary

- Ask students to recall the three angle facts from memory; give a few examples asking students which angle facts to use to find a solution.

vertically opposite angles   angles at a point   angles on a straight line   opposite angles

F

Guided practice worksheet

1 In each of the following questions work out how many more degrees you have to turn to make a full turn.

a 160° .... b 210° .... c 87° .... d 243° ....

2 In each of the following questions work out how many more degrees you have to turn to make half a turn.

a 30° .... b 140° .... c 53° .... d 112° ....

3 Work out the size of the missing angle.

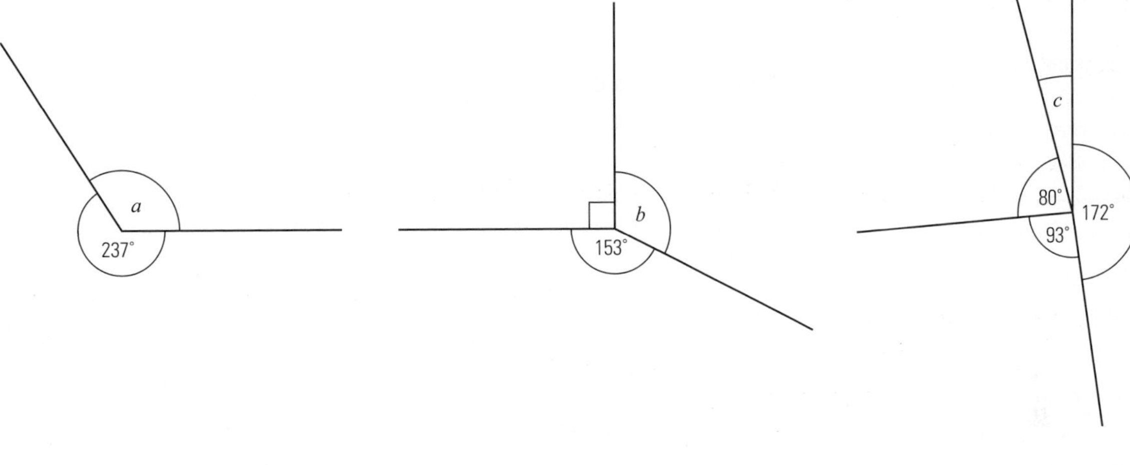

....

....

....

....

....

4 Work out the size of the missing angle.

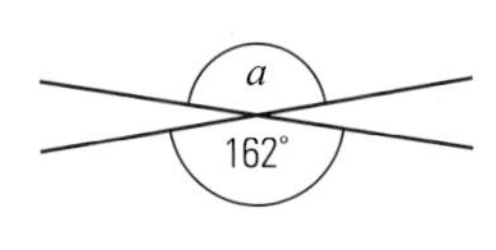

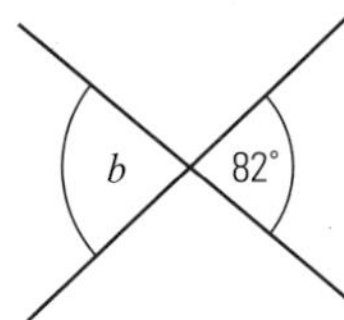

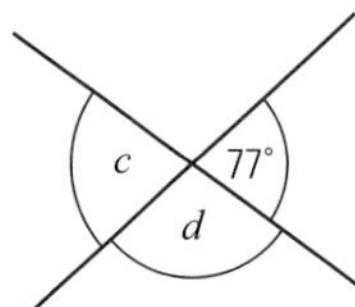

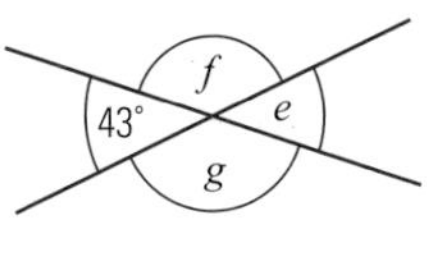

....

....

....

....

....

....

....

Specification

GCSE 2010

SP a Understand and use statistical problem solving process/handling data cycle

SP d (part) … distinguishing between different types of data

FS Process skills

Recognise that a situation has aspects that can be represented using mathematics

FS Performance

Level 2 Identify the situation or problems and identify the mathematical methods needed to solve them

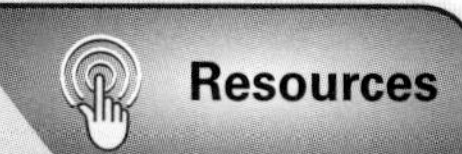

Resources

CD Resources

MS PowerPoint presentation 3.1 'Types of data'

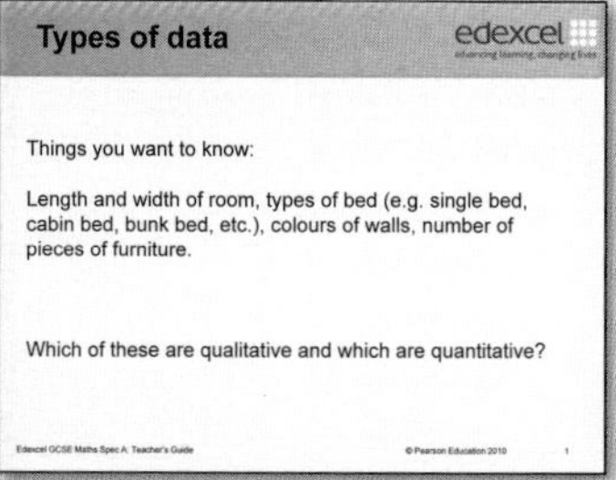

Links

http://www.mathsisfun.com/data/data.html

3.1 Introduction to data

Concepts and skills

- Specify the problem and plan.
- Decide what data to collect and what statistical analysis is needed.
- Collect data from a variety of suitable primary and secondary sources.
- Use suitable data collection techniques.
- Process and represent the data.
- Interpret and discuss the data.
- … classify (categorical or qualitative) data and discrete or continuous quantitative data.

Functional skills

- L2 Collect and represent discrete and continuous data.

Starter

- Imagine you are designing the perfect bedroom. What information do you need before starting work? Ask students to suggest some furniture they might need in their room.

Main teaching and learning

- Tell students that 'types of bed' is called a variable, and a collection of these is called data.
- Display PowerPoint 3.1, slide 1 and discuss these points:
  - They are all variables to do with a room.
  - You can describe paint colour but cannot measure it.
  - You can represent the bedroom's size as a number.
- Practise classifying variables into two types on slide 2.
  - Variables described in words, such as colour, are qualitative variables.
  - Variables with numeric values, such as height, are quantitative variables.
- Quantitative variables can then be divided into two types as shown on slide 3.
  - Those that can take on any value on a numeric scale (length of room). These are continuous variables.
  - Those that can only take certain values on a numeric scale (number of beds). These are discrete variables.

Common misconceptions

- Many students get the words qualitative and quantitative mixed up. Remind them that they come from the words quality and quantity.

Enrichment

- Ask students what test they would use to decide if data was qualitative or quantitative. (Students' own answers.)

Plenary

- *Give an example of each of the following.*
  (a) *qualitative data* (colour of hair)
  (b) *quantitative data* (distances)
  (c) *discrete data* (shoe size)
  (d) *continuous data* (weight).
- *Can data be both qualitative and discrete?* (No, 'discrete' and 'continuous' refers only to quantitative data.)

qualitative quantitative continuous discrete conclusion interpreting statistics

G

F

Guided practice worksheet

1 Wing decides to collect some data so that he can investigate the costs of meals in a restaurant. Write down two pieces of data he will need to collect.

....

2 The table gives some observations of different types of data.

Data types	Observations
Eye colour	blue, brown, green, grey
Height	176.2 cm, 165.3 cm, 182.5 cm
Breed	corgi, collie, spaniel
Number of pets	1, 0, 3, 2, 4

a Write down the names of the data types that are:

i quantitative

....

ii qualitative.

....

Hint Is the data value a number or does it describe something?

b Write down one observation that is:

i discrete data

....

ii continuous data.

....

Hint Is the data value continuous or one number?

3 State whether each of the following is continuous or discrete:

a shoe size ....

b hand span ....

c lifetime of an electric light bulb ....

d number of people in a cinema. ....

4 The table shows some information about three second-hand motor bikes.

Make	Model	Year	Engine size	Miles	Price
Yamaha	Dragster	2006	1100 cc	11 453	£4499
BMW	Adverline	2007	1200 cc	14 137	£8599
Honda	Blackbird	2005	1100 cc	9458	£4595

Write down one piece of:

a quantitative data ....

b qualitative data ....

c continuous data ....

d discrete data. ....

Specification

GCSE 2010

SP a Understand and use statistical problem solving process/handling data cycle
SP d (part) Design data-collection sheets….
SP e Extract data from printed tables and lists

FS Process skills

Select the mathematical information to use
Find results and solutions

FS Performance

Level 2 Apply a range of mathematics to find a solution

Resources

CD Resources

MS PowerPoint presentation 3.2 'Collecting data'

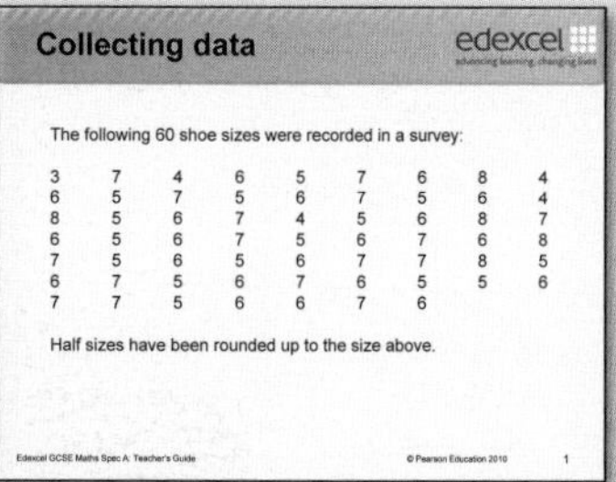

Links

http://www.mathsisfun.com/data/survey-conducting.html

3.2 Collecting data

Concepts and skills

- Collect data from a variety of suitable primary and secondary sources.
- Use suitable data collection techniques.
- Process and represent the data.
- Interpret and discuss the data.
- Design and use data-collection sheets for grouped, discrete and continuous data.
- Collect data using various methods.
- Sort, classify and tabulate data and discrete or continuous quantitative data.
- Group discrete and continuous data into class intervals of equal width.
- Extract data from lists and tables.

Functional skills

- L2 Collect and represent discrete and continuous data. …

Starter

- Imagine your school is going to open a shop selling footwear for drama and PE. You have been asked to decide how many of each shoe size to stock. Ask students what size shoe they take.

Main teaching and learning

- Tell students that what they are doing is collecting data by observation and they can use the observations to predict how many of each shoe size should be stocked.
- Display PowerPoint 3.2, slide 1 and discuss these points:
  - You need a larger sample than one class.
  - You can count how many shoes of each size there are in the sample.
  - Students don't have feet that exactly match a shoe size, but sizes between, say, $4\frac{1}{2}$ and 5 can be grouped together as size 5.
  - 5 is the class and $4\frac{1}{2}$ to 5 is the class interval.
- A sample of the variable 'shoe size' is shown on PowerPoint slide 2.
- As we run through the data we can put a stroke in the tally column opposite the relevant shoe size on slide 3.
- To make it easy to count up and find the number of shoes of each size, you can group the bars into fives so: ~~||||~~. The fifth mark is drawn through the other four.
- The total of the tallies is known as the frequency.
- The completed chart is called a tally chart.

Common misconceptions

- Many students count |||| as the same as ~~||||~~ and get the totals wrong.

Enrichment

- The school shop is going to buy 300 pairs of shoes. The number of shoes in each size should be in proportion to the number in the sample.
- Complete PowerPoint slide 3.
- Discuss other ways of collecting data – experiment, data logging.

Plenary

- *How would you collect data to investigate the following?*
  (a) *The need for a bypass through your town/village.* (Observing traffic flow over a period of time.)
  (b) *The fairness of a 4-faced die.* (By experiment, rolling and recording the frequency of each score.)
  (c) *The most popular items sold from the school vending machine.* (Observe the variety of items selected over a period of time.)
  (d) *The consistency of the number of drawing pins in boxes of equal size and cost.* (Counting the numbers of drawing pins in several boxes, i.e. by experiment.)
- *Design a data collection sheet for each of the above investigations.* (Frequency tables, showing (a) vehicle types, tallies and frequencies, (b) numbers on the die, tallies and frequencies, (c) items in vending machine, tallies and frequencies, (d) number of drawing pins per box, tallies and frequencies.)

frequency tally class interval collecting data by experiment data

Guided practice worksheet

G

1 Amaya decides to collect some data on the makes of cars passing her house. Here is a list of the data she collects:

Ford	Vauxhall	Volvo	BMW	Skoda	Jaguar	Vauxhall
Skoda	Jaguar	Volvo	Jaguar	Ford	Ford	Ford
Skoda	Vauxhall	Ford	Vauxhall	Ford	Volvo	Vauxhall
BMW	Skoda	Skoda	Skoda			

Draw up a tally chart for these data.

2 Naveed writes down the number of varieties of birds visiting his bird table for one hour every day for the 31 days in May.

On 5 of the days he sees 5 different birds. On 12 days he sees 6 different birds. On 7 days he sees 7 different birds. On the remaining days he sees 8 different birds.

Draw up a frequency table to show these data.

Guided practice worksheet

F

3 Maria records the heights of 31 children, in cm. The data she collects is shown below.

123 98 124 94 117 109 100 122 99 103 92 108 117 124 136 106
127 133 128 130 116 102 117 114 121 134 128 126 96 127 131

Complete the frequency table below for these data.

Height	Tally	Frequency
90–99		
100–109		
110–119		
120–129		
130–139		
Total		

4 Andrew decides to record the number of times a blue tit visits her nest. He sets up his camera to record timed photographs every time she enters the nesting box. What is the name given to this type of data collection?

....

....

Specification

GCSE 2010

SP a Understand and use statistical problem solving process/handling data cycle

SP c (part) Design … a survey.

FS Process skills

Draw conclusions in light of situations

FS Performance

Level 2 Interpret and communicate solutions to … practical problems in familiar and unfamiliar contexts and situations

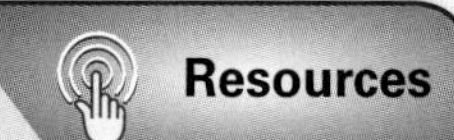

Resources

CD Resources

MS PowerPoint presentation 3.3 'Questionnaires'

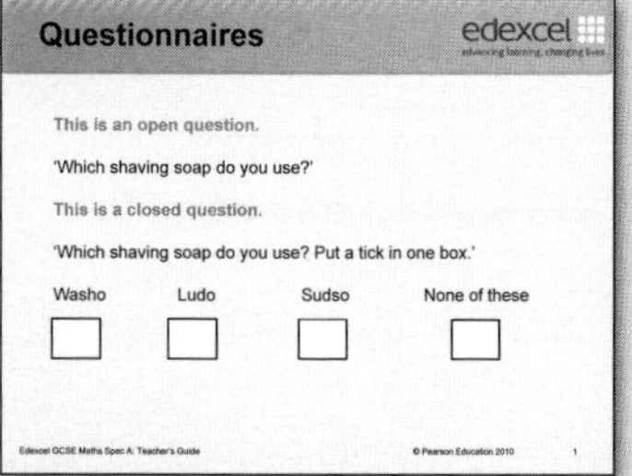

Links

http://www.bbc.co.uk/schools/gcsebitesize/maths/data/questionnairesact.shtml

3.3 Questionnaires

Concepts and skills

- Decide what data to collect and what statistical analysis is needed.
- Identify which primary data they need to collect and in what format, including grouped data.
- Consider fairness.
- Design a question, for a questionnaire.
- Criticise questions for a questionnaire.

Functional skills

- L2 Collect and represent discrete and continuous data….

Starter

- Ask students: *What do you like to eat in the mornings?*

Main teaching and learning

- Tell students that this question was used on a piece of paper sent out by a maker of breakfast cereals. A collection of questions on a piece of paper which were to be filled in were sent out to people at random. This is called a questionnaire.
- How many of the people questioned said breakfast? How many might not have breakfast?
- Ask the students: *What question would you have asked?*
- You must be careful what sort of question you ask. You might get an answer you don't expect.
- The question above is an open question, since you can give any answer to it. To limit the number of answers you expect you can use a closed question. Examples of both are shown on PowerPoint 3.3 slide 1.
- Questions should not lead the person who is filling in the answer as to what answer to give. For example, 'You do like cereal, don't you?' is likely to get the answer 'Yes'. This is a leading question.

Common misconceptions

- There are a number of mistakes that students sometimes make. Some of the common ones are shown on PowerPoint slide 2. Ask the students what is wrong in each case. Click to reveal the answers.

Enrichment

- Design a questionnaire to collect information on a person's gender, age and views about the benefits of a good education.

Plenary

- *'Men watch less TV than women.'*
  - (a) *How would you test this statement?* (Questionnaire)
  - (b) *What questions would you ask on your questionnaire?* (Gender; age; programmes watched.) Discuss as a group and talk about the response boxes that are needed.

questionnaire open question closed question

Guided practice worksheet

E

1 The following question was on a questionnaire sent out to a sample of council tenants.

'Do you agree that we need a new ring road?'

Yes Perhaps

Write down two things that are wrong with this question.

....

....

2 Here is a list of answer boxes and questions.

a Yes ☐ No ☐ Don't know ☐

b Agree ☐ Disagree ☐ Don't know ☐

c 0 ☐ 1 ☐ 2 ☐ 3 or more ☐

Choose which set of boxes should be used for each of A, B, C, D and E.

A How many brothers and sisters do you have? ....

B Statistics is fun. ....

C Everyone needs to be able to use a computer. ....

D Is Galloway a county in Scotland? ....

E How many times have you been to the doctors' surgery this year? ....

3 A company asked the following question on a questionnaire designed to find out whether or not free gym membership would be a sensible 'perk' for their employees.

Are you a sports fan? Yes/No

Write down two things that are wrong with this question.

....

....

4 Write down a question that could be used to find out the ages of people visiting an optician. Don't forget to put in the answer boxes.

....

....

5 Which of the following questions are biased? Give a reason for your choices.

A Most people enjoy chips. Do you eat chips?

B How long does it take you to travel to school each day?

C Do you agree that it is a good idea to eat five portions of fruit and vegetables a day?

D Swimming is fun for most people. Do you enjoy swimming?

E Will you, or will you not, go on holiday this year?

....

....

....

Specification

GCSE 2010

SP a Understand and use statistical problem solving process/handling data cycle
SP b Identify possible sources of bias
SP c Design an experiment or survey

FS Process skills

Draw conclusions in light of situations

FS Performance

Level 2 Interpret and communicate solutions to ... practical problems in familiar and unfamiliar contexts and situations

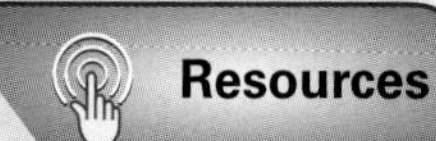

Resources

Links

http://illuminations.nctm.org/activities.aspx?grade=all&srchstr=random%20drawing
http://www.bbc.co.uk/education/mathsfile/shockwave/games/datapick.html

3.4 Sampling

Concepts and skills

- Use suitable data collection techniques.
- Understand how sources of data may be biased.
- Understand sample and population.

Functional skills

- L2 Collect and represent discrete and continuous data....

Starter

- Ask students: *Do you get too much pocket money? Tell them I know the answer is no, but how much money in coins do you have in your pocket?* Explain that during this lesson, the students will be taking two samples to find out.

Main teaching and learning

- Tell students that by taking a sample of three from the class we are going to estimate how much money in coins students have in their pockets. Discuss how accurate this will be. Ask: *How should we select the three students?* Explain that the class is the population from which a sample is to be taken.
- Select three people at random and get them to count up how much money in coins they have in their pockets. Work out how much each student would have if the total was divided between the three of them.
- Select half the class at random and get them to count their money. Work out the new figure per head.
- Tell the students that they are using a sample to estimate what the value is for the whole population.
- Discuss other methods of choosing a sample.

Common misconceptions

- Students sometimes do not understand what constitutes an unbiased sample.

Enrichment

- Work out the amount per head for the whole class and compare the three figures. Explain that the bigger the sample size the more accurate the result should be.

Plenary

- *'Men watch less TV than women.'*
  - (a) *Who would you ask?* (Variety of ages; avoid asking friends only, as they may have similar interests.)
  - (b) *Where would you ask them?* (Open to discussion.)
  - (c) *How many people would you ask?* (A sample size of 50 men and 50 women would be sufficient.)

sample population biased random sample representative chance

Guided practice worksheet

D

1 Mark wants to know what the students at his college think about the library facilities. He decides to give a questionnaire to a sample of students. Write down a reason why he is sensible to use a sample.

2 A teacher thinks that the 25 pupils in her after-school drama club don't like meeting on Thursdays and would like to try meeting on a different day of the week. She asks all the pupils for their views. What are the advantages of asking all the pupils rather than a sample?

3 An opinion poll company decides to conduct a telephone poll to find out people's views on political parties. They phone 5 people in each of 10 cities.

Write down two reasons why this is a biased poll.

4 Rowan wants to find out what people think of the new county swimming pool. She uses the first 20 people she meets at the door of the pool as a sample.

What is wrong with this sample?

5 A council is interested in the traffic flow at a particular roundabout.

Councillor Jackson goes to the roundabout one Saturday morning and notes down all the traffic using the roundabout during one hour.

Councillor Brown says that this data is biased as this is not a good sample.

Explain why Councillor Brown is right.

Specification

GCSE 2010

SP a Understand and use statistical problem solving process/handling data cycle

SP e Extract data from printed tables and lists

SP f Design and use two-way tables for discrete and grouped data

FS Process skills

Select the mathematical information to use

Find results and solutions

FS Performance

Level 2 Apply a range of mathematics to find solutions

Resources

CD Resources

MS PowerPoint presentation 3.5 'Tables'

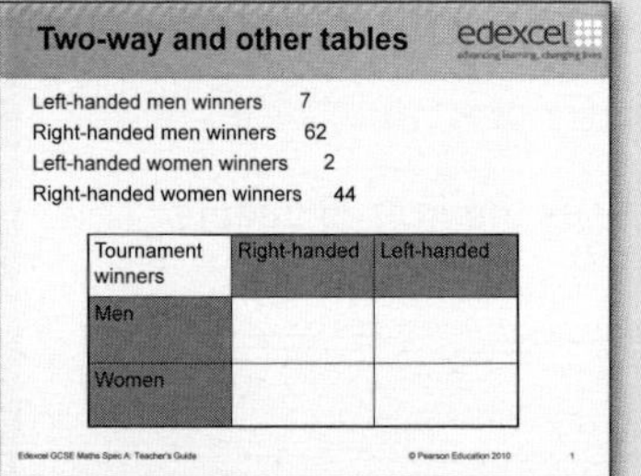

ActiveTeach resources

Counting traffic 2 video

RP KC Collecting data knowledge check

RP PS Data collection sheet problem solving

3.5 Two-way and other tables

Concepts and skills

- Collect data from a variety of suitable primary and secondary sources.
- Process and represent the data.
- Interpret and discuss the data.
- Design and use two-way tables for discrete and grouped data.
- Use information provided to complete a two-way table.
- Extract data from lists and tables.

Functional skills

- L2 Collect and represent discrete and continuous data….

Starter

- Ask students: *Are girls different from boys?* Tell them *I know the answer is yes, but do you think that the proportion of left-handed women tennis players is the same as the proportion of left-handed men tennis players?*

Main teaching and learning

- Tell students that out of 69 men winners of a particular tournament there were only seven left-handed players. Out of 46 women winners of the corresponding women's tournament there were only two left-handed players.
- Discuss how accurate this comparison will be. Explain that as this is direct observation it should be very accurate.
- Point out that here we have two categories that we can put people into:
  - men and women tennis champions
  - left- and right-handed tennis champions.
- Explain that the two categories give rise to four frequencies: men left-handers; women left-handers; men right-handers; women right-handers.
- Ask the students to suggest a way of showing this in a table.
- Display PowerPoint slide 1.
- Tell the students that most tables are made up of rows and columns, with the frequency or other value where the rows and columns cross. Display PowerPoint slide 2.
- Be sure to let the students discover the layout for themselves. The two-way table allows comparisons to be made. Draw this point out in PowerPoint slide 2.
- Explain that most tables are read in a similar way. Use PowerPoint slide 3 to discuss other tables.

Enrichment

- Work out the proportion of men left-handers and the proportion of women left-handers. Draw conclusions about left-handed tennis players.

Plenary

- *Draw a data collection sheet that could be used to record the favourite types of music of girls and boys in your class.* (Two-way tally chart.)

two-way tables database primary data secondary data

Guided practice worksheet

F

1 A kiosk on the seafront sells ice creams, drinks, ice lollies and crisps. People buying two items get a 25% reduction in price. The manager keeps a record of some of the sales he makes one Saturday. The data he collects is shown in the two-way table.

	Ice cream	Drink	Total
Ice lolly	36	28	64
Crisps	16	42	58
Total	52	70	122

a How many people are represented by this table altogether?

....

b Write down the total numbers of ice creams sold.

....

c Write down the number of people who bought an ice lolly.

....

d Write down the most popular pair of items.

....

2 The table shows some information about some medal-winning countries in past Commonwealth Games.

	Gold	Silver	Bronze	Total
Australia	732	619	555	1906
England	578	553	564	1695
Canada	414	445	459	1318
New Zealand	124	168	237	529
Scotland	82	94	154	330
South Africa	92	92	97	281

a Write down the country that won the most medals overall.

....

b Write down which of these countries won the least gold medals.

....

c Write down the country that won the most bronze medals.

....

d How many more gold medals did Australia win than England?

....

e How many more medals did Australia win than South Africa?

....

E

3 The two-way table shows information about the holiday choices of some holiday-makers.

Complete the table.

	France	Spain	Total
Self-catering	34	24	
Full board	16	48	
Total			

Specification

GCSE 2010

A a Distinguish the different roles played by letter symbols in algebra, using the correct notation

FS Process skills

Recognise that a situation has aspects that can be represented using mathematics

FS Performance

Level 2 Identify the situation or problems and identify the mathematical methods needed to solve them

Resources

Links

http://www.bbc.co.uk/schools/gcsebitesize/maths/algebra/factorisinghirev1.shtml

4.1 Using letters to represent numbers

Concepts and skills

- Use notation and symbols correctly.

Functional skills

- L2 Understand and use simple formulae and equations involving one- or two-step operations.

Prior key knowledge, skills and concepts

- Students need to remember:
  - $d + d = 2d$
  - $2g = 2 \times g$
  - $5p - 2p = 3p$
  - $4p - p = 3p$

Starter

- Go through 'Before you start' in the chapter introduction to remind students about those things they need to know.
- Check their understanding of the 'Get ready' box, possibly with real fruit.

Main teaching and learning

- Remind students that a letter (variable) is used to replace a number.
- Teach them to use expressions such as $x + 2$ or $x - 3$ when adding or subtracting from the letter.
- Teach them to use expressions such as $3 \times a$ when multiplying by a number.
- Teach them to use expressions such as $a \div 2$ or $\frac{a}{2}$ when dividing by a number.

Common misconceptions

- If you buy x bags of sweets at 20p each the total cost is $20x$ pence. You do not use the p from pence in the expression.
- Remember that you can only add and subtract the same variables (letters).

Don't forget d means $1d$.

Plenary

- Eggs are sold in boxes of six at 90p each and boxes of 12 at 160p each. Peter buys s boxes of 6 eggs and t boxes of 12 eggs. *How many eggs does he buy altogether? What is the total cost?* ($6s + 12t$, $90s + 160t$ pence)

Section 4.1 Using letters to represent numbers

Guided practice worksheet

F

1 Find these.

a $b + b$ ....

b $c + c + c + c + c$ ....

c $2a + 3a$ ....

d $a + 3a$ ....

e $7c - 2c$ ....

f $4p - p$ ....

g $6t + 2t$ ....

h $10m - m$ ....

i $20K - 10K$ ....

> Think of 2 apples plus 3 apples

> Remember that a is the same as $1a$

> Think about 4 pineapples minus 1 pineapple

2 Use algebra to write:

> Use + for plus, sum, more than, added, increased.
> Use – for minus, less than, fewer than, decreased

a t plus 5 ....

b e minus 7 ....

c 1 more than x ....

d s decreased by 5 ....

e y and 2 added together ....

f 3 fewer than g ....

> Careful which way around you write this

g the sum of d and 40 ....

h 5 less than m ....

i P increased by 99 ....

3 a There are s Smarties in a packet. Jason ate 10.

How many are left? ....

> A box contains b bolts and some matching nuts. There are 5 fewer nuts than bolts. How many nuts are there?
> '5 fewer than' means 'take away 5' which can be written – 5.
> So the number of nuts = number of bolts – 5
> $= b - 5$

b Sanjit is y years old. His brother Jamil is 2 years older.

How old is Jamil? ....

c Kit boiled an egg for k minutes. Pat boiled his egg for 1 minute less.

How long did Pat spend boiling his egg? ....

d Maria received m text messages yesterday and 4 today. How many did she receive altogether?

....

e Yuk Wah made a bracelet using m red and n blue beads. How many beads did she use? ....

f Jay charged his mobile phone with t minutes of talk time. He made calls lasting c minutes. How many minutes of talk time were left on his phone? ....

39A

Section 4.1 Using letters to represent numbers

Guided practice worksheet

F

4 a Ping pong balls are sold in packs of 3.

> 5 lots of d things is written $5d$

How many balls are there in n packs? ....

b A spider has 8 legs. How many legs do m spiders have? ....

c Manku's car petrol tank holds f litres. He used 5 full tanks on a holiday. How much petrol did he use?

....

E

d A unit of electricity costs 18 pence in the daytime and 5 pence in the night time. In one month, the Bronson family used d daytime units and n night time units of electricity. What is the cost in pence of the electricity they used?

....

e A teaspoon holds 5 ml and a dessert spoon holds 10 ml. Terry mixes b teaspoons of blackcurrant juice and a dessertspoons of apple juice together. How much juice did she mix?

....

f Farhat has 5 Maths lessons and 6 English lessons each week. A Maths lesson lasts m minutes and an English lesson lasts e minutes. How much time each week does she spend in Maths and English classes?

....

g Jane has x 5p coins and y 20p coins. What is the total value of these coins, in pence? ....

39B

Specification

GCSE 2010
A b Distinguish in meaning between the words 'equation', 'formula' and 'expression'

FS Process skills
Select the mathematical information to use

FS Performance
Level 2 Identify the situation or problems and identify the mathematical methods needed to solve them

Resources

Links
http://www.mathsisfun.com/algebra/index.html

4.2 Understanding variables, terms and expressions

Concepts and skills

- Write an expression.

Functional skills

- L2 Understand and use simple formulae and equations involving one- and two-step operations.

Prior key knowledge, skills and concepts

- Students should be able to use letters to represent numbers.

Starter

- Use Get ready to check understanding of section 4.1.

Main teaching and learning

- Explain that a letter in algebra is a variable, e.g. x, y, p.
- Explain that terms are made up from variables, e.g. $3x$, $4y$, $6p$.
- Ask the questions below, writing students' responses on the board.
  There is a car park which is full. There are 12 rows of cars in the car park and each row contains the same number of cars. We don't know how many cars are in each row. How can we write down the total number of cars in the car park?
  If 5 more cars enter the full car park and double park, how many cars are there in the car park?
  If c cars leave, how many cars will there be?

  There are x people in a cinema. Each pays £6 for a ticket. How much money has been paid in total?
- Explain that expressions are made up from terms or variables e.g. $x + y$, $3p - 4q$.
  How many terms are in the following expressions? What are the terms? (Make sure students include the + or – sign.)
  $2x + y - 4z$; $a - 56b + 9c - 6$; $4p - q + 3r + 27$
  If a school stationery set contains a pens and b pencils and a parent buys three sets at the start of the year, what expression would we write down to describe how many pens have they bought? How many terms are in this expression?
  What are the terms?
  Does it matter what order the terms are in? Why not?
  Rewrite the expression, reversing the terms. *Do we need a plus or a minus in front of the first term?*

  If a box of chocolates contains a hard centres and b soft centres and Janine eats three soft centres, what expression would describe how many soft centre chocolates are left?
  If the box originally had 6 hard centres and 10 soft centres, what expression would tell us how many of each type of chocolate are left?
  Work out the value of each of these expressions if $x = 3$ and $y = 5$
  $2x + 4y$; $5x - y - 10$; $x + y - 8$; $6x - 3y + 4$

Common misconceptions

- $6x - x = 5x$. The answer is not 6.
- x on its own means $1x$.

Plenary

- Check that students understand the difference between a variable, a term and an expression by giving them a selection to choose from e.g. $x, y, p, 3x, 4y, 6p, x + y, 3p - 4q$.

algebra term expression

Guided practice worksheet

> Remember that variables are always letters

1 Write down the letters that are variables in these expressions.

a $9p - 3r$ .... b $2 + 4b$ ....

c $s + 3t$ .... d $a + b + c$ ....

e $7d + 3p$ .... f $2m + 3n + 5t$ ....

g $2p - 8k$ .... h $7 + 2d - 5g$ ....

2 Write down the terms in these expressions.

> Remember that *terms* are separated by + or – signs. They can be letters, numbers or both

a $4m + 2y$ .... b $7p + 4$ ....

c $a + b$ .... d $9 + 3t$ ....

e $4 + 2d + 4e$ .... f $3W + 2X + 3C$ ....

3 Write down the terms in these expressions.

> $5m - 2y$ has the two terms $5m$ and $-2y$. Remember to write down the – sign of the negative term

a $4a - 2b$ .... b $w - 3s$ ....

c $12m - 10$ .... d $4 - 4j$ ....

e $2a + 2b - 2c$ .... f $8f - 2k + 3d$ ....

g $2a + 2b - 10$ .... h $8g - h - 2i$ ....

i $3q - 6 + 5k$ .... j $2n + 2 - 3n$ ....

4 Make two different expressions using the following terms together with + and – signs.

> $2y$ and t. First expression could be $2y + t$. Second expression could be $t - 2y$

a a and k .... b $2f$ and $3t$ ....

c 4 and $2e$ .... d a, b and c ....

e $5t$, $3u$ and $8v$ .... f 9, s and $3r$ ....

g $5y$, $3y$ and y ....

5 Write down the terms in these expressions.

> Remember: a term can have several letters and numbers; for example, $3mn$, gh, $5t$, b are all terms. A term can also contain powers; for example, x^2, $5t^2$, b^3

a $ab + 2d$ .... b $2pq + 4tf$ ....

c $5m + 3mn$ .... d $2d - 5ef$ ....

e $x^2 + y^2$ .... f $3c^2 - 2d$ ....

g $4rs + t^3$ .... h $k^2 + 4k - 2ks$ ....

F

Guided practice worksheet

6 Make four different terms by choosing some of the numbers, variables, + and – signs in question 1.

> Using $9p - 3r$ we can make these new terms: $9r$, $3p$, $-9p$, $3r$, pr, $-pr$, $3pr$, $-3pr$, $9pr$, $-9pr$, p^2, $4r^2$, p^3, etc.

....

....

....

....

Specification

GCSE 2010
A c (part) Manipulate algebraic expressions by collecting like terms….

FS Process skills
Use appropriate mathematical procedures

FS Performance
Level 2 Use appropriate checking procedures and evaluate their effectiveness at each stage

4.3 Collecting like terms

Concepts and skills

- Manipulate algebraic expressions by collecting like terms.

Functional skills

- L2 Understand and use simple formulae and equations involving one- and two-step operations.

Prior key knowledge, skills and concepts

- Students should be able to distinguish between variables, expressions and terms.

Starter

- Write questions from 'Get ready' on board and ask students to answer them in their books.
- Check answers to make sure they can cope with the harder examples to follow.
- *What is* $2a + 3a + b$*?* ($5a + b$) Make sure that students realise that there are no terms in ab.

Main teaching and learning

- Explain Example 8 in the Student Book. Simplify $2a + 7b + 5a - 2b$. ($7a + 5b$)
- Tell students to try Exercise 4G. Give them the answers to the first five questions after a couple of minutes.
- Explain Example 9, $2a + 7b + 9 + 5a - 2b - 6$. Make sure that students realise that the numbers are treated as separate entities.
- Explain Example 10. Simplify $2a^2 + 5ab + 3a^2 - 3ab$. ($5a^2 + 2ab$) Make sure that students realise that the powers of the same variable are treated as separate entities before doing Exercise 4I.
- Explain that sometimes one can have negative answers and that $2a - 5a = -3a$.

Common misconceptions

- $3x - x = 2x$ and not 3.
- $4p + 5p^2 = 4p + 5p^2$ and not $9p^2$ or $9p^3$
- $2ab$ and $2a + 2b$ are not the same.

Enrichment

- Tell students to check their understanding by doing Exercise 4J.

Plenary

- Check students' understanding by asking them to simplify these.
  - $3a + 5b + 4a - 2b$ ($7a + 3b$)
  - $6p + 7 - p - 5$ ($5p + 2$)
  - $2a + 2b + 2 + 5a - 5b - 6$ ($7a - 3b - 4$)
  - $5x^2 + 2y^3 - 2x^2 - 4y^3$ ($3x^2 - 2y^3$)

simplify like terms

Guided practice worksheet

F

Simplify the following expressions.

Remember: p is the same as $1p$

1 $p + p + p$ is the same as $1p + 1p + 1p$ which add up to $3p$

a $d + d + d$ ....   b $s + s + s + s + s + s$ ....

2 $4r + 2r = 6r$ (because $4 + 2 = 6$)

a $7k + k$ ....   b $9a - 6a$ ....   c $8r - r$ ....

d $8w - 7w$ ....   e $4h + 3h + 2h$ ....

k is the same as $1k$

E

3 $7m - 2m + 4m = 9m$ (because $7 - 2 + 4 = 9$)

a $8v + 2v - 3v$ ....   b $6d - d + 3d$ ....   c $5q + 2q - q$ ....

4
$3a + 2a + 5p - p$ (combine like terms only)
$= 5a + 4p$ (you cannot combine these unlike terms; think of these as 5 apples plus 4 pears)

a $4t + 2t + 7y + 2y$ ....   b $5a - 2a + 9g - 3g$ ....

c $7u + u + 4b - b$ ....   d $h + 3h + i + 2i$ ....

e $9m - m + 6t - t$ ....   f $6y - 5y + x + 3x$ ....

5
$7y + 5r - 2y + 3r$ (identify like terms)
$= 7y - 2y + 5r + 3r$ (collect like terms together, with their signs)
$= 5y + 8r$ (combine like terms)

a $5m + 6j + 2m + 3j$ b $2h + 3i + 2i + h$

c $7s + 4t - 3s + 2t$ d $9u + 5g - 7u - 2g$

e $6t + 2t + 4 + 3$ f $6 + 2k + 9f - k - 7f$

+4 and +3 are like terms

+6 is unlike the other terms

Guided practice worksheet

E

6
$3d - 7d = -4d$ (because $3 - 7 = -4$)

$2t + 3r - 6t - 4r$
$= 2t - 6t + 3r - 4r$ (collect like terms together)
$= -4t - r$ (combine like terms)

a $x - 4x$ b $4y - 6y - 2y$

c $-6t + 2t$ d $2m - 8m + 6x - x$

e $5g + 2f - 2g - 6f$ f $d + e - 5d - 5e$

D

7
$5x^2 + 2fd - 2x^2 + 3fd$
$= 5x^2 - 2x^2 + 2fd + 3fd$ (collect like terms)
$= 3x^2 + 5fd$ (combine like terms)

a $7ab - 10ab$ b $5x^2 + 2x^2 + 4mn - 2mn$

c $2pq + 4ef + 5pq - ef$ d $3x^2 + 2y^2 + 4x^2 + 3y^2$

e $2u^2 + 3u + 4u^2 - u$ f $5mn + 2m^2 - 4mn - 4m^2$

g $3x^2 + 4x + 5 + 2x^2 - x$

Hint u^2 and u are unlike terms.

Specification

GCSE 2010

A a Distinguish the different roles played by letter symbols in algebra, using the correct notation

A c (part) Manipulate algebraic expressions…

FS Process skills

Use appropriate mathematical procedures

FS Performance

Level 2 Use appropriate checking procedures and evaluate their effectiveness at each stage

Resources

ActiveTeach resources

Simplifying expressions quiz 1

4.4 Multiplying with numbers and letters
4.5 Dividing with numbers and letters

Concepts and skills

- Use notation and symbols correctly.
- Manipulate algebraic expressions….
- Write expressions using squares and cubes.

Functional skills

- L2 Understand and use simple formulae and equations involving one- and two-step operations.

Prior key knowledge, skills and concepts

- Students should be able to collect like terms.

Starter

- Check that students know multiplication tables up to 10 × 10.
- *What is 5 × 7?* (35) *How many times does 8 go into 72?* (9)
- *What numbers go into 12 and 18 exactly?* (2, 3 and 6)
- *Write these fractions in their simplest form* $\frac{8}{12}, \frac{12}{9}, \frac{10}{15}$. $\left(\frac{2}{3}, \frac{4}{3}, \frac{2}{3}\right)$

Main teaching and learning

- Explain that $a \times b = ab$ and $2a \times 3b = 2 \times 3 \times a \times b = 6ab$.
  - *How do we write* $3xm$ *in its simplest form? So how would we write* $a \times b$*?*
  - *How would we write* $a \times b \times c$*? What other acceptable solutions are there?* (There are 6 ways of arranging abc. It is conventional to write in alphabetical order.)
  - *If there are* n *students in a row, how many are there in 4 rows?* ($4n$)
  - *Does it matter which way around the number and the letter go?* (Yes (even though $4xn$ and $nx4$ give the same answer))
  - *How many students are there in* m *rows?* (mn)
  - Ask students to explain how they would calculate the answer to the following: *If the total number of students in 4 rows is* $4n$*, how many are there if we double the number of students?* ($2 \times 4n = 8n$) Discuss the possible ways of working this out.
  - Repeat the question above but treble the number of students.
- Remind students that $a \times a$ is a^2 and $a \times a \times a$ is a^3.
- $\frac{16ab}{4ab} = 4a$ because the 4 cancels into the 16 and the bs cancel out as well.

Common misconceptions

- Students forget that they can only add and subtract the same variables (letters).

Plenary

- Check students' understanding by asking them to simplify these.

  $3a \times 5b$ $\quad$ $4a \times 2b$

  $6p \times 2p$ $\quad$ $2a \times 2a \times 5a$ $\quad$ $\frac{6x}{2x}$ $\quad$ $\frac{(5x \times 4x)}{10x}$

  ($15ab$, $8ab$, $12p^2$, $20a^3$, 3, $2x$)

cancelling

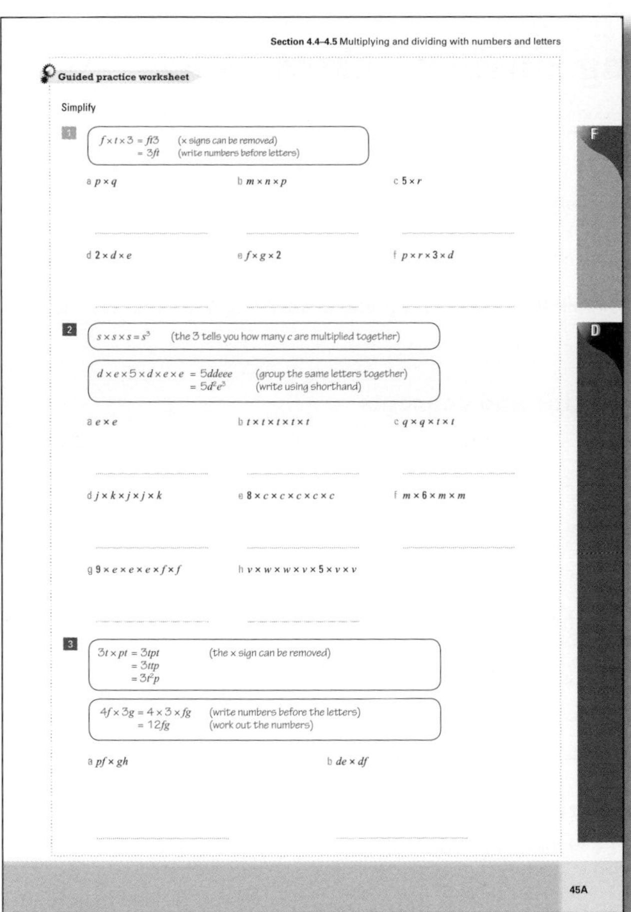

Section 4.4–4.5 Multiplying and dividing with numbers and letters

Guided practice worksheet

Simplify

1

$f \times t \times 3 = ft3$ (× signs can be removed)
$= 3ft$ (write numbers before letters)

a $p \times q$ b $m \times n \times p$ c $5 \times r$

d $2 \times d \times e$ e $f \times g \times 2$ f $p \times r \times 3 \times d$

2

$s \times s \times s = s^3$ (the 3 tells you how many c are multiplied together)

$d \times e \times 5 \times d \times e \times e = 5ddeee$ (group the same letters together)
$= 5d^2e^3$ (write using shorthand)

a $e \times e$ b $t \times t \times t \times t$ c $q \times q \times t \times t$

d $j \times k \times j \times j \times k$ e $8 \times c \times c \times c \times c \times c$ f $m \times 6 \times m \times m$

g $9 \times e \times e \times e \times f \times f$ h $v \times w \times w \times v \times 5 \times v \times v$

3

$3t \times pt = 3tpt$ (the × sign can be removed)
$= 3ttp$
$= 3t^2p$

$4f \times 3g = 4 \times 3 \times fg$ (write numbers before the letters)
$= 12fg$ (work out the numbers)

a $pf \times gh$ b $de \times df$

45A

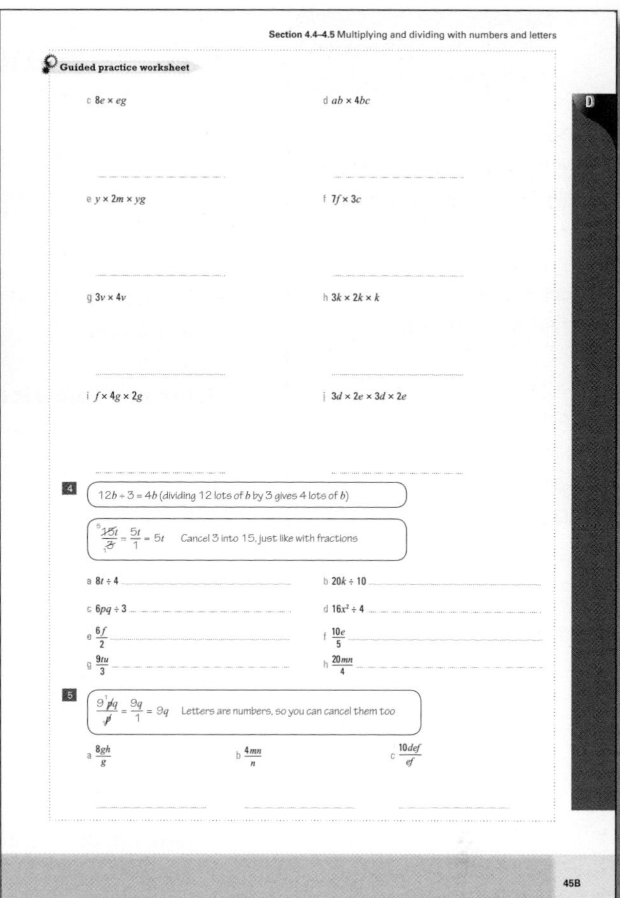

Section 4.4–4.5 Multiplying and dividing with numbers and letters

Guided practice worksheet

c $8e \times eg$ d $ab \times 4bc$

e $y \times 2m \times yg$ f $7f \times 3c$

g $3v \times 4v$ h $3k \times 2k \times k$

i $f \times 4g \times 2g$ j $3d \times 2e \times 3d \times 2e$

4

$12b \div 3 = 4b$ (dividing 12 lots of b by 3 gives 4 lots of b)

$\frac{15t}{3} = \frac{5t}{1} = 5t$ Cancel 3 into 15, just like with fractions

a $8t \div 4$ b $20k \div 10$

c $6pq \div 3$ d $16x^2 \div 4$

e $\frac{6f}{2}$ f $\frac{10e}{5}$

g $\frac{9tu}{3}$ h $\frac{20mn}{4}$

5

$\frac{9pq}{p} = \frac{9q}{1} = 9q$ Letters are numbers, so you can cancel them too

a $\frac{8gh}{g}$ b $\frac{4mn}{n}$ c $\frac{10def}{ef}$

45B

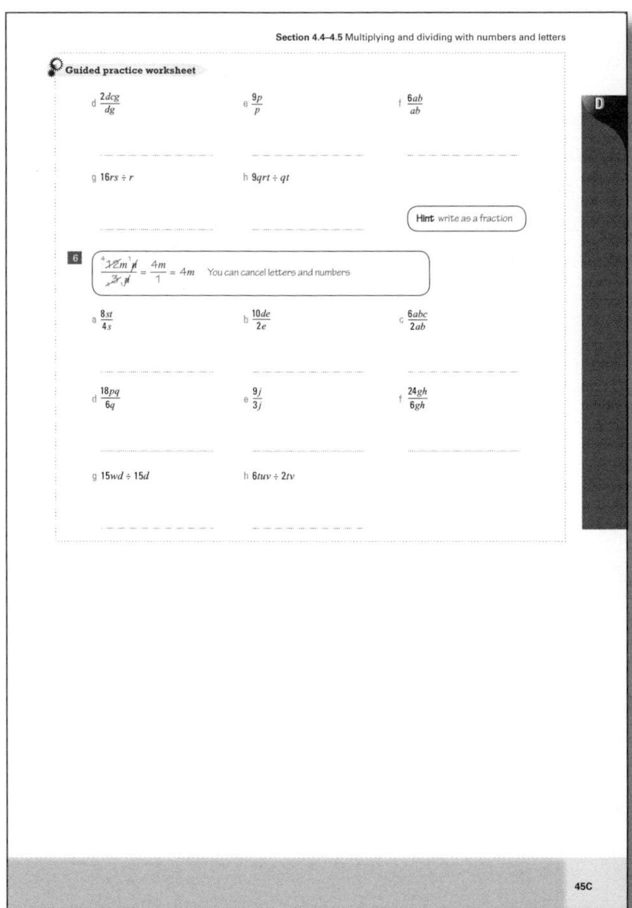

Section 4.4–4.5 Multiplying and dividing with numbers and letters

Guided practice worksheet

d $\frac{2dcg}{dg}$ e $\frac{9p}{p}$ f $\frac{6ab}{ab}$

g $16rs \div r$ h $9qrt \div qt$

Hint write as a fraction

6

$\frac{12mp}{3p} = \frac{4m}{1} = 4m$ You can cancel letters and numbers

a $\frac{8st}{4s}$ b $\frac{10de}{2e}$ c $\frac{6abc}{2ab}$

d $\frac{18pq}{6q}$ e $\frac{9j}{3j}$ f $\frac{24gh}{6gh}$

g $15wd \div 15d$ h $6tuv \div 2tv$

45C

Specification

GCSE 2010

A c Manipulate algebraic expressions by… multiplying a single term over a bracket….

FS Process skills

Use appropriate mathematical procedures

FS Performance

Level 2 Use appropriate checking procedures and evaluate their effectiveness at each stage

4.6 Expanding single brackets

Concepts and skills

- Multiply a single algebraic term over a bracket.

Functional skills

- L2 Understand and use simple formulae and equations involving one- and two-step operations.

Prior key knowledge, skills and concepts

- Students need to know that:
  - $a \times b = ab$ and $2a \times 3b = 2 \times 3 \times a \times b = 6ab$
  - $a \times a$ is a^2 and $a \times 2 = 2a$.

Starter

- *Complete the table to find what happens when you double $2a + 3$.*

×	$2a$		3		
2	a	a	1	1	1

Main teaching and learning

- Teach students that $2(3a + 6)$ means $2 \times (3a + 6)$. You multiply everything inside the bracket by the 2.
- Work on Exercise 4N.
- Teach students that $a(2a + 5)$ means $a \times (2a + 5)$. You multiply everything inside the bracket by the a.
- Work on Exercise 4O followed by Exercise 4P.

Common misconceptions

- $2(3a + 6) = 6a + 12$. Many students multiply only the first term.

Enrichment

- Explain, using this rectangle, why $3(2x + 5) = 6x + 15$.

$2x + 5$

3

Plenary

- Check understanding of this topic and the previous one on collection of like terms by asking students to simplify expressions such as $2(4a + 3) + 3(2a - 1)$. $(14a + 3)$

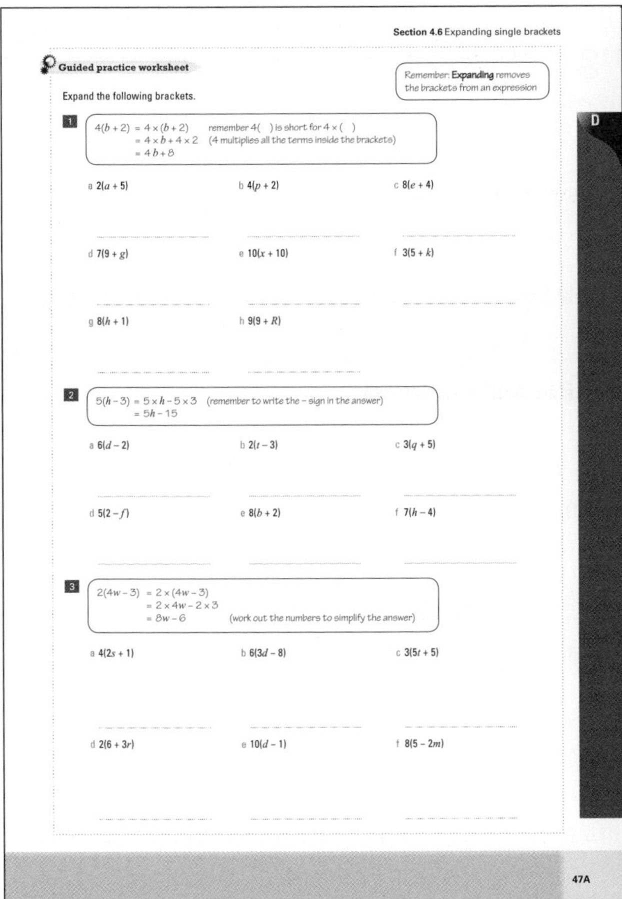

Guided practice worksheet

Remember: **Expanding** removes the brackets from an expression

Expand the following brackets.

D

1

$4(b+2) = 4 \times (b+2)$ remember 4( ) is short for 4 × ( )
$= 4 \times b + 4 \times 2$ (4 multiplies all the terms inside the brackets)
$= 4b + 8$

a $2(a+5)$ b $4(p+2)$ c $8(e+4)$

d $7(9+g)$ e $10(x+10)$ f $3(5+k)$

g $8(h+1)$ h $9(9+R)$

2

$5(h-3) = 5 \times h - 5 \times 3$ (remember to write the – sign in the answer)
$= 5h - 15$

a $6(d-2)$ b $2(t-3)$ c $3(q+5)$

d $5(2-f)$ e $8(b+2)$ f $7(h-4)$

3

$2(4w-3) = 2 \times (4w-3)$
$= 2 \times 4w - 2 \times 3$
$= 8w - 6$ (work out the numbers to simplify the answer)

a $4(2s+1)$ b $6(3d-8)$ c $3(5t+5)$

d $2(6+3r)$ e $10(d-1)$ f $8(5-2m)$

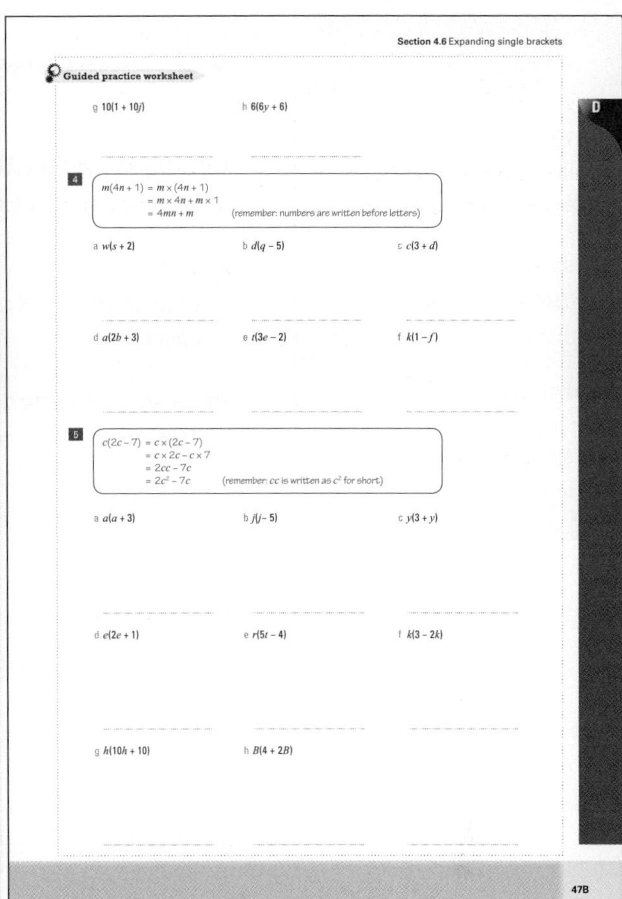

Guided practice worksheet

D

g $10(1+10j)$ h $6(6y+6)$

4

$m(4n+1) = m \times (4n+1)$
$= m \times 4n + m \times 1$
$= 4mn + m$ (remember: numbers are written before letters)

a $w(s+2)$ b $d(q-5)$ c $c(3+d)$

d $a(2b+3)$ e $t(3e-2)$ f $k(1-f)$

5

$c(2c-7) = c \times (2c-7)$
$= c \times 2c - c \times 7$
$= 2cc - 7c$
$= 2c^2 - 7c$ (remember: cc is written as c^2 for short)

a $a(a+3)$ b $j(j-5)$ c $y(3+y)$

d $e(2e+1)$ e $r(5t-4)$ f $k(3-2k)$

g $h(10h+10)$ h $B(4+2B)$

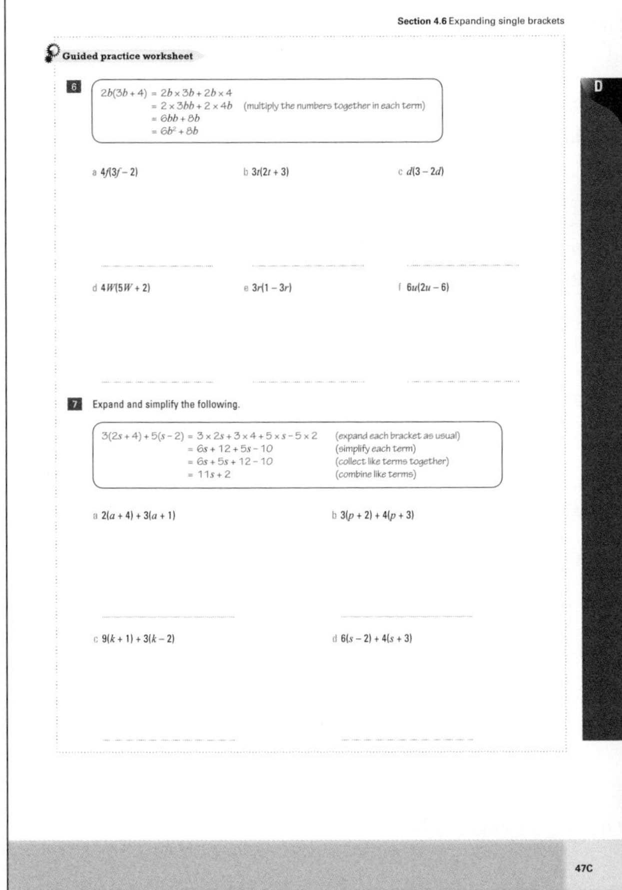

Guided practice worksheet

D

6

$2b(3b+4) = 2b \times 3b + 2b \times 4$
$= 2 \times 3bb + 2 \times 4b$ (multiply the numbers together in each term)
$= 6bb + 8b$
$= 6b^2 + 8b$

a $4f(3f-2)$ b $3t(2t+3)$ c $d(3-2d)$

d $4W(5W+2)$ e $3r(1-3r)$ f $6u(2u-6)$

7 Expand and simplify the following.

$3(2s+4) + 5(s-2) = 3 \times 2s + 3 \times 4 + 5 \times s - 5 \times 2$ (expand each bracket as usual)
$= 6s + 12 + 5s - 10$ (simplify each term)
$= 6s + 5s + 12 - 10$ (collect like terms together)
$= 11s + 2$ (combine like terms)

a $2(a+4) + 3(a+1)$ b $3(p+2) + 4(p+3)$

c $9(k+1) + 3(k-2)$ d $6(s-2) + 4(s+3)$

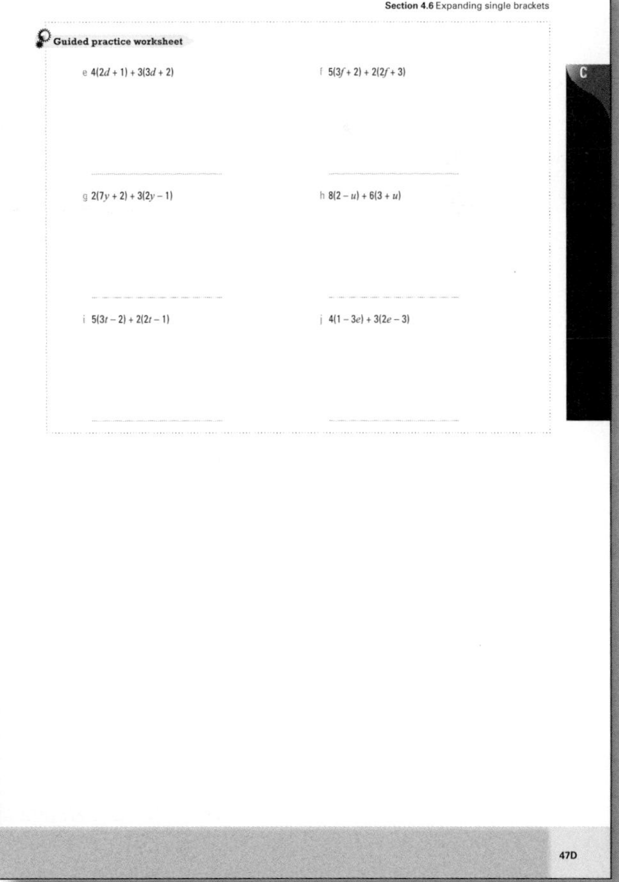

Guided practice worksheet

C

e $4(2d+1) + 3(3d+2)$ f $5(3f+2) + 2(2f+3)$

g $2(7y+2) + 3(2y-1)$ h $8(2-u) + 6(3+u)$

i $5(3t-2) + 2(2t-1)$ j $4(1-3e) + 3(2e-3)$

Specification

GCSE 2010
A c Manipulate algebraic expressions by… taking out common factors

FS Process skills
Use appropriate mathematical procedures

FS Performance
Level 2 Use appropriate checking procedures and evaluate their effectiveness at each stage

Resources

ActiveTeach resources
Simplifying expressions quiz 2

4.7 Factorising

Concepts and skills

- Factorise algebraic expressions by taking out common factors.

Functional skills

- L2 Understand and use simple formulae and equations involving one- and two-step operations.

Prior key knowledge, skills and concepts

- Students should know that:
  - $2(3a + 6)$ means $2 \times (3a + 6)$. You multiply everything inside the bracket by the 2.
  - 2, 3 and 6 divide exactly into 12 and 18.
  - 2, 3 and 6 are common factors of 12 and 18.

Starter

- *Write down the factors of 6 and 8. What is the common factor?* (1, 2, 3, 6; 1, 2, 4, 8; 1 and 2)
- *Write down the factors of 8 and 12. What are the common factors?* (1, 2, 4, 8; 1, 2, 3, 4, 6, 12; 1, 2 and 4)
- *Write down the factors of $2a$ and $5a$. What is the common factor?* (1, 2, a; $2a$; $5a$ and a)
- *Write down the factors of a and a^2. What is the common factor?* (1, a, 1, a; a^2; 1 and a)

Main teaching and learning

- Teach students to realise that 2 is a common factor in $2x$ and 6, so that $2x + 6 = 2(x + 3)$.
  - Ask the class to multiply out $2(x + 3)$ ($= 2x + 6$) and explain that writing $2x + 6$ as $2(x + 3)$ is called factorising.
  - Explain that factorising is the opposite process to multiplying out brackets.
  - Ask the class to factorise $2x + 10$.You may need to ask *What is the highest common factor of 2 and 10?*
  - Write $2x + 10 = 2 \times x + 2 \times 5$.
  - *How can this be written more simply by using brackets?* (Lower attainers may be more successful if they cover up the common '2×'.)
  - Check that $2(x + 5) = 2x + 10$ by multiplying out brackets.
- Try Exercise 4Q.
- Teach students to realise that a is a common factor in a^2 and $3a$, so that $a^2 + 3a = a(a + 3)$.
- Try Exercise 4R.
- Teach students to realise that $2a$ is a common factor in $2a^2$ and $6a$, so that $2a^2 + 6a = 2a(a + 3)$.
- Try Exercise 4S.

Common misconceptions

- $2a^2 + 6a = 2a(a + 3)$ is factorised fully.
- $2a^2 + 6a = 2(a^2 + 3a)$ and $a(2a + 6)$ are not fully factorised.

Plenary

- Check understanding by asking students to factorise:

  $3p + 6$ $\quad$ $p^2 + 2p$ $\quad$ $3p^2 + 6p$.

  ($3(p + 2)$, $p(p + 2)$, $3p(p + 2)$)

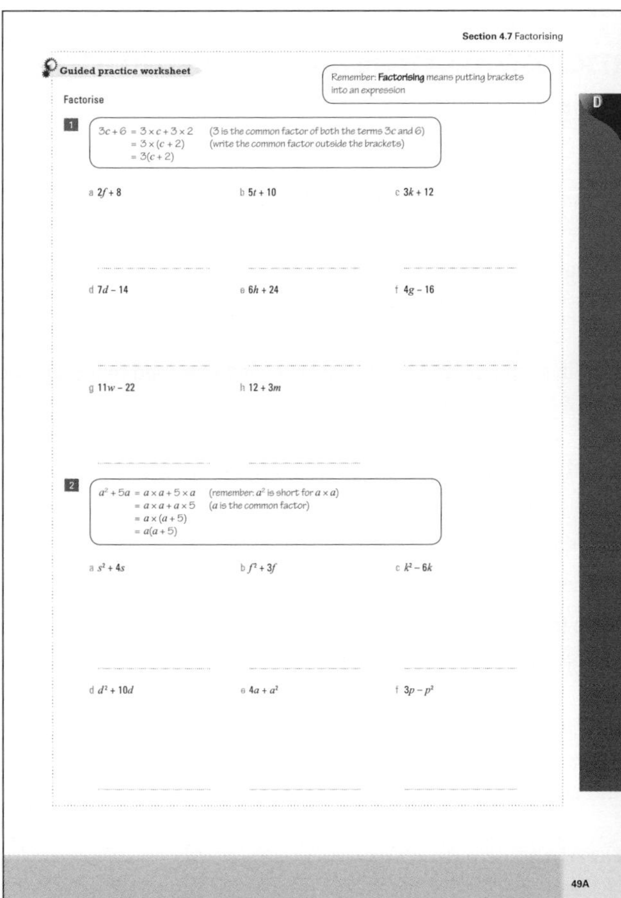

Guided practice worksheet

Remember: **Factorising** means putting brackets into an expression

Factorise

1

$3c + 6 = 3 \times c + 3 \times 2$ (3 is the common factor of both the terms 3c and 6)
$= 3 \times (c + 2)$ (write the common factor outside the brackets)
$= 3(c + 2)$

a $2f + 8$ b $5t + 10$ c $3k + 12$

d $7d - 14$ e $6h + 24$ f $4g - 16$

g $11w - 22$ h $12 + 3m$

2

$a^2 + 5a = a \times a + 5 \times a$ (remember: a^2 is short for $a \times a$)
$= a \times a + a \times 5$ (a is the common factor)
$= a \times (a + 5)$
$= a(a + 5)$

a $s^2 + 4s$ b $f^2 + 3f$ c $k^2 - 6k$

d $d^2 + 10d$ e $4a + a^2$ f $3p - p^2$

D

49A

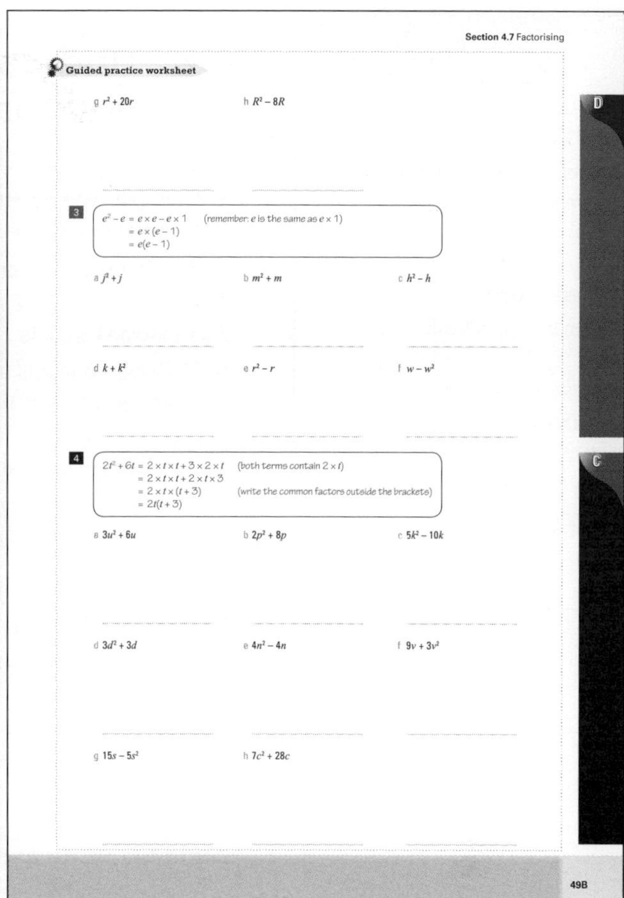

Guided practice worksheet

g $r^2 + 20r$ h $R^2 - 8R$

3

$e^2 - e = e \times e - e \times 1$ (remember: e is the same as $e \times 1$)
$= e \times (e - 1)$
$= e(e - 1)$

a $j^2 + j$ b $m^2 + m$ c $h^2 - h$

d $k + k^2$ e $r^2 - r$ f $w - w^2$

4

$2t^2 + 6t = 2 \times t \times t + 3 \times 2 \times t$ (both terms contain $2 \times t$)
$= 2 \times t \times t + 2 \times t \times 3$
$= 2 \times t \times (t + 3)$ (write the common factors outside the brackets)
$= 2t(t + 3)$

a $3u^2 + 6u$ b $2p^2 + 8p$ c $5k^2 - 10k$

d $3d^2 + 3d$ e $4n^2 - 4n$ f $9v + 3v^2$

g $15s - 5s^2$ h $7c^2 + 28c$

D C

49B

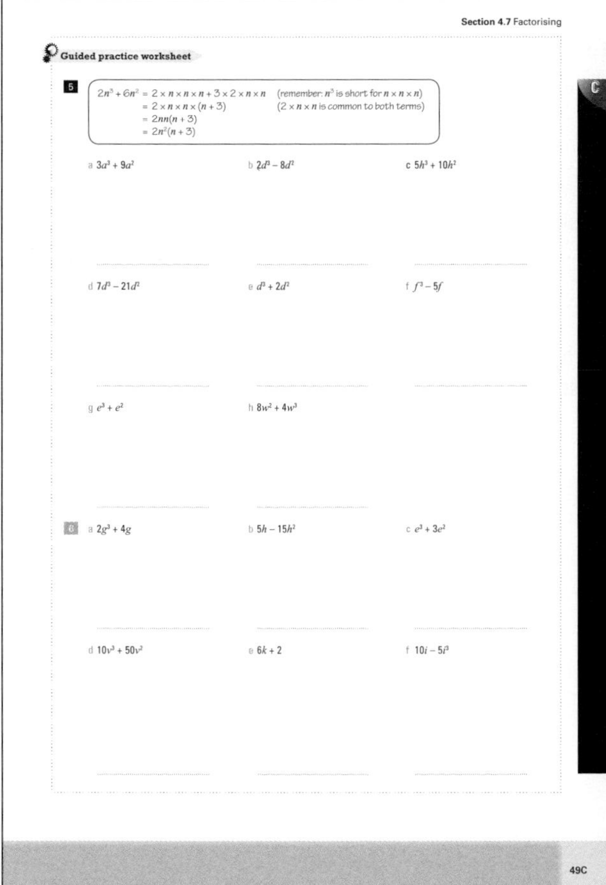

Guided practice worksheet

5

$2n^3 + 6n^2 = 2 \times n \times n \times n + 3 \times 2 \times n \times n$ (remember: n^3 is short for $n \times n \times n$)
$= 2 \times n \times n \times (n + 3)$ ($2 \times n \times n$ is common to both terms)
$= 2nn(n + 3)$
$= 2n^2(n + 3)$

a $3a^3 + 9a^2$ b $2d^3 - 8d^2$ c $5h^3 + 10h^2$

d $7d^3 - 21d^2$ e $d^3 + 2d^2$ f $f^3 - 5f$

g $e^3 + e^2$ h $8w^2 + 4w^3$

6 a $2g^3 + 4g$ b $5h - 15h^2$ c $e^3 + 3e^2$

d $10v^3 + 50v^2$ e $6k + 2$ f $10i - 5i^3$

C

49C

Guided practice worksheet

g $12 - 6p^2$ h $4d^2 + 2d$

C

49D

GCSE 2010

A b Distinguish in meaning between the words 'equation', 'formula' and 'expression'

FS Process skills

Select the mathematical information to use

FS Performance

Level 2 Identify the situation or problems and identify the mathematical methods needed to solve them

4.8 Understanding expressions, equations and formulae

Concepts and skills

- Write an expression.
- Select an expression/equation/formula from a list.

Functional skills

- L2 Understand and use simple formulae and equations involving one- and two-step operations.

Prior key knowledge, skills and concepts

- Students need to know that:
  - a letter in algebra is a variable, e.g. x, y, p
  - terms are made up from variables, e.g. $3x$, $4y$, $6p$
  - expressions are made up from terms or variables, e.g. $x + y$, $3p - 4q$.

Starter

- Draw three circles on the board and label them variable, term and expression. Give students the variables, terms and expressions from the prior knowledge list and ask them to write them into the correct circle. (By inspection.)

Main teaching and learning

- Explain the difference between expressions, identities, equations and formulae.
- Go through Example 23.
- Work on Exercise 4T.

Common misconceptions

- Identities, equations and formulae all have equals signs in them.

Enrichment

- Play a game: Working in pairs write a variable, a term, an expression, an identity, an equation or a formula and ask your partner to say what it is. The winner is the first one to get 10 correct.

Plenary

- Draw six circles on the board and label them variable, term, expression, identity, equation and formula. Give students some variables, terms, expressions, identities, equations and formulae and ask them to write them into the correct circle. (By inspection.)

identity equation formula

Guided practice worksheet

F

> Remember: An **expression** is a collection of terms. It does not contain an = sign

1 Which of the following are expressions?

a $2p + d$ ....

b $x = 5$ ....

c $9f^2 + 2f - 3$ ....

d $\frac{1}{4}w - 4$ ....

e $4p + 5p = 9p$ ....

f $3x$ ....

g $2 + 2 = 4$ ....

h 99 ....

D

> Remember: An **identity** looks like this: expression = expression
> For example: $2p + 3p = p + 4p$

2 Describe each of the following as an expression or an identity

a $9w - 4w$ ....

b $3g - g = 4g - 2g$ ....

c $8(s + t) = 8s + 8t$ ....

d $3x^2 - 2x + 1$ ....

e $2h - 2h = 0$ ....

f $f^3 = 4f^3 - 3f^3$ ....

g $2(e + 1) - e - 2$ ....

> Remember: A **formula** shows how one variable (letter) can be calculated using other variables.
> It looks like: letter = expression involving other letters
> For example: $P = 2a + 2b$

3 Describe each of the following as an expression, formula or identity.

a $v = u + at$ ....

b $5g + 2h = 3g + 2(g + h)$ ....

c $2a + 2b$ ....

d $vi = 6vi - 5vi$ ....

e $w = vi$ ....

f $G = 4G - 3G$ ....

g $u - \frac{1}{2}at^2$ ....

h $ma = F$ ....

Section 4.8 Understanding expressions, equations and formulae

Guided practice worksheet

D

> Remember: An **equation** looks like an identity but is only true for certain values of the variable (letter)
> For example: $2p = 6$ is an equation because it is only true when $p = 3$
> $2p = p + p$ is an identity because it is true for all values of p

4 Describe each of the following as an equation or an identity.

a $8t = 2t + 6t$ ....

b $7s = 14$ ....

c $w + 4 = 6$ ....

d $r + 2 = 2r - r + 2$ ....

e $q - q = 0$ ....

f $f \div 4 = 3$ ....

g $3d - 2 = 1$ ....

h $c = c$ ....

5 Describe each of the following as an expression, identity, formula or equation.

a $C = 2\pi r$ ....

b $4m = 8$ ....

c $a + b + 2a$ ....

d $4t + 5 = 2t + 2t + 5$ ....

e $n - 5 = 10$ ....

f $b = 2s^2$ ....

g $3(t - 1) = 3t - 3$ ....

h $4(2x + 3)$ ....

i $c = \sqrt{a^2 + b^2}$ ....

j $10 = 2e + 6$ ....

Specification

GCSE 2010
A c Manipulate algebraic expressions …

FS Process skills
Find results and solutions

FS Performance
Level 2 Use appropriate checking procedures and evaluate their effectiveness at each stage

Resources

Links
http://www.bbc.co.uk/education/mathsfile/shockwave/games/postie.html

ActiveTeach resources
RP KC Algebra 1 knowledge check
RP PS Algebric expressions 1 problem solving

Follow up
Chapter 9: Algebra 2

4.9 Replacing letters with numbers

Concepts and skills

The bullet below is not taken from the Specification but builds towards the other bullets in A c

- Substitute numbers into an expression.

Functional skills

- L2 Understand and use simple formulae and equations involving one- and two-step operations.

Prior key knowledge, skills and concepts

- Times tables from 1 to 9.
- Always work out the brackets first.
- $c^2 = c \times c$.

Starter

- Complete these times tables:

×	2	5
3	(6)	(15)
6	(12)	(30)

×	4	7
2	(8)	(14)
9	(36)	(63)

- Work out:
  (i) 2(7 – 5) (4)
  (ii) 3(5 + 4) (27)
  (iii) 5(5 – 1) (20)
- What are the values of 3^2, 2^3? (9, 8)

Main teaching and learning

- Letters can be replaced by numbers.
- If $g = 2$ then $3g = 3 \times 2$, since $3g$ means $3 \times g$ or $g + g + g$ or $2 + 2 + 2 = 6$.
- If $x = 7$ then $3(x - 5) = 3(7 - 5)$. Deal with the brackets first, then $3 \times 2 = 6$.

Common misconceptions

- If $g = 5$ then $3g = 3 \times 5$ or 15 and not 35.

Enrichment

- What happens if you put $c = 5$ into:
  (i) $3c$ (15) (ii) $3(c + 2)$ (21) (iii) c^2 (25)
  (iv) $2c^2$ (50) (v) c^c? (3125)

Plenary

- If $h = 10$ find the value of:
  (i) $3h$ (30) (ii) $3(h + 2)$ (36) (iii) $h \times h$ (100)
  (iv) $3h - 2$ (28) (v) $2 + 3h$. (32)

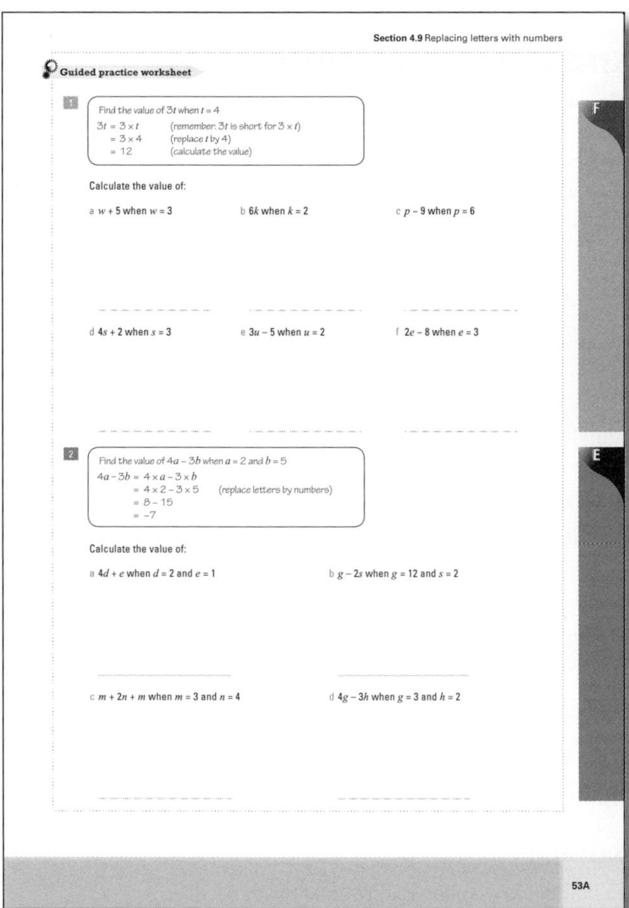

Guided practice worksheet

F

1

Find the value of $3t$ when $t = 4$

$3t = 3 \times t$ (remember: $3t$ is short for $3 \times t$)
$= 3 \times 4$ (replace t by 4)
$= 12$ (calculate the value)

Calculate the value of:

a $w + 5$ when $w = 3$ b $6k$ when $k = 2$ c $p - 9$ when $p = 6$

d $4s + 2$ when $s = 3$ e $3u - 5$ when $u = 2$ f $2e - 8$ when $e = 3$

E

2

Find the value of $4a - 3b$ when $a = 2$ and $b = 5$

$4a - 3b = 4 \times a - 3 \times b$
$= 4 \times 2 - 3 \times 5$ (replace letters by numbers)
$= 8 - 15$
$= -7$

Calculate the value of:

a $4d + e$ when $d = 2$ and $e = 1$ b $g - 2s$ when $g = 12$ and $s = 2$

c $m + 2n + m$ when $m = 3$ and $n = 4$ d $4g - 3h$ when $g = 3$ and $h = 2$

53A

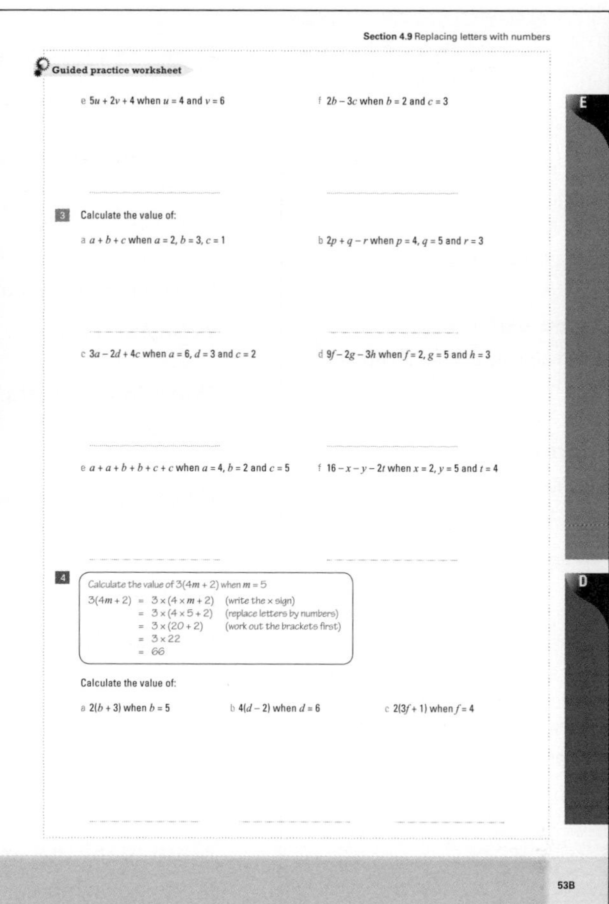

Guided practice worksheet

E

e $5u + 2v + 4$ when $u = 4$ and $v = 6$ f $2b - 3c$ when $b = 2$ and $c = 3$

3 Calculate the value of:

a $a + b + c$ when $a = 2$, $b = 3$, $c = 1$ b $2p + q - r$ when $p = 4$, $q = 5$ and $r = 3$

c $3a - 2d + 4c$ when $a = 6$, $d = 3$ and $c = 2$ d $9f - 2g - 3h$ when $f = 2$, $g = 5$ and $h = 3$

e $a + a + b + b + c + c$ when $a = 4$, $b = 2$ and $c = 5$ f $16 - x - y - 2t$ when $x = 2$, $y = 5$ and $t = 4$

D

4

Calculate the value of $3(4m + 2)$ when $m = 5$

$3(4m + 2) = 3 \times (4 \times m + 2)$ (write the × sign)
$= 3 \times (4 \times 5 + 2)$ (replace letters by numbers)
$= 3 \times (20 + 2)$ (work out the brackets first)
$= 3 \times 22$
$= 66$

Calculate the value of:

a $2(b + 3)$ when $b = 5$ b $4(d - 2)$ when $d = 6$ c $2(3f + 1)$ when $f = 4$

53B

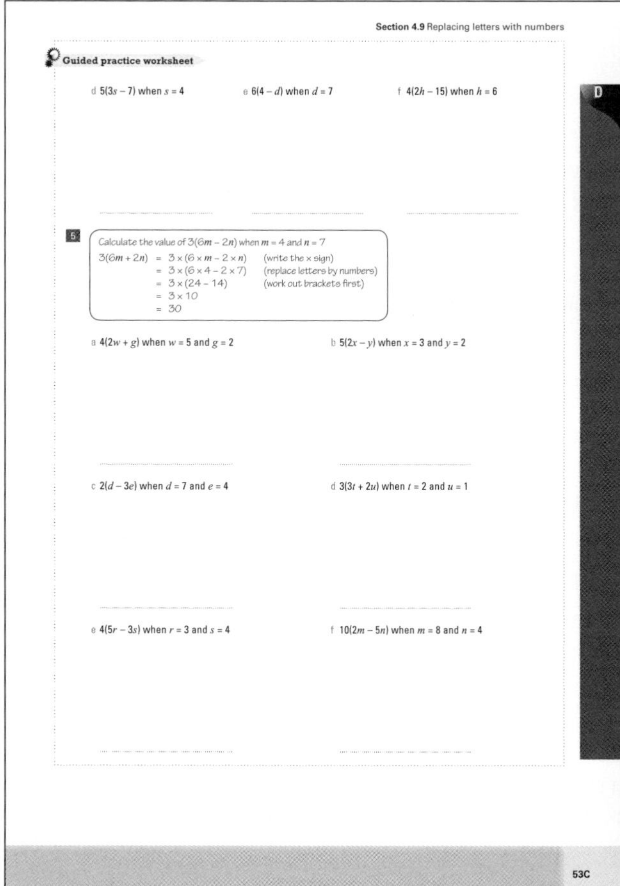

Guided practice worksheet

D

d $5(3s - 7)$ when $s = 4$ e $6(4 - d)$ when $d = 7$ f $4(2h - 15)$ when $h = 6$

5

Calculate the value of $3(6m - 2n)$ when $m = 4$ and $n = 7$

$3(6m + 2n) = 3 \times (6 \times m - 2 \times n)$ (write the × sign)
$= 3 \times (6 \times 4 - 2 \times 7)$ (replace letters by numbers)
$= 3 \times (24 - 14)$ (work out brackets first)
$= 3 \times 10$
$= 30$

a $4(2w + g)$ when $w = 5$ and $g = 2$ b $5(2x - y)$ when $x = 3$ and $y = 2$

c $2(d - 3e)$ when $d = 7$ and $e = 4$ d $3(3t + 2u)$ when $t = 2$ and $u = 1$

e $4(5r - 3s)$ when $r = 3$ and $s = 4$ f $10(2m - 5n)$ when $m = 8$ and $n = 4$

53C

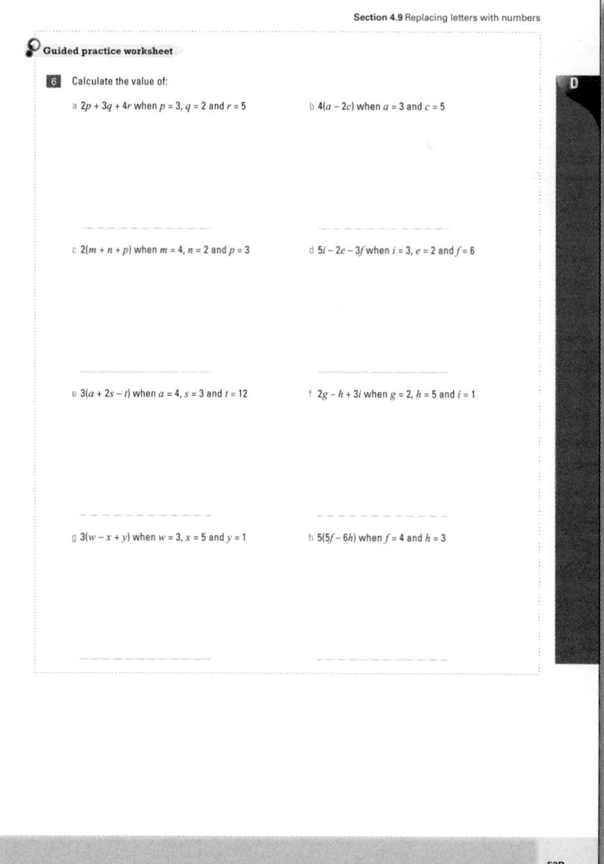

Guided practice worksheet

D

6 Calculate the value of:

a $2p + 3q + 4r$ when $p = 3$, $q = 2$ and $r = 5$ b $4(a - 2c)$ when $a = 3$ and $c = 5$

c $2(m + n + p)$ when $m = 4$, $n = 2$ and $p = 3$ d $5i - 2e - 3f$ when $i = 3$, $e = 2$ and $f = 6$

e $3(a + 2s - t)$ when $a = 4$, $s = 3$ and $t = 12$ f $2g - h + 3i$ when $g = 2$, $h = 5$ and $i = 1$

g $3(w - x + y)$ when $w = 3$, $x = 5$ and $y = 1$ h $5(5f - 6h)$ when $f = 4$ and $h = 3$

53D

Specification

GCSE 2010

N j Use decimal notation and recognise that each terminating decimal is a fraction
N b Order rational numbers

FS Process skills

Select the mathematical information to use

FS Performance

Level 1 Identify and obtain necessary information to tackle the problem

Resources

Resources

Data for plenary

Links

http://www.bbc.co.uk/schools/ks3bitesize/maths/number/index.shtml
http://nrich.maths.org/public/search.php?search=decimals

ActiveTeach resources

Decimal place value animation
Ordering numbers quiz
Ordering decimals animation

5.1 Understanding place value
5.2 Writing decimal numbers in order of size

Concepts and skills

- Understand place value.
- Identify the value of digits in a decimal or whole number.
- Order… decimals….

Functional skills

- L1 Add and subtract decimals up to two decimal places.

Prior key knowledge, skills and concepts

- Students need to know about digits and place value.

Starter

- Recap place value. Use continuous variables to establish the need for measurements between integers.
- Metres are not accurate enough, so we use centimetres.
- Centimetres are not accurate enough, so we use millimetres.
- *So how can you relate, say, 275 cm to metres?* (2.75 m)

Main teaching and learning

- You move from column to column in place value by multiplying by 10.
- Going the other way it is ÷10, so obtaining tenths, hundredths, etc.
- Extend place value to reading and writing decimals.
- Draw a number line from 4.3 to 4.5, labelled at each tenth with marks at every hundredth (i.e. marks at 4.31, 4.32 etc, but no labels). Ask students where an arrow should be placed to indicate the position of the following numbers: 4.45, 4.47, 4.31, 4.39.
- Teach students to order decimals.
- Ask students to put the following numbers in order, using a table of tens, units, tenths, hundredths and thousandths if necessary.
  1.2, 0.6, 0.9
  4.33, 4.34, 4.333, 4.3
  18.9, 18.75, 18.958, 18.98, 18.58
  0.46, 0.045, 0.446, 0.041, 0.4
  7.01, 7.003, 7.009, 7.019, 7.19
  63.4, 64.339, 64.8, 64.09, 64.89
- Encourage students to put in missing zeros when ordering and comparing decimals.

Common misconceptions

- Confusing tens with tenths and hundreds with hundredths.
- Confusing 2.35 hours with 2 hours 35 minutes and vice versa.
- 4.56 is read as 'four point fifty six' and not 'four point five six'. Saying decimals wrongly can lead to students' thinking that, for example, 4.5 is smaller than 4.23 because 5 is smaller than 23.

Plenary

- Use a context of times in sports (athletics, swimming, Formula 1, whatever is of interest to your students) and ask students to put times from races in order.

Guided practice worksheet

Make sure you know the difference between tens and tenths, hundreds and hundredths.

1 For each number write down i the tenths digit and ii the tens digit.

a 215.561

....

....

b 7476.91

....

....

c 73.21

....

....

d 103.65

....

....

e 93.4

....

....

2 For each number, say whether the underlined digit is tenths, hundredths or thousandths.

a $0.0\underline{3}67$ ....

b $0.\underline{7}83$ ....

c $0.00\underline{3}14$ ....

d $7.\underline{1}2$ ....

e $1.9\underline{0}73$ ....

3 Put these numbers in order of size. Start with the smallest.

0.32 0.4 0.093 0.317 0.326

....

4 Put these numbers in order of size. Start with the largest.

0.71 0.703 0.76 0.6993 0.714

....

GCSE 2010
N a (part) Add, subtract… any number

FS Process skills
Use appropriate mathematical procedures

FS Performance
Level 1 Apply mathematics in an organised way to find solutions to straightforward practical problems for different purposes

5.3 Adding and subtracting decimals

Concepts and skills

- Add, subtract … decimals.

Functional skills

- L1 Add and subtract decimals up to two decimal places.

Prior key knowledge, skills and concepts

- All number bonds.
- Significance of place value.

Starter

- Talk about going shopping. *How would you find the total cost of an item costing £4.95 and an item costing £1.24 (your calculator has broken!).* Discuss methods.

Main teaching and learning

- Start from the familiar integer additions and subtractions.
- Show that the same procedure applies with decimals (it might help to insert zeros to make the columns complete).
- Write the following on the board and ask students what they think the answer might be. 4.56 + 12.70, 8.00 – 6.72, 19.80 + 7.23, £10.00 – £4.95 + £2.60.
- With the class, write the numbers underneath each other on the board. Ask *Does it matter how I line the numbers up?* (Decimal points must be underneath each other.) Ask *What do you notice about the number of decimal places in the numbers in the question and those in the answer?*

Common misconceptions

- When subtracting decimals, students often don't write in zeros and consequently obtain wrong answers.
- Students often align the first digits or the last digits rather than the decimal points.

Plenary

- Give further examples like Example 6.

Guided practice worksheet

F

1 Work out:

a $\begin{array}{r} 0.3 \\ +\ 0.4 \\ \hline \end{array}$ ....

b $\begin{array}{r} 0.7 \\ +\ 0.5 \\ \hline \end{array}$ ....

c $\begin{array}{r} 2.4 \\ +\ 0.8 \\ \hline \end{array}$ ....

d $\begin{array}{r} 5.61 \\ +\ 1.47 \\ \hline \end{array}$ ....

e $\begin{array}{r} 0.379 \\ +\ 2.312 \\ \hline \end{array}$ ....

2 Work out:

a $\begin{array}{r} 0.9 \\ -\ 0.4 \\ \hline \end{array}$ ....

b $\begin{array}{r} 1.6 \\ -\ 0.7 \\ \hline \end{array}$ ....

c $\begin{array}{r} 3.1 \\ -\ 1.6 \\ \hline \end{array}$ ....

d $\begin{array}{r} 0.347 \\ -\ 0.129 \\ \hline \end{array}$ ....

e $\begin{array}{r} 0.634 \\ -\ 0.545 \\ \hline \end{array}$ ....

3 Work out:

> **Hint** Make sure the decimal points are in line so that the columns for units and tenths are in line. Fill any blank spaces with zeros (0s).

a 0.451 + 1.2 + 0.03 ....

b 3.1 + 1.907 + 0.0981 ....

c 0.031 + 0.05 + 0.0428 ....

d 2.7 + 3.670 + 1.25 ....

e 0.56 + 7.08 + 0.4 ....

f 1.92 + 2.375 + 0.008 ....

4 Work out:

a 1.8 – 0.7 ....

b 2.3 – 1.5 ....

c 0.34 – 0.2 ....

d 1.43 – 0.07 ....

e 0.923 – 0.87 ....

f 1.63 – 0.127 ....

g 0.0813 – 0.0135 ....

h 0.7 – 0.356 ....

5 Ian has £5.

He spends £1.29 on a magazine and 85p on a drink.

How much has he left? ....

Specification

GCSE 2010

N a (part) … multiply and divide any number

N d Use the terms square, positive and negative square root, cube and cube root

N q Understand and use number operations and the relationships between them, including inverse operations and hierarchy of operations

FS Process skills

Use appropriate mathematical procedures

FS Performance

Level 2 Apply a range of mathematics to find solutions

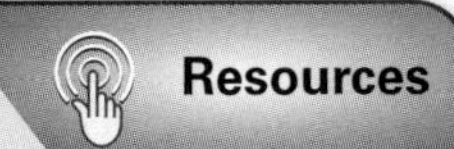

Resources

Links

http://www.bbc.co.uk/schools/gcsebitesize/maths/number/powersrootsact.shtml

5.4 Multiplying decimals
5.5 Squares and square roots, cubes and cube roots
5.6 Dividing decimals

Concepts and skills

- Add, subtract, multiply and divide whole numbers, integers, decimals, fractions and numbers in index form.
- Multiply or divide any number by powers of 10.
- Multiply or divide by any number between 0 and 1.
- Solve a problem involving division by a decimal (up to two decimal places).
- Recall integer squares up to 15 × 15 and the corresponding square roots.
- Recall the cubes of 2, 3, 4, 5 and 10.
- Find squares and cubes.
- Find square roots and cube roots.
- Multiply and divide numbers using the commutative, associative, and distributive laws and factorisation where possible, or place value adjustments.

Functional skills

- L2 Carry out calculations with numbers of any size in practical context, to a given number of decimal places.

Prior key knowledge, skills and concepts

- Place value

Starter

- Ask students to work out: 20 × 3, 2 × 30, 2 × 3, 2 × 0.3, 0.2 × 3, 0.2 × 0.3. (60, 60, 6, 0.6, 0.6, 0.06)
- Emphasise the point that multiplying by a number greater than 1 increases the value and multiplying by (a positive number) less than 1 decreases the value.

Main teaching and learning

- Teach students to multiply using the rule for total number of decimal places.
  - Ask students to say how they would multiply these numbers by ten: 5.43, 8.41, 9.002, 0.017 and write it on the board. Use column headings 'Hundreds, Tens, Units, Tenths, Hundredths' to show that the value of digits has increased by 10.
  - Repeat this exercise but now multiply these numbers by one hundred: 68.943, 0.59, 4.007, 19.02, 1.0065.
  - Ask students to say how they would multiply 3.72 and 1.4. Encourage them to ignore the decimal point. *Ask students Where do you think the decimal point would go to make this a sensible answer?* (Encourage them to use their estimating skills.)
- Teach division slowly, first with a single whole number, then progress to 2-digit whole numbers.
  - Ask students to say how they would divide these numbers by ten: 543, 841, 9002, 17 and write it on the board. Use column headings 'Hundreds, Tens, Units, Tenths, Hundredths' to show that the value of digits has decreased by 10.
  - Repeat this exercise but now divide these numbers by one hundred: 68 943, 59, 4007, 1902, 10 065.
  - Ask students to work out an estimate for the answer to each of the following before dividing: 14.5 ÷ 5, 13.96 ÷ 8, 24.9 ÷ 0.3, 19.2 ÷ 0.03, 0.048 ÷ 0.06.
  - Ask students how they might go about doing the actual division. Encourage students to ignore the decimal point at first, then ask them where they would place the decimal point in the answer.
  - Show students that dividing decimals can be made easier if both decimals are multiplied by the same power of 10. Then long division can be carried out in the usual way with the powers of 10 cancelling.
- Finally, teach dividing by a decimal (never more than 2 digits).
- Practice with the following questions
  What is the cost of 2.2 kg of potatoes at 35p per kilogram?
  What is the cost of 1.7 m of ribbon at £1.40 per metre?

Common misconceptions

- 0.2 × 0.3 = 0.06, not 0.6
- Multiplying by a number less than 1 and not getting a smaller answer is incorrect.
- When multiplying decimals, the position of the decimal point in the answer frequently causes confusion.
- Great care is needed when a calculation gives an answer that ends in a zero; it is important that this final zero is not 'lost'.

Plenary

- Ask students to explain how to divide by a decimal.

cube cube root square square root

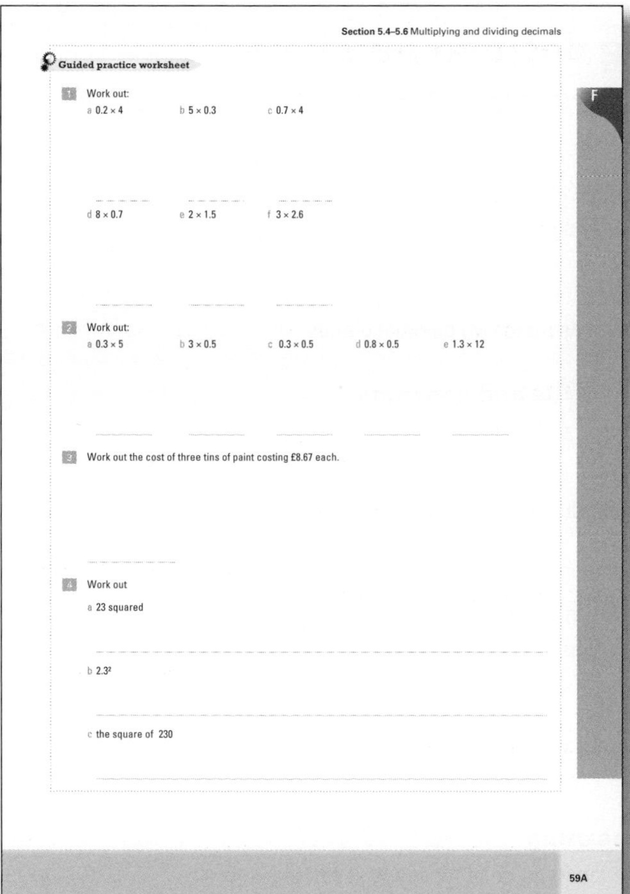

Section 5.4–5.6 Multiplying and dividing decimals

Guided practice worksheet

F

1 Work out:

a 0.2×4 b 5×0.3 c 0.7×4

d 8×0.7 e 2×1.5 f 3×2.6

2 Work out:

a 0.3×5 b 3×0.5 c 0.3×0.5 d 0.8×0.5 e 1.3×12

3 Work out the cost of three tins of paint costing £8.67 each.

4 Work out

a 23 squared

b 2.3^2

c the square of 230

59A

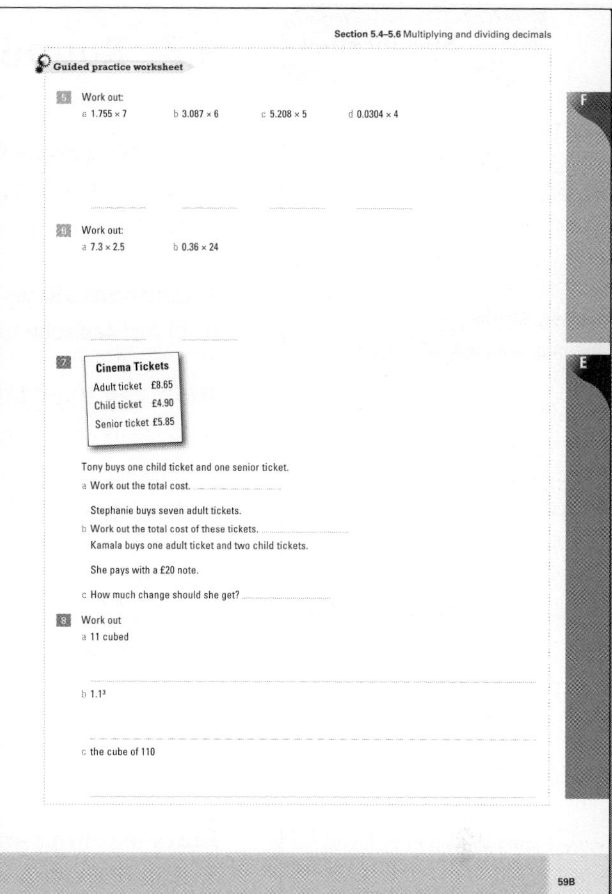

Section 5.4–5.6 Multiplying and dividing decimals

Guided practice worksheet

F

5 Work out:

a 1.755×7 b 3.087×6 c 5.208×5 d 0.0304×4

6 Work out:

a 7.3×2.5 b 0.36×24

E

7

Cinema Tickets	
Adult ticket	£8.65
Child ticket	£4.90
Senior ticket	£5.85

Tony buys one child ticket and one senior ticket.

a Work out the total cost.

Stephanie buys seven adult tickets.

b Work out the total cost of these tickets.

Kamala buys one adult ticket and two child tickets.

She pays with a £20 note.

c How much change should she get?

8 Work out

a 11 cubed

b 1.1^3

c the cube of 110

59B

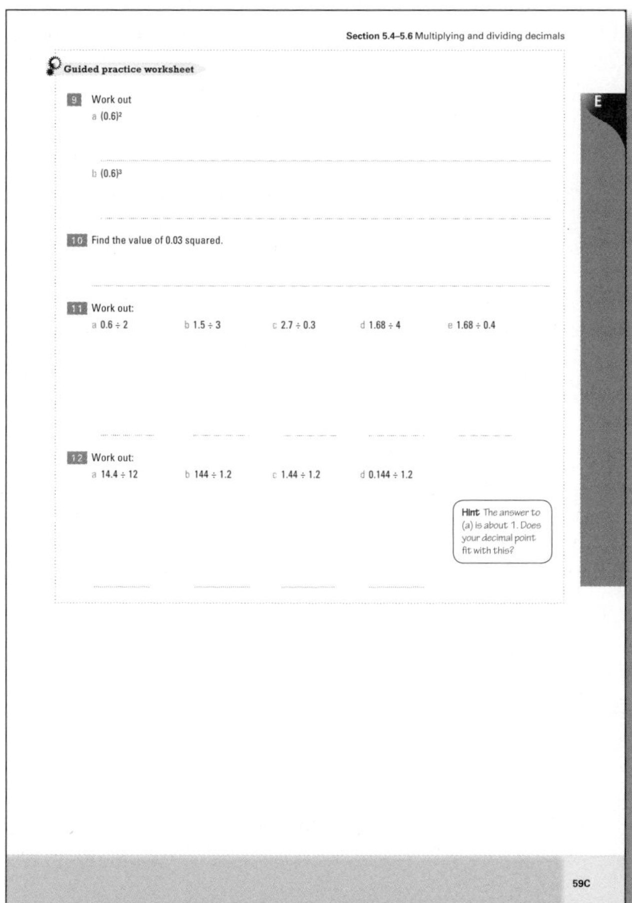

Section 5.4–5.6 Multiplying and dividing decimals

Guided practice worksheet

E

9 Work out

a $(0.6)^2$

b $(0.6)^3$

10 Find the value of 0.03 squared.

11 Work out:

a $0.6 \div 2$ b $1.5 \div 3$ c $2.7 \div 0.3$ d $1.68 \div 4$ e $1.68 \div 0.4$

12 Work out:

a $14.4 \div 12$ b $144 \div 1.2$ c $1.44 \div 1.2$ d $0.144 \div 1.2$

Hint The answer to (a) is about 1. Does your decimal point fit with this?

59C

Specification

GCSE 2010
N u (part) Approximate to specified or appropriate degrees of accuracy including a given… number of decimal places….

FS Process skills
Select the mathematical information to use
Use appropriate mathematical procedures

FS Performance
Level 1 Identify and obtain necessary information to tackle the problem

Resources

Links
http://www.mathsisfun.com/decimals-menu.html

ActiveTeach resources
Rounding interactive

5.7 Rounding decimal numbers

Concepts and skills

- Round to the nearest integer… .
- Round to a given number of decimal places.

Functional skills

- L1 Add and subtract decimals up to two decimal places.

Prior key knowledge, skills and concepts

- Students should know what a digit is.
- Students should understand decimal places.
- Students should be able to do simple mental arithmetic.

Starter

- Give examples of decimals in everyday situations:
  Price £5.99 Petrol 102.9p per litre
  Price per 100 g is 26.4p
  100 metres in 9.58 seconds
  Density of glass = 2.6 g/cm^3
  16°C = 60.8°F

Main teaching and learning

- Start with a recap of the meaning of 'to the nearest whole number'.
- Explain how to round numbers to one decimal place.
- Explain how to round numbers to any given number of decimal places.
- Ask students what they think rounding 0.549 to one decimal place means. Then repeat for two decimal places.
- Ask students to round the following numbers, to 1, 2 and 3 decimal places
  8.1432
  1.9078
  12.3934

Enrichment

Using rounding in estimations

- Ask students to estimate answers to the following by rounding the decimal to what they think would produce a sensible estimate. Ask how many decimal places they rounded to and why. 40×0.51, 10×0.275, 40×0.116, 100×0.7105, 50×0.506, 100×0.251, 80×0.7562
- Now ask students to round both of the following numbers and calculate an estimate of the answer: 59×0.36, 12 doughnuts costing 34p each, 18 tubes of paint costing £1.34 each, $78.32 \div 0.41$, 108×5.29,
- Ask students to estimate the answer to the following calculations, then use their calculators to compare answers: 16.49×2.1, $296 \div 26.43$, $\frac{2.8 \times 2.95}{4.94}$

Plenary

- Discuss Exercise 5I question 5.
- Ask students to explain the process of rounding.

Guided practice worksheet

1 Write these measurements to the nearest whole number.

a 3.6 kg .... b 4.32 cm ....

c 10.49 s .... d 909.502 m ....

e 2.63 cm .... f 9.68 s ....

g 1503.2 km .... h 8.27 g ....

2 Write these measurements to the nearest 100.

a 1520 m .... b 273 g ....

c 84 s .... d 143.5 cm ....

3 Write these numbers to 1 decimal place (1 d.p.)

a 3.54 .... b 12.07 ....

c 0.73 .... d 0.087 ....

e 9.98 ....

4 A chicken weighs 2.781 kg.
It is to be cooked according to the formula: Cooking time in minutes = (Weight in kg x 20) + 25
Rounding the weight to 1 d.p., how long would the chicken be cooked for?

....

5 Write these numbers to 2 decimal places.

a 7.7776 .... b 13.925 ....

c 0.3487 .... d 0.045 ....

e 6.0094 ....

6 Write these numbers to the number of decimal places indicated by the number in brackets.

a 0.0907 (2) .... b 0.003 (1) ....

c 0.66666 (3) .... d 1.0505 (1) ....

7 The distance between the two end posts of a fence is 876.3 cm.
Decide a suitable degree of accuracy to work out the amount of chain link fencing to be bought.

....

G

F

E

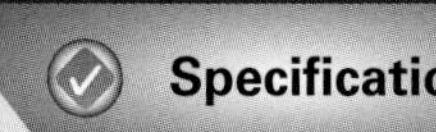

Specification

GCSE 2010
N u (part) Approximate to specified or appropriate degrees of accuracy including a given... number of... significant figures

FS Process skills
Select the mathematical information to use
Use appropriate mathematical procedures

FS Performance
Level 1 Identify and obtain necessary information to tackle the problem

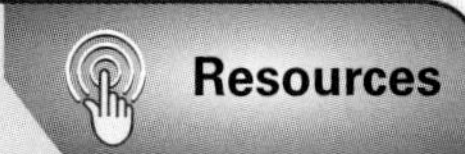

Resources

ActiveTeach resources
Significant figures interactive

5.8 Rounding to 1 significant figure
5.9 Rounding to a given number of significant figures

Concepts and skills

- Round to the nearest integer and to any given number of significant figures.

Functional skills

- L1 Add and subtract decimals up to two decimal places.

Prior key knowledge, skills and concepts

- Rounding to a given number of decimal places.

Starter

- *The height of a person is 1.73 metres to 2 decimal places. This height is also 173 centimetres to the nearest cm. Which is more accurate?* (Clearly both are equally accurate, so the number of decimal places is not necessarily a true mark of accuracy. Each of the three digits is significant, i.e. important in determining the height.)

Main teaching and learning

- Teach students what a significant figure is.
- Write the number 1781 on the board. *This is the number of people who completed a 10 mile race. Give me an estimate of the number of people who completed the race.*
- Students will offer 1780, 1800, 1000. Ask which you think is the most appropriate answer (1800). Explain that in this case, only two of the digits in 1781 are **significant** (meaningful) and another way of asking this question would be 'What is 1781 to two significant figures?'
- Teach students when 0 is significant and when it is not.
- The most common error when rounding to a number of significant figures is for students to forget to fill in places to the left of the decimal point with zeros. The need for this can be illustrated by asking students whether, for example, 2345 is close to 2000 or to 2

Common misconceptions

- Confusing decimal places with significant figures.
- Not realising that 0 can be a significant figure if surrounded by significant digits.

Plenary

- Give further examples like questions 6 and 7 of Exercise 5K.

F

E

Guided practice worksheet

1 £46 375 has been stolen in a raid on a Post Office.
As the reporter for the local newspaper, write a suitable headline.
Use as few words as possible (no more than 8).

....

2 Write these numbers to 1 significant figure.

a 2.7 ....

b 0.347 ....

c 205 ....

d 0.95 ....

e 3532 ....

f 20.09 ....

3 Write these numbers to 2 significant figures.

Hint Use a zero to keep the same order of magnitude.

a 753 ....

b 2.653 ....

c 0.0987 ....

d 4375 ....

e 403 ....

f 0.08076 ....

4 Write these numbers to the number of significant figures indicated in brackets.

a 921 (1) ....

b 971 (1) ....

c 1127 (2) ....

d 3.0781 (3) ....

e 0.005642 (3) ....

5 Write down the number of significant figures in each of the following numbers.

a 1500 ....

b 2007 ....

c 15.2 ....

d 63.076 ....

e 53 million ....

f 0.034 ....

Specification

GSCE 2010

N u Approximate to specified or appropriate degrees of accuracy including a given power of ten, number of decimal places and significant figures

FS Process skills

Use appropriate mathematical procedures

FS performance

Level 1 Use appropriate checking procedures at each stage

Resources

Resources

Starter information sheet

ActiveTeach resources

Building the course 1 video
Paper 3 video

5.10 Estimating

Concepts and skills

- Estimate answers to calculations, including use of rounding.

Functional skills

- L1 Add, subtract, multiply and divide whole numbers using a range of strategies.

Prior key knowledge, skills and concepts

- Students should be able to round to 1 significant figure.

Starter

- *Some people shopping in a supermarket keep a rough idea of how much they have spent as they pick up each item. As I go round I will tell you what I am buying and its cost. At the end, I want you to tell me roughly how much I will have to pay.*

Main teaching and learning

- Ask students to round these numbers to 1 significant figure: 18.4, 1.9, 178.3, 47.2, 16.45, 1449.9, 350.5, 69.15
- Teach students to use 1 significant figure accuracy to get a rough idea of the true answer.
- *How can you estimate answers to the following calculations?*

  18.2×48.9 $(20 \times 50 = 1000)$

  $1620 \div 4.3$ $(2000 \div 4 = 500)$

  $\frac{40.5 \times 7.7}{0.24}$ $\left(\frac{40 \times 8}{0.2} = \frac{40 \times 80}{2} = 1600\right)$
- For the last calculation discuss approximation of decimals, e.g. 0.24 could be rounded to 1 s.f. (0.2) or treated as $\frac{1}{4}$.

Common misconceptions

- Some students try to be as accurate as possible, rather than estimating.
- Students often confuse 'to 1 significant figure' with 'to 1 decimal place'.

Enrichment

- Ask students to quickly write down their estimations for the solutions to the following word problems.

  You have £60 and a cinema ticket costs £4.50. How many people can go to the cinema? (12)

  You buy 5 CDs, costing £13.99 each, how much do you spend? (£70)

  If Bodrul earns £6.78 per hour and work 18 hours one week, estimate how much he earns. (less than £140)

  If a concert ticket costs £8.50, estimate how many you can buy for £60. (at least 6)

  How many minutes in a day and in a year? (more than 1200, about 480 000)

Plenary

- Find some sporting attendance figures and ask students to estimate the total attendance at several events.

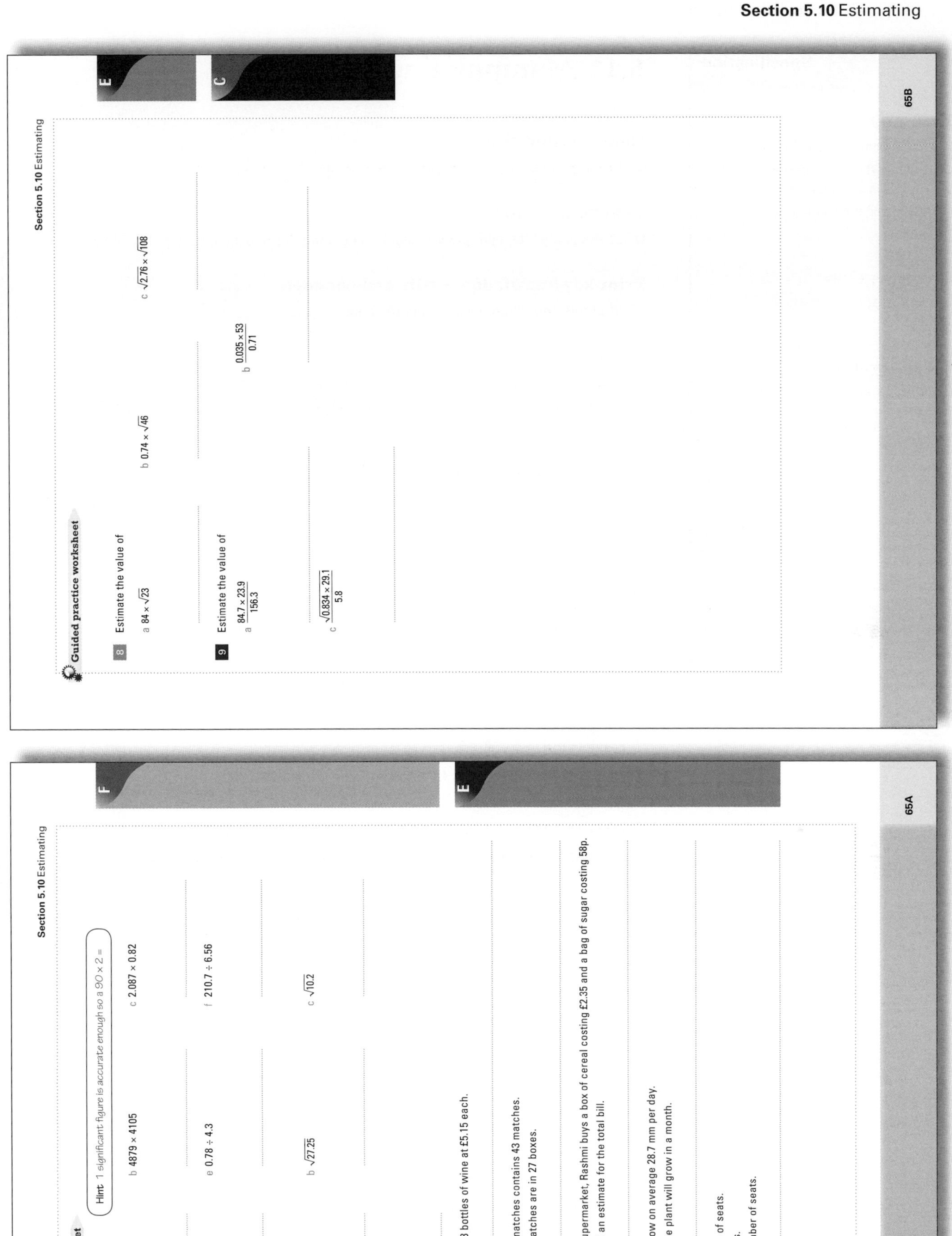

Section 5.10 Estimating

Guided practice worksheet

F

1 Estimate the value of:

Hint 1 significant figure is accurate enough so a 90 × 2 =

a 93 × 1.9　b 4879 × 4105　c 2.087 × 0.82

d 18.7 ÷ 2.9　e 0.78 ÷ 4.3　f 210.7 ÷ 6.56

2 Estimate the value of:

a $\sqrt{35.9}$　b $\sqrt{27.25}$　c $\sqrt{10.2}$

d $\sqrt{13.3}$

E

3 Estimate the cost of 18 bottles of wine at £5.15 each.

4 On average, a box of matches contains 43 matches.
Estimate how many matches are in 27 boxes.

5 While shopping in a supermarket, Rashmi buys a box of cereal costing £2.35 and a bag of sugar costing 58p.
Work out in your head an estimate for the total bill.

6 A plant is known to grow on average 28.7 mm per day.
Estimate how much the plant will grow in a month.

7 A cinema has 19 rows of seats.
Each row has 73 seats.
Estimate the total number of seats.

65A

Section 5.10 Estimating

Guided practice worksheet

E

8 Estimate the value of

a $84 \times \sqrt{23}$　b $0.74 \times \sqrt{46}$　c $\sqrt{2.76} \times \sqrt{108}$

C

9 Estimate the value of

a $\frac{84.7 \times 23.9}{156.3}$　b $\frac{0.035 \times 53}{0.71}$

c $\frac{\sqrt{0.834 \times 29.1}}{5.8}$

65B

Specification

GCSE 2010

N q Understand and use number operations and the relationships between them, including inverse operations and the hierarchy of operations

FS Process skills

Use appropriate mathematical procedures

FS Performance

Level 1 Use appropriate checking procedures at each stage

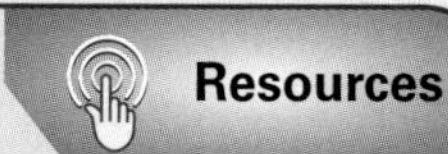

Resources

ActiveTeach resources

RP KC Decimals and rounding knowledge check

RP PS Decimals problem solving

5.11 Manipulating decimals

Concepts and skills

- Use one calculation to find the answer to another.

Functional skills

- L1 Add, subtract, multiply and divide whole numbers using a range of strategies.

Prior key knowledge, skills and concepts

- Students should understand place value.

Starter

- Use some mental agility through simple instances, such as:
  Given that 15 × 0.2 = 3, what is (a) *15 × 0.02* (b) *1.5 × 2* (c) *1.5 × 0.2* (d) *3 ÷ 0.2?*
  Write your 'given that' results on the board prior to questioning.
- Alternatively, ask students to use their calculators to work out the following.
  (a) 57.3 × 16 = (916.8)
  (b) 5.73 × 1.6 = (9.168)
  (c) 0.573 × 1600 = (91.68)
  (d) 0.0573 × 0.16 = (0.009168)
  (e) 573 × 16 = (9168)
  What have your answers in common? (The same digits.)

Main teaching and learning

- 7 × 8 = 56, 7 × 80 = 560, 70 × 80 = 5600, 700 × 0.8 = 560
- The product of 7 and 8, regardless of the place value of the 7 and of the 8, will always result in the digits 56.
- Hence, since 57.2 × 219 = 12 526.8, you can complete
  (a) 5.72 × 2.19 =
  (b) 572 × 0.219 =
  (c) 0.0572 × 0.0219 =
  just by considering place value.
  (a) this is about 6 × 2 = 12, so the answer is 12.5268
  (b) this is about 600 × 0.2 = 120, so the answer is 125.268
  (c) this is about 0.06 × 0.02 = 0.0012, so the answer is 0.001 25268

Plenary

- You can also work out inverses as follows.
  Given 23.7 × 0.31 = 7.47, work out
  (a) 310 × 2.37
  (b) 74.7 ÷ 0.237
  (a) The sequence of digits is 747. The question is where to put the decimal place.
  Since 310 × 2.37 is about 300 × 2 = 600, the answer must be 747.
  (b) Since 23.7 × 0.31 = 7.47, it follows that 7.47 ÷ 23.7 = 0.31
  74.7 ÷ 0.237 is about 70 ÷ 0.2 = 350, so the answer must be 310.

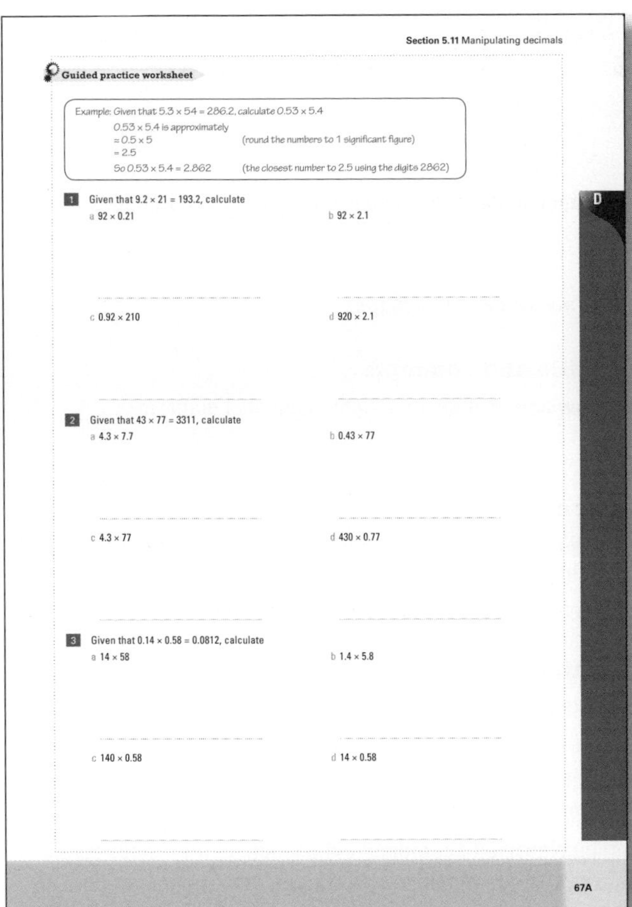

Guided practice worksheet

Example: *Given that* $5.3 \times 54 = 286.2$, *calculate* 0.53×5.4

0.53×5.4 is approximately

$= 0.5 \times 5$ (round the numbers to 1 significant figure)

$= 2.5$

So $0.53 \times 5.4 = 2.862$ (the closest number to 2.5 using the digits 2862)

1 Given that $9.2 \times 21 = 193.2$, calculate

a 92×0.21

b 92×2.1

c 0.92×210

d 920×2.1

2 Given that $43 \times 77 = 3311$, calculate

a 4.3×7.7

b 0.43×77

c 4.3×77

d 430×0.77

3 Given that $0.14 \times 0.58 = 0.0812$, calculate

a 14×58

b 1.4×5.8

c 140×0.58

d 14×0.58

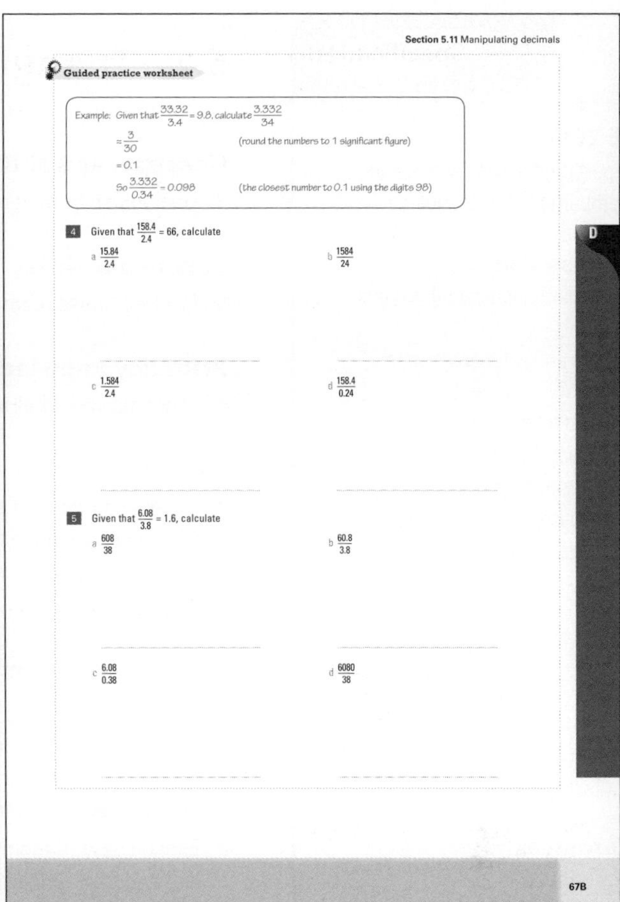

Guided practice worksheet

Example: *Given that* $\frac{33.32}{3.4} = 9.8$, *calculate* $\frac{3.332}{34}$

$\approx \frac{3}{30}$ (round the numbers to 1 significant figure)

$= 0.1$

So $\frac{3.332}{0.34} = 0.098$ (the closest number to 0.1 using the digits 98)

4 Given that $\frac{158.4}{2.4} = 66$, calculate

a $\frac{15.84}{2.4}$

b $\frac{1584}{24}$

c $\frac{1.584}{2.4}$

d $\frac{158.4}{0.24}$

5 Given that $\frac{6.08}{3.8} = 1.6$, calculate

a $\frac{608}{38}$

b $\frac{60.8}{3.8}$

c $\frac{6.08}{0.38}$

d $\frac{6080}{38}$

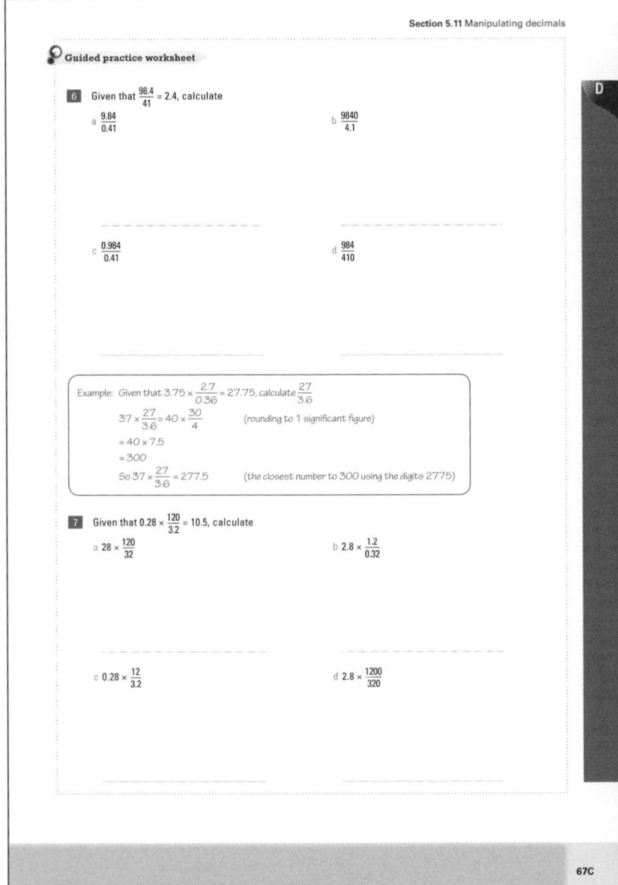

Guided practice worksheet

6 Given that $\frac{98.4}{41} = 2.4$, calculate

a $\frac{9.84}{0.41}$

b $\frac{9840}{4.1}$

c $\frac{0.984}{0.41}$

d $\frac{984}{410}$

Example: *Given that* $3.75 \times \frac{2.7}{0.36} = 27.75$, *calculate* $\frac{27}{3.6}$

$37 \times \frac{27}{3.6} \approx 40 \times \frac{30}{4}$ (rounding to 1 significant figure)

$= 40 \times 7.5$

$= 300$

So $37 \times \frac{27}{3.6} = 277.5$ (the closest number to 300 using the digits 2775)

7 Given that $0.28 \times \frac{120}{3.2} = 10.5$, calculate

a $28 \times \frac{120}{32}$

b $2.8 \times \frac{1.2}{0.32}$

c $0.28 \times \frac{12}{3.2}$

d $2.8 \times \frac{1200}{320}$

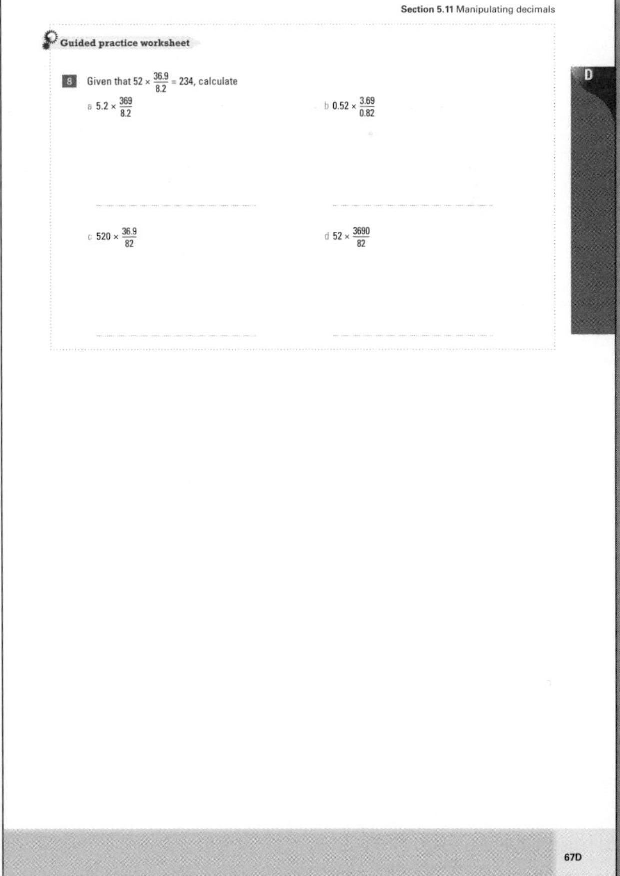

Guided practice worksheet

8 Given that $52 \times \frac{36.9}{8.2} = 234$, calculate

a $5.2 \times \frac{369}{8.2}$

b $0.52 \times \frac{3.69}{0.82}$

c $520 \times \frac{36.9}{82}$

d $52 \times \frac{3690}{82}$

Specification

GCSE 2010
GM b (part) Understand and use the angle properties of… triangles.

FS Process skills
Select the mathematical information to use
Find results and solutions

FS Performance
Entry 3 Select mathematics to obtain answers to simple given practical problems that are clear and routine

Resources

Resources
Pieces of card with 90° corners

CD Resources
Resource sheet 6.1

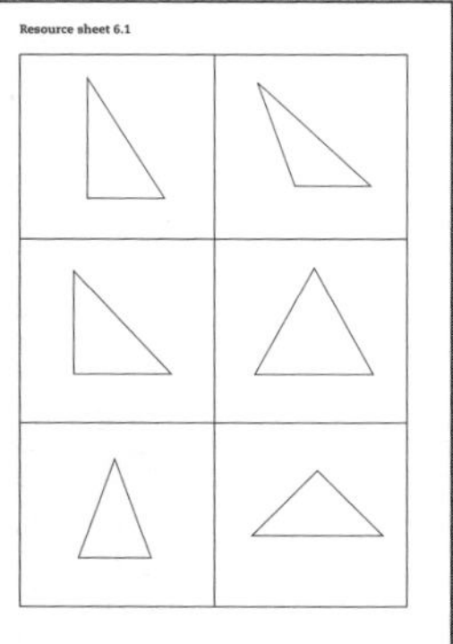

Resource sheet 6.1 cont.

acute-angled	isosceles
right-angled	scalene
obtuse-angled	equilateral
acute-angled	isosceles
right-angled	scalene
obtuse-angled	isosceles

Links
http://nrich.maths.org/public/search.php?search=triangles

ActiveTeach resources
Estimating angles quiz 2
Triangle break up animation
Triangles interactive
Fairground shapes 1 video

6.1 Triangles

Concepts and skills

- Distinguish between scalene, equilateral, isosceles and right-angled triangles.

Functional skills

- EL3 Recognise, name and draw simple 2D… shapes.

Prior key knowledge, skills and concepts

- Students should already know how to indicate a right angle on a diagram.

Starter

- Have a selection of triangles drawn and give each student a piece of card that has a 90° angle. Students have to estimate whether the largest angle is less than 90°, equal to 90° or greater than 90° and then use the 90° corner on the piece of card to check if they are correct.

Main teaching and learning

- Tell students they are going to find out about the properties of different three-sided shapes, called triangles.
- Go through all of 6.1 and ask students where they might find these shapes in everyday life. (e.g. ▲ = end of a Toblerone chocolate, ◣ = a slide ▲ = front of a roof of a house.)
- Explain how triangles can be classified according to the length of their sides (scalene, isosceles or equilateral) or by the size of their angles (acute, right-angled or obtuse).
- Discuss why it is not possible to have more than one right angle or more than one obtuse angle in a triangle.

Common misconceptions

- Students often assume that lines or angles are the same size just because they look the same size. They cannot assume this unless they are given as equal or marked as equal.

Enrichment

- Distinguish between scalene, equilateral, isosceles and right-angled triangles.

Plenary

- Divide the class into three groups. Use Resource sheet 6.1. Students in group A are given pieces of card with various triangles drawn on them. Group B students are given pieces of card with either 'acute-angled', 'right-angled' or 'obtuse-angled' written on them. Students in group C are given pieces of card with either 'scalene', 'isosceles' or 'equilateral' written on them. They then have to get themselves into appropriate groups of three – one from each group – so that the descriptions match the triangle drawn.

triangle scalene isosceles right-angled equilateral

Guided practice worksheet

G

1 Here is a list of the names of some types of triangles:

Scalene triangle	*Isosceles triangle*	*Acute-angled triangle*
Right-angled triangle	*Equilateral triangle*	*Obtuse-angled triangle*

Use the list to help you write down the names of these shapes.

Each shape can have two different names.

a

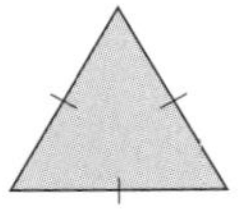

b

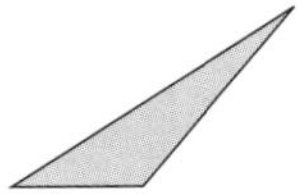

c

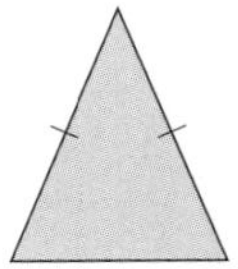

d

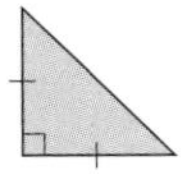

e

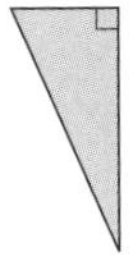

f

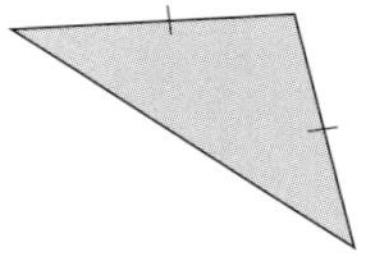

2

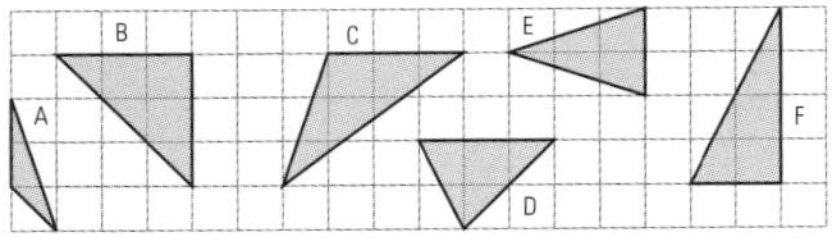

A B C D E F

a Two of these triangles are right-angled triangles. Which two? ......

b Which of the above triangles are isosceles triangles? ......

c Which triangles are obtuse-angled triangles? ......

d Which triangle is scalene and right-angled? ......

e Two of these triangles are acute-angled triangles. Which two? ......

Guided practice worksheet

G

3 a Draw a triangle that is both scalene and obtuse-angled.

b Draw a triangle that is both right-angled and isosceles.

F

4 Write down the name of a triangle with:

a only two of its angles equal ......

b one of its angles greater than 90° ......

c all of its sides the same length. ......

5 Melissa says she can draw a triangle that is both right-angled and equilateral.

Melissa is wrong. Explain why.

Specification

GCSE 2010

GM d Recall the properties and definitions of special types of quadrilateral, including square, rectangle, parallelogram, trapezium, kite and rhombus

FS Process skills

Select the mathematical information to use

Find results and solutions

FS Performance

Entry 3 Select mathematics to obtain answers to simple given practical problems that are clear and routine

Resources

Resources

Scissors

Links

http://www.ies.co.jp/math/java/geo/quadri.html

ActiveTeach resources

Angles in a quadrilateral animation

Quadrilaterals interactive

6.2 Quadrilaterals

Concepts and skills

- Recall the properties and definitions of special types of quadrilateral, including symmetry properties.
- List the properties of each, or identify (name) a given shape.
- Name all quadrilaterals that have a specific property.
- Identify quadrilaterals from everyday usage.
- Classify quadrilaterals by their geometric properties.

Functional skills

- EL3 Recognise, name and draw simple 2D… shapes.

Prior key knowledge, skills and concepts

- Students should know the concepts of parallel lines and perpendicular lines and how to indicate a right angle in a diagram.
- Students should know how to sketch shapes.

Starter

- Demonstrate folding a piece of paper in half, then cutting off a corner at 45°. *What shape will the cut-out piece make?*
- Then do the same, cutting out an angle at a slant.
- Repeat by folding in half and then in half again or even adding an extra fold.

Main teaching and learning

- Tell students they are going to find out about the properties of different four-sided shapes, called quadrilaterals.
- Go through all of Section 6.2 in the Student Book and ask where they might find these shapes in everyday life. (e.g. ■ = chest, ▲ = front of a roof, ⬟ = shape of a field.

Common misconceptions

- Students sometimes measure the angles and lines of diagrams that have the words 'Diagram NOT accurately drawn'.

Enrichment

- Draw the two diagonals of some special quadrilaterals, showing if they bisect each other, if they meet at 90°, etc. Students have to identify the shapes and give reasons for their answers.

Plenary

- Put the students in pairs and give each student a different list of quadrilaterals, for example, trapezium, square, parallelogram, and so on. They should then take turns to describe a shape to their partner without naming the shape: for example, 'My shape has one pair of parallel sides'. The partner has to correctly identify the shape.

diagonal quadrilateral square rectangle parallelogram adjacent bisect kite

Guided practice worksheet

G

1 Here is a list of the names of some shapes:

Rhombus *Rectangle* *Parallelogram* *Square* *Kite* *Trapezium*

Use the list to help you write down the names of these shapes:

a 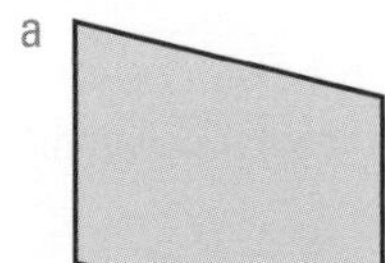

b 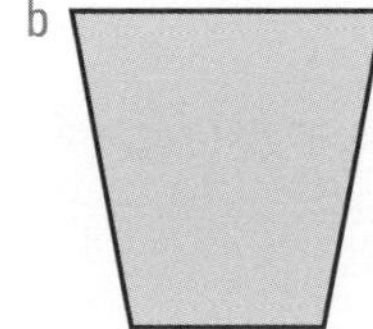

c 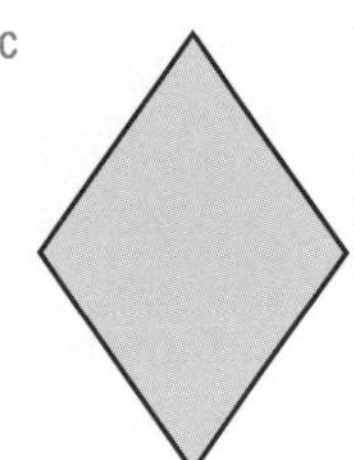

....

2 Write down the names of all the shapes on the grid below labelled A to J.

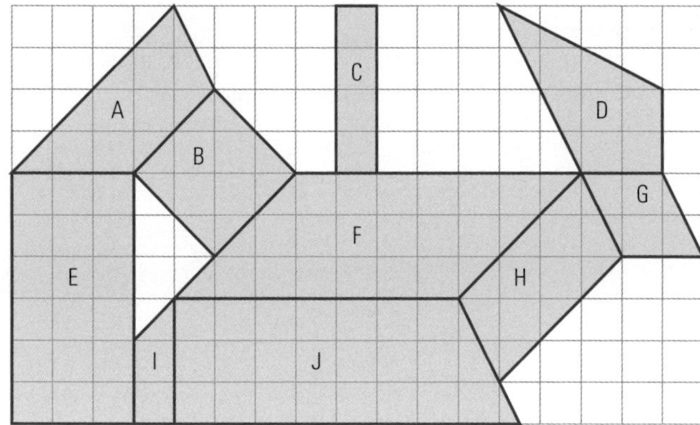

A .... B .... C ....

D .... E .... F ....

G .... H .... I ....

J ....

F

3 Write down the name of the quadrilateral that could have the following properties:

a only two of its angles equal and two pairs of sides the same length ....

b only one pair of opposite sides are parallel ....

c all 4 angles equal to 90° but the sides not all the same length. ....

4 Write down the name of a quadrilateral where:

a it has 4 lines of reflection symmetry ....

b all sides are the same length but only opposite angles are equal ....

c only one diagonal bisected by the other diagonal. ....

Specification

GCSE 2010

GM f Understand congruence and similarity

FS Process skills

Select the mathematical information to use

Find results and solutions

FS Performance

Entry 3 Select mathematics to obtain answers to simple given practical problems that are clear and routine

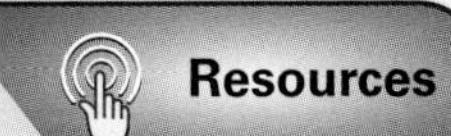

Resources

Resources

Tracing paper

Centimetre-square spotty paper

Links

http://www.ies.co.jp/math/java/geo/congruent.html

http://www.bbc.co.uk/schools/gcsebitesize/maths/shapes/congruencysimilarityact.shtml

6.3 Congruent and similar shapes

Concepts and skills

- Understand congruence.
- Identify shapes which are congruent.
- Understand similarity.
- Identify shapes which are similar; including all circles or all regular polygons with equal number of sides.

Functional skills

- EL3 Recognise, name and draw simple 2D… shapes.

Prior key knowledge, skills and concepts

- Students should know that if you take a shape and turn it over or turn it around, the properties of the shape remain unchanged.

Starter

- Draw some shapes on the board and ask individual students to draw in a line to divide the shape into two shapes that are identical. For example:

Main teaching and learning

- Give students some tracing paper so that they can trace shapes and see they are the same size.
- Give students some sheets of centimetre-square spotty paper. Draw a shape on the board, e.g. and ask them to draw a shape congruent to this but in a different orientation.

Common misconceptions

- Students sometimes measure the angles and lines of diagrams that have the words 'Diagram NOT accurately drawn'.

Enrichment

- Draw a range of polygons on the board. Join some of the vertices with straight lines and discuss what shapes can be found, for example, pentagon = rectangle + isosceles triangle.

Plenary

- Ask students to say which two shapes or objects in the classroom are congruent. (e.g. 2 table tops, 2 windows, 2 rulers.)

congruent similar

Guided practice worksheet

1 Write down which of the shapes is congruent with the first shape drawn.
There may be more than one answer to each part.

a A B C D

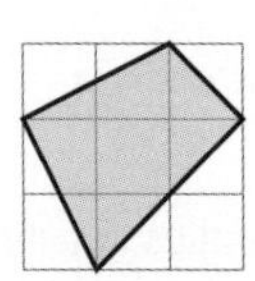
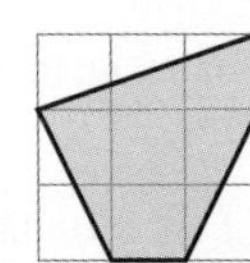
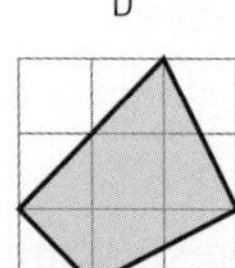

....

b A B C D

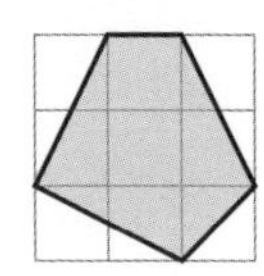
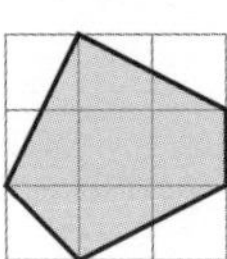
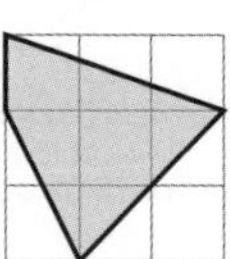

....

c A B C D

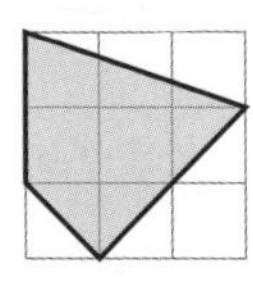
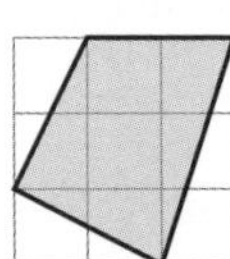
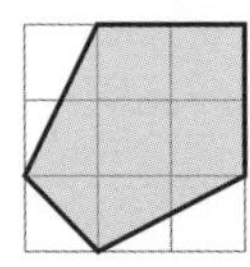
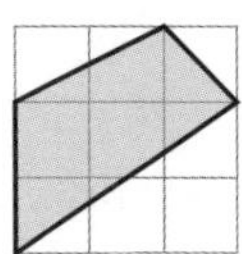
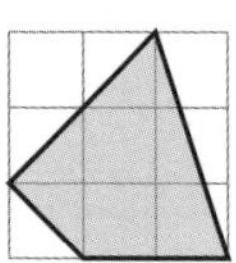

....

d A B C D

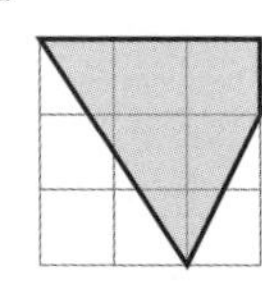
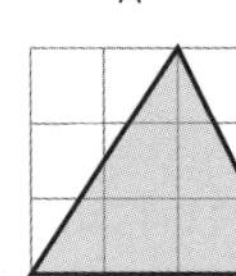
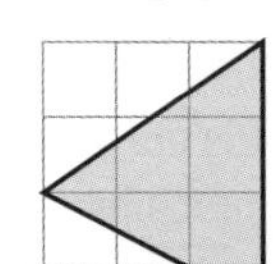
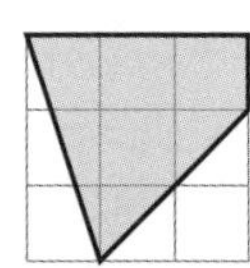
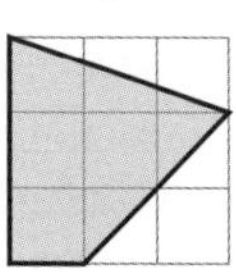

....

2 Here are some 4-sided shapes with a diagonal line drawn.
In each case say whether the diagonal has divided the shape into two congruent triangles.

a 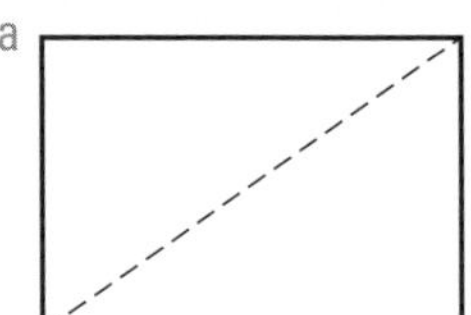
b 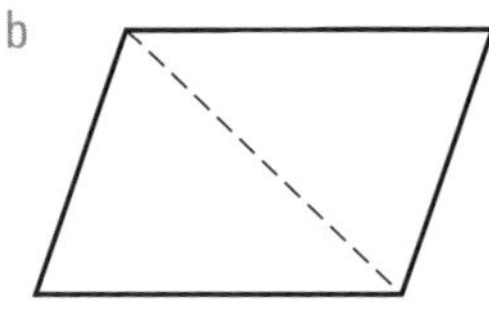
c 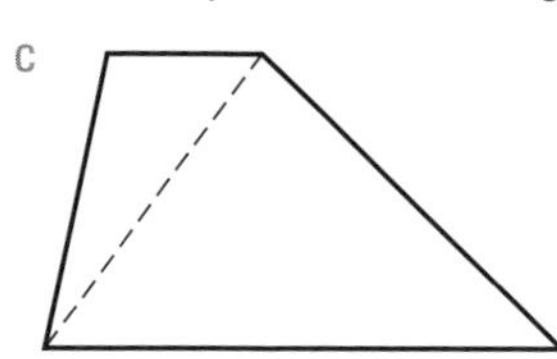
d 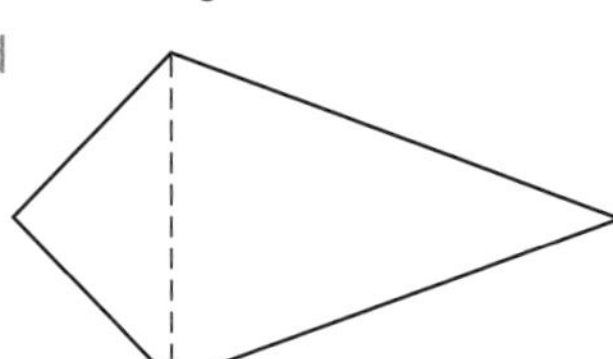

....

3 Debbie says that all equilateral triangles are congruent to each other.
Debbie is not correct. Explain why.

....

....

Specification

GCSE 2010

GM u Draw triangles and other 2D shapes using ruler and protractor
GM v Use straight edge and a pair of compasses to carry out constructions

FS Process skills

Use appropriate mathematical procedures

FS Performance

Level 1 Apply mathematics in an organised way to find solutions to straightforward practical problems for different purposes

Resources

Resources

Pencil, ruler, compasses, protractor

6.4 Accurate drawings

Concepts and skills

- Make accurate drawings of triangles and other 2D shapes using a ruler and a protractor.
- Use straight edge and a pair of compasses to do standard constructions.
- Construct a triangle.
- Understand, from the experience of constructing them, that triangles satisfying SSS, SAS, ASA and RHS are unique, but SSA triangles are not.
- Draw parallel lines.
- Draw and construct diagrams from given instructions.

Functional skills

- L1 Construct geometric diagrams, models and shapes.

Prior key knowledge, skills and concepts

- Students should know how to draw lines accurately and draw angles accurately.
- Students should also know how to use a protractor and a pair of compasses.

Starter

- Divide the students into pairs. Ask one student from each pair to draw a line accurately to a measurement of their choice. The other student should then estimate the length of the line in centimetres. The same student then draws an angle accurately and the other estimates its size. Students should then swap over and repeat the activity.

Main teaching and learning

- Ensure students can use compasses correctly by first showing them that when the pencil is in the compasses the tip of the pencil and the tip of the compasses should be level. Let students practise drawing arcs.
- Ensure students know how to read accurately from a protractor. They need to know when to use the outer numbers and the inner numbers and where to position the centre of the protractor on the angle being measured.
- Direct students to draw a triangle, and specify the lengths of the three sides of the triangle to be drawn. Then ask them to measure all three angles and see that they add up to $180° \pm 6°$.
- This is a good topic for pairing students and getting them to check each other's answers.

Common misconceptions

- Students should always estimate what an angle will look like before drawing it as it is not uncommon for an angle of e.g. 73° to look obtuse and an angle of e.g. 110° to look acute.

Enrichment

- Alex draws an isosceles triangle so that one of the angles is 80°. *Must one of the other angles also be 80°? Give reasons for your answer.*

Plenary

- Draw on the board a number of triangles that all look like equilateral triangles but that have different measurements marked on them, for example, 135°, 9.2 cm and 12.4 cm, and so on. Ask students to draw what they think each triangle will look like without using any measuring tools. Then ask them to measure the lines and angles in their triangles. How accurate were their initial drawings?

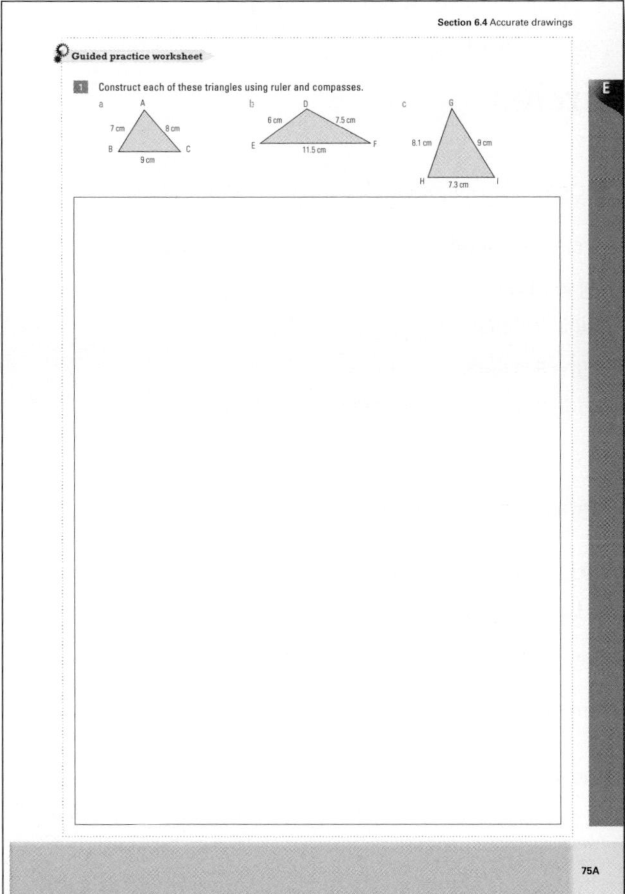
Section 6.4 Accurate drawings
Guided practice worksheet
1 Construct each of these triangles using ruler and compasses.
a A 7 cm 8 cm B C 9 cm
b D 6 cm 7.5 cm E F 11.5 cm
c G 8.1 cm 9 cm H I 7.3 cm
75A

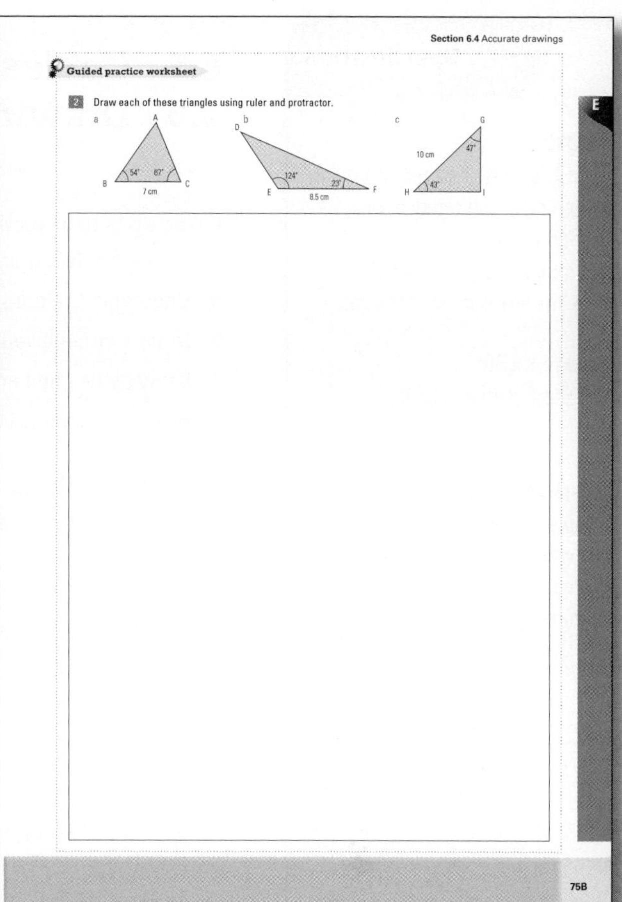
Section 6.4 Accurate drawings
Guided practice worksheet
2 Draw each of these triangles using ruler and protractor.
a A 54° 87° B C 7 cm
b D 124° 23° E F 8.5 cm
c G 47° 10 cm 43° H I
75B

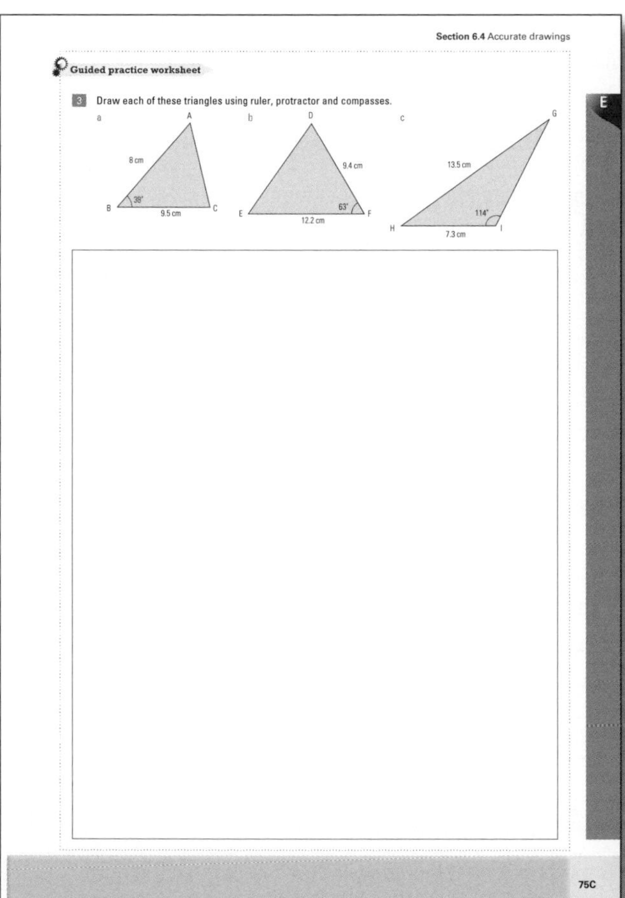
Section 6.4 Accurate drawings
Guided practice worksheet
3 Draw each of these triangles using ruler, protractor and compasses.
a A 8 cm 38° B C 9.5 cm
b D 9.4 cm 63° E F 12.2 cm
c G 13.5 cm 114° H I 7.3 cm
75C

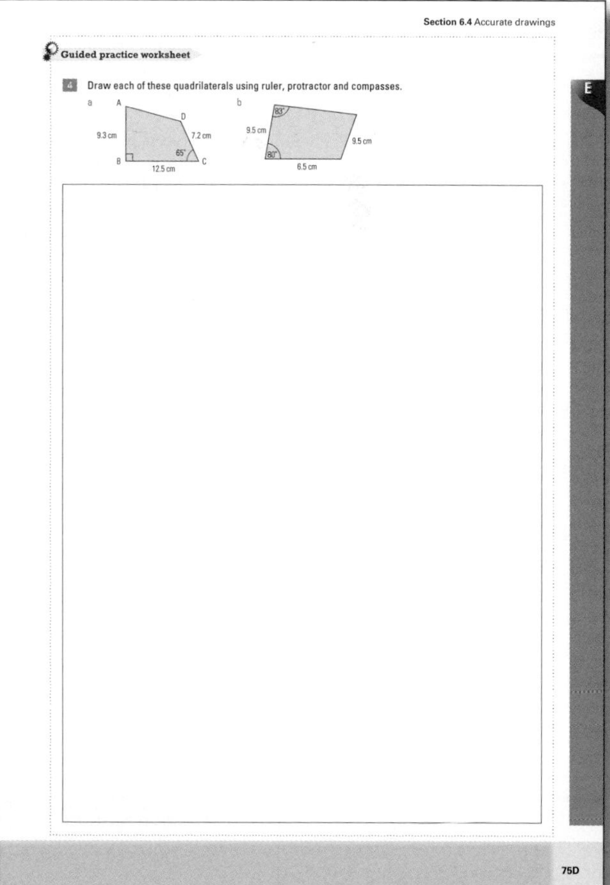
Section 6.4 Accurate drawings
Guided practice worksheet
4 Draw each of these quadrilaterals using ruler, protractor and compasses.
a A D 9.3 cm 7.2 cm 65° B C 12.5 cm
b 9.5 cm 9.5 cm 6.5 cm
75D

Specification

GCSE 2010
GM i Distinguish between centre, radius, chord, diameter, circumference, tangent, arc, sector and segment
GM v Use straight edge and a pair of compasses to carry out constructions

FS Process skills
Use appropriate mathematical procedures

FS Performance
Level 1 Apply mathematics in an organised way to find solutions to straightforward practical problems for different purposes

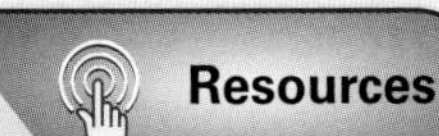

Resources

Resources
Pencil, ruler, compasses

CD Resources
Resource sheet 6.5

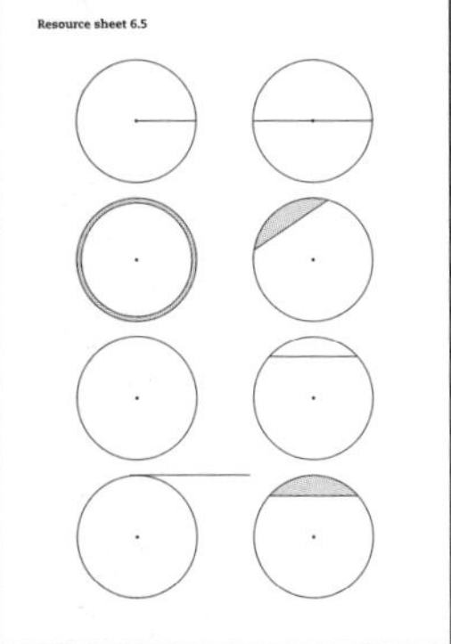

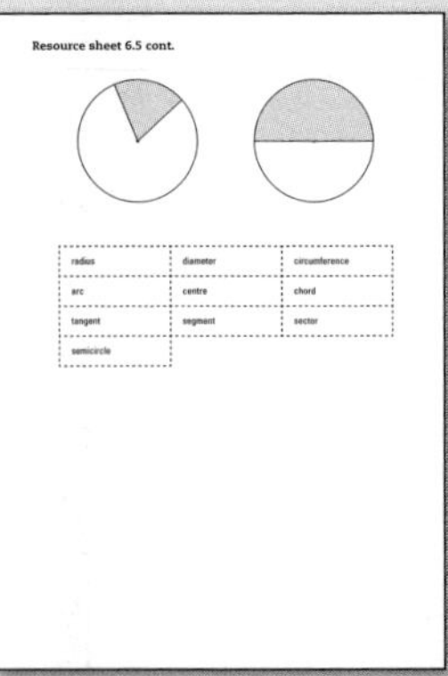

Links
http://www.mathsisfun.com/quadrilaterals.html
http://www.mathsisfun.com/geometry/circle.html

6.5 Circles
6.6 Drawing circles

Concepts and skills

- Recall the definition of a circle and identify (name) and draw parts of a circle.
- Understand related terms of a circle.
- Draw a circle given the radius or diameter.
- Draw circles and arcs to a given radius.
- Draw and construct diagrams from given instructions.

Functional skills

- L1 Construct geometric diagrams, models and shapes.

Prior key knowledge, skills and concepts

- Students should know how to use a pair of compasses.

Starter

- Discuss with students where circles are to be found in everyday life.

Main teaching and learning

- Tell students they are going to find out about circles and parts of a circle (arc, centre, chord, circumference, diameter, radius, sector, segment, semicircle, tangent).
- As students need to learn the various names in this section, they will need as much practice as possible just using the names, so that they become part of their vocabulary. This could be done by getting students to make posters, doing matching exercises, testing each other and any other exercise in which the names are used.
- Tell students they are going to learn to draw circles accurately using a pair of compasses.

Common misconceptions

- Students sometimes hold on to the pencil end of the compass when drawing circles. Explain that they should not do this as it tends to make the end move, resulting in an inaccurately drawn circle.

Enrichment

- Give students diagrams of circles with a radius drawn on. Ask them to explain why this is not a diameter.
- Give students diagrams of circles with a segment shaded. Ask them to explain why this is not a sector.
- Draw circles and arcs to a given radius.

Plenary

- Divide the students into two teams, with each team having a group A and a group B.
- Give each team's group A cards with diagrams of a circle and one of the following drawn on:

radius	diameter	circumference	arc	centre
chord	tangent	segment	sector	semicircle

- Each student in group A will have one or two cards.
- Give each team's group B cards with just the above names written on the card.
- Each student has to find his or her matching partner.
- The first team to do all the correct matchings wins.

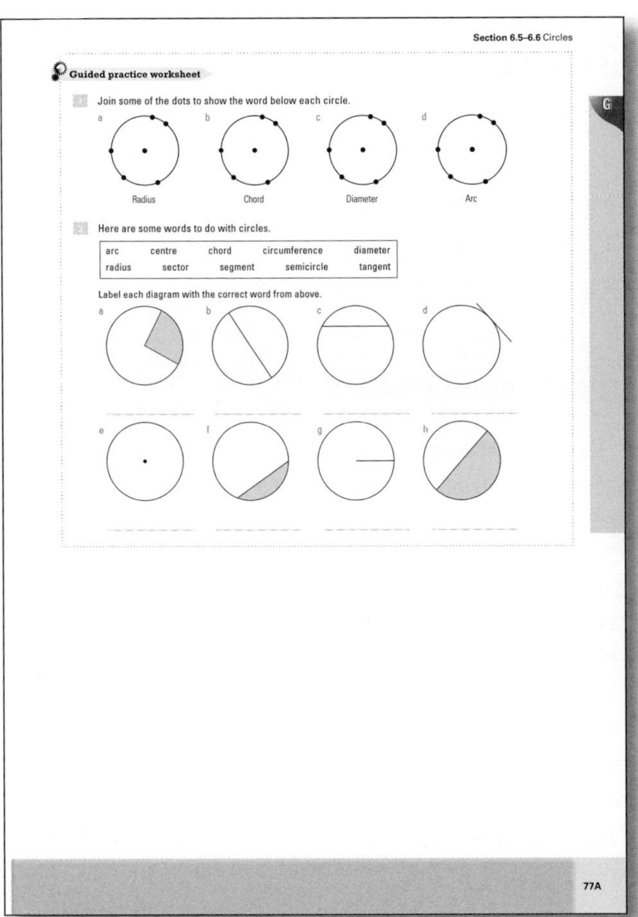

Section 6.5–6.6 Circles

Guided practice worksheet

Join some of the dots to show the word below each circle.

a Radius b Chord c Diameter d Arc

Here are some words to do with circles.

arc	centre	chord	circumference	diameter
radius	sector	segment	semicircle	tangent

Label each diagram with the correct word from above.

a b c d

e f g h

77A

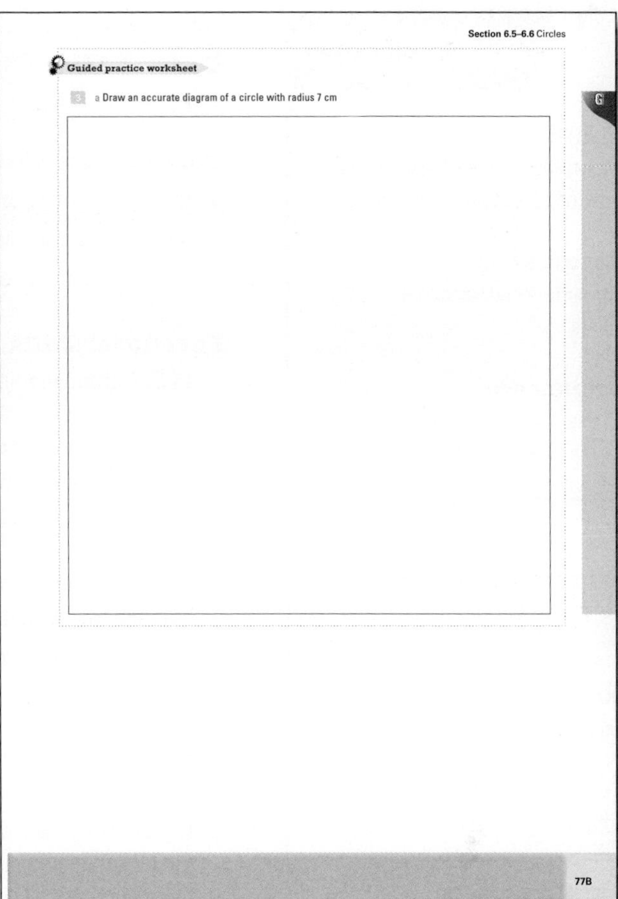

Section 6.5–6.6 Circles

Guided practice worksheet

a Draw an accurate diagram of a circle with radius 7 cm

77B

Section 6.5–6.6 Circles

Guided practice worksheet

b Draw an accurate diagram of a circle with diameter 12 cm.

77C

Section 6.5–6.6 Circles

Guided practice worksheet

c Draw an accurate diagram of a circle with radius 4.7 cm.

77D

Specification

GCSE 2010
GM e (part) Recognise reflection… symmetry of 2D shapes

FS Process skills
Use appropriate mathematical procedures

FS Performance
Level 1 Use appropriate checking procedures at each stage

Resources

Resources
Two-way mirrors

CD Resources
Resource sheet 6.7

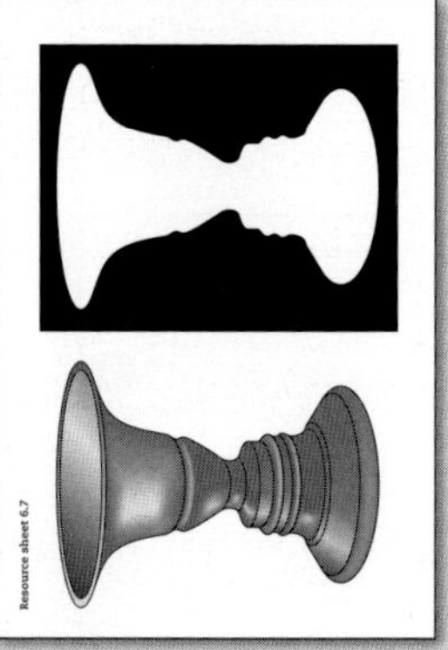

Links
http://www.mathsisfun.com/puzzles/jigsaw-puzzles-index.html

ActiveTeach resources
Line symmetry interactive

6.7 Line symmetry

Concepts and skills

- Recognise reflection symmetry of 2D shapes.
- Identify and draw lines of symmetry on a shape.
- Draw or complete diagrams with a given number of lines of symmetry.

Functional skills

- L1 Construct geometric diagrams, models and shapes.

Prior key knowledge, skills and concepts

- Students should have experience of using a mirror to see if a shape is symmetrical.

Starter

- Ask each student to fold a piece of paper over once. Then tell them to cut out a shape over the fold. Can they see the line symmetry when they open the piece of paper?
- Next ask students to do the same thing with two folds to demonstrate more than one line of symmetry.

Main teaching and learning

- Tell students they are going to find out about line symmetry.
- Explain how one side of the shape is exactly the same as the other side when folded on the mirror line so that if you could look through both halves, one half would be sitting directly on the other half.
- Discuss what happens when you put a two-way mirror on the mirror line and what happens when you reflect a shape that has bits on either side of the mirror line, using a two-way mirror.

Common misconceptions

- When students reflect a shape about a line sloping at 45° to the horizontal they often draw the shape as if the mirror line is vertical. They should be advised to actually turn their diagram around so that the mirror line is vertical in front of them. This often eliminates errors.

Enrichment

A02/A03 focus

- Give students an open shape and ask them to predict what the shape will be after it has been reflected.

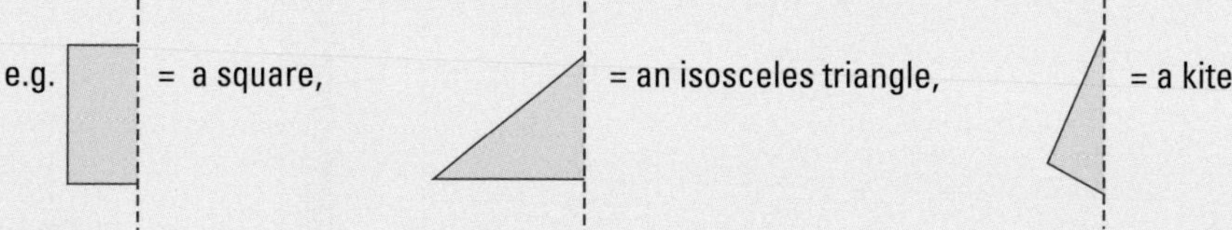

Plenary

- Show students the example of Rubin's vase on Resource sheet 6.7, where you can see two faces and a vase, and ask them to try to draw their own symmetrical optical illusion.

symmetrical line of symmetry mirror line mirror image

Guided practice worksheet

F

1 Draw all the lines of symmetry on each of these letters.
If there are no lines of symmetry write NONE.

B H S V C

2 Complete each drawing so that it has line symmetry.

a b c

3

d e f

4 Add one square so that each shape has line symmetry.

a

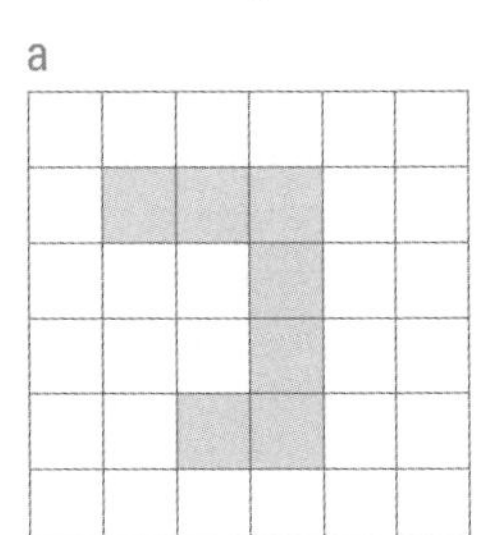

b

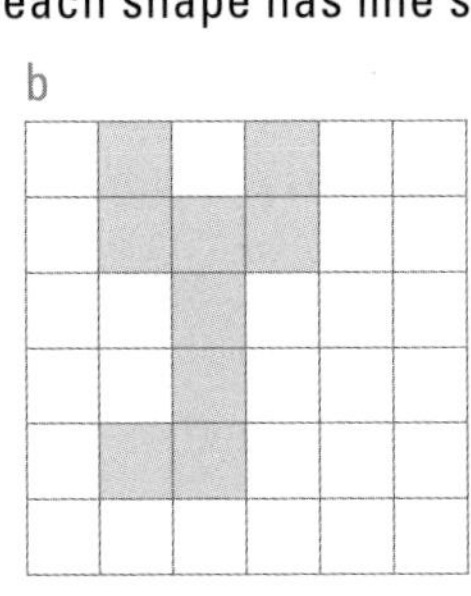

c

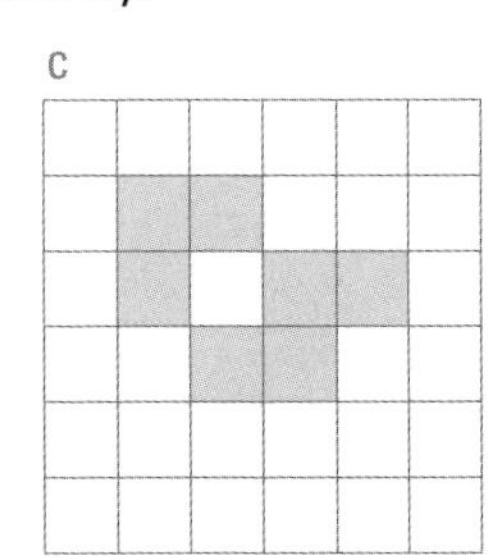

Specification

GCSE 2010
GM e (part) Recognise… rotation symmetry of 2D shapes

FS Process skills
Use appropriate mathematical procedures

FS Performance
Level 1 Use appropriate checking procedures at each stage

Resources

Resources
Board puzzles with cut-out geometric shapes
Tracing paper
Cut-outs of various shapes (or card and scissors)

Links
http://nrich.maths.org/public/search.php?search=congruent+shapes

ActiveTeach resources
RP KC 2D shapes knowledge check
RP PS Symmetry problem solving

6.8 Rotational symmetry

Concepts and skills

- Recognise rotation symmetry of 2D shapes.
- Identify the order of rotational symmetry of a 2D shape.
- Draw or complete diagrams with a given order of rotational symmetry.

Functional skills

- L1 Construct geometric diagrams, models and shapes.

Prior key knowledge, skills and concepts

- Students should know what 90° and 180° turns are and should understand which direction you go in when you turn clockwise or anticlockwise.
- Students should have some experience of drawing shapes on isometric paper.

Starter

- Show students some young children's board puzzles with cut-out geometric shapes that fit into the shapes on the board. Ask students in how many ways each shape can be put back into its slot on the board so that it fits exactly. This exercise will give students a good introduction to the concept of rotational symmetry.

Main teaching and learning

- Tell students they are going to find out about rotational symmetry.
- Explain the difference between line symmetry and rotational symmetry.
- Explain how with line symmetry we use tracing paper and just turn it over to see if the shape is the same, but with rotational symmetry we rotate the tracing paper to do this.

Common misconceptions

- When students trace a shape on tracing paper and then rotate about a point they often forget to also draw ┼ to represent the start before rotating. If they do not do this they often get the angle of rotation incorrect when working on plain paper (as in their GCSE examination).

Enrichment

- Ask students to write down the difference between line symmetry and rotational symmetry.

Plenary

- Give students cut-outs of various shapes such as a pentagon, a trapezium, etc., or get students to cut out their own shapes on card. Ask students to mark one of the corners on their shape. Then ask them to stand it upright and draw the shape in this position. They should then roll it once and draw what they see. They continue to do this until the shape is back where it started. They can then say if the shape has rotational symmetry or not and the order of rotational symmetry.

e.g.

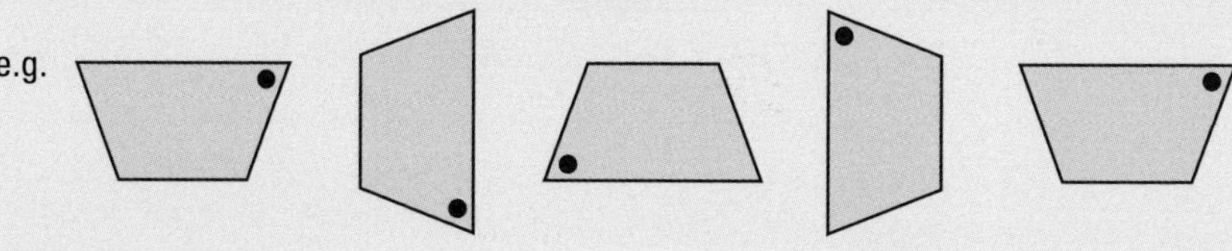

= No rotational symmetry

rotation symmetry order of rotational symmetry

F

Guided practice worksheet

1 These shapes all have rotational symmetry.

Write down the order of rotational symmetry for each.

a

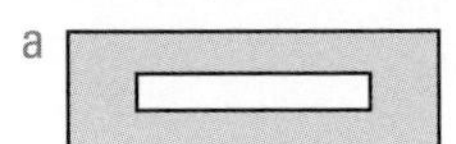

b

c

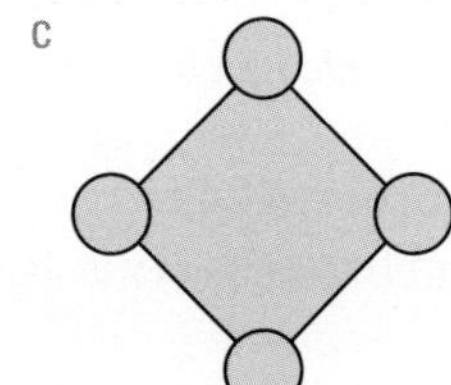

d

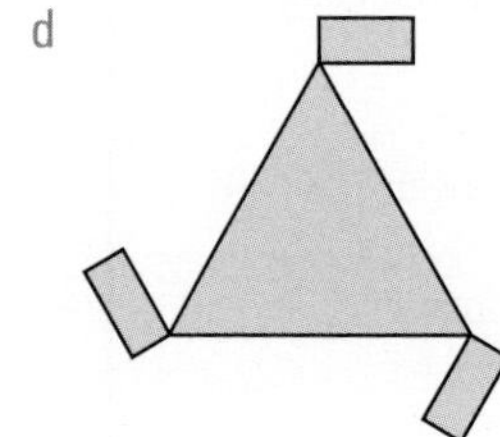

2 Add one square so that each shape has rotational symmetry.

a

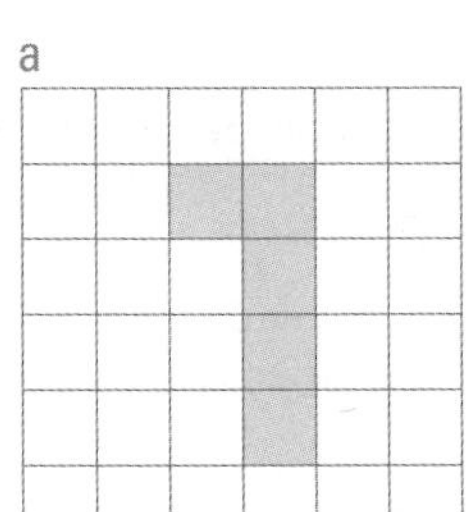

b

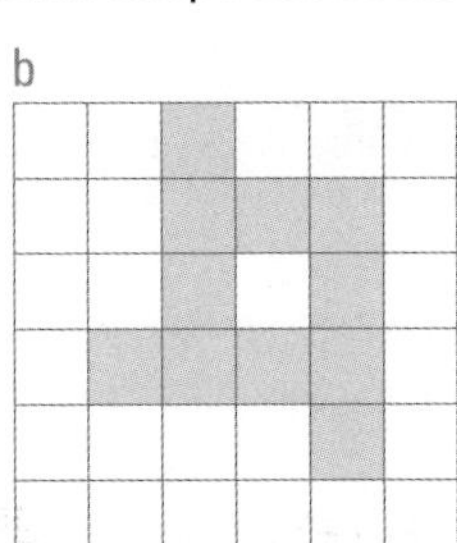

c

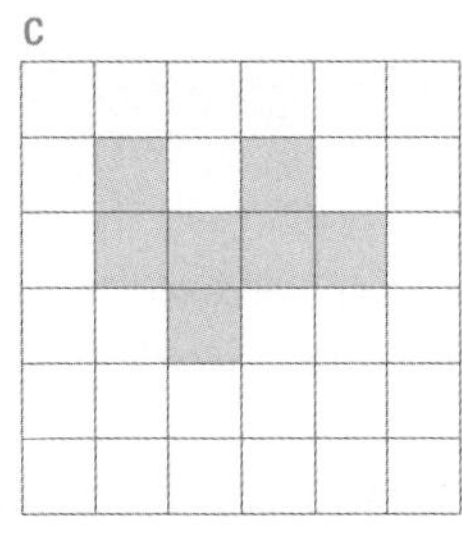

3 Some of these shapes have rotational symmetry and some do not.

For each shape, say if it has rotational symmetry.

If it does, give the order of rotational symmetry.

a

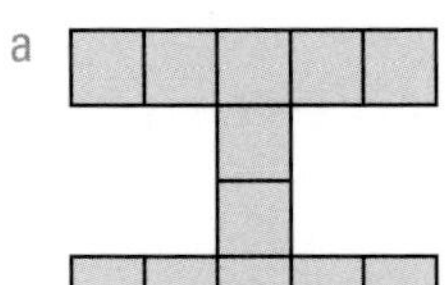

b

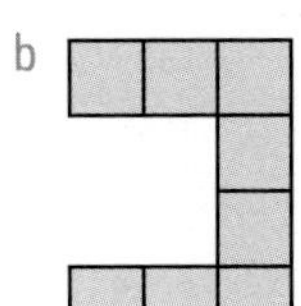

c

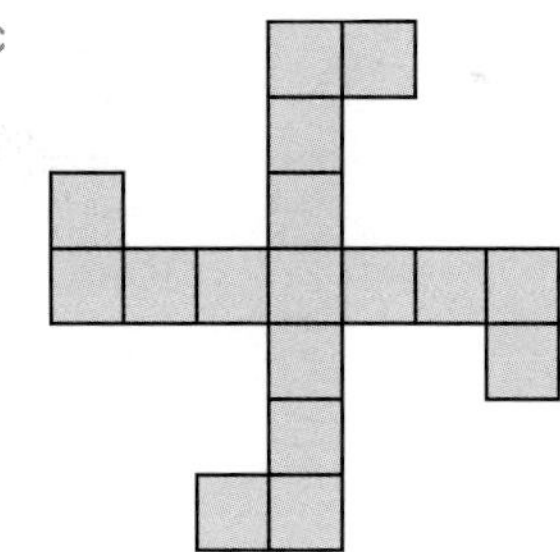

d

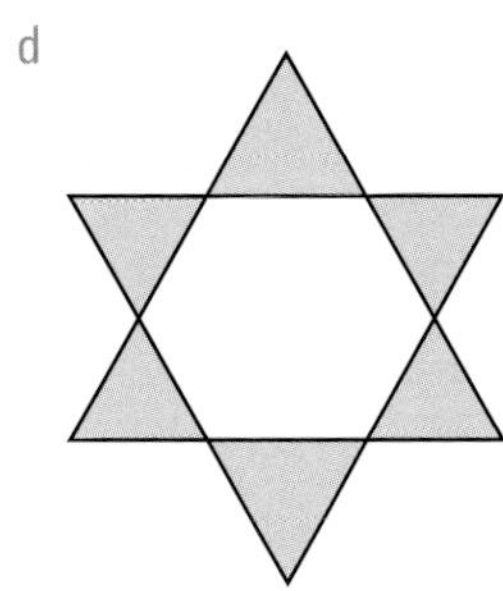

e

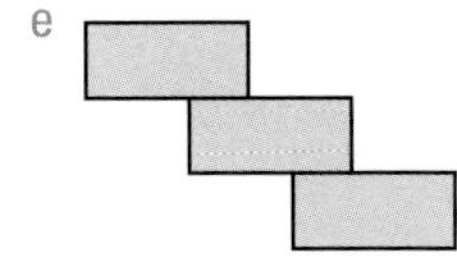

f

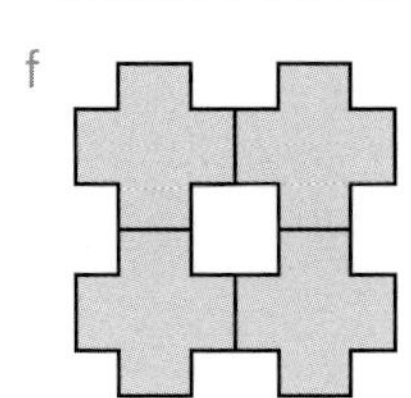

Specification

GCSE 2010

GM b (part) Understand and use the angle properties of … quadrilaterals

FS Process skills

Select the mathematical information to use

Find results and solutions

FS Performance

Level 1 Select mathematics in an organised way to find solutions

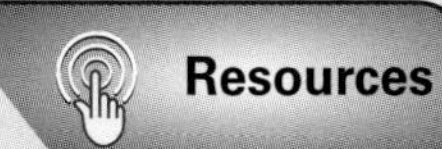

Resources

Resources

Rulers, scissors

ActiveTeach resources

Missing angles quiz

7.1 Angles in quadrilaterals

Concepts and skills

- Understand and use the angle properties of quadrilaterals.
- Use the fact that the angle sum of a quadrilateral is 360°.

Functional skills

- L1 Use simple formulae … for one- or two-step operations.

Prior key knowledge, skills and concepts

- Students should know that the sum of the angles at a vertex equals 360°.

Starter

- Ask students to list words starting with the prefix 'quad', for example, quad bike and quadruple. In discussion, establish that the common element is the number four.

Main teaching and learning

- Introduce the term quadrilateral as meaning literally '4-sided' and hence the name for any shape with four straight sides.
- Ask students to draw a 'random' quadrilateral, cut it out and tear off the corners. Fitting the angles together, demonstrate that all of their quadrilaterals have angles that add up to 360°.
- Test students with some examples of solving problems using the fact that the angles of a quadrilateral equal 360°.

Common misconceptions

- Students fail to recognise that a quadrilateral can have the properties of more than one special quadrilateral at the same time, e.g a rhombus is also a parallelogram.

Enrichment

- Ask students to find other ways of demonstrating that the angle sum of a quadrilateral equals 360°, for example by dividing it into two triangles.

Plenary

- Ask students to recall the literal meaning of quadrilateral as a way of memorising what a quadrilateral is.

Guided practice worksheet

1 Measure all the angles in the following quadrilateral, write down the total.

DAB = ...
ABC = ...
BCD = ...
CDA = ...
Total = ...

2 Work out the size of the missing angles in these quadrilaterals.

a

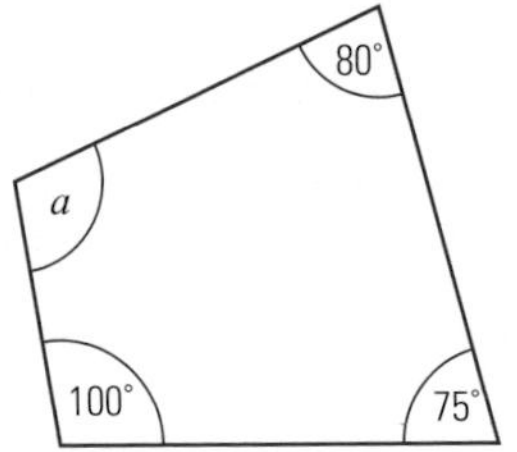

....

b

....

c

....

d

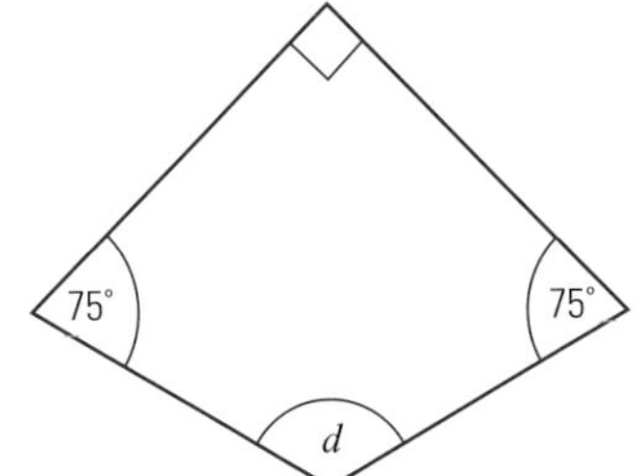

....

Specification

GCSE 2010
GM c (part) Calculate and use the sums of the interior… angles of polygons

FS Process skills
Select the mathematical information to use
Find results and solutions

FS Performance
Level 2 Apply a range of mathematics to find solutions

Resources

Resources
Protractor, calculator

Links
http://www.bbc.co.uk/schools/gcsebitesize/maths/shapes/polygonsact.shtml

ActiveTeach resources
Polygon interactive

7.2 Polygons

Concepts and skills

- Calculate and use the sums of the interior angles of polygons.
- Use geometrical language appropriately and recognise and name pentagons, hexagons, heptagons, octagons and decagons.
- Use the sum of angles of irregular polygons.
- Calculate and use the angles of regular polygons.
- Use the sum of the interior angles of an n-sided polygon.

Functional skills

- L2 Understand and use simple equations and simple formulae for one- or two-step operations.

Prior key knowledge, skills and concepts

- Students should know the properties of triangles and quadrilaterals.

Starter

- Ask students to write down the mathematical names for three- and four-sided shapes and the sum of their interior angles.
- Ask students to find the missing angle in a number of triangles and quadrilaterals.

Main teaching and learning

- Draw shapes with 3, 4, 5, 6, 7, 8 and 10 sides. Ask students to name each shape (if necessary explain that a five-sided shape is a pentagon and ask students to deduce the rest).
- Tell the students they will need to learn each of these names for the exam.
- Use the Guided practice worksheet to get students to establish the number of degrees in each polygon and the pattern, i.e. +180° per side added.
- Demonstrate that the total of the interior angles is equal to $(n - 2) \times 180°$. This can also be demonstrated by dividing polygons into triangles.
- Explain how if you know the angle sum of a polygon you can establish the number of sides.

Common misconceptions

- Students sometimes think that triangles and quadrilaterals do not count as polygons.
- Sometimes students believe that polygons are always regular.

Enrichment

- Ask students what the pentathlon, heptathlon and decathlon are. Explain that the prefix 'pent' means five, 'hept' means seven and 'dec' means ten.
- Discuss the meaning of the prefix 'poly' – many. Hence a polygon is the name for any closed shape with straight sides. Explain that a regular polygon has equal sides and angles.
- Ask students for other words in everyday life that use 'pent-', 'hex-', 'oct-' and 'dec-', e.g. The Pentagon (in USA), octopus, decade, etc.

Plenary

- Ask students to write down the names of all the shapes with 3–10 sides (excluding nine).
- Put the students in pairs and give each student a different list of polygons, for example, equilateral triangle, square, parallelogram, regular pentagon, and so on. They should then take turns to describe a shape to their partner without naming the shape, for example, 'My shape has three sides all the same length'. The partner has to correctly identify the shape.

polygon pentagon hexagon heptagon octagon decagon regular

Guided practice worksheet

F

1. Use a protractor to measure the interior angles of these polygons. Fill your answers in the table.

1 2 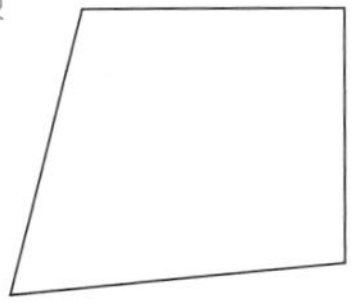 3

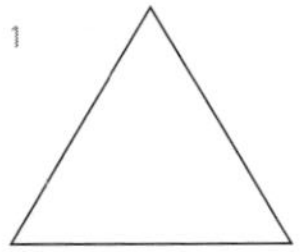

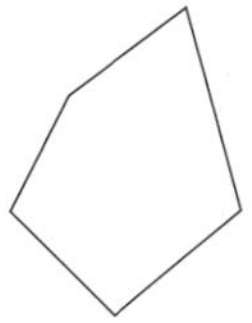

4 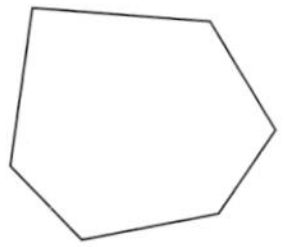 5 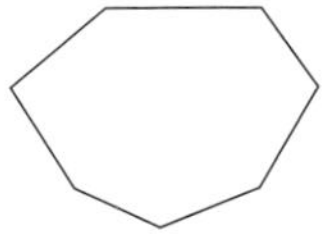 6

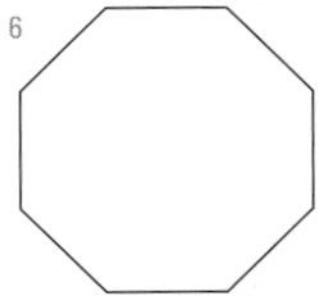

	Name of shape	Size of angles	Sum of interior angles
1			
2			
3			
4			
5			
6			

2. By how many degrees do the totals increase with each side added?

D

3. What would the sum of the interior angles be for a decagon?

Section 7.2 Polygons

Guided practice worksheet

D

4. What would be the sum of the interior angles for a 20-sided shape?

5. Complete the following.

The sum of the interior angles for a n-sided polygon is ($n-$..........) × 180°

Specification

GCSE 2010

GM c Calculate and use the sums of the interior and exterior angles of polygons
GM f Understand congruence and similarity.

FS Process skills

Select the mathematical information to use
Find results and solutions

FS Performance

Level 2 Apply a range of mathematics to find solutions

Resources

Resources

Rulers

7.3 Exterior and interior angles

Concepts and skills

- Use the sum of the exterior angles of any polygon is 360°.
- Use the sum of the interior angle and the exterior angle is 180°.
- Identify shapes which are similar; including … all regular polygons with equal numbers of sides.

Functional skills

- L2 Understand and use simple equations and simple formulae for one- or two-step operations.

Prior key knowledge, skills and concepts

- Students should know the names of polygons and the sum of their interior angles.
- They should also know that the angles on a straight line add up to 180°.

Starter

- Draw a regular polygon with the sides extended. Ask students to recall the size of the interior angles and thus calculate the size of the exterior angle. Then ask students to find the sum of the exterior angles.

Main teaching and learning

- Using further examples, establish that the sum of the exterior angles of any polygon is 360° and that the interior angle and the exterior angle sum to 180°.
- Work through examples of n-sided regular polygons, establishing the exterior angle by using the formula exterior angle = $\frac{360^\circ}{n}$.
- Again using the formula exterior angle = $\frac{360^\circ}{n}$ show how, given the exterior angle, the number of sides of a regular polygon can be obtained.

Common misconceptions

- Students sometimes think that the formula exterior angle = $\frac{360^\circ}{n}$ can be used for irregular polygons.

Enrichment

- Students could use ICT packages (e.g. logo) to draw regular polygons.

Plenary

- Ask students to summarise all the angle facts relating to polygons.

exterior angle

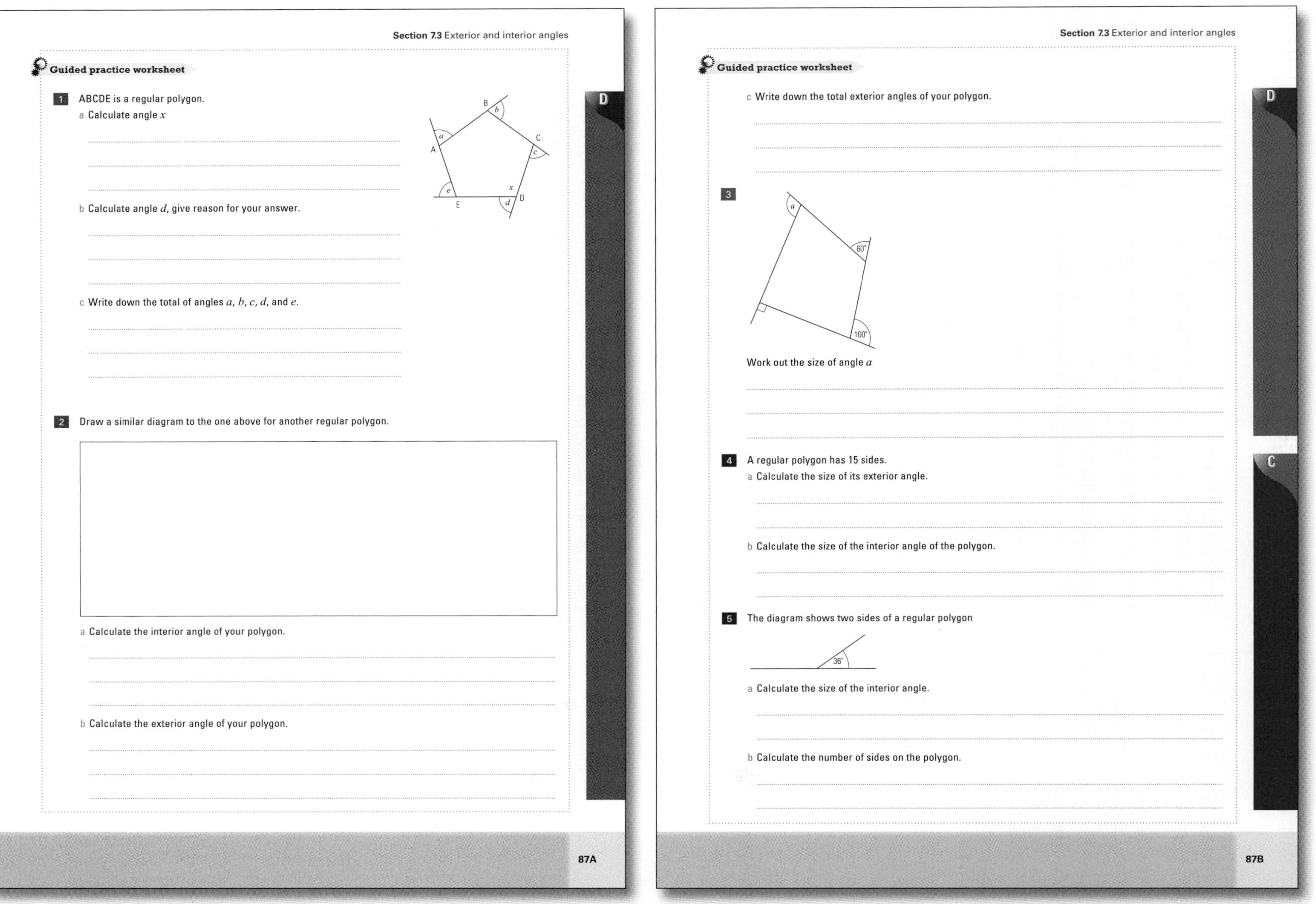

Guided practice worksheet

D

1 ABCDE is a regular polygon.

a Calculate angle x

b Calculate angle d, give reason for your answer.

c Write down the total of angles a, b, c, d, and e.

2 Draw a similar diagram to the one above for another regular polygon.

a Calculate the interior angle of your polygon.

b Calculate the exterior angle of your polygon.

Section 7.3 Exterior and interior angles

Guided practice worksheet

c Write down the total exterior angles of your polygon.

3

Work out the size of angle a

4 A regular polygon has 15 sides.

a Calculate the size of its exterior angle.

b Calculate the size of the interior angle of the polygon.

C

5 The diagram shows two sides of a regular polygon

a Calculate the size of the interior angle.

b Calculate the number of sides on the polygon.

GCSE 2010
GM c Calculate and use the sums of the interior and exterior angles of polygons

FS Process skills
Select the mathematical information to use

FS Performance
Level 1 Select mathematics in an organised way to find solutions

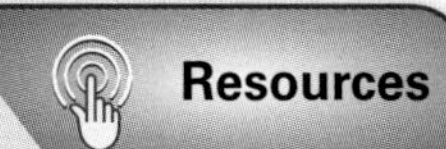

Resources
Ruler, scissors, paper or card, adhesive tape

Links
http://nrich.maths.org/4832

ActiveTeach resources
Angles quiz
Tessellations interactive

7.4 Tessellations

Concepts and skills

- Understand tessellations of regular and irregular polygons.
- Tessellate combinations of polygons.
- Explain why some shapes tessellate when other shapes do not.

Functional skills

- L1 Construct geometric diagrams, models and shapes.

Prior key knowledge, skills and concepts

- Students should know properties of polygons.

Starter

- Check that students can recall that angles around a point add up to 360°.
- Check that students can calculate the interior and exterior angles of a regular polygon.

Main teaching and learning

- Explain how tessellation is similar to tiling a floor with one shape of tile so that there are no gaps.
- Demonstrate that all triangles and all quadrilaterals tessellate.
- Show that for polygons having more than four sides, the interior angles must be a factor of 360.
- Ask students if a regular octagon can tessellate. *What is the interior angle of a regular octagon?* (135°) Look at the vertex where two identical regular octagons meet. Angles round a point sum to 360°, but the two octagons make 270°, so a third octagon will not fit. However, 360 – 270 = 90, so a square with same side length can complete the tessellation.

Common misconceptions

- Students do not draw enough shapes to demonstrate that their tessellation can carry on infinitely.

Enrichment

- Create 'artistic' tessellations from regular shapes by cutting out shapes from an edge and attaching them to other sides.

Plenary

- Ask students to explain why a parallelogram will always tessellate, but a pentagon will not.

E

Guided practice worksheet

1 Show how each of the following shapes tessellates.

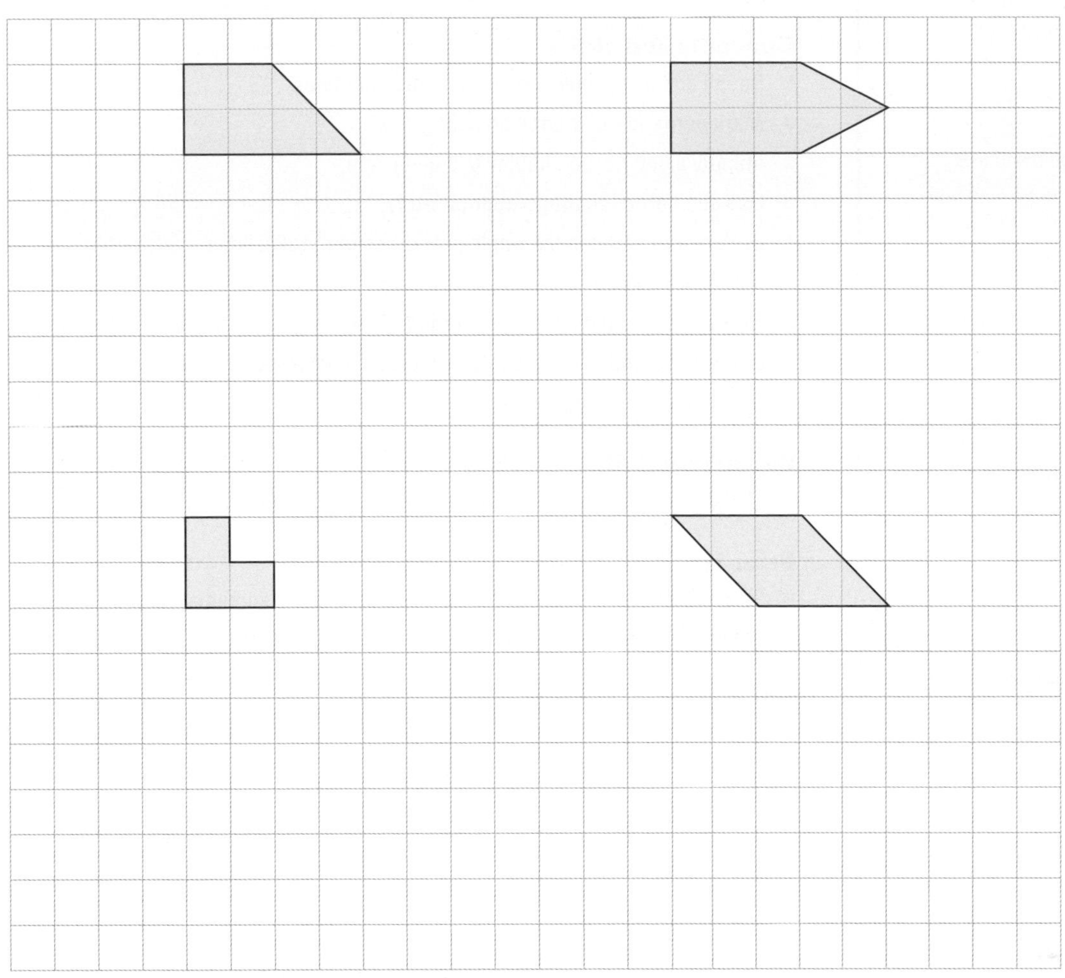

2 Which of the following polygons tessellate? Give a reason for your answer.

a hexagon ....

b square ....

c decagon ....

d pentagon ....

3 A regular octagon can be tessellated when combined with another shape.
Write down the name of the other shape.

....

Specification

GCSE 2010

GM a Recall and use properties of angles at a point, angles on a straight line (including right angles), perpendicular lines, and opposite angles at a vertex

GM b (part) Understand and use the angle properties of parallel and intersecting lines...

FS Process skills

Select the mathematical information to use

Find results and solutions

FS Performance

Level 1 Select mathematics in an organised way to find solutions

Resources

Resources

Ruler, tracing paper

Links

http://www.bbc.co.uk/schools/gcsebitesize/maths/shapes/anglesact.shtml

7.5 Perpendicular and parallel lines
7.6 Corresponding and alternate angles

Concepts and skills

- Recall and use properties of perpendicular lines.
- Mark perpendicular lines on a diagram.
- Identify a line perpendicular to a given line.
- Use geometric language appropriately.
- Understand and use the angle properties of parallel lines.
- Mark parallel lines on a diagram.
- Find missing angles using properties of corresponding and alternate angles.
- Understand and use the angle properties of intersecting lines.
- Give reasons for angle calculations.

Functional skills

- L1 Use simple formulae for one- or two-step operations.

Prior key knowledge, skills and concepts

- Students should be able to find the size of missing angles around a point or on a straight line.

Starter

- Check students can recall that angles around a point sum to 360°, and on a straight line sum to 180°. Also, ensure that they know how to name angles and lines using letters.

Main teaching and learning

- Using pairs of converging, diverging and parallel lines discuss what will happen if lines are extended. Establish that parallel lines will never meet. Introduce dashed marks to indicate parallel lines.
- Tell students that lines that meet at 90° are called perpendicular lines.
- Provide a number of examples so that students can practise identifying parallel and perpendicular lines.
- Tell students that diagrams and shapes containing parallel lines have certain properties that will allow them to work out missing angles.
- Ask students to draw a pair of parallel lines with an intersecting line on tracing paper. Cut the diagram across the transect and show through translation that corresponding angles are equal. Introduce the term 'corresponding'.
- Repeat the above exercise but show through rotation that alternate angles are equal. Introduce the term 'alternate'.
- Work through a number of examples identifying corresponding and alternate angles. Emphasise the importance of giving reasons when identifying angles.

Common misconceptions

- Students do not always give a full explanation or provide reasons in full. For example, they might say 'alternate angles' rather than stating that 'alternate angles are equal'.

Enrichment

- Ask students to 'prove' that 'u-angles' add up to 180°.

Plenary

- Summarise the work by asking the class to identify all the angles, and provide reasons for their answers, on a pair of parallel lines with an intersect and one angle marked as x.

perpendicular parallel corresponding angles alternative angles

Guided practice worksheet

1 a Identify all the pairs of parallel lines in this diagram.

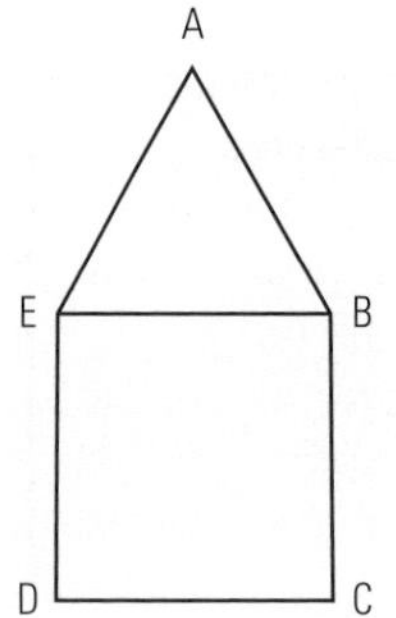

....

....

b Identify all the pairs of perpendicular lines in this diagram.

....

....

2 Complete the following statements. Use one of the following words:
Equal, alternate, corresponding

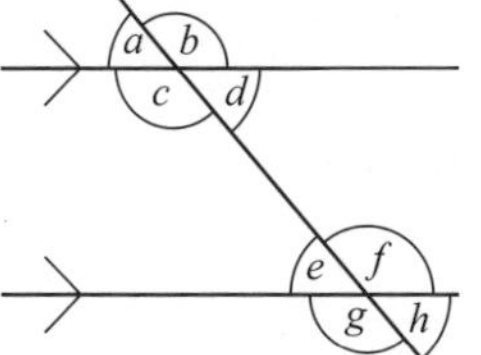

a Angles d and e are .... angles.

b Angles a and e are .... angles.

c Angles c and f are .... angles.

d Angles h and d are .... angles.

e Corresponding angles are ....

f Alternate angles are ....

3 Find all the missing angles in this diagram.

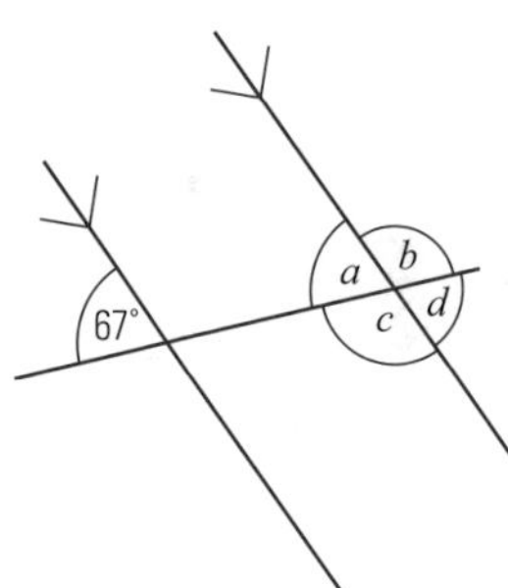

....

....

....

....

....

....

4 Find all the missing angles in this diagram. Give reasons for your answers.

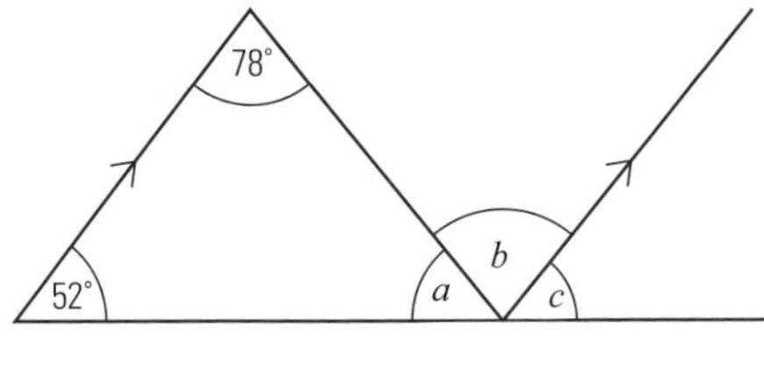

....

....

....

....

GCSE 2010
GM b (part) Understand and use the angle properties of parallel lines….

FS Process skills
Not applicable

FS Performance
Not applicable

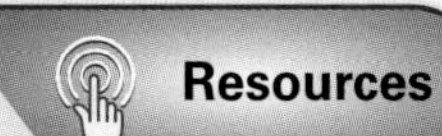

Resources
Ruler

ActiveTeach resources
Angles in a triangle quiz

7.7 Proofs

Concepts and skills

- Understand the proof that the angle sum of a triangle is 180°.
- Understand a proof that the exterior angle of a triangle is equal to the sum of the interior angles at the other two vertices.

Functional skills

- Not applicable

Prior key knowledge, skills and concepts

- Students should know the properties of parallel lines, including alternate and corresponding angles.

Starter

- Discuss the meaning and importance of proof in mathematics and explain that students will be shown three angle proofs. Emphasise that they will be expected to recall these proofs in the examination.

Main teaching and learning

- Take the students through each of the proofs:
  - the exterior angle of a triangle is equal to the sum of the interior angles at the other two vertices;
  - the sum of the angles of a triangle is equal to 180°;
  - the opposite angles of a parallelogram are equal.
- After each demonstration ask students to repeat the proof in their books.

Common misconceptions

- Some students find it difficult to understand the difference between a proof and a specific example. Emphasise the difference between the generalised nature of proof and demonstration through specific examples.

Plenary

- Ask students to go through their proofs and to correct work in their books, if necessary.

Guided practice worksheet

C

Write down a reason after each line of working, e.g. angle sum of a triangle.

1 Use the angle of a straight line (180°) to prove that opposite angles are equal.

You must prove that $a = c$

$a + b =$ .... because ....

$b + c =$ .... because ....

So $a + b = b + c$

So $a = c$ (subtract b from both sides)

Opposite angles are equal.

2 The base angles of an isosceles triangles are equal.
Prove that the bisector of the top angle meets the base at right angles.

You must show that $c = 90°$

$a + b + c =$ .... because ....

$a + b + d =$ .... because ....

So $c = d$ because the left sides of the equations are equal

$c + d =$ .... because ....

So $c = 90°$ because ....

The bisector of the top angle meets the base at right angles.

Guided practice worksheet

C

3 Prove that the diagonals of a square cross at right angles.

Hint: Look for isosceles triangles

You must show that d = 90°

$b = c$ because ....

$b + c = 90°$ because ....

So $c = 45°$ because ....

$a = e$ because ....

$a + c = 90°$ because ....

So $a = 45°$ because ....

So $d = 90°$ because ....

The diagonals of a square cross at right angles.

4 The quadrilateral on the left has been split into two triangles on the right.

Prove that the angle sum of a quadrilateral is 360°.
You must show that $a + b + c + d = 360°$

$a + p + r =$ .... because ....

$c + q + s =$ .... because ....

$a + p + q + c + r + s =$ .... (add the equations together)

$a + b + c + d = 360°$ because ....

The angle sum of a quadrilateral is 360°.

Specification

GCSE 2010
GM r Understand and use bearings

FS Process skills
Select the mathematical information to use
Find results and solutions

FS Performance
Level 1 Apply mathematics in an organised way to find solutions to straightforward practical problems for different purposes

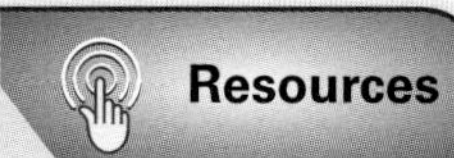

Resources

Resources
Protractor

CD Resources
Resource sheet 7.8 for drawing bearings

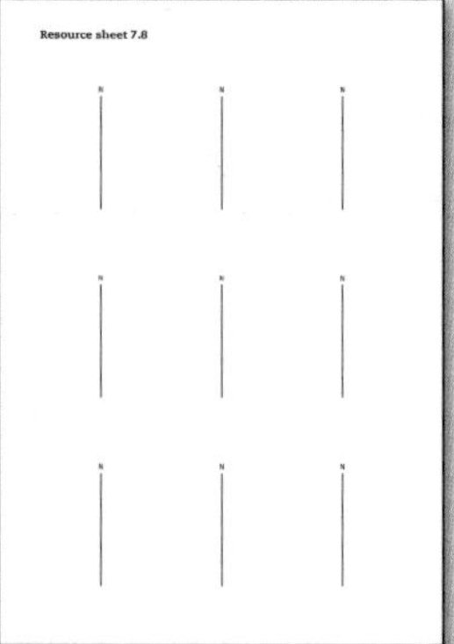
Resource sheet 7.8

Links
http://www.bbc.co.uk/schools/gcsebitesize/maths/shapes/coordinatesandbearingsact.shtml

ActiveTeach resources
Bearings interactive

7.8 Bearings

Concepts and skills

- Use three-figure bearings to specify direction.
- Mark on a diagram the position of point B given its bearing from point A.
- Give a bearing between the points on a map or scaled plan.
- Given the bearing of a point A from Point B, work out the bearing of B from A.

Functional skills

- L1 Construct geometric diagrams, models and shapes.

Prior key knowledge, skills and concepts

- Students should be able to use a protractor to draw and measure angles.
- They should also be able to recall and use properties of parallel lines, and mark perpendicular and parallel lines on a diagram.
- They should also be able to find missing angles using properties of corresponding and alternate angles.

Starter

- Ask students a few questions which require them to find missing angles using properties of corresponding and alternate angles.

Main teaching and learning

- Tell the students that bearings are used to communicate the direction of one point from another, usually used in navigation.
- Explain that in order to avoid any confusion in communication, bearings are always measured clockwise from north and given as three-figure numbers.
- Go through a few examples, emphasising the placement of the zero for bearings less than 100°.
- Demonstrate how, when measuring bearings greater than 180°, the smaller angle can be measured and subtracted from 360°.
- Explain how, when working with problems involving bearings, drawing lines representing north creates parallel lines which can be used to solve the problem.
- Work through a few examples showing how to use the properties of corresponding and alternate angles to solve problems.

Common misconceptions

- Students sometimes drop the zero for bearings less than 100°.
- Some students may also measure/read angles in an anticlockwise direction.
- Emphasise that bearings should be taken at the 'from' point.

Enrichment

- Ask students to draw simple scale drawings using bearings and distance. (By inspection.)

Plenary

- Go through a few examples making deliberate errors, for example measuring anticlockwise. Ask students to identify the errors that you make.

bearing

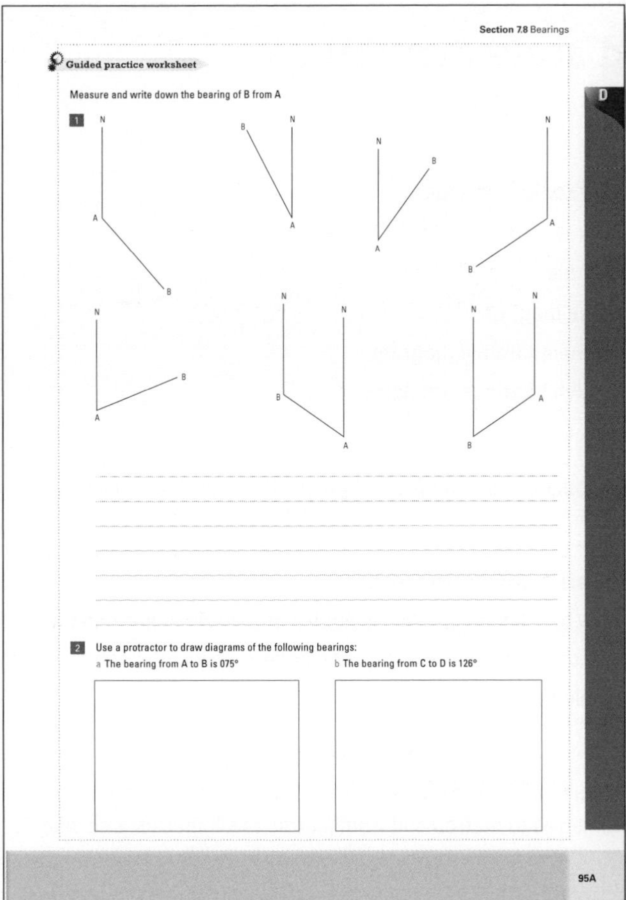

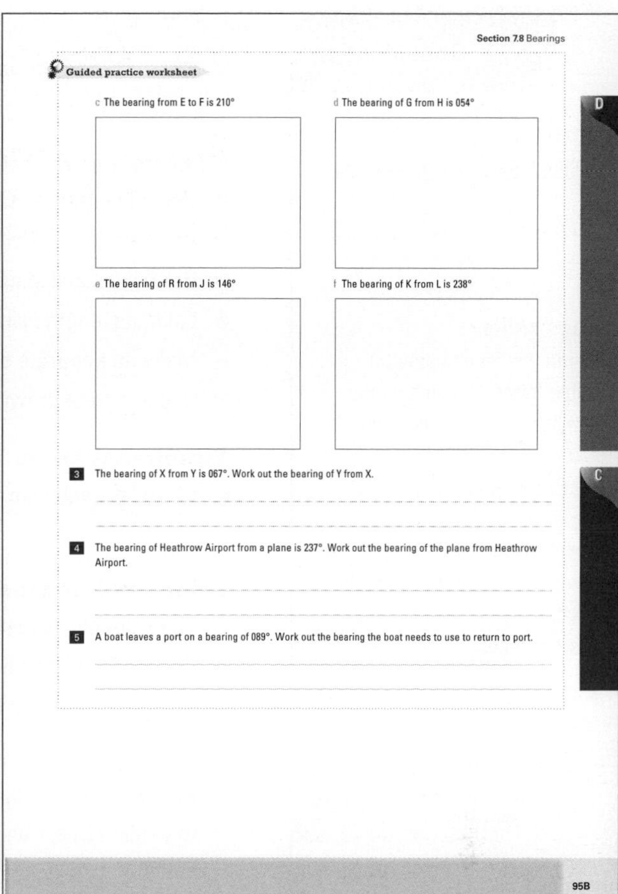

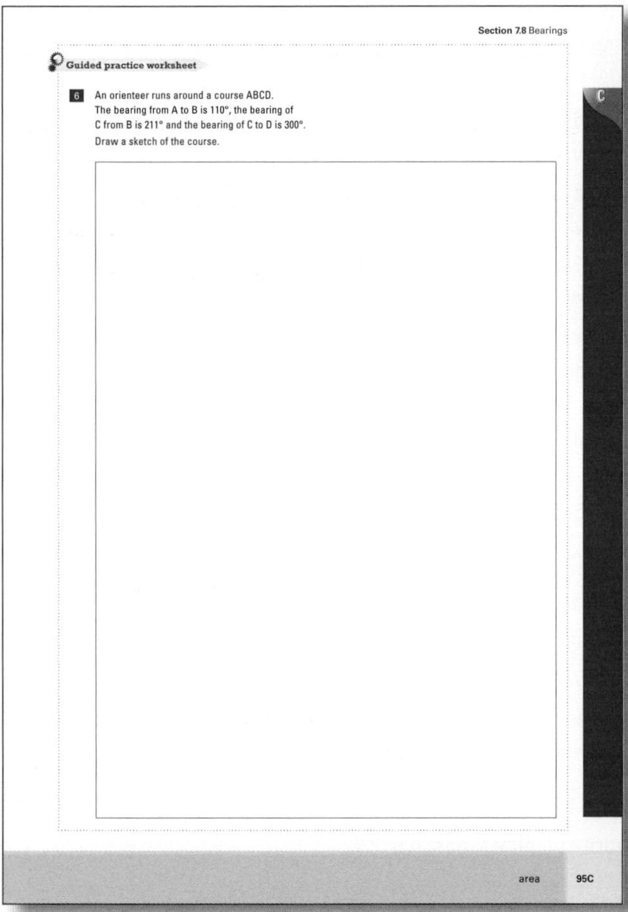

Specification

GCSE 2010

GM m Use and interpret maps and scale drawings

GM u (part) Draw… shapes using ruler and protractor

FS Process skills

Make an initial model of a situation using suitable forms of representation

Select the mathematical information to use

Find results and solutions

FS Performance

Level 2 Identify the situation or problems and identify the mathematical methods needed to solve them

Resources

Resources

Ruler, protractor

CD Resources

Resource sheet 7.9a

Resource sheet 7.9b

Resource sheet 7.9c

Resource sheet 7.9d

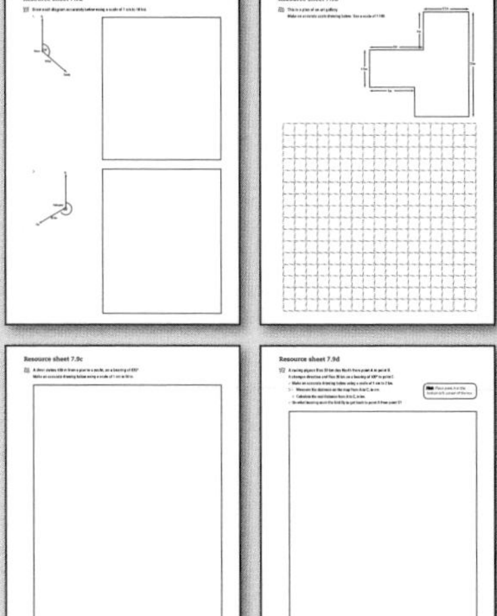

ActiveTeach resources

Building the course 2a video

Setting up the fair 1 video

RP KC Angles 2 knowledge check

RP PS Angles 2 problem solving

7.9 Maps and scale drawings

Concepts and skills

- Use and interpret maps and scale drawings.
- Read and construct scale drawings.
- Draw lines and shapes to scale.
- Estimate length using a scale diagram.
- Make an accurate scale drawing from a diagram.
- Use accurate drawing to solve bearings problems.

Functional skills

- L2 Understand, use and calculate ratio and proportion, including problems involving scale.

Prior key knowledge, skills and concepts

- The students should be able to draw and measure lines to the nearest millimetre.
- They should also be able to convert between units of measurement in the same system.
- Students also need to be able to use bearings.

Starter

- Ask students a number of questions covering examples of converting from millimetres to centimetres, from centimetres to metres and from metres to kilometres, and vice versa.

Main teaching and learning

- Explain that maps and scale drawings are accurate drawings from which the true measurements can be taken.
- Explain that a scale of 1:50 means that every 50 units is represented by one unit on the map or scale drawing.
- Discuss various scales used in maps, e.g. 1:25 000, and explain that, in this example, one centimetre on the map will equal 250 m.
- Explain that when drawing a scale drawing to the scale of $1:n$, the lengths on the diagram can be found by dividing the 'real' length by n.
- Discuss the fact that a 'real' distance from a map or scale drawing drawn to a ratio of $1:n$ can be found by multiplying the measured distance by n.
- Explain that a scale of $1:n$ implies that both sides of the ratio are in the same unit and that students may have to convert measurements into other units in order to give sensible answers.
- Demonstrate how the size of an angle is preserved when represented in a scale drawing.
- Illustrate how problems involving bearings can be represented and solved using a scale drawing.

Common misconceptions

- Students sometimes mix units when working with scale drawings.
- They may also drop the zero for bearings less than 100°.
- Some students may also measure/read angles in an anticlockwise direction and forget that bearings should be taken at the 'from' point.

Enrichment

- Scale drawings using more complex ratios, e.g. 2:7.

Plenary

- Go though a few examples that require students to use scale. For example, a building is 15 m high; how big would it be drawn using a scale of 1:50? (30 cm)

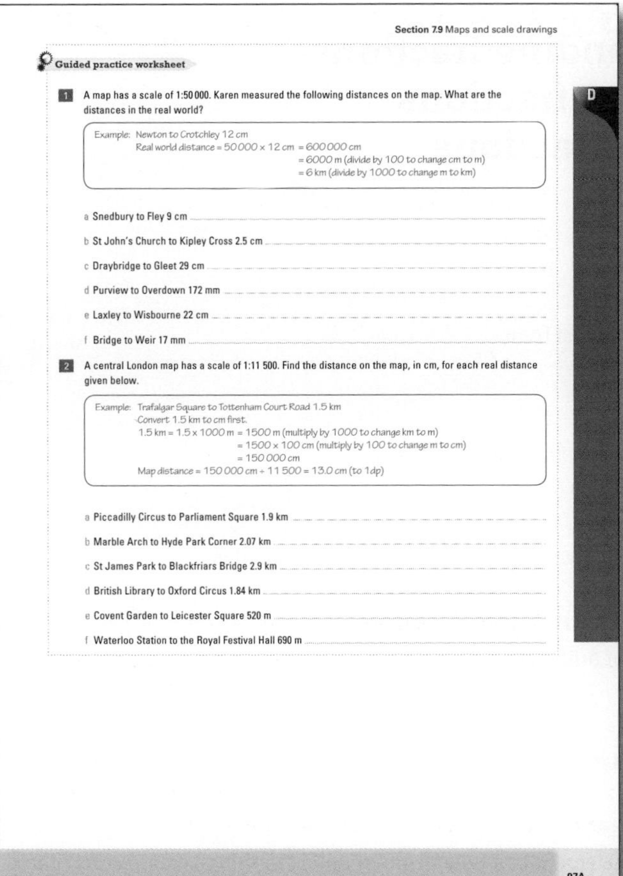

Section 7.9 Maps and scale drawings

Guided practice worksheet

1 A map has a scale of 1:50 000. Karen measured the following distances on the map. What are the distances in the real world?

Example: Newton to Crotchley 12 cm
Real world distance = 50 000 × 12 cm = 600 000 cm
= 6000 m (divide by 100 to change cm to m)
= 6 km (divide by 1000 to change m to km)

a Snedbury to Fley 9 cm ……

b St John's Church to Kipley Cross 2.5 cm ……

c Draybridge to Gleet 29 cm ……

d Purview to Overdown 172 mm ……

e Laxley to Wisbourne 22 cm ……

f Bridge to Weir 17 mm ……

2 A central London map has a scale of 1:11 500. Find the distance on the map, in cm, for each real distance given below.

Example: Trafalgar Square to Tottenham Court Road 1.5 km
Convert 1.5 km to cm first.
1.5 km = 1.5 x 1000 m = 1500 m (multiply by 1000 to change km to m)
= 1500 × 100 cm (multiply by 100 to change m to cm)
= 150 000 cm
Map distance = 150 000 cm ÷ 11 500 = 13.0 cm (to 1dp)

a Piccadilly Circus to Parliament Square 1.9 km ……

b Marble Arch to Hyde Park Corner 2.07 km ……

c St James Park to Blackfriars Bridge 2.9 km ……

d British Library to Oxford Circus 1.84 km ……

e Covent Garden to Leicester Square 520 m ……

f Waterloo Station to the Royal Festival Hall 690 m ……

97A

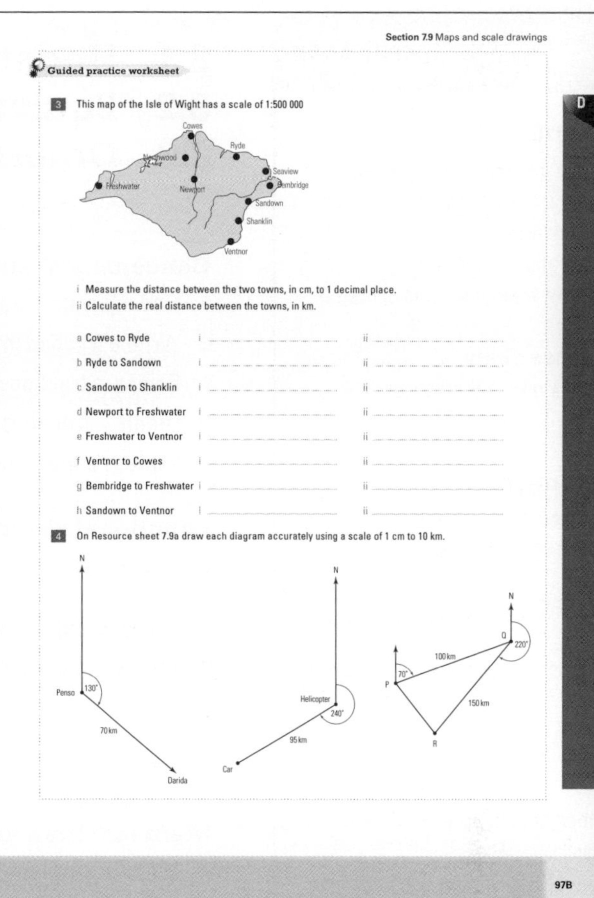

Section 7.9 Maps and scale drawings

Guided practice worksheet

3 This map of the Isle of Wight has a scale of 1:500 000

i Measure the distance between the two towns, in cm, to 1 decimal place.
ii Calculate the real distance between the towns, in km.

a Cowes to Ryde i …… ii ……

b Ryde to Sandown i …… ii ……

c Sandown to Shanklin i …… ii ……

d Newport to Freshwater i …… ii ……

e Freshwater to Ventnor i …… ii ……

f Ventnor to Cowes i …… ii ……

g Bembridge to Freshwater i …… ii ……

h Sandown to Ventnor i …… ii ……

4 On Resource sheet 7.9a draw each diagram accurately using a scale of 1 cm to 10 km.

97B

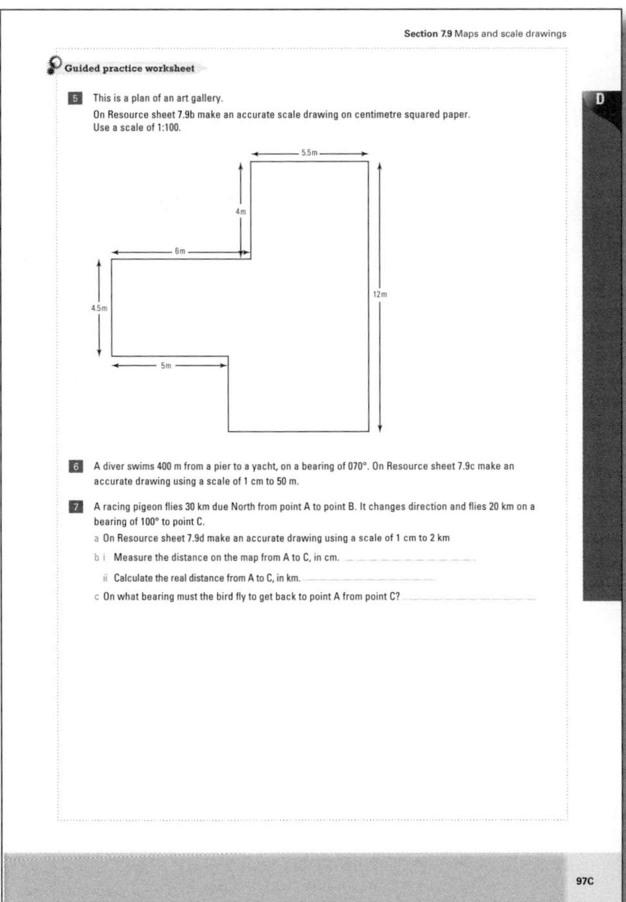

Section 7.9 Maps and scale drawings

Guided practice worksheet

5 This is a plan of an art gallery.
On Resource sheet 7.9b make an accurate scale drawing on centimetre squared paper.
Use a scale of 1:100.

6 A diver swims 400 m from a pier to a yacht, on a bearing of 070°. On Resource sheet 7.9c make an accurate drawing using a scale of 1 cm to 50 m.

7 A racing pigeon flies 30 km due North from point A to point B. It changes direction and flies 20 km on a bearing of 100° to point C.

a On Resource sheet 7.9d make an accurate drawing using a scale of 1 cm to 2 km

b i Measure the distance on the map from A to C, in cm. ……

ii Calculate the real distance from A to C, in km. ……

c On what bearing must the bird fly to get back to point A from point C? ……

97C

Specification

GCSE 2010

N h Understand equivalent fractions, simplifying a fraction by cancelling all common factors
N b Order rational numbers
N o Interpret fractions … as operators

FS Process skills

Use appropriate mathematical procedures

FS Performance

Level 1 Use appropriate checking procedures at each stage

Resources

Links

http://nrich.maths.org/public/search.php?search=fractions
http://www.mathsisfun.com/fractions-menu.html

ActiveTeach resources

Multiplication and division quiz
Fractions of shapes interactive
Fraction and percentage finder interactive
Fraction quiz
Equivalent fractions interactive
Simplest form fractions interactive
Simplifying fractions quiz

8.1 Understanding fractions
8.2 Equivalent fractions
8.3 Ordering fractions

Concepts and skills

- Find equivalent fractions.
- Write a fraction in its simplest form.
- Compare fractions.
- Order … fractions.
- Express a given number as a fraction of another.

Functional skills

- L1 Understand and use equivalences between common fractions …

Prior key knowledge, skills and concepts

- Tables and basic rules of arithmetic.

Starter

- Lead a discussion about instances of fractions in common use (e.g. $\frac{1}{2}$ price, etc.).

Main teaching and learning

- *What is a fraction?* Make sure that students understand that fractions are equal parts of a unit.
- Show students equivalent fractions by ongoing subdivision of a rectangle. Build a family.
- Compare fractions using a rectangle divided into an appropriate number of squares to accommodate both fractions. For example, a 6×5 rectangle to compare $\frac{2}{3}$ and $\frac{3}{5}$.
- Change fractions to ones with a common denominator.

Plenary

- Discuss how students tackled Exercise 8C question 4.

numerator denominator equivalent fractions simplest form common denominator

Guided practice worksheet

1 In the diagrams, what fraction is shaded?

a

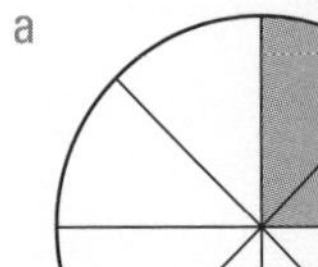

b

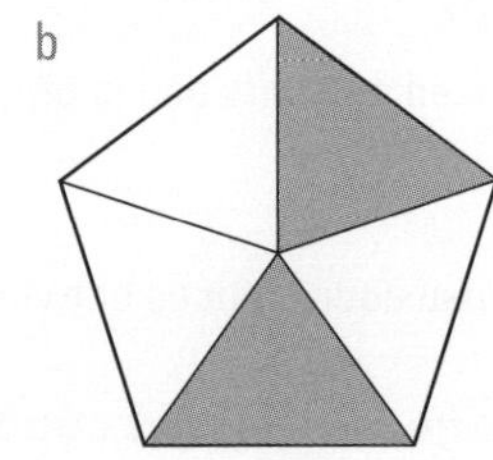

c

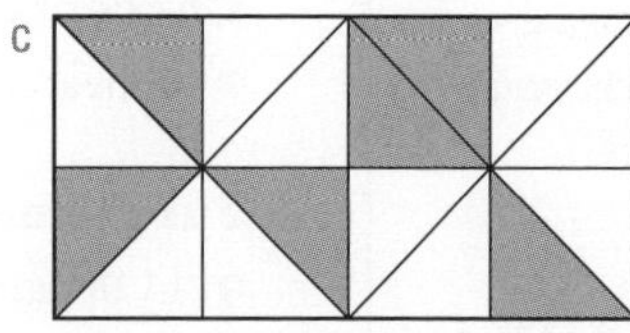

....

2 There are 500 beads in a jar. Eighty of the beads are green.
Work out 80 as a fraction of 500 giving your answer in its simplest form.

....

3 Use this diagram to help you find some fractions equivalent to $\frac{1}{3}$.
Use the fact that each column has $\frac{1}{3}$ shaded.

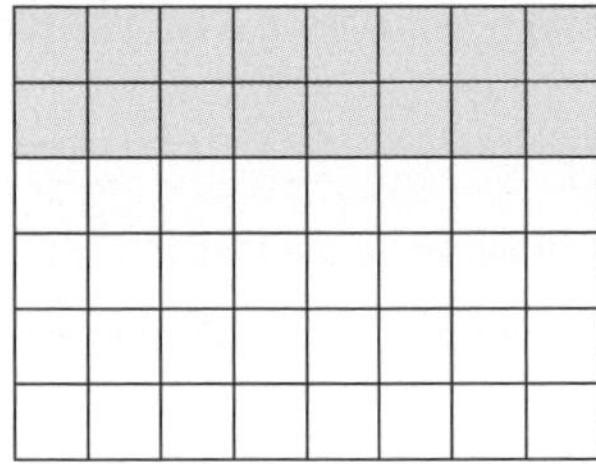

....

....

4 Complete the fractions so that each is equivalent to $\frac{3}{5}$.

$\frac{\square}{10}$ $\frac{18}{\square}$ $\frac{24}{\square}$ $\frac{\square}{45}$ $\frac{21}{\square}$ $\frac{\square}{120}$ $\frac{90}{\square}$

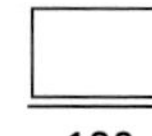

5 Write the following fractions in their simplest form.

a $\frac{8}{18}$ ....

b $\frac{27}{36}$ ....

c $\frac{18}{60}$ ....

d $\frac{50}{80}$ ....

e $\frac{33}{132}$ ....

f $\frac{48}{60}$ ....

Specification

GCSE 2010
N h Understand equivalent fractions, simplifying a fraction by cancelling all common factors

FS Process skills
Use appropriate mathematical procedures

FS Performance
Level 1 Use appropriate checking procedures at each stage

Resources
Road sign(s) for plenary

8.4 Improper fractions and mixed numbers

Concepts and skills

- Convert between mixed numbers and improper fractions.

Functional skills

- L1 Understand and use equivalences between common fractions …

Prior key knowledge, skills and concepts

- Tables to 9×9

Starter

- Discuss where mixed numbers are seen in real life (see Why do this?). Ask students to give further examples.
- *Write the first question in the Get ready box as a fraction.* $\left(\frac{23}{4}\right)$. Explain that this is an improper fraction.

Main teaching and learning

- Teach students how to:
  - Turn an improper fraction into a mixed number by dividing.
  - Draw a rectangle on the board and ask *How many quarters in a whole?* Write $\frac{4}{4}$ on the board and divide the rectangle into 4.
  - *What does* $\frac{9}{4}$ *mean?* (There are nine quarters.)
  - Draw the diagram below and ask *How else can we write the fraction* $\frac{9}{4}$*?* $\left(\frac{9}{4} = 2\frac{1}{4}\right)$

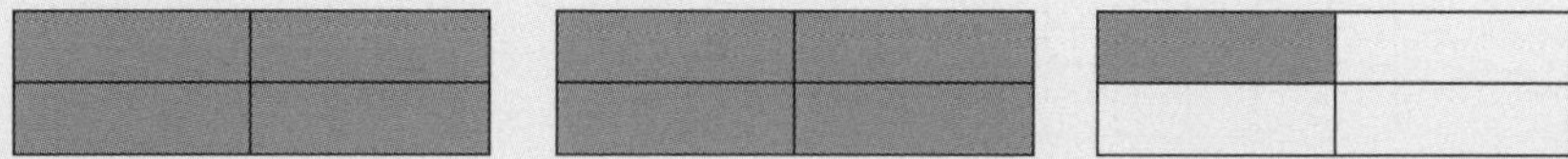

- *What is the name of a fraction where the numerator is bigger than the denominator?* (improper)
- *What is the name given to a number with a whole number part and a fractional part?* (mixed number)
- turn a mixed number into an improper fraction by splitting the integer into matching fractional pieces.

Common misconceptions

- When converting from a mixed number students sometimes take the numerator of the fraction part as a whole number, e.g. $\frac{9}{4} = 2.1$.

Plenary

- Make up a road sign using local place names, with distances using mixed numbers. Ask students to convert these distances to improper fractions. (You could do this the other way round as well.)

improper fractions mixed numbers

G

Guided practice worksheet

1 Change these improper fractions into mixed numbers (by doing the division with a remainder).

a $\frac{6}{5}$ b $\frac{17}{10}$ c $\frac{24}{5}$

d $\frac{37}{6}$ e $\frac{19}{7}$ f $\frac{43}{8}$

2 Change these mixed numbers into improper fractions (by splitting the whole numbers into fractional parts).

a $3\frac{1}{4}$ b $2\frac{2}{5}$ c $1\frac{9}{16}$

d $4\frac{3}{8}$ e $5\frac{3}{10}$ f $5\frac{5}{12}$

Specification

GCSE 2010
N a (part) … multiply and divide any number
N o Interpret fractions … as operators

FS Process skills
Use appropriate mathematical procedures

FS Performance
Level 2 Apply a range of mathematics to find solutions

Resources

ActiveTeach resources
Mixed multiplication quiz
Multiplying a fraction animation
Mixed division quiz
Dividing a fraction

8.5 Multiplying fractions
8.6 Dividing fractions

Concepts and skills

- … multiply and divide… fractions.
- Find a fraction of a quantity.

Functional skills

- L2 Carry out calculations with numbers of any size …

Prior key knowledge, skills and concepts

- Tables to 9 × 9

Starter

- Ask questions involving 'half of', 'quarter of', 'third of' etc.
- Extend to explain 'two-thirds of' as 2 × a third of.

Main teaching and learning

- Teach students to:
  - Multiply a proper fraction by a proper fraction.
    - *How would you calculate* $\frac{3}{4} \times \frac{1}{2}$*?*
  - Multiply a fraction by an integer by writing the integer as $\frac{n}{1}$
  - Multiply with improper fractions.
  - Multiply mixed numbers by changing them to improper fractions.
  - Ask students to make up their own examples of multiplying by fractions. Write these on the board and work through them as a class. Remember to include mixed fractions as well as proper fraction and unit fractions. Encourage them to find the simplest form.
  - Divide a fraction by an integer.
    - Ask a student to draw on the board a diagram to illustrate $\frac{1}{3}$. Ask another to draw lines on the same diagram to show
    - $\frac{3}{4} \div 2$
    - $\frac{5}{12} \div 5$
    - $\frac{6}{7} \div 3$
  - Divide a fraction by a fraction.

Common misconceptions

- Students sometimes invert the wrong fraction.

Plenary

- Discuss students' methods for Exercise 8E question 6 and Exercise 8F question 4.

Section 8.5–8.6 Multiplying and dividing fractions

E

Guided practice worksheet

1 Work out.

a $\frac{2}{5} \times \frac{1}{3}$ b $\frac{1}{5} \times \frac{2}{3}$ c $\frac{3}{8} \times \frac{3}{5}$ d $\frac{7}{12} \times \frac{5}{6}$

2 Work out, giving your answer in its simplest form.

a $\frac{5}{14} \times \frac{2}{15}$ b $\frac{3}{8} \times \frac{2}{9}$ c $\frac{4}{5} \times \frac{5}{8}$ d $\frac{7}{15} \times \frac{5}{21}$

3 Work out.

a $\frac{2}{3} \times 2$ b $\frac{3}{10} \times 5$ c $4 \times \frac{5}{12}$ d $\frac{2}{15} \times 6$

4 Work out.

a $\frac{1}{2} \div 2$ b $\frac{3}{5} \div 3$ c $\frac{4}{9} \div 2$ d $\frac{5}{8} \div 4$

5 Work out.

a $\frac{2}{3} \div \frac{4}{5}$ b $\frac{7}{15} \div \frac{3}{5}$ c $\frac{18}{25} \div \frac{4}{5}$ d $\frac{8}{21} \div \frac{2}{3}$

Section 8.5–8.6 Multiplying and dividing fractions

C

Guided practice worksheet

6 Work out.

a $1\frac{1}{2} \times 2\frac{1}{4}$ b $3\frac{2}{5} \times 2\frac{1}{2}$ c $4\frac{2}{3} \times 1\frac{1}{10}$

d $2\frac{2}{7} \times 4\frac{1}{5}$ e $5\frac{1}{4} \times 3\frac{3}{7}$

Hint Change mixed numbers to improper fractions.

7 Work out, giving your answer in its simplest form.

a $2\frac{4}{5} \div 2\frac{1}{10}$ b $4\frac{1}{6} \div 3\frac{1}{3}$ c $1\frac{1}{8} \div 6\frac{3}{4}$ d $2\frac{2}{15} \div 2\frac{14}{25}$

Hint Change mixed numbers to improper fractions.

Specification

GCSE 2010
N a Add, subtract … any number
N i Add and subtract fractions

FS Process skills
Use appropriate mathematical procedures

FS Performance
Level 2 Apply a range of mathematics to find solutions

Resources

ActiveTeach resources
Adding and subtracting quiz
Adding fractions 2 interactive

8.7 Adding and subtracting fractions

Concepts and skills
- Add and subtract fractions.

Functional skills
- L2 Carry out calculations with numbers of any size …

Prior key knowledge, skills and concepts
- Lowest (least) common multiple

Starter
- Give students examples where they need to add and subtract fractions with the same denominator.

Main teaching and learning
- Teach students to:
  - add/subtract fractions where one denominator needs changing
  - add/subtract fractions where a common denominator is needed (although any common denominator will work, the LCM is best)
    - Example

$\frac{2}{3} + \frac{3}{4} = 1\frac{5}{12}$

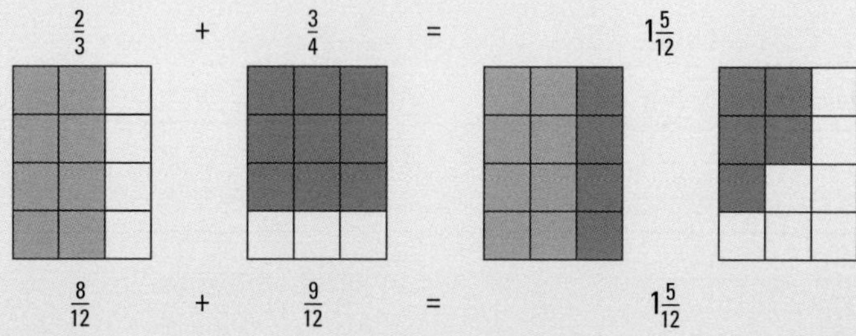

$\frac{8}{12} + \frac{9}{12} = 1\frac{5}{12}$

  - Ask students to add the following, illustrating each with a similar diagram:
  - $\frac{2}{3} + \frac{1}{2}$
  - $\frac{3}{4} + \frac{4}{5}$
  - $\frac{1}{3} + \frac{5}{8}$
  - add/subtract mixed numbers.

Common misconceptions
- Students sometimes add the denominators as well as the numerators.

Plenary
- Discuss how to tackle Worksheet 8.7 questions 4 and 5.

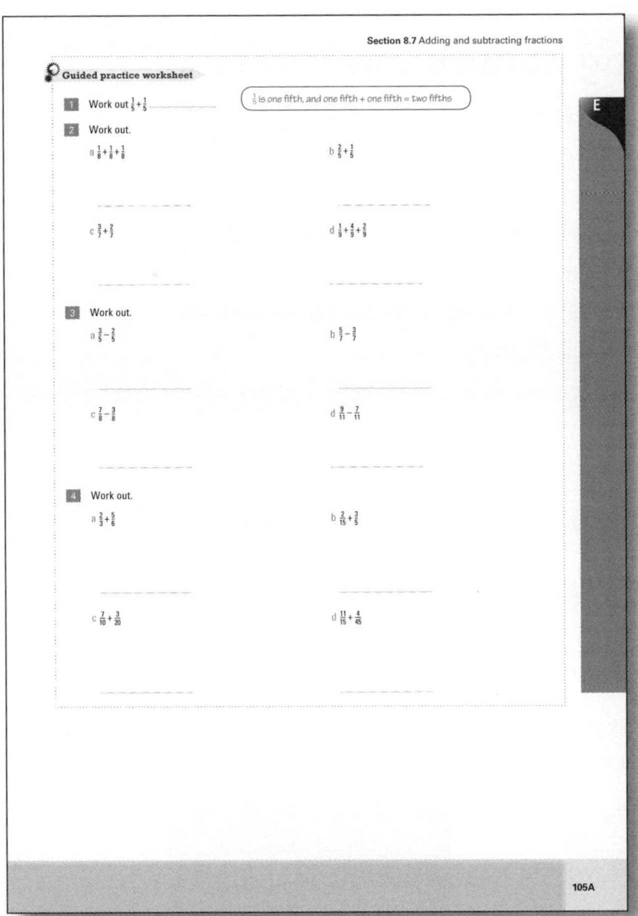

Guided practice worksheet

E

1 Work out $\frac{1}{5}+\frac{1}{5}$ ....

$\frac{1}{5}$ *is one fifth, and one fifth + one fifth = two fifths*

2 Work out.

a $\frac{1}{8}+\frac{1}{8}+\frac{1}{8}$

b $\frac{2}{5}+\frac{1}{5}$

c $\frac{3}{7}+\frac{2}{7}$

d $\frac{1}{9}+\frac{4}{9}+\frac{2}{9}$

3 Work out.

a $\frac{3}{5}-\frac{2}{5}$

b $\frac{5}{7}-\frac{3}{7}$

c $\frac{7}{8}-\frac{3}{8}$

d $\frac{9}{11}-\frac{7}{11}$

4 Work out.

a $\frac{2}{3}+\frac{5}{6}$

b $\frac{2}{15}+\frac{3}{5}$

c $\frac{7}{10}+\frac{3}{20}$

d $\frac{11}{15}+\frac{4}{45}$

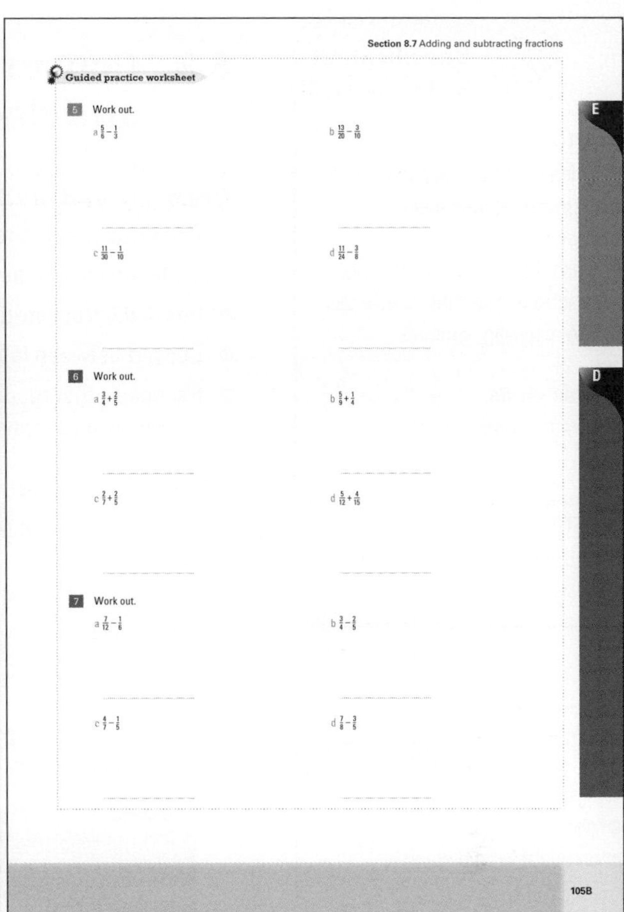

Guided practice worksheet

E

5 Work out.

a $\frac{5}{6}-\frac{1}{3}$

b $\frac{13}{20}-\frac{3}{10}$

c $\frac{11}{30}-\frac{1}{10}$

d $\frac{11}{24}-\frac{3}{8}$

D

6 Work out.

a $\frac{3}{4}+\frac{2}{5}$

b $\frac{5}{9}+\frac{1}{4}$

c $\frac{2}{7}+\frac{2}{5}$

d $\frac{5}{12}+\frac{4}{15}$

7 Work out.

a $\frac{7}{12}-\frac{1}{6}$

b $\frac{3}{4}-\frac{2}{5}$

c $\frac{4}{7}-\frac{1}{5}$

d $\frac{7}{8}-\frac{3}{5}$

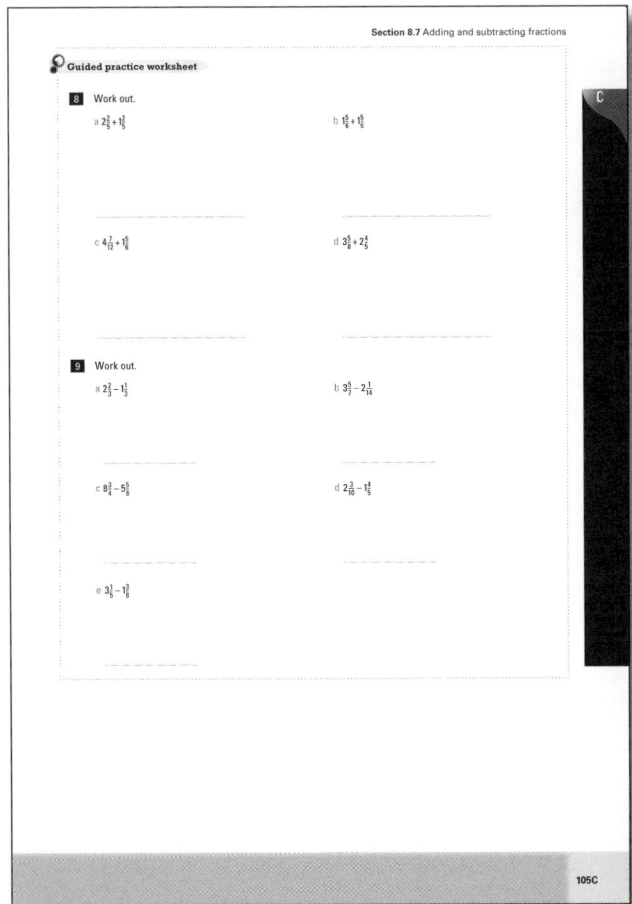

Guided practice worksheet

C

8 Work out.

a $2\frac{2}{5}+1\frac{2}{5}$

b $1\frac{5}{6}+1\frac{5}{6}$

c $4\frac{7}{12}+1\frac{5}{6}$

d $3\frac{5}{8}+2\frac{4}{5}$

9 Work out.

a $2\frac{2}{3}-1\frac{1}{3}$

b $3\frac{5}{7}-2\frac{1}{14}$

c $8\frac{3}{4}-5\frac{5}{8}$

d $2\frac{3}{10}-1\frac{4}{5}$

e $3\frac{1}{5}-1\frac{3}{8}$

Specification

GCSE 2010

N j Use decimal notation and recognise that each terminating decimal is a fraction

N k Recognise that recurring decimals are exact fractions, and that some exact fractions are recurring decimals.

FS Process skills

Use appropriate mathematical procedures

FS Performance

Level 2 Apply a range of mathematics to find solutions

Resources

Resources

Information about local distances

Links

http://www.bbc.co.uk/schools/gcsebitesize/maths/number/fracsdecpersact.shtml

ActiveTeach resources

RP KC Fraction knowledge check

RP PS Fraction problem solving

8.8 Converting between fractions and decimals

Concepts and skills

- Recall the fraction-to-decimal conversion of familar simple fractions.
- Write terminating decimals as fractions.
- Recall the fraction-to-decimal conversion of familiar simple fractions.
- Convert between factions and decimals.
- Recognise that recurring decimals are exact fractions, and that some exact fractions are recurring decimals.

Functional skills

- L2 Understand and use equivalences between fractions, decimals…

Prior key knowledge, skills and concepts

- Place value

Starter

- Display two road signs like these (substitute local place names). *Is the information on the signs equivalent?* (yes)

Cardiff	22.2
Bristol	31.4
Bath	60.5

Cardiff	$22\frac{1}{5}$
Bristol	$31\frac{2}{5}$
Bath	$60\frac{1}{2}$

Main teaching and learning

- Show students that dividing the numerator by the denominator converts a fraction to a decimal. Only use simple cases at this stage.
- As a class convert the following fractions to decimals by first writing them as fractions with a denominator of 10 or 100.
  $\frac{1}{10}$ $\frac{2}{5}$ $\frac{7}{10}$ $\frac{7}{25}$ $\frac{1}{100}$ $\frac{8}{20}$ $\frac{7}{5}$ $\frac{20}{80}$ $\frac{13}{100}$
- As a class convert the following fractions into decimals using a calculator.
  $\frac{1}{3}$ $\frac{7}{9}$ $\frac{2}{3}$ $\frac{5}{11}$ $\frac{19}{28}$ $\frac{79}{124}$ $\frac{1}{7}$ $\frac{7}{16}$ $\frac{3}{9}$
- Point out that dividing by 1 converts a decimal to a fraction, but it will be necessary to find an equivalent fraction where the numerator is an integer. Lining up the decimal point is essential.
  - Identify the place value of each of the digits in the following numbers and ask *How would we write this number as a fraction?*
  - 0.1, 0.04, 0.45, 0, 2.5, 14.2, 1.5, 0.99, 0.606, 5.677, 10.1
  - *When is it easier/quicker to write numbers as fractions?*

Plenary

- Discuss question 10 in the review exercise.

terminating decimals recurring decimals

F

Guided practice worksheet

1 Turn these decimals into fractions in their simplest form.

a 0.32 b 0.05 c 0.175 d 0.025

2 By turning these fractions into decimals put them in order of size. Start with the smallest.

$\frac{5}{8}$ $\frac{3}{5}$ $\frac{7}{11}$ $\frac{2}{3}$ $\frac{4}{7}$

Specification

GCSE 2010
N a Add, subtract, multiply and divide any number
N e Use index notation for squares, cubes and powers of 10

FS Process skills
Examine patterns and relationships

FS Performance
Level 1 Use appropriate checking procedures at each stage

9.1 Calculating with powers

Concepts and skills

- Add, subtract, multiply and divide … numbers in index form.
- Use index notation for squares and cubes.
- Use index notation for powers of 10.
- Find the value of calculations using indices.

Functional skills

- L1 Add, subtract, multiply and divide whole numbers using a range of strategies.

Prior key knowledge, skills and concepts

- Students should already understand square numbers.
- Students should already understand cube numbers.
- Students should already know times tables up to 10×10.

Starter

- *Find the value of: (i) 5 squared* (25) *(ii) 3 cubed* (27) *(iii)* 2^2 (4) *(iv)* 2^3 (8) *(v)* 4^2 (16)

Main teaching and learning

- Explain that the index squared comes from the area of a square (e.g. the area of a square of side 4 is $4 \times 4 = 16$) and the index cubed comes from the volume of a cube (e.g. the volume of a cube of side 3 is $3 \times 3 \times 3 = 27$).
- Explain that a power or an index is the number of times you multiply a number by itself.
- $4^x = 64$ means find the power to which 4 must be raised to get 64.

  $4 \times 4 = 16$ $16 \times 4 = 64$ so $x = 3$.
- Work on Exercise 9A.

Common misconceptions

- 4^3 does not mean 4×3 but $4 \times 4 \times 4$.

Enrichment

- *Using powers, explain why* $2^6 = 4^3 = 8^2 = 64$.
- *How many squares are there on a chessboard? The answer is not 64. Think about squares of side 1, 2, 3…* (204)

Plenary

- Check that students can work out the answers to these:

  (i) 3^4 (81)

  (ii) $2^3 \times 3^2$ (72)

  (iii) Write 100 000 as a power of 10. (10^5)

base index power

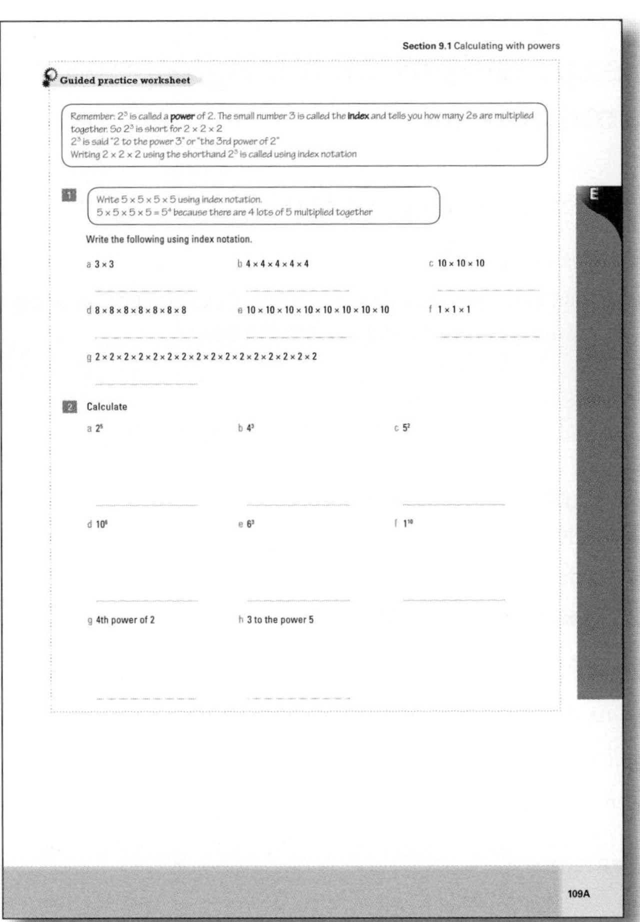

Section 9.1 Calculating with powers

Guided practice worksheet

Remember: 2^3 is called a **power** of 2. The small number 3 is called the **index** and tells you how many 2s are multiplied together. So 2^3 is short for $2 \times 2 \times 2$
2^3 is said "2 to the power 3" or "the 3rd power of 2"
Writing $2 \times 2 \times 2$ using the shorthand 2^3 is called using index notation

1 Write $5 \times 5 \times 5 \times 5$ using index notation.
$5 \times 5 \times 5 \times 5 = 5^4$ because there are 4 lots of 5 multiplied together

Write the following using index notation.

a 3×3
b $4 \times 4 \times 4 \times 4 \times 4$
c $10 \times 10 \times 10$
d $8 \times 8 \times 8 \times 8 \times 8 \times 8 \times 8$
e $10 \times 10 \times 10 \times 10 \times 10 \times 10 \times 10 \times 10$
f $1 \times 1 \times 1$
g $2 \times 2 \times 2 \times 2 \times 2 \times 2 \times 2 \times 2 \times 2 \times 2 \times 2 \times 2 \times 2 \times 2 \times 2 \times 2$

2 Calculate

a 2^5
b 4^3
c 5^2
d 10^6
e 6^3
f 1^{10}
g 4th power of 2
h 3 to the power 5

109A

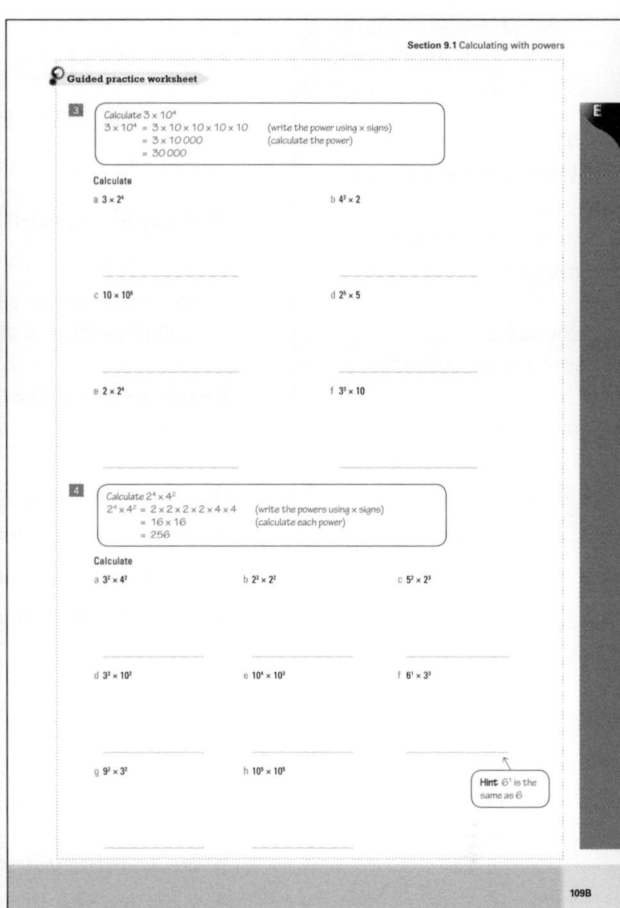

Section 9.1 Calculating with powers

Guided practice worksheet

3 Calculate 3×10^4
$3 \times 10^4 = 3 \times 10 \times 10 \times 10 \times 10$ (write the power using × signs)
$= 3 \times 10\,000$ (calculate the power)
$= 30\,000$

Calculate

a 3×2^4
b $4^2 \times 2$
c 10×10^6
d $2^5 \times 5$
e 2×2^4
f $3^3 \times 10$

4 Calculate $2^4 \times 4^2$
$2^4 \times 4^2 = 2 \times 2 \times 2 \times 2 \times 4 \times 4$ (write the powers using × signs)
$= 16 \times 16$ (calculate each power)
$= 256$

Calculate

a $3^2 \times 4^2$
b $2^3 \times 2^2$
c $5^2 \times 2^3$
d $3^3 \times 10^2$
e $10^4 \times 10^3$
f $6^1 \times 3^3$
g $9^2 \times 3^2$
h $10^5 \times 10^5$

Hint 6^1 is the same as 6

109B

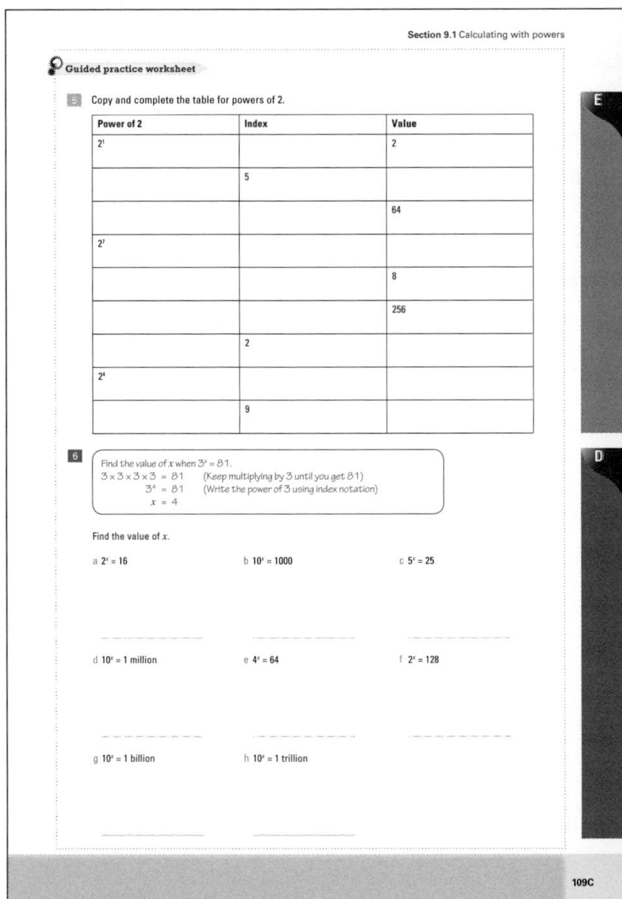

Section 9.1 Calculating with powers

Guided practice worksheet

5 Copy and complete the table for powers of 2.

Power of 2	Index	Value
2^1		2
	5	
		64
2^7		
		8
		256
	2	
2^4		
	9	

6 Find the value of x when $3^x = 81$.
$3 \times 3 \times 3 \times 3 = 81$ (Keep multiplying by 3 until you get 81)
$3^4 = 81$ (Write the power of 3 using index notation)
$x = 4$

Find the value of x.

a $2^x = 16$
b $10^x = 1000$
c $5^x = 25$
d $10^x = 1$ million
e $4^x = 64$
f $2^x = 128$
g $10^x = 1$ billion
h $10^x = 1$ trillion

109C

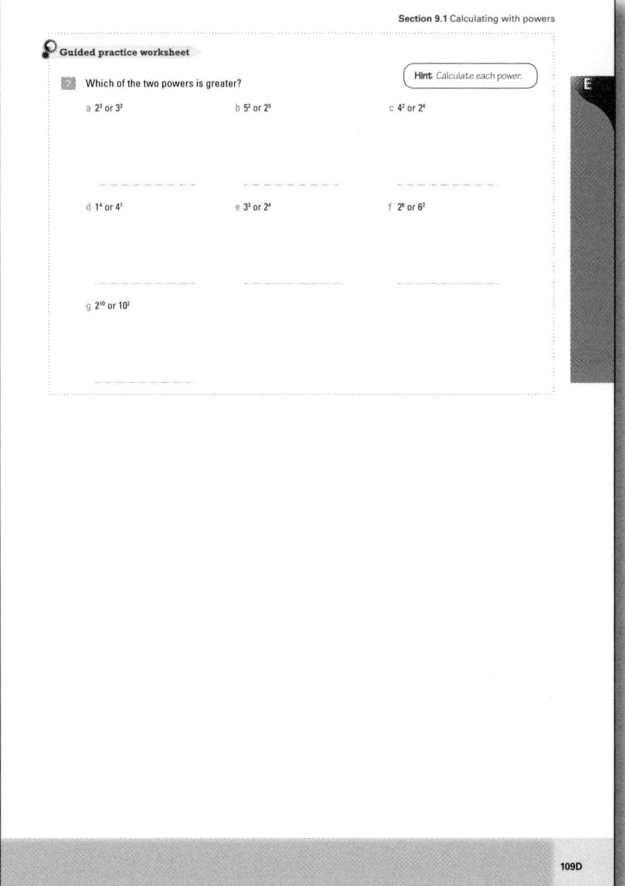

Section 9.1 Calculating with powers

Guided practice worksheet

7 Which of the two powers is greater?

Hint Calculate each power.

a 2^3 or 3^2
b 5^2 or 2^5
c 4^2 or 2^4
d 1^4 or 4^1
e 3^3 or 2^4
f 2^6 or 6^2
g 2^{10} or 10^2

109D

Specification

GCSE 2010

N e Use index notation for squares, cubes and powers of 10.

N f Use index laws for multiplication and division of integer powers

FS Process skills

Examine patterns and relationships

FS Performance

Level 1 Use appropriate checking procedures at each stage

9.2 Writing expressions as a single power of the same number

Concepts and skills

- Find the value of calculations using indices.
- Use index laws to simplify and calculate the value of numerical expressions involving multiplication and division of integer powers, and powers of a power.

Functional skills

- L1 Add, subtract, multiply and divide whole numbers using a range of strategies.

Prior key knowledge, skills and concepts

- Students should already understand square numbers.
- Students should already understand cube numbers.
- Students should already know times tables up to 10 × 10.

Starter

- *Write as a power of 2: (i) 4* (2^2) *(ii) 8* (2^3) *(iii) 16* (2^4) *(iv) 64* (2^6)
- *Write as a power of 3: (i) 3* (3^1) *(ii) 9* (3^2) *(iii) 27* (3^3) *(iv) 81* (3^4)
- *Write as a power of 10: (i) one hundred* (10^2) *(ii) one thousand* (10^3)

Main teaching and learning

- Write down the rules for multiplying, dividing and raising a power to a power for numbers.
- Go through an example for each.
- Work on Exercise 9B.

Common misconceptions

- $3^2 \times 3^4 = 3^8$, as students multiply the powers rather than adding them.
- $4^5 \div 4^2 = 4^{2.5}$, as students divide the powers rather than subtracting them.
- $(2^3)^2 = 2^5 = 32$, as students add the powers rather than multiplying to give $2^6 = 64$.

Enrichment

- *Show that 4000 can be written as $2^2 \times 10^3$.*
- *Write, using powers of two numbers: (i) 800* ($2^3 \times 10^2$) *(ii) 27 000* ($3^3 \times 10^2$) *(iii) 256 000* ($2^8 \times 10^3$ or $4^4 \times 10^3$ or $16^2 \times 10^3$) *(iv) 144* ($3^2 \times 4^2$ or $2^4 \times 3^2$)

Plenary

- Check that students can do the examples in the common misconceptions section correctly.

Guided practice worksheet

Simplify by writing each expression as a single power.

1 $2^3 \times 2^4 = 2^{3+4}$
$= 2^7$ (when multiplying powers of a number, add the indices)

a $3^2 \times 3^4$ b $2^3 \times 2^5$ c $10^2 \times 10^3$ d $8^4 \times 8^2$

e $5^1 \times 5^3$ f 3×3^4 g $7^3 \times 7$ h $10^{10} \times 10^{10}$

Hint Write 3 as the power 3^1.

2 $6^3 \times 6^3 \times 6^4 = 6^{3+3+4}$
$= 6^{10}$ (add all the indices together)

a $2^3 \times 2^4 \times 2^5$ b $5^2 \times 5^5 \times 5^3$ c $10^2 \times 10^4 \times 10^6$

d $4^1 \times 4^3 \times 4^2$ e $6^2 \times 6^4 \times 6$ f $8 \times 8^3 \times 8^2$

g $10^4 \times 10 \times 10^2$ h $9 \times 9^3 \times 9$

Hint Write 6 as the power 6^1.

Guided practice worksheet

3 $2^7 \div 2^4 = 2^{7-4}$
$= 2^3$ (when dividing powers of a number, subtract the indices)

$\frac{4^6}{4^2} = 4^6 \div 4^2$ (you can write the fraction as a division)
$= 4^{6-2}$
$= 4^4$

a $5^4 \div 5^2$ b $2^8 \div 2^3$ c $\frac{8^6}{8^4}$ d $10^9 \div 10^5$

e $\frac{4^6}{4^2}$ f $7^4 \div 7^1$ g $10^{10} \div 10$ h $\frac{3^5}{3}$

Hint Write 10 as the power 10^1.

4 $(3^2)^4 = 3^{2\times4}$
$= 3^8$ (when raising a power to a further power, multiply the indices)

a $(2^3)^4$ b $(5^2)^3$ c $(10^4)^2$ d $(2^{10})^{10}$

5 a $4^3 \times 4^3 \times 4$ b $6^3 \div 6$ c $10^5 \times 10$

d $2^7 \div 2^7$ e $3^3 \times 3^3 \times 3^3$ f $\frac{12^9}{12^7}$

Hint You don't need to use indices to work this out.

Hint Combine the first two powers, then the last power. Work from left to right.

g $4^3 \times 4^7 \div 4^4$ h $3^6 \times \frac{3^5}{3^2}$

Specification

GCSE 2010
A c (part) Manipulate algebraic expressions…

FS Process skills
Use appropriate mathematical procedures

FS Performance
Level 2 Use appropriate checking procedures and evaluate their effectiveness at each stage

9.3 Using powers in algebra to simplify expressions

Concepts and skills

- Use simple instances of index laws.

Functional skills

- L2 Understand and use simple formulae and equations involving one- or two-step operations.

Prior key knowledge, skills and concepts

- Students should already know that when you multiply you add powers: $2^3 \times 2^4 = 2^7$.
- Students should already know that when you divide you subtract powers: $3^6 \div 3^2 = 3^4$.
- Students should already know that when you raise a power to a power you multiply powers: $(5^2)^3 = 5^6$.

Starter

- *Work out: (i)* 10^3 (1000) *(ii)* 5^2 (25) *(iii)* 3^4 (81) *(iv)* 2^5 (32)
- *Write as a power of 10: (i) 1000* (10^3) *(ii) 100 000* (10^5) *(iii) 10 000* (10^4)

Main teaching and learning

- Write down the rules for multiplying, dividing and raising a power to a power for algebraic terms. Go through an example for each.
- Work on Exercise 9C.

Common misconceptions

- $a^2 \times a^4 = a^8$, as students multiply the powers rather than adding them.
- $b^6 \div b^2 = b^3$, as students divide the powers rather than subtracting them.
- $(c^3)^2 = c^5$, as students add the powers rather than multiplying them.

Plenary

- Check that students can do the examples in the Common misconceptions section correctly.

Guided practice worksheet

C

Remember: Use the same rules for powers of letters as for powers of numbers

Simplify

1 $a^2 \times a^4 = a^{2+4}$ (when multiplying powers, add the indices)
$= a^6$

a $r^3 \times r^5$

b $p^2 \times p^7$

c $e^{10} \times e^{10}$

d $w^3 \times w$

e $m^2 \times m^3 \times m^2$

f $h^2 \times h \times h^5$

Hint Write w as the power w^1.

2 $c^6 \div c^3 = c^{6-3}$ (when dividing powers, subtract the indices)
$= c^3$

$\frac{n^7}{n^2} = n^7 \div n^2$ (write the fraction as a division)
$= n^{7-2}$
$= n^5$

a $d^7 \div d^3$

b $s^8 \div s^2$

c $k^5 \div k$

Hint Write k as the power k^1.

d $b^{99} \div b^{98}$

e $w^5 \div w^5$

f $\frac{d^8}{d^3}$

g $\frac{b^{10}}{b^9}$

h $\frac{V^5}{V}$

Hint You do not need to use indices here.

Guided practice worksheet

C

3 $3d^2 \times 5d^3 = 3 \times 5 \times d^2 \times d^3$ (group the numbers and letters)
$= 15 \times d^2 \times d^3$ (work out the numbers)
$= 15 \times d^{2+3}$ (work out the powers)
$= 15d^5$

a $2c^3 \times c^4$

b $g^5 \times 4g^2$

c $r^2 \times r^3 \times 7$

d $3m^3 \times 2m^2$

e $8G^2 \times 3G^6$

f $2h^3 \times 4h$

Hint Write h as the power h^1.

4 $12w^5 \div 4w^2 = 12 \div 4 \times w^5 \div w^2$ (divide the numbers and powers separately)
$= 3 \times w^5 \div w^2$ (work out the numbers)
$= 3 \times w^{5-2}$ (work out the powers)
$= 3w^3$

a $8u^6 \div 2u^3$

b $6h^4 \div 3h^2$

c $15y^5 \div 3y$

Hint Write y as the power y^1.

d $30p^5 \div 6p^2$

e $\frac{8t^6}{4t^3}$

f $\frac{20p^7}{5p^3}$

g $a^3 \times \frac{a^6}{a^2}$

h $m \times \frac{m^7}{m^5} \times m^3$

Hint Write the fraction as the division $8t^6 \div 4t^3$.

Hint Work out the division first.

Specification

GCSE 2010
N q Understand and use number operations and the relationships between them, including inverse operations and hierarchy of operations

FS Process skills
Use appropriate mathematical procedures

FS Performance
Level 1 Use appropriate checking procedures at each stage

Resources

ActiveTeach resources
BIDMAS animation

9.4 Understanding order of operations

Concepts and skills

- Use brackets and the hierarchy of operations.

Functional skills

- L1 Add, subtract, multiply and divide whole numbers using a range of strategies.

Prior key knowledge, skills and concepts

- 4 rules of number

Starter

- *Find the value of:*
  (i) *5 squared* (25) (ii) *3 cubed* (27) (iii) $2 \times 3 \times 4$ (24) (iv) $2 + 3 + 4$ (9) (v) $4^2 + 5^2$ (41)

Main teaching and learning

- Explain the mnemonic BIDMAS using Key point in book.
- Work through the examples and explain the main idea especially with brackets and indices.

Get students to attempt Exercise 9D.

Common minconceptions

- $2 \times 3^2 = 6^2$ or 36 because students multiply before finding the index.
- $2(3 + 4) = 6 + 4 = 10$ because students only multiply the first number in the bracket.

Enrichment

- Get students to set up a game of snap with common mistakes and the right answer. Use cards e.g. 3×2^2 with number cards 12 and 36 and $2(3 + 4) = 10$ and 14 etc. They can then play the game in pairs.

Plenary

- Check that students can work out the answers to
  (i) 5×3^2 (45) (ii) $2^3 \times 3^2$ (72) (iii) $3(2^2 + 4)$ (24) (iv) $5(3^3 - 4^2) \div 10$ (5.5)

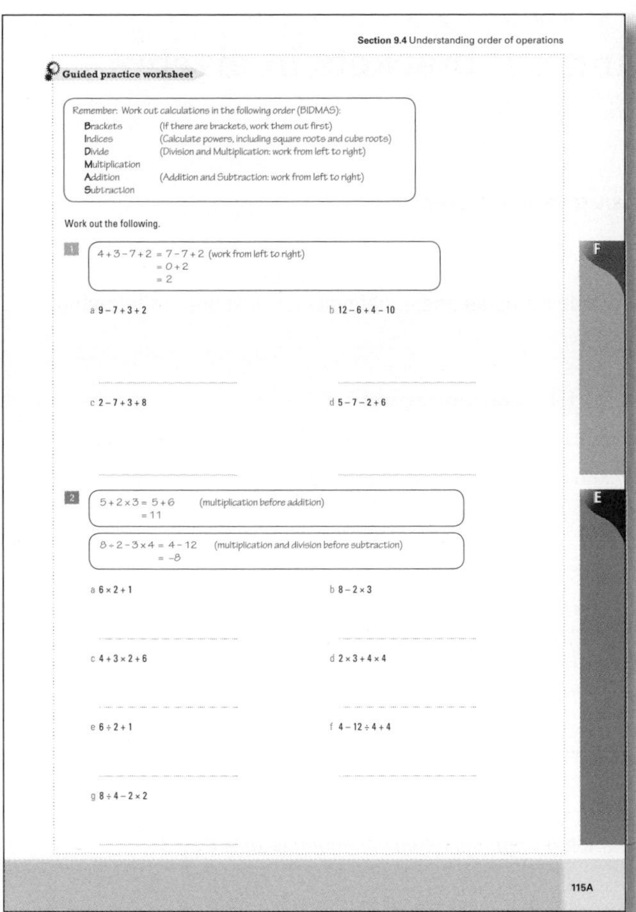

Guided practice worksheet

Remember: Work out calculations in the following order (BIDMAS):

Brackets	(If there are brackets, work them out first)
Indices	(Calculate powers, including square roots and cube roots)
Divide	(Division and Multiplication: work from left to right)
Multiplication	
Addition	(Addition and Subtraction: work from left to right)
Subtraction	

Work out the following.

F

1

$4 + 3 - 7 + 2 = 7 - 7 + 2$ (work from left to right)
$= 0 + 2$
$= 2$

a $9 - 7 + 3 + 2$ b $12 - 6 + 4 - 10$

c $2 - 7 + 3 + 8$ d $5 - 7 - 2 + 6$

E

2

$5 + 2 \times 3 = 5 + 6$ (multiplication before addition)
$= 11$

$8 \div 2 - 3 \times 4 = 4 - 12$ (multiplication and division before subtraction)
$= -8$

a $6 \times 2 + 1$ b $8 - 2 \times 3$

c $4 + 3 \times 2 + 6$ d $2 \times 3 + 4 \times 4$

e $6 \div 2 + 1$ f $4 - 12 \div 4 + 4$

g $8 \div 4 - 2 \times 2$

115A

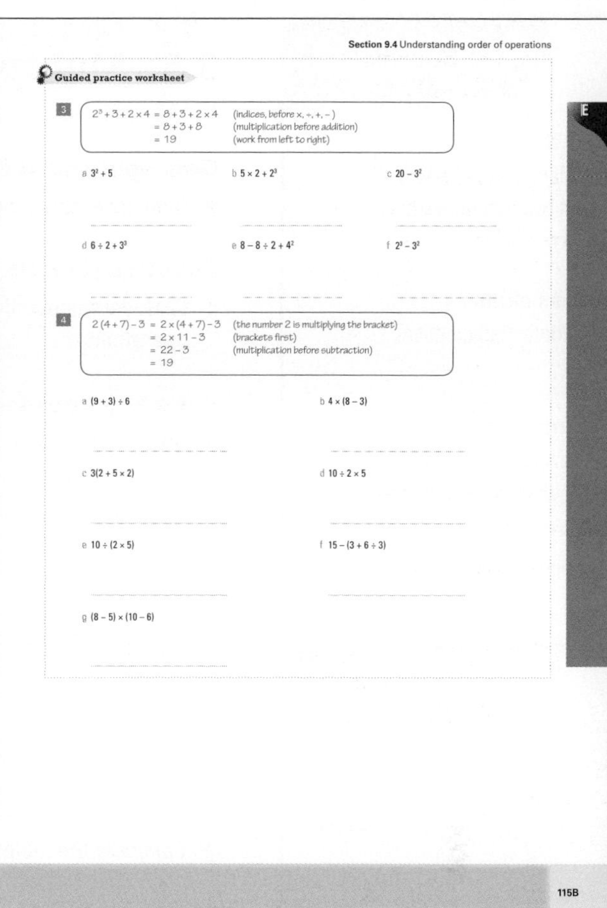

Guided practice worksheet

E

3

$2^3 + 3 + 2 \times 4 = 8 + 3 + 2 \times 4$ (indices, before ×, ÷, +, −)
$= 8 + 3 + 8$ (multiplication before addition)
$= 19$ (work from left to right)

a $3^2 + 5$ b $5 \times 2 + 2^3$ c $20 - 3^2$

d $6 \div 2 + 3^3$ e $8 - 8 \div 2 + 4^2$ f $2^3 - 3^2$

4

$2(4 + 7) - 3 = 2 \times (4 + 7) - 3$ (the number 2 is multiplying the bracket)
$= 2 \times 11 - 3$ (brackets first)
$= 22 - 3$ (multiplication before subtraction)
$= 19$

a $(9 + 3) \div 6$ b $4 \times (8 - 3)$

c $3(2 + 5 \times 2)$ d $10 \div 2 \times 5$

e $10 \div (2 \times 5)$ f $15 - (3 + 6 \div 3)$

g $(8 - 5) \times (10 - 6)$

115B

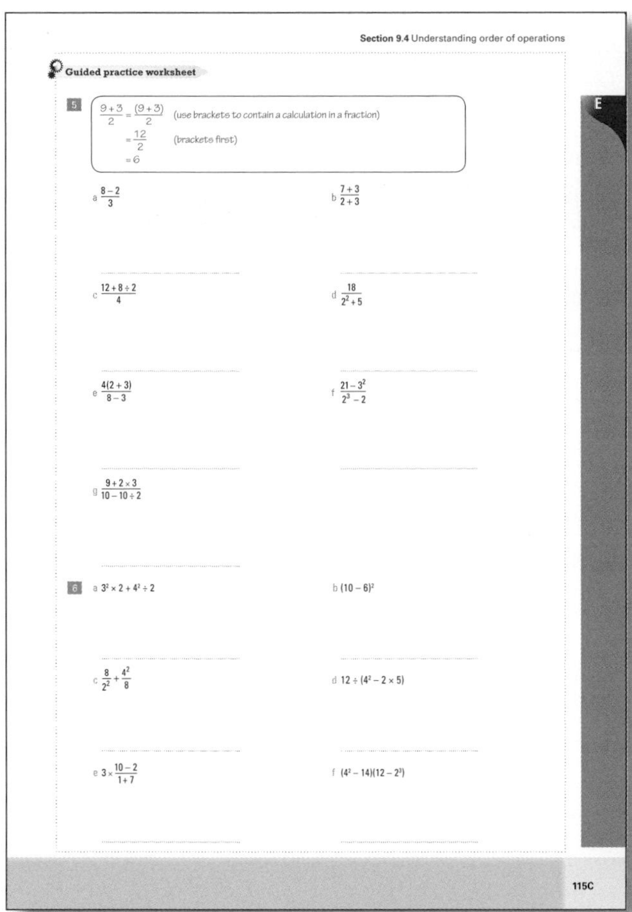

Guided practice worksheet

E

5

$\frac{9+3}{2} = \frac{(9+3)}{2}$ (use brackets to contain a calculation in a fraction)
$= \frac{12}{2}$ (brackets first)
$= 6$

a $\frac{8-2}{3}$ b $\frac{7+3}{2+3}$

c $\frac{12+8\div 2}{4}$ d $\frac{18}{2^2+5}$

e $\frac{4(2+3)}{8-3}$ f $\frac{21-3^2}{2^3-2}$

g $\frac{9+2\times 3}{10-10\div 2}$

6

a $3^2 \times 2 + 4^2 \div 2$ b $(10 - 6)^2$

c $\frac{8}{2^2} + \frac{4^2}{8}$ d $12 \div (4^2 - 2 \times 5)$

e $3 \times \frac{10-2}{1+7}$ f $(4^2 - 14)(12 - 2^3)$

115C

Specification

GCSE 2010

A c (part) Manipulate algebraic expressions by… multiplying a single term over a bracket…

FS Process skills

Use appropriate mathematical procedures

FS Performance

Level 2 Use appropriate checking procedures and evaluate their effectiveness at each stage

Resources

Links

http://www.bbc.co.uk/schools/gcsebitesize/maths/algebra/symbolsact.shtml

http://www.bbc.co.uk/schools/gcsebitesize/maths/algebra/symbolsrev3.shtml

9.5 Multiplying out brackets in algebra

Concepts and skills

- Multiply a single algebraic term over a bracket.

Functional skills

- L2 Understand and use simple formulae and equations involving one- or two-step operations.

Prior key knowledge, skills and concepts

- Students should already know that $a \times b = ab$ and $2a \times 3b = 2 \times 3 \times a \times b = 6ab$.
- Students should already know that $a \times a$ is a^2 and $a \times 2 = 2a$.

Starter

×	**2*a***		**4**			
	a	a	1	1	1	1
3						

- *Complete the table to find what happens when you multiply 2a + 4 by 3.*

Main teaching and learning

- $2(3a + 5)$ means $2 \times (3a + 5)$. You multiply everything inside the bracket by the 2.
- $a(3a + 5)$ means $a \times (3a + 5)$. You multiply everything inside the bracket by the a.
- $2a(3a + 5)$ means $2a \times (3a + 5)$. You multiply everything inside the bracket by the $2a$.
- Work on Exercise 9E.

Common misconceptions

- $2(3a + 6) = 6a + 12$. Many students multiply only the first term.

Enrichment

- Get students to explain, using a rectangle like this, why $2x(3x + 5) = 6x^2 + 10x$.

$3x + 5$

$2x$ [rectangle]

Plenary

- Check understanding of this topic and collection of like terms using questions such as $2a(4a + 3) + 3a(2a - 1)$.

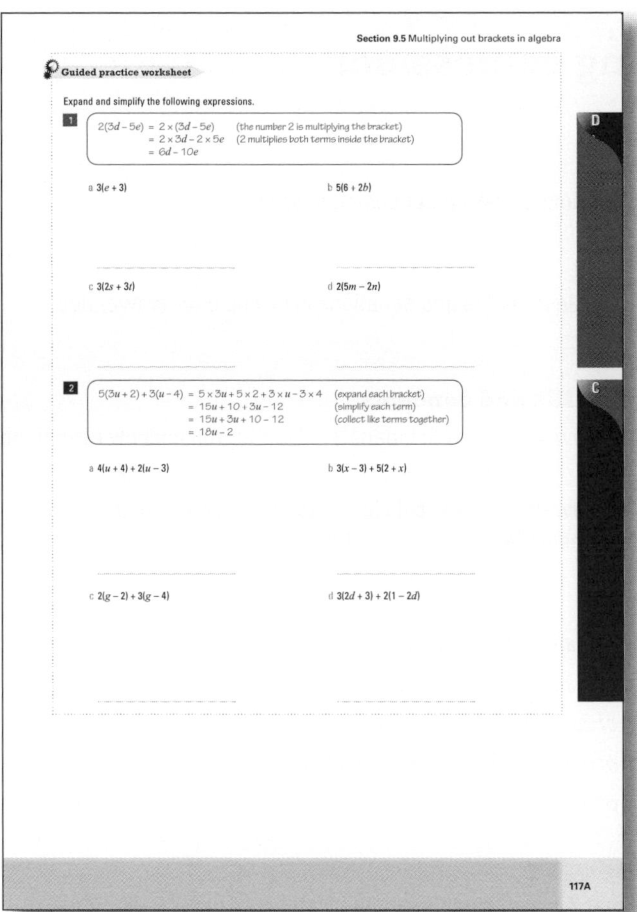
Section 9.5 Multiplying out brackets in algebra

Guided practice worksheet

Expand and simplify the following expressions.

1
$2(3d - 5e) = 2 \times (3d - 5e)$ (the number 2 is multiplying the bracket)
$= 2 \times 3d - 2 \times 5e$ (2 multiplies both terms inside the bracket)
$= 6d - 10e$

a $3(e + 3)$
b $5(6 + 2b)$
c $3(2s + 3t)$
d $2(5m - 2n)$

2
$5(3u + 2) + 3(u - 4) = 5 \times 3u + 5 \times 2 + 3 \times u - 3 \times 4$ (expand each bracket)
$= 15u + 10 + 3u - 12$ (simplify each term)
$= 15u + 3u + 10 - 12$ (collect like terms together)
$= 18u - 2$

a $4(u + 4) + 2(u - 3)$
b $3(x - 3) + 5(2 + x)$
c $2(g - 2) + 3(g - 4)$
d $3(2d + 3) + 2(1 - 2d)$

D C

117A

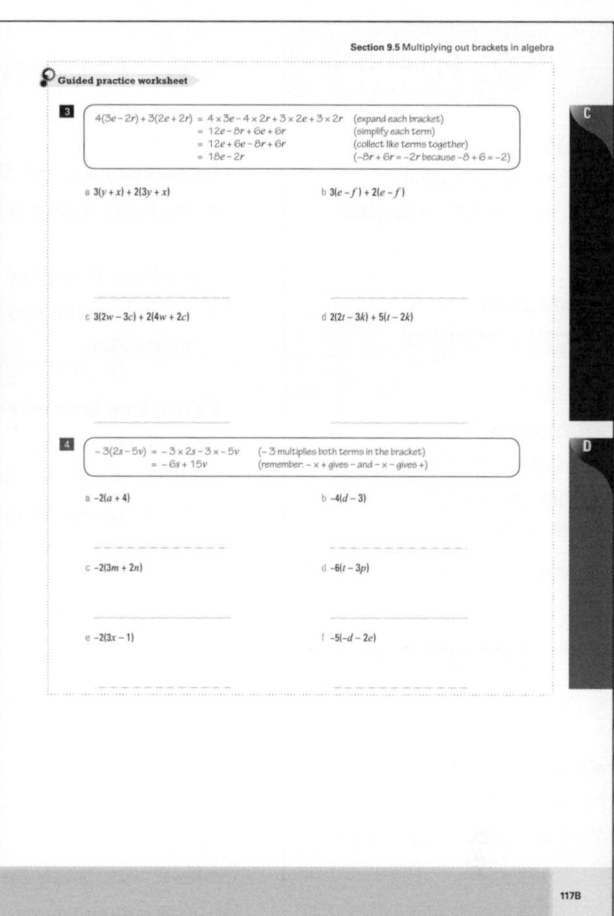
Section 9.5 Multiplying out brackets in algebra

Guided practice worksheet

3
$4(3e - 2r) + 3(2e + 2r) = 4 \times 3e - 4 \times 2r + 3 \times 2e + 3 \times 2r$ (expand each bracket)
$= 12e - 8r + 6e + 6r$ (simplify each term)
$= 12e + 6e - 8r + 6r$ (collect like terms together)
$= 18e - 2r$ ($-8r + 6r = -2r$ because $-8 + 6 = -2$)

a $3(y + x) + 2(3y + x)$
b $3(e - f) + 2(e - f)$
c $3(2w - 3c) + 2(4w + 2c)$
d $2(2t - 3k) + 5(t - 2k)$

4
$-3(2s - 5v) = -3 \times 2s - 3 \times -5v$ (-3 multiplies both terms in the bracket)
$= -6s + 15v$ (remember: $- \times +$ gives $-$ and $- \times -$ gives $+$)

a $-2(a + 4)$
b $-4(d - 3)$
c $-2(3m + 2n)$
d $-6(t - 3p)$
e $-2(3x - 1)$
f $-5(-d - 2e)$

C D

117B

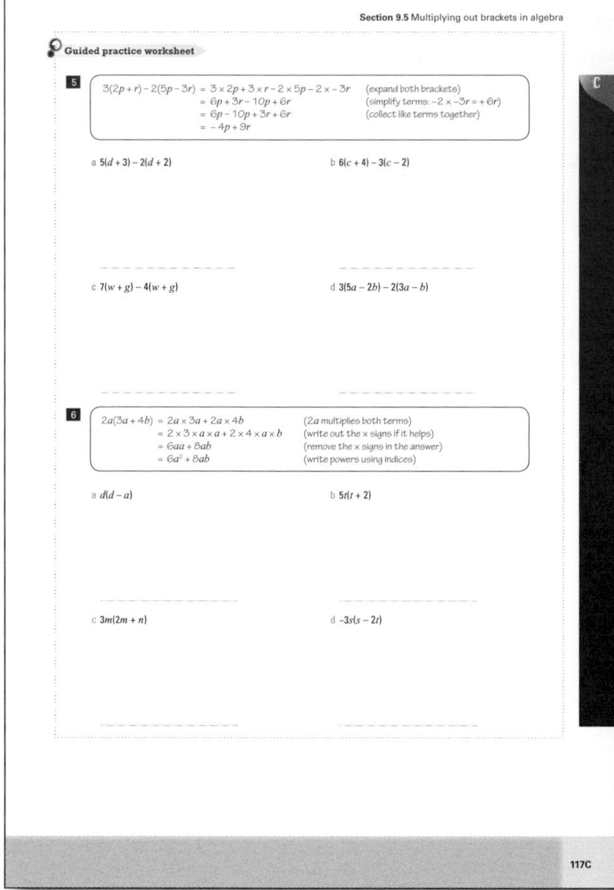
Section 9.5 Multiplying out brackets in algebra

Guided practice worksheet

5
$3(2p + r) - 2(5p - 3r) = 3 \times 2p + 3 \times r - 2 \times 5p - 2 \times -3r$ (expand both brackets)
$= 6p + 3r - 10p + 6r$ (simplify terms: $-2 \times -3r = +6r$)
$= 6p - 10p + 3r + 6r$ (collect like terms together)
$= -4p + 9r$

a $5(d + 3) - 2(d + 2)$
b $6(c + 4) - 3(c - 2)$
c $7(w + g) - 4(w + g)$
d $3(5a - 2b) - 2(3a - b)$

6
$2a(3a + 4b) = 2a \times 3a + 2a \times 4b$ ($2a$ multiplies both terms)
$= 2 \times 3 \times a \times a + 2 \times 4 \times a \times b$ (write out the × signs if it helps)
$= 6aa + 8ab$ (remove the × signs in the answer)
$= 6a^2 + 8ab$ (write powers using indices)

a $d(d - a)$
b $5t(t + 2)$
c $3m(2m + n)$
d $-3s(s - 2t)$

C

117C

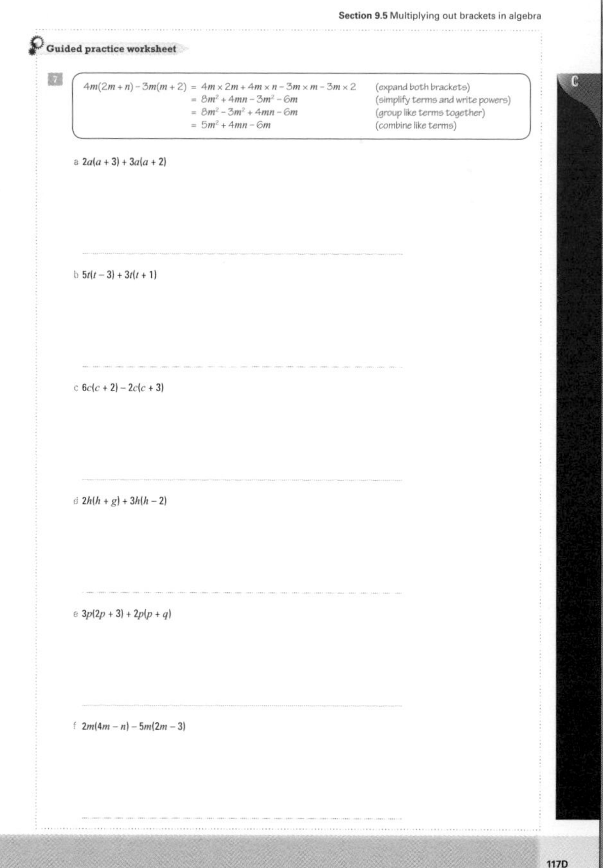
Section 9.5 Multiplying out brackets in algebra

Guided practice worksheet

7
$4m(2m + n) - 3m(m + 2) = 4m \times 2m + 4m \times n - 3m \times m - 3m \times 2$ (expand both brackets)
$= 8m^2 + 4mn - 3m^2 - 6m$ (simplify terms and write powers)
$= 8m^2 - 3m^2 + 4mn - 6m$ (group like terms together)
$= 5m^2 + 4mn - 6m$ (combine like terms)

a $2a(a + 3) + 3a(a + 2)$
b $5t(t - 3) + 3t(t + 1)$
c $6c(c + 2) - 2c(c + 3)$
d $2h(h + g) + 3h(h - 2)$
e $3p(2p + 3) + 2p(p + q)$
f $2m(4m - n) - 5m(2m - 3)$

C

117D

Specification

GCSE 2010

A c (part) Manipulate algebraic expressions by… taking out common factors

FS Process skills

Use appropriate mathematical procedures

FS Performance

Level 2 Use appropriate checking procedures and evaluate their effectiveness at each stage

Resources

ActiveTeach resources

RP KC Algebra 2 knowledge check
RP PS Simplified expressions problem solving

9.6 Factorising expressions

Concepts and skills

- Factorise algebraic expressions by taking out common factors.

Functional skills

- L2 Understand and use simple formulae and equations involving one- or two-step operations.

Prior key knowledge, skills and concepts

- Students should already know that $2(3a + 6)$ means $2 \times (3a + 6)$. You multiply everything inside the bracket by the 2.
- Students should already know that 2, 3 and 6 divide exactly into 12 and 18 and, therefore, 2, 3 and 6 are common factors of 12 and 18.

Starter

- *Write down the factors of 6 and 8. What is the common factor?* (2)
- *Write down the factors of 8 and 12. What are the common factors?* (2, 4)
- *Write down the factors of $2a$ and $5a$. What is the common factor?* (a)
- *Write down the factors of a and a^2. What is the common factor?* (a)
- *Write down the factors of $4pq$ and $6p^2q^3$* ($2pq$)

Main teaching and learning

- Get students to realise that 2 is a common factor in $2x$ and 6, so that $2x + 6 = 2(x + 3)$. (Because $2x = 2 \times x$ and $6 = 2 \times 3$.)
- Get students to realise that a is a common factor in a^2 and $3a$, so that $a^2 + 3a = a(a + 3)$.
- Get students to realise that $2a$ is a common factor in $2a^2$ and $6a$, so that $2a^2 + 6a = 2a(a + 3)$. (Because $2a^2 = 2a \times a$ and $6a = 2a \times 3$.)
- Try Exercise 9F.

Common misconceptions

- Some students, when asked to factorise $2a^2 + 6a$, give the answer $2(a^2 + 3a)$ or $a(2a + 6)$. These are not fully factorised. The correct answer is $2a^2 + 6a = 2a(a + 3)$.

Plenary

- Check understanding by asking students to factorise these: (i) $3p + 6$ ($3(p + 2)$), (ii) $p^2 + 2p$ ($p(p + 2)$), (iii) $3p^2 + 6p$ ($3p(p + 2)$), (iv) $6p^2q - 8pq^2$ ($2pq(3p - 4q)$).

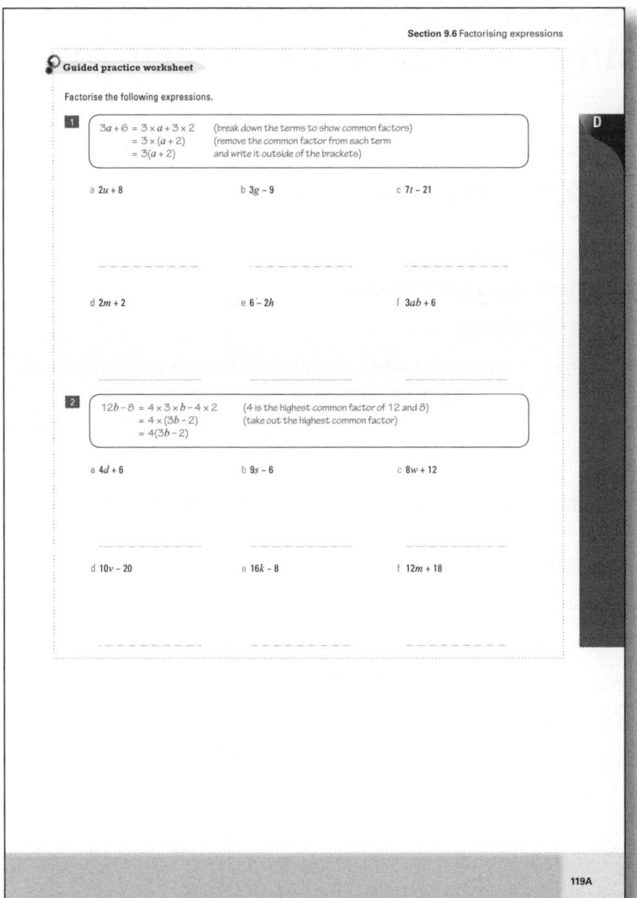

Guided practice worksheet

Factorise the following expressions.

1

$3a + 6 = 3 \times a + 3 \times 2$ (break down the terms to show common factors)
$= 3 \times (a + 2)$ (remove the common factor from each term
$= 3(a + 2)$ and write it outside of the brackets)

a $2u + 8$ b $3g - 9$ c $7t - 21$

d $2m + 2$ e $6 - 2h$ f $3ab + 6$

2

$12b - 8 = 4 \times 3 \times b - 4 \times 2$ (4 is the highest common factor of 12 and 8)
$= 4 \times (3b - 2)$ (take out the highest common factor)
$= 4(3b - 2)$

a $4d + 6$ b $9s - 6$ c $8w + 12$

d $10v - 20$ e $16k - 8$ f $12m + 18$

D

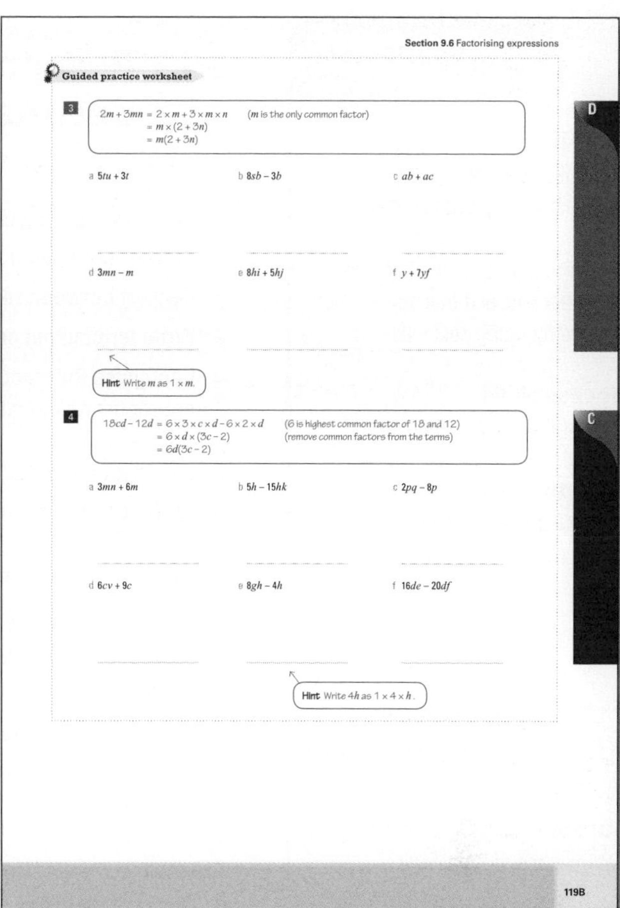

Guided practice worksheet

3

$2m + 3mn = 2 \times m + 3 \times m \times n$ (m is the only common factor)
$= m \times (2 + 3n)$
$= m(2 + 3n)$

a $5tu + 3t$ b $8sb - 3b$ c $ab + ac$

d $3mn - m$ e $8hi + 5hj$ f $y + 7yf$

Hint Write m as $1 \times m$.

4

$18cd - 12d = 6 \times 3 \times c \times d - 6 \times 2 \times d$ (6 is highest common factor of 18 and 12)
$= 6 \times d \times (3c - 2)$ (remove common factors from the terms)
$= 6d(3c - 2)$

a $3mn + 6m$ b $5h - 15hk$ c $2pq - 8p$

d $6cv + 9c$ e $8gh - 4h$ f $16de - 20df$

Hint Write $4h$ as $1 \times 4 \times h$.

D

C

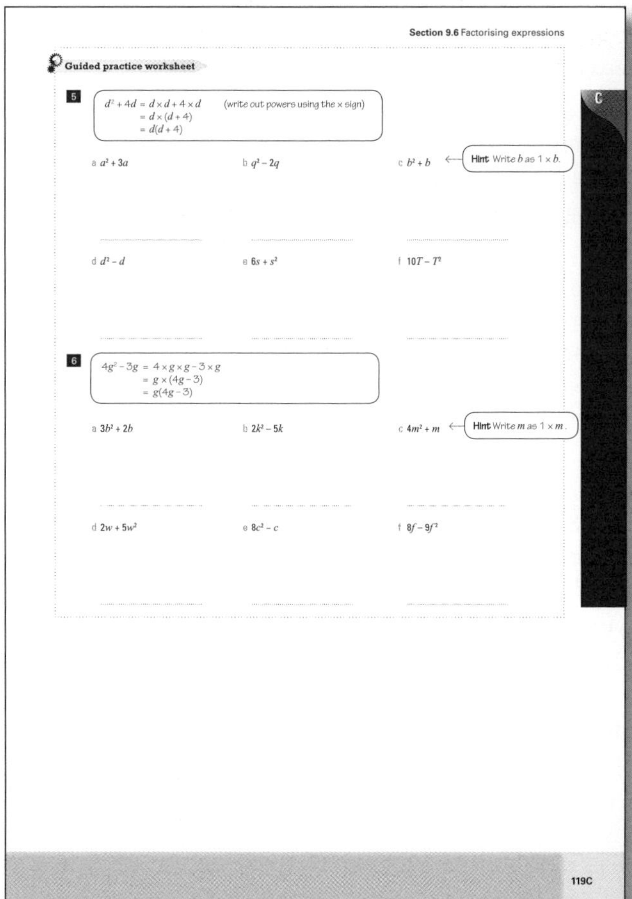

Guided practice worksheet

5

$d^2 + 4d = d \times d + 4 \times d$ (write out powers using the × sign)
$= d \times (d + 4)$
$= d(d + 4)$

a $a^2 + 3a$ b $q^2 - 2q$ c $b^2 + b$ ← **Hint** Write b as $1 \times b$.

d $d^2 - d$ e $6s + s^2$ f $10T - T^2$

6

$4g^2 - 3g = 4 \times g \times g - 3 \times g$
$= g \times (4g - 3)$
$= g(4g - 3)$

a $3b^2 + 2b$ b $2k^2 - 5k$ c $4m^2 + m$ ← **Hint** Write m as $1 \times m$.

d $2w + 5w^2$ e $8c^2 - c$ f $8f - 9f^2$

C

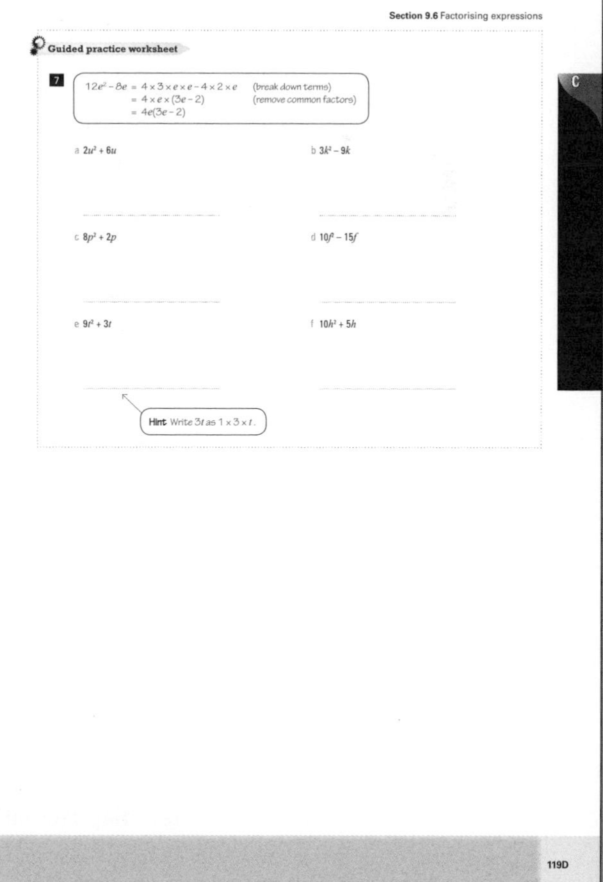

Guided practice worksheet

7

$12e^2 - 8e = 4 \times 3 \times e \times e - 4 \times 2 \times e$ (break down terms)
$= 4 \times e \times (3e - 2)$ (remove common factors)
$= 4e(3e - 2)$

a $2u^2 + 6u$ b $3k^2 - 9k$

c $8p^2 + 2p$ d $10f^2 - 15f$

e $9t^2 + 3t$ f $10h^2 + 5h$

Hint Write $3t$ as $1 \times 3 \times t$.

C

GCSE 2010

N j Use decimal notation and recognise that each terminating decimal is a fraction

N k Recognise that recurring decimals are exact fractions, and that some exact fractions are recurring decimals

FS Process skills

Examine patterns and relationships

FS Performance

Level 2 Use appropriate checking procedures and evaluate their effectiveness at each stage

Resources

Calculators, paper (for posters)

10.1 Recognising terminating and recurring decimals

Concepts and skills

- Convert between fractions and decimals.
- Convert between recurring decimals and fractions.
- Write terminating decimals as fractions.
- Recognise that recurring decimals are exact fractions, and that some exact fractions are recurring decimals.

Functional skills

- L2 Understand and use equivalences between fractions, decimals and percentages.

Prior key knowledge, skills and concepts

- Students should be able to write a fraction as a decimal.
- Students should be able to work out powers, including squares and cubes.
- Students should be able to work out square roots and cube roots.
- Students should be able to round to one decimal place.
- Students should be able to use the correct order of operations when carrying out a calculation.

Starter

- Check that students know the decimal equivalents of simple fractions.
- *What is* $\frac{1}{2}$ *as a decimal?* (0.5). *What is* $\frac{1}{4}$ *as a decimal?* (0.25), etc.
- Use students' responses to make a list of fractions and their decimal equivalents.

Main teaching and learning

- Ask students how a fraction such as $\frac{1}{40}$ can be changed into a decimal.
- Ask students to suggest different fractions and show how each one is converted to a decimal. Compile a list of the results on the board.
- Discuss, using the results obtained, the difference between a terminating decimal and a recurring decimal.
- Explain how dots are used to indicate the recurring nature of a decimal.

Common misconceptions

- Some calculators round the final digit. For $\frac{2}{3}$, for example, the calculator display might show 0.6666667 rather than 0.6666666. Discuss this with the students.

Enrichment

- Following on from Question 3 in Exercise 10B, students could explore other sets of fractions that lead to recurring decimals – those with a denominator of 9, for example, or a denominator of 11, or 12, or 13,…. They could produce a poster of their findings.
- Students could practise using a written method for changing a fraction into a decimal.

Plenary

- Display a variety of fractions, and for each one ask whether it gives a terminating decimal or a recurring decimal.
- Can students find a rule for determining whether a fraction will give a terminating or a recurring decimal?
- Display a decimal (e.g. 0.45, 0.175, 0.0625, 0.63636363…) and challenge students to see how quickly they can find a fraction that gives that decimal.

Guided practice worksheet

1 Write $\frac{1}{4}$ as a decimal.

Remember: To change a fraction into a decimal, divide the numerator by the denominator.

....

2 Write $\frac{5}{8}$ as a decimal.

....

3 Change these fractions to decimals.

a $\frac{7}{8}$ ....

b $\frac{5}{16}$ ....

c $\frac{7}{20}$ ....

d $\frac{18}{25}$ ....

4 Change these fractions to decimals.

a $\frac{13}{40}$ ....

b $\frac{37}{80}$ ....

c $\frac{14}{32}$ ....

d $\frac{23}{50}$ ....

5 Write $\frac{1}{3}$ as a decimal.

Remember: You can use a dot to indicate that a figure recurs.

....

6 Write $\frac{1}{9}$ as a decimal.

....

7 For each statement, say whether it is true or false.

a 0.55555555… is written as $0.\dot{5}$ ....

b 0.83333333… is written as $0.8\dot{3}$ ....

c 0.37373737… is written as $0.\dot{3}7\dot{3}$ ....

d 0.12312312… is written as $0.\dot{1}2\dot{3}$ ....

8 Change these fractions to decimals.

a $\frac{3}{11}$ ....

b $\frac{7}{12}$ ....

c $\frac{19}{22}$ ....

d $\frac{46}{99}$ ....

G

F

E

Specification

GCSE 2010

N q (part) Understand and use number operations and the relationships between them, including inverse operations…

N v (part) Use calculators effectively and efficiently…

FS Process skills

Examine patterns and relationships

FS Performance

Level 2 Use appropriate checking procedures and evaluate their effectiveness at each stage

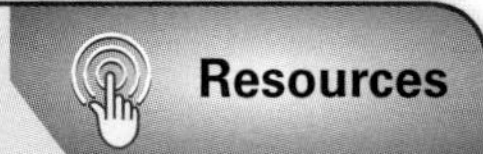

Resources

Resources

Calculators

10.2 Finding reciprocals

Concepts and skills

- Use inverse operations.
- Understand 'reciprocal' as multiplicative inverse, knowing that any non-zero number multiplied by its reciprocal is 1 (and that zero has no reciprocal because division by zero is not defined).
- Find reciprocals.
- Understand and use unit fractions as multiplicative inverses.
- Know how to enter complex calculations.
- Use a range of calculator functions including $+$, $-$, $\times$, $\div$, x^2, $\sqrt{x}$, memory, x^y, $x^{\frac{1}{y}}$, brackets.

Functional skills

- L2 Carry out calculations with numbers of any size in practical contexts, to a given number of decimal places.

Prior key knowledge, skills and concepts

- Students should already be able to use a calculator to enter numbers and carry out the four operations.

Starter

- Quick-fire questions on complements of 1, starting with numbers with 1 decimal place, then 2 decimal places and then 3 decimal places.

Main teaching and learning

- Ask students to find the reciprocal key on their calculators. Ask them to key in several numbers and write down the result. Can they work out what the key does?
- Establish that the reciprocal of a number is 1 divided by the number.
- Find the reciprocals of several numbers, giving the answers as decimals and also, when appropriate, as fractions.
- Discuss how to find the reciprocal of a fraction.

Common misconceptions

- Some students might not have a scientific calculator and will need to key in 1 divided by the number.

Enrichment

- *What is the reciprocal of 0? What happens when you try to work this out on your calculator? Can you explain why this happens?* (0 has no reciprocal. You get an error on your calculator because you can't divide by 0.)

Plenary

- *What happens when you multiply a number by its reciprocal?* (The answer is always 1.)

reciprocal

Guided practice worksheet

1 Find the reciprocal of 5.

> **Hint** Use the reciprocal key on your calculator.

....

2 Find the reciprocal of 20.

....

3 Find the reciprocal of 3.

....

4 Find the reciprocal of 0.2.

....

5 Which is bigger, the reciprocal of 4 or the reciprocal of 40?

....

6 Find the reciprocal of $\frac{3}{4}$.

> Remember: To find the reciprocal of a fraction turn it upside down.

....

7 Find the reciprocal of $\frac{2}{5}$.

....

8 The reciprocal of 32 is 0.03125.
What is the reciprocal of 0.03125?

....

9 Match each number with its reciprocal.

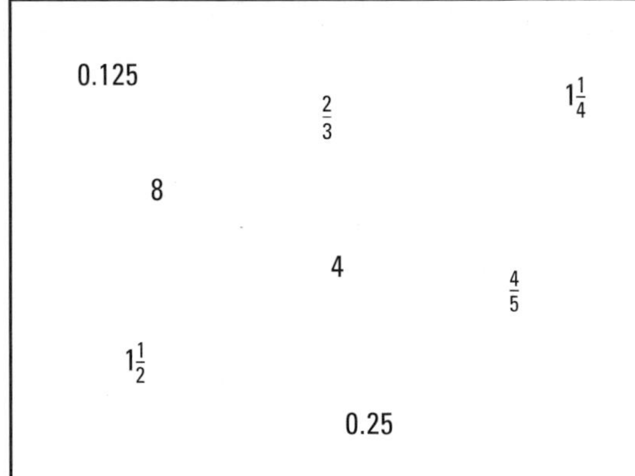

Specification

GCSE 2010

N v (part) Use calculators effectively and efficiently…

FS Process skills

Decide on the methods, operations and tools, including ICT, to use in a situation

Interpret results and solutions

FS Performance

Level 2 Identify the situation or problems and identify the mathematical methods needed to solve them

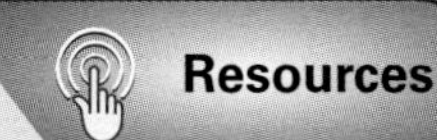

Resources

Resources

Calculators

ActiveTeach resources

The audience video

10.3 Interpreting a calculator display

Concepts and skills

- Use a range of calculator functions including +, −, ×, ÷, x^2, $\sqrt{x}$, memory, x^y, $x^{\frac{1}{y}}$, brackets.
- Enter a range of calculations, including those involving time and money.
- Understand how to interpret the calculator display, particularly when the display has been rounded by the calculator, and not to round during the intermediate steps of a calculation.

Functional skills

- L2 Carry out calculations with numbers of any size in practical contexts, to a given number of decimal places.

Prior key knowledge, skills and concepts

- Students should already be able to use a calculator to enter numbers and carry out the four operations.

Starter

- Use the 'Get ready' questions to check that students can solve simple problems on a calculator using the four operations. Make up other similar questions.

Main teaching and learning

- Display a price list (e.g. panini £1.80, bowl of soup £1.65, salad £2.10, fruit juice 85p). Ask students to find the total cost of 3 panini and 2 salads. *What does the calculator display show?* Establish that 8.7 means £8.70.
- Ask students to find the total cost of different orders from the same price list.
- Work through some examples in which the calculator display is not the final answer, e.g.:
  - *A crate holds 24 bottles. How many crates are needed for 300 bottles?*
  - *A box weighs 30 kg. A van can carry a maximum load of 1000 kg. What is the greatest number of boxes that the van can safely carry?*

Common misconceptions

- Emphasise that answers involving pounds and pence should be written with two figures after the decimal point. Check that students have written £8.90, not £8.9, as the answer to Question 1 of Exercise 10E. In Questions 7, 8, 9 and 10 make sure that students have given answers that are whole numbers.

Enrichment

- Ask students to work out their age in days; in minutes; in seconds.

Plenary

- *A group of people decide to share a prize of £400 equally. If there are 3 people in the group how much should each person receive?* Repeat for groups of different sizes.

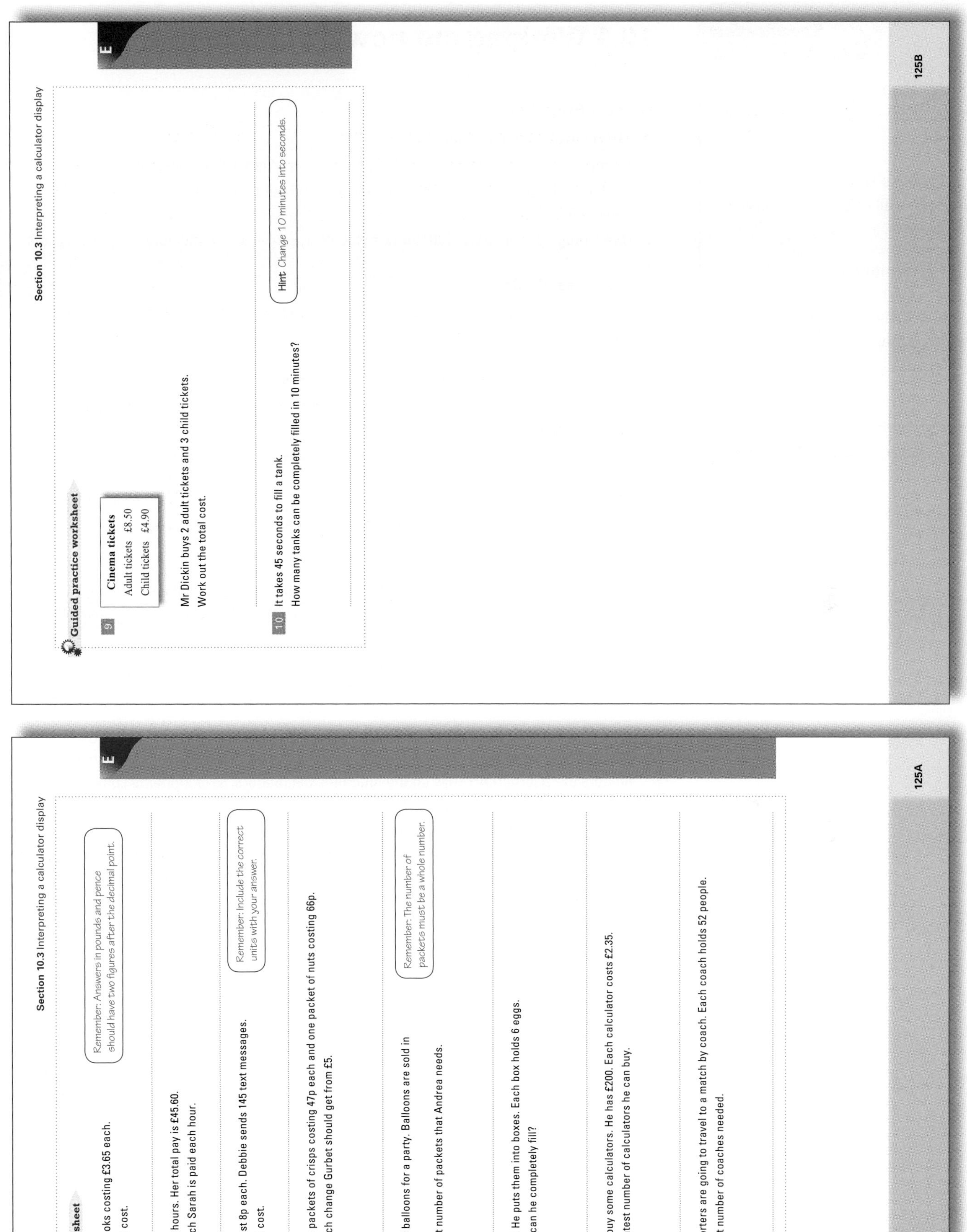

E

Section 10.3 Interpreting a calculator display

Guided practice worksheet

1 Jean buys four books costing £3.65 each.
Work out the total cost.

Remember: Answers in pounds and pence should have two figures after the decimal point.

2 Sarah works for 8 hours. Her total pay is £45.60.
Work out how much Sarah is paid each hour.

3 Text messages cost 8p each. Debbie sends 145 text messages.
Work out the total cost.

Remember: Include the correct units with your answer.

4 Gurbet buys three packets of crisps costing 47p each and one packet of nuts costing 66p.
Work out how much change Gurbet should get from £5.

5 Andrea needs 200 balloons for a party. Balloons are sold in packets of 15.
Work out the least number of packets that Andrea needs.

Remember: The number of packets must be a whole number.

6 Rob has 267 eggs. He puts them into boxes. Each box holds 6 eggs.
How many boxes can he completely fill?

7 Mr Beg wants to buy some calculators. He has £200. Each calculator costs £2.35.
Work out the greatest number of calculators he can buy.

8 450 football supporters are going to travel to a match by coach. Each coach holds 52 people.
Work out the least number of coaches needed.

125A

E

Section 10.3 Interpreting a calculator display

Guided practice worksheet

9

Cinema tickets	
Adult tickets	£8.50
Child tickets	£4.90

Mr Dickin buys 2 adult tickets and 3 child tickets.
Work out the total cost.

10 It takes 45 seconds to fill a tank.
How many tanks can be completely filled in 10 minutes?

Hint: Change 10 minutes into seconds.

125B

Specification

GCSE 2010
N v (part) Use calculators effectively and efficiently…

FS Process skills
Select the mathematical information to use

FS Performance
Level 2 Identify the situation or problems and identify the mathematical methods needed to solve them

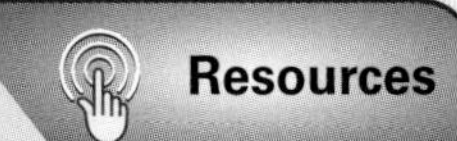

Resources

Resources
Calculators, mini whiteboards

10.4 Working out powers and roots

Concepts and skills

- Know how to enter complex calculations.
- Understand how to interpret the calculator display, particularly when the display has been rounded by the calculator, and not to round during the intermediate steps of a calculation.
- Use a range of calculator functions including +, –, ×, ÷, x^2, $\sqrt{x}$, memory, x^y, $x^{\frac{1}{y}}$, brackets.

Functional skills

- L2 Carry out calculations with numbers of any size in practical contexts, to a given number of decimal places.

Prior key knowledge, skills and concepts

- Students should already be able to work out the square of a number and the cube of a number.
- Students should already be familiar with index notation.
- Students should already be able to find square roots and cube roots.
- Students should already be able to round to one decimal place.

Starter

- Use the 'Get ready' questions and other similar questions to check that students can work out squares, cubes, square roots and cube roots. Students could use mini whiteboards to respond to quick-fire questions.

Main teaching and learning

- Tell students that they are going to use some of the function keys on a calculator to work out powers and roots.
- Discuss how squares, cubes and larger powers can be worked out on a calculator and identify the appropriate keys on the students' calculators. Give students some squares, cubes and larger powers to work out.
- Discuss why calculators have square root and cube root keys (e.g. can quickly find roots that are not integers) and identify these keys on the students' calculators.
- Ask students to find the square root and cube root of various numbers. Check that they can remember how to round to one decimal place.

Common misconceptions

- In questions requiring rounding, encourage students to write down the full calculator display before rounding their answer. Rounding at an intermediate step can make the final answer wrong.

Enrichment

- $2^4 = 4^2$. Challenge students to find other pairs of numbers that behave in this way. (Student's own answers.)

Plenary

- *Faisal has 500 small square tiles. He wants to make a square pattern. What is the largest number of tiles he can use?* (484)
- Students work in pairs. One writes down five whole numbers between 1 and 100 and the other estimates (to 1 decimal place) the square root of each number. They use a calculator to check the estimates and award 1 point for a correct units digit and 1 point for a correct tenths digit (after the display is rounded). They then swap roles.

Guided practice worksheet

1 Work out.

a 18^2 ....   b 2.7^2 ....   c 32^2 ....

Hint Use the x^2 key on your calculator.

2 Work out.

a 1.2^3 ....   b 7^3 ....   c 2.6^3 ....

Hint Use the x^3 key on your calculator.

3 Which is smaller, 3.1^2 or 2.1^3?

....

4 Work out.

a 2^7 ....   b 5^4 ....   c 6^5 ....

Hint Use the power key on your calculator.

5 Which is bigger, 8^2 or 2^8?

....

6 Work out.

a $\sqrt{10.24}$ ....   b $\sqrt{37.21}$ ....   c $\sqrt{1.69}$ ....

Hint Use the square root key on your calculator.

7 Work out, giving your answers to one decimal place.

a $\sqrt{140}$ ....   b $\sqrt[3]{300}$ ....   c $\sqrt{84}$ ....

8 Work out $\sqrt{33.64} + 4.2$

....

9 Which is bigger, $\sqrt{70}$ or $\sqrt[3]{200}$?

....

10 Work out.

a $\sqrt[3]{125}$ ....   b $\sqrt[3]{512}$ ....   c $\sqrt[3]{2197}$ ....

Hint Use the cube root key on your calculator.

Specification

GCSE 2010

N v (part) Use calculators effectively and efficiently…

FS Process skills

Select the mathematical information to use

FS Performance

Level 2 Identify the situation or problems and identify the mathematical methods needed to solve them

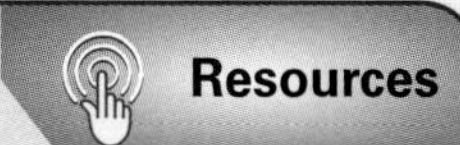

Resources

Resources

Calculators, paper (for posters)

ActiveTeach resources

Extreme 2 video
RP KC Calculator knowledge check
RP PS Calculator problem solving

10.5 Using a calculator to work out complex calculations

Concepts and skills

- Know how to enter complex calculations.
- Use a range of calculator functions including +, −, ×, ÷, x^2, $\sqrt{x}$, memory, x^y, $x^{\frac{1}{y}}$, brackets.
- Understand how to interpret the calculator display, particularly when the display has been rounded by the calculator, and not to round during the intermediate steps of a calculation.

Functional skills

- L2 Carry out calculations with numbers of any size in practical contexts, to a given number of decimal places.

Prior key knowledge, skills and concepts

- Students should already be able to use brackets and the hierarchy of operations (BIDMAS).

Starter

- Use the 'Get ready' questions to check that students can recall and use BIDMAS. Once the answer to the third question has been agreed, discuss possible ways of keying the calculation into a calculator.

Main teaching and learning

- Tell students that they are going to use a calculator to work out complex calculations.
- Discuss how to key in calculations such as $(2.3 + 4.9)^2$ and $\sqrt{14.12 - 2.87}$.
- Consider the expression used in Example 7. Discuss what is wrong with keying in $16.3 + 7.82 \div 7.7 - 4.7$.
- Discuss the different methods for evaluating expressions that are fractions.

Common misconceptions

- When working out expressions that are fractions many students do not realise that the calculator will give them the wrong answer if they do not either put brackets around the numerator and denominator or work out the numerator and denominator separately and then divide.
- Encourage students to write down their working and to use estimation to check that each answer is of the right magnitude.

Enrichment

- Ask students to make up calculations of their own (and the answers).
- Students could produce a poster of the different calculator keys that have been used in this chapter and devise one or two examples for each one.

Plenary

- Use a selection of the calculations made up by the students (see Enrichment, above) for the rest of the class to solve.

Guided practice worksheet

Hint Use the bracket keys on your calculator.

1 Work out.

a $(4.3 + 2.8)^2$ ....

b $(8.2 - 3.9)^2$ ....

2 Work out.

a $13^2 + 7^3$ ....

b $9^3 - 21^2$ ....

3 Work out.

Remember: You need to find the square root of the whole calculation.

a $\sqrt{15.7 - 14.79}$ ....

b $\sqrt{486 - 197}$ ....

4 Work out the value of each of these.

Write down all the figures on your calculator display.

a $\frac{5.29 - 1.37}{2.3}$ ....

b $\frac{128.5}{4.76 + 8.17}$ ....

5 Work out the value of each of these.

Write down all the figures on your calculator display.

a $\frac{14.1 + 7.26}{5.8 - 2.91}$ ....

b $\frac{9.2 - 3.47}{2.5 \times 7.1}$ ....

Remember: You could work out the numerator and denominator separately or you could use brackets.

E

D

Specification

GCSE 2010

GM o Interpret scales on a range of measuring instruments and recognise the inaccuracy of measurements

GM q Make sensible estimates of a range of measures

FS Process skills

Recognise that a situation has aspects that can be represented using mathematics

Find results and solutions

FS Performance

Level 1 Understand practical problems in familiar and unfamiliar contexts and situations, some of which are non-routine

Resources

Resources

Rulers, tape measures, graph paper

Links

http://nrich.maths.org/5979

ActiveTeach resources

Scales interactive

11.1 Reading scales

Concepts and skills

- Interpret scales on a range of measuring instruments – mm, cm, m, km, ml, cl, l, mg, g, kg, tonnes, °C.
- Indicate given values on a scale.
- Make sensible estimates of a range of measures in everyday settings.

Functional skills

- L1 Convert units of measure in the same system.

Prior key knowledge, skills and concepts

- Students need to be able to use numbers written up to two decimal places, to read simple scales. They should also be able to use a ruler to carry out measurements.

Starter

- A useful exercise is to get the students to do some in-class estimates of length, and then check their estimates using rulers, tape measures and so on.

Main teaching and learning

- Recap how to use rulers to measure accurately, measuring lines in both mm and cm. Introduce the simple conversion between mm and cm at this stage.
- Discuss how to read simple scales and dials. Compare dials that have a scale involved, and those that do not. *What should you do when you have a scale?*
- When taking estimates, explain that students could divide the gap into halves, quarters or another appropriate division to help with the estimate.

Common misconceptions

- Some students will measure from the edge of the ruler rather than the '0 cm' mark.
- Students might misinterpret the mm and cm scales.
- Sometimes students misread the scales and dials or misread the scale on a dial.
- Students sometimes mix fractions and decimals, for example $5.1\frac{1}{2}$.

Enrichment

- Ask students to compare measurements in cm and mm, and other dials that have two units used. They could also draw conversion graphs using plotted points from readings taken from the scales and dials.

Plenary

- Ask students to carry out a series of measurements with rulers, measuring in mm and cm. They could then make some further estimates from given dials.

G

Guided practice worksheet

1 Write down the reading on these centimetre rulers.

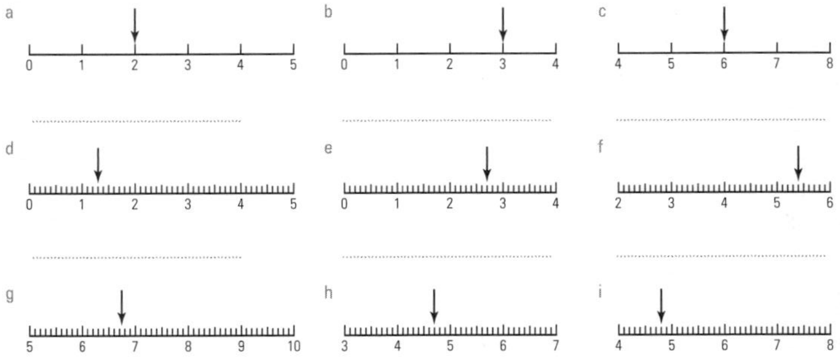

a 0 1 2 3 4 5 ....

b 0 1 2 3 4 ....

c 4 5 6 7 8 ....

d 0 1 2 3 4 5 ....

e 0 1 2 3 4 ....

f 2 3 4 5 6 ....

g 5 6 7 8 9 10 ....

h 3 4 5 6 7 ....

i 4 5 6 7 8 ....

2 Measure and write down the length of these lines in centimetres.

Make sure the '0' on the ruler is at the start of the line on the left.

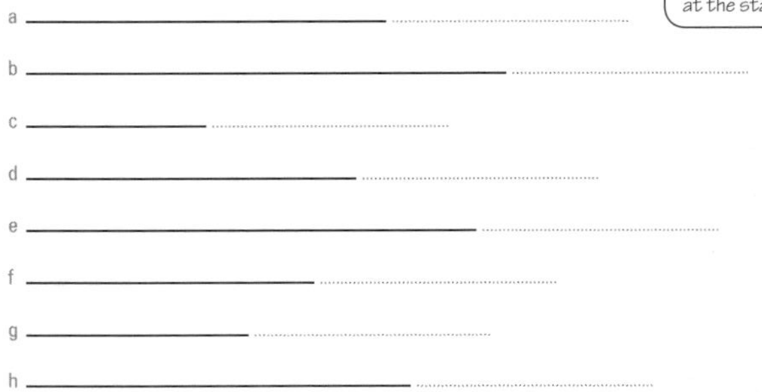

a ....

b ....

c ....

d ....

e ....

f ....

g ....

h ....

3 Measure and write down the length of these lines in millimetres.

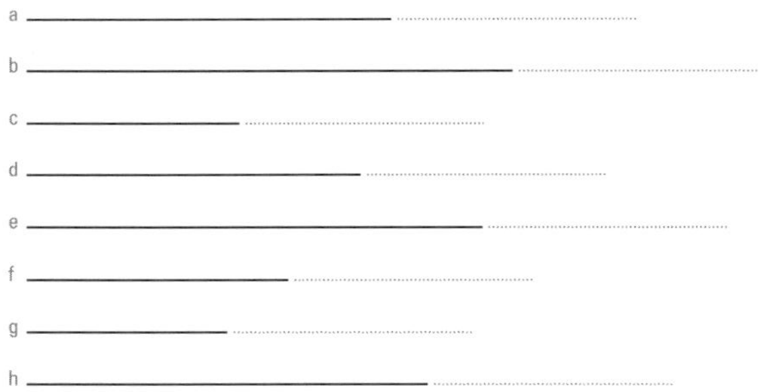

a ....

b ....

c ....

d ....

e ....

f ....

g ....

h ....

F

Guided practice worksheet

4 Write down the readings shown on these scales.

Count the divisions carefully.

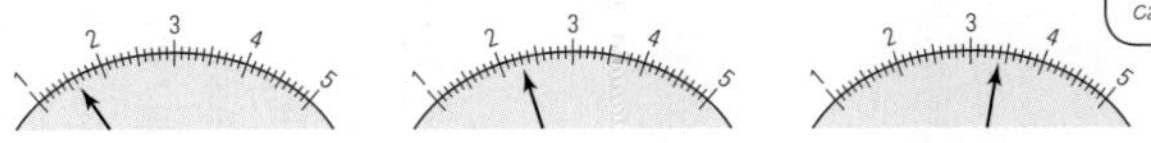

1 2 3 4 5 .... 1 2 3 4 5 .... 1 2 3 4 5 ....

5 Estimate the reading shown on these scales.

Where is the half point? Where is the $\frac{1}{4}$, 0.25, $\frac{3}{4}$, 0.75 point?

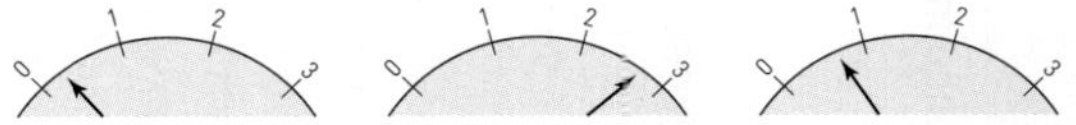

0 1 2 3 .... 0 1 2 3 .... 0 1 2 3 ....

Specification

GCSE 2010

GM o (part) Interpret scales on a range of measuring instruments…

FS Process skills

Recognise that a situation has aspects that can be represented using mathematics

Find results and solutions

FS Performance

Level 1 Identify and obtain necessary information to tackle the problem

Resources

Resources

Timetables, TV schedules

Links

http://nrich.maths.org/4806

11.2 Time

Concepts and skills

- Interpret scales on a range of measuring instruments – seconds, minutes, hours, days, weeks, months and years.
- Use correct notation for time, 12- and 24-hour clock.
- Work out time intervals.

Functional skills

- L1 Solve problems requiring calculation, with common measures including … time …
- L1 Convert units of measure in the same system.

Prior key knowledge, skills and concepts

- Students should be able to read the time from analogue or digital clocks or watches, working out simple durations of time. They should be able to use a calendar to read off dates, and work out simple durations of time using a calendar.

Starter

- A useful starter for students is to practise reading the time from analogue and/or digital clocks. They can practise reading times from timetables (for example, online timetables).
- Writing down the times they each have their meals is a useful exercise. They can either work out the duration of time between each meal, or write down the time it takes them to eat each meal. The duration of TV programmes is a further rich source of material for easy starter questions.

Main teaching and learning

- Go through all the units of time.
- Discuss changing between 12-hour and 24-hour time. Emphasise the different notation used.
- Discuss problems involving the calculation of time before/time after a certain time, for example: *Work out the time 4 hours before 6.15*, and so on.
- Discuss how to work out durations of time, for example between two times, and using times in timetables. Encourage students to share their methods of solution.
- Consider the use of timetables for problem solving. You could extend this to dealing with real and local timetables.

Common misconceptions

- Students sometimes try to use calculators to calculate time differences.
- Sometimes students have a poor knowledge of time units (e.g. thinking there are 54 weeks in a year, or 20 hours in a day).
- Some students have an inability to read correctly from a clock, or use language such as 'quarter to 5'.
- Students might have an inability to calculate time duration (difference between two times).

Enrichment

- Provide students with a timetable, or a set of timetables, and ask them to plan a journey to/from somewhere, making a list of all the crucial times of events during that journey. This could be with real timetables.
- Ask students to investigate the regulations with regard to the maximum minutes of adverts per hour allowed on television, comparing the regulations in the UK with those in the EU.

Plenary

- Organise a quick quiz centred on the units of time (how many weeks in a year, minutes in an hour, and so on). For mental agility you could extend this to minutes in a day and so on.
- Provide students with a TV programme schedule for one day or evening and ask them to calculate the durations of the programmes.

convert

Guided practice worksheet

Write the times using figures or words.

1 These clocks show times in the morning.
Write down the times on these clocks: i in 12-hour time ii in 24-hour time.

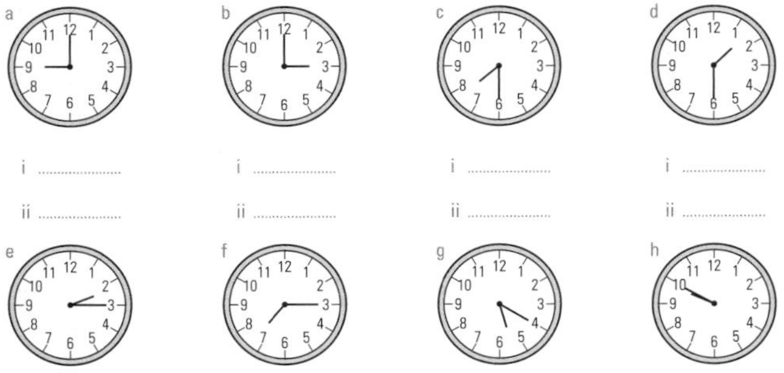

a i .... ii ....
b i .... ii ....
c i .... ii ....
d i .... ii ....
e i .... ii ....
f i .... ii ....
g i .... ii ....
h i .... ii ....

2 These clocks show times in the afternoon.
Write down the times on these clocks: i in 12-hour time ii in 24-hour time.

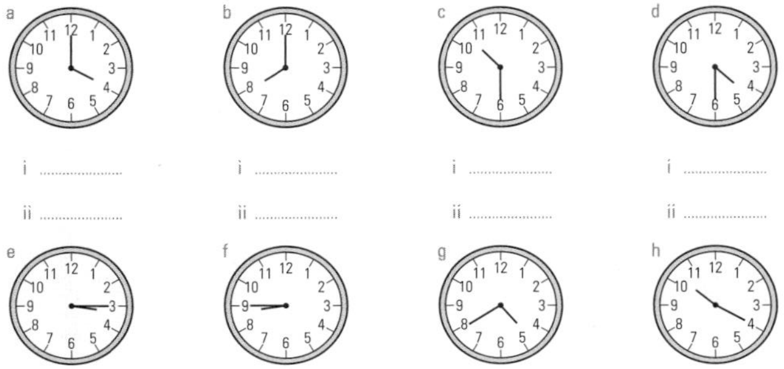

a i .... ii ....
b i .... ii ....
c i .... ii ....
d i .... ii ....
e i .... ii ....
f i .... ii ....
g i .... ii ....
h i .... ii ....

3 Use the clock faces in Question 1 to find the time:

i from b to a .... ii from d to c ....
iii from e to f .... iv from g to h ....

4 Use the clock faces in Question 2 to find the time:

i from a to b .... ii from d to c ....
iii from e to f .... iv from g to h ....

Guided practice worksheet

5 How long is it, in hours and minutes, between these times?
You may wish to draw clock faces to help you.

Count up the hours and then the minutes.

a 10.30 am to 11.40 am ....

b 2.30 pm to 5.50 pm ....

c 11.15 am to 1.30 pm ....

d 3.40 pm to 6.00 pm ....

e 0800 hours to 1150 hours ....

f 0120 hours to 0330 hours ....

g 0430 hours to 1250 hours ....

h 1650 hours to 2000 hours ....

Specification

GCSE 2010

GM o (part) Interpret scales on a range of measuring instruments…
GM p Convert measurements from one unit to another
GM q Make sensible estimates of a range of measures

FS Process skills

Decide on the methods, operations and tools … to use in a situation
Examine patterns and relationships

FS Performance

Level 1 Identify and obtain necessary information to tackle the problem

Resources

Links

http://www.bbc.co.uk/schools/gcsebitesize/maths/shapes/measuresact.shtml

ActiveTeach resources

Metric units quiz
Unit equivalents interactive
Paper 1 video

11.3 Metric units

Concepts and skills

- Know that measurements using real numbers depend upon the choice of unit.
- Convert between units of measure within one system.
- Convert metric units to metric units.
- Make sensible estimates of a range of measures in everyday settings.
- Choose appropriate units for estimating or carrying out measurement.

Functional skills

- L1 Solve problems requiring calculation, with common measures including … length, weight, capacity …
- L1 Convert units of measure in the same system.

Prior key knowledge, skills and concepts

- Students should be familiar with common metric units.
- They should be able to choose an appropriate unit to carry out a practical measurement.
- They should be able to make some simple estimates with regard to measuring using metric units.

Starter

- Students could undertake oral work in describing things they could measure, and the units they would use to undertake the measurement. Start with simple items in the classroom, then move onto things you describe. You could also set students a number of *Which is heavier…?* problems.

Main teaching and learning

- Start by going through all the metric units. Comparing them visually where possible might help, as will giving real-life examples of objects that have a particular length, weight or capacity.
- Discuss which units are appropriate for measuring different things; stress the importance of stating units with any answers.
- Go through the process of changing units: discuss the difference between multiplying and dividing by multiples of 10.
- Emphasise the need for sensible answers: *How do you judge whether an answer is appropriate for the problem set?*
- Explain to students the need to convert to the same unit before ordering, and the need to change the units back for the final answer, always stating the units used.

Common misconceptions

- Some students fail to give units with answers that involve units.
- Students sometimes misplace decimal points, or draw them faintly so that they are ambiguous.

Enrichment

- Ask students to investigate other units not stated here, and those used in science.
- You could demonstrate how to convert between uncommon metric units.

Plenary

- Hold a class quiz to judge whether or not students have understood the topic of measure: you could ask students to guess the length/height/capacity of various objects, then ask them to convert their estimates into a different metric measurement.

metric unit

G

Guided practice worksheet

1 Write down the metric unit that you would use to measure:

a the capacity of a kitchen mug ....

b the diameter of a £1 coin ....

c the weight of an ipod ....

d the capacity of a bucket ....

e the length of a car ....

f the weight of a bag of cement ....

g the distance from London to Paris ....

h the weight of a bus ....

If you are changing to a larger unit you **divide**. If you are changing to a smaller unit you **multiply**.

2 Change these lengths to centimetres.

a 2 m .... b 3000 mm ....

c 5.5 m .... d 40 mm ....

3 Change these lengths to millimetres.

a 7 cm .... b 4.5 cm ....

c 80 cm .... d 24 cm ....

4 Change these lengths to metres.

a 4 km .... b 700 cm ....

c 30 km .... d 20 cm ....

5 Change these weights to grams.

a 6 kg .... b 40 kg ....

c 2.5 kg .... d 35 kg ....

6 Change these capacities to litres.

a 8000 ml .... b 30 000 ml ....

c 50 ml .... d 900 ml ....

7 Change these capacities to millilitres.

a 4 l .... b 70 l ....

c 2.5 l .... d 0.5 l ....

8 Change these lengths to kilometres.

a 4000 m .... b 20 000 m ....

c 500 m .... d 2500 m ....

Specification

GCSE 2010
GM p Convert measurements from one unit to another

FS Process skills
Decide on the methods, operations and tools… to use in a situation
Examine patterns and relationships
Consider the appropriateness and accuracy of the results and conclusions

FS Performance
Level 2 Identify the situation or problems and identify the mathematical methods needed to solve them

Resources

Resources
Graph paper
Rulers that show both centimetres and inches

ActiveTeach resources
Building the course 2b video
Setting up the fair 1 video

11.4 Imperial units

Concepts and skills

- Convert imperial units to imperial units.
- Convert between metric and imperial measures.
- Know rough metric equivalents of pounds, feet, miles, pints and gallons.
- Estimate conversions.

Functional skills

- L2 Use, convert and calculate using metric and, where appropriate, imperial measures.

Prior key knowledge, skills and concepts

- Students should have a working knowledge of metric units.

Starter

- Do some practical measurement using imperial and metric measure, for comparison. Using rulers that show both centimetres and inches is useful, as are scales in metric and imperial measure. Drawing conversion graphs is also a useful task.

Main teaching and learning

- Start by emphasising where we still use imperial units in our lives, and why it is important that we still study them.
- Also emphasise the history behind imperial units: they were in common use until our relationship grew with the EU, but the USA still uses imperial units.
- Work through the conversion of common imperial units.
- Discuss approximate equivalents and how to change between units.

Common misconceptions

- Students sometimes misunderstand the relationship between imperial units.
- Some students may forget the common imperial–metric equivalents.
- Sometimes students try to convert imperial units using a calculator.

Enrichment

- Ask students to investigate the evolution of measurement and units. Ask them: *Which other imperial units have been used in the past (and are no longer used)? How did they relate to the units used today? What units were used in Roman, Egyptian, Babylonian times?*

Plenary

- Have a class quiz to test the students' knowledge of imperial–metric equivalents.
- Give students some additional metric–imperial conversions.

Guided practice worksheet

G

1 The following scales represent part of an imperial ruler marked off in inches. Write down the measurement shown on each of the rulers.

$1 + \frac{1}{4} = 1\frac{1}{4}$ inches.

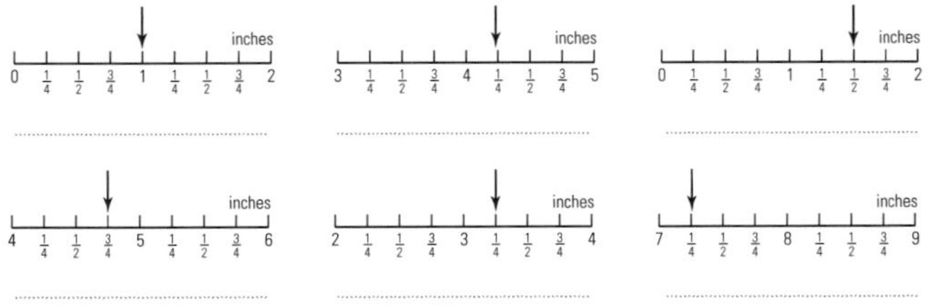

....

....

F

2 The dials below are from bathroom scales, showing a weight in stones and pounds.

a Write down, in stones and pounds, the measurement shown on each of the scales.

b Change each of your answers in part a in stones and pounds to an answer in just pounds.

1 stone = 14 pounds.

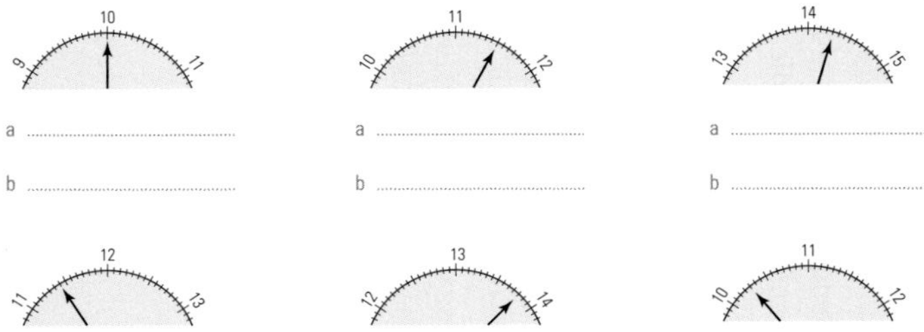

a .... a .... a ....

b .... b .... b ....

a .... a .... a ....

b .... b .... b ....

10 stone 4 pounds = $(10 \times 14) + 4$
= $140 + 4 = 144$ pounds.

3 Change these imperial measurements.

a 2 feet into inches ....

b 3 yards into feet ....

c 16 pints into gallons ....

d 12 feet into yards ....

e 48 inches into feet ....

f 3 stone into pounds ....

g 3 gallons into pints ....

Guided practice worksheet

F

h 140 pounds into stones ....

i 2 pounds into ounces ....

Imperial unit conversions
12 inches = 1 foot
3 feet = 1 yard
16 ounces = 1 pound
14 pounds = 1 stone
8 pints = 1 gallon

Metric–imperial approximate equivalent conversions

Metric		Imperial	Metric		Imperial
8 km	⟶	5 miles	1 kg	⟶	2.2 pounds
1 m	⟶	39 inches	25 g	⟶	1 ounce
30 cm	⟶	1 foot	4.5 litres	⟶	1 gallon
2.5 cm	⟶	1 inch	1 litre	⟶	1.75 pints

4 Change these measurements.

a 60 cm into feet ....

b 9 litres into gallons ....

c 10 cm into inches ....

d 5 kg into pounds ....

e 10 ounces into grams ....

f 3 feet into cm ....

g 8 inches into cm ....

h 10 miles into km ....

i 5 gallons into litres ....

Specification

GCSE 2010

GM p Convert measurements from one unit to another

GM s Understand and use compound measures

FS Process skills

Decide on the methods, operations and tools… to use in a situation

Use appropriate mathematical procedures

Find results and solutions

FS Performance

Level 2 Apply a range of mathematics to find solutions

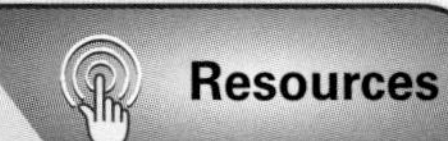

Resources

Resources

Graph paper

Internet access

ActiveTeach resources

Swimming 2 video

Traffic flows 2 video

11.5 Speed

Concepts and skills

- Convert between metric speed measures.
- Understand and use compound measures, including speed.

Functional skills

- L2 Use, convert and calculate using metric and, where appropriate, imperial measures.

Prior key knowledge, skills and concepts

- Students should be able to change between durations of time and be aware that time calculations cannot usually be performed on a calculator.

Starter

- Students can discuss situations where they have met speed, for example the speedometer of a car. Also discuss relative speeds: what is the speed of a person walking, a bicycle, a car, a plane, and so on. Discuss speed records.

Main teaching and learning

- Describe to students the relationship between speed, distance and time. Outline the units associated with these three variables.
- Discuss speed as a measure of how far you travel per unit of time (for example, 30 mph means you travel 30 miles every 1 hour).
- Cover how to calculate speed (average speed).
- Now explain how to calculate time taken and distance travelled.
- Elaborate on the concept of time, explaining how to convert time into a decimal, if appropriate, for use in calculating speed. Allow the students to practise this concept to ensure a full understanding.

Common misconceptions

- Some students use multiplication when they should use division and vice versa.
- Students sometimes give answers that are inappropriate since they do not fit the context.
- Sometimes students encounter problems with using division of hours in speed calculations, and in relation to the use of a calculator.

Enrichment

- Ask students to compare speeds given in different units: miles per hour and miles per second, or km per hour and m/s.
- Students could investigate speed records and draw graphs to show how particular records have changed over time.
- Ask students to use the internet to investigate the average speed of various trains between two locations during one day.

Plenary

- Students could find how the speed changes as the distance becomes greater.
- Ask students to find how the speed changes as the time changes.

Guided practice worksheet

E

1 A car is travelling at a speed of 50 mph (miles per hour).
Write down how far the car will have travelled in:

Car speed = distance travelled each hour.

a 1 hour ....

b 2 hours ....

c 3 hours ....

d 4 hours ....

e 5 hours ....

2 A car covers the distance of 1 mile in exactly 1 minute.

a If it continues to travel at the same speed, how far will it travel in:

Speed: $\frac{\text{Distance}}{\text{Time}}$

Time = $\frac{\text{Distance}}{\text{Speed}}$

Distance = Speed × Time

D / S T

i 5 minutes ....

ii 10 minutes ....

iii 30 minutes ....

iv 1 hour ....

v 2 hours? ....

b At what speed is the car travelling? ....

D

3 A plane is travelling at a speed of 200 km/h.
How far will the plane have flown after:

a $\frac{1}{2}$ hour ....

b 1 hour ....

c 2 hours ....

d $2\frac{1}{2}$ hours ....

e 7 hours? ....

4 What is the speed of a car that takes 4 hours to travel 120 miles?

Hint: Units are miles and hours, so speed is given as miles per hour (MPH)

....

5 What is the speed of a man who takes 3 hours to travel 9 miles?

....

6 What is the speed of a cyclist who takes 5 hours to ride a distance of 200 miles?

....

7 A car is travelling at a speed of 45 mph.
How far will it travel in 3 hours?

....

Guided practice worksheet

D

8 A car is travelling at a speed of 90 mph.
How far will it travel in $2\frac{1}{2}$ hours?

....

9 A man runs at a speed of 6 mph.
How long will it take him to run a distance of 9 miles?

....

10 A plane is travelling at a speed of 200 mph.
How long will it take to fly a distance of 900 miles?

....

Specification

GCSE 2010
GM o Interpret scales on a range of measuring instruments and recognise the inaccuracy of measurements

FS Process skills
Decide on the methods, operations and tools... to use in a situation
Examine patterns and relationships
Consider the appropriateness and accuracy of the results and conclusions

FS Performance
Level 2 Identify the situation or problems and identify the mathematical methods needed to solve them

Resources

Resources
ruler

ActiveTeach resources
Running 2 video
Setting up the fair 3 video
RP KC Measure knowledge check
RP PS Measure problem solving

11.6 Accuracy of measurements

Concepts and skills

- Recognise that measurements given to the nearest whole unit may be inaccurate by up to one half in either direction.

Functional skills

- L2 Use, convert and calculate, using metric and, where appropriate, imperial measures.

Prior key knowledge, skills and concepts

- Students should already be able to measure lengths, using a ruler, and read scales.

Starter

- Ask students to explain how they would use a ruler to measure the length of their textbooks.
  The textbook is not an exact number of cm. What are the divisions between each cm? (millimetres) *How do you read these divisions to get an accurate measurement of the book?*

Main teaching and learning

- Ask students to measure the length and width of a sheet of A4 paper and then give their answers. Compare answers to show that not all students have got the same result. Tell students, in this case it has been difficult to obtain an accurate answer. *What would be another way of giving the answer to show there is variation in our measurements?* (Give the measurements to the nearest millimetre or centimetre.)
- Ask students to name metric units of measurement (millimetre, centimetre, metre, gram, kilogram, ton, litre, km/h).
- Work through Examples 15 and 16. Note that in Example 16, the length of the calculator is measured in centimetres, but is correct to the nearest millimetre.

Common misconceptions

- Students sometimes think that the greatest possible value should be rounded up, rather than thinking of it as an upper limit to the measurement given.
- Students sometimes don't spot that the unit of accuracy may not the same as the unit of measurement, e.g. a length given in cm that is accurate to the nearest mm.

Plenary

- Work through Exercise 11O. Discuss in particular Questions 5–7, which apply what they have found about greatest and least measurements to real-life situations.

Section 11.6 Accuracy of measurements

Guided practice worksheet

C

Example: A coin is placed on a digital weighing scale, accurate to the nearest gram (g). The reading is 26 g. What is the lightest and heaviest possible weight of the coin?
'To the nearest gram (g)' means the true weight could be 0.5 grams more or less than the measurement.

So lightest possible weight of coin = 26 g − 0.5 g = 15.5 g
And heaviest possible weight of coin = 26 g + 0.5 g = 26.5 g

1 A garden centre fills bags of compost to the nearest kilogram.

a What is the lightest possible weight of a bag marked 12 kg? ....

b What is the heaviest possible weight of a bag marked 25 kg? ....

2 Estelle recorded the temperature of her greenhouse to be 29°C to the nearest °C (degrees Centigrade). Write down the lowest and highest possible temperature of the greenhouse.

....

3 A spoon is manufactured to hold 10 ml of liquid, to the nearest ml (millilitre).

a What is the most amount of liquid it could hold? ....

b If you found that it could only hold 9.7 ml, could you complain to the manufacturer?

....

4 The coverage of a can of paint is 8 m^2, to the nearest m^2 (square metre).

a What is the biggest area that the can of paint will cover? ....

b Tariq estimates the area of his wall is 7.6 m^2. Can he be sure that a single can of paint will be enough?

....

Example: An estate agent measured the width of a room to be 3.74 m, to the nearest cm. What is the greatest possible width of the room?

3.74 m = 374 cm (convert to units used for accuracy)
Greatest possible width of room = 374 cm + 0.5 cm = 374.5 cm
Write the answer in the original units, i.e. 3.745 m

5 An elastic band was stretched to 19.4 cm, to the nearest mm. What is the furthest possible distance it was stretched?

....

6 The diagram shows the dimensions of a table tennis table, to the nearest cm.
What are the smallest and biggest dimensions of the table?

2.74 m
1.52 m
table tennis table

....

7 A can contains 2.65 litres of oil, to the nearest centilitre (cl).
What is the most oil it contains?

Hint 1 litre = 100 cl

....

Section 11.6 Accuracy of measurements

Guided practice worksheet

C

8 Better Batteries claim one of their AA batteries will run a toy car for at least 12 hours, to the nearest hour. Jean finds that her toy car runs for 11 hours and 40 minutes. Is the claim of Better Batteries correct?

....

9 1 foot is 30.5 cm, to the nearest mm.
From this information, what can you say about the length of 1 foot in millimetres?

....

Example: Gus's weighing scales showed he weighed 32.4 kg, to the nearest 100g. What was his lightest possible weight?

32.4 kg = 32 400 g (convert to units used for accuracy)
Lightest possible weight = 32 400 g − 50 g (subtract half degree of accuracy)
= 31 350 g
= 32.35 kg (convert back to original units)

10 Karl's weighing scales are accurate to the nearest 10 g. What are the lightest and heaviest weights of letters with these scale readings?

a 40 g ....

b 100 g ....

c 200 g ....

d 10 g ....

11 An explorer recorded the distances between three ancient monuments to the nearest 100 m. Find the shortest and longest distances between them.

a Burial Ground to Temple = 4.2 km ....

b Temple to Granary = 1.6 km ....

c Granary to Burial Ground = 0.7 km ....

Specification

GCSE 2010

SP g Produce charts and diagrams for various data types

SP i Interpret a wide range of graphs and diagrams and draw conclusions

FS Process skills

Make an initial model of a situation using suitable forms of representation

Find results and solutions

FS Performance

Level 2 Identify the situation or problems and identify the mathematical methods needed to solve them.

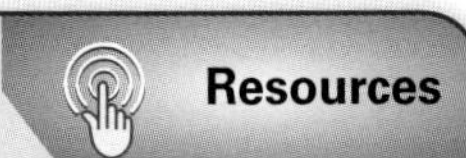

Resources

CD Resources

Resource sheet 12.1

MS PowerPoint presentation 12.1 'Pictograms'

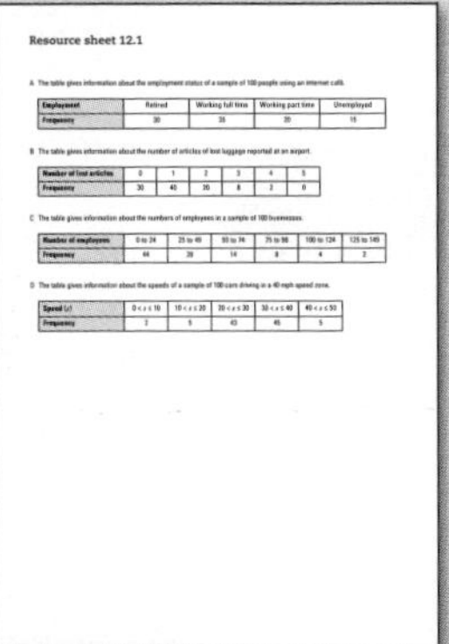

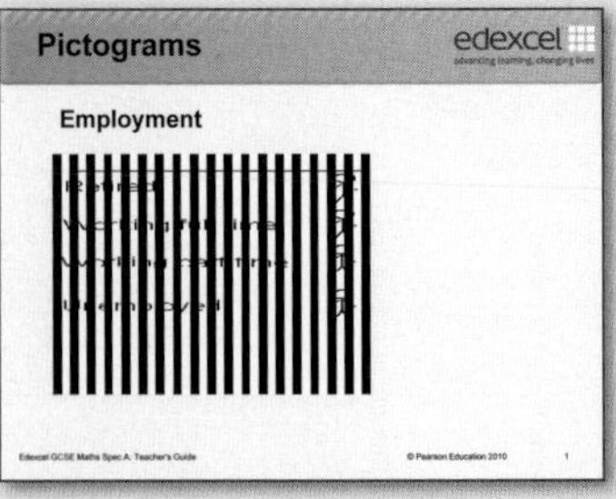

Links

http://nrich.maths.org/2341

12.1 Pictograms

Concepts and skills

- Produce pictograms.
- From pictograms ...:
  - read off frequency values
  - calculate total population
  - find greatest and least values.

Functional skills

- L2 Collect and represent discrete continuous data...

Starter

- Remind students about the different types of data. Discuss the data on Resource sheet 12.1 and which type of data each of the examples falls into.
- The type of representation of data depends on the type of data.

Main teaching and learning

- Tell students that they are going to look at **pictograms**.
  - The word 'pictogram' comes from the word 'picture'.
  - A picture is used to represent a number of articles.
  - *What picture could represent the data in A on Resource sheet 12.1?*
- As a class, complete the pictogram for data A in PowerPoint 12.1 slide 1.
- Having drawn a pictogram, you can find out the total number of the population.
  - You add together the individual frequencies.
- You can find the greatest and least categories.
  - The greatest has the highest frequency; the least has the lowest frequency.

Common misconceptions

- Students sometimes forget to add a key.

Enrichment

- Tell the students to draw a pictogram for data B on the Resource sheet. Use a square to represent 4 pieces of luggage. Slide 3 gives the solution.
- In a pictogram, one symbol represents 3 TVs. How many symbols will be needed to represent:
  (a) 12 TVs (3) (b) 4 TVs $\left(1\frac{1}{3}\right)$ (c) 14 TVs? $\left(4\frac{2}{3}\right)$
- In a pictogram, one symbol represents 4 CDs. How many parcels are represented by:
  (a) 5 symbols (20) (b) $1\frac{1}{2}$ symbols (6) (c) $2\frac{1}{4}$ symbols? (9)
- Aruna is drawing a pictogram showing the number of hours of instant messaging each of her friends spent one night. She decides to use a picture of a smiley face to represent 3 hours. Imran says that it would be better to use the symbol to represent 4 hours. Is Imran correct? Give a reason for your answer. (Imran: easier to divide a picture into quarters.)

Plenary

- In a pictogram, one symbol represents 3 TVs. How many symbols will be needed to represent
  (a) 12 TVs (3) (b) 4 TVs $\left(1\frac{1}{3}\right)$ (c) 14 TVs? $\left(4\frac{2}{3}\right)$
- In a pictogram, one symbol represents 4 CDs. How many CDs are represented by
  (a) 5 symbols (20) (b) $1\frac{1}{2}$ symbols (6) (c) $2\frac{1}{4}$ symbols? (9)
- Aruna is drawing a pictogram showing the number of hours of instant messaging each of her friends spent one night. She decides to use a picture of a smiley face to represent 3 hours. Imran says that it would be better to use the symbol to represent 4 hours. Is Imran correct? Give a reason for your answer? (Imran: easier to divide a picture into quarters.)

Guided practice worksheet

G

1 The pictogram gives information about the shoe sizes of a sample of students.

Shoe size	
35	1 symbol
36	2 symbols
37	4 symbols
38	3 symbols
39	2 symbols

Key
symbol = 2 students

a Write down the shoe size that was most common.

....

b Write down the shoe size that was least common.

....

c How many people took size 38 shoes?

....

d Work out the number of people in the sample.

....

2 The pictogram gives some information about the number of times students were absent from school last term.

Times absent	
0	1 symbol
1	2 symbols
2	3½ symbols
3	
4	

symbol = 2 people

a How many were absent twice?

....

There were five people absent 3 times and three people absent 4 times.

b Complete the pictogram.

3 The table shows the number of telephone calls made last night by students.
Draw a pictogram for these data. Use a phone symbol as a symbol.

Number	0	1	2	3	4
Frequency	4	6	8	9	6

Specification

GCSE 2010

SP g Produce charts and diagrams for various data types

SP i Interpret a wide range of graphs and diagrams and draw conclusions

SP l Compare distributions and make inferences

FS Process skills

Make an initial model of a situation using suitable forms of representation

Find results and solutions

FS Performance

Level 2 Identify the situation or problems and identify the mathematical methods needed to solve them.

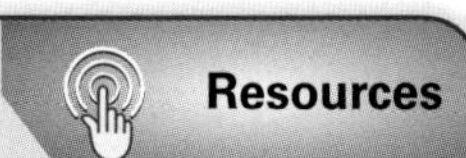

Resources

CD Resources

Resource sheet 12.1

PowerPoint presentation 12.2 'Pie charts'

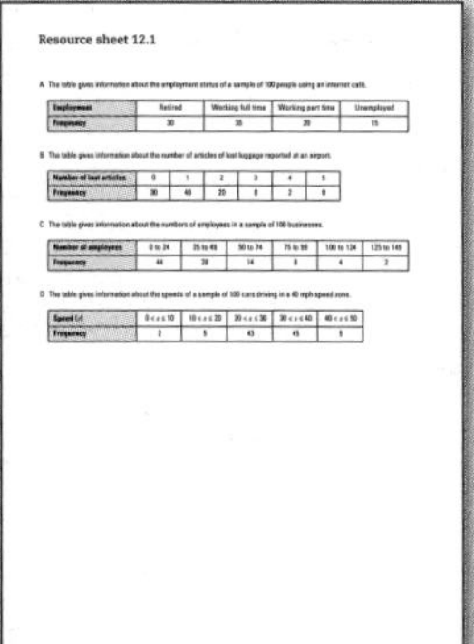

Pie charts edexcel

Employment

Category	Frequency	Angle
Retired	30	$\frac{30 \times 360}{100} = 108°$
Working full time	35	$\frac{35 \times 360}{100} = 126°$
Working part time	20	$\frac{20 \times 360}{100} = 72°$
Unemployed	15	$\frac{15 \times 360}{100} = 36°$
Total	100	360°

Edexcel GCSE Maths Spec A: Teacher's Guide © Pearson Education 2010 1

Links

http://nlvm.usu.edu/en/nav/frames_asid_183_g_4_t_5.html?open=activities&from=category_g_4_t_5.html

12.2 Pie charts

Concepts and skills

- Produce pie charts.
- Interpret pie charts.
- From pie charts:
  - find the total frequency
  - find the size of each category.
- Understand that the frequency represented by corresponding sectors in two pie charts is dependent upon the total populations represented by each of the pie charts.

Functional skills

- L2 Collect and represent discrete continuous data…

Starter

- Remind students of the different types of data.
- The type of representation of data depends on the type of data.

Main teaching and learning

- Tell students that they are going to look at pie charts.
- The word 'pie' is familiar to everyone. When serving a pie it is cut into slices and each person is given a slice. Some slices might be bigger than others.
- Tell the students that each category is represented by a slice of pie. The size of the slice is proportional to the frequency of the category.
- As a class, draw the pie chart, for data A on Resource sheet 12.1. PowerPoint 12.2 slides 1 and 2 give the solution.
- Having drawn the pie chart, you can find out the frequency of a particular category.
- You can find the greatest and least categories.
  - The greatest has the highest frequency; the least has the lowest frequency.

Common misconceptions

- Students sometimes forget to add a key.

Enrichment

- Get the students to draw a pie chart for data B on the Resource sheet. PowerPoint 12.2 slide 3 gives the solution.

Plenary

- *A pie chart is being drawn to represent 36 shops. How many degrees will represent 1 shop?* (10)
- *A pie chart is used to represent 60 people. How many people are represented by:* (a) 90°(15) (b) 180°? (30)
- *180° on a pie chart represents 20 people. How many people does the whole pie chart represent?* (40)
- *90° on a pie chart represents 15 people. How many people does the whole pie chart represent?* (60)
- *30° on a pie chart represents 50 people. How many people does the whole pie chart represent?* (600)
- *A pie chart to represent 1080 people needs to be drawn. Ahmed says that 1 degree will represent 3 people. Sahid says that 3 degrees will represent 1 person. Who is correct, why?* (Ahmed; if 3°represented 1 person, then 3 × 1080 = 3240° would be needed which is more than the number of degrees in a circle.)

Guided practice worksheet

1 The pie chart shows the populations of the countries in the United Kingdom.

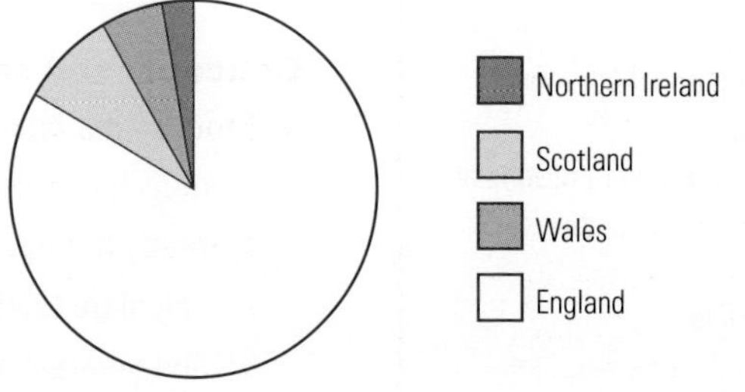

a Write down the country that has the largest population.

....

b Write down the name of the country that has the second smallest population.

....

2 The pie chart gives information about the frequency of the number of accidents per day on a town's bypass over a period of 36 days.

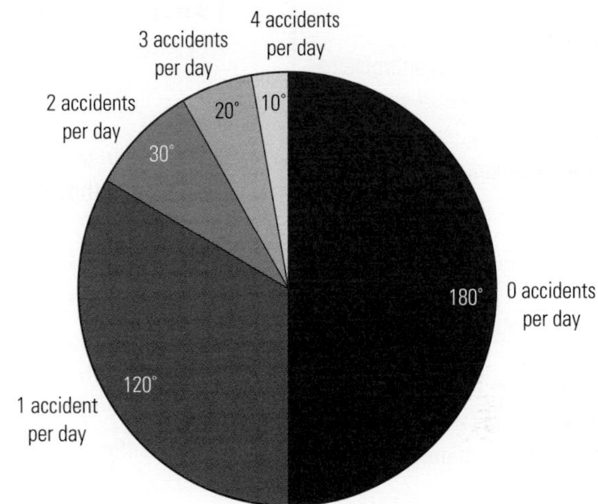

a On how many days were there no accidents?

....

b Work out the number of days on which there were 3 accidents.

....

3 The table gives some information about the ages of 120 cars in a survey.

a Complete this table.

b Draw the pie chart for these data.

Age	Frequency	Angle of pie chart
over 10 years	48	
7 to 10 years	24	
3 to 6 years	30	
less than 3 years	18	

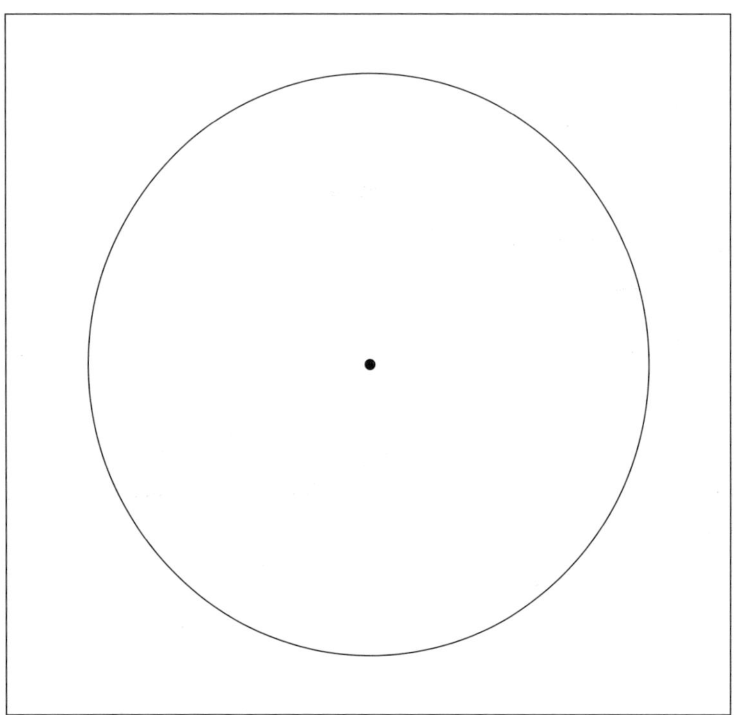

F

E

Specification

GCSE 2010

SP g Produce charts and diagrams for various data types

SP i Interpret a wide range of graphs and diagrams and draw conclusions

FS Process skills

Make an initial model of a situation using suitable forms of representation

Find results and solutions

FS Performance

Level 2 Identify the situation or problems and identify the mathematical methods needed to solve them

Resources

CD Resources

Resource sheet 12.1

MS PowerPoint presentation 12.3 'Bar charts'

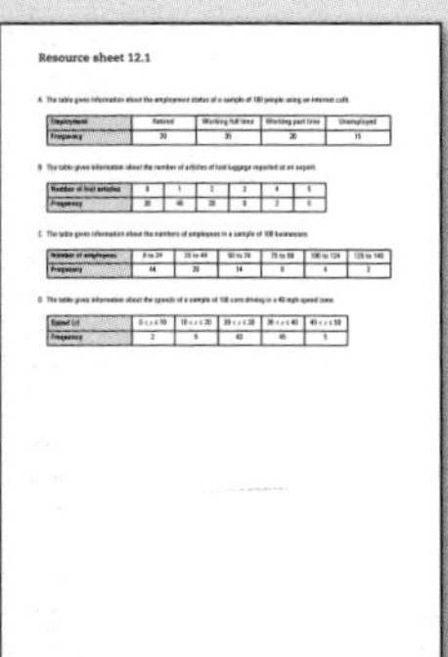

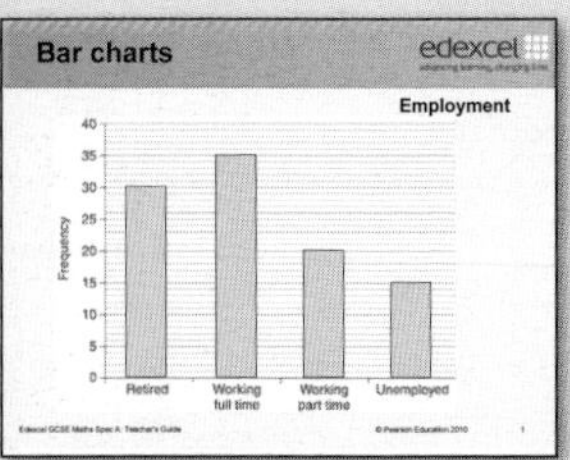

Links

http://nlvm.usu.edu/en/nav/frames_asid_323_g_4_t_5.html?from=category_g_4_t_5.html

12.3 Bar charts

Concepts and skills

- Produce bar charts.
- From … bar charts…:
  - read off frequency values
  - calculate total population
  - find greatest and least values.
- Recognise simple patterns, characteristics relationships in bar charts….

Functional skills

- L2 Collect and represent discrete continuous data…

Starter

- *Who can tell me what a bar is?* The dictionary gives seven definitions of what a bar is: we need the definition 'a long, shaped, rigid piece of material'.

Main teaching and learning

- Tell students that they are going to look at bar charts.
- The idea of a bar chart is that we represent each category by a bar and we make the length of the bar proportional to its frequency. If we stood these next to each other we could compare them.
- It is difficult to take a load of bars around to show people, so what you do is to make a drawing of the bars on a chart. The result is a bar chart.
- Because the categories are separate, we leave a gap between each of the bars.
- A frequency scale is added so the lengths of the bars can be determined.
- The bars may be vertical or horizontal.
- Draw a bar chart for Example A on Resource sheet 12.1. PowerPoint 12.3 slide 1.
- You can find the greatest and least categories (slide 2).
  - The greatest has the longest bar; the least has the shortest bar.
- Example B on Resource sheet 12.1 is discrete numerical data.
- You can still use the idea of sticks but because you have single consecutive values on a scale, the bars are reduced to a line. We call the result a line diagram (slide 3).
- In Example C on the Resource sheet you have grouped discrete data.
- Since you have grouped values a bar chart is used (slide 4).

Common misconceptions

- Students sometimes do not leave gaps between the lines.

Enrichment

- Discuss the different types of data on Resource sheet 12.1 and why the diagrams are as they are.

Plenary

- Look back at the bar charts given in the introduction to Chapter 12. Which month is the mode? (August)
- Look at September. How much rain fell? (250mm)
- Look at Question 3 in Exercise 12D.

  (a) How many cars did Garage C sell? (4 cars)

  (b) How many cars did Garage B sell? (5 cars)

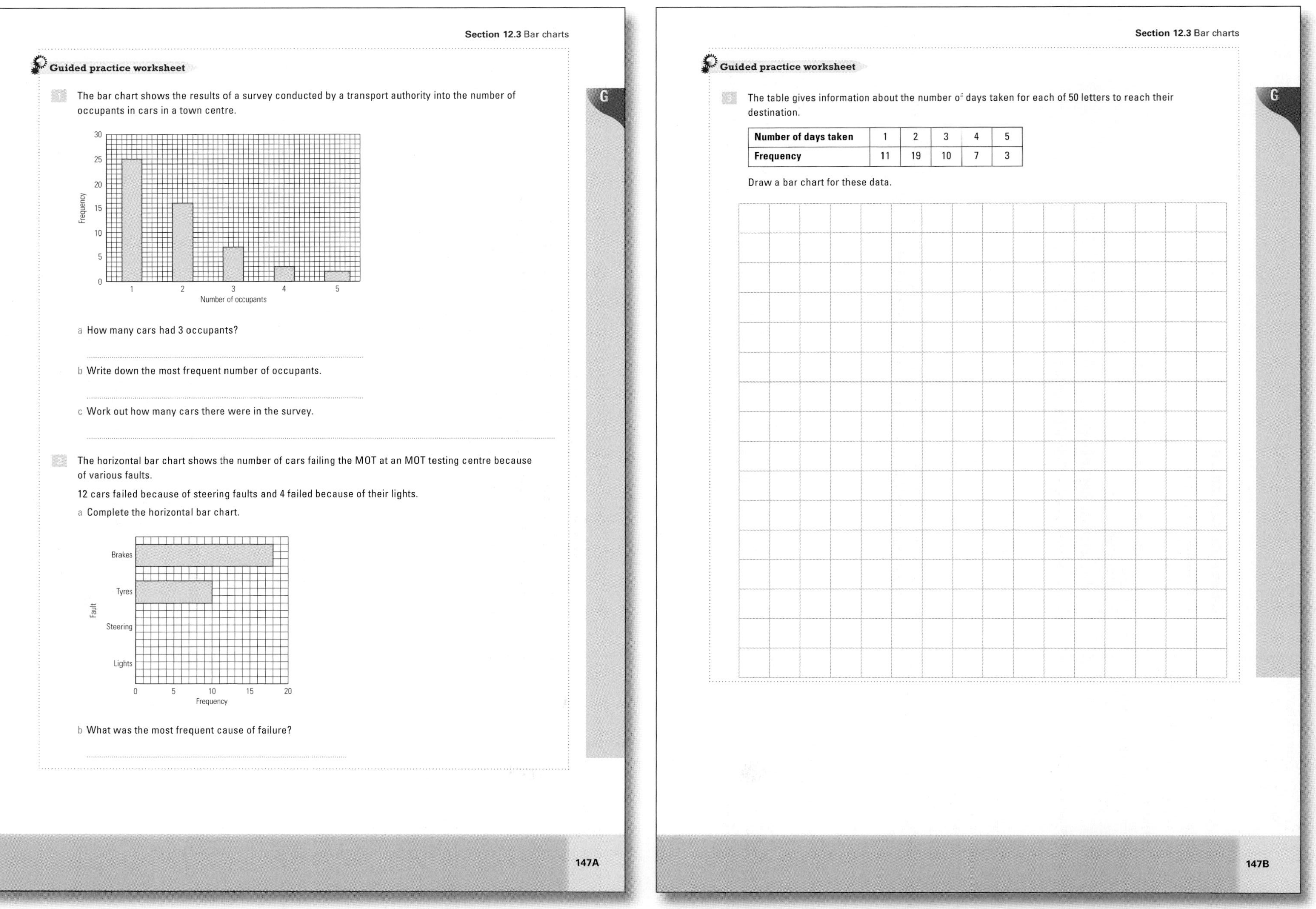

Guided practice worksheet

1 The bar chart shows the results of a survey conducted by a transport authority into the number of occupants in cars in a town centre.

a How many cars had 3 occupants?

b Write down the most frequent number of occupants.

c Work out how many cars there were in the survey.

2 The horizontal bar chart shows the number of cars failing the MOT at an MOT testing centre because of various faults.

12 cars failed because of steering faults and 4 failed because of their lights.

a Complete the horizontal bar chart.

b What was the most frequent cause of failure?

Guided practice worksheet

3 The table gives information about the number of days taken for each of 50 letters to reach their destination.

Number of days taken	1	2	3	4	5
Frequency	11	19	10	7	3

Draw a bar chart for these data.

Specification

GCSE 2010

SP g Produce charts and diagrams for various data types

SP i Interpret a wide range of graphs and diagrams and draw conclusions

SP l Compare distributions and make inferences

FS Process skills

Make an initial model of a situation using suitable forms of representation

Find results and solutions

FS Performance

Level 2 Identify the situation or problems and identify the mathematical methods needed to solve them

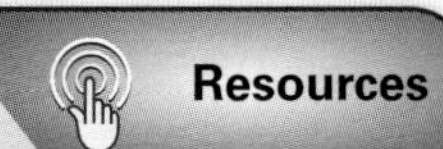

Resources

CD Resources

MS PowerPoint presentation 12.4 'Bar charts'

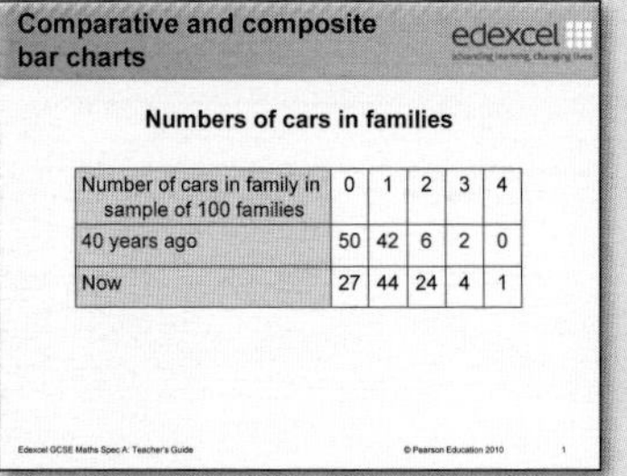

Comparative and composite bar charts

edexcel

Numbers of cars in families

Number of cars in family in sample of 100 families	0	1	2	3	4
40 years ago	50	42	6	2	0
Now	27	44	24	4	1

Links

http://nrich.maths.org/5424

12.4 Comparative and composite bar charts

Concepts and skills

- Produce:
  - composite bar charts
  - comparative and dual bar charts.
- Interpret:
  - composite bar charts
  - comparative and dual bar charts.
- From... bar charts...:
  - read off frequency values
  - calculate total population
  - find greatest and least values.
- Recognise simple patterns, characteristics relationships in bar charts....
- Use comparative bar charts to compare distributions.

Functional skills

- L2 Collect and represent discrete continuous data...

Starter

- Discuss how modes of transport have changed over the last 40 years or so. For example, more people drive and flights are more common.

Main teaching and learning

- Tell students that they are going to look at how the number of cars owned by families has changed over the years.
- We are going to use bar charts to make comparisons between then and now.
- Display PowerPoint 12.4, slide 1 and discuss these points.
  - You need a bar for each variable, each year.
- As a class, draw the comparative (in this case dual) bar chart (slide 2).
  - In the past there were more people with 0 cars, and fewer with 1, 2, 3 or 4 cars.
  - There were none with 4 cars.
  - This chart allows you to compare actual numbers.
- As a class, draw a composite bar chart (slide 3).
  - The greatest proportion of people had 0 cars in the past. The greatest proportion have 1 car now.
  - This chart allows you to see the proportions of each number of cars.

Common misconceptions

- Sometimes students do not leave a gap between categories, or they leave a gap between pairs of values on dual bar charts.
- Sometimes students do not stack categories in the same order on a composite bar chart.

Enrichment

- Find how many students came to school by car, cycling, walking, or by other means when they were at infant school, and how they travel to school now. Draw composite and comparative charts for these data.

Plenary

- *In Example 6, who sold more houses?* (Agent B sold 13 more houses.)
- *Clare has drawn a bar chart. Tom says it is wrong because the bars are all different widths. Is he right?* (Yes, bars should all be the same width.)

compare dual bar chart

F

Guided practice worksheet

1 The dual bar chart gives information about the shoes sizes of 16 boys and 16 girls.

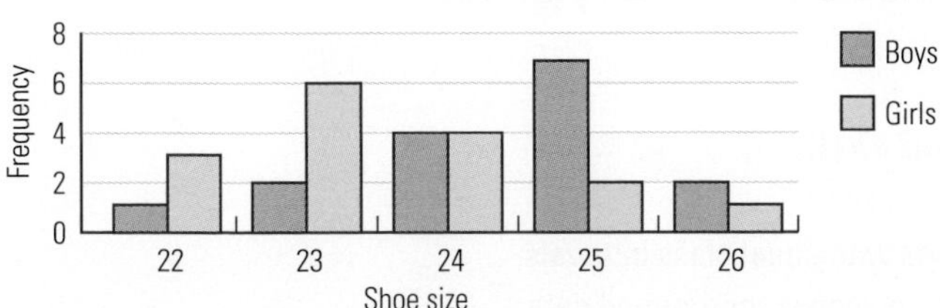

a Write down the most common size for the boys' shoes.

....

b Work out how many more boys than girls wore size 25 shoes.

....

c Compare the distributions of boys' and girls' shoes.

....

2 The composite bar chart shows the blood groups of a sample of 100 British and 100 Danish people.

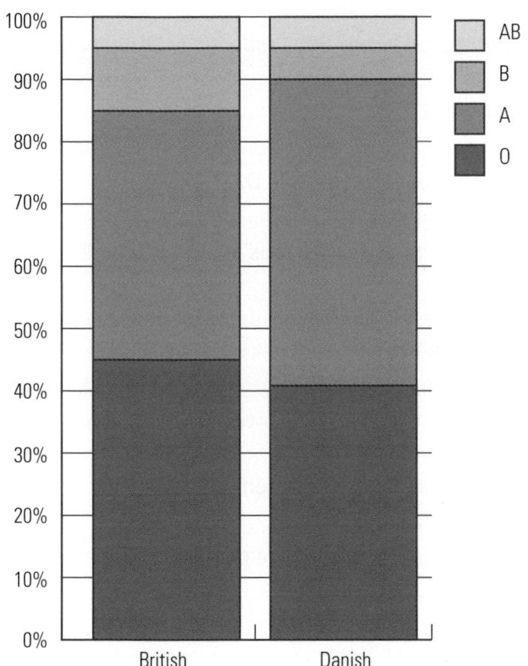

a Write down the blood group that was most common in the British sample.

....

b Write down the blood group that was had by 50% of the Danish sample.

....

c Work out how many more of the Danish sample had blood group A compared to the British sample.

....

....

Specification

GCSE 2010

SP g Produce charts and diagrams for various data types

SP i Interpret a wide range of graphs and diagrams and draw conclusions

FS Process skills

Make an initial model of a situation using suitable forms of representation

Find results and solutions

FS Performance

Level 2 Identify the situation or problems and identify the mathematical methods needed to solve them

Resources

CD Resources

Resource sheet 12.1

MS PowerPoint presentation 12.5 'Histograms'

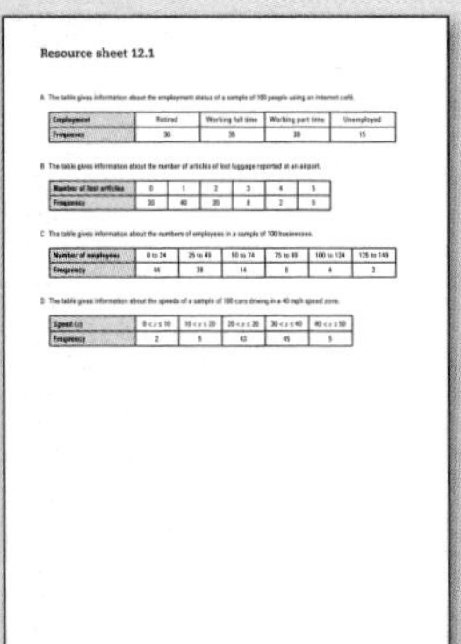

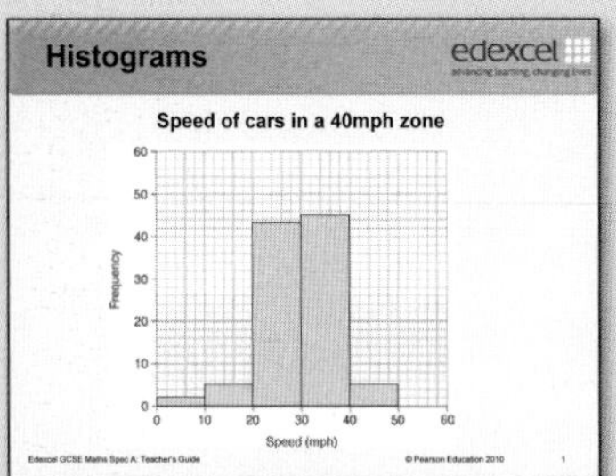

Links

http://nlvm.usu.edu/en/nav/frames_asid_145_g_4_t_5.html?open=instructions&from=category_g_4_t_5.html

ActiveTeach resources

More or less quiz

Frequency polygons interactive

RP KC Processing data knowledge check

RP PS Processing data problem solving

12.5 Line diagrams for discrete data and histograms for continuous data
12.6 Frequency polygons

Concepts and skills

- Produce
  - histograms with equal class intervals
  - frequency polygons for grouped data
- Interpret frequency polygons.
- From… line graphs, frequency polygons, frequency diagrams and histograms with equal class intervals:
  - read off frequency values
  - calculate total population
  - find greatest and least values.
- Recognise simple patterns, characteristics relationships in… line graphs and frequency polygons.

Functional skills

- L2 Collect and represent discrete continuous data…

Starter

- *Why are speed limits important? Why are limits reduced to 20 mph around schools?*

Main teaching and learning

- *Today we are going to look at the speeds people do in a 40 mph zone.*
- Look at the data on Resource sheet 12.1 Example D.
  - The variable, speed, is continuous data.
  - When doing a chart, you will have a continuous scale horizontally and a frequency scale vertically.
  - You can still use bars to represent continuous data, but because it is continuous you do not leave spaces between the bars.
  - When the variable is continuous the chart is known as a histogram.
- As a class, draw the histogram for Example D. PowerPoint 12.5 slide 1 shows the solution.
  - You can see that most cars travelled at between 30 and 40 mph.
  - Few cars travelled at under 20 or over 40 mph.
- You can create a frequency polygon by joining the mid-points of the tops of the bars (slide 2).
  - You do not have to draw a histogram to get a frequency polygon (slide 3).
- Frequency polygons can be used to compare frequency distributions (slide 4).
  - You can see from the diagram that speeds just before the 30 mph limit have increased and those just after have decreased.

Enrichment

- Discuss how the type of data affects the type of diagram used (slide 5).

Plenary

- *Look at the line graph given in Example 8. How many families were included in the survey?* (36)
- Refer to Question 4 in Exercise 12F.
  (a) *In which class interval would a speed of 20 mph be recorded?* ($20 \leqslant s < 175$)
  (b) *In which class interval would a speed of 55 mph be recorded* ($50 \leqslant s < 60$)
  (c) *Draw a frequency polygon to show the information in the table.*
  (d) *How many cars travelled at 75mph?* (Not possible to tell as data has been grouped.)

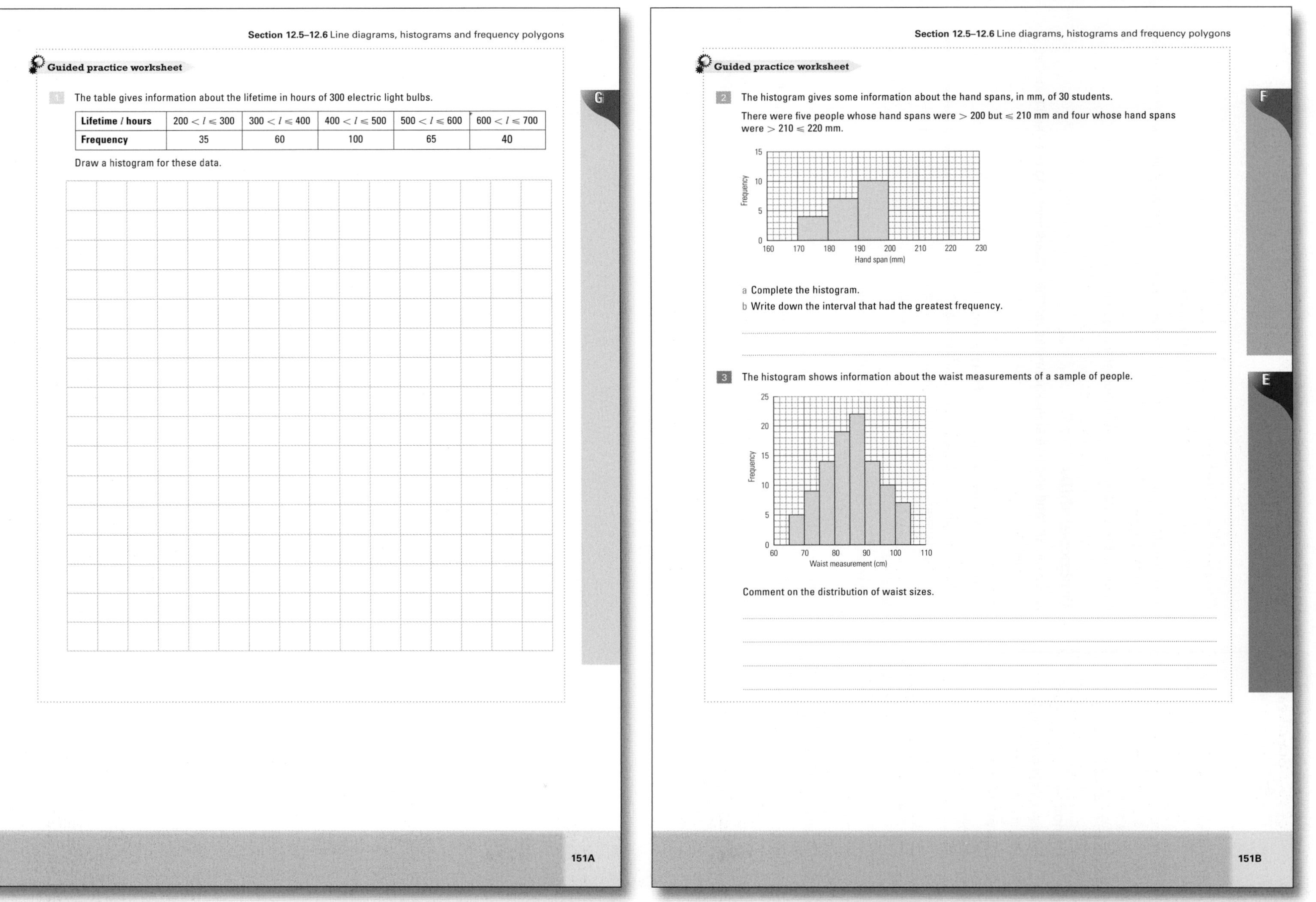

Guided practice worksheet

G

1 The table gives information about the lifetime in hours of 300 electric light bulbs.

Lifetime / hours	$200 < l \leqslant 300$	$300 < l \leqslant 400$	$400 < l \leqslant 500$	$500 < l \leqslant 600$	$600 < l \leqslant 700$
Frequency	35	60	100	65	40

Draw a histogram for these data.

Section 12.5–12.6 Line diagrams, histograms and frequency polygons

Guided practice worksheet

F

2 The histogram gives some information about the hand spans, in mm, of 30 students.

There were five people whose hand spans were > 200 but ⩽ 210 mm and four whose hand spans were > 210 ⩽ 220 mm.

a Complete the histogram.

b Write down the interval that had the greatest frequency.

E

3 The histogram shows information about the waist measurements of a sample of people.

Comment on the distribution of waist sizes.

Specification

GCSE 2010
A i (part) Generate terms of a sequence using term-to-term… definitions of the sequence

FS Process skills
Examine patterns and relationships

FS Performance
Level 2 Use appropriate checking procedures and evaluate their effectiveness at each stage

Resources

Links
http://nrich.maths.org/241

13.1 Sequences

Concepts and skills

- Recognise sequences of odd and even numbers.
- Generate arithmetic sequences of numbers, squared integers and sequences derived from diagrams.
- Write the term-to-term definition of a sequence in words.

Functional skills

- L2 Understand and use simple formulae and equations involving one- and two-step operations.

Prior key knowledge, skills and concepts

- Students should be able to spot differences from one member to the next in a number pattern using addition, subtraction, multiplication and division (term-to-term rule).

Starter

- *Write down five even numbers.* (Students' own answers.)
- *Write down five odd numbers.* (Students' own answers.)
- *Write down the first five multiples of 5.* (5, 10, 15, 20, 25)
- *Write down 50. Count down in 4s until you get to 30. How many numbers have you written down?* (6)

Main teaching and learning

- Explain each concept and get students to work through each exercise in turn.

Common misconceptions

- None really, as students cope quite well with this topic.

Plenary

- Find the next two members of these patterns.

a	3	7	11	15	19 … (23, 27)
b	60	55	50	45	40 … (35, 30)
c	2	4	8	16	32 … (64, 128)
d	100	10	1	0.1	0.01 … (0.001, 0.0001)

Section 13.1 Sequences

Guided practice worksheet

F

Remember: the term-to-term rule tells you how to find the next number in a sequence.

1 You are given the first term of a sequence and the term-to-term rule.
Write down the first five terms of the sequence.

a first term 3, rule "add 4" ....

b first term 17, rule "subtract 2" ....

c first term 4, rule "multiply by 10" ....

d first term 16, rule "divide by 2" ....

> first term is 4, rule is 'add 3'
> 4 → 7 → 10 → 13 → 16 (+3 +3 +3 +3)

For questions 2–5, i find the term-to-term rule for each sequence, ii write down the next two terms.

2 The rule is 'add a number'.

> 7, 12, 17, 22 ...
> (i) $12 - 7 = 5$ so the rule is 'add 5'
> (ii) The next term is $22 + 5$ which is 27. The next term is $27 + 5$ which is 32.

a 5, 7, 9, 11 ... i .... ii ....

b 2, 6, 10, 14 ... i .... ii ....

c 9, 17, 25, 33 ... i .... ii ....

d 15, 40, 65 ... i .... ii ....

e 170, 210, 250, 290 ... i .... ii ....

3 The rule is 'subtract a number'.

> 78, 71, 64, 57 ...
> (i) $78 - 71 = 7$ so the rule is 'subtract 7'
> (ii) The next two numbers are 50 and 43.

a 22, 20, 18, 16 ... i .... ii ....

b 50, 45, 40, 35 ... i .... ii ....

c 109, 98, 87 ... i .... ii ....

d 2000, 1930, 1860, 1790 ... i .... ii ....

e 6, 3, 0, −3 ... i .... ii ....

Section 13.1 Sequences

Guided practice worksheet

F

4 The rule is 'multiply by a number'.

> 2, 6, 18 ...
> (i) $6 \div 2 = 3$ so the rule is 'multiply by 3'
> (ii) The next two numbers are $18 \times 3 = 54$, $54 \times 3 = 162$.

a 4, 8, 16 ... i .... ii ....

b 1, 5, 25 ... i .... ii ....

c 10, 100, 1000 ... i .... ii ....

d 1, 20, 400 ... i .... ii ....

e 3, 15, 75 ... i .... ii ....

5 The rule is 'divide by a number'.

> 200 000, 20 000, 2 000 ...
> (i) $200\,000 \div 20\,000 = 10$ so the rule is 'divide by 10'
> (ii) The next two numbers are 200 and 20.

a 384, 192, 96 ... i .... ii ....

b 512, 256, 128 ... i .... ii ....

c 4 500 000, 450 000, 45 000 ... i .... ii ....

d 4096, 1024, 256 ... i .... ii ....

e 480, 240, 120 ... i .... ii ....

6 Fill in the missing numbers. The type of rule is shown.

a ......, 20, 18, 16, ..., ..., ... (subtract)

b 8, 13, ..., ..., 28 ... (add)

c 1, ..., 9, 27, ..., 243, ... (multiply)

d 96, 48, ..., 12, ... (divide)

e 2, ..., 50, 250, ..., ... (multiply)

f ......, ..., 36, 30, 24 ... (subtract)

g 12, ..., ..., ..., 40, 47 ... (add)

h ......, 400, 40, ..., ... (divide)

E

7 Dan started with £10 savings and asked his dad to give him £5 each week.
Joanne started with 25p savings and asked her dad to double her savings each week.

a Who do you think will end up with the most savings after 8 weeks?

....

....

....

b Complete the table below.

Savings at beginning of week	1	2	3	4	5	6	7	8	9
Dan	£10								
Joanne	25p								

Section 13.1 Sequences

Guided practice worksheet

E

8 i Draw the next two shapes for each of the three patterns
ii Find the number of lines in the 7th shape of each of the three patterns.

a

b

c

ii a .... lines

b .... lines

c .... lines

Specification

GCSE 2010
A i Generate terms of a sequence using term-to-term and position-to-term definitions of the sequence

FS Process skills
Examine patterns and relationships

FS Performance
Level 2 Use appropriate checking procedures and evaluate their effectiveness at each stage

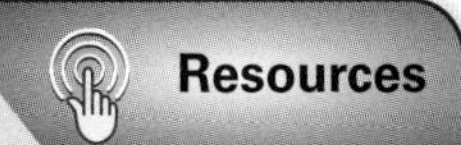

Resources

CD Resources
Resource sheet 13.2a
Resource sheet 13.2b

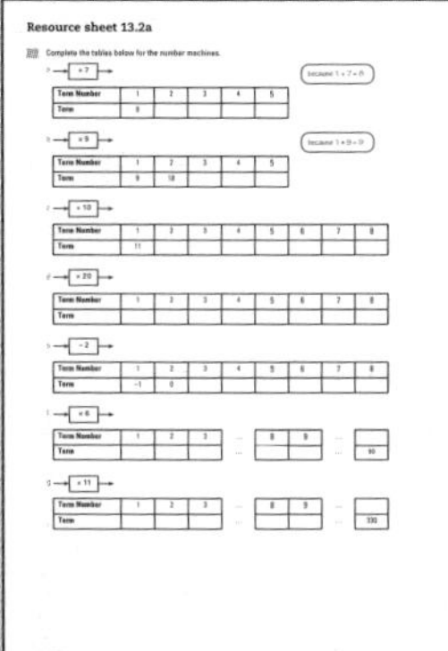

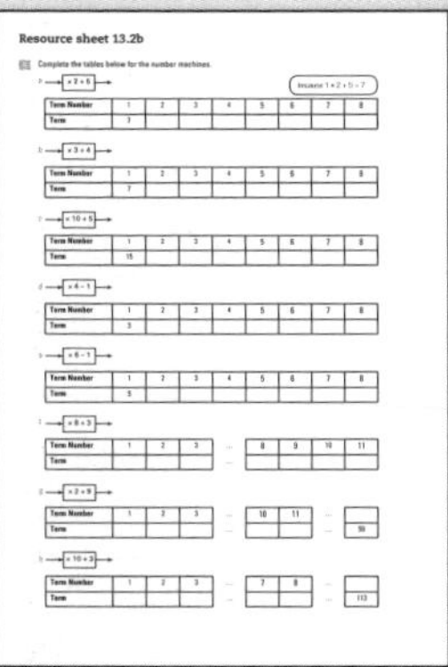

ActiveTeach resources
Operations quiz
Function machine interactive

13.2 Using input and output machines to investigate number patterns

Concepts and skills

- Generate arithmetic sequences of numbers, squared integers and sequences derived from diagrams.
- Find a specific term in the sequence using position-to-term… rules.

Functional skills

- L2 Understand and use simple formulae and equations involving one- and two-step operations.

Prior key knowledge, skills and concepts

- Students should be able to understand number machines.

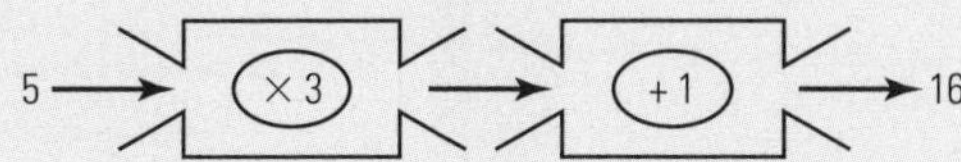

Starter

- Use the 'Get ready' exercise to introduce the topic.
- *Complete this table for the $2x + 1$ machine.*

Input	Output
1	3
2	(5)
5	(11)
(10)	21

Main teaching and learning

- Introduce the idea that if the first four terms of a sequence are 4, 7, 10, 13 then the terms are labelled term 1, 2, 3, 4, etc.
- Check that students can complete a table of values from term number-to-term.
- Explain how to find the 10th term in a sequence.
- Explain that, given a term, you can work backwards to find the term number.

Common misconceptions

- When students look at the term numbers they should check that they are going up in numerical order.

Enrichment

- Draw a table of values for:
  - even numbers
  - odd numbers
  - square numbers
  - 5 times table.

Plenary

- Write the sequence 5, 9, 13, 17 … on the board. Ask students to write down the first 10 terms and then the 20th term. *What term number has 101 as its term?* (25)

one-stage input and output machine   two-stage input and output machine

Guided practice worksheet

G

Remember: The **term number** tells you the position of the term in the sequence.

1 Write down the term number for the term written in bold.

1, 4, **7**, 10, 13 … The 3rd term is **7**. So the term number is 3.

a 2, 4, 6, **8**, 10, 12 … ……

b 1, 2, 4, 8, 16, 32, **64** … ……

c **0**, 5, 10, 15, 20, 25 … ……

d 96, 48, 24, 12, 6, **3**, 1,5 … ……

F

2 On Resource sheet 13.2a, complete the tables for the number machines.

3 In question 2, use words to write down the rule for finding the term from the term number. 2 a is given.

a add 7 to the term number

b ……

c ……

d ……

e ……

f ……

g ……

4 Write down the term-to-term rule for each sequence in question 2.

Remember: the **term-to-term** rule tells you how to get from one term to the next term.

The terms in Question 2b are 9 → 18 (+ 9) so the term-to-term rule is + 9.

a ……

b +9

c ……

d ……

e ……

f ……

g ……

5 What is the 20th term for each sequence in question 2?

a ……

b ……

c ……

d ……

e ……

f ……

g ……

Section 13.2 Using input and output machines to investigate number patterns

Guided practice worksheet

E

6 On Resource sheet 13.2b, complete the tables for the number machines.

7 In question 6, use words to write down the rule for finding the term from the term number.

a ……

b ……

c ……

d ……

e ……

f ……

g ……

h ……

8 Write down the term-to-term rule for each sequence in question 6.

a ……

b ……

c ……

d ……

e ……

f ……

g ……

h ……

9 What is the 15th term for each sequence in question 6?

a ……

b ……

c ……

d ……

e ……

f ……

g ……

h ……

Specification

GCSE 2010

A i Generate terms of a sequence using term-to-term and position-to-term definitions of the sequence

A j Use linear expressions to describe the nth term of an arithmetic sequence

FS Process skills

Examine patterns and relationships

FS Performance

Level 2 Use appropriate checking procedures and evaluate their effectiveness at each stage

Resources

CD Resources

Resource sheet 13.3a
Resource sheet 13.3b
Resource sheet 13.3c
Resource sheet 13.3d

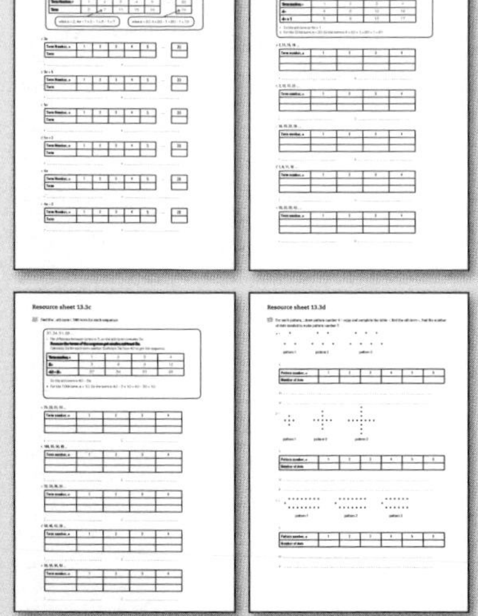

Links

http://www.bbc.co.uk/schools/gcsebitesize/maths/algebra/sequencesact.shtml

13.3 Finding the nth term of a number pattern

Concepts and skills

- Find a specific term in the sequence using position-to-term or term-to-term rules.
- Find the nth term of an arithmetic sequence.
- Use the nth term of an arithmetic sequence.

Functional skills

- L2 Understand and use simple formulae and equations involving one- and two-step operations.

Prior key knowledge, skills and concepts

- Students should know how to:
  - generate a number pattern using term-to-term rules
  - generate a number pattern using position-to-term rules.

Starter

- Tell students to work through the 'Get ready' section.

Main teaching and learning

- Go through Example 9 to explain how to work out the nth term of a number sequence.
- Explain how to find any term in the sequence once the nth term has been found.

Common misconceptions

- If the difference between terms is 3 the nth term is $n + 3$. Emphasise that the +3 should go in front of the n as $3n$. Then you find out what number you add and subtract to find the nth term.

Enrichment

- Find the nth term for the number of matches in each of these patterns of matchsticks.

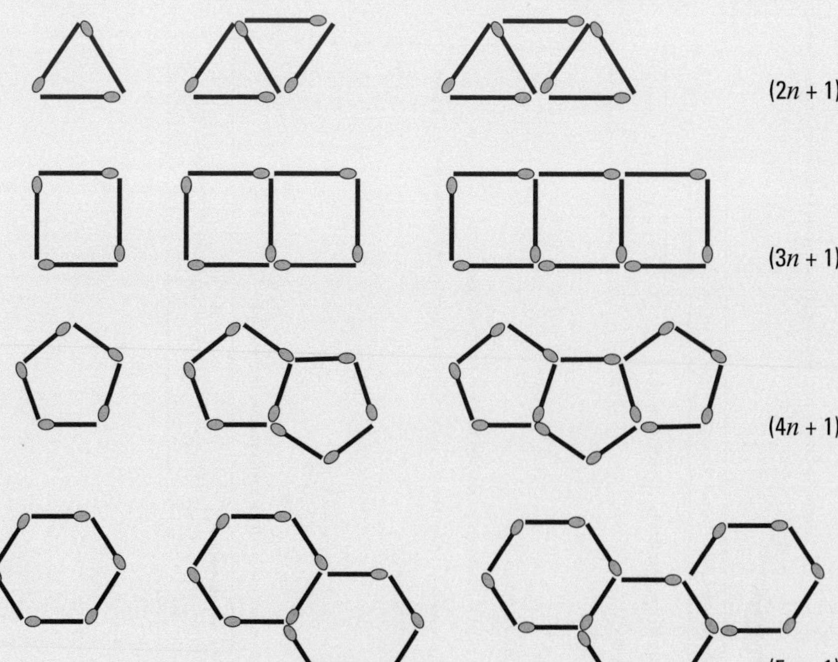

- What is the nth term for a regular polygon with p sides? ($(p - 1)n + 1$)

Plenary

- *Find the nth term of this sequence:*

  2 8 14 20 26 ... ($6n - 4$)

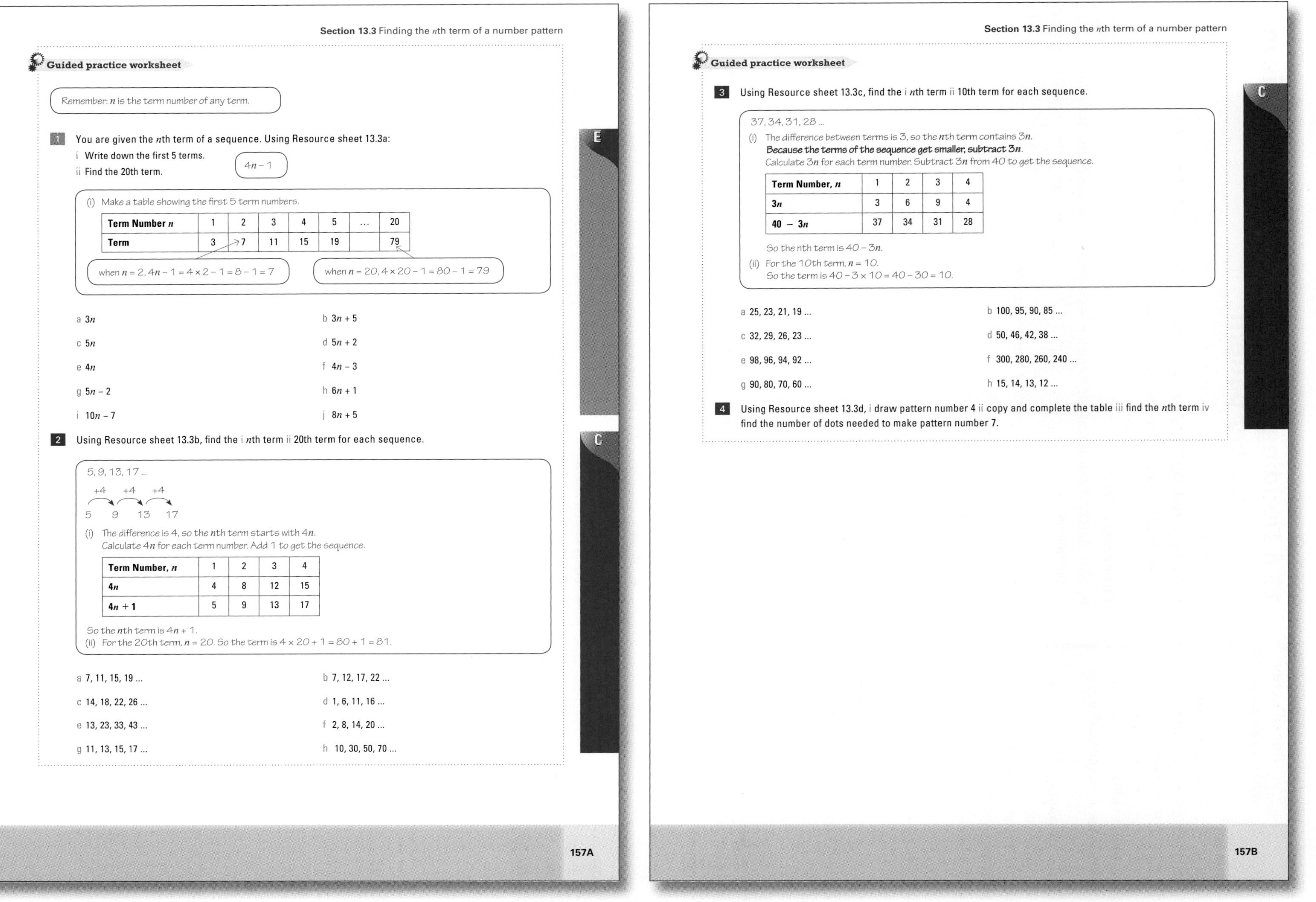

Guided practice worksheet

Remember: n is the term number of any term.

1 You are given the nth term of a sequence. Using Resource sheet 13.3a:
i Write down the first 5 terms.
ii Find the 20th term.

$4n - 1$

(i) Make a table showing the first 5 term numbers.

Term Number n	1	2	3	4	5	...	20
Term	3	7	11	15	19		79

when $n = 2$, $4n - 1 = 4 \times 2 - 1 = 8 - 1 = 7$

when $n = 20$, $4 \times 20 - 1 = 80 - 1 = 79$

a $3n$ b $3n + 5$

c $5n$ d $5n + 2$

e $4n$ f $4n - 3$

g $5n - 2$ h $6n + 1$

i $10n - 7$ j $8n + 5$

2 Using Resource sheet 13.3b, find the i nth term ii 20th term for each sequence.

5, 9, 13, 17 ...

+4 +4 +4

5 9 13 17

(i) The difference is 4, so the nth term starts with $4n$.
Calculate $4n$ for each term number. Add 1 to get the sequence.

Term Number, n	1	2	3	4
$4n$	4	8	12	15
$4n + 1$	5	9	13	17

So the nth term is $4n + 1$.
(ii) For the 20th term, $n = 20$. So the term is $4 \times 20 + 1 = 80 + 1 = 81$.

a 7, 11, 15, 19 ... b 7, 12, 17, 22 ...

c 14, 18, 22, 26 ... d 1, 6, 11, 16 ...

e 13, 23, 33, 43 ... f 2, 8, 14, 20 ...

g 11, 13, 15, 17 ... h 10, 30, 50, 70 ...

157A

Guided practice worksheet

3 Using Resource sheet 13.3c, find the i nth term ii 10th term for each sequence.

37, 34, 31, 28 ...

(i) The difference between terms is 3, so the nth term contains $3n$.
Because the terms of the sequence get smaller, subtract $3n$.
Calculate $3n$ for each term number. Subtract $3n$ from 40 to get the sequence.

Term Number, n	1	2	3	4
$3n$	3	6	9	4
$40 - 3n$	37	34	31	28

So the nth term is $40 - 3n$.
(ii) For the 10th term, $n = 10$.
So the term is $40 - 3 \times 10 = 40 - 30 = 10$.

a 25, 23, 21, 19 ... b 100, 95, 90, 85 ...

c 32, 29, 26, 23 ... d 50, 46, 42, 38 ...

e 98, 96, 94, 92 ... f 300, 280, 260, 240 ...

g 90, 80, 70, 60 ... h 15, 14, 13, 12 ...

4 Using Resource sheet 13.3d, i draw pattern number 4 ii copy and complete the table iii find the nth term iv find the number of dots needed to make pattern number 7.

157B

Specification

GCSE 2010

A i Generate terms of a sequence using term-to-term and position-to-term definitions of the sequence

FS Process skills

Examine patterns and relationships

FS Performance

Level 2 Use appropriate checking procedures and evaluate their effectiveness at each stage

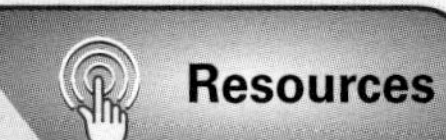

Resources

ActiveTeach resources

RP KC Sequence knowledge check
RP PS Sequence problem solving

Follow up

Chapter 15: Graphs 1

13.4 Deciding whether or not a number is in a number pattern

Concepts and skills

- Identify which terms can or cannot be in a sequence.

Functional skills

- L2 Understand and use simple formulae and equations involving one- and two-step operations.

Prior key knowledge, skills and concepts

- Students should know how to:
  - generate a number pattern using term-to-term rules
  - generate a number pattern using position-to-term rules.

Starter

- Go through examples in the 'Get ready' box.
- Tell students to work in pairs and write down another five patterns, each with another number that is or is not in the pattern.

Main teaching and learning

- *Either,* go through some number patterns and point out some key features such as:
  - if patterns go up by even numbers, e.g. 2, 4, 6 etc, then all the members of the pattern will be all even, or all odd
  - if patterns go up in odd numbers, e.g. 3, 5, 7 etc, then the members of the pattern will alternate even and odd
  - if patterns go up in 5s then the alternate numbers will end with the same digit
  - if patterns go up in 10s the members will end in the same digit.
- *or,* try to find the nth term of some number patterns and see if you can find the term number.

Common misconceptions

- If the difference between terms is 3, the nth term is $n + 3$. Emphasise that the +3 should go in front of the n as $3n$. Then you find out what number you add and subtract to find the nth term.

Enrichment

- *Working in pairs write down five sequences of numbers and two other numbers with each sequence, one that is in the sequence and one that isn't in the sequence. Swap sequences and say which of the numbers is in the sequence and which one isn't.* (Students' own answer.)

Plenary

- *Explain why 85 is not a member of the sequence 4, 8, 12, 16, 22, ….* (Since all members of the pattern end in an even number then 85 cannot be in the pattern as it ends in a 5, which is an odd number. *Or* the nth term of the pattern is $4n$. If $4n = 85$ then $n = 85 \div 4$ which is not a whole number so n is not a whole number, which means that 85 is not a member of the pattern.)

Guided practice worksheet

C

1 Are any of the numbers in brackets part of the given sequence?

> 4, 9, 14, 19, 24, 29 … {79, 58}
> The odd terms of the sequence are 9, 19, 29, 39 … which include 79.
> The even terms are 4, 14, 24, 34 … and end in 4, and so do not include 58.
> 79 is part of the sequence, 58 is not.

a 6, 11, 16, 21, 26, 31 … {76, 67} ……………………

b 10, 15, 20, 25, 30 … {120, 95} ……………………

c 8, 10, 12, 14, 16 … {51, 52} ……………………

d 13, 23, 33, 43, 53 … {130, 103} ……………………

e 21, 23, 25, 27, 29 … {63, 73} ……………………

f 25, 50, 75, 100, 125 … {200, 85} ……………………

g 41, 39, 37, 35, 33 … {10, 7} ……………………

h 94, 89, 84, 79, 74 … {24, 11} ……………………

i 13, 18, 23, 28, 33 … {77, 88} ……………………

2 One of the numbers in the sequence is not part of a pattern. Which number?

> 2, 5, 8, 10, 11, 14, 17 …
> The term-to-term rule is "add 3", so 10 is not part of the pattern because 10 + 1 = 11.

a 10, 12, 13, 14, 16, 18 … ……………………

b 6, 9, 11, 13, 15, 17 … ……………………

c 30, 40, 50, 60, 70, 75 … ……………………

d 20, 23, 26, 28, 29, 32, 35 … ……………………

e 41, 40, 38, 36, 34 … ……………………

f 110, 99, 88, 77, 60 … ……………………

g 80, 75, 70, 66, 65, 60 … ……………………

h 62, 57, 52, 47, 44, 42, 37 … ……………………

Specification

GCSE 2010
GM x (part) Calculate perimeters… of shapes made from triangles and rectangles

FS Process skills
Select the mathematical information to use

FS Performance
Level 2 Identify the situation or problems and identify the mathematical methods needed to solve them

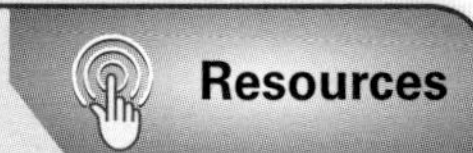

Resources

Resources
Paper with squares of side 1 cm, tape measures, rulers

ActiveTeach resources
Addition quiz
Area interactive

14.1 Perimeter

Concepts and skills

- Measure shapes to find perimeters….
- Find the perimeter of rectangles and triangles.
- Find the perimeter of compound shapes.

Functional skills

- L2 Find … perimeter … of common shapes.

Prior key knowledge, skills and concepts

- Students should be able to measure the lengths of lines to the nearest millimetre.

Starter

- Check that students understand what is meant by the length and width of a rectangle by showing them some rectangles on a squared grid and asking them to identify the length and width.
- Check that students can measure length and give their answer to the nearest millimetre. For example, ask them to measure the length and width of a book, the desk, a poster on the notice board or the lengths of the sides of a triangle, rectangle or other polygon.

Main teaching and learning

- Tell students they are going to find out about the perimeter of a shape. Explain that the perimeter is the total distance around the edge of a shape.
- Discuss what information is needed to work out the perimeter of a shape. Explain that they might find out this information by counting the units along the sides of the shape.
- Ask students to find the perimeter of some rectangles and squares drawn on a centimetre-square grid by counting. Remind them to write down the units with their answers.
- Explain that, alternatively, they might find the perimeter of a shape by measuring the lengths of the sides using a ruler.
- Ask students to find the perimeter of some 2D shapes by measuring the lengths of all the sides. Again, remind them to state their units.
- Discuss the possible units of perimeter – mm, cm, m, km. Stress that all the sides must be in the same units before they are added together to find the perimeter.
- Cover shapes where the lengths of some of the sides are not known and need to be worked out before the perimeter is calculated.
- Ask students to find any missing lengths on a shape drawn on the board and work out the perimeter of the shape.

Common misconceptions

- If a diagram is given with the lengths of only some of the sides indicated, students often forget to find and include the lengths of the missing sides.
- Students often include the lengths of internal lines shown in their calculation of the perimeter of a compound shape.

Enrichment

- Ask students to find the perimeter of some of the following: the classroom, the school building, the school grounds, their bedroom, their house, their garden. *Who might need to know these measurements and why?* Ask them to work out how much it might cost to put a fence around the school perimeter, for example.
- Using a plan drawn to scale, work out the perimeter of a building.
- Ask students to draw as many rectangles as they can with a perimeter of 24 cm. Tell them that the lengths of the sides must be whole numbers.

Plenary

- Ask students to write down one thing they have learned in the lesson, then go round the class making a list that everyone can see.

Guided practice worksheet

F

1 Here are some rectangles drawn on a centimetre-square grid.

a Write down the length and the width of each rectangle.

b Work out the perimeter of each rectangle.

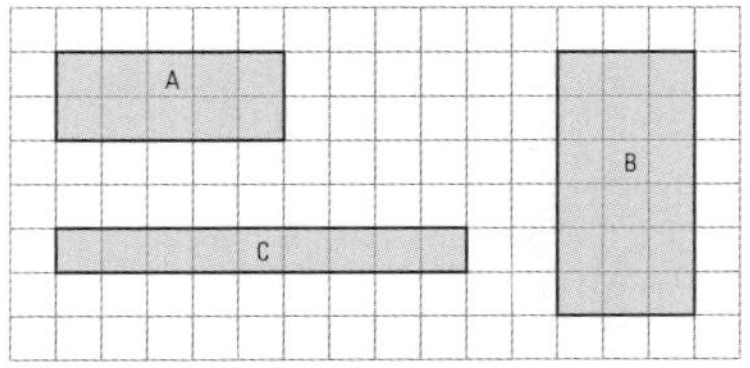

A Length = ... cm Width = ... cm Perimeter = ... cm

B Length = ... cm Width = ... cm Perimeter = ... cm

C Length = ... cm Width = ... cm Perimeter = ... cm

2 Here are some rectangles.
Measure the length and width of each rectangle.
Give your answer to the nearest mm.

Remember to give the units with your answers.

.... cm .... cm .... cm

.... cm .... cm .... cm

3

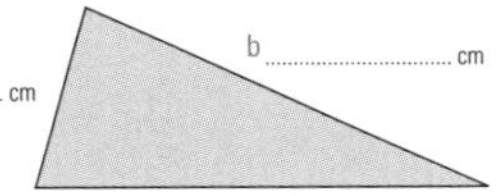

a .... cm b .... cm c .... cm

Measure the length of each side of this triangle.

Work out the perimeter of the triangle. ....

4 a Find the perimeter of this shape.

....

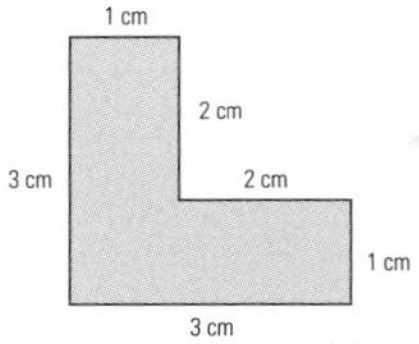

b Draw a square with the same perimeter as the shape in part a

1 cm, 2 cm, 2 cm, 1 cm, 3 cm, 3 cm

Guided practice worksheet

E

5 Work out the perimeter of shapes A, B and C.
In each case all the sides are of length 10 cm.

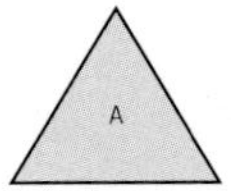

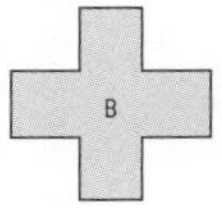

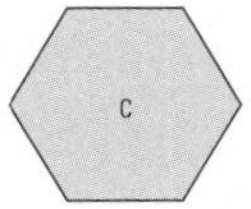

A B C

6 Work out the perimeter of this shape.

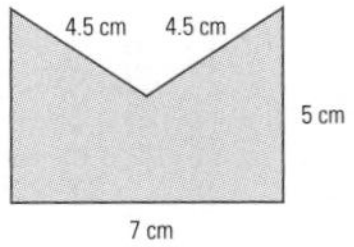

4.5 cm, 4.5 cm, 5 cm, 7 cm

D

7 Here is a shape.

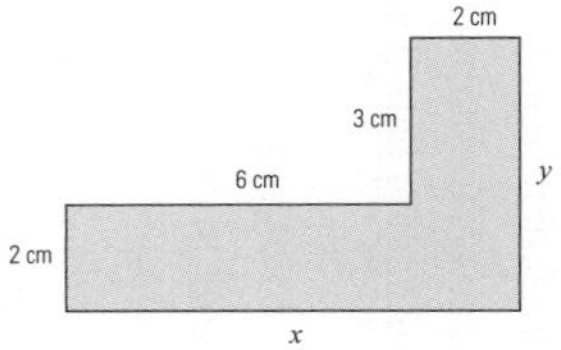

2 cm, 3 cm, 6 cm, 2 cm, x, y

a Work out the length of the side marked x.

b Work out the length of the side marked y.

c Work out the perimeter of the shape.

8 The perimeter of a rectangular field is 680 m.
The length of the field is 190 m.
Work out the width of the field.

Specification

GCSE 2010
GM x (part) Calculate… areas of shapes made from triangles and rectangles

FS Process skills
Select the mathematical information to use

FS Performance
Level 2 Identify the situation or problems and identify the mathematical methods needed to solve them

Resources

Resources
Paper with squares of side 1 cm
Plan of a classroom or other room drawn to scale on a centimetre-square grid

ActiveTeach resources
Perimeter quiz

14.2 Area

Concepts and skills

- Find the area of a rectangle and traingle.

Functional skills

- L2 Find area … of common shapes.

Prior key knowledge, skills and concepts

- Students should already understand the concept of area.

Starter

- Check that students understand what is meant by 'finding the number of squares that cover a shape' by using the diagrams in the 'Get ready' questions and any additional ones if you feel further practice is needed.
- You could use the number of complete square tiles on the classroom floor or the number of ceiling tiles if appropriate.

Main teaching and learning

- Tell students they are going to find out about the area of a shape. Explain that the area of a shape is given by the number of squares needed to cover the shape and that square centimetres or square metres are used as standard units of measurement.
- Show students how to write units of area, i.e. square centimetres or cm^2, square metres or m^2.
- Ask students to find the area of some rectangles and squares drawn on a centimetre-square grid by counting the number of squares of side 1 cm. Remind them to write cm^2 with their answers.
- Discuss how an estimate for the area of a shape that is not covered by an exact number of squares is found. Demonstrate how parts of a square can be put together to count as one complete square by drawing a closed curve on a square grid and estimating the area it covers. Count the whole squares and then find out roughly how many complete squares would be covered by all the parts. Add your answers to give an estimate for the area of the shape.
- Ask students to find an estimate for the area of some 2D shapes drawn on centimetre-squared paper. Include some shapes that are made from rectangles and triangles and some that include curves.

Common misconceptions

- Students frequently think that $3\,cm^2$ means a square with side 3 cm. You might have to reinforce the fact that $3\,cm^2$ means an area covering the equivalent of three squares each with side 1 cm.

Enrichment

- Using a plan of a classroom or other room drawn to scale on a centimetre-square grid, ask students to work out the area covered by the plan.
- Ask students to draw as many rectangles as they can with an area of $24\,cm^2$. Tell them that the lengths of the sides must be whole numbers. Extend the investigation by looking at other areas, e.g. $30\,cm^2$, $36\,cm^2$.
- Ask students to work out how many cm^2 there are in $1\,m^2$ or how many mm^2 there are in $1\,cm^2$. They should explain how they worked out their answers.

Plenary

- Ask students to explain the difference between perimeter and area and how they would know whether a written quantity was a perimeter or an area.
- Ask students to give you an example of where area occurs in real life. List these examples for everyone to see.

G

Guided practice worksheet

1 Here are some shapes drawn on a centimetre-square grid.

Find the area of each shape.

Hint How do you count part of a square?.

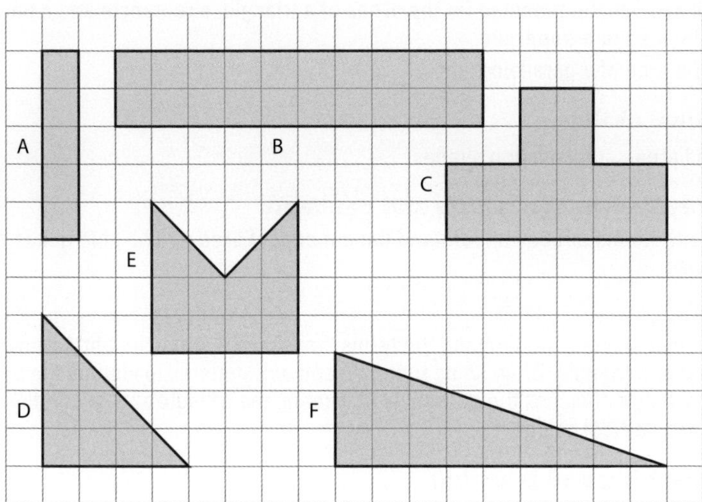

A .... B .... C ....

D .... E .... F ....

2 Estimate the area of the following shapes drawn on a centimetre-square grid.

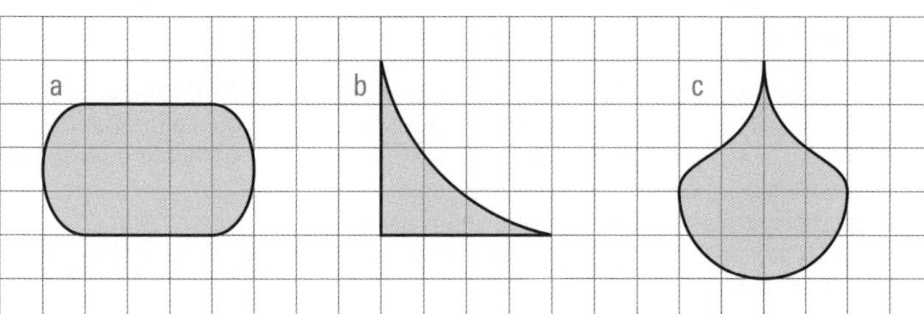

A .... B .... C ....

Specification

GCSE 2010

GM x (part) Calculate… areas of shapes made from triangles and rectangles

FS Process skills

Use appropriate mathematical procedures

FS Performance

Level 2 Apply a range of mathematics to find solutions

Resources

Resources

Paper with squares of side 1 cm

CD Resources

Resource sheet 14.3

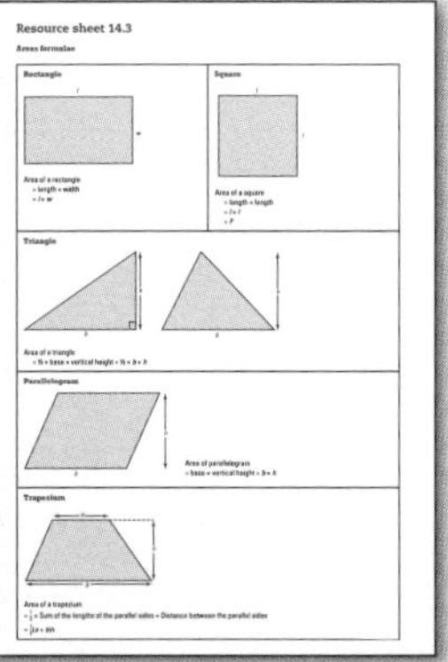

ActiveTeach resources

Perimeter and area quiz

Parallelogram area animation

Triangle area animation

14.3 Finding areas using formulae

Concepts and skills

- Measure shapes to find… areas.
- Recall and use the formulae for the areas of a triangle, a rectangle and a parallelogram.
- Find the area of a trapezium.
- Find the area of a parallelogram.

Functional skills

- L2 Find area … of common shapes.

Prior key knowledge, skills and concepts

- Students should already understand the concept of area and be able to use simple formulae.

Starter

- Check that students understand the terms 'base' and 'vertical height' when used in the context of a triangle. Draw some triangles and ask students to identify the base and vertical height. Discuss the possibility of rotating the triangle and so identify a different base and vertical height.

Main teaching and learning

- Tell students they are going to learn how to find the area of rectangles, triangles, parallelograms and trapeziums by calculation rather than by counting squares.
- Show students the formula that can be used for working out the area of a rectangle. Start by using a rectangle divided up into centimetre squares and then move on to rectangles where the length and width are given or have to be measured.
- Explain that the formula can be used when the length and width are not whole numbers, e.g. with a rectangle measuring 4 cm by 3.5 cm, and demonstrate why this would give the same answer as the method of counting squares. (Answer 14 cm^2.)
- Discuss how the formula for a rectangle can be adapted to give a formula for the area of a square.
- Ask students to use the formula to work out the area of a page in their books, the area of a classroom floor or wall, or other rectangular or square objects. Remind them to include the correct units with their answers.
- Discuss how to find the area of a triangle by halving the area of the rectangle that surrounds it and show students how this leads to the formula for the area of a triangle.
- Demonstrate how to get the formula for the area of a parallelogram by showing that a parallelogram covers the same area as that of the rectangle made by cutting a triangle off one side of the parallelogram and sticking it onto the other side.
- Show students how to get the formula for the area of a trapezium by showing that a trapezium covers the same area as that of the rectangle made by cutting a triangle of the appropriate size off the sides of the trapezium and using them to form a rectangle.

Common misconceptions

- Some students might forget to multiply by $\frac{1}{2}$ when finding the area of a triangle.
- When calculating the area of an obtuse-angled triangle some students might use the length of a side rather than the vertical (or perpendicular) height. A demonstration comparing the calculation for right-angled triangles and obtuse-angled triangles should help students appreciate the need for care here.
- It is common for students using the formula $\frac{1}{2}bh$ to multiply together $\frac{1}{2}b$ and $\frac{1}{2}h$ when evaluating their expression. Some students prefer to use the formula in the form $\dfrac{b \times h}{2}$
- When calculating the area of a parallelogram, a common mistake is for students to multiply the lengths of the sides.

Enrichment

- Students may be introduced to other units of area such as the hectare (10 000 square metres) which is commonly used for measuring land area. They could research other units of area used in other parts of the world and their equivalences.

Plenary

- In pairs, ask one student to draw diagrams of a rectangle, square, triangle and parallelogram all with area 36 cm^2. Tell them to mark on their diagrams the lengths needed to work out their areas. Ask the other student in the pair to do the same thing for an area of 64 cm^2. Students then check each other's diagrams by using the formulae to work out the area of each shape.

Guided practice worksheet

Use the formulae on Resource sheet 14.3 to work out the areas of the following shapes.

1

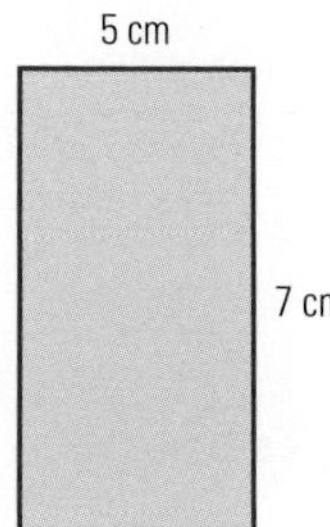

2

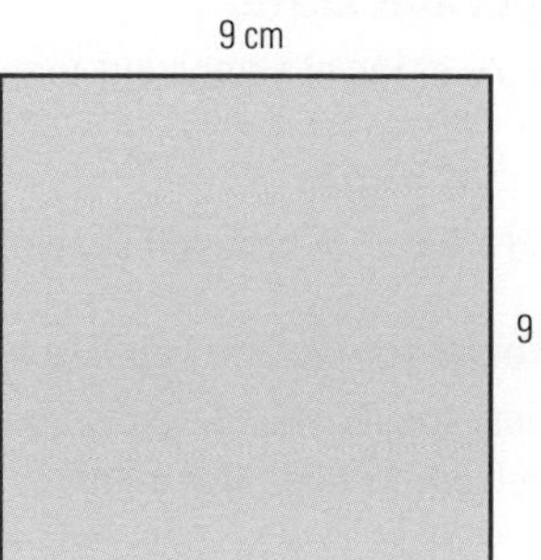

3

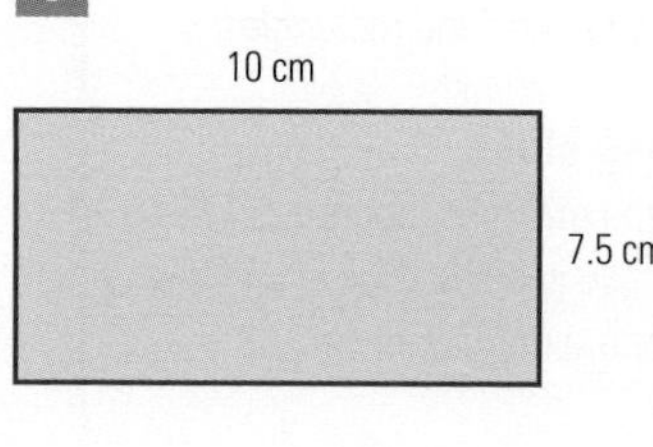

E

4

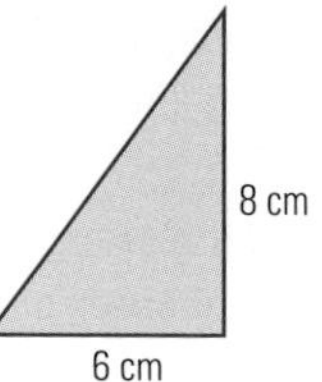

5

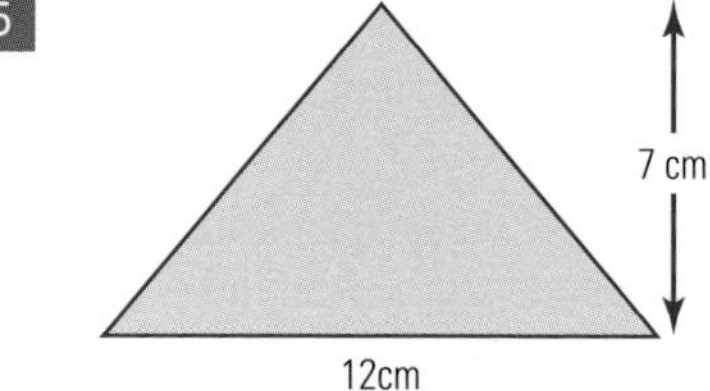

6

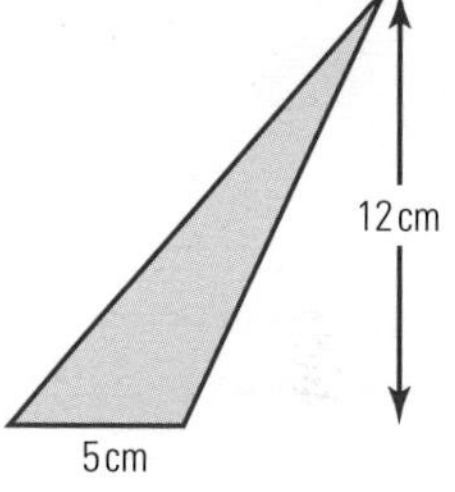

D

7

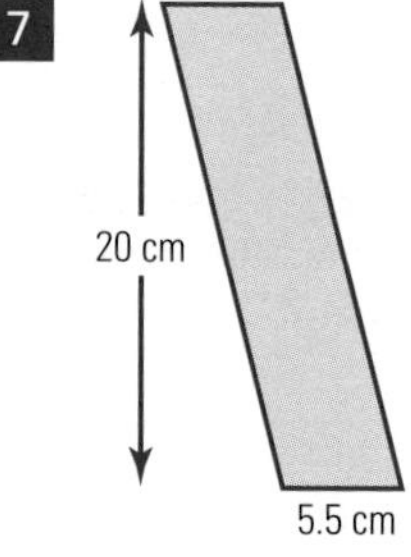

8

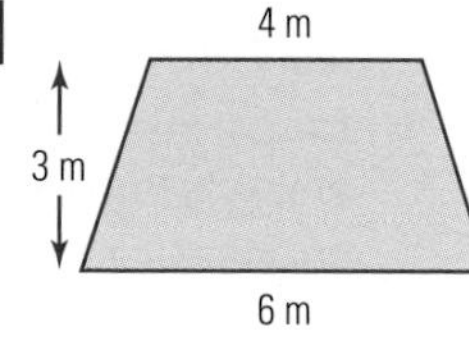

9

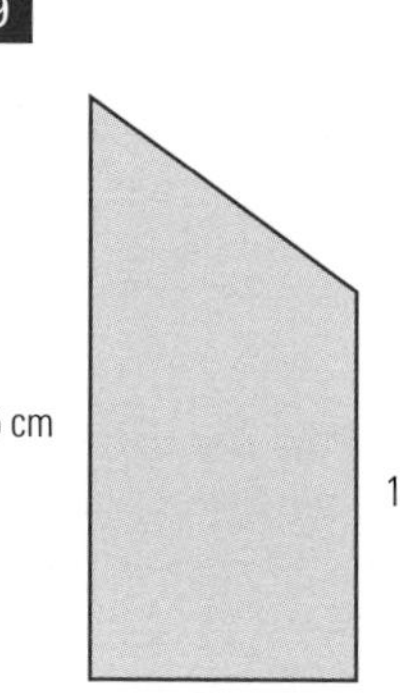

10

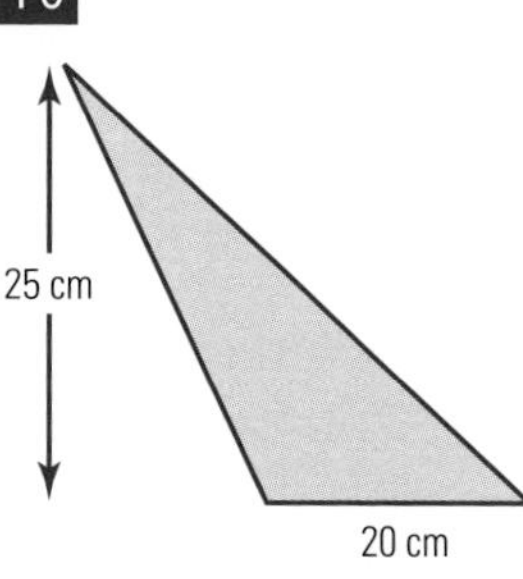

C

Specification

GCSE 2010
GM x (part) Calculate... areas of shapes made from triangles and rectangles

FS Process skills
Decide on the methods, operations and tools... to use in a situation
Use appropriate mathematical procedures

FS Performance
Level 2 Apply a range of mathematics to find solutions

Resources

Links
http://www.bbc.co.uk/schools/gcsebitesize/maths/shapes/areaandperimeteract.shtml

ActiveTeach resources
Dodgems video
Seats video
RP KC Perimeter knowledge check
RP PS Perimeter problem solving

14.4 Problems involving areas

Concepts and skills

- Calculate areas of compound shapes made from triangles and rectangles.

Functional skills

- L2 Find area ... of common shapes.

Prior key knowledge, skills and concepts

- Students should already know how to find the area of rectangles, triangles, parallelograms and trapeziums.

Starter

- Draw compound shapes on the board and ask students to draw lines to show how the shapes can be split up into simpler shapes – i.e. rectangles, triangles, parallelograms or trapeziums. Discuss any different ways to divide up the shapes.

Main teaching and learning

- Tell students they are going to learn how to find the area of more complicated shapes by splitting them up into simple shapes and how to solve other real-life problems involving areas.
- Using some of the shapes from the starter exercise, discuss how the area of a complicated shape can be found by finding and adding together the areas of its constituent parts.
- Draw a simple 'L' shape on the board and mark on its dimensions.
- Ask students to split the shape into two rectangles, work out their areas and hence find the area of the 'L' shape. Suggest that it may help to draw the simpler shapes separately and mark on their dimensions before calculating the areas.
- Discuss how splitting the shape up in different ways still leads to the same answer.
- Explain that sometimes when compound shapes are split up there is a need to find missing lengths before working out the area.
- Tell the students that sometimes, to find the area of a complicated shape, they might need to subtract one area from another. Show examples of this.
- Explain that there are many everyday situations where area is needed to solve a problem, e.g. tiling a floor, wall or ceiling, carpeting a floor, sowing seeds to make a lawn or spreading fertiliser on farmland. (See Example 12, page 273 of the Student Book).

Common misconceptions

- It is common for students to think that two sides of a trapezium must be equal and consequently that the area of any trapezium can be found by splitting it up into a rectangle and two congruent triangles.
- Some students might work out the area of a region between two rectangles by subtracting the lengths and subtracting the widths before multiplying to find their answer. Students might need reminding that they must work out the area of the outer rectangle and the area of the inner rectangle, then subtract these two areas to find the area between them.

Enrichment

- Students could combine their drawing and measuring skills with the use of formulae to find the area of regular polygons. With the added restriction that all the regular polygons have a perimeter of 40 cm, students can investigate what happens to the area of the polygon as the number of sides increases.

Plenary

- Draw one or more composite shapes on the board and ask students to find the area of the shape(s). Some of the letters of the alphabet could be used, with appropriate lengths marked on the diagram(s).

Guided practice worksheet

D

Split the shapes up, work out the areas of these parts of the shapes and add them together.

1 Work out the areas of the following shapes.

a

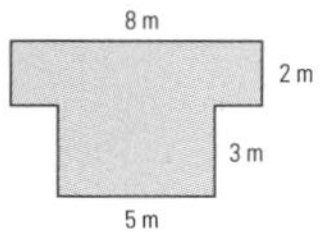

8 m
2 m
3 m
5 m

b

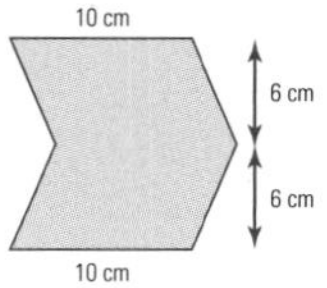

10 cm
6 cm
6 cm
10 cm

c

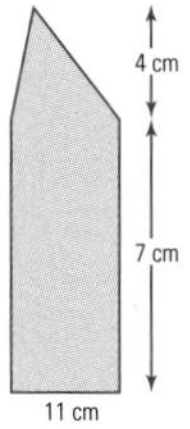

4 cm
7 cm
11 cm

d

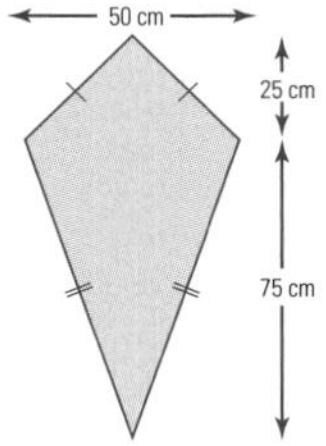

50 cm
25 cm
75 cm

2 John wants to replace the lawn in his garden.
His lawn is a rectangle measuring 6.8 m by 3 m.
Lawn turf is sold in pieces measuring 1.7 m by 0.6 m.
One piece of turf costs £9.45.

a How many pieces of turf will John need?

b Find the total cost of the turf John will need.

Guided practice worksheet

C

3 Work out the shaded area in the shapes below.

a

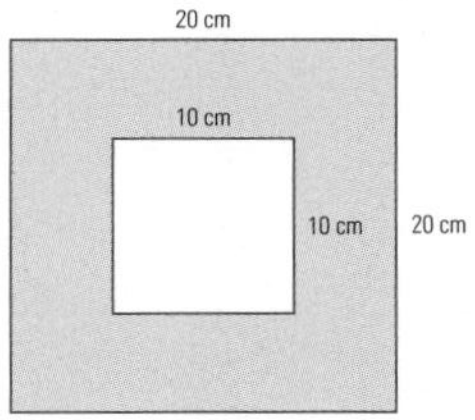

20 cm
10 cm
10 cm
20 cm

b

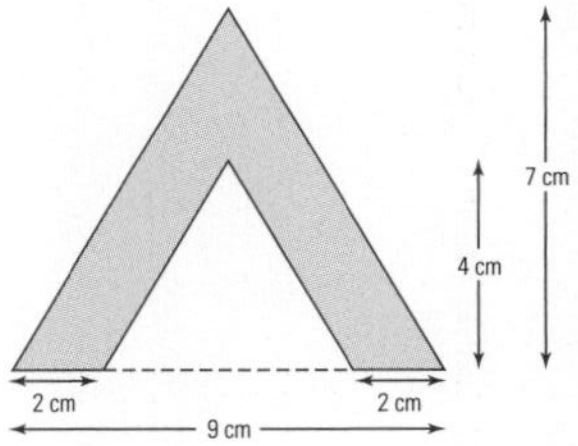

7 cm
4 cm
2 cm
2 cm
9 cm

c

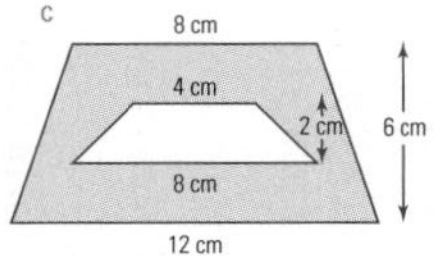

8 cm
4 cm
2 cm
6 cm
8 cm
12 cm

You will need to work out the areas of the holes in the shapes.

Specification

GCSE 2010
A k (part) Use the conventions for coordinates in the plane and plot points…, including using geometric information

FS Process skills
Select the mathematical information to use

FS Performance
Level 1 Identify and obtain necessary information to tackle the problem

Resources

CD Resources
Resource sheet 15.1

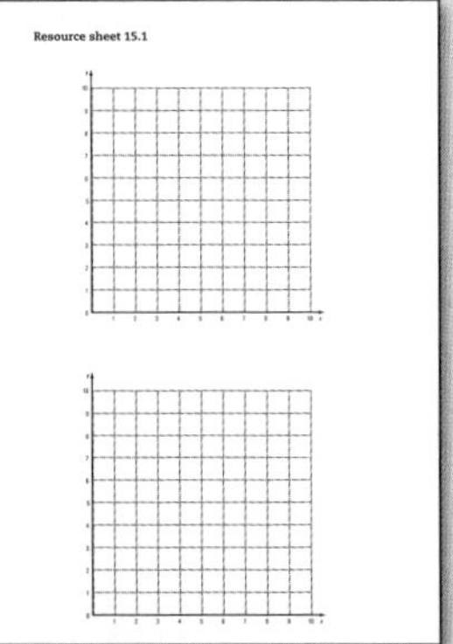

Links
http://nrich.maths.org/6288

ActiveTeach resources
Midpoints interactive

15.1 Coordinates of points in the first quadrant

Concepts and skills

- Use axes and coordinates to specify points….
- Identify points with given coordinates.
- Identify coordinates of given points.
- Draw, label and scale axes.

Functional skills

- L1 Extract and interpret information from tables, diagrams, charts and graphs.

Prior key knowledge, skills and concepts

- Know that in an ordered pair you carry out the first operation before the second.

Starter

- Go through 'Get ready' questions.
- Remind students about the fact that the x-coordinate always comes first and the y-coordinate always comes second.
- Use a form of mnemonic to help, e.g. x comes before y in the alphabet, along the corridor and up the stairs, etc.

Main teaching and learning

- Explain the concept and tell students to work through each question in turn.
- Use Resource sheet 15.1 for questions 4, 6, 7 and 8 or tell the students to draw the grid themselves.

Common misconceptions

- Swapping the y- and the x-coordinates, e.g. plotting (2, 3) as (3, 2).

Enrichment

- *Draw the plan of a treasure island on a coordinate grid.*
- *Write down the coordinates of all the points of interest you put on the island.*
- *Give some mathematical clues to work out the coordinates of the treasure.* (By inspection.)

Plenary

- On squared paper draw a coordinate grid and number it from 0 to 6 across the page and 0 to 6 up the page.
  (a) *Plot the points P at (1, 5), Q at (2, 1) and R at (6, 2).*
  (b) *Mark the position of point S so that $PQRS$ is a square.*
  (c) *Write down the coordinates of point S.* (5, 6)

coordinates x-coordinate y-coordinate

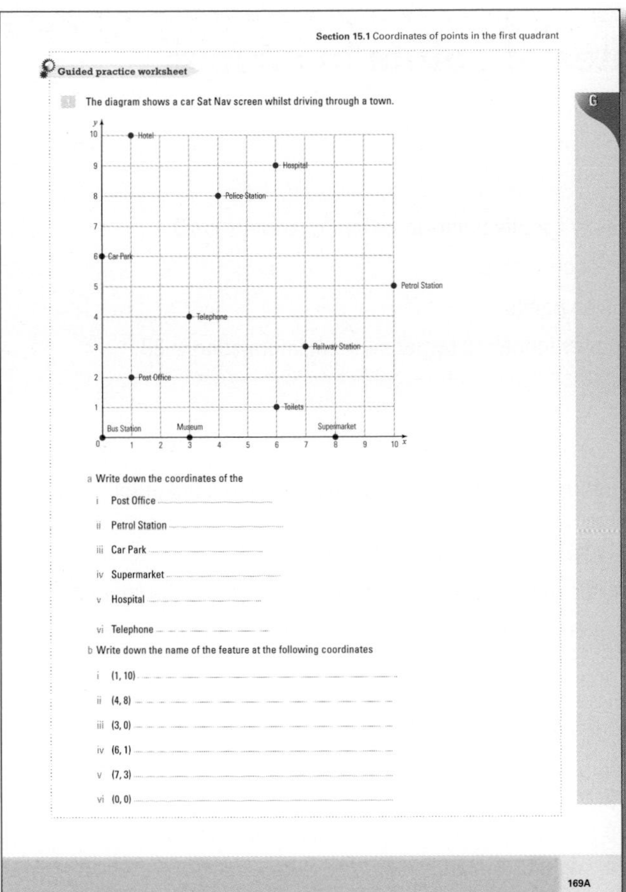

Guided practice worksheet

1 The diagram shows a car Sat Nav screen whilst driving through a town.

a Write down the coordinates of the

i Post Office ....

ii Petrol Station ....

iii Car Park ....

iv Supermarket ....

v Hospital ....

vi Telephone ....

b Write down the name of the feature at the following coordinates

i (1, 10) ....

ii (4, 8) ....

iii (3, 0) ....

iv (6, 1) ....

v (7, 3) ....

vi (0, 0) ....

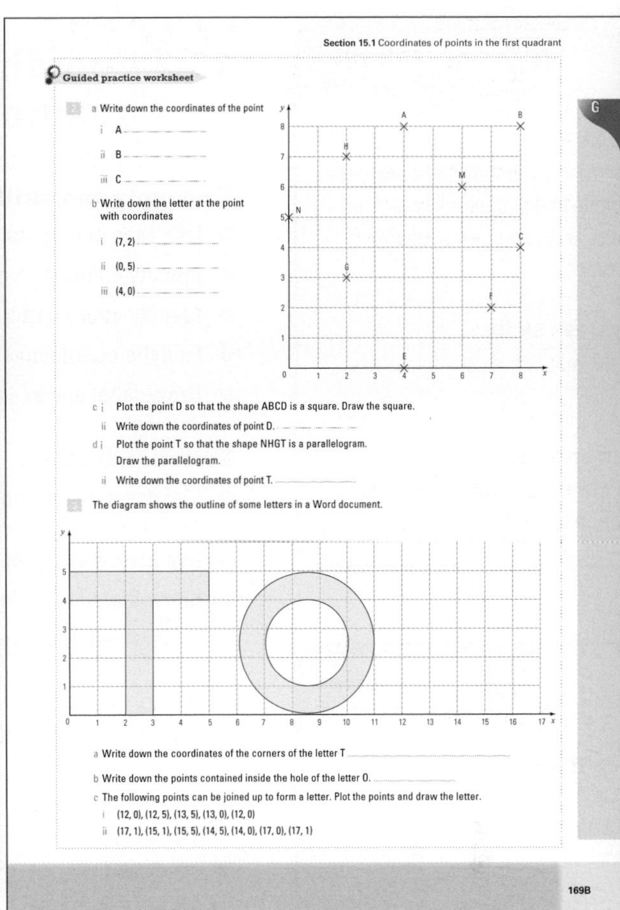

Guided practice worksheet

2 a Write down the coordinates of the point

i A ....

ii B ....

iii C ....

b Write down the letter at the point with coordinates

i (7, 2) ....

ii (0, 5) ....

iii (4, 0) ....

c i Plot the point D so that the shape ABCD is a square. Draw the square.

ii Write down the coordinates of point D. ....

d i Plot the point T so that the shape NHGT is a parallelogram. Draw the parallelogram.

ii Write down the coordinates of point T. ....

3 The diagram shows the outline of some letters in a Word document.

a Write down the coordinates of the corners of the letter T ....

b Write down the points contained inside the hole of the letter O. ....

c The following points can be joined up to form a letter. Plot the points and draw the letter.

i (12, 0), (12, 5), (13, 5), (13, 0), (12, 0)

ii (17, 1), (15, 1), (15, 5), (14, 5), (14, 0), (17, 0), (17, 1)

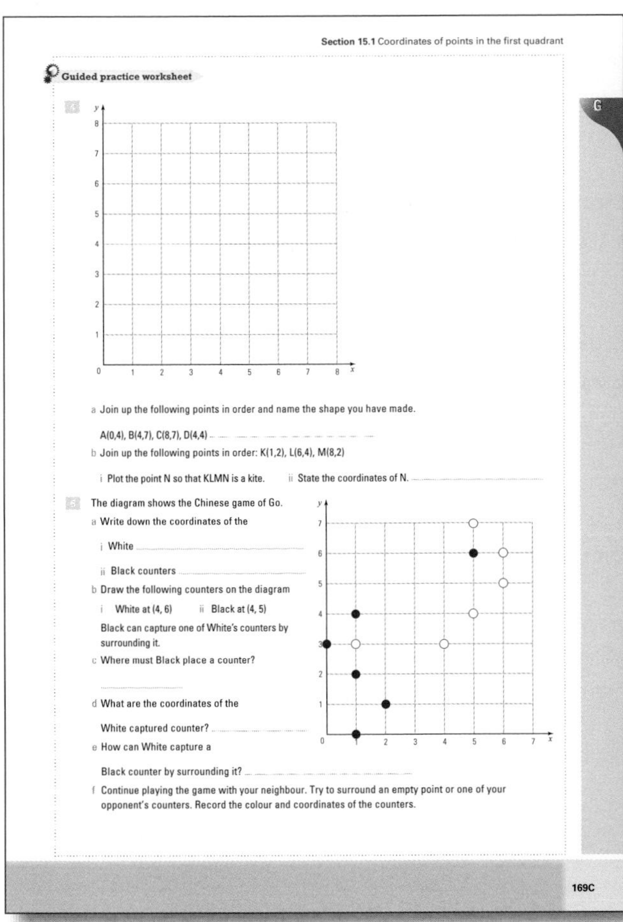

Guided practice worksheet

4

a Join up the following points in order and name the shape you have made.

A(0,4), B(4,7), C(8,7), D(4,4) ....

b Join up the following points in order: K(1,2), L(6,4), M(8,2)

i Plot the point N so that KLMN is a kite. ii State the coordinates of N. ....

5 The diagram shows the Chinese game of Go.

a Write down the coordinates of the

i White ....

ii Black counters ....

b Draw the following counters on the diagram

i White at (4, 6) ii Black at (4, 5)

Black can capture one of White's counters by surrounding it.

c Where must Black place a counter?

....

d What are the coordinates of the

White captured counter? ....

e How can White capture a

Black counter by surrounding it? ....

f Continue playing the game with your neighbour. Try to surround an empty point or one of your opponent's counters. Record the colour and coordinates of the counters.

Specification

GCSE 2010

A k Use the conventions for coordinates in the plane and plot points in all four quadrants, including using geometric information

FS Process skills

Select the mathematical information to use

FS Performance

Level 1 Identify and obtain necessary information to tackle the problem

Resources

CD Resources

Resource sheet 15.2

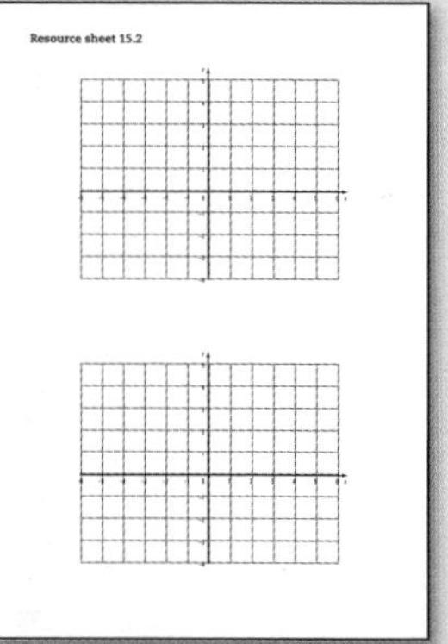

ActiveTeach resources

Positive coordinates quiz

15.2 Coordinates of points in all four quadrants

Concepts and skills

- Use axes and coordinates to specify points in all four quadrants in 2D.
- Identify points with given coordinates.
- Identify coordinates of given points.
- Find the coordinates of points identified by geometrical information in 2D.
- Draw, label and scale axes.

Functional skills

- L1 Extract and interpret information from tables, diagrams, charts and graphs.

Prior key knowledge, skills and concepts

- Know that in an ordered pair you carry out the first operation before the second.
- Understand negative numbers and know that –4 is smaller than –3 etc.

Starter

- *Which one of these sets of numbers is in order?*

–1	–4	–5	0	2	3	6	
0	–1	2	3	–4	–5	6	
–5	–4	–1	0	2	3	6	(Answer: this set)
0	–1	–4	–5	2	3	6	
6	–5	–4	3	2	–1	0	

- *Working in pairs, write three similar questions to Question 1 and see if your partner gets them right.*

Main teaching and learning

- Explain the concept and get students to work through each question in turn.
- Use Resource sheet 15.2 or tell the students to draw the grid themselves.

Common misconceptions

- Swapping the y- and the x-coordinates, e.g. plotting (–2, 3) as (3, –2).

Enrichment

- *Draw the plan of a theme park with exciting rides on a coordinate grid.*
- *Write down the coordinates of all the rides you put in the park.*
- *Give some mathematical clues to work out the coordinates of the entrance.* (By inspection.)

Plenary

- Use Resource sheet 15.2, or tell the students to draw the grid themselves.
  a *Plot the points P at (–3, –4), Q at (3, –2) and R at (1, 4).*
  b *Mark the position of point S so that $PQRS$ is a square.*
  c *Write down the coordinates of point S.* (–5, 2)
- *Working in pairs, write two similar questions to the one above, using different shapes.* (Students' own answers.)

axis origin x-axis y-axis

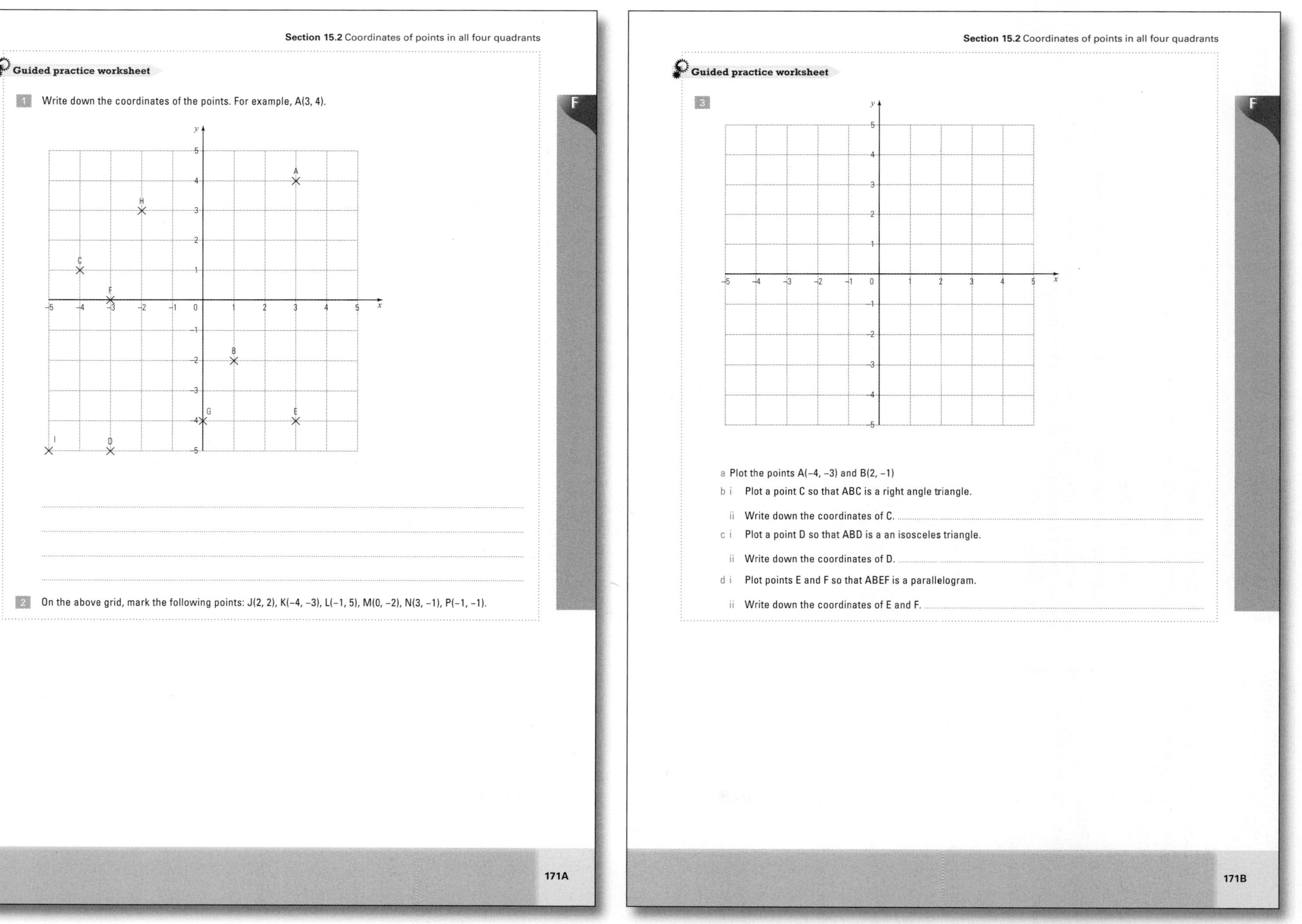

Section 15.2 Coordinates of points in all four quadrants

Guided practice worksheet

F

1 Write down the coordinates of the points. For example, A(3, 4).

2 On the above grid, mark the following points: J(2, 2), K(−4, −3), L(−1, 5), M(0, −2), N(3, −1), P(−1, −1).

171A

Section 15.2 Coordinates of points in all four quadrants

Guided practice worksheet

F

3

a Plot the points A(−4, −3) and B(2, −1)

b i Plot a point C so that ABC is a right angle triangle.

ii Write down the coordinates of C.

c i Plot a point D so that ABD is a an isosceles triangle.

ii Write down the coordinates of D.

d i Plot points E and F so that ABEF is a parallelogram.

ii Write down the coordinates of E and F.

171B

Specification

GCSE 2010
A k Use the conventions for coordinates in the plane and plot points in all four quadrants, including using geometric information

FS Process skills
Select the mathematical information to use
Use appropriate mathematical procedures

FS Performance
Level 1 Identify and obtain necessary information to tackle the problem

Resources

ActiveTeach resources
Mixed coordinates quiz

15.3 Finding the midpoint of a line segment

Concepts and skills

- Find the coordinates of the midpoint of a line segment.

Functional skills

- L1 Extract and interpret information from tables, diagrams, charts and graphs.

Prior key knowledge, skills and concepts

- Know how to add positive and negative numbers.

Starter

- *Work out:*

  (i) $3 + 4$ (7) (ii) $3 - 1$ (2) (iii) $-2 + 5$ (3) (iv) $2 - 5$ (−3)
  (v) $-2 - 1$ (−3) (vi) $2 + -3$ (−1) (vii) $3 + -2$ (1) (viii) $-2 + -3$ (−5)
  (ix) $-1 + -2$ (−3) (x) $2 + -5$ (−3)
- Go through and explain the results of the 'sums'.
- Get students to work through the 'Get ready' section.

Main teaching and learning

- Explain how to find the coordinates of the midpoint of a line in the first quadrant by adding the corresponding x-coordinates and dividing by 2, then adding the corresponding y-coordinates and dividing by 2.
- Go through examples and tell students to attempt Exercise 15C.
- Explain how to find the coordinates of the midpoint of a line in any of the four quadrants by adding the corresponding x-coordinates and dividing by 2, then adding the corresponding y-coordinates and dividing by 2.
- Go through examples and get students to attempt Exercise 15D.

Common misconceptions

- Subtracting the coordinates and dividing by 2.
- Dividing the coordinates by 2.
- Adding the digits and ignoring the signs, e.g. adding −2 and 3 and getting 5.

Enrichment

- *Draw a square on a coordinate grid.*
  Find the coordinates of the midpoint of the opposite corners.
  Check that the answers are the same.
  This shows that the diagonals of a square cut each other in half.
- *Repeat for all other quadrilaterals to find which ones have the same property.*
  (By inspection.)

Plenary

- *Work out the coordinates of the midpoint of each of these line segments:*
  - AB when A is (1, 1) and B is (7, 5). (4, 3)
  - PQ when P is (3, −2) and Q is (−6, 8). (−1.5, 3)

mid-point

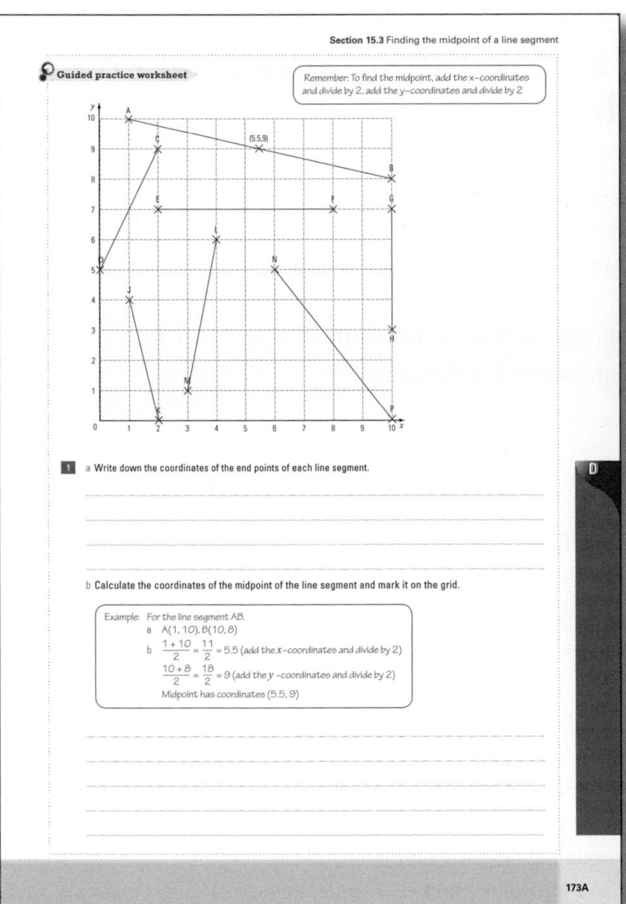
Section 15.3 Finding the midpoint of a line segment
Guided practice worksheet
Remember: To find the midpoint, add the x-coordinates and divide by 2, add the y-coordinates and divide by 2
(5.5,9)
1 a Write down the coordinates of the end points of each line segment.
b Calculate the coordinates of the midpoint of the line segment and mark it on the grid.
Example: For the line segment AB.
a A(1, 10), B(10, 8)
b (1 + 10)/2 = 11/2 = 5.5 (add the x-coordinates and divide by 2)
(10 + 8)/2 = 18/2 = 9 (add the y-coordinates and divide by 2)
Midpoint has coordinates (5.5, 9)
173A

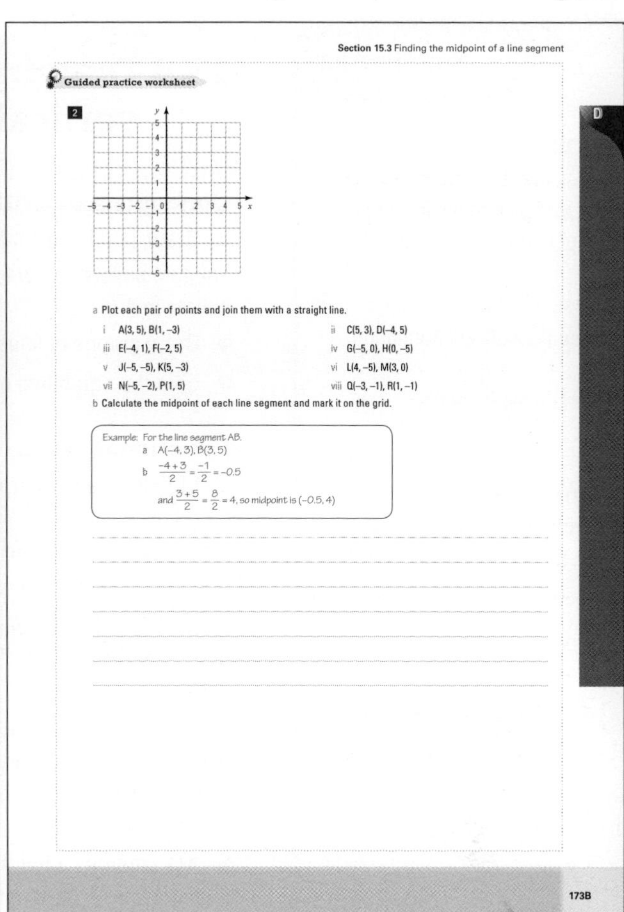
Section 15.3 Finding the midpoint of a line segment
Guided practice worksheet
2
a Plot each pair of points and join them with a straight line.
i A(3, 5), B(1, −3)
ii C(5, 3), D(−4, 5)
iii E(−4, 1), F(−2, 5)
iv G(−5, 0), H(0, −5)
v J(−5, −5), K(5, −3)
vi L(4, −5), M(3, 0)
vii N(−5, −2), P(1, 5)
viii Q(−3, −1), R(1, −1)
b Calculate the midpoint of each line segment and mark it on the grid.
Example: For the line segment AB.
a A(−4, 3), B(3, 5)
b (−4 + 3)/2 = −1/2 = −0.5
and (3 + 5)/2 = 8/2 = 4, so midpoint is (−0.5, 4)
173B

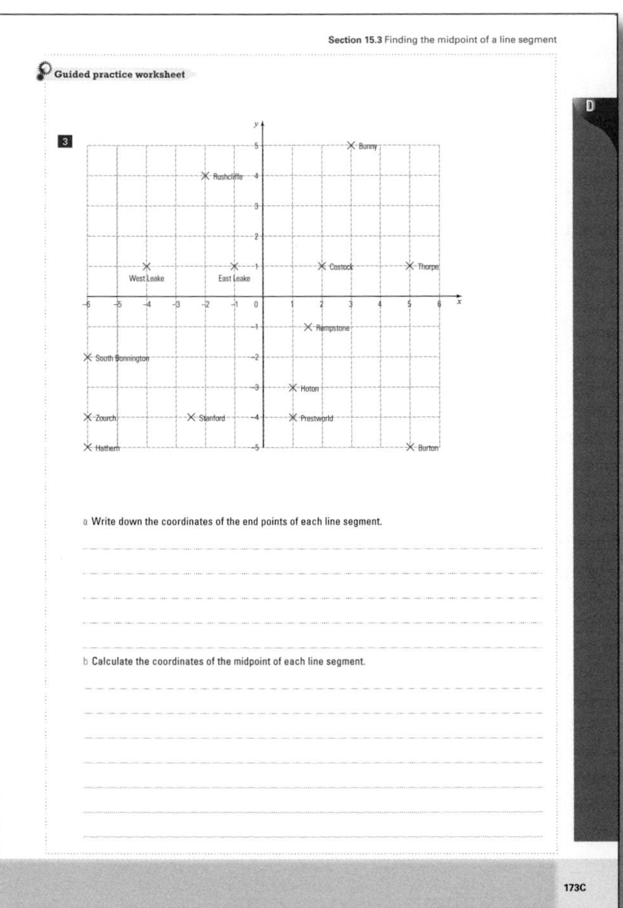
Section 15.3 Finding the midpoint of a line segment
Guided practice worksheet
3
Bunny
Rushcliffe
West Leake
East Leake
Costock
Thorpe
Rempstone
South Bonnington
Hoton
Zouch
Stanford
Prestwold
Hathern
Burton
a Write down the coordinates of the end points of each line segment.
b Calculate the coordinates of the midpoint of each line segment.
173C

Specification

GCSE 2010

A I Recognise and plot equations that correspond to straight-line graphs in the coordinate plane....

FS Process skills

Select the mathematical information to use

Use appropriate mathematical procedures

FS Performance

Level 1 Identify and obtain necessary information to tackle the problem

Resources

CD Resources

Resource sheet 15.4

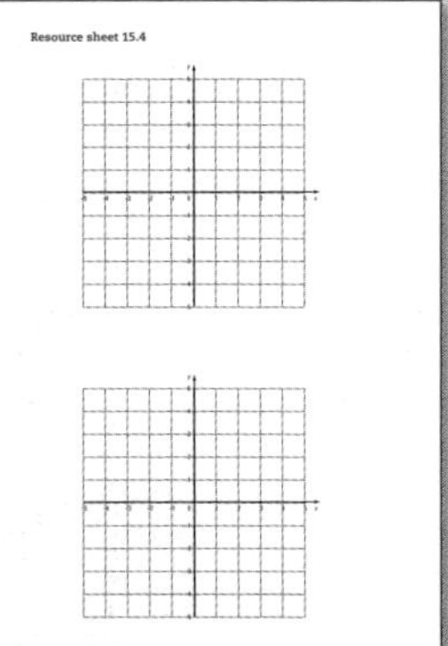

ActiveTeach resources

Coordinates quiz

Straight-line graphs interactive

15.4 Drawing and naming horizontal and vertical lines

Concepts and skills

- Draw, label and scale axes.

The two bullets below are not taken from the Specification but build towards the other bullets in A I.

- Draw graphs of lines with equations $y = n$ and $x = m$.
- Give the equations of horizontal and vertical lines.

Functional skills

- L1 Extract and interpret information from tables, diagrams, charts and graphs.

Prior key knowledge, skills and concepts

- Plotting coordinate pairs (x, y).
- How to substitute numbers in equations.

Starter

- Go through 'Get ready' questions and remind students about the fact that the x-coordinate always comes first and the y-coordinate always comes second. Use a form of mnemonic to help, e.g. x comes before y in the alphabet, along the corridor and up the stairs etc.
- Ask students what they notice about the coordinates of the two lines, i.e. in vertical lines the x-coordinate stays the same and in horizontal lines the y-coordinate stays the same.

Main teaching and learning

- Go through the 'Key points'.
- Ask students to complete Exercise 15E.
- Use Resource sheet 15.4 for questions 3–5 or tell the students to draw the grid themselves.

Common misconceptions

- Swapping the y and the x, and calling lines with equations x = constant y = constant, and vice versa.
- Not realising that the x-axis has equation $y = 0$ and the y-axis has equation $x = 0$.

Enrichment

- Draw straight lines of the form $y = p$ and $x = q$ and realise that they intersect at (p, q).

Plenary

- Check understanding of x lines being vertical and y lines being horizontal and that the x-axis has equation $y = 0$ and the y-axis has equation $x = 0$.

Guided practice worksheet

E

1 Write down the equation of each line. The first one has been done for you.

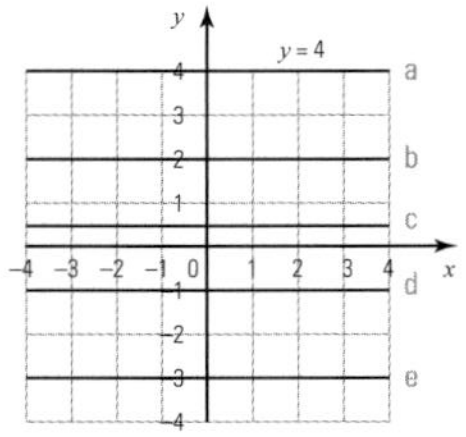

a $y = 4$

b ....

c ....

d ....

e ....

2 Write down the equation of each line.

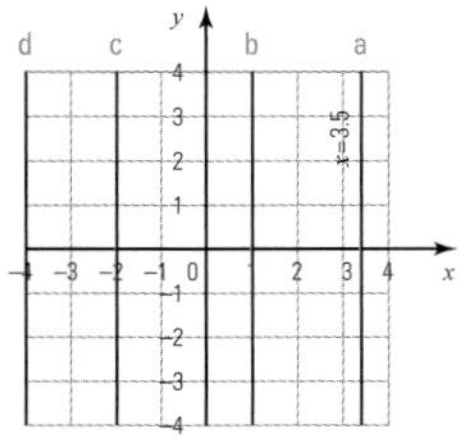

a $x = 3.5$

b ....

c ....

d ....

3 On the grid below, draw the lines with these equations. Write the equation on the line.

a $x = 3$

b $y = -2$

c $y = 3.5$

d $x = -1.5$

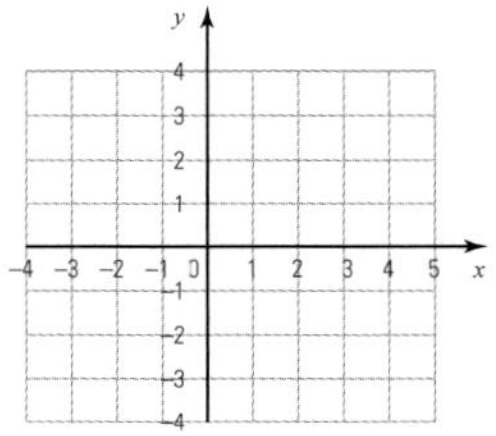

4 a Write down the equation of each line.

....

....

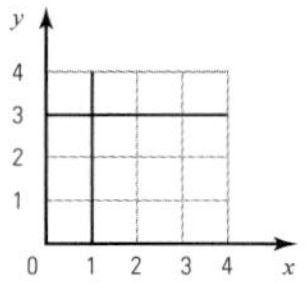

b Write down the coordinates of their point of intersection.

....

Guided practice worksheet

E

5 Write down the equation of the i vertical ii horizontal line passing through each point.

a (4, 5) i .... ii ....

b (−7, 1) i .... ii ....

c (0, 5) i .... ii ....

d (−10, 0) i .... ii ....

6 Write down the equation of the i x–axis .... ii y–axis. ....

Specification

GCSE 2010
A I Recognise and plot equations that correspond to straight-line graphs in the coordinate plane, including finding gradients

FS Process skills
Select the mathematical information to use
Use appropriate mathematical procedures

FS Performance
Level 1 Identify and obtain necessary information to tackle the problem

Resources

CD Resources
Resource sheet 15.5

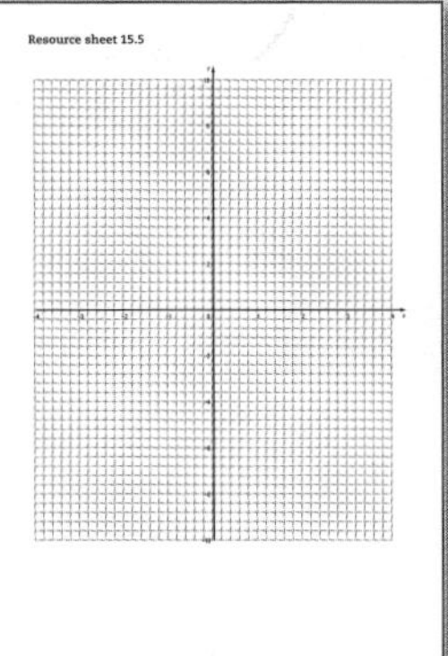

Links
http://www.bbc.co.uk/education/mathsfile/shockwave/games/planethop.html

15.5 Drawing slanting lines

Concepts and skills

- Recognise that equations of the form $y = mx + c$ correspond to straight-line graphs in the coordinate plane.
- Plot and draw graphs of functions.
- Plot and draw graphs of straight lines of the form $y = mx + c$.
- Plot and draw graphs of straight lines of the form $x + y = c$.

Functional skills

- L1 Extract and interpret information from tables, diagrams, charts and graphs.

Prior key knowledge, skills and concepts

- Completing a table of values using a number machine.
- Plotting coordinate pairs.

Starter

- *Work out the answer to:*

(a) $3 \times 2 + 1$ (7)	(b) $3 \times -2 + 1$ (–5)
(c) $1 + 2 \times 4$ (9)	(d) $-2 + 2 \times 3$ (4)
(e) $-2 \times 2 + 3$ (–1)	(f) $-2 \times -3 + 1$ (7)
(g) $-3 - 2 \times 1$ (–5)	(h) $-2 \times -3 - 4$ (2)

Don't forget BIDMAS.

Main teaching and learning

- Explain the example and get students to work through each question in turn for Exercises 15F and then 15G.
- Use Resource sheet 15.5 or, alternatively, get the students to draw the grid themselves.

Common misconceptions

- Swapping the y and the x, e.g. plotting (–2, 3) as (3, –2).
- Getting in a muddle with the order of operations when substituting values.

Enrichment

- Work with gradients that are fractions.
- Find the coordinates of points where two straight lines cross.

Plenary

- *On a grid, plot and draw the graphs of four lines that have a gradient of 2.*
- *On a separate grid, plot and draw the graphs of four lines with gradient –2.*
- *Write down their equations.* (Lines with gradient 2 have equations $y = 2x = c$, where c is the y-intercept. Lines with gradient –2 have equations $y = -2x + c$, where c is the y-intercept.)

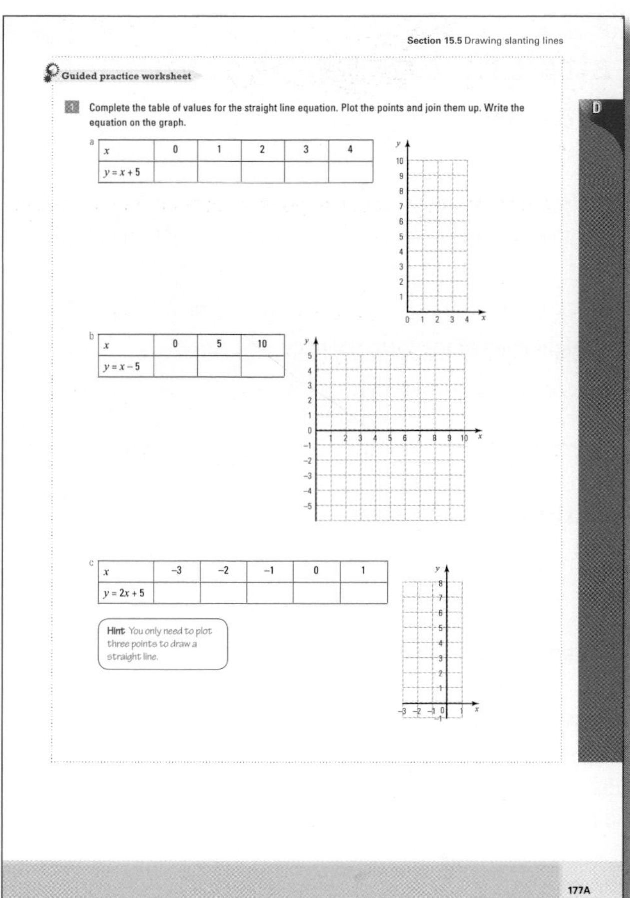

Guided practice worksheet

1 Complete the table of values for the straight line equation. Plot the points and join them up. Write the equation on the graph.

a

x	0	1	2	3	4
$y = x + 5$					

b

x	0	5	10
$y = x - 5$			

c

x	−3	−2	−1	0	1
$y = 2x + 5$					

Hint You only need to plot three points to draw a straight line.

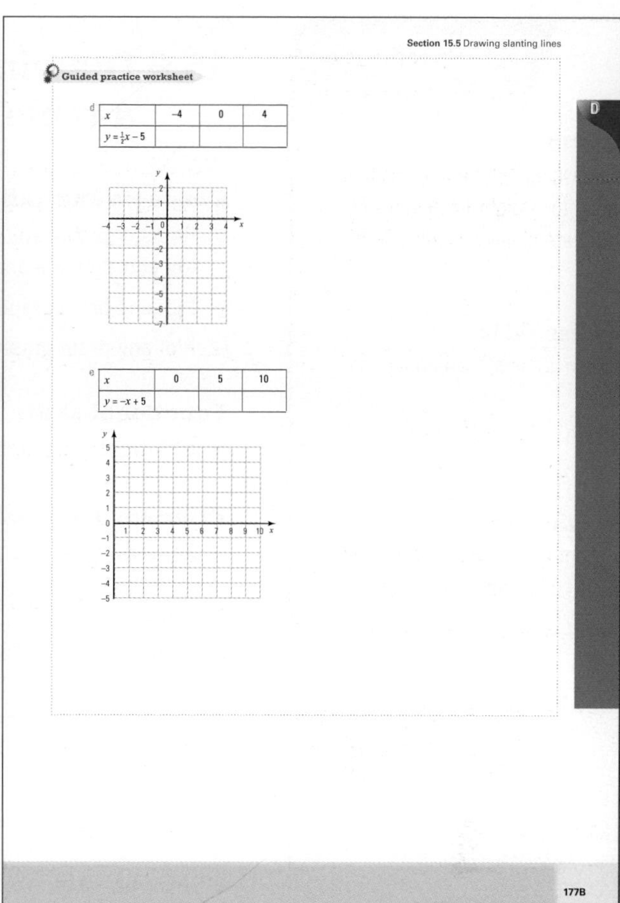

Guided practice worksheet

d

x	−4	0	4
$y = \frac{1}{2}x - 5$			

e

x	0	5	10
$y = -x + 5$			

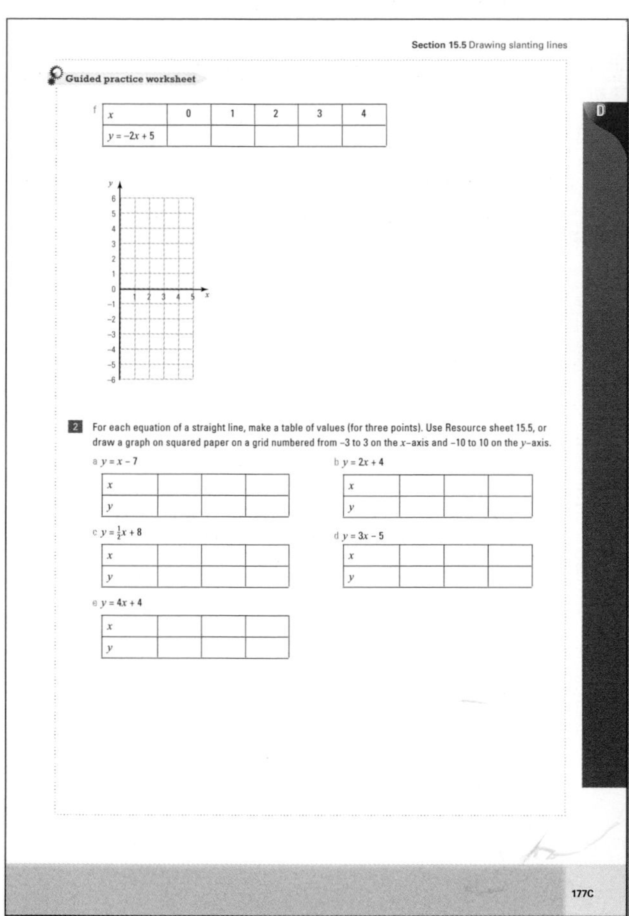

Guided practice worksheet

f

x	0	1	2	3	4
$y = -2x + 5$					

2 For each equation of a straight line, make a table of values (for three points). Use Resource sheet 15.5, or draw a graph on squared paper on a grid numbered from −3 to 3 on the x-axis and −10 to 10 on the y-axis.

a $y = x - 7$

x			
y			

b $y = 2x + 4$

x			
y			

c $y = \frac{1}{2}x + 8$

x			
y			

d $y = 3x - 5$

x			
y			

e $y = 4x + 4$

x			
y			

Specification

GCSE 2010

A I Recognise and plot equations that correspond to straight-line graphs in the coordinate plane, including finding gradients

FS Process skills

Select the mathematical information to use

Use appropriate mathematical procedures

FS Performance

Level 1 Identify and obtain necessary information to tackle the problem

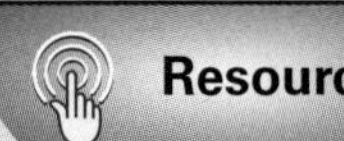

Resources

CD Resources

Resource sheets 15.5 and 15.6

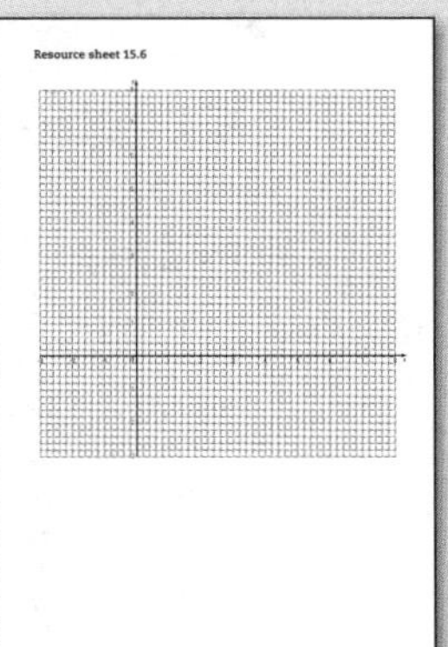

15.6 Drawing straight-line graphs without a table of values

Concepts and skills

- Recognise that equations of the form $y = mx + c$ correspond to straight-line graphs in the coordinate plane.
- Plot and draw graphs of functions.
- Plot and draw graphs of straight lines of the form $y = mx + c$.

Functional skills

- L1 Extract and interpret information from tables, diagrams, charts and graphs.

Prior key knowledge, skills and concepts

- Plotting coordinate pairs.

Starter

- Check understanding of plotting points on the y-axis.

Main teaching and learning

- Explain the examples and get students to work through each question in turn for Exercises 15H, 15I and 15J. Use Resource sheet 15.5 and/or 15.6 or, alternatively, get the students to draw the grid themselves.

Common misconceptions

- Misreading the coordinate on the y-axis.
- Misreading the scales on the axes.

Enrichment

- Work with gradients that are fractions.
- Find the coordinates of points where two straight lines cross.

Plenary

- Check understanding by getting students to draw the graphs of:
  (a) $y = x + 2$ (b) $y = 2x - 1$ (c) $x + y = 3$. (By inspection.)

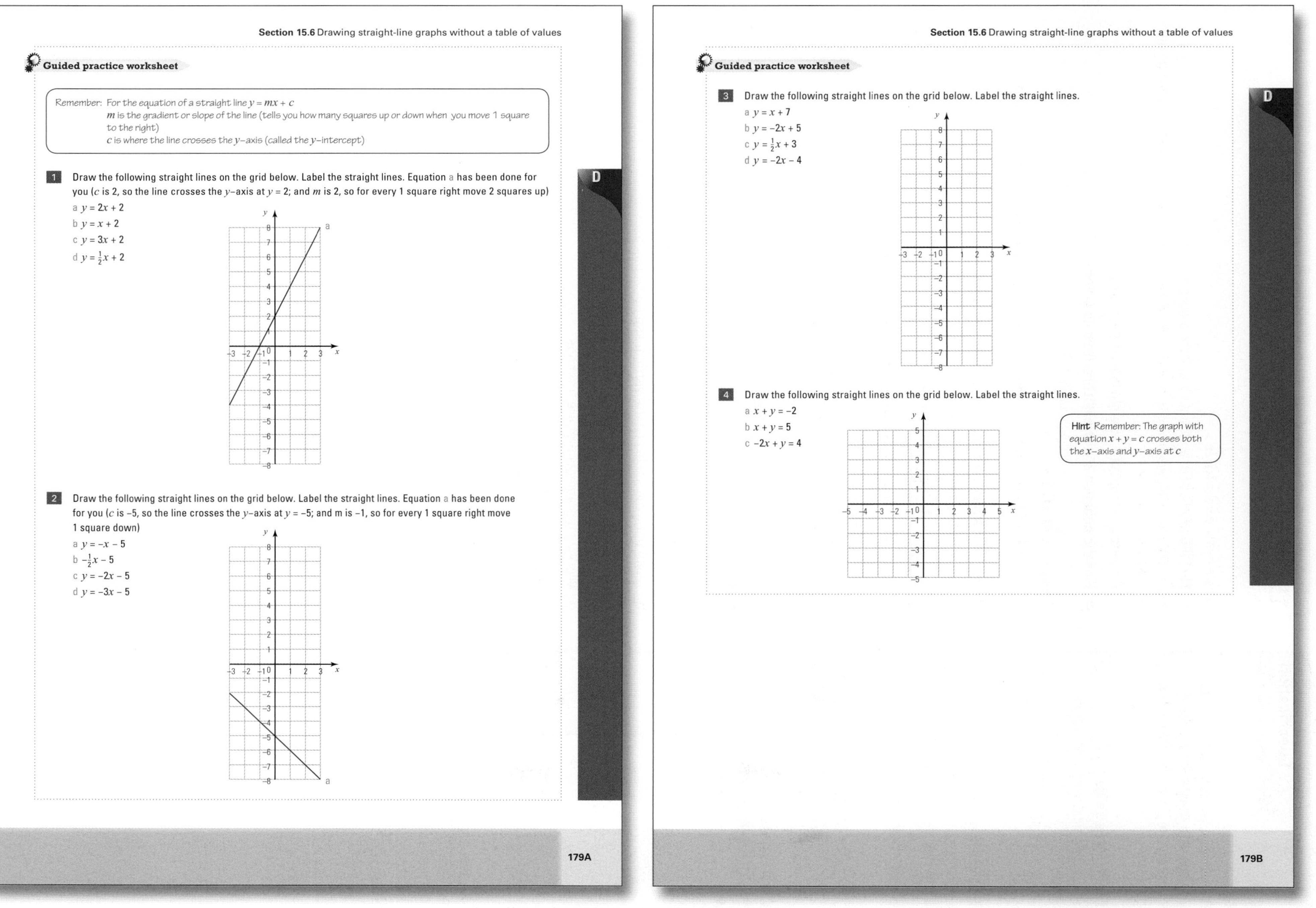

Guided practice worksheet

Remember: For the equation of a straight line $y = mx + c$
m is the gradient or slope of the line (tells you how many squares up or down when you move 1 square to the right)
c is where the line crosses the y-axis (called the y-intercept)

1 Draw the following straight lines on the grid below. Label the straight lines. Equation a has been done for you (c is 2, so the line crosses the y-axis at $y = 2$; and m is 2, so for every 1 square right move 2 squares up)

a $y = 2x + 2$
b $y = x + 2$
c $y = 3x + 2$
d $y = \frac{1}{2}x + 2$

2 Draw the following straight lines on the grid below. Label the straight lines. Equation a has been done for you (c is –5, so the line crosses the y-axis at $y = -5$; and m is –1, so for every 1 square right move 1 square down)

a $y = -x - 5$
b $-\frac{1}{2}x - 5$
c $y = -2x - 5$
d $y = -3x - 5$

Section 15.6 Drawing straight-line graphs without a table of values

Guided practice worksheet

3 Draw the following straight lines on the grid below. Label the straight lines.

a $y = x + 7$
b $y = -2x + 5$
c $y = \frac{1}{2}x + 3$
d $y = -2x - 4$

4 Draw the following straight lines on the grid below. Label the straight lines.

a $x + y = -2$
b $x + y = 5$
c $-2x + y = 4$

Hint Remember: The graph with equation $x + y = c$ crosses both the x-axis and y-axis at c

Specification

GCSE 2010

A I Recognise and plot equations that correspond to straight-line graphs in the coordinate plane, including finding gradients

FS Process skills

Select the mathematical information to use

Use appropriate mathematical procedures

FS Performance

Level 1 Identify and obtain necessary information to tackle the problem

Resources

CD Resources

Resource sheet 15.7

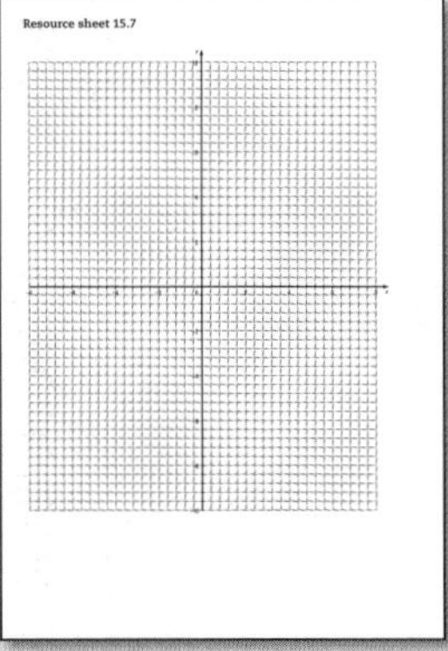

ActiveTeach resources

RP KC Graphs 1 knowledge check

RP PS Coordinates problem solving

15.7 Naming straight-line graphs

Concepts and skills

- Find the gradient of a straight line from a graph.

The two bullets below are not in the Specification but are useful guides for the learning in this section.

- Find the intercept of a straight line on the y-axis.
- Find the equation of a straight line from its graph.

Functional skills

- L1 Extract and interpret information from tables, diagrams, charts and graphs.

Prior key knowledge, skills and concepts

- Know how to read coordinates.
- Know how to read scales from the axes.

Starter

- Check understanding of reading off points from the y-axis.
- Check understanding of reading scales off the x- and y-axes.

Main teaching and learning

- Go through examples on how to find the equations of straight lines.
- Work on Exercise 15K.

Common misconceptions

- Misreading the y-intercept.
- Misreading the scales on the vertical and horizontal axes.

Enrichment

- Work with gradients that are fractions.
- Find the coordinates of points where two straight lines cross.

Plenary

- Students work in pairs to plot two points, join them with a straight line and find the equation of the line. (By inspection.)

Guided practice worksheet

Each of these straight lines has an equation that looks like $y = mx + c$.

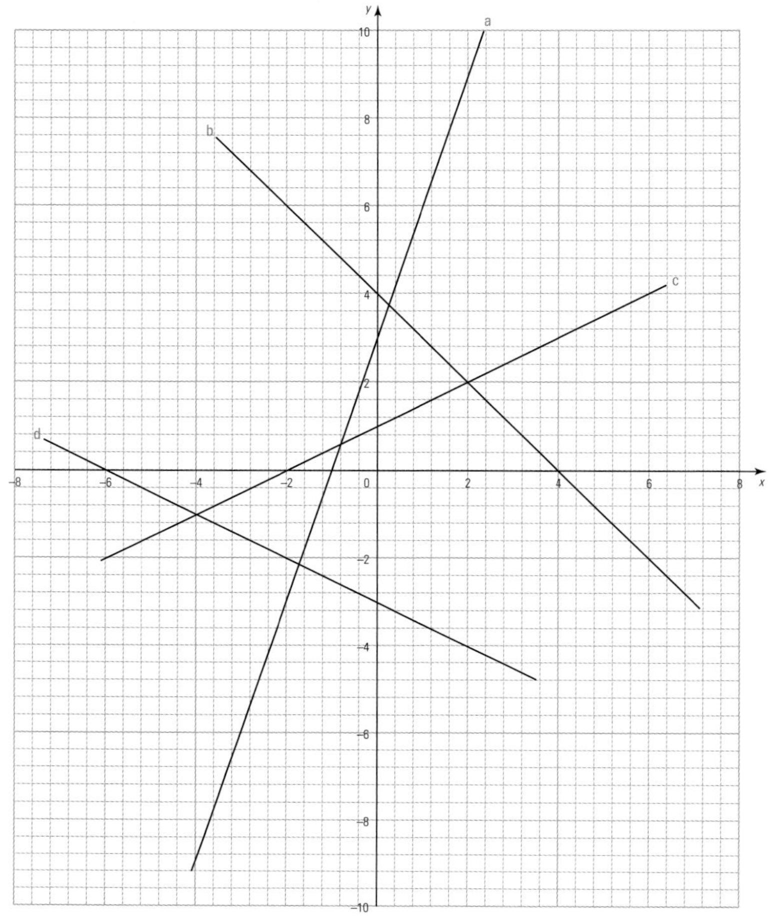

Section 15.7 Naming straight-line graphs

Guided practice worksheet

1 Write down the value of c (the y-intercept)

a ....

b ....

c ....

d ....

2 Find the gradient, m.

a ....

b ....

c ....

d ....

3 Use your answers to questions 1 and 2 to write down the equations of the straight lines.

a ....

b ....

c ....

d ....

4 Write down the equations of these straight lines.

a ....

b ....

c ....

d ....

e ....

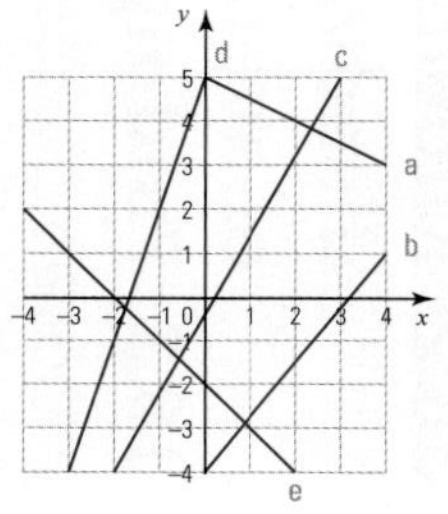

Specification

GCSE 2010

SP h (part) Calculate median, mean, range, mode…

SP l Compare distributions and make inferences

SP u Use calculators efficiently and effectively, including statistical functions

FS Process skills

Recognise that a situation has aspects that can be represented using mathematics

Use appropriate mathematical procedures

Interpret results and solutions

FS Performance

Level 1 Apply mathematics in an organised way to find solutions to straightforward practical problems for different purposes

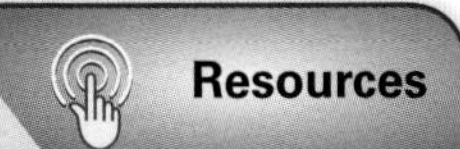

Resources

CD resources

Examples of averages

MS PowerPoint presentation 16.1 'Mean, mode, median and range'

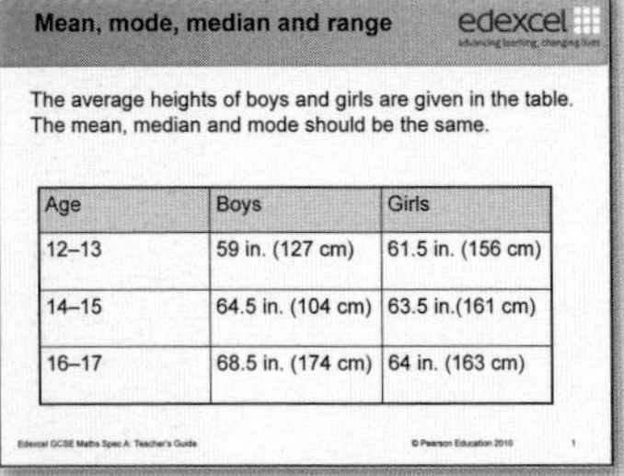

Mean, mode, median and range

The average heights of boys and girls are given in the table. The mean, median and mode should be the same.

Age	Boys	Girls
12–13	59 in. (127 cm)	61.5 in. (156 cm)
14–15	64.5 in. (104 cm)	63.5 in.(161 cm)
16–17	68.5 in. (174 cm)	64 in. (163 cm)

Links

http://nrich.maths.org/public/search.php?search=average

http://nrich.maths.org/6267

http://www.bbc.co.uk/schools/gcsebitsize/maths/data/measuresofaverageact.shtml

ActiveTeach resources

Mental calculation quiz 1

Traffic flows 1 video

Counting traffic 1 video

16.1 Finding the mode, the median and the mean
16.2 Knowing the advantages and disadvantages of the three types of average
16.3 Finding the range

Concepts and skills

- Calculate:
  - mean
  - mode
  - median
  - range.
- Recognise the advantages and disadvantages between measures of average.
- Calculate the mean of a small data set, using the appropriate key on a scientific calculator.

Functional skills

- L1 Find mean and range.

Starter

- *Are you average? It depends what you mean by average.* Discuss 'average'. Bring examples of uses of the word 'average', for example, batting averages, average scores, 67% of students are 'above average', etc.

Main teaching and learning

- Tell the students you are going to look at whether they have **average** height.
- Display PowerPoint 16.1 slide 1 and discuss these points.
  - The height given is a measure of where the middle amount might be (the average).
- To give an accurate picture you need to know the smallest and greatest height of a group of people (the difference between them is called the **range** of values).
- Tell the class to write on the white board what height they are.
- Tell the class there are three possible averages.
  - *'What number is most common?'* This is called the **mode**.
  - *'If we arrange the numbers from smallest to largest, which number will be in the middle?'* There will be one value in the middle if there is an odd number of people, two values if there is an even number. This is called the **median**.
  - *'If we shared all the heights out so that we were all the same height, what would that height be?'* Add all the numbers and divide by the number of people. This is called the **mean**.
- Display PowerPoint 16.1 slide 2 and discuss how it compares with the findings of the class.

Common misconceptions

- Students sometimes mix up the mean, mode and median.
- Students sometimes refer to a figure as an average rather than the mean, mode or median, as the case may be.

Enrichment

- Work out the class's mean, mode, median and range. Tell students they might have to pick the most suitable average. Discuss the advantages of each.

Plenary

- *Is the mode always a number in the original list of numbers?* (Yes)
- *Given the numbers 2, 4, 6, 6, 8, what is the mode?* (6)
- *Given the numbers 4, 4, 6, 8, 8, what is the mode?* (4 and 8; more than one mode is possible.)
- *When would the median be a number in the original ordered list?* (Odd number of numbers in the list, or the two middle numbers being the same in the ordered list.)
- *Give three different sets of numbers where the median is 8 and the range is 5.* (4, 8, 9; or 5, 8, 10; or 6, 8, 11). *Are these the only three alternative answers?* (No, e.g. 8, 8, 13. Some higher attaining students may introduce decimal numbers.)

mean mode median range average spread

Guided practice worksheet

F

1 Jasmine is learning to word process. She records the number of errors she makes on each page of typing. They are as follows:

6 9 5 6 8 2 4 9 6 1

a Write down her best score. ....

b Write down her worst score. ....

c Work out the range of her scores.

d Write down the mode.

E

2 Haycroft farm grows redcurrants. They collect them in boxes. The following are the numbers of boxes they collected each day during the three weeks of harvesting.

4 7 8 8 8 8 9 9 9 9 9 5 5 5 4 4 4 3 2 2

a Work out the range.

b Write down the mode.

c Work out the median number of boxes.

3 A factory owner records the number of employees absent in the first 7 days of the new year. The results are shown below.

8 10 9 5 10 3 11

a Write down the mode. ....

b Work out the median number of employees absent.

c Work out the mean number of employees absent.

d Work out the range of absentees.

Guided practice worksheet

E

4 When is it a good idea to use the mode as a measure of average?

5 When is it not a good idea to use the mean as a measure of average?

6 Only one average can be used for qualitative data. Which one is it?

7 Five people work in an office. They do not all work the same number of hours. Their wages for one particular week are: £156 £100 £454 £160 £100

a Write down the mode. ....

b Work out the median wage.

c Work out the mean wage.

d Which of the three averages best describes the wages of these office workers? Explain your answer.

Specification

GCSE 2010

SP g Produce charts and diagrams for various data types

SP i Interpret a wide range of graphs and diagrams and draw conclusions

FS Process skills

Select the mathematical information to use

Find results and solutions

FS Performance

Level 1 Select mathematics in an organised way to find solutions

Resources

CD resources

MS PowerPoint presentation 16.4 'Stem and leaf diagrams'

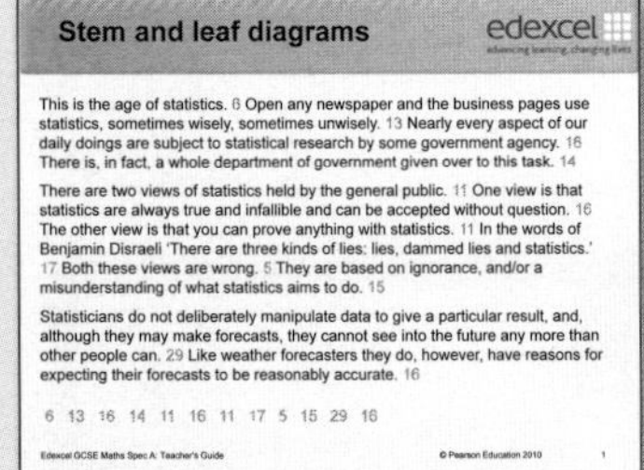

ActiveTeach resources

Stem and leaf quiz

Stem and leaf interactive

16.4 Using stem and leaf diagrams to find averages and range

Concepts and skills

- Produce ordered stem and leaf diagrams.
- Interpret stem and leaf diagrams.
- Find range, mode, median and greatest and least values from stem and leaf diagrams.

Functional skills

- L1 Find mean and range.
- L1 Collect and record discrete data and organise and represent information in different ways.

Starter

- *How long should a sentence be?* Marcel Proust once wrote one 958 words long.

Main teaching and learning

- Tell students they are going to investigate sentence lengths.
- Display PowerPoint 16.4 slide 1 and discuss these points:
  - The variable is sentence length. Check the lengths on the slide.
  - In a sentence letters are grouped into words so that sense can be made of the sentence.
  - You can put these numbers into groups according to their first digit (slide 2).
  - The first digit of a number is called its stem, the second digit is called the leaf. A group has 1 stem and several leaves.
  - When we arrange these in a diagram it is called a stem and leaf diagram (slide 3). If we put the leaves in order it is called an ordered stem and leaf diagram (slide 4).
- The mode, median and range can be readily seen (slide 5).
  - The mode has the most identical leaves in the same group.
  - The median is the middle one (or halfway between the middle two).
  - The range is the last number minus the first.

Common misconceptions

- Sometimes students call the median the mean.

Enrichment

- *What sort of data is required for a stem and leaf diagram?*

Plenary

- Divide the students in the class into two groups.

  Their heights, to the nearest centimetre, are going to be shown on a stem and leaf diagram.

  What numbers should go in the stem?

  (a) Students in each group arrange themselves in order of height and, starting with the shortest, measure their height and record it on the stem and leaf diagram displayed on the board for each group. For each group ask the following questions.

  (i) *What is the range?*

  (ii) *What is the median?*

  (iii) *How many students are over/under a height of … cm?*

  (b) *Can you swap pairs of students between groups so that the ranges are the same?*

  (c) *Can you swap pairs of students between groups so that the medians are the same?*

  (d) *Can you swap pairs of students between groups so that the ranges and the medians are the same?*

stem and leaf diagram ordered stem and leaf diagram

Guided practice worksheet

D

1 The stem and leaf diagram shows the time, in minutes, it takes a mechanic to change the tyres on 15 cars.

Key 1|4 is 14 minutes

1	4	5	6	7	
2	1	3	3	8	8
3	1	6	3	3	3
4	0				

a Write down the modal time.

....

b Work out the range.

....

c Write down the median time.

....

2 The stem and leaf diagram shows the time, in minutes, it takes a postman to sort the mail he is to deliver.

Key 2|4 is 24 minutes

2	4	6	6	8	9	
3	0	2	2	7	8	8
4	1	3	3	3	3	9
5	1	1	2			

a Write down the modal time.

....

b Work out the range.

....

c Write down the median time.

....

Guided practice worksheet

D

3 The unordered stem and leaf diagram shows the number of lessons required by 18 adults before they passed their driving test.

Key 2|4 is 24 lessons

1	2	9	3	6	8	
2	6	2	4	3	9	8
3	2	0	3	0	4	0
4	0					

a Draw an ordered stem and leaf diagram for these data.

b Use the ordered stem and leaf diagram to find:

i the modal number of lessons

....

ii the median number of lessons

....

iii the range.

....

Specification

GCSE 2010

SP g Produce charts and diagrams for various data types

SP h Calculate median, mean, range, mode and modal class

FS Process skills

Use appropriate mathematical procedures

FS Performance

Level 2 Use appropriate checking procedures and evaluate their effectiveness at each stage

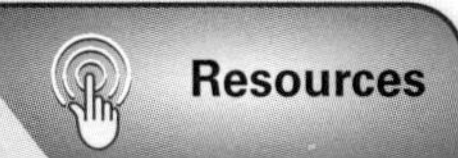

Resources

CD resources

MS PowerPoint presentation 16.5 'Frequency tables'

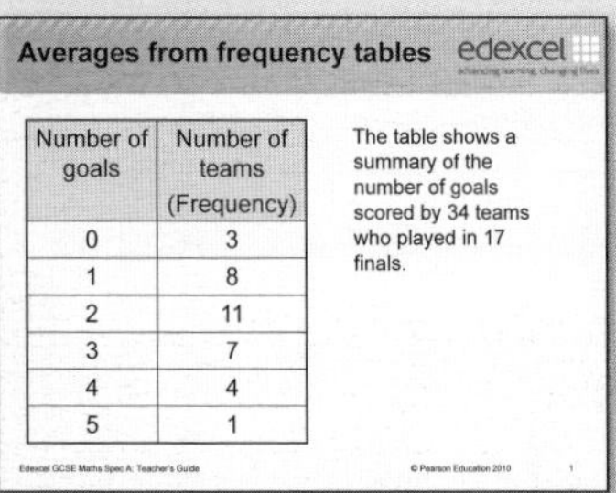

Averages from frequency tables

Number of goals	Number of teams (Frequency)
0	3
1	8
2	11
3	7
4	4
5	1

The table shows a summary of the number of goals scored by 34 teams who played in 17 finals.

16.5 Using frequency tables to find averages for discrete data

Concepts and skills

- Produce frequency diagrams for grouped discrete data.
- Find the median for large data sets....

Functional skills

- L2 Use and interpret statistical measures, tables and diagrams, for discrete and continuous data...

Prior key knowledge, skills and concepts

- Students should already know what is meant by mode, median and range of a set of data.

Starter

- Lots of people want to go to a cup final. *'What makes a game worth watching? Is it the number of goals scored?'* Ask students to guess what the average number of goals scored by teams playing in a cup final might be and the range of scores. Write down their guesses.

Main teaching and learning

- Tell students that they are going to investigate goals scored in finals.
- Display PowerPoint 16.5 slide 1. This is a frequency table.
  - The variable is number of goals.
  - The mode is obvious. It has the highest frequency.
  - There are 34 teams, so the median will be the $\frac{34+1}{2}$ = 17.5th value.
  - Explain how to find the 17.5th value.
- The mean is not obvious.
  - mean = sum of all values/number of values.
  - Show how to extend the frequency diagram with another column for these totals (slide 2).
  - Show how to find the sum of all values. (There are 3 noughts which add to 0, 8 ones which add to 8, 11 twos which add to 22, etc.) The range is the last number – the first number = 5 – 0 = 5.

Common misconceptions

- Students sometimes try to find the mean of the data by dividing the total of the second column by the total of the first column $\left(\frac{34}{15} = \text{mean}\right)$.

Enrichment

- Discuss how the students' guesses compare with the actual figures.

Plenary

- Divide the class into two groups (e.g. boys and girls). Draw a tally chart showing number of children in a family. Ask each member of one group for the number of children in their family. Complete the frequency table. Repeat with a new frequency table for the second group.

  For each group answer the following.

  (a) *What is the range?*

  (b) *What is the total number of children in the families?*

  (c) *What are the median and the mean?*

  (d) *What is the mean of the two groups combined?* (A common error will be to give the mean of the two means, which is only true if the group sizes are equal.)

Guided practice worksheet

D

1 The table gives information about the number of letters received daily by Jason.

Number of letters *x*	Frequency *f*	*fx*
0	0	
1	8	
2	7	
3	4	
4	2	
Total		

a Complete the table.

b Write down the modal class.

....

c Write down the median number of letters.

....

d Work out the mean number of letters.

....

2 The table gives information about the number of goals scored by Burnham Rangers over a season.

a Complete the table.

b Write down the modal class.

....

Number of goals scored *x*	0	1	2	3	4	5
Frequency *f*	4	8	9	6	8	2
fx						

c Write down the median number of goals scored.

....

d Work out the mean number of goals scored.

....

3 Lucy carried out a survey. She asked each person coming out of a newsagent's how many papers and magazines they had bought. She did this for an hour. The data she collected is shown in the table.

a Write down the modal class.

....

Number of items bought *x*	0	1	2	3	4	5	6
Frequency *f*	5	5	7	9	3	1	1

b Write down the median number of items bought.

....

c Work out the mean number of items bought. Give your answer to one decimal place.

....

....

....

Add an extra row to the table to help with your calculations.

Specification

GCSE 2010

SP g Produce charts and diagrams for various data types

SP h Calculate median, mean, range, mode and modal class

FS Process skills

Use appropriate mathematical procedures

FS Performance

Level 2 Use appropriate checking procedures and evaluate their effectiveness at each stage

Resources

Resources

Resource sheet 16.6

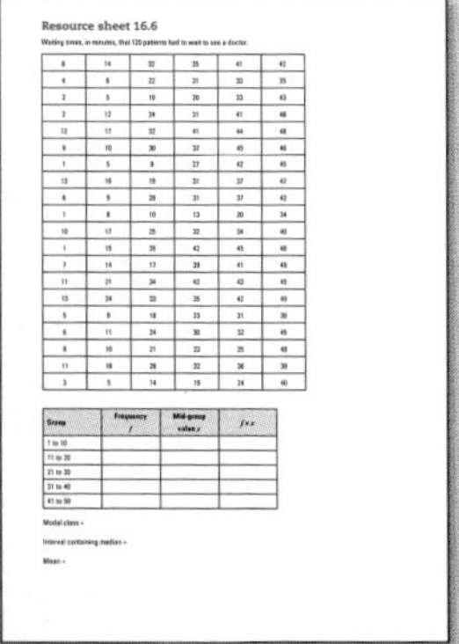

ActiveTeach resources

RP KC Averages and range knowledge check

RP PS Averages and range problem solving

16.6 Working with grouped data
16.7 Estimating the mean of grouped data

Concepts and skills

- Produce frequency diagrams for grouped discrete data.
- Calculate:
  - modal class
  - interval containing the median.
- Estimate the mean of grouped data using the mid-interval value.
- Find the median for large data sets with grouped data.
- Estimate the mean for large data sets with grouped data.
- Understand that the expression 'estimate' will be used where appropriate, when finding the mean of grouped data using mid-interval values.

Functional skills

- L2 Use and interpret statistical measures, tables and diagrams, for discrete and continuous data…

Prior key knowledge, skills and concepts

- Students should already know what is meant by the mean, mode, median and range of a set of data.

Starter

- *If you go to the doctor's, how long do you expect to wait in the waiting room? Is it possible to predict how long you could be waiting? What data could surgery managers collect to help them to answer this question?* (Students' own answers.)

Main teaching and learning

- Tell students that they are going to investigate waiting times.
- The Resource sheet shows the number of minutes that 120 patients had to wait to see a doctor. Tell the students to complete the frequency table.
  - *The class interval that has the highest frequency is called the modal class. Find the modal class.* (31 to 40)
  - There are 120 numbers. The median will be the average of the 60th and 61st numbers. *How can we find the group they come into? We call this the median class. Find the median class.* (21 to 30)
- When you group numbers you lose the details of the individual numbers. Explain that when dealing with groups you assume that the mean of each class is in the middle of that class. You can only estimate the mean.
  - mean × frequency = total for class
  - *What is the overall total?* (3120)
  - Use the Resource sheet to find the overall total.
  - Mean $= \dfrac{\text{overall total}}{\text{total number}} = \dfrac{\Sigma f \times x}{\Sigma f}$.
  - Use the Resource sheet to estimate the mean. (26)

Common misconceptions

- Sometimes students do not use the class mid-point when estimating the mean.

Enrichment

- Discuss what information each of the averages gives you about the waiting times. Is one more useful than another? Will this information be helpful to patients?

Plenary

- *What are the middle values of the class intervals 1 to 5 and 5 to 11?* (3, 8)
- *What are the middle values of the class intervals 2 to 7 and 9 to 16?* (4.5, 12.5)
- *What are the middle values of the class intervals* $0 < x \leqslant 10$ *and* $10 < x \leqslant 20$*?* (5, 15)
- *What are the middle values of the class intervals* $80 < x \leqslant 120$ *and* $120 < x \leqslant 160$*?* (100, 140)
- The table shows the number of visitors under 21 to a sweet shop in one day
  - (a) *How many people visited altogether?* (153)
  - (b) *Which is the modal group?* (11 to 15 inclusive)
  - (c) *Which is the median class?* (11 to 15)
  - (d) *Joan says that an estimate for the age is 21.5. Why must this answer be wrong?* (Greater than the highest value.)

Age (years)	Frequency
1 to 5	20
6 to 10	46
11 to 15	58
16 to 20	29

modal class

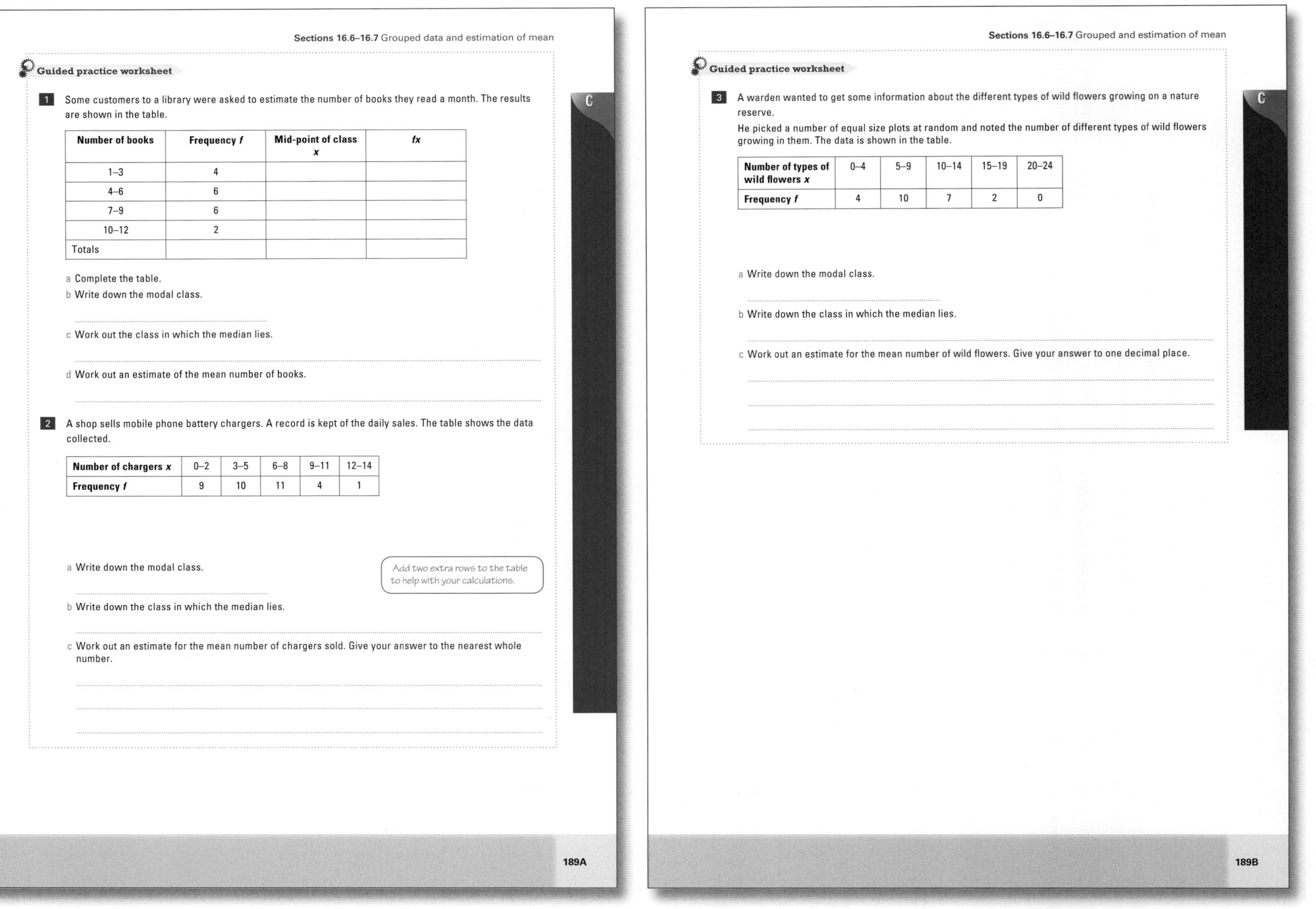

Guided practice worksheet

C

1 Some customers to a library were asked to estimate the number of books they read a month. The results are shown in the table.

Number of books	Frequency f	Mid-point of class x	fx
1–3	4		
4–6	6		
7–9	6		
10–12	2		
Totals			

a Complete the table.

b Write down the modal class.

c Work out the class in which the median lies.

d Work out an estimate of the mean number of books.

2 A shop sells mobile phone battery chargers. A record is kept of the daily sales. The table shows the data collected.

Number of chargers x	0–2	3–5	6–8	9–11	12–14
Frequency f	9	10	11	4	1

Add two extra rows to the table to help with your calculations.

a Write down the modal class.

b Write down the class in which the median lies.

c Work out an estimate for the mean number of chargers sold. Give your answer to the nearest whole number.

Guided practice worksheet

C

3 A warden wanted to get some information about the different types of wild flowers growing on a nature reserve.

He picked a number of equal size plots at random and noted the number of different types of wild flowers growing in them. The data is shown in the table.

Number of types of wild flowers x	0–4	5–9	10–14	15–19	20–24
Frequency f	4	10	7	2	0

a Write down the modal class.

b Write down the class in which the median lies.

c Work out an estimate for the mean number of wild flowers. Give your answer to one decimal place.

Specification

GCSE 2010
GM z (part) Find circumferences… of circles

FS Process skills
Use appropriate mathematical procedures

FS Performance
Level 2 Apply a range of mathematics to find solutions

Resources

Resources
Compasses, string and scissors

ActiveTeach resources
Cycling 2 video

Follow up
Student Book Section 17.1 and Exercises 17A and 17B

17.1 Circumference of a circle

Concepts and skills

- Find circumferences… of circles.
- Recall and use the formulae for the circumference of a circle….
- Use $\pi = 3.142$ or use the π button on a calculator.

Functional skills

- L2 Find … perimeters… of common shapes.

Prior key knowledge, skills and concepts

- Students should know the simple properties of a circle.
- They should know how to find the π button on their calculator and use it.

Starter

- Ask students to draw a circle using compasses. They should then cut a piece of string so that its length is the same as the length of the diameter and see how many times they can fit it around the circumference of the circle. Students could try this with circles of different sizes. Ask the students what they notice.

Main teaching and learning

- Tell students they are going to find a formula to work out the circumference of a circle if they know the length of the diameter.
- Explain how we can do all this when we are given the radius instead of the diameter.
- Discuss how, many years ago, the Hebrews and the Babylonians believed that the diameter fitted into the circumference exactly three times. In 250 BCE Archimedes calculated the real value and found it was closer to 3.14. Today, we still use this value, which we call pi. There is no pattern to the decimals in the exact value of pi and it can be written to millions of decimal places starting 3.141 592 653 589 793 238 462 643 383 279 …
- A student might like to prepare a poster that goes round the classroom stating π to many decimal places.

Common misconceptions

- Many students round their final answer before showing the unrounded answer to 4 or 5 significant figures. If they round incorrectly without showing their unrounded answer, they could lose marks in an examination.

Enrichment

- Draw circles in squares and squares in circles and discuss how they would find the perimeter of the shaded parts.

Plenary

- Draw some circles with either the radius or the diameter or the circumference marked and ask students to estimate the circumference (given the radius or the diameter) or estimate the radius and diameter (given the circumference).

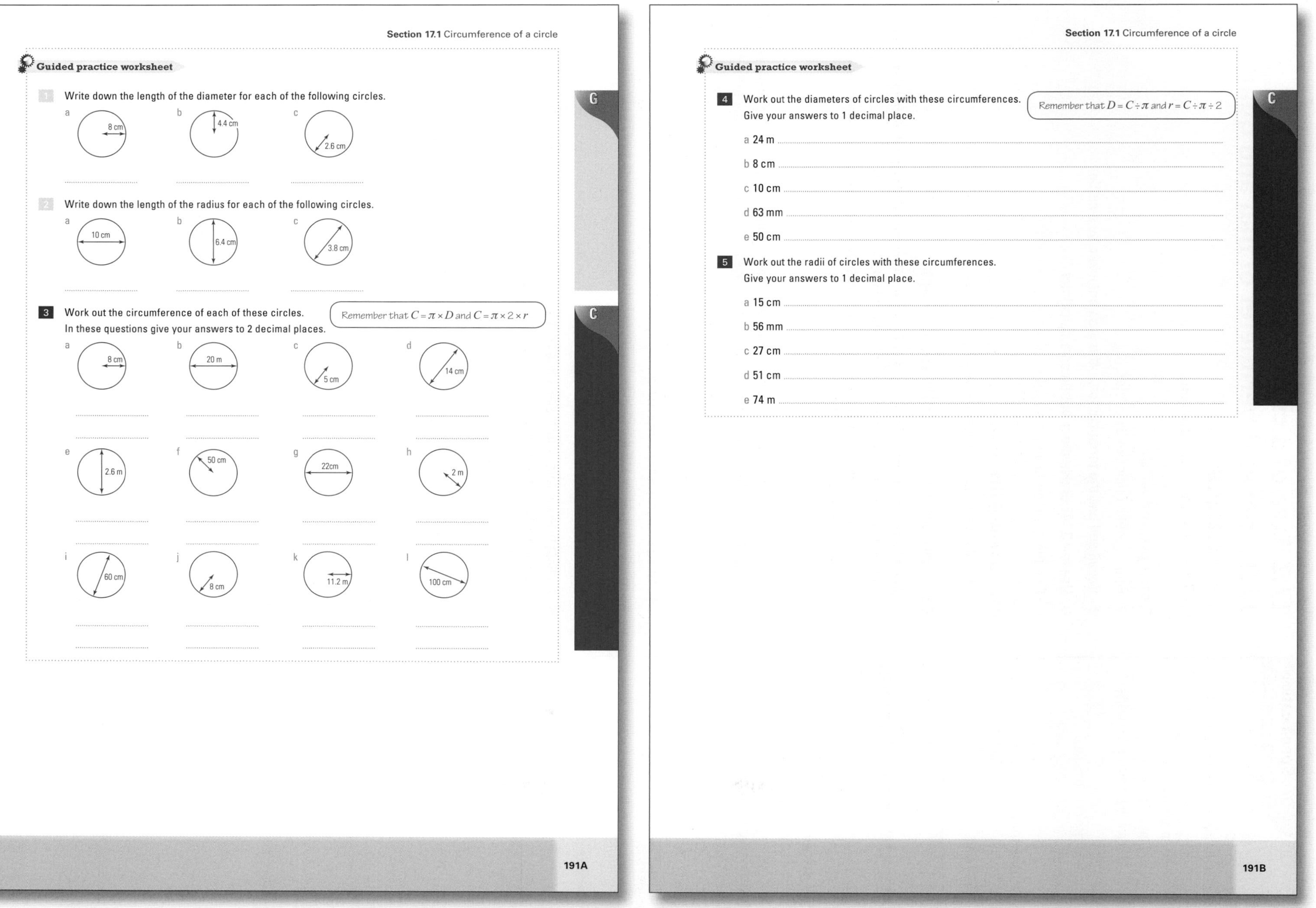

Guided practice worksheet

G

1 Write down the length of the diameter for each of the following circles.

a 8 cm b 4.4 cm c 2.6 cm

2 Write down the length of the radius for each of the following circles.

a 10 cm b 6.4 cm c 3.8 cm

C

3 Work out the circumference of each of these circles. In these questions give your answers to 2 decimal places.

Remember that $C = \pi \times D$ and $C = \pi \times 2 \times r$

a 8 cm b 20 m c 5 cm d 14 cm

e 2.6 m f 50 cm g 22cm h 2 m

i 60 cm j 8 cm k 11.2 m l 100 cm

Guided practice worksheet

C

4 Work out the diameters of circles with these circumferences. Give your answers to 1 decimal place.

Remember that $D = C \div \pi$ and $r = C \div \pi \div 2$

a 24 m ....

b 8 cm ....

c 10 cm ....

d 63 mm ....

e 50 cm ....

5 Work out the radii of circles with these circumferences. Give your answers to 1 decimal place.

a 15 cm ....

b 56 mm ....

c 27 cm ....

d 51 cm ....

e 74 m ....

Specification

GCSE 2010
GM z (part) Find… areas of circles.

FS Process skills
Recognise that a situation has aspects that can be represented using mathematics
Use appropriate mathematical procedures

FS Performance
Level 2 Apply a range of mathematics to find solutions

Resources

Resources
Centimetre-squared paper, compasses

ActiveTeach resources
Area of a circle animation
Waltzer video
Asymmetric bars 3 video
Running 1 video
RP KC Circles knowledge check
RP PS Circles problem solving

17.2 Area of a circle
17.3 Area and perimeter of half and quarter circles

Concepts and skills

- Find … areas enclosed by circles.
- Recall and use the formulae for… the area enclosed by a circle.
- Use $\pi \approx 3.142$ or use the π button on a calculator.
- Find the perimeters and areas of semicircles and quarter circles.

Functional skills

- L2 Find area … of common shapes.

Prior key knowledge, skills and concepts

- Students should know how to use the π button on their calculator and know how to work out πr^2 for different values of r using their calculators.
- Remind students how to write a number correct to two decimal places and three significant figures.

Starter

- Ask students to draw a circle with radius 3 cm on centimetre-squared paper using compasses. They should then count up the squares in the circle to find the area. Make a table with columns r, r^2 and Area. Repeat for circles with radius 4 cm, 5 cm, 6 cm and 7 cm. Ask the students what they notice.

Main teaching and learning

- Tell students they are going to find a formula to work out the area of a circle if they know the length of the radius.
- Explain how we can do all this when we are given the diameter instead of the radius.
- Explain that a circle is actually a line that connects each end to make a loop. The line itself does not have an area but the space inside the loop does. So a circle does not really have an area, but when we say 'area of a circle' we really mean the area of the space inside the circle.

Common misconceptions

- Many students multiply π by r and then square their answer. Explain to students the difference between calculating πr^2 and $(\pi r)^2$. Some students might find it easier to use $A = \pi \times r \times r$.

Enrichment

- Draw circles in squares and squares in circles and discuss how they would find the area of the shaded parts.

Plenary

- Draw some circles with either the radius or the diameter given and ask students to estimate the area.

semicircle

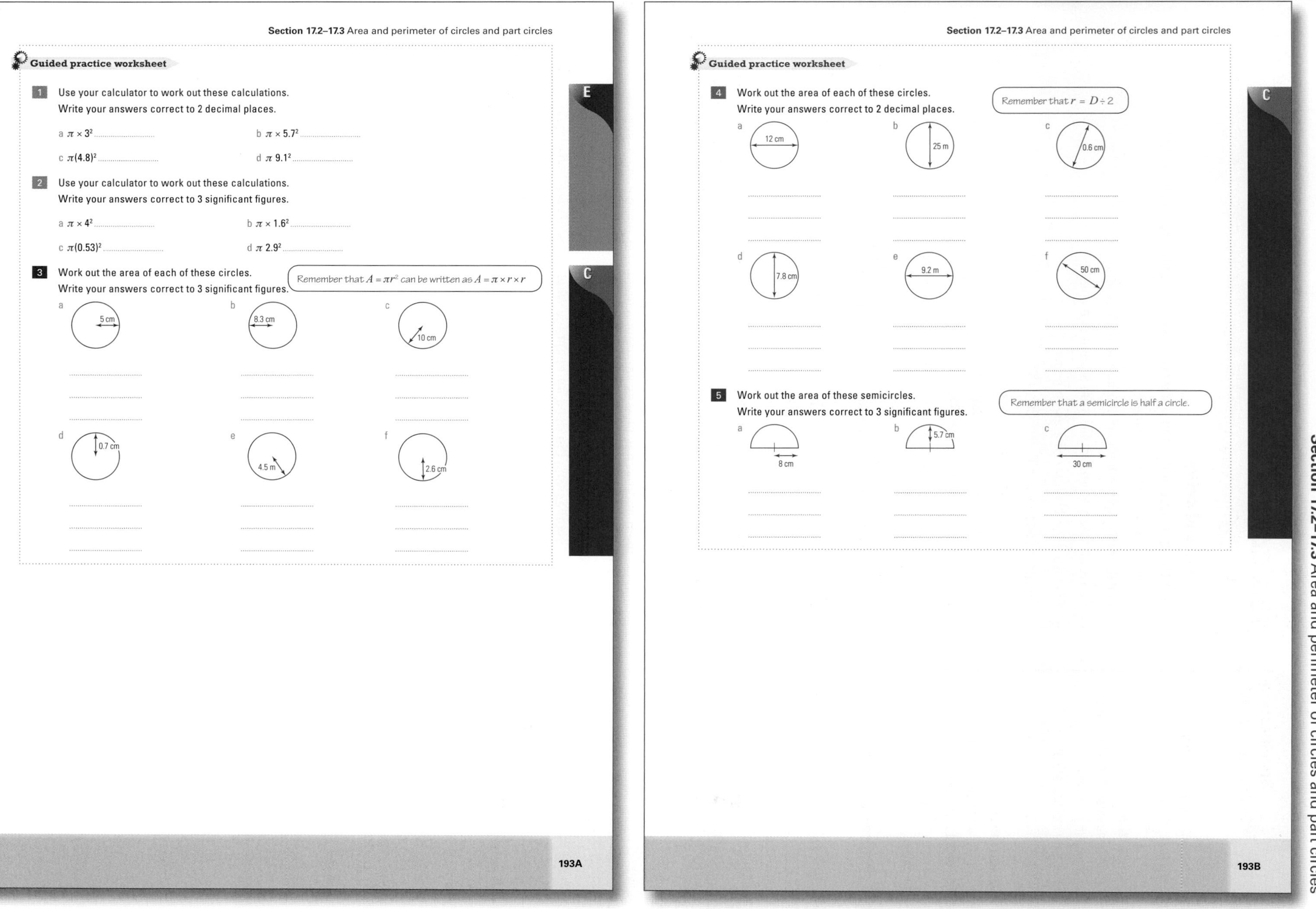

Guided practice worksheet

E

1 Use your calculator to work out these calculations.
Write your answers correct to 2 decimal places.

a $\pi \times 3^2$ .... b $\pi \times 5.7^2$ ....

c $\pi(4.8)^2$ .... d π 9.1^2 ....

2 Use your calculator to work out these calculations.
Write your answers correct to 3 significant figures.

a $\pi \times 4^2$ .... b $\pi \times 1.6^2$ ....

c $\pi(0.53)^2$ .... d π 2.9^2 ....

C

3 Work out the area of each of these circles.
Write your answers correct to 3 significant figures.

Remember that $A = \pi r^2$ can be written as $A = \pi \times r \times r$

Guided practice worksheet

C

4 Work out the area of each of these circles.
Write your answers correct to 2 decimal places.

Remember that $r = D \div 2$

5 Work out the area of these semicircles.
Write your answers correct to 3 significant figures.

Remember that a semicircle is half a circle.

Specification

GCSE 2010

GM v Use straight edge and a pair of compasses to do constructions

FS Process skills

Decide on the methods, operations and tools … to use in a situation

Use appropriate mathematical procedures

FS Performance

Level 1 Apply mathematics in an organised way to find solutions to straightforward practical problems for different purposes

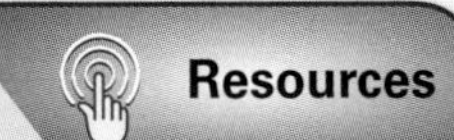

Resources

Links

http://nrich.maths.org/public/search.php?search=constructions

ActiveTeach resources

Constructions interactive

18.1 Constructions

Concepts and skills

- Use straight edge and a pair of compasses to do standard constructions.
- Construct an equilateral triangle.
- Construct the perpendicular bisector of a given line.
- Construct the perpendicular from a point to a line.
- Construct the bisector of a given angle.
- Construct angles of 60°, 90°, 30°, 45°.
- Construct a regular hexagon inside a circle.
- Construct diagrams of everyday 2-D situations involving rectangles, triangles, perpendicular and parallel lines.
- Draw and construct diagrams from given instructions.

Functional skills

- L1 Construct geometric diagrams, models and shapes.

Prior key knowledge, skills and concepts

- Students need to know that 'bisect' means 'cut in half', and should be able to carry out measurement and drawing of lines accurately.
- They should also be able to use a pair of compasses accurately.

Starter

- Ask students to draw circles accurately to practise using compasses. You could then discuss ways of drawing an equilateral triangle and explore whether trial and improvement approaches give as accurate a triangle as using compasses.

Main teaching and learning

- Begin by emphasising the need for accuracy when students are completing constructions.
- Tell students they must be able to use compasses accurately. Setting them to a given radius and maintaining that radius is vital in all construction work.
- Work through each of the main constructions with the students.
- Discuss how the basic constructions can be used creatively to perform other tasks – e.g. an angle of 30° is 60° bisected; squares can be constructed using four 90° constructions, and so on.
- Stress that students should not guess angles and should not use a protractor when completing constructions.

Common misconceptions

- Some students misuse their compass by not having it tight enough.
- Students also sometimes do not complete, or they erase, the arcs demonstrating their construction method.

Enrichment

- Ask students to construct a variety of regular polygons.

Plenary

- Summarise the steps that need to be followed in order to produce common constructions.

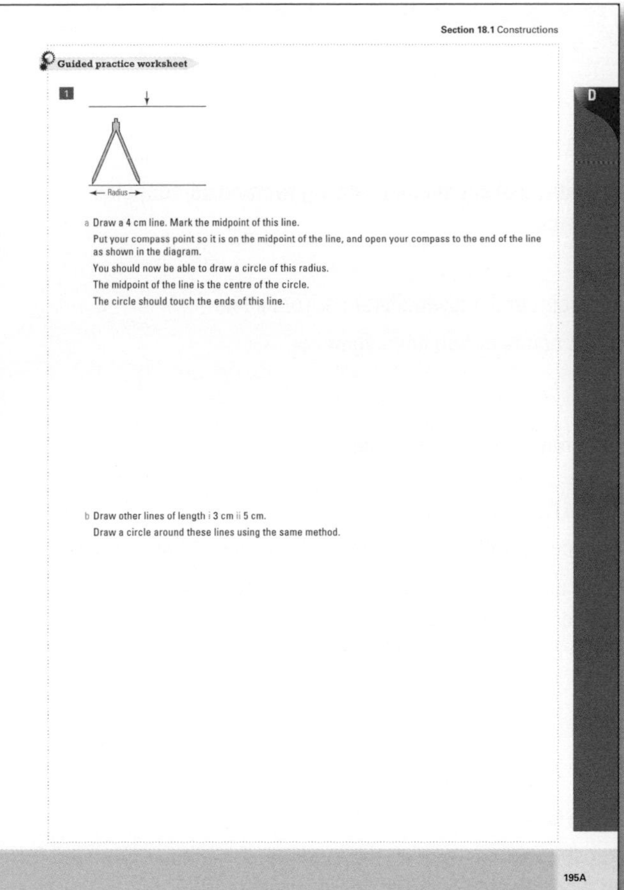
Section 18.1 Constructions

Guided practice worksheet

D

1

a Draw a 4 cm line. Mark the midpoint of this line.
Put your compass point so it is on the midpoint of the line, and open your compass to the end of the line as shown in the diagram.
You should now be able to draw a circle of this radius.
The midpoint of the line is the centre of the circle.
The circle should touch the ends of this line.

b Draw other lines of length i 3 cm ii 5 cm.
Draw a circle around these lines using the same method.

195A

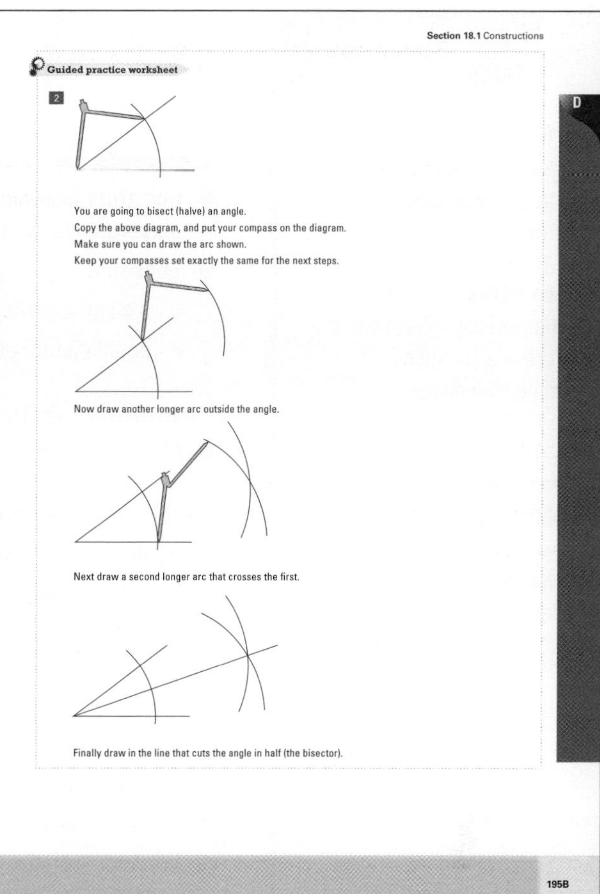
Section 18.1 Constructions

Guided practice worksheet

D

2

You are going to bisect (halve) an angle.
Copy the above diagram, and put your compass on the diagram.
Make sure you can draw the arc shown.
Keep your compasses set exactly the same for the next steps.

Now draw another longer arc outside the angle.

Next draw a second longer arc that crosses the first.

Finally draw in the line that cuts the angle in half (the bisector).

195B

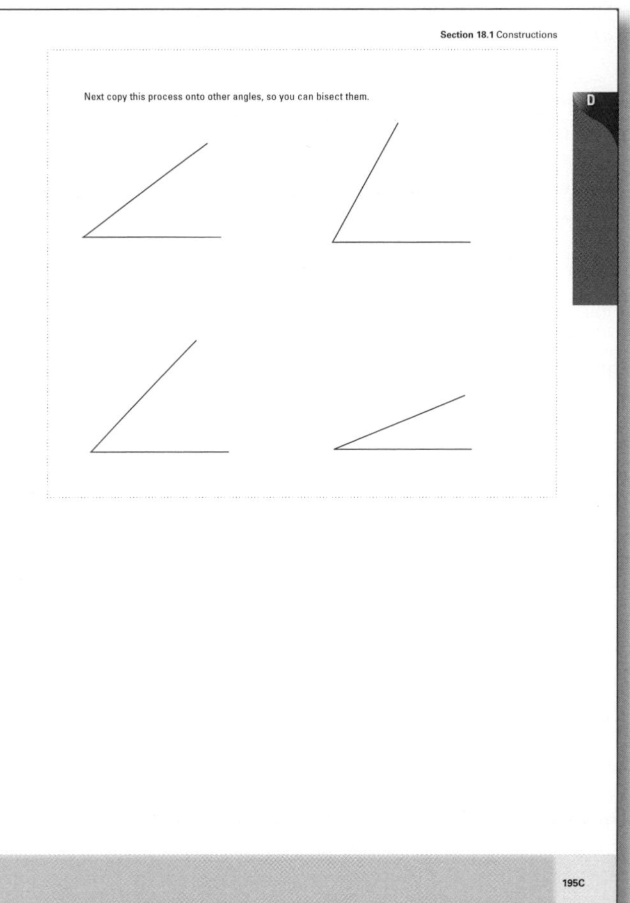
Section 18.1 Constructions

D

Next copy this process onto other angles, so you can bisect them.

195C

Specification

GCSE 2010

GM v Use straight edge and a pair of compasses to do constructions

GM w Construct loci

FS Process skills

Decide on the methods, operations and tools … to use in a situation

Use appropriate mathematical procedures

FS Performance

Level 1 Apply mathematics in an organised way to find solutions to straightforward practical problems for different purposes

Resources

Links

http://nrich.maths.org/public/search.php?search=loci

ActiveTeach resources

Hi-energy video

18.2 Loci

Concepts and skills

- Construct diagrams of everyday 2-D situations involving rectangles, triangles, perpendicular and parallel lines.
- Construct:
  - a given distance from a point and a given distance from a line
  - equal distances from two points or two line segments.

Functional skills

- L1 Construct geometric diagrams, models and shapes.

Prior key knowledge, skills and concepts

- Students need to be able to carry out measurement and drawing of lines accurately.
- They also need to be able to use a pair of compasses accurately and have a working knowledge of the constructions detailed in Section 18.1.

Starter

- Ask students to draw circles of different sizes. Can they draw concentric circles accurately?

Main teaching and learning

- Work through the three most common loci with the students. Emphasise the need for accuracy, building on the work already covered on constructions.
- Explain the principle of adding individual points until the locus becomes clear.
- Students could discuss possible methods of determining what a particular locus looks like, before moving on to a formal construction stage.

Common misconceptions

- Some students draw loci using a dashed, dotted or incomplete line/curve; rather than a continuous line/curve.

Enrichment

- Ask students to produce loci around more complex shapes, for example an L shape.

Plenary

- Recap the three most common loci, ensuring that students have a thorough knowledge of each one.

locus bisector equidistant perpendicular bisector

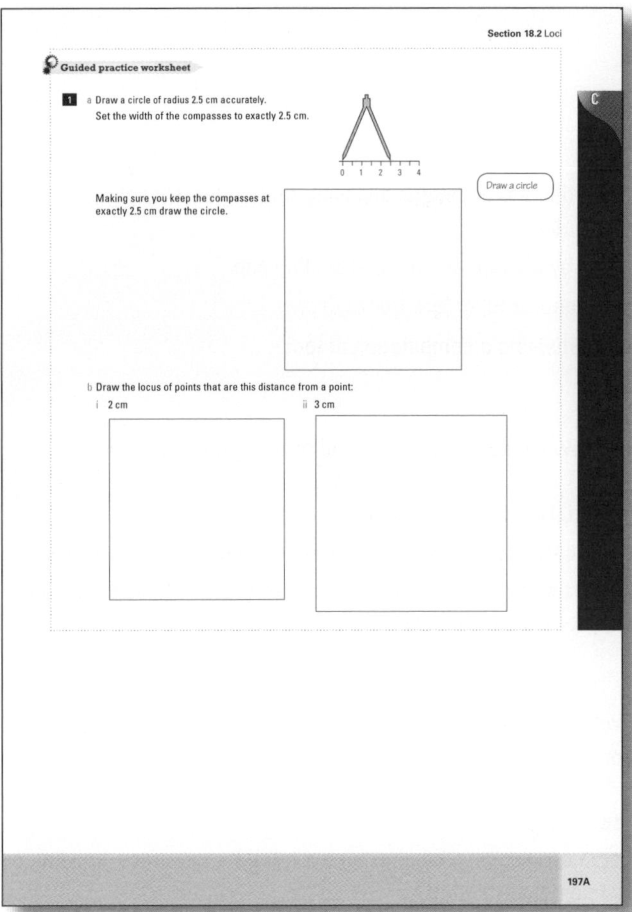

Section 18.2 Loci

Guided practice worksheet

1 a Draw a circle of radius 2.5 cm accurately.
Set the width of the compasses to exactly 2.5 cm.

Making sure you keep the compasses at exactly 2.5 cm draw the circle.

Draw a circle

b Draw the locus of points that are this distance from a point:

i 2 cm

ii 3 cm

197A

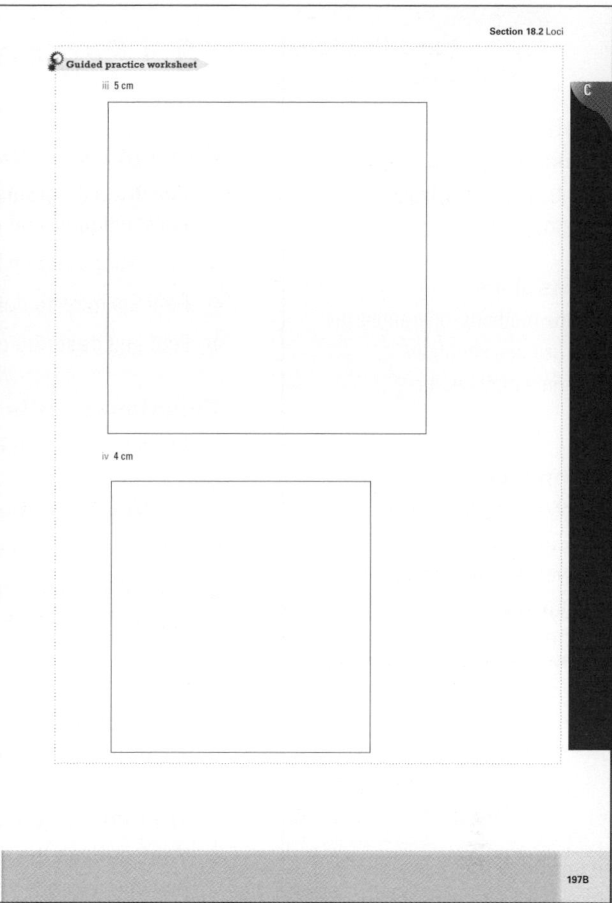

Section 18.2 Loci

Guided practice worksheet

iii 5 cm

iv 4 cm

197B

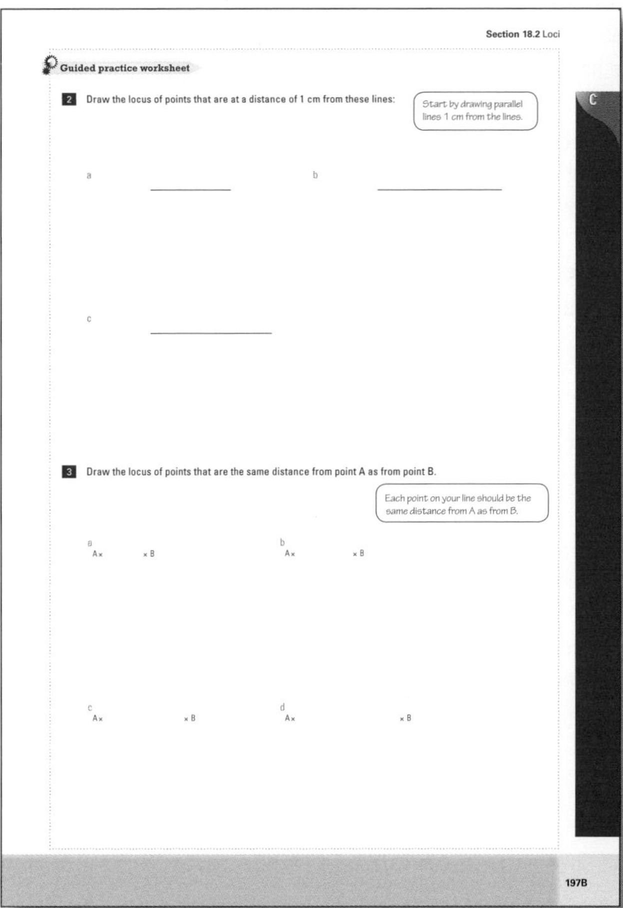

Section 18.2 Loci

Guided practice worksheet

2 Draw the locus of points that are at a distance of 1 cm from these lines:

Start by drawing parallel lines 1 cm from the lines.

a

b

c

3 Draw the locus of points that are the same distance from point A as from point B.

Each point on your line should be the same distance from A as from B.

a A× ×B

b A× ×B

c A× ×B

d A× ×B

197B

Specification

GCSE 2010
GM v Use straight edge and a pair of compasses to do constructions
GM w Construct loci

FS Process skills
Decide on the methods, operations and tools … to use in a situation
Use appropriate mathematical procedures

FS Performance
Level 1 Apply mathematics in an organised way to find solutions to straightforward practical problems for different purposes

Resources

ActiveTeach resources
RP KC Constructions and loci knowledge check
RP PS Loci problem solving

18.3 Regions

Concepts and skills

- Construct diagrams of everyday 2-D situations involving rectangles, triangles, perpendicular and parallel lines.
- Construct a region bounded by a circle and an intersecting line.
- Regions may be defined by 'nearer to' or 'greater than'.
- Find and describe regions satisfying a combination of loci.

Functional skills

- L1 Construct models and draw shapes, measuring and drawing angles….

Prior key knowledge, skills and concepts

- Students need to be able to carry out measurement and drawing of lines accurately.
- They also need to be able to use a pair of compasses accurately and have a working knowledge of the three most common loci covered in Section 18.2.

Starter

- Ask students to draw circles of different sizes, and then shade the inside of the circles. They could also draw concentric circles and shade alternate circles.

Main teaching and learning

- Work through the most common regions. Emphasise the need for accuracy, building on the work already covered on constructions.
- Reiterate the principle of adding individual points until the locus becomes clear.
- Again students could discuss possible methods of determining what a particular locus looks like, before moving on to a formal construction stage.
- Emphasise the language associated with this topic, e.g. maximum, minimum, nearer to, and so on.
- Ensure students shade the correct region. When overlapping regions are needed, ensure that distinctive shading is used, and that the final overlapping region is also distinctly clear from any other shading and clearly identified as the answer.

Common misconceptions

- Sometimes students either fail to shade the region or shade the wrong part of the diagram.

Enrichment

- Ask students to produce loci and regions related to more complex shapes, for example an L shape.

Plenary

- Recap the most common regions, ensuring that students have a thorough knowledge of each one.
- Go over each of the common misconceptions outlined within Sections 18.1–18.3 and ensure that students know how to avoid these pitfalls.

Guided practice worksheet

1 a Shade the region inside the circle.

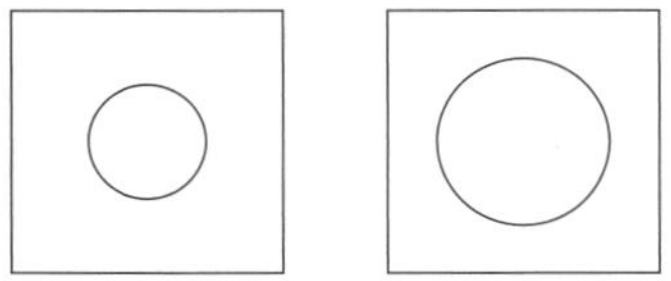

b Shade the region outside the circle.

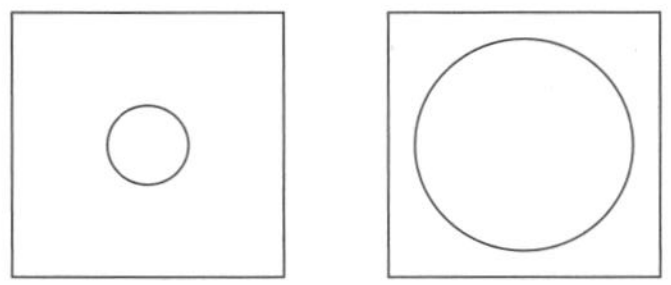

2 Draw the region of points that are each less than the following distances from a point:

a 2 cm

b 2.5 cm

c 3 cm

d 3.5 cm

Draw a circle and shade the inside of it.

Section 18.3 Regions

Guided practice worksheet

3 Shade the region of points that are closer to AD than DC in each of the following rectangles.

a A B D C

b A B D C

c A B D C

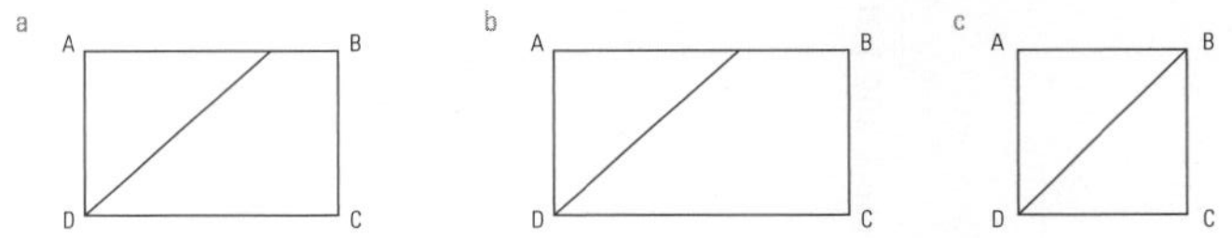

4 Shade the region of points that are closer to DC than AD in each of the following rectangles.

a A B D C

b A B D C

c A B D C

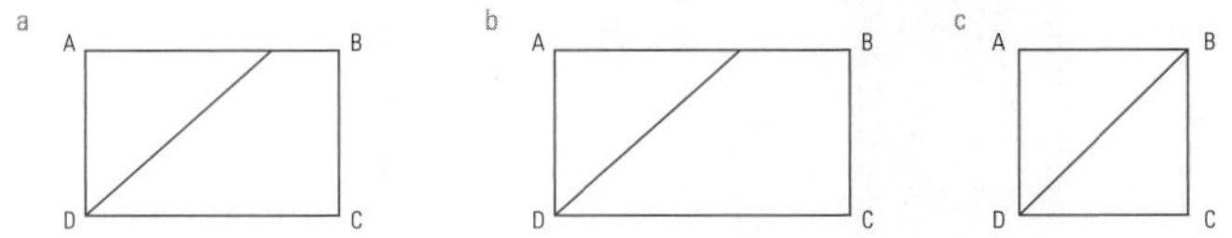

5 Shade the region of points that are closer to AD than DC in each of the following rectangles.

a A B D C

b A B D C

c A B D C

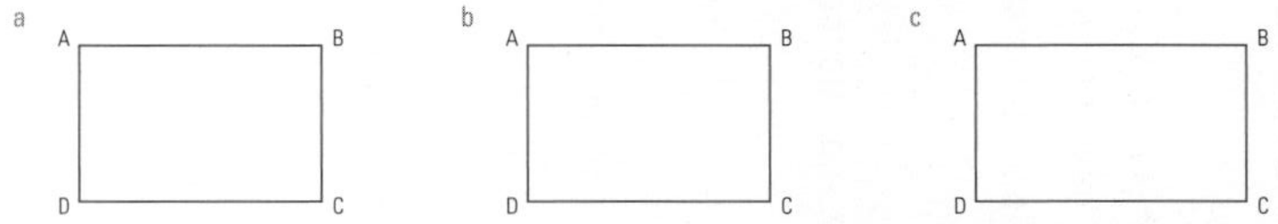

You will need to add a line to the rectangle.

Specification

GCSE 2010

N l Understand that 'percentage' means 'number of parts per 100' and use this to compare proportions

N m Use percentage

FS Process skills

Recognise that a situation has aspects that can be represented using mathematics

Use appropriate mathematical procedures

Find results and solutions

FS Performance

Level 2 Apply a range of mathematics to find solutions

Resources

Resources

Calculators

Links

http://nrich.maths.org/public/search.php?search=percentages

http://www.bbc.co.uk/education/mathsfile/shockwave/games/saloonsnap.html

19.1 Converting between percentages, fractions and decimals and ordering them

Concepts and skills

- Order fractions, decimals and percentages.
- Convert between fractions, decimals and percentages.

Functional skills

- L2 Understand and use equivalences between fractions, decimals and percentages.

Prior key knowledge, skills and concepts

- Students should already be able to multiply and divide by an integer, simplify a fraction, change a fraction into a decimal, find a fraction of a quantity, and write one quantity as a fraction of another quantity.

Starter

- Check that students can remember how to simplify a fraction and write a fraction as a decimal.
- *What is $\frac{60}{100}$ in its simplest form?* $\left(\frac{3}{5}\right)$ *What is $\frac{45}{100}$ in its simplest form?* $\left(\frac{9}{20}\right)$
  What is $\frac{30}{100}$ as a decimal? (0.3) *What is $\frac{3}{100}$ as a decimal?* (0.03)

Main teaching and learning

- Tell students that they are going to find out about percentages and how they are linked to fractions and decimals.
- Explain that a percentage is a fraction with a denominator of 100, so 70%, for example, means 70 out of 100 or $\frac{70}{100}$.
- Use a 100 square. Shade in the first five columns. 50 out of 100 or 50% is shaded. Show that 50% = $\frac{50}{100} = \frac{1}{2}$ and that as a decimal it is 0.5. What percentage is not shaded? (50%) Repeat with different numbers of squares shaded.
- Check that students remember how to write a fraction in its simplest form.
- Display $\frac{3}{8}$, 0.4 and 35%. Discuss how these can be placed in order of size.

Common misconceptions

- Emphasise the difference between, for example, 0.03 as a percentage (3%) and 0.3 as a percentage (30%).

Enrichment

- Ask students to collect examples of the use of percentages from newspapers and magazines. These could be used to make a poster.

Plenary

- Display a rectangle divided into 10 parts, with 5 red, 3 blue and 2 white. Ask students to write sentences about the diagram, e.g. 30% is blue, $\frac{1}{2}$ is red, etc.
- Ask students to write 48% as a fraction and as a decimal and explain their answers. $\left(\frac{12}{25}; 0.48\right)$
- Students could make up questions like Question 3 in Exercise 19D, which involve ordering a list of fractions, decimals and percentages.

Guided practice worksheet

G

1 What percentage of each shape is shaded?

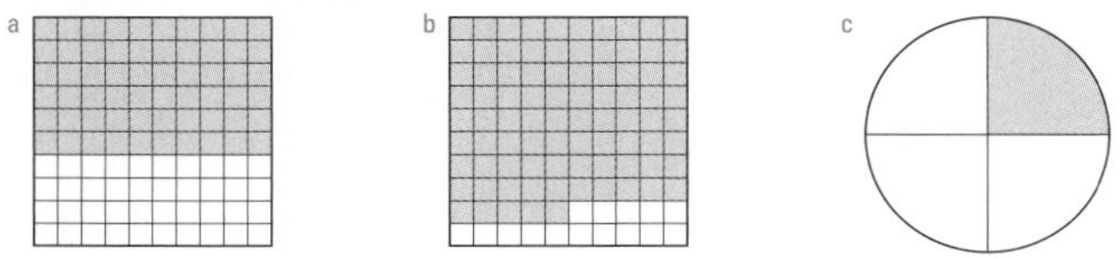

a .... b .... c ....

2 30% of the cars in a car park are red.
What percentage of the cars are not red?

....

3 Damien got 75% of the questions in a test correct.
What percentage of the questions did Damien not get correct?

Remember: Per cent means out of 100.

....

4 Write these percentages as decimals.

a 60% .... b 35% ....

c 27% .... d 80% ....

e 8% ....

5 VAT is charged at a rate of 17.5%. Write 17.5% as a decimal.

....

6 Choose a fraction from the box to complete each statement.

$\frac{1}{10}$	$\frac{1}{2}$	$\frac{1}{4}$	$\frac{3}{10}$	$\frac{3}{4}$

a 50% = ... b 25% = ...

c 75% = ... d 10% = ...

e 30% = ...

Remember: 70% means 70 out of 100 or $\frac{70}{100}$.

7 Write these percentages as fractions in their simplest form.

a 70% .... b 20% ....

c 60% .... d 45% ....

e 64% ....

Section 19.1 Converting between percentages, fractions and decimals and ordering them

Guided practice worksheet

G

8 36% of the students in a class are boys. What fraction of the students are boys?
Give your fraction in its simplest form.

....

9 Which is bigger, $\frac{3}{4}$ or 70%?

....

F

10 Write each list in order of size, start with the smallest number.

Hint: First, write all the numbers as decimals. You can read more about this in 19.1 Example 4.

a 27% 0.3 $\frac{1}{4}$ b 0.42 45% $\frac{2}{5}$ c 0.64 $\frac{2}{3}$ 60% $\frac{5}{8}$

Specification

GCSE 2010

N m Use percentage

N o Interpret fractions, decimals and percentages as operators

FS Process skills

Recognise that a situation has aspects that can be represented using mathematics

Use appropriate mathematical procedures

Find results and solutions

FS Performance

Level 2 Apply a range of mathematics to find solutions

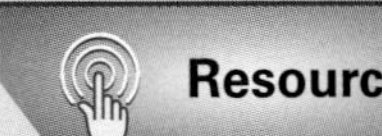

Resources

Resources

Calculators, mini whiteboards, paper (for posters and dominoes for enrichment activity)

Links

www.hmrc.gov.uk/rates

ActiveTeach resources

FDP equivalents quiz

Fraction and percentage finder interactive

19.2 Finding percentages of quantities

Concepts and skills

- Use percentages to solve problems.
- Find a percentage of a quantity.
- Use percentages in real-life situations:
  - price after VAT
  - value of profit or loss
  - simple interest
  - income tax calculations.

Functional skills

- L2 Understand and use equivalences between fractions, decimals and percentages.

Prior key knowledge, skills and concepts

- Students should already be able to find a fraction of a quantity.

Starter

- Use a number of questions similar to the 'Get ready' questions to check that students know how to find a simple fraction of a quantity.
- *What is* $\frac{1}{2}$ *of 36?* (18) *What is* $\frac{1}{4}$ *of 28?* (7) *What is* $\frac{3}{4}$ *of 48?* (36) *What is* $\frac{1}{10}$ *of 80?* (8)

Main teaching and learning

- Tell students that they are going to find percentages of quantities.
- Establish common equivalences such as $50\% = \frac{1}{2}$, $25\% = \frac{1}{4}$, $10\% = \frac{1}{10}$ and $1\% = \frac{1}{100}$.
- Discuss how to find 50%, 25% and 10% of a quantity and practise these orally.
- Extend to finding multiples of 10%.
- Students should answer the questions in Exercise 19F without using a calculator.
- Explain that harder percentages of amounts can be worked out using a calculator and discuss appropriate methods.

Common misconceptions

- Some of the questions in this section require students to work out a percentage increase or decrease but at this stage they are not asked to add it on to, or subtract it from, the original amount.

Enrichment

- Students could produce a poster explaining how to work out two or three different percentages. Differentiate by allocating appropriate percentages to students or to groups of students.
- Students can work in pairs to make sets of percentage dominoes, where the left-hand side of each domino has a percentage of a quantity (e.g. 25% of 60) and the right-hand side has an answer. They can work in groups to play dominoes.
- Give students different amounts of taxable income and ask them to calculate the income tax payable. (For 2009/2010, income tax is paid at the basic rate of 20% on the first £37 400 of taxable income and at the higher rate of 40% for taxable income over £37 400.) The personal allowance on which no tax is paid is £6 475. Up-to-date tax rates can be found at www.hmrc.gov.uk/rates.

Plenary

- Display a variety of questions, e.g. 15% of 60, 23% of 65, and for each one ask whether it is best tackled by a mental method or by using a calculator.
- Students can use mini whiteboards to respond to quick-fire questions, e.g. 20% of £40.
- *'To find 10% of a quantity you divide it by 10, so to find 20% you must divide it by 20.' What is wrong with this statement?*

F

Guided practice worksheet

Remember: $50\% = \frac{1}{2}$ and $25\% = \frac{1}{4}$

1 Work out.

a 50% of £40 .... b 50% of 24 cm ....

c 25% of £20 .... d 25% of 48 km ....

2 Work out.

a 75% of 40 kg .... b 75% of £16 ....

c 75% of 24 g .... d 75% of £60 ....

3 Work out.

Remember: To work out 10% you divide by 10.

a 10% of 30 kg .... b 10% of £50 ....

c 10% of £80 .... d 10% of £65 ....

4 Work out.

Hint To work out 5% first work out 10%

a 5% of 20 cm .... b 20% of £60 ....

c 30% of 200 m .... d 15% of £40 ....

E

5 There are 260 students in Year 7. 5% of these students were absent on Friday. How many students were absent on Friday?

Section 19.2 Finding percentages of quantities

D

Guided practice worksheet

6 Last year a garage sold 270 cars. 35% of these cars were new cars. Work out how many new cars the garage sold last year.

7 In a street there are 180 houses. 85% of the houses are semi-detached. Work out the number of semi-detached houses in the street.

8 Use a calculator to work out:

Note: You can find out how to do this in 19.2 Example 6.

a 37% of £20 .... b 23% of 40 km ....

c 56% of £80 .... d 7% of 320 kg ....

e 19% of 80 kg .... f 74% of £360 ....

g 43% of 240 m .... h 83% of £650 ....

9 Farjad earns £450. He saves 12% of this. How much does he save?

10 A packet contains 25 biscuits. 32% of the biscuits are covered with chocolate. Work out how many biscuits are covered with chocolate.

11 An oil tank holds 175 litres when it is full. The tank is 44% full. How many litres of oil are in the tank?

12 Tamsin bought a flat costing £120 000. When she sold the flat she made a profit of 17%. Work out how much profit Tamsin made.

Specification

GCSE 2010
N m Use percentage
N o Interpret fractions, decimals and percentages as operators

FS Process skills
Recognise that a situation has aspects that can be represented using mathematics
Use appropriate mathematical procedures
Find results and solutions

FS Performance
Level 2 Apply a range of mathematics to find solutions

Resources

Resources
Calculators
Pictures of items for sale (see Plenary)
Access to internet for enrichment activity research

19.3 Using percentages

Concepts and skills

- Use percentages to solve problems.
- Use decimals to find quantities.
- Understand the multiplicative nature of percentages as operators.
- Use a multiplier to increase or decrease by a percentage in any scenario where percentages are used.

Functional skills

- L2 Understand and use equivalences between fractions, decimals and percentages.

Prior key knowledge, skills and concepts

- Students should already be able to find a percentage of a quantity.

Starter

- Display a spider diagram with £60 at the centre and various percentages as the 'legs' (e.g. 50%, 25%, 10%, 15%, 35%) and ask students to find the values one at a time.

Main teaching and learning

- Tell students that they are going to increase or decrease an amount by a given percentage and ask for real-life situations in which this happens.
- Discuss how you would reduce £125 by 12%. (Two methods are given in Example 7, but with lower-attaining students you may decide to focus on method 1.)
- Ask students what the multiplier would be for different percentage increases and decreases.

Common misconceptions

- Make sure students understand that VAT is *added* to the cost of an item.
- Some students might feel more comfortable using a non-calculator method to work out VAT (10% + 5% + 2.5%). Provide opportunities for them to work out VAT using a calculator.

Enrichment

- Students could research the interest rates being offered by banks and building societies. Choose an amount to invest and, for each rate, work out how much interest they would get after one year.
- Discuss whether, in Question 12 Exercise 19H, the super-sale price would be the same if the 10% reduction is applied before the price is halved.
- More able students could be given a reverse percentage problem (e.g. *If the sale price of a shirt is £12 after a 20% discount, what is the normal price?*).

Plenary

- Discuss how to find VAT (e.g. Question 5 Exercise 19H) using a mental method and using a calculator method.
- Display pictures of several items for sale, each with a price. Ask students to work out the price of each after a 20% reduction or after VAT at $17\frac{1}{2}$% is added.

Guided practice worksheet

E

1 In a sale normal prices are reduced by 10%. The normal price of a shirt is £30.

a Work out 10% of £30. ....

b What is the sale price of the shirt? ....

2 Linda's bus fare for her journey to school and back is £2.40.
All bus fares are increased by 10%.

a Work out 10% of £2.40. ....

b What will be Linda's bus fare after the increase? ....

3 Peter puts £500 in a savings account. The interest rate is 6% per year.
How much will Peter have in his account at the end of one year?

Remember: Interest is added to the account.

....

....

D

4 Work out the sale price of each item.

a
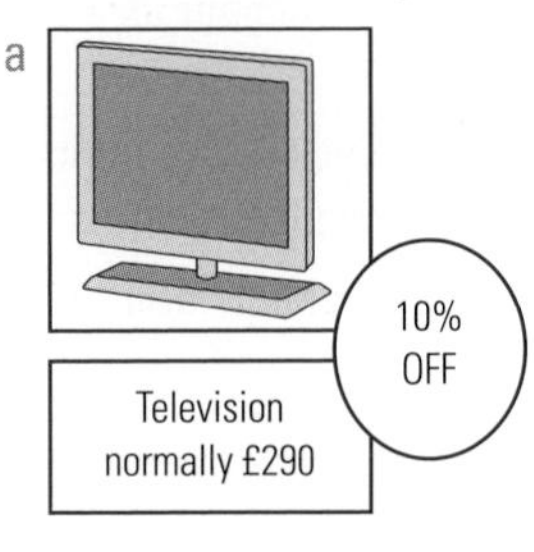

b
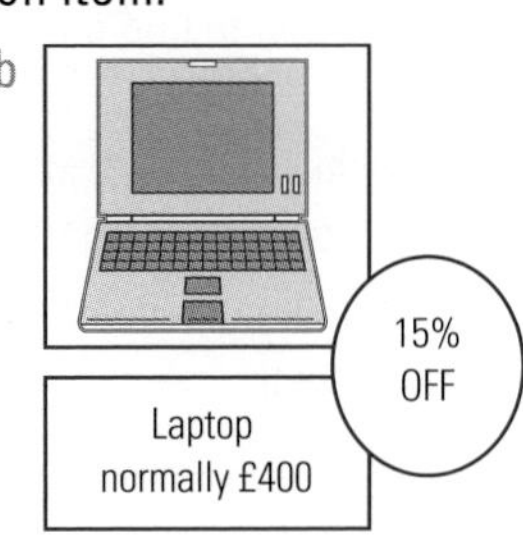

c
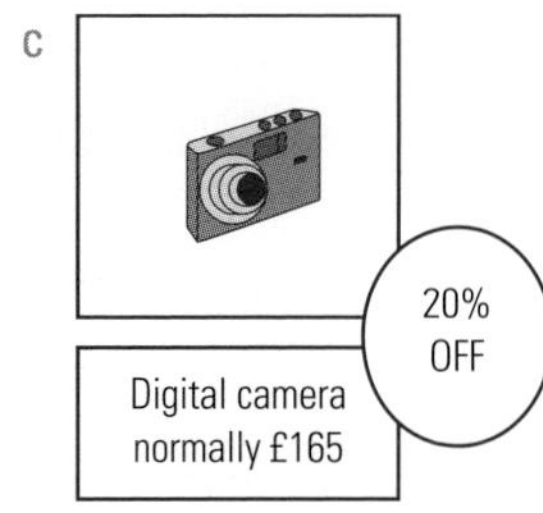

Remember: Work out the reduction and subtract it from the normal price.

....

....

5 A holiday costing £780 is reduced by 15% in a sale.
Work out the sale price of the holiday.

....

....

6 Adam's monthly salary is £1860.
His salary is increased by 4%.
Work out Adam's new monthly salary.

....

....

7 A camera costs £360 plus VAT at 17½%.
Work out the total cost of the camera.

Remember: Work out VAT and add it to the cost.

....

....

Specification

GCSE 2010
N m Use percentage
N o Interpret fractions, decimals and percentages as operators

FS Process skills
Recognise that a situation has aspects that can be represented using mathematics
Use appropriate mathematical procedures
Find results and solutions

FS Performance
Level 2 Apply a range of mathematics to find solutions

Resources

Resources
Calculators

ActiveTeach resources
Production costs video
RP KC Percentages knowledge check
RP PS Percentages problem solving

19.4 Writing one quantity as a percentage of another

Concepts and skills

- Use percentages to solve problems.
- Express a given number as a percentage of another number.
- Use decimals to find quantities.

Functional skills

- L2 Understand and use equivalences between fractions, decimals and percentages.

Prior key knowledge, skills and concepts

- Students should already be able to write one quantity as a fraction of another quantity.
- Students should already be able to find equivalent fractions.

Starter

- Discuss how to write 16 as a fraction of 20 $\left(\frac{16}{20} = \frac{4}{5}\right)$.
- Discuss how to find equivalent fractions. Ask students to give examples.

Main teaching and learning

- Tell students that they are going to find out how to write one number as a percentage of another.
- Explain that sometimes, as in Example 8, an equivalent fraction with a denominator of 100 can be found. This method should be used for the questions in Exercise 19I.
- Discuss what happens when an equivalent fraction with a denominator of 100 cannot be found easily, as in Example 9.

Common misconceptions

- Students often struggle to change a fraction into a percentage when the denominator is neither a factor nor a multiple of 100. Give students ample opportunity to practise calculator methods.

Enrichment

- *What is 60 as a percentage of 40?* (150%) Discuss situations that could lead to percentages greater than 100%.

Plenary

- *Sophie scored 16 out of 25 in a science test, 13 out of 20 in a business test and 31 out of 50 in an ICT test. In which test did she do best?* $\left(\frac{16}{25} = 64\%, \frac{13}{20} = 65\%, \frac{31}{50} = 62\%.\right)$
- *How many boys are there in the class? What percentage of the class are boys?*
- *How many students in the class have brown eyes? What percentage is this?*

Guided practice worksheet

F

1 A box contains 10 pens. 6 pens are black and 4 pens are blue.
What percentage of the pens are blue?

2 Safiyah got 7 out of 20 in a spelling test.
What is 7 out of 20 as a percentage?

3 In a survey, 170 out of 200 people said they used a computer.
What percentage of the people used a computer?

4 A cricket team played 24 matches. They won 18 matches.
What percentage of the matches did the team win?

Note: You will need to use a calculator for questions 4, 5, 6, 7 and 9.

5 In a class of 32 students, 12 students have blue eyes.
What percentage of the students have blue eyes?

6 There are 24 passengers on a bus. 16 of the passengers are female.
What percentage of the passengers are female?

7 In a maths test, Laura scored 45 out of 60 and in a science test she scored 23 out of 50.
In which test did she do best?

Hint Write both scores as percentages.

8 a Write £23 out of £50 as a percentage.

b Write £3 out of £10 as a percentage.

c Write 9 kg out of 10 kg as a percentage.

d Write 12 cm out of 20 cm as a percentage.

e Write 14 km out of 25 km as a percentage.

Hint Write the first number as a fraction of the second number and make the denominator 100.

9 a Write £27 out of £45 as a percentage.

b Write 14 m out of 35 m as a percentage.

c Write £75 out of £120 as a percentage.

d Write 63 kg out of 180 kg as a percentage.

e Write 112 km out of 140 km as a percentage.

Specification

GCSE 2010
GM k Use 2D representations of 3D shapes

FS Process skills
Select the mathematical information to use

FS Performance
Entry 3 Select mathematics to obtain answers to simple given practical problems that are clear and routine

Resources

Resources
Collection of 3D solids
Real objects in a variety of shapes, for example food tins, cartons, etc.

Links
http://www.ies.co.jp/math/java/geo/Solomon/Solomon.html

ActiveTeach resources
Expanding cube animation
Prism animation
Pyramid animation
3D Graphics video

20.1 Recognising three-dimensional shapes

Concepts and skills

- Identify and name common solids: cube, cuboid, cylinder, prism, pyramid, sphere and cone.
- Know the terms face, edge and vertex.
- Use 2D representations of 3D shapes.

Functional skills

- 3 Recognise and name simple … 3D shapes and their properties.

Prior key knowledge, skills and concepts

- Students should be able to recognise and name 2D shapes.

Starter

- Ask students to write down the names of as many shapes as they can remember.
- Ask them to describe the shapes, for example: square, rectangle, circle, triangle, parallelogram, hexagon, octagon, etc.
- Encourage students to describe examples of any 3D shapes that they already know.
- Important – have a selection of 3D solids and allow students to handle the shapes.

Main teaching and learning

- Show students a cuboid and ask them to name it.
- Discuss the names of various 3D shapes with the group.
- Now ask students to attempt Exercise 20A from the Student Book.
- Describe a shape to the class, for example: *The shape I am thinking of has 6 square faces.* Ask students to name the shape.
- Hold up a cube and ask students how many faces, edges and vertices it has.
- Now show students a cuboid and ask them, *What is the difference between the cube and the cuboid?*
- Discuss different shapes with the students. Make sure you insist on students using the correct terminology.
- Show students a prism and discuss its properties. Ask: *Is a cuboid a prism?*
- Now ask students to complete Exercise 20B from the Student Book.
- Although it is possible to teach the work in this chapter using pictures and diagrams, teachers should be aware that giving students the opportunity to handle models of solids and use multilink is invaluable in developing a depth of understanding.

Common misconceptions

- Sometimes students display a lack of precision and inability to realise there is a difference between cubes and cuboids.
- Students sometimes think that all of the faces must be regular.
- Some students forget to include hidden faces (e.g. the face between the solid and the table).

Enrichment

- Use real objects and discuss why they are particular shapes. For example, you could use a chocolate orange, cereal packet, Toblerone, tin of beans and so on.

Plenary

- Have a class quiz in which you describe features of a 3D shape and the students must name the shape that you are describing. For example:
  6 equal square sides – cube
  2 parallel triangular sides and 3 rectangular sides – triangular prism
  4 triangular faces – tetrahedron
  1 circular side – cone
  A pentagon and 5 triangles
  2 circular faces
  2 shapes with 8 vertices
  A shape with 6 vertices.

cone cube cuboid cylinder prism pyramid sphere three-dimensional (3-D) vertices

F

Guided practice worksheet

Name the shape and complete the table.

	Name	Faces	Edges	Vertices
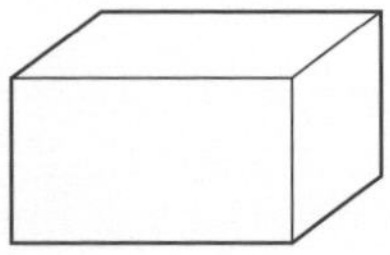				
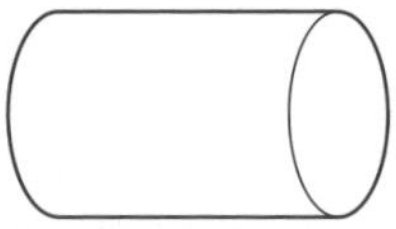				
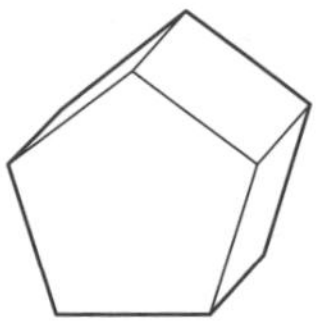				
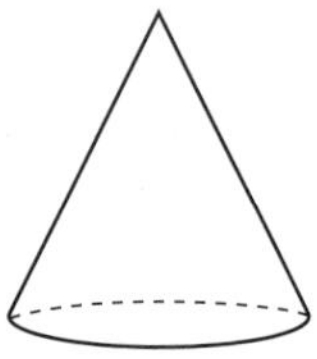				
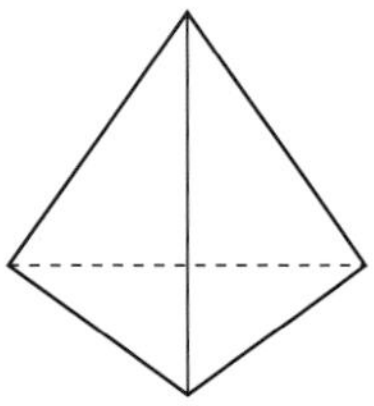				
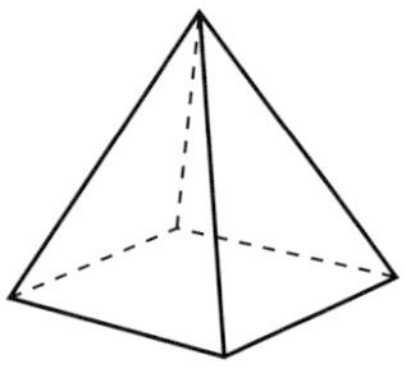				

Hint Don't forget the hidden faces, edges and vertices.

Hint The shape of the face will help you to name this prism.

Challenge: Can you find a connection between the number of faces, edges and vertices?

Specification

GCSE 2010
GM k Use 2D representations of 3D shapes

FS Process skills
Use appropriate mathematical procedures
Interpret results and solutions

FS Performance
Level 2 Apply a range of mathematics to find solutions

Resources

Resources
4 cubes and a cuboid
Isometric paper
The nets of a variety of cuboids, some of which can be folded to make the 3D shape, some of which will not make a cuboid
Pencils and rulers
Card

CD resources
PowerPoint 20.2 'Using isometric paper'

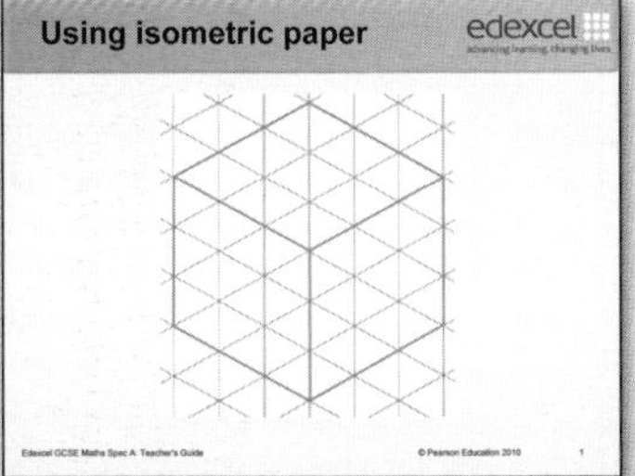

Links
http://www.mathsnet.net/geometry/solid/
http://illuminations.nctm.org/Activities.aspx?grade=all&srchstr=solids

ActiveTeach resources
Prism or not quiz

20.2 Drawing 3D shapes

Concepts and skills

- Use 2D representations of 3D shapes.
- Use isometric grids.
- Draw nets and show how they fold to make a 3D solid.

Functional skills

- L2 Recognise and use 2D representations of 3D objects.

Prior key knowledge, skills and concepts

- Recognise and name 3D shapes.
- Recognise and draw squares.
- Recognise equilateral triangles.

Starter

- Show students a cube and ask them to draw it on plain paper.
- *It is easy to draw a square but difficult to ensure that all sides are parallel for the cube. It is easier if you use isometric paper.*
- Ask if anyone knows what 'isometric' means (equal measure).
- Ask students what shapes make up the pattern on the paper (equilateral triangles). *So all of the sides are* -------- (equal).
- Show students a 3-cm cube drawn on isometric paper. (See PowerPoint 20.2.)
- Explain that the sides of the equilateral triangles ensure that lengths remain the same.
- Ask students to draw the cube on isometric paper. Isometric paper must be the right way up: vertical lines but no horizontal lines.

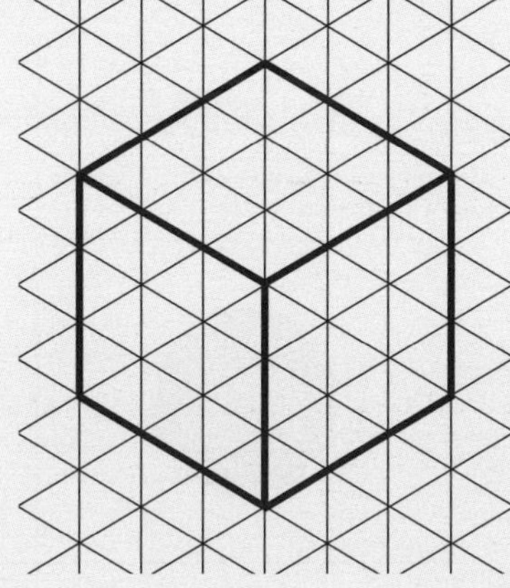

Main teaching and learning

- Ask students to draw different sized cubes – 1 cm and 2 cm.
- Continue with cuboids and prisms.
- Now ask students to practise using isometric paper by completing Exercise 20C from the Student Book.
- Show students a cuboid and then unfold the shape to show them the net.
- Explain to the students that most packaging begins as a flat piece of material which is then folded.
- Now ask students to draw the net and make a cube of sides 6 cm.
- Discuss with the students the shapes of the nets of other possible solids.

Common misconceptions

- Students sometimes fail to understand that they must use the angles on the isometric paper and not draw horizontal lines.
- Many students have problems in visualising which sides must be equal to fit together when the net is folded.

Enrichment

- Most of the packets that contain food or other materials begin as flat sheets of card, metal or plastic material, which is then folded into the appropriate shape.

Plenary

- Hold a quick quiz showing students the nets of a variety of cuboids. Students must identify which of the nets will fold to make cuboids.

horizontal vertical solid isometric net

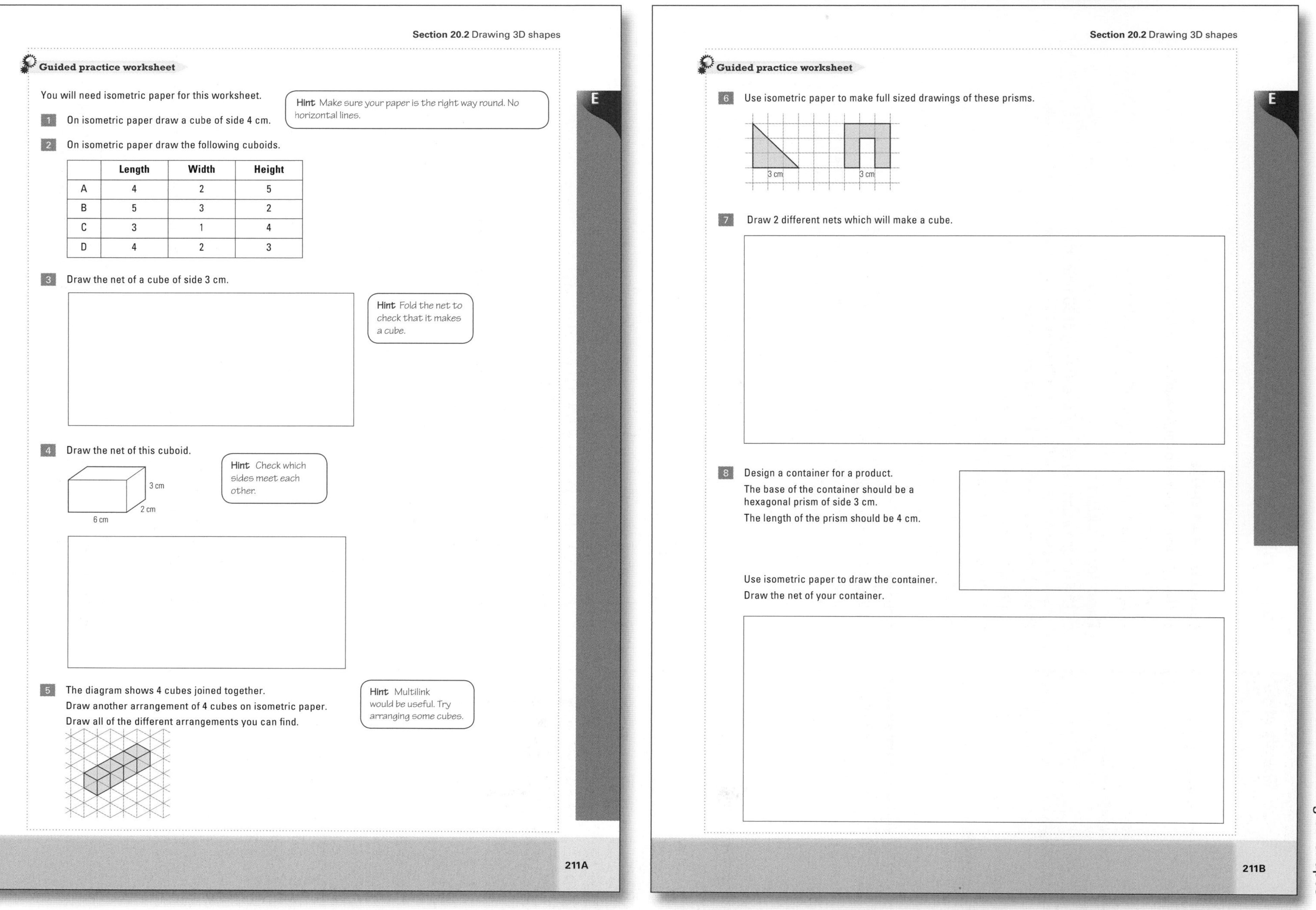

Guided practice worksheet

You will need isometric paper for this worksheet.

Hint Make sure your paper is the right way round. No horizontal lines.

1 On isometric paper draw a cube of side 4 cm.

2 On isometric paper draw the following cuboids.

	Length	Width	Height
A	4	2	5
B	5	3	2
C	3	1	4
D	4	2	3

3 Draw the net of a cube of side 3 cm.

Hint Fold the net to check that it makes a cube.

4 Draw the net of this cuboid.

Hint Check which sides meet each other.

5 The diagram shows 4 cubes joined together.
Draw another arrangement of 4 cubes on isometric paper.
Draw all of the different arrangements you can find.

Hint Multilink would be useful. Try arranging some cubes.

E

Guided practice worksheet

6 Use isometric paper to make full sized drawings of these prisms.

7 Draw 2 different nets which will make a cube.

8 Design a container for a product.
The base of the container should be a hexagonal prism of side 3 cm.
The length of the prism should be 4 cm.

Use isometric paper to draw the container.
Draw the net of your container.

E

Specification

GCSE 2010
GM k Use 2D representations of 3D shapes

FS Process skills
Use appropriate mathematical procedures

FS Performance
Level 2 Apply a range of mathematics to find solutions

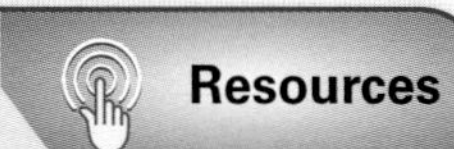

Resources

Resources
A coffee mug
Squared paper
A cuboid and a cone
Multilink
Rulers, pencils and paper

CD resources
PowerPoint 20.3 'Maps, plans and elevations'

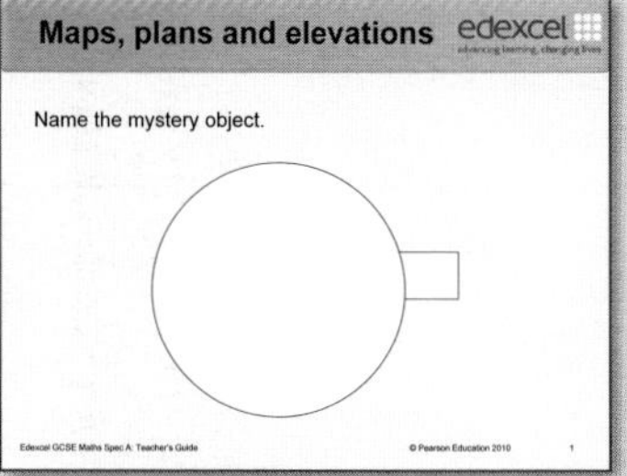

ActiveTeach resources
Volume and area quiz
Rings and blocks 2 video

20.3 Plans and elevations

Concepts and skills
- Understand and draw front and side elevations and plans of shapes made from simple solids.
- Given the front and side elevations and the plan of a solid, draw a sketch of the 3D solid.

Functional skills
- L2 Recognise and use 2D representations of 3D objects.

Prior key knowledge, skills and concepts
- Recognise and name 3D shapes.
- Recognise and name 2D shapes.

Starter
- Show students the plan view of a coffee mug (PowerPoint 20.3) and ask them to identify it.
- Explain that the view from vertically above an object is called the plan view. Ask what other views there are.
- Ask someone to sketch a front elevation and then a side elevation of a coffee mug.
- Show the students how to use dotted lines to show how the different views fit together.

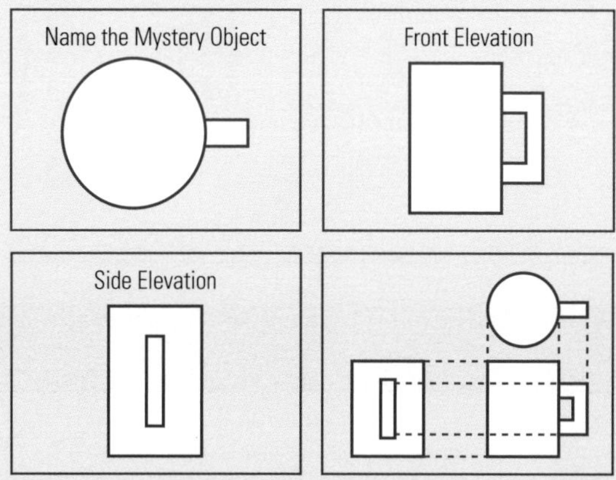

- Tell students that designers in all walks of life draw 3D objects from different views. For example, an architect will draw the front and side view (called an elevation) of a house; an engineer might draw the plan, front and side view of the wing of an aircraft.

Main teaching and learning
- Hold up a cuboid and discuss which is going to be the front elevation.
- Ask all students to draw the plan, front and side elevations and to use dotted lines to show how their three diagrams fit together.
- Hold up a cone and discuss what the plan will look like.
- Ask students to draw the front and side elevations.
- Now ask students to practise drawing plans and elevations by completing Exercise 20E from the Student Book. Squared paper might help in keeping lines parallel.

Common misconceptions
- Students sometimes fail to draw all of their diagrams to the same scale.
- Many students have problems in visualising which sides fit together.

Enrichment
- Ask students working in pairs to build 3D models using multilink or other building materials then ask their partner to sketch the plan, front and side elevations.

Plenary
- Ask students to draw an unusual view of a familiar object on paper.
- Pass the papers round the class and ask students to write down the name of the object and then draw an alternative view of it.

plan elevation front elevation side elevation

Guided practice worksheet

D

1 Use squared paper to make an accurate drawing of the plan, front and side elevations for this cuboid.

Hint Use the squares to represent 1 cm^2.

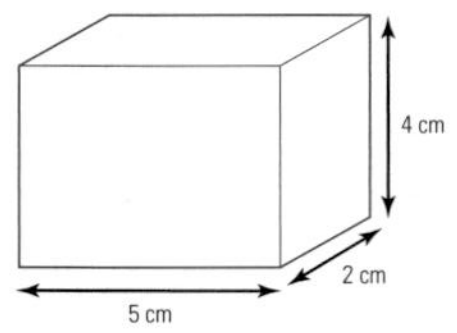

4 cm

2 cm

5 cm

2 Sketch the plan, front and side elevations of these shapes.

a

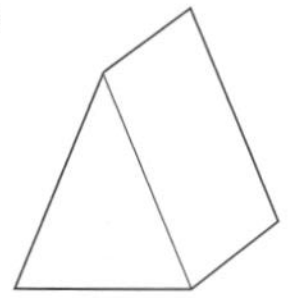

b

c

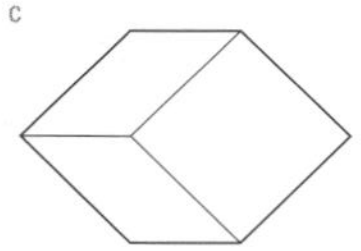

d

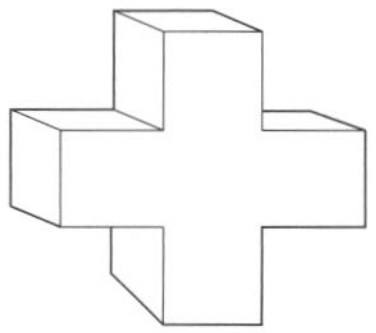

Guided practice worksheet

D

3 Use multilink cubes to construct this solid.

Hint Start with the plan then build the elevation.

Plan

Front elevation

Side elevation

4 Make accurate drawings of the plan, front elevation and side elevation of this wedge.

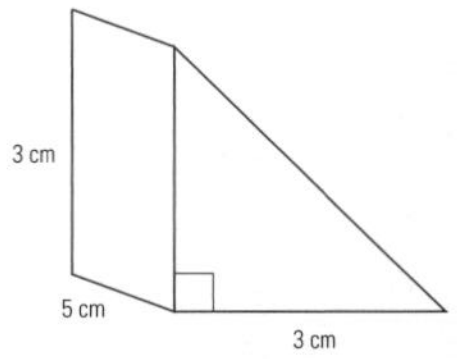

3 cm

5 cm

3 cm

Specification

GCSE 2010

GM aa Calculate volumes of right prisms and shapes made from cubes and cuboids

FS Process skills

Decide on the methods, operations and tools … to use in a situation

Use appropriate mathematical procedures

Find results and solutions

FS Performance

Level 2 Apply a range of mathematics to find solutions

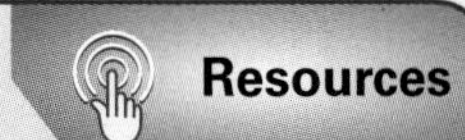

Resources

Resources

Multilink

Models of cuboids

Hexagonal prism

CD Resources

PowerPoint 20.4 'Volumes'

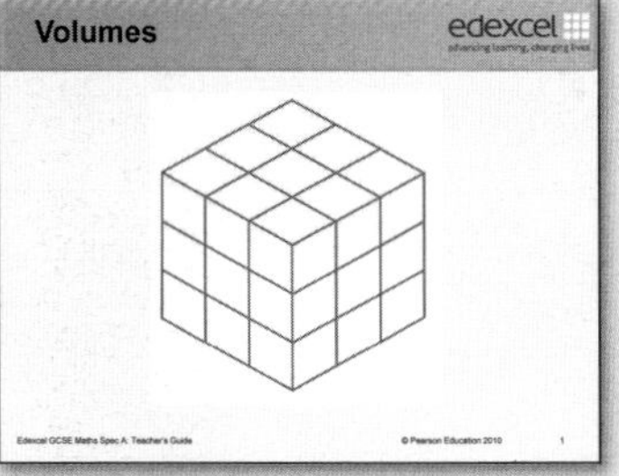

ActiveTeach resources

Multiplying 3 numbers quiz

Paper 2 video

20.4 Volumes

Concepts and skills

- Find the volume of a prism, including a triangular prism, cube and cuboid.
- Calculate volumes of right prisms and shapes made from cubes and cuboids.
- Recall and use the formula for the volume of a cuboid.
- Find the volume of a cylinder.

Functional skills

- L2 Find… volume of common shapes.

Prior key knowledge, skills and concepts

- Students should be able to find the area of a square and rectangle.

Starter

- Show students a 3-cm cube made from multilink (slide 1 from PowerPoint 20.4).
- Ask them to make the cube.
- Ask students, *What is the length of a side? What is the area of the side? How many multilink cubes did it take to build the cube?*
- Explain that volume is the amount of space taken up.
- Discuss what facts students need to know about a cuboid to work out its volume.
- With the class, devise a table on which to record their results. Show the students slide 2 from PowerPoint 20.4.
- Establish that the volume of a cuboid = length × width × height.

Main teaching and learning

- Ask the class to work in pairs to build five cuboids. Use the table to record their results.
- Ask students to look for a pattern that will save them having to build the models.
- Show students slide 3 from PowerPoint 20.4 and ask for a strategy to find the volume.
- Discuss the units that are used in measurement.
- Use Exercise 20F for practice.
- Show students slide 4 from PowerPoint 20.4. Ask, *What is this solid?* (hexagonal prism). *How would we find its volume?* (consider 1-cm slices).
- Establish that the volume of a prism = face area × length.
- Discuss the units that are used in measurement.
- Use Exercise 20G for practice.

Common misconceptions

- Students sometimes confuse area with volume.
- Some students do not ensure that all of the units are the same, while others do not provide the correct units with their answer.

Enrichment

Functional skills focus

- A lot of different commodities are packaged in containers which are prisms. Cuboids can be fitted together to give larger cuboids and are easy to stack. Triangles are stronger than rectangles. Other shapes are used for novelty or to give impact in a display.
- Ask students to give as many examples as they can.

Plenary

- Revisit how to find the volume of a cuboid, a prism and a cylinder.
- Ask the students to think about a container that could hold 200 cm^3. Working in groups, ask them to find as many possible shapes for the container as they can.
- Discuss which would be the best shapes for packing a number of the containers together.

volume cross-section

E

Guided practice worksheet

1 Find the volumes of the following cuboids.

a

6.5 cm, 2.3 cm, 1.8 cm

b

4.3 cm, 3.3 cm, 2.8 cm

Hint *The volume of a cuboid is length × width × height.*

2 Work out the volumes of the following cuboids.

a Length 4.3 cm, width 2.4 cm, height 1.7 cm

b Length 2 m, width 3 m, height 500 cm

c Length 0.5 m, width 0.6 m, height 400 cm

3 Calculate the volume of this prism which is made up of two cuboids.

9.4 cm, 7.4 cm, 2.4 cm, 3.8 cm, 12.3 cm

Hint *Find the area of the face and multiply by the length.*

4 Find the volumes of these prisms.

a

Area 15 cm², 6.3 cm

b

Area 12 cm², 4.5 cm

c

Area 30 cm², 4.5 cm

C

Guided practice worksheet

5 A tin of soup has a diameter of 7.5 cm and a height of 10 cm.
Calculate the volume of the tin.

6 A triangular prism has volume 40 cm³.
The area of the triangular face of the cuboid is 6.4 cm².
Calculate the length of the prism.

7 A large carton which has length 0.5 m width, 0.35 m and height 0.2 m is used to pack tins of beans. The cans of beans have a diameter of 7.5 cm and a height of 9 cm.
Work out how many cans will fit into the carton.
Work out the volume of beans in each can
Calculate the volume of space in the carton which is not filled with beans.

Hint *How many cans will fit along the length and how many will fit along the width. How many layers will fit into the box?*

8 A large carton which has length 1.5 m width 0.9 m and height 0.8 m is used to contain packets of soap powder.
Each packet has length 30 cm width 20 cm and depth 10 cm.
Work out maximum number of packets the carton contains when it is full.

9 A cuboid measures 5 m by 3 m by 60 cm.
Explain why the volume of the cuboid is not 900 cm³.
Work out the correct volume of the cuboid in m³.
Work out the correct volume of the cuboid in cm³.

Specification

GCSE 2010
GM x Calculate perimeters and areas of shapes made from triangles and rectangles and other shapes
GM z Find circumferences and areas of circles

FS Process skills
Make an initial model of a situation using suitable forms of representation
Use appropriate mathematical procedures

FS Performance
Level 2 Aapply a range of mathematics to find solutions

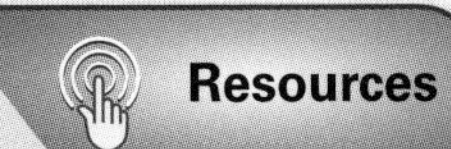

Resources

Resources
Calculator

ActiveTeach resources
Fairground shapes 2 video

20.5 Surface area

Concepts and skills

- Find surface area using rectangles and triangles.
- Find the surface area of a prism.
- Find the surface area of a cylinder.

Functional skills

- L2 Find area... of common shapes.

Prior key knowledge, skills and concepts

Students should already be able to:

- find areas of 2D shapes
- find the circumference and area of a circle.

Starter

- Work through some examples to demonstrate how to calculate the area of rectangles and triangles.

Main teaching and learning

- Explain that the surface area of any shape is the total area of its net and can found by adding the areas of all its sides.
- Demonstrate how the surface area of a cube and a prism can be calculated by calculating the areas of the sides and adding them together.
- Emphasise that all measurements must be in the same units.
- Demonstrate that the surface area of a cylinder is the area of the two end circles plus a rectangle with a width equal to the circumference of the end circle and height of the cylinder; hence the formula for the surface area of a cylinder is $2\pi r^2 + 2\pi rl$.

Common misconceptions

- Students sometimes use mixed units when calculating surface area.
- Some students confuse the formulae for volume and surface area.

Enrichment

- Students could use ICT to investigate the relationship of volume to surface area to find the largest or smallest volume enclosed by a given surface area or vice versa.

Plenary

- Consolidate students' learning by asking them to recall the formulae for calculating the surface area of a prism and cylinder.

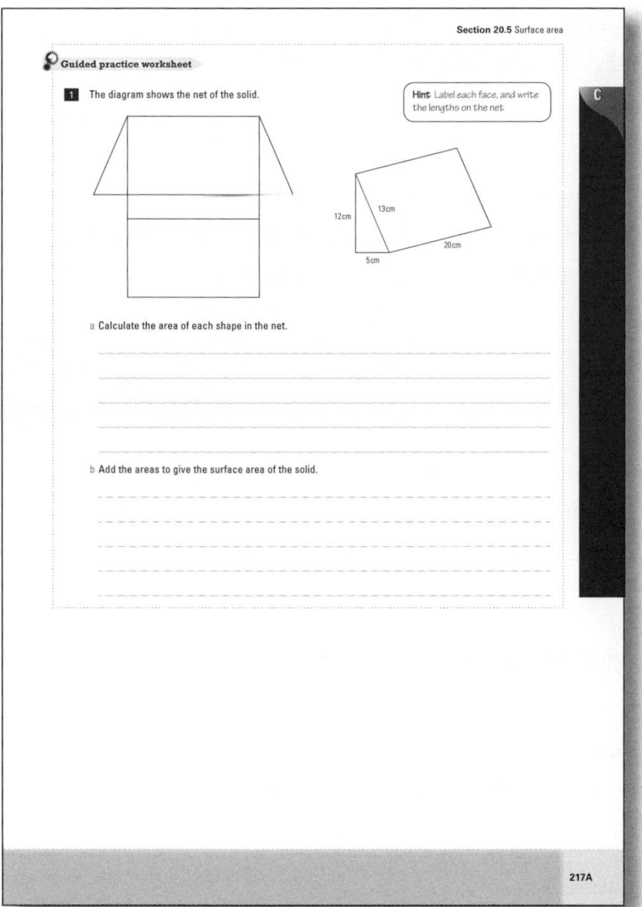
Section 20.5 Surface area

Guided practice worksheet

1 The diagram shows the net of the solid.

Hint: Label each face, and write the lengths on the net.

a Calculate the area of each shape in the net.

b Add the areas to give the surface area of the solid.

217A

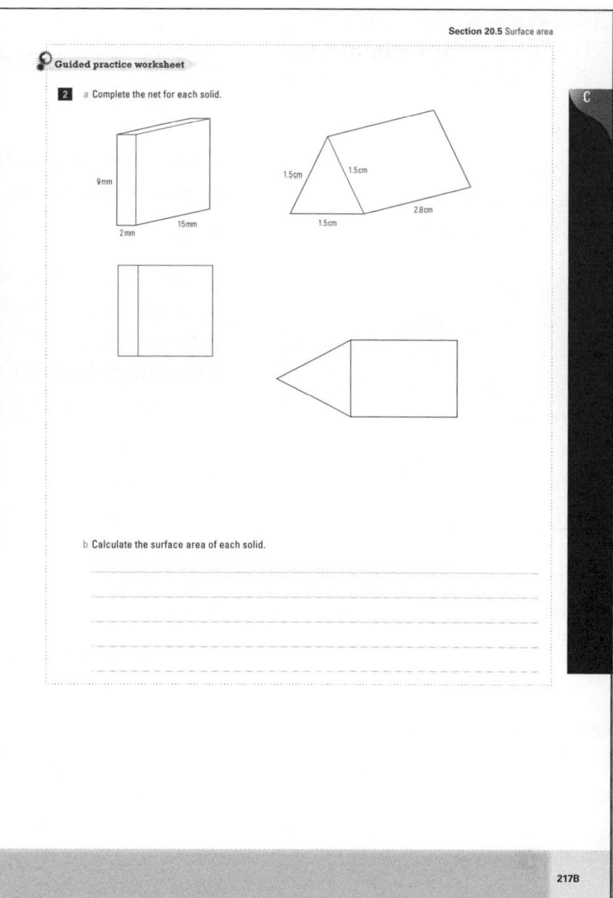
Section 20.5 Surface area

Guided practice worksheet

2 a Complete the net for each solid.

b Calculate the surface area of each solid.

217B

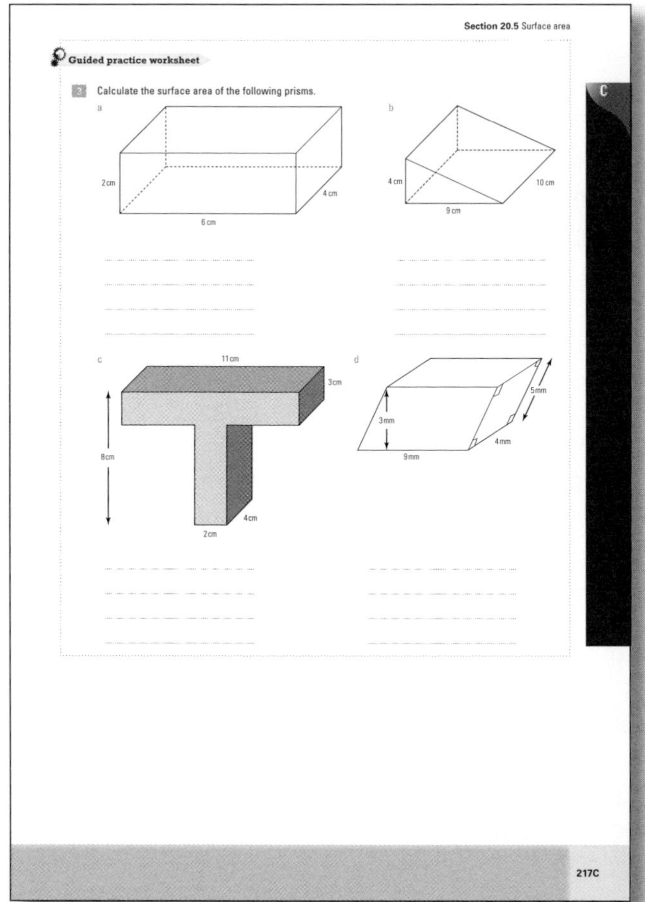
Section 20.5 Surface area

Guided practice worksheet

3 Calculate the surface area of the following prisms.

217C

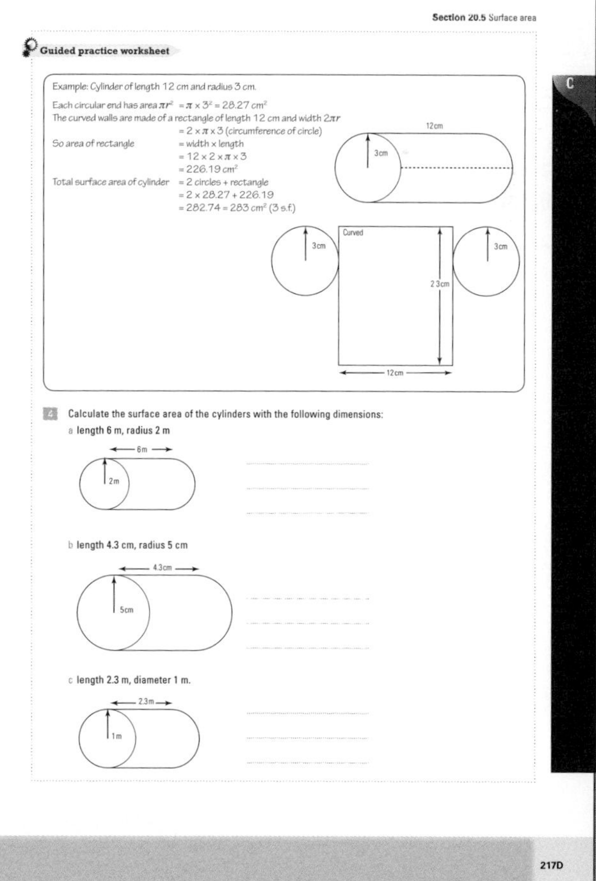
Section 20.5 Surface area

Guided practice worksheet

Example: Cylinder of length 12 cm and radius 3 cm.

Each circular end has area $\pi r^2 = \pi \times 3^2 = 28.27$ cm²

The curved walls are made of a rectangle of length 12 cm and width $2\pi r$

$= 2 \times \pi \times 3$ (circumference of circle)

So area of rectangle = width × length

$= 12 \times 2 \times \pi \times 3$

$= 226.19$ cm²

Total surface area of cylinder = 2 circles + rectangle

$= 2 \times 28.27 + 226.19$

$= 282.74 = 283$ cm² (3 s.f.)

4 Calculate the surface area of the cylinders with the following dimensions:

a length 6 m, radius 2 m

b length 4.3 cm, radius 5 cm

c length 2.3 m, diameter 1 m.

217D

Specification

GCSE 2010

GM n Understand the effect of enlargement for perimeter, area and volume of shapes and solids

FS Process skills

Use appropriate mathematical procedures

FS Performance

Level 2 Apply a range of mathematics to find solutions

Resources

CD resources

PowerPoint 20.6 'Perimeter, area and volume'

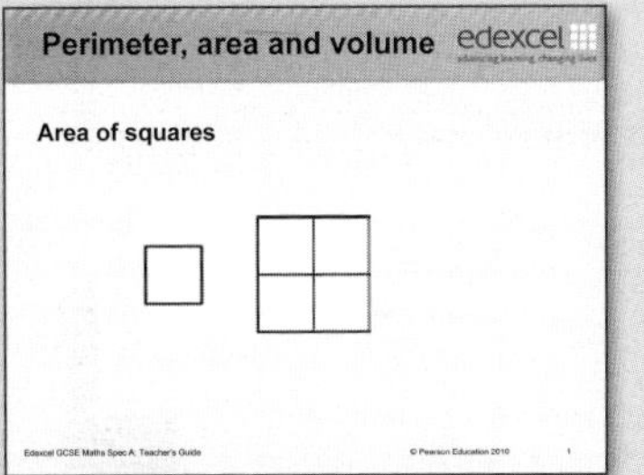

ActiveTeach resources

Setting up the fair 2 video

20.6 Perimeter, area and volume

Concepts and skills

- Understand the effect of enlargement for perimeter, area and volume of shapes and solids.
- Understand that enlargement does not have the same effect on area and volume.
- Use simple examples of the relationship between enlargement and areas and volumes of simple shapes and solids.

Functional skills

- L2 Understand, use and calculate ratio and proportion, including problems involving scale.

Prior key knowledge, skills and concepts

- Students should already understand area and volume and be able to find the areas of rectangles and triangles and the volumes of prisms, cuboids and cylinders.

Starter

Area

- Display PowerPoint 20.6 slides 1–3, which show a square being enlarged.
  What is the scale factor? How much bigger is the area after each enlargement?
- Consolidate the results using PowerPoint 20.6 slide 4.
- Discuss the results and the key fact that if the ratio of the corresponding sides is k the ratio of the areas is k^2.

Main teaching and learning

Area

- Use PowerPoint 20.6 slide 5 to go through Example 8 from the student book. Practise the skills using Exercise 20K.

Volume

- Ask students to use multilink to build cubes. This will really help to consolidate these difficult concepts.
- Display PowerPoint 20.6 slides 6–7, which show a cube being enlarged.
  What is the scale factor? How much bigger is the volume after each enlargement?
- Consolidate the results using PowerPoint 20.6 slide 8.
- Discuss the results and the key fact that if the ratio of the corresponding sides is k the ratio of the volumes is k^3.
- Use PowerPoint 20.6 slide 9 to go through Example 9 from the student book. Practise the skills using Exercise 20L.

Common misconceptions

- Students should be encouraged to take care with units and be reminded that scale factors are not measures and do not have units.
- Students must take care not to mix length, area and volume.
- Remind students that solids are only similar if the enlargement takes place in all three dimensions.

Plenary

- Recap the lesson, stressing the terms **scale factor** and **area factor**.
- Display PowerPoint 20.6 slide 10. Pentagons A and B are similar. The perimeter of A is 25 cm. The perimeter of B is 100 cm. The area of pentagon A is 30 cm^2.
  Calculate the area of pentagon B (480 cm^2).

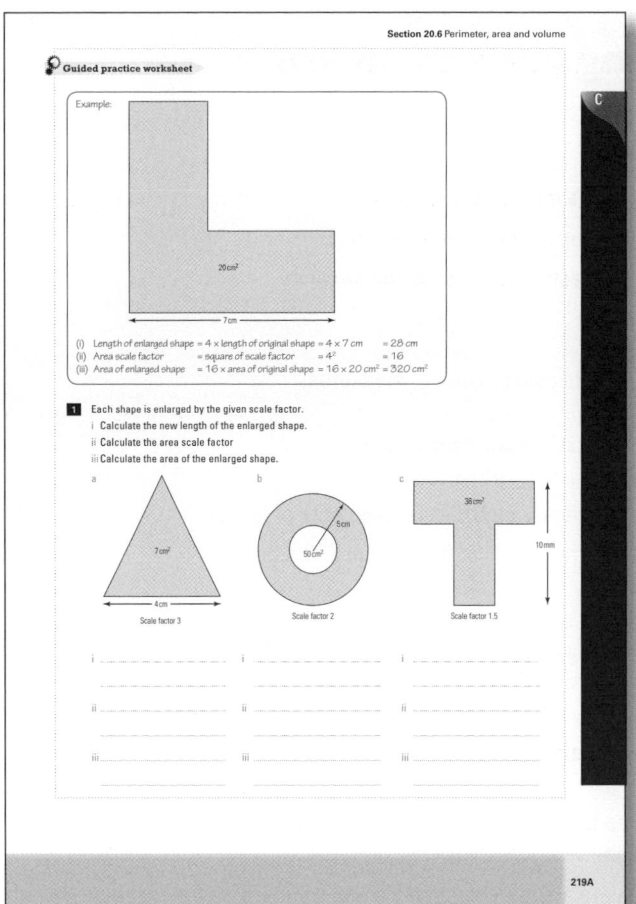

Guided practice worksheet

Example:

(i) Length of enlarged shape = 4 × length of original shape = 4 × 7 cm = 28 cm
(ii) Area scale factor = square of scale factor = 4^2 = 16
(iii) Area of enlarged shape = 16 × area of original shape = 16 × 20 cm² = 320 cm²

1 Each shape is enlarged by the given scale factor.
i Calculate the new length of the enlarged shape.
ii Calculate the area scale factor
iii Calculate the area of the enlarged shape.

i .... i .... i ....
ii .... ii .... ii ....
iii .... iii .... iii ....

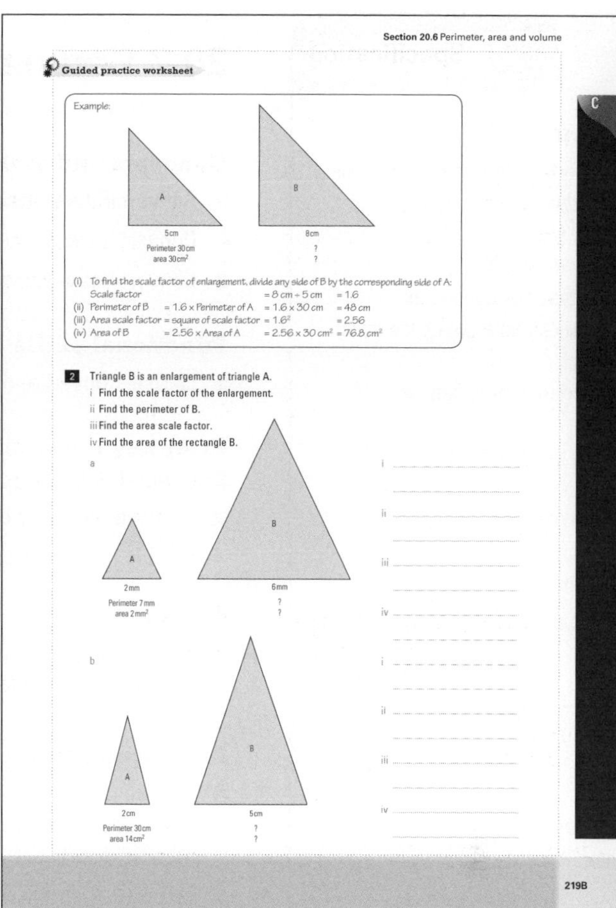

Guided practice worksheet

Example:

(i) To find the scale factor of enlargement, divide any side of B by the corresponding side of A:
Scale factor = 8 cm ÷ 5 cm = 1.6
(ii) Perimeter of B = 1.6 × Perimeter of A = 1.6 × 30 cm = 48 cm
(iii) Area scale factor = square of scale factor = 1.6^2 = 2.56
(iv) Area of B = 2.56 × Area of A = 2.56 × 30 cm² = 76.8 cm²

2 Triangle B is an enlargement of triangle A.
i Find the scale factor of the enlargement.
ii Find the perimeter of B.
iii Find the area scale factor.
iv Find the area of the rectangle B.

i ....
ii ....
iii ....
iv ....

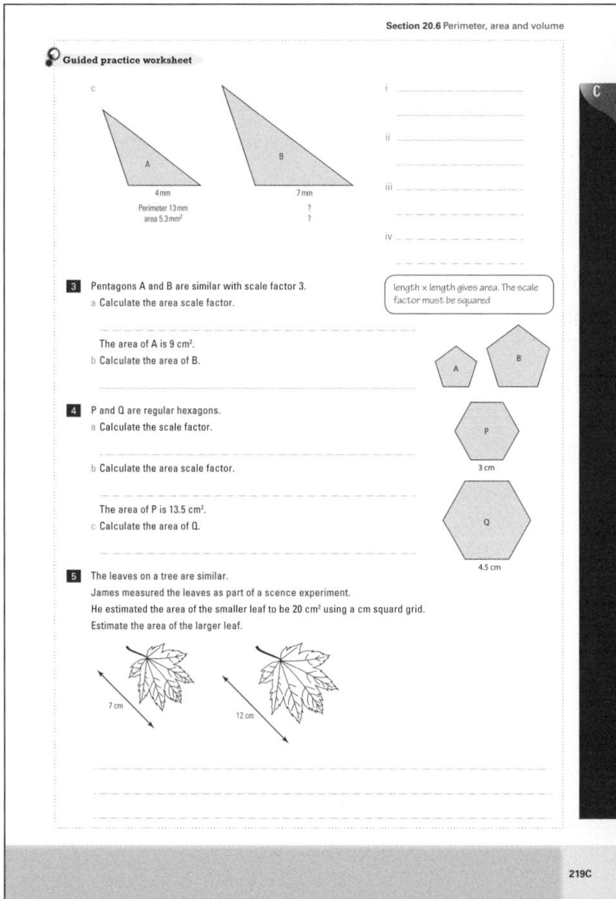

Guided practice worksheet

i ....
ii ....
iii ....
iv ....

3 Pentagons A and B are similar with scale factor 3.
a Calculate the area scale factor.

length × length gives area. The scale factor must be squared

The area of A is 9 cm².
b Calculate the area of B.

4 P and Q are regular hexagons.
a Calculate the scale factor.

b Calculate the area scale factor.

The area of P is 13.5 cm².
c Calculate the area of Q.

5 The leaves on a tree are similar.
James measured the leaves as part of a scence experiment.
He estimated the area of the smaller leaf to be 20 cm² using a cm squard grid.
Estimate the area of the larger leaf.

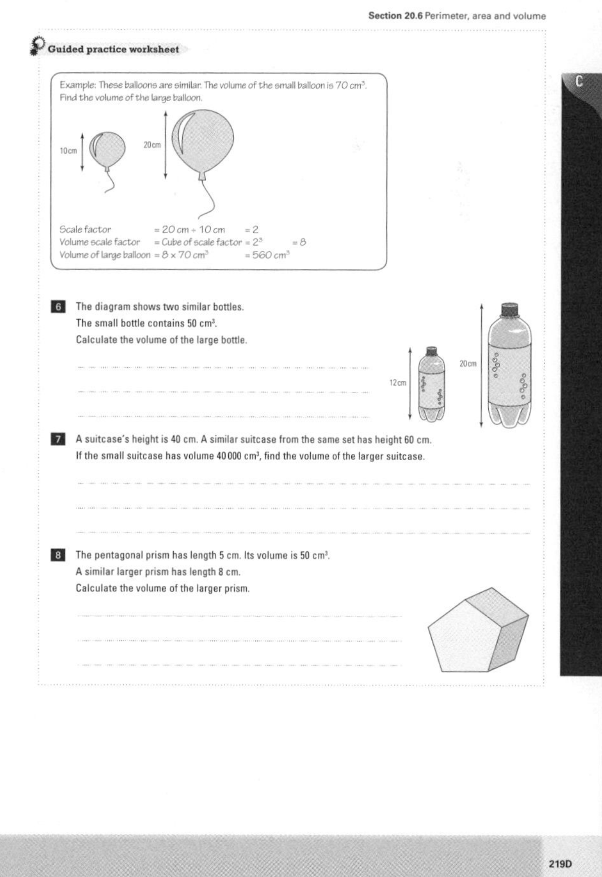

Guided practice worksheet

Example: These balloons are similar. The volume of the small balloon is 70 cm³.
Find the volume of the large balloon.

Scale factor = 20 cm ÷ 10 cm = 2
Volume scale factor = Cube of scale factor = 2^3 = 8
Volume of large balloon = 8 × 70 cm³ = 560 cm³

6 The diagram shows two similar bottles.
The small bottle contains 50 cm³.
Calculate the volume of the large bottle.

7 A suitcase's height is 40 cm. A similar suitcase from the same set has height 60 cm.
If the small suitcase has volume 40 000 cm³, find the volume of the larger suitcase.

8 The pentagonal prism has length 5 cm. Its volume is 50 cm³.
A similar larger prism has length 8 cm.
Calculate the volume of the larger prism.

Specification

GCSE 2010
GM p Convert measurements from one unit to another

FS Process skills
Recognise that a situation has aspects that can be represented using mathematics
Use appropriate mathematical procedures
Find results and solutions

FS Performance
Level 2 Apply a range of mathematics of find solutions

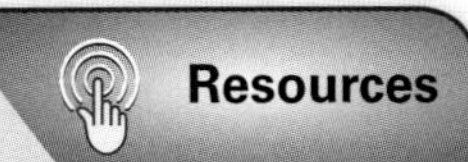
Resources

Resources
Calculator

ActiveTeach resources
RP KC 3-D shapes knowledge check
RP PS 3-D shapes: nets and elevations problem solving

Follow up
Any area work

20.7 Converting units of measure

Concepts and skills

- Convert between metric area measures.
- Convert between metric volume measures.
- Convert between metric measures of volume and capacity.

Functional skills

- L2 Use, convert and calculate using metric… measures.

Prior key knowledge, skills and concepts

Students should already:

- know conversions between linear metric measurements of length
- be able to find the area of a rectangle and the volume of a cube.

Starter

- Ask a series of quick-fire questions to test students' understanding of conversions between metric units.

Main teaching and learning

Area

- Ask students to calculate the area of two squares, one with sides of 10 mm and the other with sides of 100 cm.
- Establish that that these are a square centimetre and a square metre, respectively, and hence provide the conversion factors.
- Work through some examples converting between different volumes expressed in mm^2, cm^2 and m^2.

Volume

- Ask students to calculate the volume of cubes with sides of 10 mm and 100 cm.
- Establish that these are also a cube centimetre and metre respectively, and hence establish the conversion factors.
- Work through examples converting between volumes expressed in mm^3, cm^3 and m^3.

Enrichment

- Students could explore further conversions, e.g. imperial measurements.

Plenary

- Consolidate students' understanding of the key points that have been covered by asking more quick-fire questions.

Guided practice worksheet

1 Convert the areas by multiplying.

> Example: *Convert* $0.54\ m^2$ *to* mm^2
> $1\ m = 1000\ mm$ so $1\ m^2 = 1000\ mm \times 1000\ mm = 1\,000\,000\ mm^2$
> So $0.54\ m^2 = 0.54 \times 1\,000\,000\ mm^2 = 540\,000\ mm^2$

a $0.25\ m^2$ to mm^2 ....

b $1.4\ m^2$ to cm^2 (use $1\ m = 100\ cm$) ....

c $3.4\ cm^2$ to mm^2 (use $1\ cm = 10\ mm$) ....

d $0.024\ m^2$ to cm^2 ....

e $0.03\ m^2$ to mm^2 ....

f $0.7\ cm^2$ to mm^2 ....

g $4\ cm^2$ to mm^2 ....

h $0.0066\ m^2$ to mm^2 ....

2 Convert the areas by dividing.

> Example: $3500\ cm^2$ to m^2
> $1\ m = 100\ cm$ so $1\ m^2 = 100\ cm \times 100\ cm = 10\,000\ cm^2$ so divide by $10\,000$
> So $3500\ cm^2 = 3500 \div 10\,000\ m^2 = 0.35\ m^2$

a $4500\ cm^2$ to m^2 ....

b $34\,000\ cm^2$ to m^2 ....

c $320\ mm^2$ to cm^2 (use $1\ cm = 10\ mm$) ....

d $4000\ mm^2$ to cm^2 ....

e $34\,000\ mm^2$ to m^2 (use $1\ m = 1000\ mm$) ....

f $500\,000\ mm^2$ to m^2 ....

g $40\,000\ cm^2$ to m^2 ....

h $2650\ mm^2$ to cm^2 ....

3 Convert the following areas by multiplying or dividing.

a $0.42\ cm^2$ to mm^2 (multiply because cm are bigger than mm) ....

b $62\,000\ mm^2$ to m^2 (divide because mm are smaller than m) ....

c $237\ mm^2$ to cm^2 ....

d $5200\ cm^2$ to m^2 ....

e $0.0044\ m^2$ to cm^2 ....

f $0.24\ cm^2$ to mm^2 ....

g $350\ mm^2$ to cm^2 ....

h $420\,000\ mm^2$ to m^2 ....

> Remember: Multiply if converting to a smaller unit, divide if converting to a larger unit

221A

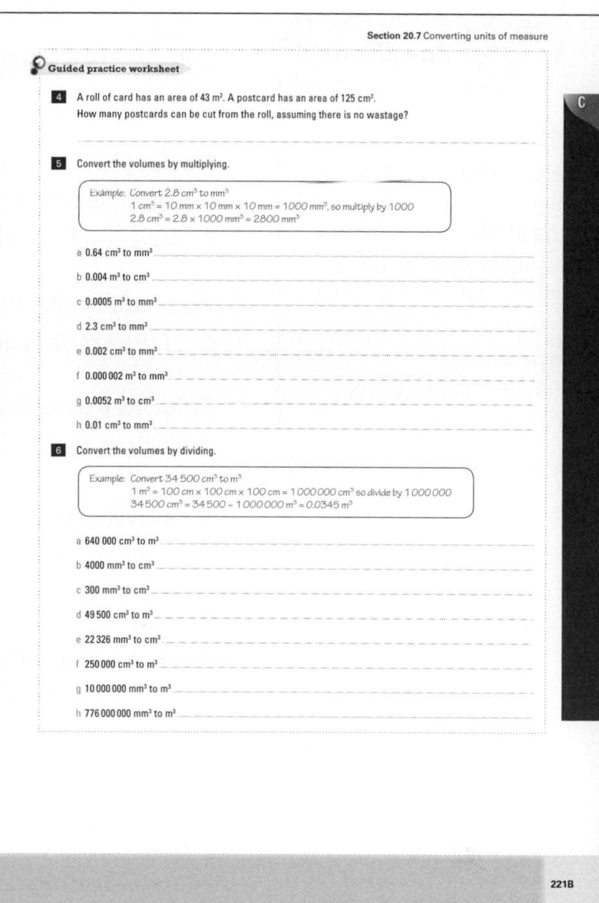

Section 20.7 Converting units of measure

Guided practice worksheet

4 A roll of card has an area of $43\ m^2$. A postcard has an area of $125\ cm^2$.
How many postcards can be cut from the roll, assuming there is no wastage?

....

5 Convert the volumes by multiplying.

> Example: *Convert* $2.8\ cm^3$ *to* mm^3
> $1\ cm^3 = 10\ mm \times 10\ mm \times 10\ mm = 1000\ mm^3$, so multiply by 1000
> $2.8\ cm^3 = 2.8 \times 1000\ mm^3 = 2800\ mm^3$

a $0.64\ cm^3$ to mm^3 ....

b $0.004\ m^3$ to cm^3 ....

c $0.0005\ m^3$ to mm^3 ....

d $2.3\ cm^3$ to mm^3 ....

e $0.002\ cm^3$ to mm^3 ....

f $0.000\,002\ m^3$ to mm^3 ....

g $0.0052\ m^3$ to cm^3 ....

h $0.01\ cm^3$ to mm^3 ....

6 Convert the volumes by dividing.

> Example: *Convert* $34\,500\ cm^3$ *to* m^3
> $1\ m^3 = 100\ cm \times 100\ cm \times 100\ cm = 1\,000\,000\ cm^3$ so divide by $1\,000\,000$
> $34\,500\ cm^3 = 34\,500 \div 1\,000\,000\ m^3 = 0.0345\ m^3$

a $640\,000\ cm^3$ to m^3 ....

b $4000\ mm^3$ to cm^3 ....

c $300\ mm^3$ to cm^3 ....

d $49\,500\ cm^3$ to m^3 ....

e $22\,326\ mm^3$ to cm^3 ....

f $250\,000\ cm^3$ to m^3 ....

g $10\,000\,000\ mm^3$ to m^3 ....

h $776\,000\,000\ mm^3$ to m^3 ....

221B

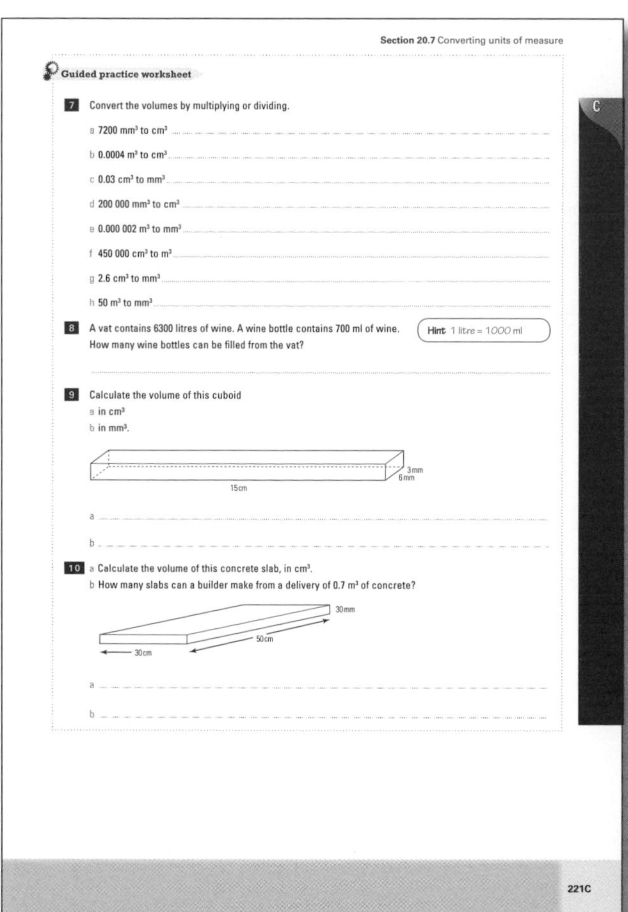

Section 20.7 Converting units of measure

Guided practice worksheet

7 Convert the volumes by multiplying or dividing.

a $7200\ mm^3$ to cm^3 ....

b $0.0004\ m^3$ to cm^3 ....

c $0.03\ cm^3$ to mm^3 ....

d $200\,000\ mm^3$ to cm^3 ....

e $0.000\,002\ m^3$ to mm^3 ....

f $450\,000\ cm^3$ to m^3 ....

g $2.6\ cm^3$ to mm^3 ....

h $50\ m^3$ to mm^3 ....

8 A vat contains 6300 litres of wine. A wine bottle contains 700 ml of wine.
How many wine bottles can be filled from the vat?

> **Hint:** 1 litre = 1000 ml

....

9 Calculate the volume of this cuboid
a in cm^3
b in mm^3.

3mm
6mm
15cm

a ....

b ....

10 a Calculate the volume of this concrete slab, in cm^3.
b How many slabs can a builder make from a delivery of $0.7\ m^3$ of concrete?

30mm
50cm
30cm

a ....

b ....

221C

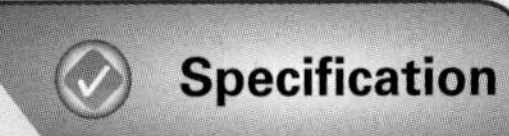

GCSE 2010

A d Set up and solve simple equations

FS Process skills

Select the mathematical information to use

FS Performance

Level 1 Identify and obtain necessary information to tackle the problem

21.1 Using simple equations

Concepts and skills

- Set up simple equations.
- Solve simple equations.

Functional skills

- L1 Use simple formulae expressed in words for one- or two-step operations.

Prior key knowledge, skills and concepts

- Students should already know number bonds for +, −, × and ÷ for all numbers from 0 to 10.
- Students should already know that letters can represent numbers.
- Students should be able to collect like terms.

Starter

- Use mental arithmetic to answer questions such as these:
  What number do you add to 5 to get 8? (3)
  What number do you take away from 7 to get 3? (4)
  What number do you multiply by 3 to get 15? (5)
  What do you divide 12 by to get 2? (6)

Main teaching and learning

- Use students' basic mathematical knowledge to set up some simple equations.
- Solve the equations using number bonds.
- Work through Examples 1 and 2 before students tackle Exercise 21A.

Common misconceptions

- Some students might not realise that the letters stand for numbers.
- Sometimes students do not realise that $2x$ is $x + x$ or $2 \times x$.
- If $x = 3$, then $2x = 6$ and not 23.

Plenary

- Check understanding of the topic by using pair work and getting students to make up five questions like questions 11 to 15 of Exercise 21A to give their partner to solve and see who gets more correct.

Section 21.1 Using simple equations

Guided practice worksheet

1 Fill in the box to make the equation true.

a 5 + □ = 9　　b □ − 3 = 2　　c 10 − □ = 1　　d 2 × □ = 8

e □ ÷ 2 = 5　　f 12 ÷ □ = 3　　g □ × 5 = 20　　h 0 − □ = − 9

2 Replace the box □ in Question 1 by a letter to make a simple equation. You can use any letter. Solve the equation.

> Example: a □ + 5 = 12 becomes a + 5 = 12. The solution is $a = 7$
> b 6 × □ = 18 becomes $6 \times p = 18$ which you can write as $6p = 18$
> The solution is $p = 3$
> c □ ÷ 4 = 2 becomes $t \div 4 = 5$ which you can write as $\frac{t}{4} = 2$
> The solution is $t = 8$

3 Express each problem as an equation. Then solve the equation to find the number.

> Example: John thinks of a number, multiplies it by 5. The answer is 20. What is the number?
> 5 × number = 20 (use arithmetic to find the number, 4)
> $5 \times p = 20$ (replace the missing number by a letter)
> $5p = 20$ (you don't need to write the × sign)
> $p = 4$ (you have now solved the equation $5p = 20$)

a Rex thinks of a number and adds 3 to it. The answer is 11.

b Toi Fung thinks of a number and divides it by 2. The answer is 8.

c Brian thinks of a number and subtracts 10 from it. The answer is 12.

G

Section 21.1 Using simple equations

Guided practice worksheet

d Kim thinks of a number and multiplies it by 7. The answer is 28.

e Gusta thinks of a number and adds 50 to it. The answer is 65.

f Val thinks of a number and divides it by 10. The answer is 7.

g Darius divides 12 by a number. The answer is 4.

4 Fill in the box to make the equation true. Try out different numbers until you find the one that works.

> Remember BIDMAS: Work out brackets first, then ÷, × then +, −

a 2 × □ + 1 = 7　　b 4 × □ − 3 = 5　　c 10 − 2 × □ = 4

d □ ÷ 2 + 5 = 8　　e □ × 3 + 2 = 11　　f 12 ÷ □ + 1 = 7

g 30 − □ × 5 = 20　　h 5 + 2 × □ = 7　　i 4 × (□ + 1) = 12

5 Replace the box □ in Question 4 by a letter to make a simple equation. You can use any letter. Solve the equation.

> Example: a 3 × □ + 5 = 17 becomes $3 \times a + 5 = 17$ or simply $3a + 5 = 17$
> The solution is $a = 4$ (because $3 \times 4 + 5 = 17$)
> b 6 + □ ÷ 3 = 10 becomes $6 + u \div 3 = 10$ or $6 + \frac{u}{3} = 10$
> The solution is $u = 12$ (because $6 + 12 \div 3 = 6 + 4 = 10$)

G

Section 21.1 Using simple equations

Guided practice worksheet

6 Express each problem as an equation. Then solve the equation to find the number.

> Example: Amy thinks of a number, multiplies it by 2 and adds 3. The answer is 15.
> What is the number?
> 2 × number + 3 = 15 (use arithmetic to find the number, 6)
> $2 \times d + 3 = 15$ (replace the missing number by a letter)
> $2d + 3 = 15$ (you don't need to write the × sign)
> $d = 6$ (you have now solved the equation)

a Marcia thinks of a number, multiplies it by 2 and adds 3. The answer is 7.

b Jason thinks of a number, divides it by 2 and adds 4. The answer is 9.

c Steve thinks of a number, multiplies by 4 and subtracts 1. The answer is 11.

d Remi thinks of a number, multiplies by 3 and subtracts 2. The answer is 19.

e Dillon thinks of a number, divides by 5 and adds 3. The answer is 6.

f Sharon thinks of a number, multiplies by 10 and subtracts 30. The answer is 40.

g Franz thinks of a number, adds 1, then multiplies by 3. The answer is 15.

> Hint: Use brackets.

h Dom thinks of a number, subtracts 2, then multiplies by 4. The answer is 12.

G

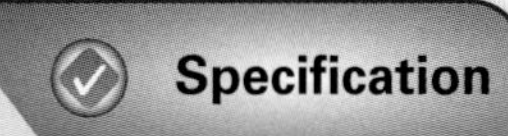

Specification

GCSE 2010
A d Set up and solve simple equations

FS Process skills
Use appropriate mathematical procedures

FS Performance
Level 1 Use appropriate checking procedures

Resources

ActiveTeach resources
Equations quiz

21.2 Solving equations with one operation

Concepts and skills

- Rearrange simple equations.
- Solve simple equations.

Functional skills

- L1 Use simple formulae expressed in words for one- or two-step operations.

Prior key knowledge, skills and concepts

- Students should already know that + and – are the inverse of one another.
- Students should already know that × and ÷ are the inverse of one another.

Starter

- Use mental arithmetic to answer questions such as these:
  What number do you add to 4 to total 9? (5)
  What number do you subtract from 12 to get 5? (7)
  What number do you multiply by 3 to get a product of 12? (4)
  What number do you divide 15 by to get the answer 3? (5)

Main teaching and learning

- Go through Example 3 on addition, then work on Exercise 21B.
- Go through Example 4 on subtraction, then work on Exercise 21C.
- Go through Example 5 on multiplication, then work on Exercise 21D.
- Go through Example 6 on division, then work on Exercise 21E.
- Students should then do Exercise 21F.

Common misconceptions

- Some students do not realise that $x + 3 = 5$ is the same as $3 + x = 5$.
- Some students think that $x - 7 = 4$ is the same as $7 - x = 4$.

Plenary

- Check understanding of the topic by using pair work and getting students to make up five equations with one operation similar to those in Exercise 21F to give their partner and see who gets more correct.

Section 21.2 Solving equations with one operation

Guided practice worksheet

Remember the balance method of solving an equation: You can add, subtract, multiply or divide both sides by the same number. The equation will still be true.

1 Solve these equations. Show your working. Write each step on a new line. Don't just write down the answer.

Example: $c + 2 = 10$
$c + 2 - 2 = 10 - 2$ (subtract 2 from both sides to get *c* on its own)
$c = 8$

Example: $9 = 3 + p$
$9 - 3 = 3 - 3 + p$ (subtract 3 from both sides to get *p* on its own)
$6 = p$
$p = 6$ (it doesn't matter which way around you write an equation)

a $m + 5 = 12$

b $k + 7 = 18$

c $h + 2 = 5$

d $3 + w = 7$

e $10 = h + 4$

f $16 = 7 + a$

2 Solve these equations. Show your working.

Example: $d - 10 = 60$
$d - 10 + 10 = 60 + 10$ (add 10 to both sides to get *d* on its own)
$d = 70$

a $y - 3 = 4$

b $e - 10 = 20$

c $n - 4 = 4$

d $f - 13 = 22$

e $8 = u - 5$

f $10 = b - 25$

Section 21.2 Solving equations with one operation

Guided practice worksheet

3 Solve these equations. Show your working.

a $s + 3 = 7$

b $t - 6 = 6$

c $r - 12 = 9$

d $3 + d = 9$

e $9 = e - 3$

f $24 = p + 12$

4 Solve these equations. Show your working.

Example: $3r = 12$ (*r* is multiplied by 3)
$\frac{3 \times r}{3} = \frac{12}{3}$ (divide both sides by 3 to get *r* on its own)
$r = \frac{12}{3}$ (multiplying by 3 and dividing by 3 cancel each other out, leaving *r* on its own)
$r = 4$

a $5m = 15$

b $4w = 20$

c $3k = 27$

d $18 = 6y$

e $9j = 90$

f $2u = 36$

Section 21.2 Solving equations with one operation

Guided practice worksheet

5 Solve these equations. Show your working.

Example: $\frac{a}{2} = 5$ (*a* is divided by 2)
$\frac{a \times 2}{2} = 5 \times 2$ (multiply both sides by 2 to get *a* on its own)
$a = 5 \times 2$
$a = 10$

a $\frac{u}{3} = 2$

b $\frac{y}{5} = 3$

c $2 = \frac{p}{8}$

d $c \div 6 = 2$

Hint this is the same as $\frac{c}{6} = 2$

e $k \div 9 = 11$

f $\frac{x}{10} = 10$

6 Solve these equations. Show your working.

a $w + 5 = 9$

b $4t = 12$

c $u - 10 = 35$

d $\frac{h}{3} = 7$

e $14 = f - 6$

f $q + 9 = 12$

g $32 = 8n$

h $3 = t \div 10$

i $3g = 0$

j $p - 5 = 0$

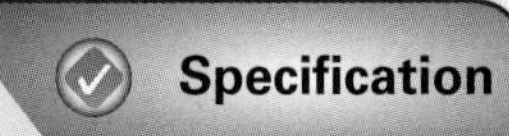

GCSE 2010
A d Set up and solve simple equations

FS Process skills
Use appropriate mathematical procedures

FS Performance
Level 1 Use appropriate checking procedures at each stage

21.3 Solving equations with two operations

Concepts and skills
- Solve linear equations in one unknown, with integer or fractional coefficients.

Functional skills
- L1 Use simple formulae expressed in words for one- or two-step operations.

Prior key knowledge, skills and concepts
- Students should already know that + and – are the inverse of one another.
- Students should already know that × and ÷ are the inverse of one another.

Starter
- Check understanding of inverses by asking questions such as these:

  What do you add to 3 to get to zero? (–3)

  What do you take away from 5 to get to zero? (5)

  What do you divide 4 by to get to 1? (4)

  What do you multiply 5 by to get to 1? (0.2)

Main teaching and learning
- Go through Example 7 then work on Exercise 21G.
- Go through Example 8 then work on Exercise 21H.
- Go through Example 9 then work on Exercise 21I.
- Students should then tackle Exercise 21J.
- Emphasise the principle that you deal with the + or – first (so that the letter is on its own on one side of the equation), then deal with the × and ÷.

Common misconceptions
- Students sometimes do not remember to get rid of the + and – first before dealing with the × and ÷.

Plenary
- Check understanding of the topic by using pair work and getting students to make up five equations with two operations like those in Exercise 21J to give their partner and see who gets more correct.

Guided practice worksheet

Remember: When solving equations with two operations, add or subtract from both sides first

1 Solve these equations. Show your working.
Write each step on a new line.

Example: $2d - 7 = 9$
$2d - 7 + 7 = 9 + 7$ (add 7 to both sides first ...)
$2d = 16$
$2 \times d \div 2 = 16 \div 2$ (... then divide by 2 both sides)
$d = 8$

a $3p + 2 = 11$ b $2w - 5 = 9$

c $5t + 1 = 21$ d $4x - 7 = 1$

e $3n - 6 = 0$ f $6g + 10 = 40$

2 Solve these equations. Show your working.

Example: $\frac{t}{5} + 3 = 4$
$\frac{t}{5} + 3 - 3 = 4 - 3$ (subtract 3 from both sides first ...
$\frac{t}{5} = 1$
$5 \times \frac{t}{5} = 5 \times 1$ (... then multiply both sides by 5)
$t = 5$

a $\frac{p}{2} + 1 = 5$ b $\frac{h}{3} + 2 = 7$

c $\frac{u}{5} + 6 = 9$ d $d \div 4 + 2 = 8$

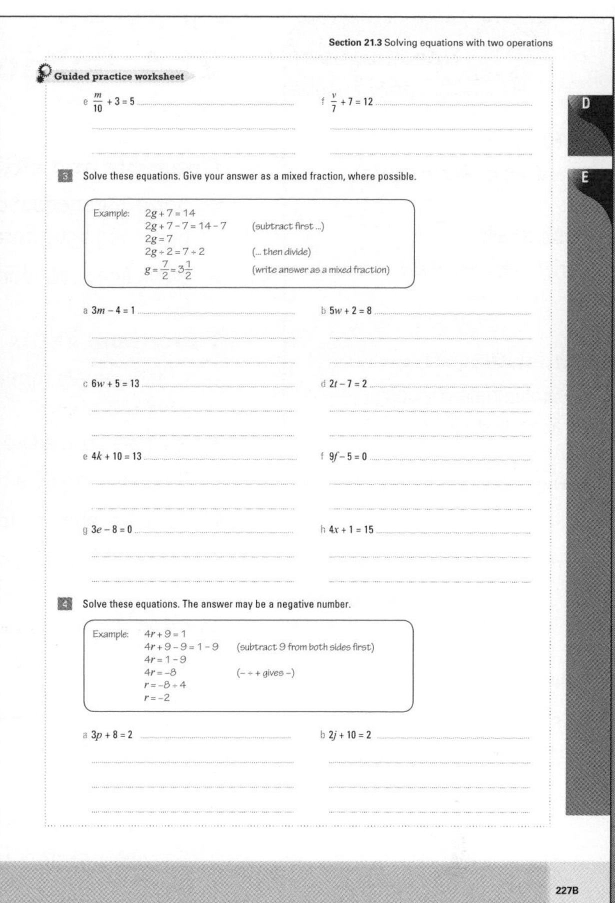

Guided practice worksheet

e $\frac{m}{10} + 3 = 5$ f $\frac{v}{7} + 7 = 12$

3 Solve these equations. Give your answer as a mixed fraction, where possible.

Example: $2g + 7 = 14$
$2g + 7 - 7 = 14 - 7$ (subtract first ...)
$2g = 7$
$2g \div 2 = 7 \div 2$ (... then divide)
$g = \frac{7}{2} = 3\frac{1}{2}$ (write answer as a mixed fraction)

a $3m - 4 = 1$ b $5w + 2 = 8$

c $6w + 5 = 13$ d $2t - 7 = 2$

e $4k + 10 = 13$ f $9f - 5 = 0$

g $3e - 8 = 0$ h $4x + 1 = 15$

4 Solve these equations. The answer may be a negative number.

Example: $4r + 9 = 1$
$4r + 9 - 9 = 1 - 9$ (subtract 9 from both sides first)
$4r = 1 - 9$
$4r = -8$ ($- \div +$ gives $-$)
$r = -8 \div 4$
$r = -2$

a $3p + 8 = 2$ b $2j + 10 = 2$

Guided practice worksheet

c $3w + 7 = 1$ d $\frac{r}{2} + 9 = 3$

e $2d + 7 = -3$ f $\frac{g}{5} + 2 = -3$

5 Solve these equations. Show your working. The answers may be fractions or negative.

a $3t - 5 = 6$ b $\frac{r}{6} + 3 = 1$

c $5y + 4 = 0$ d $\frac{h}{4} + 5 = 2$

e $4s + 3 = -2$ f $9c + 3 = 0$

g $e \div 2 + 6 = 1$ h $6y + 7 = 7$

Specification

GCSE 2010
A d Set up and solve simple equations

FS Process skills
Use appropriate mathematical procedures

FS Performance
Level 1 Use appropriate checking procedures at each stage

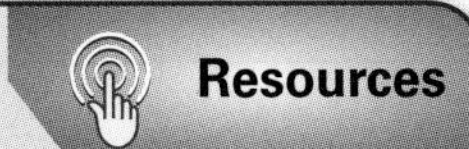

Resources

ActiveTeach resources
Solving equations quiz

21.4 Solving equations with brackets

Concepts and skills

- Solve linear equations which contain brackets, including those that have negative signs occurring anywhere in the equation, and those with a negative solution.
- Solve linear equations in one unknown, with integer or fractional coefficients.

Functional skills

- L1 Use simple formulae expressed in words for one- or two-step operations.

Prior key knowledge, skills and concepts

- Students should already know how to multiply out a single bracket.
- Students should already know that + and – are the inverse of one another.
- Students should already know that × and ÷ are the inverse of one another.

Starter

- *Work out:*
  (a) $2 \times (3 + 4)$ (14) (b) $3(5 - 2)$ (9)
  (c) $(3 + 5) \times 4$ (32) (d) $(6 - 4)5$ (10)
- *Expand:*
  (a) $2(a + 3)$ ($2a + 6$) (b) $3(b - 3)$ ($3b - 9$)
  (c) $3(2b + 5)$ ($6b + 15$) (d) $5(3a - 2)$ ($15a - 10$)

Main teaching and learning

- Go through Examples 10 and 11, then work on Exercise 21K.
- Emphasise that $\frac{x + 2}{5} = 3$ is the same as $(x + 2) \div 5 = 3$.

Common misconceptions

- Students sometimes do not remember to multiply out the bracket first.
- Students sometimes do not remember to get rid of the + and – first, then deal with the × and ÷.

Plenary

- Check understanding of the topic by using pair work and getting students to make up five equations with brackets like those in Exercise 21K to give their partner and see who gets more correct.

Section 21.4 Solving equations with brackets

Guided practice worksheet

Remember: In an equation with brackets, expand (remove) the brackets first, then add or subtract, then multiply or divide

D

1 Expand the following brackets.

Example: $5(3s - 2) = 5 \times 3s - 5 \times 2$
$= 15s - 10$

a $2(f + 5)$ .... b $3(p - 2)$ ....

c $4(2y + 1)$ .... d $7(g - 4)$ ....

e $5(3r - 6)$ .... f $4(2w + 7)$ ....

2 Solve the equations. Show your working. Write each step on a new line.

Example: $2(5r - 6) = 8$
$2 \times 5r - 2 \times 6 = 8$ (Expand the brackets first)
$10r - 12 = 8$ (Simplify)
$10r - 12 + 12 = 8 + 12$ (Add 12 to both sides)
$10r = 20$ (Simplify)
$\frac{10r}{10} = \frac{20}{10}$ (Divide both sides by 10)
$r = 2$

a $3(x + 2) = 15$ .... b $2(a - 3) = 4$ ....

c $4(d - 5) = 12$ .... d $6(f + 1) = 24$ ....

e $3(2m + 1) = 15$ .... f $2(3r - 8) = 14$ ....

229A

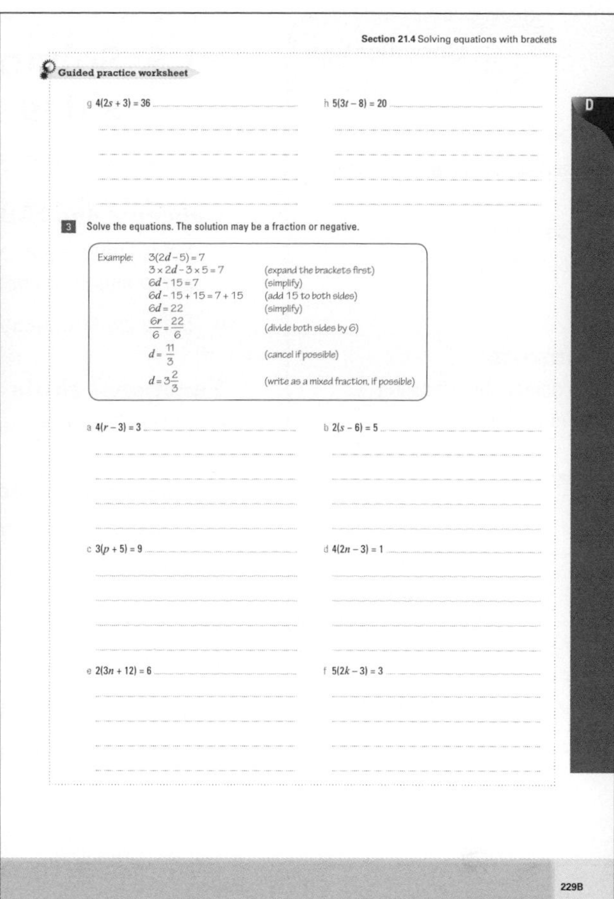

Section 21.4 Solving equations with brackets

Guided practice worksheet

D

g $4(2s + 3) = 36$ .... h $5(3t - 8) = 20$ ....

3 Solve the equations. The solution may be a fraction or negative.

Example: $3(2d - 5) = 7$
$3 \times 2d - 3 \times 5 = 7$ (expand the brackets first)
$6d - 15 = 7$ (simplify)
$6d - 15 + 15 = 7 + 15$ (add 15 to both sides)
$6d = 22$ (simplify)
$\frac{6r}{6} = \frac{22}{6}$ (divide both sides by 6)
$d = \frac{11}{3}$ (cancel if possible)
$d = 3\frac{2}{3}$ (write as a mixed fraction, if possible)

a $4(r - 3) = 3$ .... b $2(s - 6) = 5$ ....

c $3(p + 5) = 9$ .... d $4(2n - 3) = 1$ ....

e $2(3n + 12) = 6$ .... f $5(2k - 3) = 3$ ....

229B

Section 21.4 Solving equations with brackets

Guided practice worksheet

D

g $3(t + 5) = 4$ .... h $2(3y + 4) = 1$ ....

C

4 Solve the equations.

Example: $\frac{2r - 5}{2} = 3$ (here, $2r - 5$ is being divided by 2, so ...)
$2 \times \frac{2r - 5}{2} = 2 \times 3$ (... multiply both sides by 2 to get rid of the fraction)
$2r - 5 = 6$
$2r - 5 + 5 = 6 + 5$ (add 5 to both sides)
$2r = 11$
$\frac{2r}{2} = \frac{11}{2}$ (divide both sides by 2)
$r = 5.5$

a $\frac{s - 2}{2} = 4$ .... b $\frac{h - 5}{3} = 3$ ....

c $\frac{k + 1}{4} = 3$ .... d $\frac{2e - 1}{3} = 5$ ....

e $\frac{3y + 4}{5} = 5$ .... f $\frac{m + 5}{2} = 1$ ....

g $\frac{3m - 2}{2} = 4$ .... h $\frac{5d + 9}{4} = 2$ ....

229C

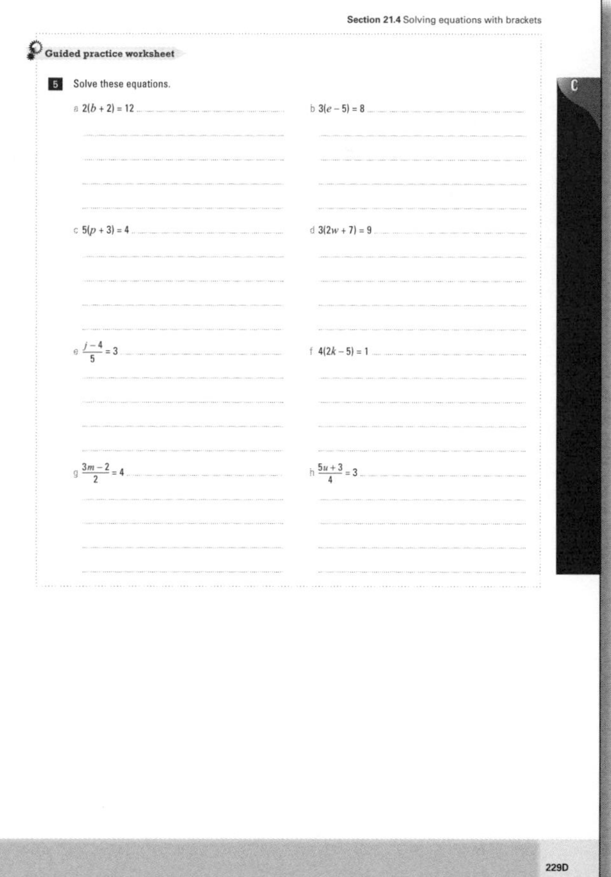

Section 21.4 Solving equations with brackets

Guided practice worksheet

C

5 Solve these equations.

a $2(b + 2) = 12$ .... b $3(e - 5) = 8$ ....

c $5(p + 3) = 4$ .... d $3(2w + 7) = 9$ ....

e $\frac{j - 4}{5} = 3$ .... f $4(2k - 5) = 1$ ....

g $\frac{3m - 2}{2} = 4$ .... h $\frac{5u + 3}{4} = 3$ ....

229D

Specification

GCSE 2010
A d Set up and solve simple equations

FS Process skills
Use appropriate mathematical procedures

FS Performance
Level 1 Use appropriate checking procedures at each stage

Resources

ActiveTeach resources
Solving linear equations quiz

21.5 Solving equations with letters on both sides

Concepts and skills

- Solve linear equations, with integer coefficients, in which the unknown appears on either side or on both sides of the equation.
- Solve linear equations in one unknown, with integer or fractional coefficients.

Functional skills

- L1 Use simple formulae expressed in words for one- or two-step operations.

Prior key knowledge, skills and concepts

- Students should already know that + and – are the inverse of one another.
- Students should already know that × and ÷ are the inverse of one another.

Starter

- *Work out:*

  (a) $5a - 2a$ ($3a$) (b) $6p + 2p$ ($8p$) (c) $4b - 3b$ (b) (d) $3t - 4t$ ($-t$)
- *Which of these is bigger?*

  (a) $4p$ *or* $2p$ (if p is positive, $4p$ is bigger)

  (b) $2t$ *or* $-3t$ (if t is positive, $2t$ is bigger)

  (c) $-2a$ *or* $3a$ (if a is positive, $3a$ is bigger)

  (d) $4j$ *or* j (if j is positive, $4j$ is bigger)

Main teaching and learning

- Go through Example 12 and then work on Exercise 21L.
- Emphasise that you should move the letters to the side of the equation that has the greater number of the letters.

Common misconceptions

- Students sometimes end up with a negative number in front of the variable.

Plenary

- Check understanding of the topic by using pair work and getting students to make up five equations with letters on both sides like those in Exercise 21L to give their partner and see who gets more correct.

Guided practice worksheet

Remember: When an equation has letters on both sides, use the balance method to get the terms with letters on one side.

1 Solve the equations. Show your working. Write each step on a new line.

Example:
$8d = 5d + 12$
$8d - 5d = 5d - 5d + 12$ (subtract 5d from both sides)
$8d - 5d = 12$ (now the terms containing d are all on one side)
$3d = 12$ (combine terms)
$\frac{3d}{3} = \frac{12}{3}$ (divide both sides by 3)
$d = 4$

a $9u = 5u + 8$

b $8e = 5e + 9$

c $7s = 2s + 20$

d $10c = 9c + 4$

e $6f = f + 10$

f $8g = 6g + 5$

g $6w = 3w - 12$

h $9h = 4h + 11$

Guided practice worksheet

2 Solve the equations. Show your working. Write each step on a new line.

Example:
$7b + 9 = 4b + 15$
$7b - 4b + 9 = 4b - 4b + 15$ (subtract 4b from both sides)
$7b - 4b + 9 = 15$ (terms containing b are all on one side)
$3b + 9 = 15$ (combine terms)
$3b + 9 - 9 = 15 - 9$ (subtract 9 from both sides)
$3b = 6$
$b = 2$ (divide both sides by 3)

a $9d + 2 = 7d + 8$

b $7v + 1 = 4v + 7$

c $8k - 3 = 2k + 9$

d $5p - 1 = 2p + 14$

e $6t + 3 = t + 13$

f $6f - 8 = 3f - 2$

g $2w + 5 = w - 6$

h $5t + 2 = 3t + 7$

Guided practice worksheet

3 Solve the equations. Show your working. Write each step on a new line.

Example:
$2g + 7 = 5g - 5$
$2g - 2g + 7 = 5g - 2g - 5$ (subtract 2g from both sides)
$7 = 5g - 2g - 5$ (terms containing g are all on one side)
$7 = 3g - 5$ (combine terms)
$7 + 5 = 3g - 5 + 5$ (add 5 to both sides)
$12 = 3g$
$4 = g$ (divide both sides by 3)
$g = 4$

a $3t + 8 = 5t$

b $2e + 10 = 7e$

c $2u + 9 = 4u + 3$

d $r + 6 = 4r$

e $3h + 8 = h - 2$

f $5f + 12 = 7f + 4$

g $2d - 7 = 5d - 10$

h $2k = 7k - 15$

Guided practice worksheet

4 Solve the equations. Write solutions as mixed fractions, where possible.

a $6p = 2p + 15$

b $r + 9 = 5r$

c $2e - 10 = 6e + 2$

d $3m + 12 = 7m - 2$

e $10a - 7 = a - 1$

f $b = 10b + 3$

5 Solve the equations. Expand the brackets first.

a $2(m + 1) = 5m$

b $3(2w - 4) = 2w$

c $7v = 2(v + 5)$

d $3(e - 1) = 2(e + 6)$

Specification

GCSE 2010
A d Set up and solve simple equations

FS Process skills
Use appropriate mathematical procedures

FS Performance
Level 1 Use appropriate checking procedures at each stage

21.6 Solving equations with negative coefficients

Concepts and skills

- Solve linear equations, with integer coefficients, in which the unknown appears on either side or on both sides of the equation.
- Solve linear equations which contain brackets, including those that have negative signs occurring anywhere in the equation, and those with a negative solution.
- Solve linear equations in one unknown, with integer or fractional coefficients.

Functional skills

- L1 Use simple formulae expressed in words for one- or two-step operations.

Prior key knowledge, skills and concepts

- Students should already know that + and – are the inverse of one another.
- Students should already know that × and ÷ are the inverse of one another.
- Students should already be able to order negative numbers.

Starter

- *Work out:*

  (a) $4a - 2a$ ($2a$) (b) $3p + 2p$ ($5p$) (c) $4b - b$ ($3b$) (d) $2t - 4t$ ($-2t$)
- *Which of these is bigger?*

  (a) $3p$ *or* $2p$ (if p is positive, $3p$ is bigger)

  (b) $2t$ *or* $-3t$ (if t is positive, $2t$ is bigger)

  (c) $-2a$ *or* $3a$ (if a is positive, $3a$ is bigger)

  (d) $4j$ *or* j (if j is positive, $4j$ is bigger)

Main teaching and learning

- Go through Example 13.
- Get students to work on Exercise 21M.

Common misconceptions

- Students need to realise that $-x = 7$ means that $x = -7$ and $-x = -7$ means that $x = 7$.

Plenary

- Check understanding of the topic by using pair work and getting students to make up five equations with negative coefficients like those in Exercise 21M to give their partner and see who gets more correct.

Guided practice worksheet

1 Solve the equations. Show your working. Write each step on a new line.

Example:
$15 - 2d = 1$
$15 - 2d + 2d = 1 + 2d$ (add $2d$ to both sides)
$15 = 1 + 2d$
$15 - 1 = 1 - 1 + 2d$ (take 1 from both sides)
$14 = 2d$
$d = 7$ (divide both sides by 2)

a $16 - 3f = 1$

b $10 - 2g = 2$

c $20 - 5e = 10$

d $14 = 2 - 4m$

e $8 = 6 - 2y$

f $24 = 8 - 2f$

2 Solve the equations. Show your working. Write each step on a new line.

Example:
$10 - 4t = 6t$
$10 - 4t + 4t = 6t + 4t$ (add $4t$ to both sides)
$10 = 6t + 4t$ (now the terms with t are all on one side)
$10 = 10t$ (add like terms)
$1 = t$ (divide both sides by 10)
$t = 1$

a $8 - 2e = 2e$

b $12 - 3b = b$

c $20 - 2k = 3k$

d $5t = 16 - 3t$

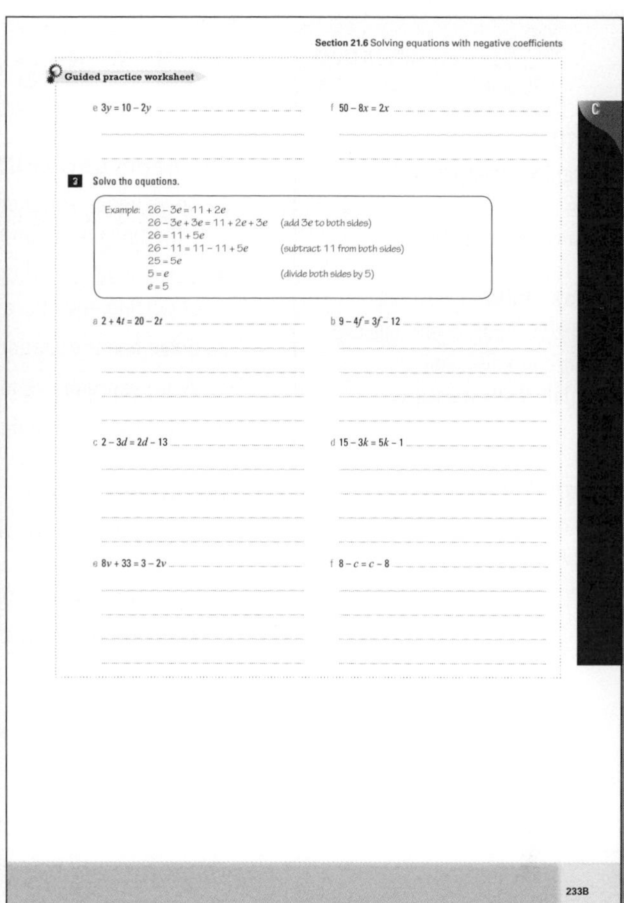

Guided practice worksheet

e $3y = 10 - 2y$

f $50 - 8x = 2x$

3 Solve the equations.

Example:
$26 - 3e = 11 + 2e$
$26 - 3e + 3e = 11 + 2e + 3e$ (add $3e$ to both sides)
$26 = 11 + 5e$
$26 - 11 = 11 - 11 + 5e$ (subtract 11 from both sides)
$25 = 5e$
$5 = e$ (divide both sides by 5)
$e = 5$

a $2 + 4t = 20 - 2t$

b $9 - 4f = 3f - 12$

c $2 - 3d = 2d - 13$

d $15 - 3k = 5k - 1$

e $8v + 33 = 3 - 2v$

f $8 - c = c - 8$

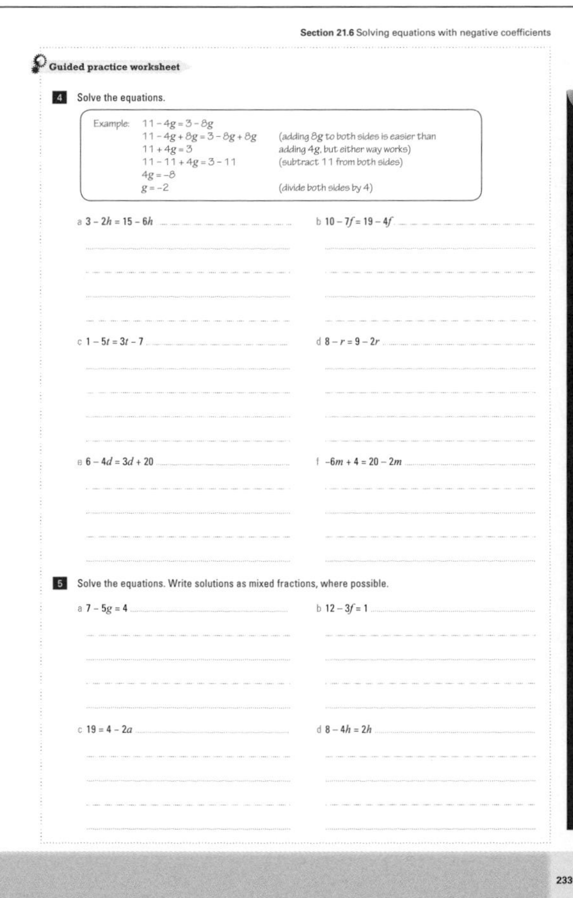

Guided practice worksheet

4 Solve the equations.

Example:
$11 - 4g = 3 - 8g$
$11 - 4g + 8g = 3 - 8g + 8g$ (adding $8g$ to both sides is easier than adding $4g$, but either way works)
$11 + 4g = 3$
$11 - 11 + 4g = 3 - 11$ (subtract 11 from both sides)
$4g = -8$
$g = -2$ (divide both sides by 4)

a $3 - 2h = 15 - 6h$

b $10 - 7f = 19 - 4f$

c $1 - 5t = 3t - 7$

d $8 - r = 9 - 2r$

e $6 - 4d = 3d + 20$

f $-6m + 4 = 20 - 2m$

5 Solve the equations. Write solutions as mixed fractions, where possible.

a $7 - 5g = 4$

b $12 - 3f = 1$

c $19 = 4 - 2a$

d $8 - 4h = 2h$

Guided practice worksheet

e $9 + 2s = 17 - s$

f $4 - b = b + 4$

g $10 - 6j = 23 - j$

h $3f + 18 = 4(2 - f)$

Specification

GCSE 2010

A c (part) Manipulate algebraic expressions …

A d Set up and solve simple equations

FS Process skills

Decide on the methods, operations and tools … to use in a situation

Use appropriate mathematical procedures

FS Performance

Level 1 Use appropriate checking procedures at each stage

21.7 Using equations to solve problems

Concepts and skills

- Solve linear equations, with integer coefficients, in which the unknown appears on either side or on both sides of the equations.
- Solve linear equations which contain brackets, including those that have negative signs occurring anywhere in the equation, and these with a negative solution.
- Solve linear equations in one unknown, with integer and fractional coefficients.
- Write expressions to solve problems.
- Use algebraic manipulation to solve problems.

Functional skills

- L1 Use simple formulae expressed in words for one- or two-step operations.

Prior key knowledge, skills and concepts

- Students should already be able to solve equations.

Starter

- *Solve these equations:*

(a) $a + 5 = 7$ ($a = 2$)

(b) $b - 4 = 2$ ($b = 2$)

(c) $3c = 12$ ($c = 4$)

(d) $\frac{x}{6} = 2$ ($x = 12$)

(e) $2b + 3 = 11$ ($b = 4$)

(f) $3c - 7 = 2$ ($c = 3$)

(g) $3(x + 2) = 12$ ($x = 2$)

(h) $5(2p - 1) = 10$ ($p = 1.5$)

(i) $3t + 2 = t - 5$ ($t = -3.5$)

(j) $4p + 5 = 3 - 2p$ $\left(p = \frac{1}{3}\right)$

Main teaching and learning

- Go through Example 14.
- Get students to work on Exercise 21N.

Enrichment

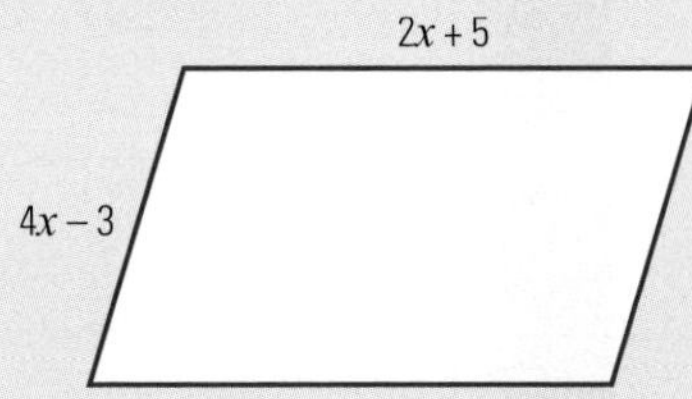

- *Two sides of a rhombus have sides of length $2x + 5$ and $4x - 3$. Find the perimeter of the rhombus.* ($12x + 4$)

Plenary

- Check understanding of the topic by using pair work and getting students to make up two questions like those in Exercise 21N that can be solved using equations to give to their partner and seeing who gets more correct.

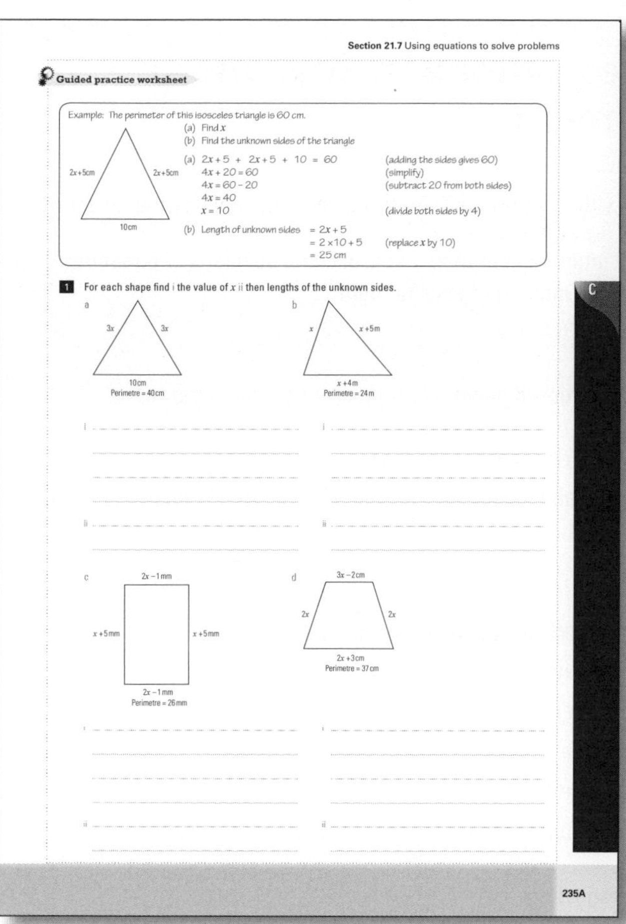

Section 21.7 Using equations to solve problems

Guided practice worksheet

Example: The perimeter of this isosceles triangle is 60 cm.
(a) Find x
(b) Find the unknown sides of the triangle

(a) $2x+5 + 2x+5 + 10 = 60$ (adding the sides gives 60)
$4x + 20 = 60$ (simplify)
$4x = 60 - 20$ (subtract 20 from both sides)
$4x = 40$
$x = 10$ (divide both sides by 4)

(b) Length of unknown sides $= 2x + 5$
$= 2 \times 10 + 5$ (replace x by 10)
$= 25$ cm

1 For each shape find i the value of x ii then lengths of the unknown sides.

a

b

i

ii

c

d

i

ii

235A

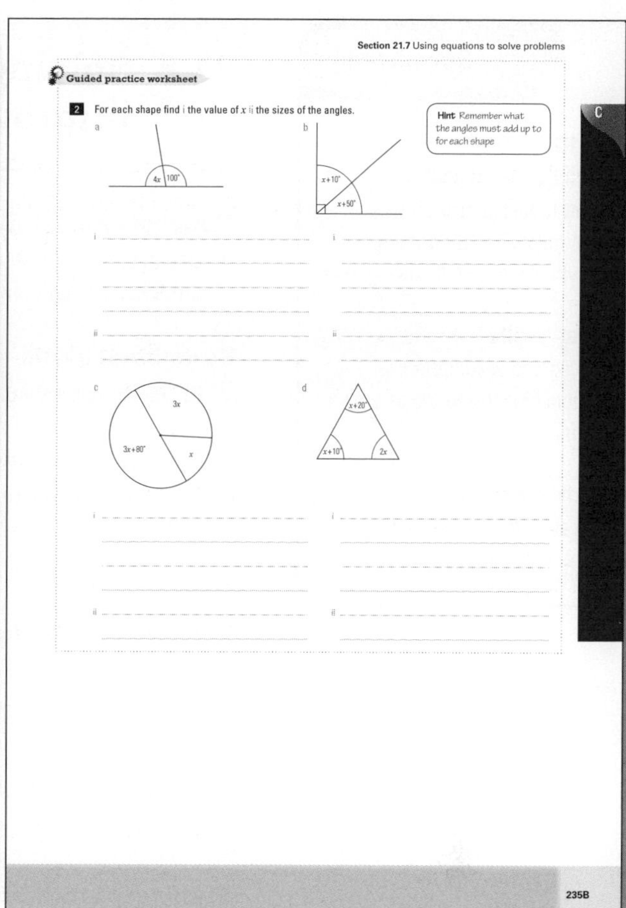

Section 21.7 Using equations to solve problems

Guided practice worksheet

2 For each shape find i the value of x ii the sizes of the angles.

Hint Remember what the angles must add up to for each shape

a

b

i

ii

c

d

i

ii

235B

Section 21.7 Using equations to solve problems

Guided practice worksheet

Example: Warren has saved £6 more than his sister Kate. He has saved four times the amount Kate has saved. If k is the amount Kate has saved
(a) write an equation involving k
(b) find the value of k
(c) find the amount Warren saved.

(a) Write the equation in words first:
£6 more than Kate = four times Kate
Then write the equation using letters:
$k + 6 = 4k$
(b) $6 = 3k$ (subtract k from both sides)
$2 = k$ (divide both sides by 3)
$k = 2$ (Kate saved £2)
(c) Warren saved £6 more than Kate. He saved £8.

For questions 3–4 a write down an equation involving the given letter b solve the equation c solve the problem.

3 Caroline walked three miles more than Terry. Caroline walked three times the distance Terry walked. Let t be the distance Terry walked. Find how far each person walked.

a

b

c

4 Gavin is 16 years older than Daljit. Gavin is twice as old as Daljit. Let d be the age of Daljit. Find the age of each person.

a

b

c

5 The two equal sides of an isosceles triangle can be calculated by $3x + 5$ or by $6x - 13$. Find the length of the equal sides.

235C

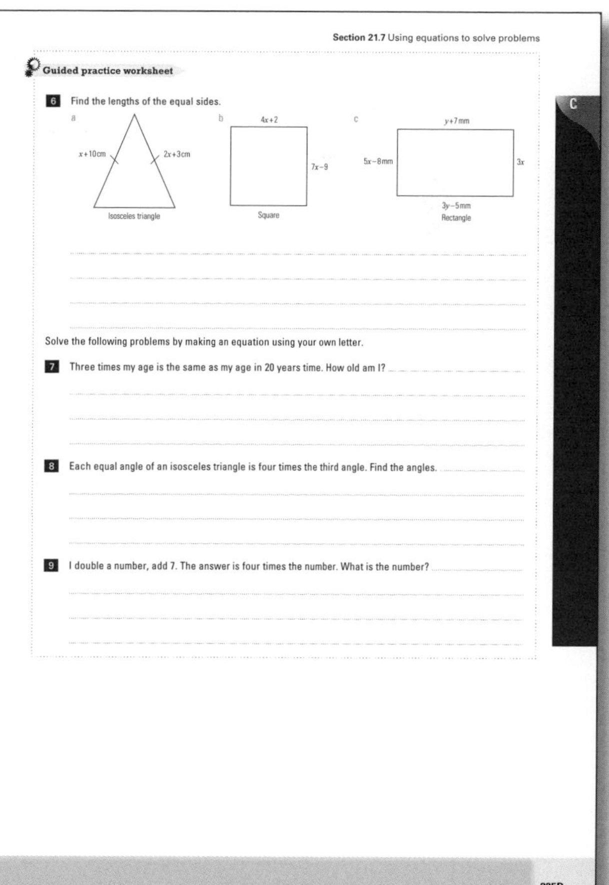

Section 21.7 Using equations to solve problems

Guided practice worksheet

6 Find the lengths of the equal sides.

a

b

c

Solve the following problems by making an equation using your own letter.

7 Three times my age is the same as my age in 20 years time. How old am I?

8 Each equal angle of an isosceles triangle is four times the third angle. Find the angles.

9 I double a number, add 7. The answer is four times the number. What is the number?

235D

Specification

GCSE 2010
A h Use systematic trial and improvement to find approximate solutions to equations where there is no simple analytical method of solving them

FS Process skills
Change values and assumptions or adjust relationships to see the effect on answers in model

FS Performance
Level 1 Use appropriate checking procedures at each stage

21.8 Solving equations by trial and improvement

Concepts and skills

- Use systematic trial and improvement to find approximate solutions of equations where there is no simple analytical method of solving them.

Functional skills

- L1 Use simple formulae expressed in words for one- or two-step operations.

Prior key knowledge, skills and concepts

- Students should already be able to substitute values into a formula involving squares and cubes.

Starter

- *What number when multiplied by itself gives you 25?* (5)
- *What number when multiplied by itself gives you 36?* (6)
- *Find the number that when it is multiplied by itself gives you 30.* (5.48)
- *What is the length of the side of a cube that has a volume of 8?* (2)
- *What is the length of the side of a cube that has a volume of 27?* (3)
- *What is the length of the side of a cube that has a volume of 16?* (2.52)

Main teaching and learning

- Go through Example 15.
- Get students to work on Exercise 21O.

Common misconceptions

- Students sometimes forget to check the halfway value in the next decimal place.

Enrichment

- *Find the perimeter of the rectangle if the area is 45 cm².* (28 cm)

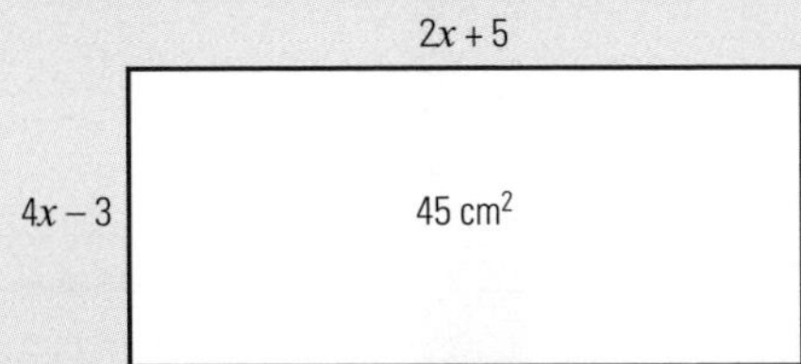

- Here is the formula for finding how much you owe a credit card company if you pay £5 off each month on an original spend of £100.

  Amount owed = $100(1 + 0.025)^n - 5n$

  where n is the number of months

  How many months does it take to clear the debt? (The debt will never be cleared. It decreases during the first 29 months, but then increases.)

Plenary

- Check understanding by asking students to solve $x^2 + x = 5$ correct to 1 d.p. ($x = 1.8$ or -2.8)

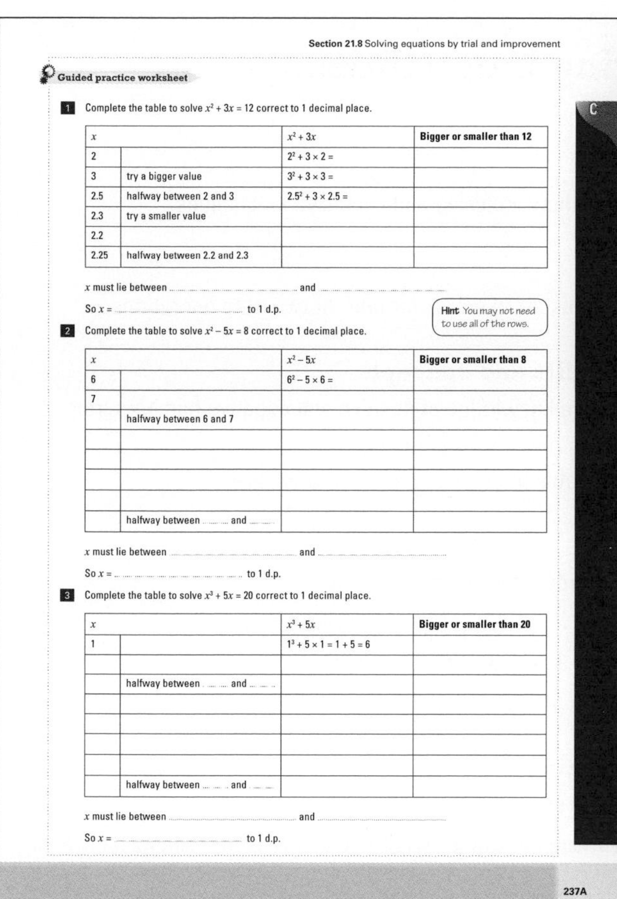

Guided practice worksheet

1 Complete the table to solve $x^2 + 3x = 12$ correct to 1 decimal place.

x		$x^2 + 3x$	Bigger or smaller than 12
2		$2^2 + 3 \times 2 =$	
3	try a bigger value	$3^2 + 3 \times 3 =$	
2.5	halfway between 2 and 3	$2.5^2 + 3 \times 2.5 =$	
2.3	try a smaller value		
2.2			
2.25	halfway between 2.2 and 2.3		

x must lie between .... and ....

So x = ... to 1 d.p.

Hint: You may not need to use all of the rows.

2 Complete the table to solve $x^2 - 5x = 8$ correct to 1 decimal place.

x		$x^2 - 5x$	Bigger or smaller than 8
6		$6^2 - 5 \times 6 =$	
7			
	halfway between 6 and 7		
	halfway between ...... and		

x must lie between .... and ....

So x = ... to 1 d.p.

3 Complete the table to solve $x^3 + 5x = 20$ correct to 1 decimal place.

x		$x^3 + 5x$	Bigger or smaller than 20
1		$1^3 + 5 \times 1 = 1 + 5 = 6$	
	halfway between ...... and		
	halfway between ...... and		

x must lie between .... and ....

So x = ... to 1 d.p.

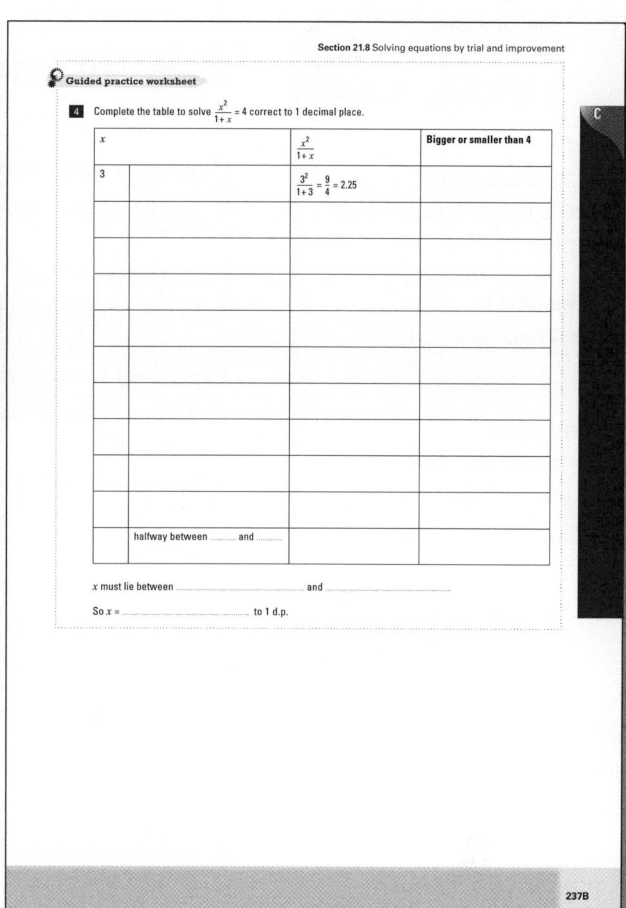

Guided practice worksheet

4 Complete the table to solve $\frac{x^2}{1+x} = 4$ correct to 1 decimal place.

x		$\frac{x^2}{1+x}$	Bigger or smaller than 4
3		$\frac{3^2}{1+3} = \frac{9}{4} = 2.25$	
	halfway between ...... and		

x must lie between .... and ....

So x = ... to 1 d.p.

Guided practice worksheet

5 Complete the table to solve $\frac{x^2+1}{x} = 5$ correct to 2 decimal places.

x		$\frac{x^2+1}{x}$	Bigger or smaller than 5
4		$\frac{4^2+1}{4} = \frac{16+1}{4} = 17 \div 4 = 4.25$	
5			
4.5	halfway between 4 and 5		
4.7			
4.8			
4.75	halfway between 4.7 and 4.8		
	halfway between ...... and		

x must lie between .... and ....

So x = ... to 1 d.p.

6 Complete the table to solve $x^2 - 4x = 7$ correct to 2 decimal places.

x		$x^3 - 4x$	Bigger or smaller than
5			

x must lie between .... and ....

So x = ... to 1 d.p.

Specification

GCSE 2010
A g Solve linear inequalities in one variable, and represent the solution set on a number line

FS Process skills
Use appropriate mathematical procedures

FS Performance
Level 1 Use appropriate checking procedures at each stage

Resources

ActiveTeach resources
Inequalities interactive

21.9 Introducing inequalities

Concepts and skills

- Use the correct notation to show inclusive and exclusive inequalities.

Functional skills

- L1 Use simple formulae expressed in words for one- or two-step operations.

Prior key knowledge, skills and concepts

- Students should already have knowledge of positive and negative numbers from −50 to +50.
- Students should already be able to put numbers in order of size.

Starter

- Arrange these numbers in order of size, smallest first:
  (a) *5, 2, 9, 12, 7* (2, 5, 7, 9, 12)
  (b) *−5, −2, −9, −12, −7* (−12, −9, −7, −5, −2)
  (c) *2, −3, 5, −4, 0* (−4, −3, 0, 2, 5)

Main teaching and learning

- Go through key points in this section and reinforce the 4 signs: $<$, $>$, $\leq$, $\geq$.
- Test understanding by working through Examples 16 and 17 with students before they tackle Exercise 21P.

Common misconceptions

- Some students do not realise that −2 is bigger than −3 and 1 is bigger than −3.

Plenary

- Check understanding of the topic by using pair work and getting students to make up five questions like those in Exercise 21P, where they have to put inequality signs between numbers so that they make a true statement.

greater than greater than or equal to less than less than or equal to

Guided practice worksheet

D

Remember: $<$ means "less than", and $>$ means "greater than"

1 Put the correct sign between each pair of numbers to make a true statement.

Example: 6, 4
6 is greater than 4, so we can write $6 > 4$
4 is less than 6, so we can also write $4 < 6$
Both inequalities are true.

a 5, 8 ....
b 10, 1 ....
c 4, 4 ....
d 9, 2 ....
e 0.7, 1 ....
f $\frac{1}{3}$, $\frac{2}{3}$ ....
g 8.3, 8.03 ....
h $\frac{1}{2}$, 0.5 ....

2 Maria said "You can always turn an inequality around. So $3 < 10$ can be turned around to make $10 > 3$."
Is Maria correct? Explain your answer.

....

....

....

3 Some of the following inequalities are not true. Find them and write them with the correct sign.

a $5 < 5$ ....
b $2 > -3$ ....
c $0 < 6$ ....
d $-3 > -2$ ....
e $6 > -6$ ....
f $-9 > 8$ ....
g $1.5 = \frac{5}{2}$ ....
h $-3 > 0$ ....

4 Write down three whole numbers that satisfy the following inequalities.

Example: $x > 4$
x is any whole number greater than 4. Choose any three you like.
5, 10, 99

a $x < 7$ ....
b $x > -3$ ....
c $x < 0$ ....
d $x < 0.5$ ....
e $x > 1\,000\,000$ ....
f $x < -200$ ....

Section 21.9 Introducing inequalities

Guided practice worksheet

C

Remember: $\leqslant$ means "less than or equal to", and $\geqslant$ means "greater than or equal to"

5 Write down the three whole values of x closest to the number in the inequality.

Example: $x \leqslant 8$
x is any number less than 8 or equal to 8
6, 7, 8 are the three values of x closest to 8 that satisfy the inequality

a $x \geqslant 4$ ....
b $x < 10$ ....
c $x \leqslant 0$ ....
d $x > -3$ ....
e $x \geqslant 999$ ....
f $x \leqslant -8$ ....
g $x \leqslant 1.5$ ....
h $x > -3.2$ ....

6 Write down the values of x that are whole numbers and satisfy the inequality.

Example: $4 < x \leqslant 8$
This means that x is greater than 4 but less than or equal to 8.
The whole numbers are: 5, 6, 7, 8

a $1 \leqslant x < 5$ ....
b $4 < x < 10$ ....
c $6 \leqslant x \leqslant 8$ ....
d $0 < x \leqslant 5$ ....
e $-4 < x \leqslant 0$ ....
f $99 < x \leqslant 100$ ....
g $0 \leqslant x < 3$ ....
h $-7 \leqslant x < -4$ ....
i $0.5 < x \leqslant 6$ ....
j $-3 \leqslant x < 0.5$ ....

7 Write down an inequality that satisfies these values of x, where x is a whole number.

Example: 5, 6, 7, 8
x is greater than 4 and less than 9, which can be written $4 < x < 9$
Other possible inequalities are: $5 \leqslant x \leqslant 8$
$5 \leqslant x < 9$
$4 < x \leqslant 8$

a 2, 3, 4, 5 ....
b 4, 5, 6, 7 ... .
c ... 6, 7, 8, 9 ....
d 0, 1, 2, 3, 4 ... .
e −2, −1, 0 ....
f −3, −2, −1, 0, 1, 2, 3 ... .
g 0, 1, 2, 3, 4, 5, 6, 7 ....
h ... −6, −5, −4, −3 ....

Specification

GCSE 2010

A g Solve linear inequalities in one variable, and represent the solution set on a number line

FS Process skills

Use appropriate mathematical procedures

FS Performance

Level 1 Use appropriate checking procedures at each stage

Resources

CD resources

Resource sheet 21.10

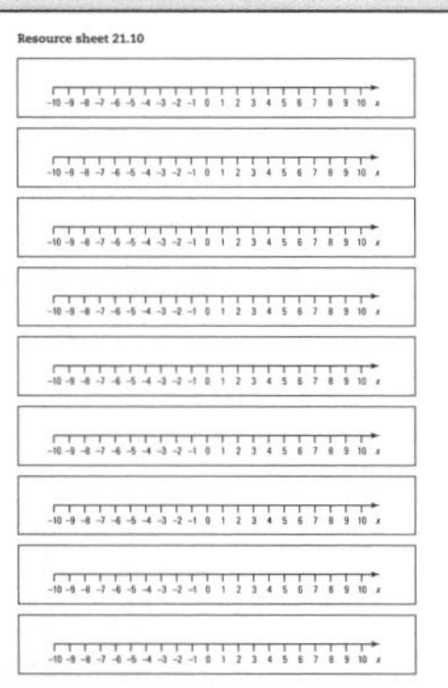

21.10 Representing inequalities on a number line

Concepts and skills

- Solve simple linear inequalities in one variable, and represent the solution set on a number line.
- Use the correct notation to show inclusive and exclusive inequalities.

Functional skills

- L1 Use simple formulae expressed in words for one- or two-step operations.

Prior key knowledge, skills and concepts

- Students should already know how to read and draw number lines.
- Students should already know how to put positive and negative integers in order.

Starter

- *Arrange these numbers in order of size, smallest first.*

  (a) *3, −2, 5, 0, −4* (−4, −2, 0, 3, 5)

  (b) $-2\frac{1}{2}, -2, -3, -2\frac{1}{4}, -2\frac{3}{4}$ ($-3, -2\frac{3}{4}, -2\frac{1}{2}, -2\frac{1}{4}, -2$)

  (c) *−3.7, −3, −2.97, −2.5, −3.57* (−3.7, −3.57, −3, −2.97, −2.5)

Main teaching and learning

- Go through key points and work through Examples 18, 19 and 20.
- Test understanding by asking students to work on Exercise 21Q.

Common misconceptions

- Students sometimes do not realise that −2 is bigger than −3 and 1 is bigger than −3.
- Students sometimes do not realise that $-2\frac{1}{2}$ is smaller than $-2\frac{1}{4}$.

Plenary

- Check understanding of the topic by using pair work and getting students to make up five questions like those in Exercise 21Q, where they have to complete a number line that represents inequalities.

inequality

Section 21.10 Representing inequalities on a number line

Guided practice worksheet

1 Show each inequality on the number line.

Example: The filled circle shows that 7 is included

0 1 2 3 4 5 6 7 8 9 10 $x \leq 7$

The empty circle shows that −2 is not included

−5 −4 −3 −2 −1 0 1 2 3 4 5 $x > -2$

a 0 1 2 3 4 5 6 7 8 9 10 $x \leq 2$

b 0 1 2 3 4 5 6 7 8 9 10 $x < 8.5$

c −5 −4 −3 −2 −1 0 1 2 3 4 5 $x < 0$

d −5 −4 −3 −2 −1 0 1 2 3 4 5 $x \geq -3$

e 0 1 2 3 4 5 6 7 8 9 10 $x > 0$

f −5 −4 −3 −2 −1 0 1 2 3 4 5 $x \leq -1.5$

2 Write down the inequality represented on these number lines.

a 0 1 2 3 4 5 6 7 8 9 10

b −5 −4 −3 −2 −1 0 1 2 3 4 5

c 0 1 2 3 4 5 6 7 8 9 10

d −5 −4 −3 −2 −1 0 1 2 3 4 5

e 16

f −30

Section 21.10 Representing inequalities on a number line

Guided practice worksheet

3 Show each inequality on the number line.

Example: −2 is included, 3 is not

−5 −4 −3 −2 −1 0 1 2 3 4 5 $-2 \leq x < 3$

a 0 1 2 3 4 5 6 7 8 9 10 $4 < x < 8$

b −5 −4 −3 −2 −1 0 1 2 3 4 5 $-1 \leq x \leq 5$

c 0 1 2 3 4 5 6 7 8 9 10 $0 \leq x < 4.5$

d 0 1 2 3 4 5 6 7 8 9 10 $6 < x \leq 10$

e −5 −4 −3 −2 −1 0 1 2 3 4 5 $-4 < x \leq 0$

f −5 −4 −3 −2 −1 0 1 2 3 4 5 $-3 < x < 2$

4 Write down the inequality represented on these number lines.

a 0 1 2 3 4 5 6 7 8 9 10

b −5 −4 −3 −2 −1 0 1 2 3 4 5

c 0 1 2 3 4 5 6 7 8 9 10

d −5 −4 −3 −2 −1 0 1 2 3 4 5

e −20 1

f 0 150

Section 21.10 Representing inequalities on a number line

Guided practice worksheet

5 Show each inequality using a simple number line.

a $x > 7$

b $x \leq -3$

c $0 < x \leq 18$

d $-5 \leq x \leq 10$

e $x \leq 200$

f $x > 1.25$

g $200 < x \leq 300$

h $-5.4 < x < -2.2$

Specification

GCSE 2010

A g Solve linear inequalities in one variable, and represent the solution set on a number line

FS Process skills

Use appropriate mathematical procedures

FS Performance

Level 1 Use appropriate checking procedures at each stage

Resources

Links

http://www.bbc.co.uk/schools/gcsebitesize/maths/algebra/inequalitiesact.shtml

ActiveTeach resources

Inequalities quiz 1

RP KC Equations and inequalities knowledge check

RP PS Equations problem solving

21.11 Solving inequalities

Concepts and skills

- Solve simple linear inequalities in one variable, and represent the solution set on a number line.
- Use the correct notation to show inclusive and exclusive inequalities.

Functional skills

- L1 Use simple formulae expressed in words for one- or two-step operations.

Prior key knowledge, skills and concepts

- Students should already be able to solve linear equations of any type, e.g.:

  (a) $x \pm 3 = 5$ (b) $ax \pm 3 = 7$ (c) $2(ax \pm 3) = 7$ (d) $ax \pm 3 = bx \pm c$

Starter

- *Solve the equations*:

  1 (a) $a + 4 = 7$ ($a = 3$) (b) $b + 7 = 2$ ($b = -5$)
  (c) $c - 5 = 2$ ($c = 7$)

  2 (a) $2d + 3 = 7$ ($d = 2$) (b) $3e + 7 = 1$ ($e = -2$)
  (c) $5f - 4 = 6$ ($f = 2$)

  3 (a) $3(g + 5) = 21$ ($g = 2$) (b) $2(3h + 5) = 4$ ($h = -1$)
  (c) $5(2j - 3) = 25$ ($j = 4$)

  4 (a) $3k + 5 = k + 2$ ($k = -1.5$) (b) $4l + 5 = 7l - 4$ ($l = 3$)
  (c) $5m - 7 = 3m - 2$ ($m = 2.5$)

Main teaching and learning

- Go through Examples 21, 22 and 23; then students should work on Exercise 21R.

Common misconceptions

- Sometimes students try to multiply or divide inequalities by a negative number.

Plenary

- Check understanding of the topic by using pair work and getting students to make up five inequalities with increasing difficulty like those in Exercise 21R and check if their partner can get them correct.

Guided practice worksheet

Remember: Solve inequalities using the rules for equations but do not multiply or divide both sides by a negative number.

1 Solve the inequality and show the solution on the number line.

Example: $2x + 5 \leq 11$
$2x \leq 11 - 5$ (subtract 5 from both sides)
$2x \leq 6$
$x \leq 3$ (divide both sides by 2)
(show the solution on a simple number line) 3

a $5x \geq 30$

b $x - 7 < 2$

c $x + 3 \geq 1$

d $\frac{x}{2} < 4$

e $3x - 2 > 0$

f $3 > 2x - 5$

g $10x - 200 < 400$

h $5x + 4 \leq 8$

2 Solve the inequality and show the solution on a number line.

Example: $8 \leq 4x < 18$
$2 \leq x < 4.5$ (divide each term by 4)
(show the solution on a simple number line) 2 4.5

a $4 \leq 2x < 8$

b $6 < 3x < 12$

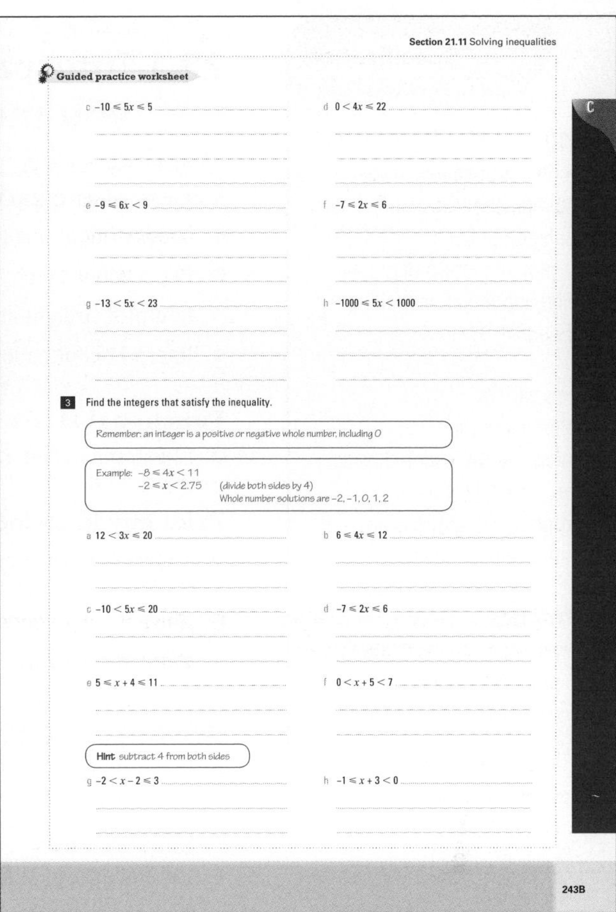

Guided practice worksheet

c $-10 \leq 5x \leq 5$

d $0 < 4x \leq 22$

e $-9 \leq 6x < 9$

f $-7 \leq 2x \leq 6$

g $-13 < 5x < 23$

h $-1000 \leq 5x < 1000$

3 Find the integers that satisfy the inequality.

Remember: an integer is a positive or negative whole number, including 0

Example: $-8 \leq 4x < 11$
$-2 \leq x < 2.75$ (divide both sides by 4)
Whole number solutions are $-2, -1, 0, 1, 2$

a $12 < 3x \leq 20$

b $6 \leq 4x \leq 12$

c $-10 < 5x \leq 20$

d $-7 \leq 2x \leq 6$

e $5 \leq x + 4 \leq 11$

f $0 < x + 5 < 7$

Hint subtract 4 from both sides

g $-2 < x - 2 \leq 3$

h $-1 \leq x + 3 < 0$

Guided practice worksheet

4 Solve the inequality and show the solution on a number line.

Example: $5x - 5 \leq 3x + 9$
$2x - 5 \leq 9$ (subtract $3x$ from both sides)
$2x \leq 14$ (add 5 to both sides)
$x \leq 7$ (divide both sides by 2)
7

a $4x > 2x + 8$

b $6x < x - 10$

c $2x + 7 \geq 3x$

d $9x \leq 5x + 10$

e $5x + 2 > 2x + 11$

f $7x - 1 \geq x - 7$

g $4 - 3x > 3 - 5x$

h $2x + 4 < 7x - 5$

5 Write down the largest integer that satisfies $6x - 3 < 4x + 2$

6 Write down the smallest integer that satisfies $3 - x \geq 6 - 2x$

Specification

GCSE 2010

A r Construct linear functions from real-life problems and plot their corresponding graphs

A s Discuss, plot and interpret graphs (which may be non-linear) modelling real-life situations

FS Process skills

Recognise that a situation has aspects that can be represented using mathematics

Examine patterns and relationships

Interpret results and solutions

FS Performance

Level 1 Interpret and communicate solutions to practical problems, drawing simple conclusions and giving explanations

Resources

ActiveTeach resources

Bath time animation

Extreme 3 video

22.1 Interpreting and drawing the graphs you meet in everyday life

Concepts and skills

- Draw straight-line graphs for real-life situations.
- Plot a linear graph.
- Interpret straight-line graphs for real-life situations.
- Interpret information presented in a range of linear and non-linear graphs.

Functional skills

- L1 Extract and interpret information from tables, diagrams, charts and graphs.

Prior key knowledge, skills and concepts

- Know how to plot coordinates.

Starter

- Work through the 'Get ready' box.

Main teaching and learning

- Go through the concepts of the types of graph that go through the origin and those that have an intercept on the positive y-axis.
- Explain Examples 1 and 2.
- Tell students to attempt Exercise 22A.
- Go through the concepts of water filling different-shaped containers, explaining the difference between:
  - shapes that have sides that are straight up, flare out or become narrower
  - shapes that are wide and shapes that are narrow
  - shapes with curves that go out and shapes that go in.
- Explain how these attributes translate into the graphs by going through Example 3.
- Tell students to attempt Exercise 22B.

Common misconceptions

- Not realising that when shapes flare outwards the graph will be curved with a decreasing gradient.
- Not realising that when shapes narrow inwards then the graph will be curved with an increasing gradient.

Enrichment

- *Use extra examples of computer-generated graphs from different-shaped containers being filled.* (Students' own answers.)
- *Use the internet to find the best mobile phone deal for a person who uses 200 minutes and 200 texts per month. Graph the results to explain the reasoning. NB the phone must be the same for each tariff.* (Students' own answers.)

Plenary

- *Draw a graph of the level of water in a water butt that is used to water a garden when the weather is dry.* (By inspection.)
- *One summer it rained a lot in April, May was dry and the weather in June started with showers and then was dry. Draw a graph to show the level of the water in the butt.* (By inspection.)

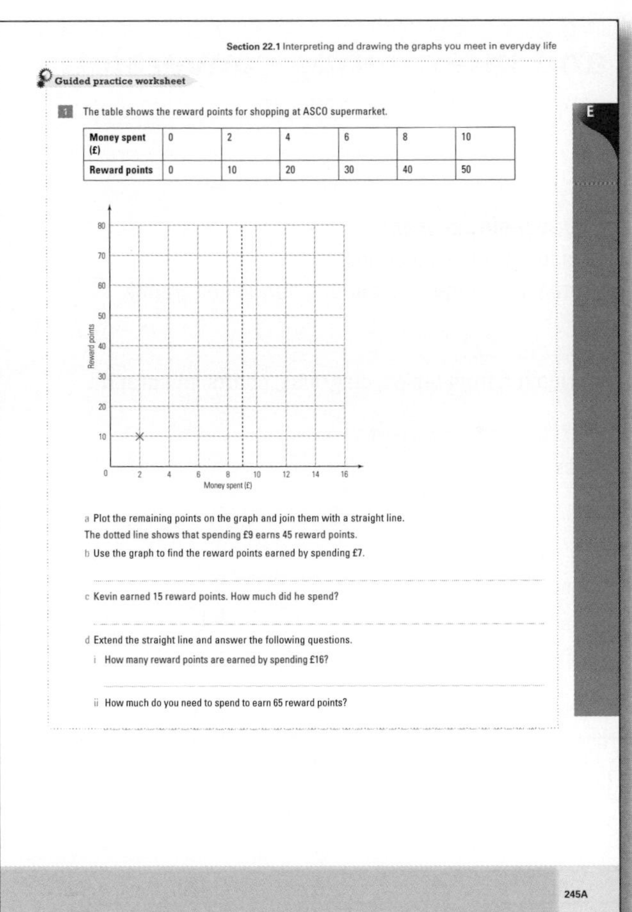

Section 22.1 Interpreting and drawing the graphs you meet in everyday life

Guided practice worksheet

1 The table shows the reward points for shopping at ASCO supermarket.

Money spent (£)	0	2	4	6	8	10
Reward points	0	10	20	30	40	50

a Plot the remaining points on the graph and join them with a straight line.
The dotted line shows that spending £9 earns 45 reward points.

b Use the graph to find the reward points earned by spending £7.

c Kevin earned 15 reward points. How much did he spend?

d Extend the straight line and answer the following questions.

i How many reward points are earned by spending £16?

ii How much do you need to spend to earn 65 reward points?

245A

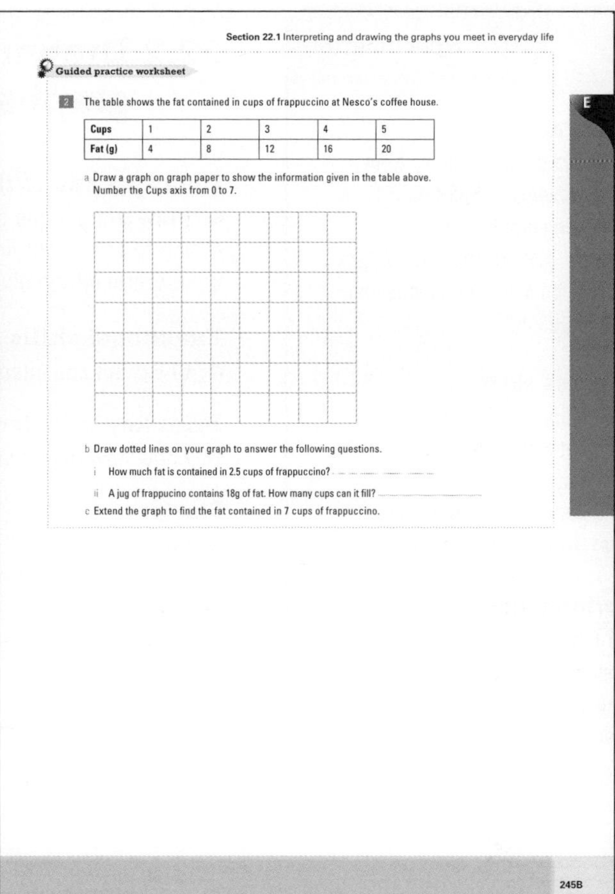

Section 22.1 Interpreting and drawing the graphs you meet in everyday life

Guided practice worksheet

2 The table shows the fat contained in cups of frappuccino at Nesco's coffee house.

Cups	1	2	3	4	5
Fat (g)	4	8	12	16	20

a Draw a graph on graph paper to show the information given in the table above.
Number the Cups axis from 0 to 7.

b Draw dotted lines on your graph to answer the following questions.

i How much fat is contained in 2.5 cups of frappuccino?

ii A jug of frappucino contains 18g of fat. How many cups can it fill?

c Extend the graph to find the fat contained in 7 cups of frappuccino.

245B

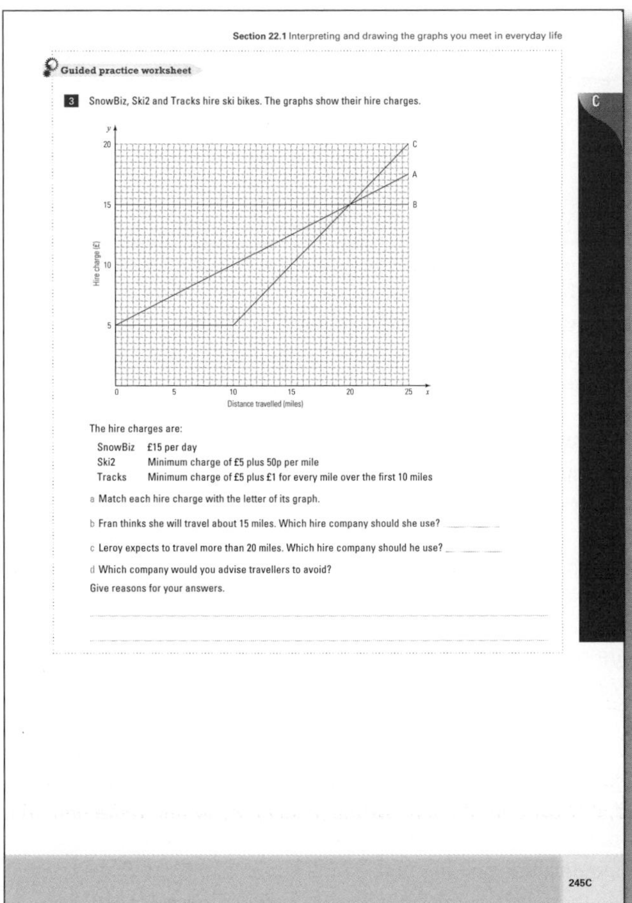

Section 22.1 Interpreting and drawing the graphs you meet in everyday life

Guided practice worksheet

3 SnowBiz, Ski2 and Tracks hire ski bikes. The graphs show their hire charges.

The hire charges are:

SnowBiz £15 per day
Ski2 Minimum charge of £5 plus 50p per mile
Tracks Minimum charge of £5 plus £1 for every mile over the first 10 miles

a Match each hire charge with the letter of its graph.

b Fran thinks she will travel about 15 miles. Which hire company should she use?

c Leroy expects to travel more than 20 miles. Which hire company should he use?

d Which company would you advise travellers to avoid?
Give reasons for your answers.

245C

Specification

GCSE 2010

A r Construct linear functions from real-life problems and plot their corresponding graphs

A s Discuss, plot and interpret graphs (which may be non-linear) modelling real-life situations

FS Process skills

Recognise that a situation has aspects that can be represented using mathematics

Examine patterns and relationships

Interpret results and solutions

FS Performance

Level 1 Interpret and communicate solutions to practical problems, drawing simple conclusions and giving explanations

22.2 Drawing and interpreting conversion graphs

Concepts and skills

- Draw straight-line graphs for real-life situations.
- Interpret straight-line graphs for real-life situations.
- Interpret information presented in a range of linear and non-linear graphs.

Functional skills

- L1 Extract and interpret information from tables, diagrams, charts and graphs.

Prior key knowledge, skills and concepts

- Know how to plot coordinates.

Starter

- Work through the 'Get ready' box.
- Read the numbers on these scales.

(a) (i) (ii) (iii) (iv) (v)

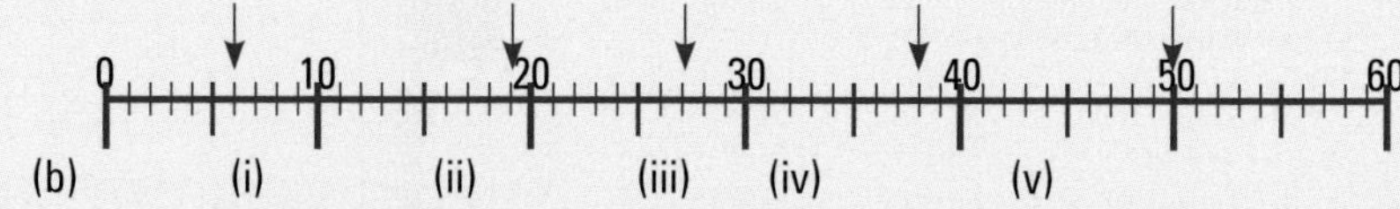

(b) (i) (ii) (iii) (iv) (v)

(c) (i) (ii) (iii) (iv) (v)

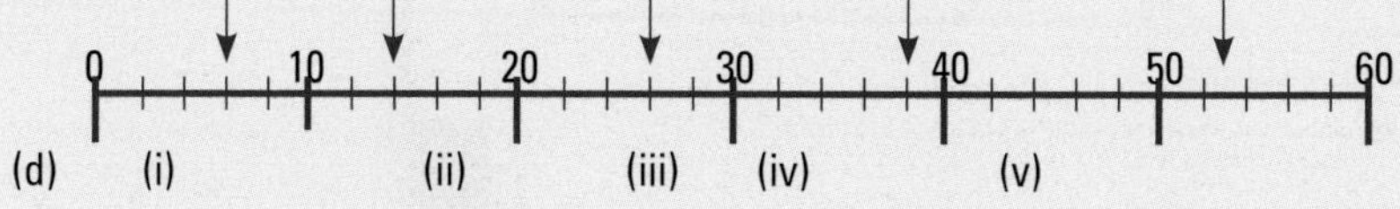

(d) (i) (ii) (iii) (iv) (v)

Main teaching and learning

- Go through key points on how to read values off a conversion graph.
- Emphasise that when you draw a conversion graph you need to plot only two points.
- If the graph is converting currencies, then (0, 0) is always on the graph.

Common misconceptions

- Reading the graphs the wrong way round.
- Reading the scales on the graph incorrectly.

Enrichment

- *Use the internet to find the exchange rate between £ and € and £ and US$.*
- *Draw one graph to show both exchange rates: from £ to € and £ to US$.*
- *Use the graphs to change some values between all three currencies.*
- *Find the exchange rate from US$ to €.*
  (By inspection.)

Plenary

- Check understanding by asking other questions on exchange rate graphs that are printed in the Student Book.
- Check that students can find values that are outside the scope of the graph by using values from the graph and then multiplying them up, e.g. read off value for £20 then multiply by 100 to find value for £2000.

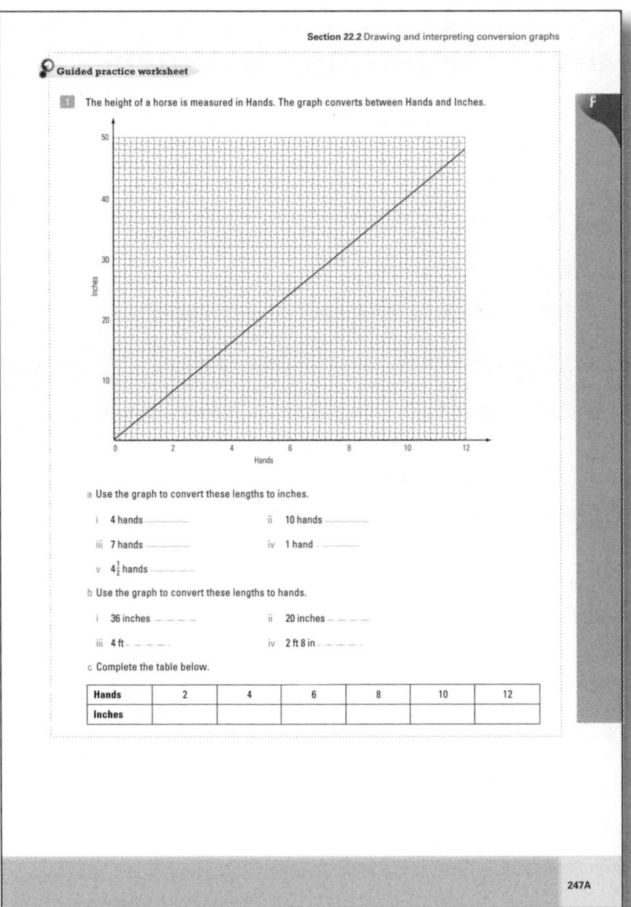

Section 22.2 Drawing and interpreting conversion graphs

Guided practice worksheet

F

1 The height of a horse is measured in Hands. The graph converts between Hands and Inches.

a Use the graph to convert these lengths to inches.

i 4 hands .... ii 10 hands ....

iii 7 hands .... iv 1 hand ....

v $4\frac{1}{2}$ hands ....

b Use the graph to convert these lengths to hands.

i 36 inches .... ii 20 inches ....

iii 4 ft .... iv 2 ft 8 in ....

c Complete the table below.

Hands	2	4	6	8	10	12
Inches						

247A

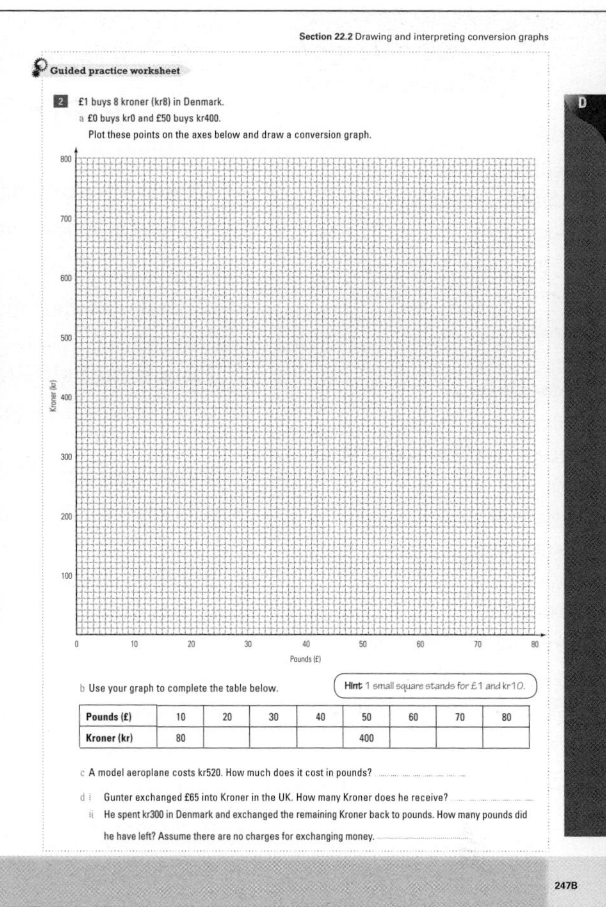

Section 22.2 Drawing and interpreting conversion graphs

Guided practice worksheet

D

2 £1 buys 8 kroner (kr8) in Denmark.

a £0 buys kr0 and £50 buys kr400.

Plot these points on the axes below and draw a conversion graph.

b Use your graph to complete the table below.

Hint: 1 small square stands for £1 and kr10.

Pounds (£)	10	20	30	40	50	60	70	80
Kroner (kr)	80				400			

c A model aeroplane costs kr520. How much does it cost in pounds? ....

d i Gunter exchanged £65 into Kroner in the UK. How many Kroner does he receive? ....

ii He spent kr300 in Denmark and exchanged the remaining Kroner back to pounds. How many pounds did he have left? Assume there are no charges for exchanging money. ....

247B

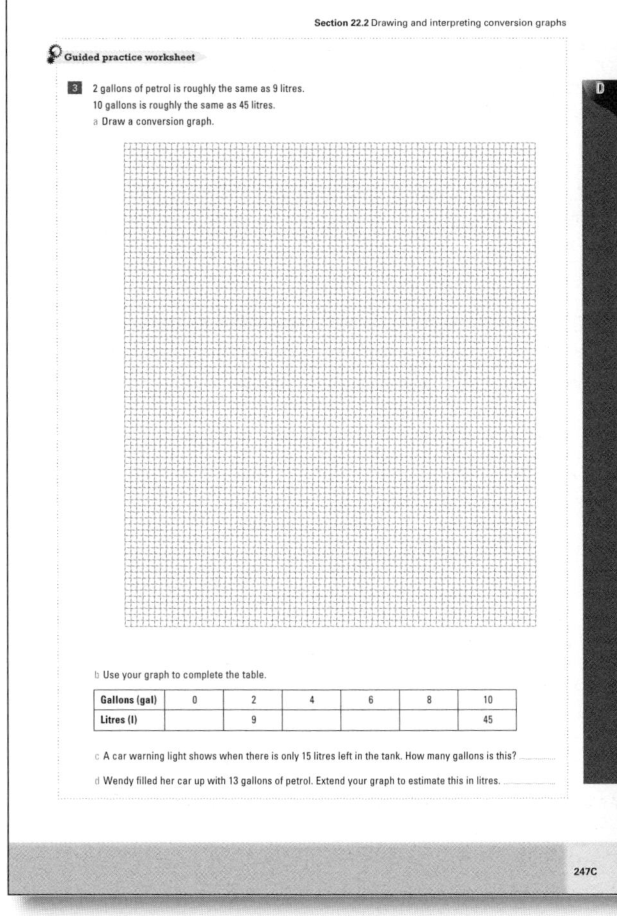

Section 22.2 Drawing and interpreting conversion graphs

Guided practice worksheet

D

3 2 gallons of petrol is roughly the same as 9 litres.

10 gallons is roughly the same as 45 litres.

a Draw a conversion graph.

b Use your graph to complete the table.

Gallons (gal)	0	2	4	6	8	10
Litres (l)		9				45

c A car warning light shows when there is only 15 litres left in the tank. How many gallons is this? ....

d Wendy filled her car up with 13 gallons of petrol. Extend your graph to estimate this in litres. ....

247C

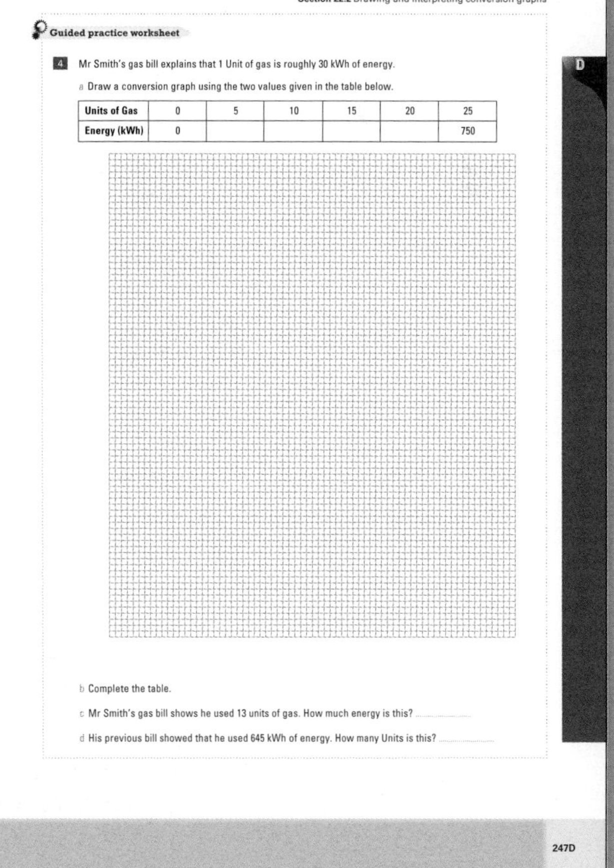

Section 22.2 Drawing and interpreting conversion graphs

Guided practice worksheet

D

4 Mr Smith's gas bill explains that 1 Unit of gas is roughly 30 kWh of energy.

a Draw a conversion graph using the two values given in the table below.

Units of Gas	0	5	10	15	20	25
Energy (kWh)	0					750

b Complete the table.

c Mr Smith's gas bill shows he used 13 units of gas. How much energy is this? ....

d His previous bill showed that he used 645 kWh of energy. How many Units is this? ....

247D

Specification

GCSE 2010

A r Construct linear functions from real-life problems and plot their corresponding graphs
A s Discuss, plot and interpret graphs (which may be non-linear) modelling real-life situations

FS Process skills

Recognise that a situation has aspects that can be represented using mathematics
Examine patterns and relationships
Interpret results and solutions

FS Performance

Level 1 Interpret and communicate solutions to practical problems, drawing simple conclusions and giving explanations

Resources

ActiveTeach resources

Distance-time graphs animation
Swimming 1 video

22.3 Drawing and interpreting distance–time graphs

Concepts and skills

- Draw distance–time graphs.
- Interpret distance–time graphs.
- Interpret information presented in a range of linear and non-linear graphs.

Functional skills

- L1 Extract and interpret information from tables, diagrams, charts and graphs.

Prior key knowledge, skills and concepts

- Know how to plot coordinates and draw straight-line graphs.

Starter

- Work through the 'Get ready' box.

Main teaching and learning

- Go through the examples in the Student Book, making sure that you bring out the key points listed in the book.
- Tell students to tackle the straight-line questions in Exercise 22D.
- Go through the example in the Student Book on curved-line graphs.
- Tell students to tackle the curved-line questions in Exercise 22D.

Common misconceptions

- Errors in dividing by time, e.g. writing 1 minute 30 seconds as 1.3 minutes.

Enrichment

- Tell students to tackle questions such as:
  Write 60 km per hour in m per second. (1000 m per second)
  Write 100 m in 10 seconds in km per hour. (36 km per hour)
- Tell students to translate the speed that various animals win races into km per hour, e.g. horses, dogs, humans.

Plenary

- Check understanding by asking other questions on distance–time graphs that are printed in the Student Book.

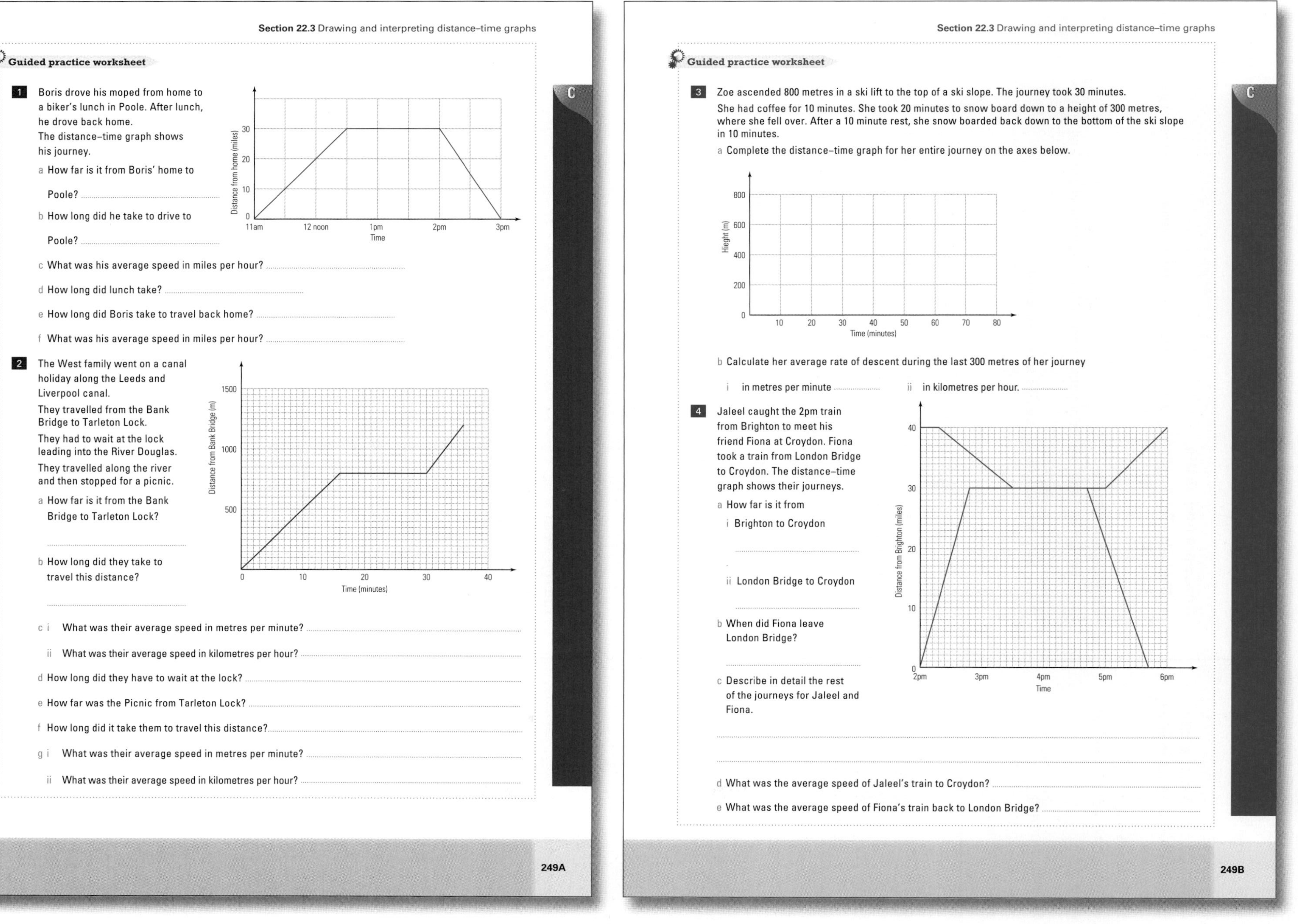

Guided practice worksheet

C

1 Boris drove his moped from home to a biker's lunch in Poole. After lunch, he drove back home.
The distance–time graph shows his journey.

a How far is it from Boris' home to Poole? ....

b How long did he take to drive to Poole? ....

c What was his average speed in miles per hour? ....

d How long did lunch take? ....

e How long did Boris take to travel back home? ....

f What was his average speed in miles per hour? ....

2 The West family went on a canal holiday along the Leeds and Liverpool canal.
They travelled from the Bank Bridge to Tarleton Lock.
They had to wait at the lock leading into the River Douglas.
They travelled along the river and then stopped for a picnic.

a How far is it from the Bank Bridge to Tarleton Lock?

....

b How long did they take to travel this distance?

....

c i What was their average speed in metres per minute? ....

ii What was their average speed in kilometres per hour? ....

d How long did they have to wait at the lock? ....

e How far was the Picnic from Tarleton Lock? ....

f How long did it take them to travel this distance? ....

g i What was their average speed in metres per minute? ....

ii What was their average speed in kilometres per hour? ....

Section 22.3 Drawing and interpreting distance–time graphs

Guided practice worksheet

C

3 Zoe ascended 800 metres in a ski lift to the top of a ski slope. The journey took 30 minutes.
She had coffee for 10 minutes. She took 20 minutes to snow board down to a height of 300 metres, where she fell over. After a 10 minute rest, she snow boarded back down to the bottom of the ski slope in 10 minutes.

a Complete the distance–time graph for her entire journey on the axes below.

b Calculate her average rate of descent during the last 300 metres of her journey

i in metres per minute .... ii in kilometres per hour. ....

4 Jaleel caught the 2pm train from Brighton to meet his friend Fiona at Croydon. Fiona took a train from London Bridge to Croydon. The distance–time graph shows their journeys.

a How far is it from

i Brighton to Croydon

....

ii London Bridge to Croydon

....

b When did Fiona leave London Bridge?

....

c Describe in detail the rest of the journeys for Jaleel and Fiona.

....

....

d What was the average speed of Jaleel's train to Croydon? ....

e What was the average speed of Fiona's train back to London Bridge? ....

Specification

GCSE 2010
A t (part) Generate points and plot graphs of simple quadratic functions…

FS Process skills
Use appropriate mathematical procedures

FS Performance
Level 1 Use appropriate checking procedure at each stage

Resources

Resources
Resource sheets 22.4a and 22.4b

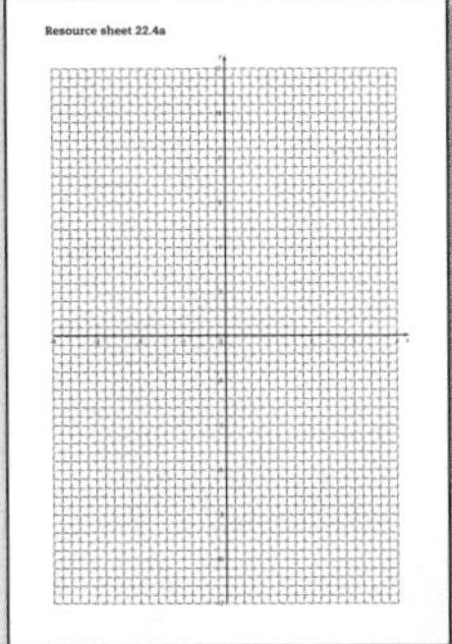

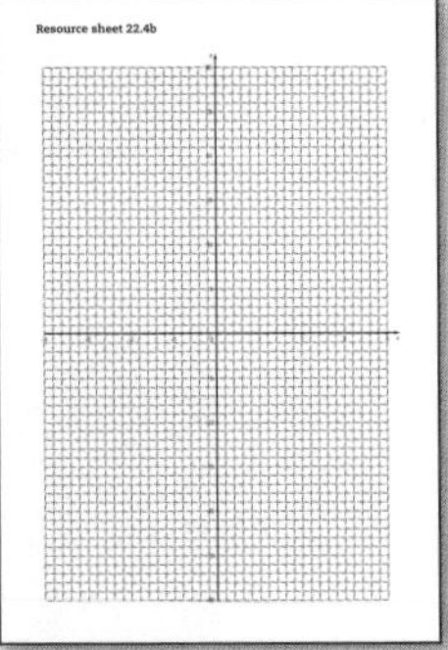

Links
http://nrich.maths.org/773

ActiveTeach resources
Squaring quiz
Building the course 3 video
Hammer throwing video

22.4 Drawing quadratic graphs

Concepts and skills

- Generate points and plot graphs of simple quadratic functions, then more general quadratic functions.

Functional skills

- L1 Extract and interpret information from tables, diagrams, charts and graphs.

Prior key knowledge, skills and concepts

- Know how to set up a table of values.
- Know how to plot coordinates.

Starter

- Use the 'Get ready' exercise to remind students about order of operations regarding indices.

Main teaching and learning

- Go through Examples 7, 8 and 9 which deal with graphs of the form $y = \mathrm{A}x^2 + \mathrm{B}$.
- Work on Exercise 22E and use Resource sheets 22.4a or 22.4b as appropriate or tell the students to draw the grids themselves.
- Go through Example 10 which deals with graphs of the form $y = \mathrm{A}x^2 + \mathrm{B}x + \mathrm{C}$.
- Work on Exercise 22F and use Resource sheets 22.4a or 22.4b as appropriate or tell the students to draw the grids themselves.

Common misconceptions

- Reading the scales on the graph incorrectly.
- Errors in calculations involving BIDMAS.

Enrichment

- Investigate, using ICT, the effect of changing the values of A, B and C in quadratic equations of the form $y = \mathrm{A}x^2 + \mathrm{B}x + \mathrm{C}$ where A, B and C are integers.
- Give students a hint to start with $y = \mathrm{A}x^2$, then move onto $y = \mathrm{A}x^2 + \mathrm{C}$, then $y = \mathrm{A}x^2 + \mathrm{B}x$, before moving onto $y = \mathrm{A}x^2 + \mathrm{B}x + \mathrm{C}$.

Plenary

- Get students to draw the graphs of $y = x^2$, $y = 2x^2$, $y = x^2 - 5$ and $y = -x^2 + 3$ all on the same grid (use Resource sheet 22.4b) and find all the points of intersection. (By inspection.)

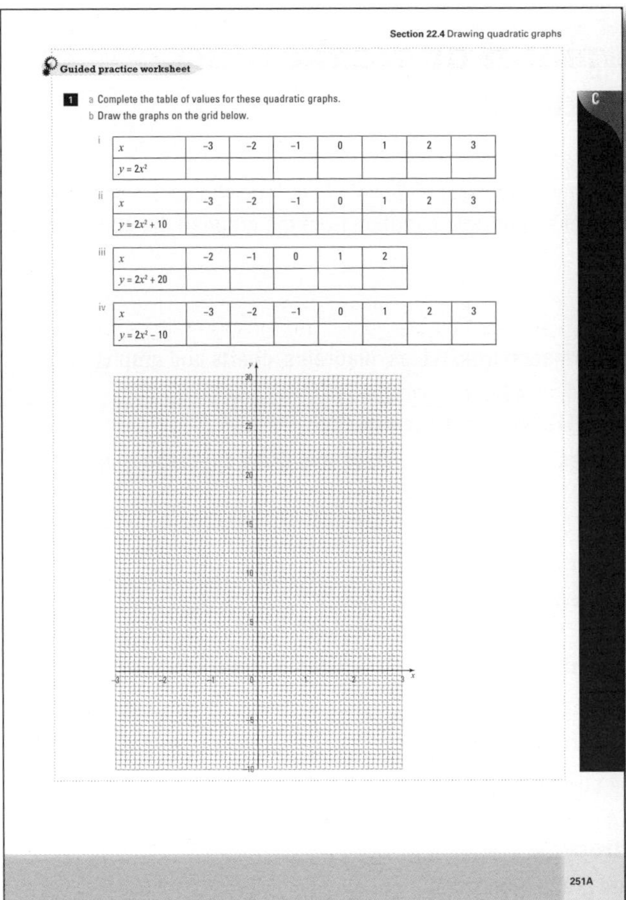

Section 22.4 Drawing quadratic graphs

Guided practice worksheet

1 a Complete the table of values for these quadratic graphs.
b Draw the graphs on the grid below.

i

x	−3	−2	−1	0	1	2	3
$y = 2x^2$							

ii

x	−3	−2	−1	0	1	2	3
$y = 2x^2 + 10$							

iii

x	−2	−1	0	1	2
$y = 2x^2 + 20$					

iv

x	−3	−2	−1	0	1	2	3
$y = 2x^2 - 10$							

251A

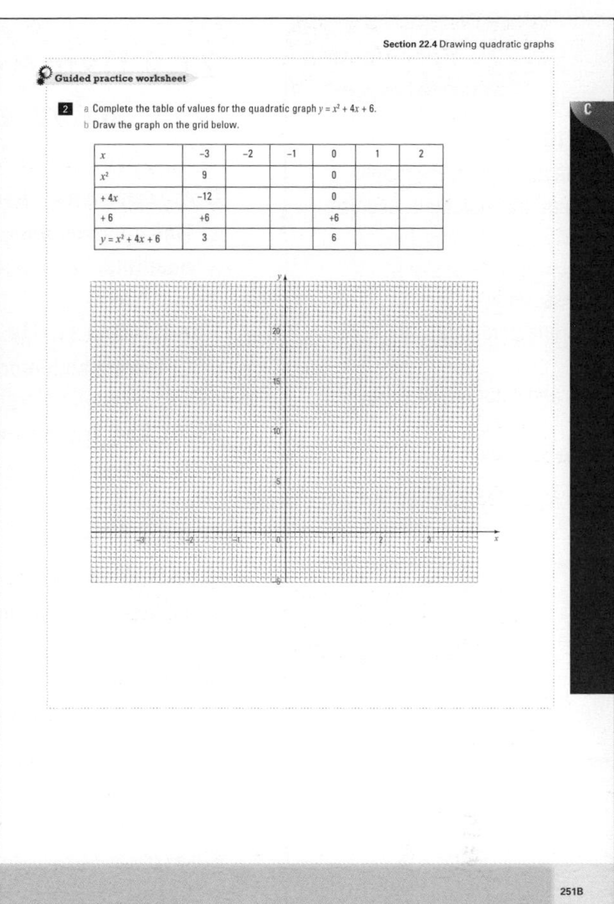

Section 22.4 Drawing quadratic graphs

Guided practice worksheet

2 a Complete the table of values for the quadratic graph $y = x^2 + 4x + 6$.
b Draw the graph on the grid below.

x	−3	−2	−1	0	1	2
x^2	9			0		
$+ 4x$	−12			0		
$+ 6$	+6			+6		
$y = x^2 + 4x + 6$	3			6		

251B

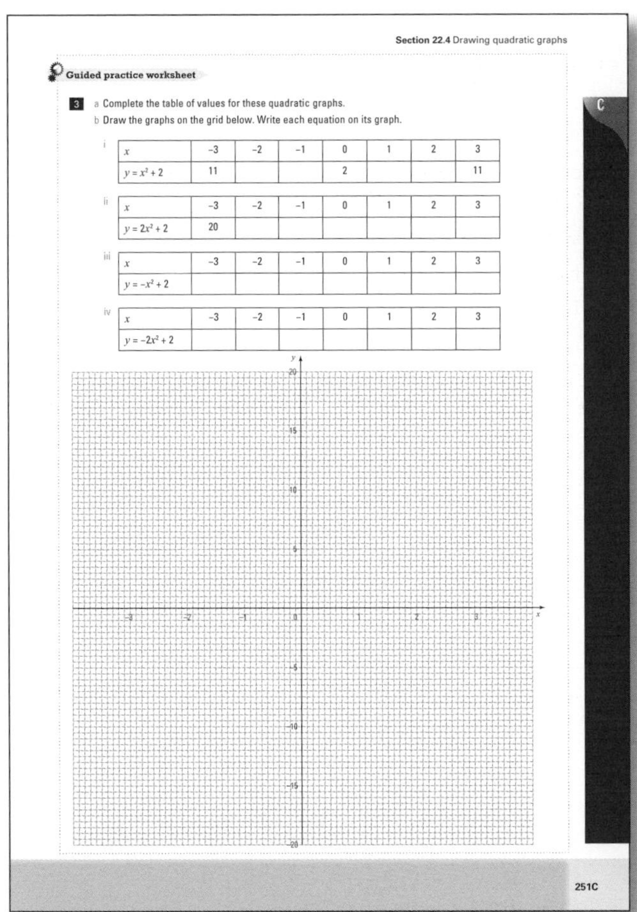

Section 22.4 Drawing quadratic graphs

Guided practice worksheet

3 a Complete the table of values for these quadratic graphs.
b Draw the graphs on the grid below. Write each equation on its graph.

i

x	−3	−2	−1	0	1	2	3
$y = x^2 + 2$	11			2			11

ii

x	−3	−2	−1	0	1	2	3
$y = 2x^2 + 2$	20						

iii

x	−3	−2	−1	0	1	2	3
$y = -x^2 + 2$							

iv

x	−3	−2	−1	0	1	2	3
$y = -2x^2 + 2$							

251C

Specification

GCSE 2010
A t Generate points and plot graphs of simple quadratic functions, and use these to find approximate solutions

FS Process skills
Use appropriate mathematical procedures
Find results and solutions

FS Performance
Level 1 Use appropriate checking procedure at each stage

Resources

CD Resource
Resource sheet 22.5

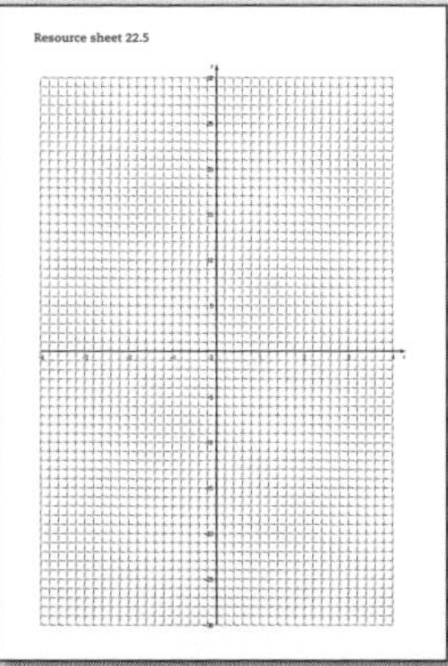

ActiveTeach resources
RP KC Graphs 2 knowledge check
RP PS Graphs 2 problem solving

22.5 Using graphs of quadratic functions to solve equations

Concepts and skills

- Find approximate solutions of a quadratic equation from the graph of the corresponding quadratic function.

Functional skills

- L1 Extract and interpret information from tables, diagrams, charts and graphs.

Prior key knowledge, skills and concepts

- Know how to plot coordinates from a table of values and draw quadratic graphs.

Starter

- *Draw the graph of $y = x^2 - 2x + 1$.*
- *Where does the curve cross the x-axis?* (1, 0)

Main teaching and learning

- Go through Example 11.
- Get students to work on Exercise 22G.
- Remind students that the equation of the x-axis is $y = 0$.

Common misconceptions

- Reading the scales on the graph incorrectly.
- Errors in calculations involving BIDMAS.
- Errors in reading off the wrong axis.

Enrichment

- Investigate the solutions of quadratic functions that are cut by horizontal lines and slanting lines of the form $y = mx + c$.
- Investigate when quadratic equations have two solutions, one solution or no solutions.

Plenary

- Check understanding of the concept that solving a quadratic equation is the same as finding where the quadratic function cuts the x-axis.

quadratic equation

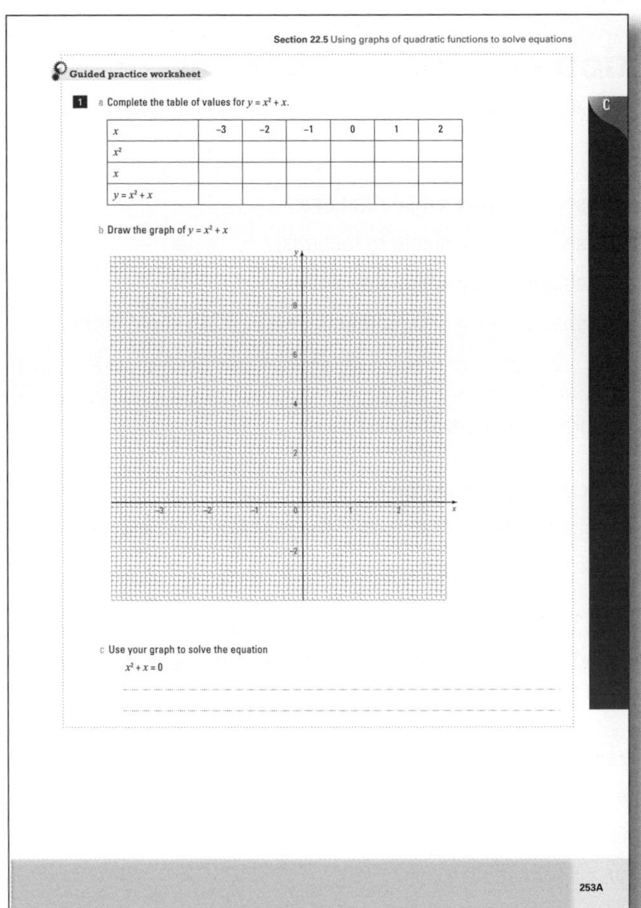

Section 22.5 Using graphs of quadratic functions to solve equations

Guided practice worksheet

1 a Complete the table of values for $y = x^2 + x$.

x	−3	−2	−1	0	1	2
x^2						
x						
$y = x^2 + x$						

b Draw the graph of $y = x^2 + x$

c Use your graph to solve the equation

$x^2 + x = 0$

253A

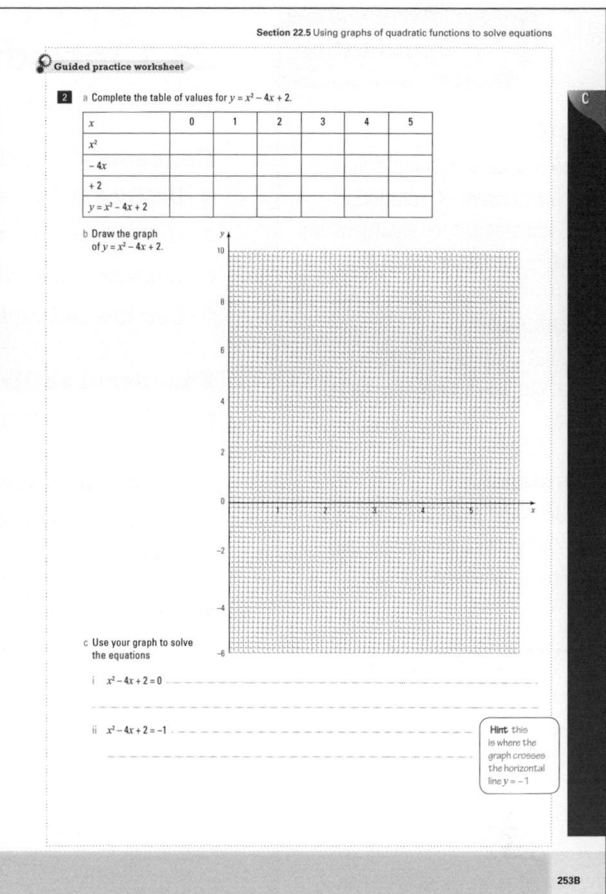

Section 22.5 Using graphs of quadratic functions to solve equations

Guided practice worksheet

2 a Complete the table of values for $y = x^2 - 4x + 2$.

x	0	1	2	3	4	5
x^2						
$-4x$						
$+2$						
$y = x^2 - 4x + 2$						

b Draw the graph of $y = x^2 - 4x + 2$.

c Use your graph to solve the equations

i $x^2 - 4x + 2 = 0$

ii $x^2 - 4x + 2 = -1$

Hint this is where the graph crosses the horizontal line $y = -1$

253B

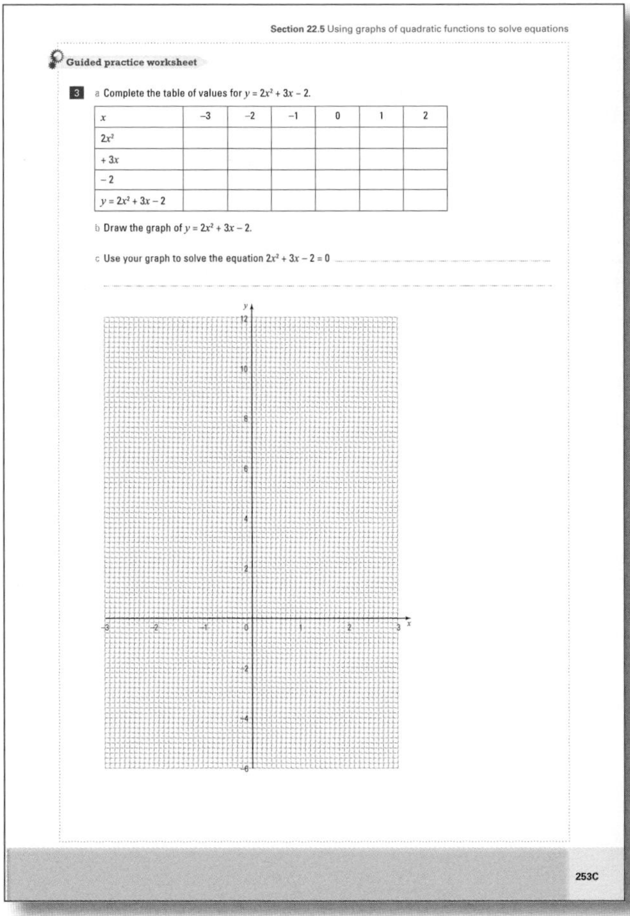

Section 22.5 Using graphs of quadratic functions to solve equations

Guided practice worksheet

3 a Complete the table of values for $y = 2x^2 + 3x - 2$.

x	−3	−2	−1	0	1	2
$2x^2$						
$+3x$						
-2						
$y = 2x^2 + 3x - 2$						

b Draw the graph of $y = 2x^2 + 3x - 2$.

c Use your graph to solve the equation $2x^2 + 3x - 2 = 0$

253C

Specification

GCSE 2010

GM I (part) Describe and transform 2D shapes using single… rotations, reflections, translations, or enlargements by a positive scale factor….

FS Process skills

Recognise that a situation has aspects that can be represented using mathematics

FS Performance

Level 1 Understand practical problems in familiar and unfamiliar context and situations, some of which are non-routine

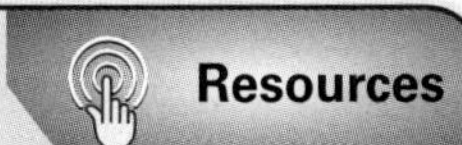

Resources

Links

http://nrich.maths.org/public/search.php?search=transformations
http://snowflakes.barkleyus.com/

23.1 Introduction

Concepts and skills

- Describe and transform 2D shapes using single rotations.
- Describe and transform 2D shapes using single reflections.
- Describe and transform 2D shapes using single translations.
- Describe and transform 2D shapes using enlargements by a positive scale factor.

Functional skills

- L1 Construct geometric diagrams, models and shapes.

Prior key knowledge, skills and concepts

- Students should be able to spot patterns in shapes in the real world, for example wallpaper.

Starter

- Discuss with the students which letters of the alphabet have both rotational and line symmetry.

Main teaching and learning

- Describe to students the four main transformations:
  - Translation – movement up and across.
  - Rotation – circular movements about a point.
  - Reflection – reflection in a line.
  - Englargement – shapes made bigger.
- Give some examples of each as they occur in real life.
- Give students the opportunity to name other examples of each type of transformation.

Common misconceptions

- Students sometimes confuse the different types of transformation.

Enrichment

- Ask students to draw a shape and then complete a transformation. Repeat for a number of different shapes and transformations.

Plenary

- Ask students to suggest differences between the four transformations. Compile the students' ideas into a class list.

Guided practice worksheet

E

1 The four main transformations are called:

reflection   rotation   translation   enlargement

For each diagram write down one of these words to describe what transformation has taken place.

a

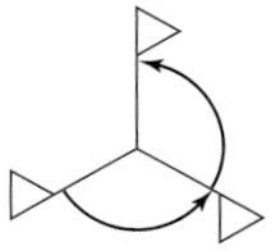

b

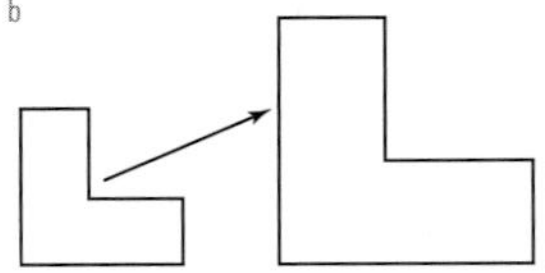

c

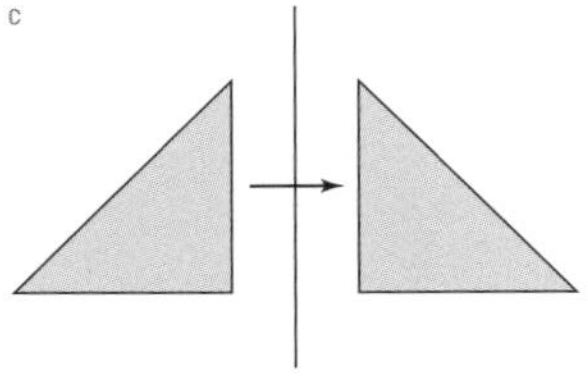

d

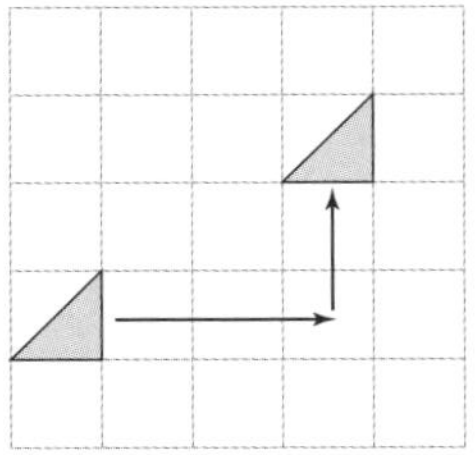

2 For each of the following identify which of the four transformations is being shown.

a

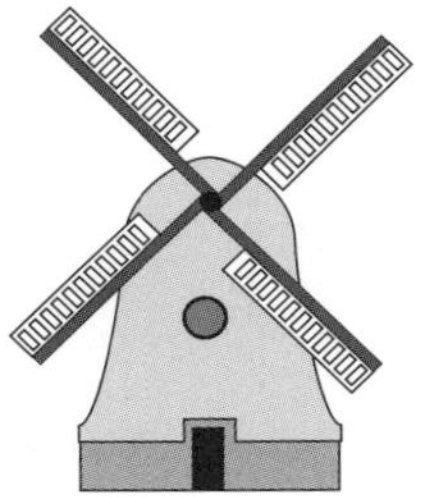

b

Guided practice worksheet

E

c

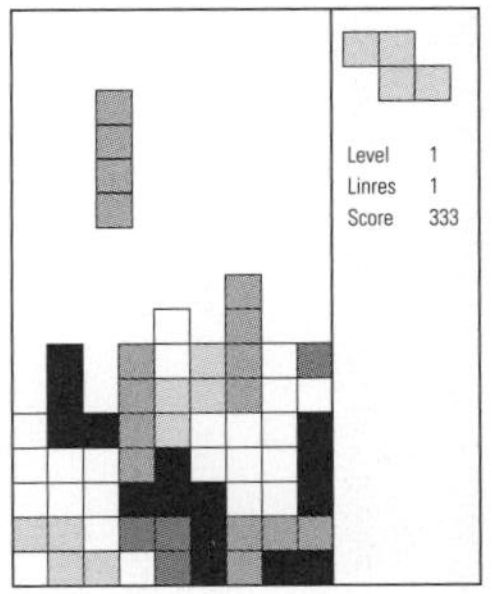

Level 1
Linres 1
Score 333

d

e

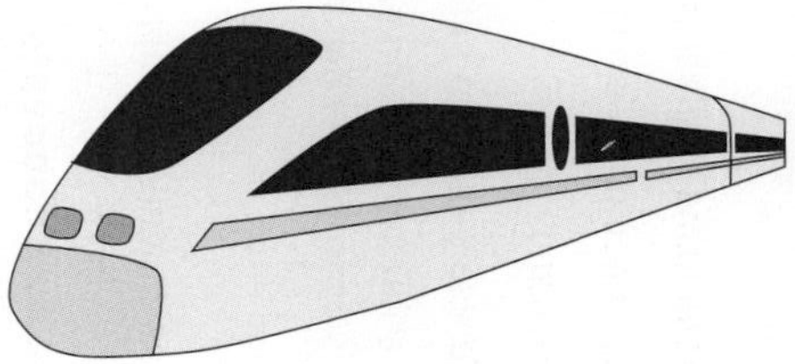

f

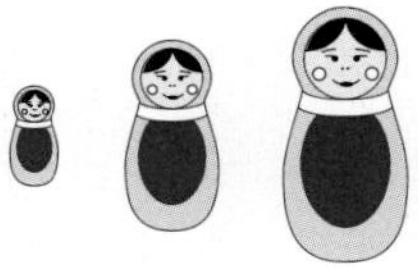

g

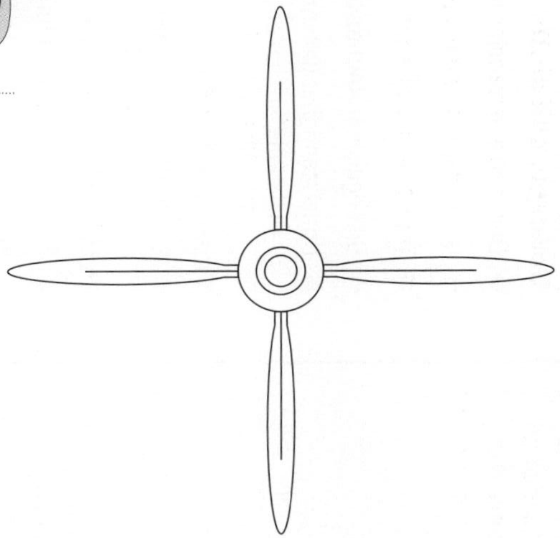

h

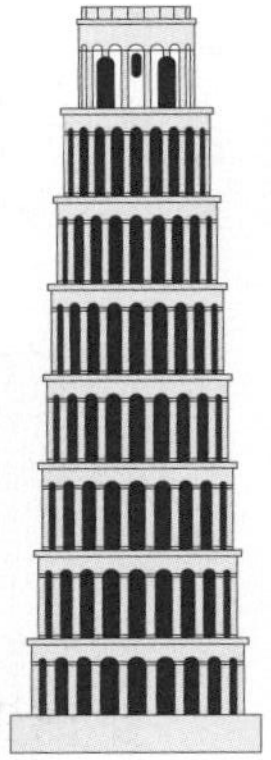

Specification

GCSE 2010
GM I (part) Describe and transform 2D shapes using single… translations… and distinguish properties that are preserved under particular transformations

FS Process skills
Use appropriate mathematical procedures
Find results and solutions

FS Performance
Level 1 Apply mathematics in an organised way to find solutions to straightforward practical problems for different purposes

Resources

Resources
Tracing paper

ActiveTeach resources
Transformations quiz
Transformations 2 interactive

23.2 Translations

Concepts and skills

- Describe and transform 2D shapes using single translations.
- Understand that translations are specified by a distance and direction (using a vector).
- Translate a given shape by the vector $\begin{pmatrix} 2 \\ -3 \end{pmatrix}$.
- Distinguish properties that are preserved under particular transformations.
- Understand that distances and angles are preserved under rotations, reflections and translations, so that any figure is congruent under any of these transformations.

Functional skills

- L1 Construct geometric diagrams, models and shapes.

Prior key knowledge, skills and concepts

- Students need to understand basic instructions with regard to direction, for example, up, down, left, right.

Starter

- Provide students with a set of moves. Working in pairs, one student describes the set of moves to their partner. Can the partner replicate the moves?

Main teaching and learning

- Explain to the students that a translation is a sliding movement.
- Emphasise that 'right' and 'up' are both positive movements, while 'left' and 'down' are both negative.
- To begin, demonstrate moving individual points. Then progress to moving shapes.
- Ensure practice by using tracing paper.
- Start with simple translations and then move on to more complex ones.
- When describing translations, ensure that students provide a full description.

Common misconceptions

- Students sometimes miscount when deciding moves.
- In deducing or using column vectors, some students forget the negative signs.
- Students can sometimes attempt translations of shapes without tracing paper, sometimes resulting in distorted or misplaced shapes.

Enrichment

- Describe a translation for a move from A to B, and then ask students to provide the translation back from B to A. *Is there a common rule for all such 'reverse' moves?*
- Ask students to perform combinations of translations and then ask them to replace these moves with just one translation from start to finish. Alternatively, ask them to set their own problems in pairs.

Plenary

- Give students a number of translations, either by word or by column vector. Provide some examples that require students to complete the translation and others where they need to describe the translation that has taken place.

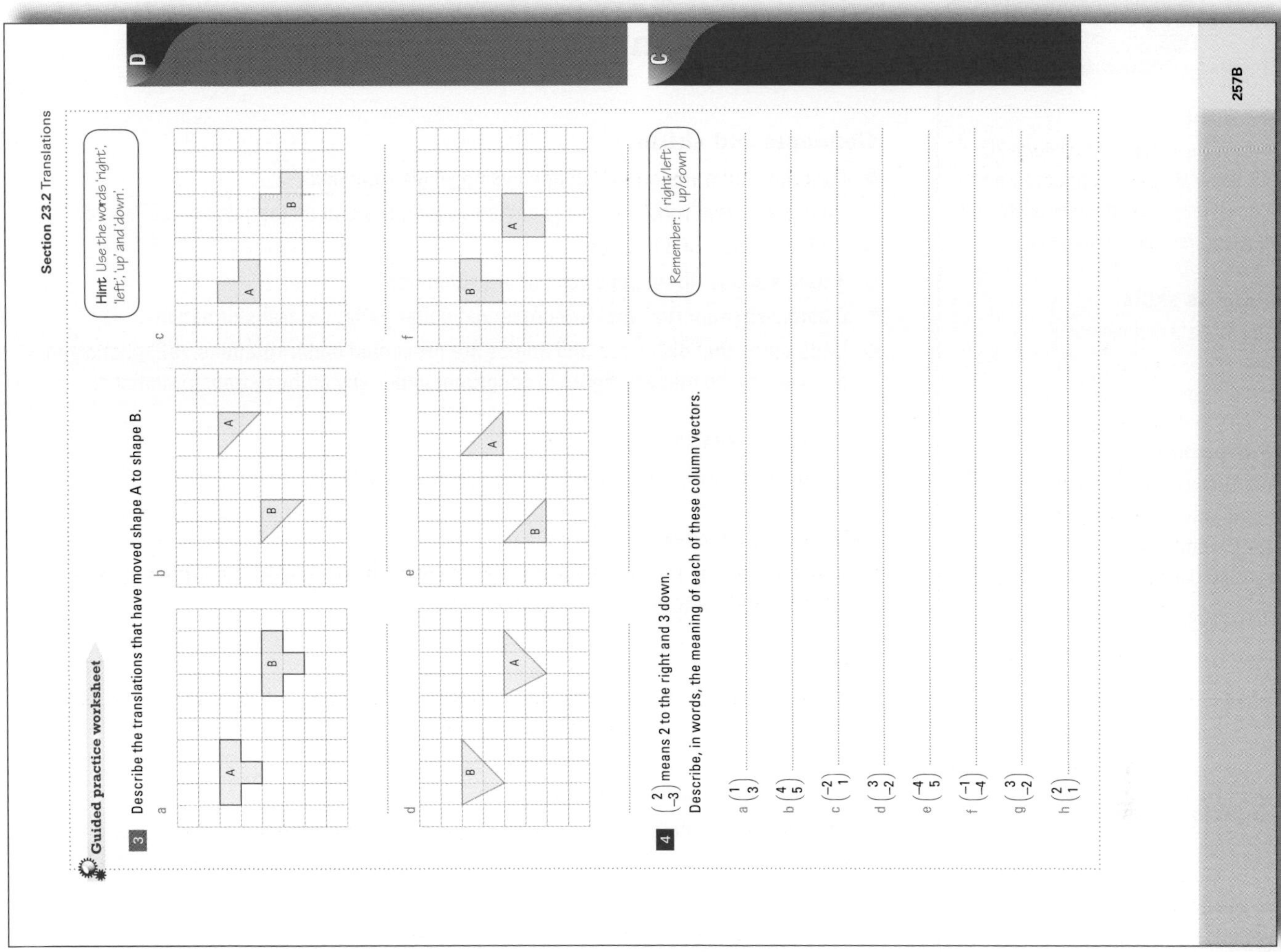

Guided practice worksheet

D

1 Translate each shape as requested.

a 3 squares right

b 2 squares up

c 4 squares down

2 Translate each shape as requested.

a 3 squares right, 1 square down

b 2 squares up, 2 squares left

c 4 squares left, 2 squares down

Guided practice worksheet

D

Hint Use the words 'right', 'left', 'up' and 'down'.

3 Describe the translations that have moved shape A to shape B.

a

b

c

d

e

f

C

4 $\begin{pmatrix} 2 \\ -3 \end{pmatrix}$ means 2 to the right and 3 down.

Describe, in words, the meaning of each of these column vectors.

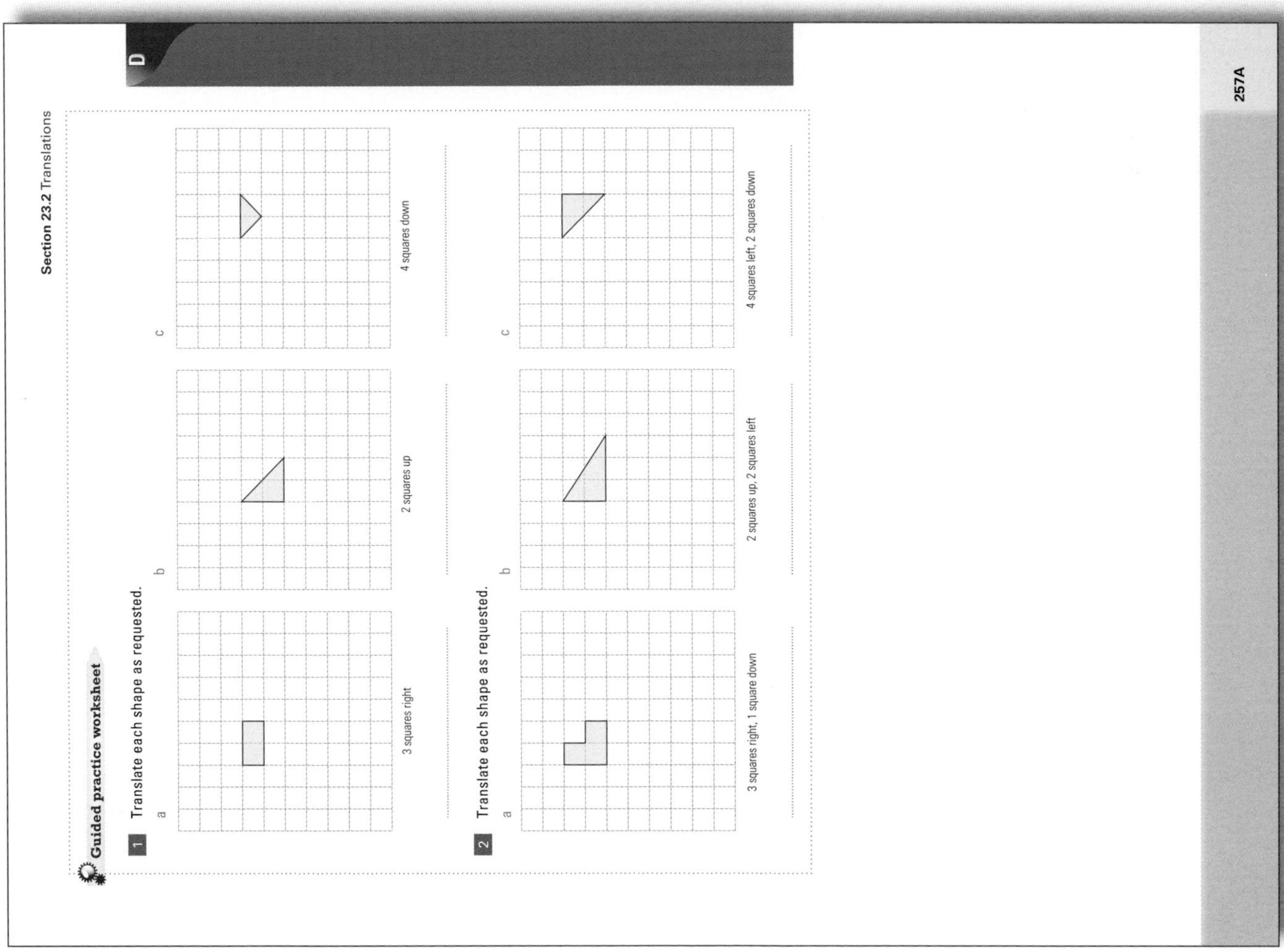

Remember: $\begin{pmatrix} \text{right/left} \\ \text{up/down} \end{pmatrix}$

a $\begin{pmatrix} 1 \\ 3 \end{pmatrix}$

b $\begin{pmatrix} 4 \\ 5 \end{pmatrix}$

c $\begin{pmatrix} -2 \\ 1 \end{pmatrix}$

d $\begin{pmatrix} 3 \\ -2 \end{pmatrix}$

e $\begin{pmatrix} -4 \\ 5 \end{pmatrix}$

f $\begin{pmatrix} -1 \\ -4 \end{pmatrix}$

g $\begin{pmatrix} 3 \\ -2 \end{pmatrix}$

h $\begin{pmatrix} 2 \\ 1 \end{pmatrix}$

Specification

GCSE 2010

GM I (part) Describe and transform 2D shapes using single… rotations… and distinguish properties that are preserved under particular transformations

FS Process skills

Use appropriate mathematical procedures

Find results and solutions

FS Performance

Level 1 Apply mathematics in an organised way to find solutions to straightforward practical problems for different purposes

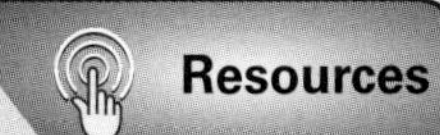

Resources

Resources

Tracing paper

ActiveTeach resources

Asymmetric bars 2 video

Floor exercises video

23.3 Rotations

Concepts and skills

- Describe and transform 2D shapes using single rotations.
- Understand that rotations are specified by a centre and an (anticlockwise) angle.
- Find the centre of a rotation.
- Rotate a shape about the origin, or any other point.
- Distinguish properties that are preserved under particular transformations.
- Understand that distances and angles are preserved under rotations, reflections and translations, so that any figure is congruent under any of these transformations.

Functional skills

- L1 Construct geometric diagrams, models and shapes.

Prior key knowledge, skills and concepts

- Students need to be aware of the language of rotation, for example left rotation, right rotation, quarter turn, clockwise, anticlockwise.

Starter

- Experiments with cards as described in the Student Book. Ask students to describe common objects that have rotational symmetry.

Main teaching and learning

- Explain how to rotate a shape to help judge its order of rotational symmetry, and discuss how it must have order >1 to have symmetry.
- Ensure students understand clockwise and anticlockwise directions.
- Consider common turns, for example half, quarter, 180°, 90°.
- Start with rotations about a central point such as the centre of the shape or the origin of a grid, before moving on to use other points.
- Discuss with students the effect of having a point of rotation in a position other than central.
- Explain all the aspects required in a description of a rotation, and ensure students include these in any descriptions of rotations that they give.
- Ask students to discuss effective ways of finding the centre of rotation for their descriptions.

Common misconceptions

- Students sometimes fail to use tracing paper, which can result in errors.
- Some students rotate clockwise rather than anticlockwise (or vice versa).
- Another common error that some students make is always using a point that is central rather than one that is given.
- Students might incorrectly draw a rotation when it overlaps.
- Some students might fail to include all aspects in the required description of a rotation.

Enrichment

- Give students a shape on a square grid. Ask them to add shaded squares so that it has rotational symmetry of 2, 4, 8. Make the shapes progressively more complex.
- Give students a shape to rotate. Ask them to produce rotations from a given point that are 45°, 90°, 135°, and so on.

Plenary

- Give students a number of shapes and ask them to produce rotations, both from a central point and by using a number of vertices as points of rotation. Use different directions of rotation.

rotation centre of rotation clockwise anticlockwise

F

Guided practice worksheet

→ = clockwise; ← = anticlockwise

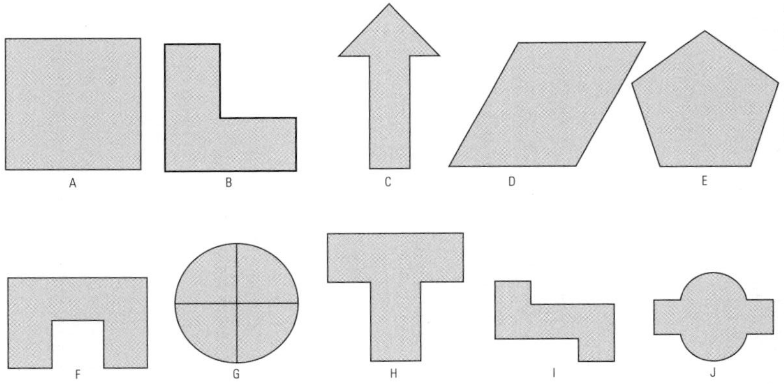

1 Which of these shapes have rotational symmetry?

A B C D E

F G H I J

2 Write down the order of rotational symmetry of each of these shapes.

a 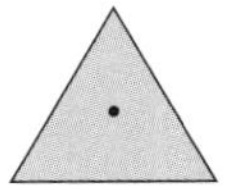 .... b 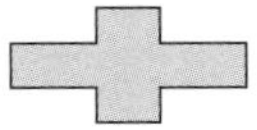 .... c ....

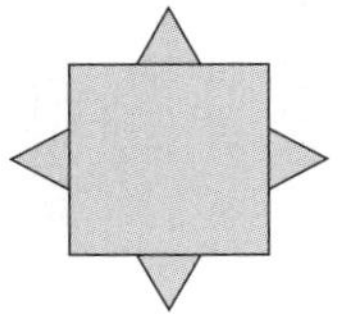

d 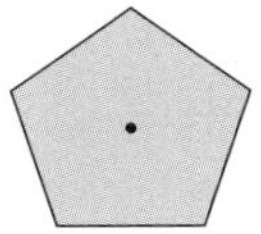 .... e 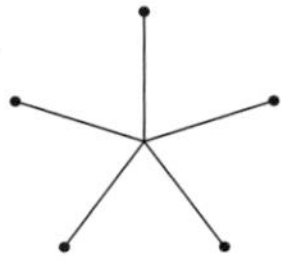 .... f ....

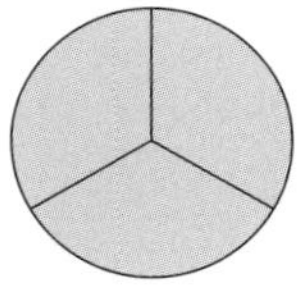

g 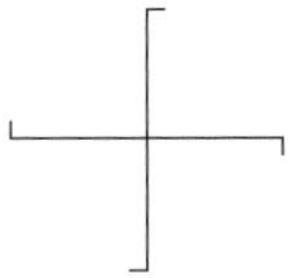 .... h 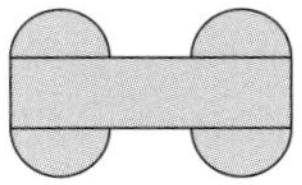 .... i ....

F

Guided practice worksheet

3 Rotate each of these shapes as requested, about the origin.

a Rotation 90° clockwise

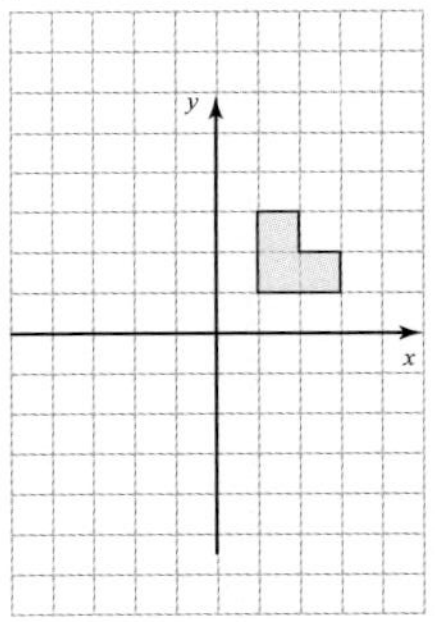

b Rotation 180°

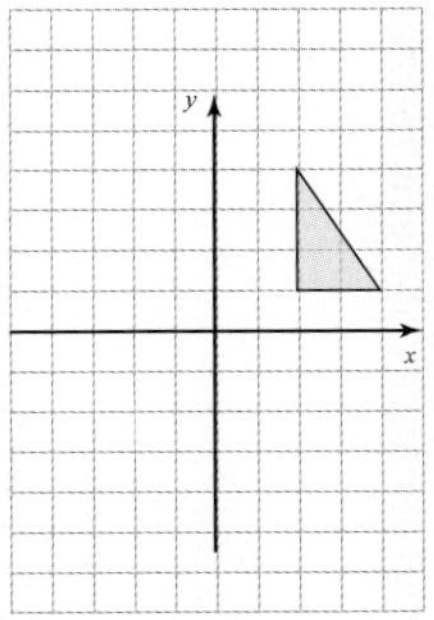

c Rotation 90° anticlockwise

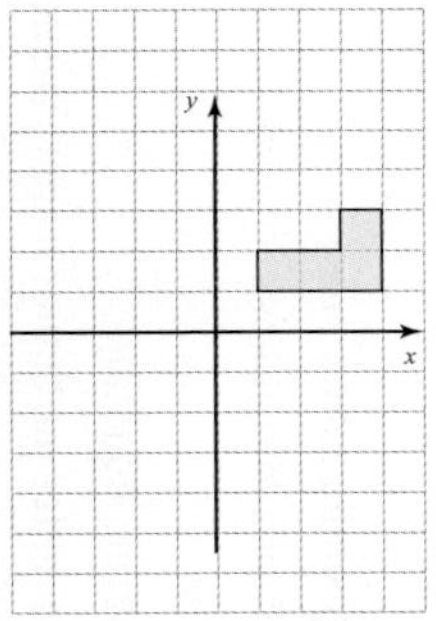

d Rotation 180°

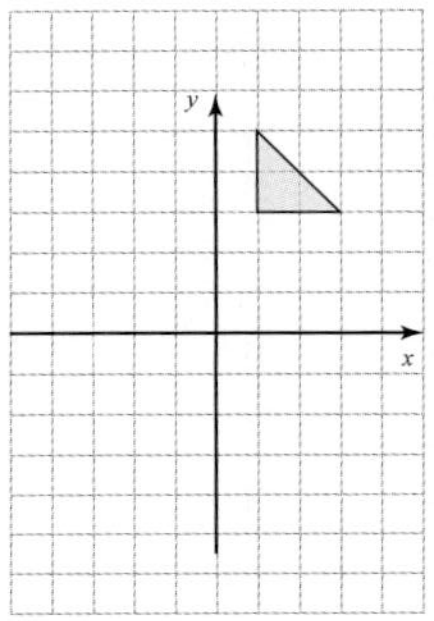

e Rotation 90° anticlockwise

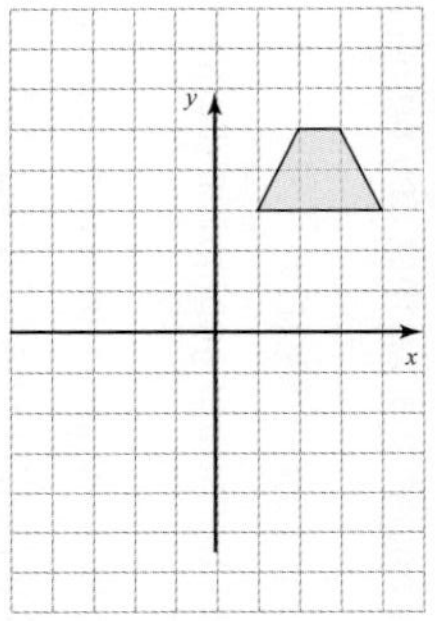

f Rotation 90° clockwise

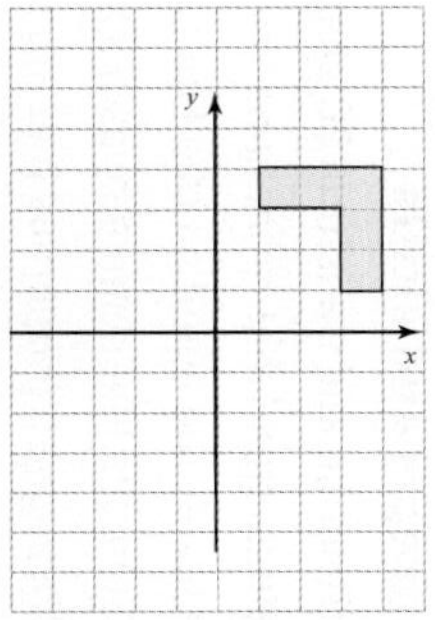

Specification

GCSE 2010

GM e (part) Recognise reflection… symmetry of 2D shapes

GM l (part) Describe and transform 2D shapes using single… reflections… and distinguish properties that are preserved under particular transformations

FS Process skills

Use appropriate mathematical procedures

Find results and solutions

FS Performance

Level 1 Apply mathematics in an organised way to find solutions to straightforward practical problems for different purposes

Resources

Links

http://www.bbc.co.uk/schools/gcsebitesize/maths/shapes/symmetryact.shtml

ActiveTeach resources

Straight lines quiz

Reflection interactive

23.4 Reflections

Concepts and skills

- Describe and transform 2D shapes using single reflections.
- Understand that reflections are specified by a mirror line.
- Identify the equation of a line of symmetry.
- State the line symmetry as a simple algebraic equation.
- Distinguish properties that are preserved under particular transformations.
- Understand that distances and angles are preserved under rotations, reflections and translations, so that any figure is congruent under any of these transformations.

Functional Skills

- L1 Construct geometric diagrams, models and shapes.

Prior key knowledge, skills and concepts

- Students need to understand work on coordinate grids, the x- and y-axes, and be able to read and plot coordinates in all four quadrants.

Starter

- Discuss with the students some common examples of objects or things that have reflective symmetry.

Main teaching and learning

- Ask students to work on identifying shapes that have reflective symmetry, and putting in mirror lines.
- Compare common shapes such as the square and the rectangle; the parallelogram and the rhombus.
- Begin by discussing simple reflections where the shape is against the mirror line, and then move on to reflections where the shape is apart from the mirror line.
- Discuss what types of shape will have reflective symmetry; students could try drawing their own shapes.
- Explain the common lines of symmetry on a grid (x- and y-axes, $y = x$ and $y = -x$).
- Explain all the aspects required in a description of a reflection, and ensure students include these in descriptions of reflections given.
- Discuss with students effective ways of finding the line of symmetry for their descriptions.

Common misconceptions

- Students sometimes insert too many mirror lines in shapes: e.g. 8 lines on a rectangle.
- Some students fail to use tracing paper, which can result in badly drawn reflections.
- Students might produce the correct shape, but with incorrect spacing from the mirror line.
- Sometimes students produce a reflection on a grid, using an axis as a mirror line rather than the given line of symmetry.
- Some students might use the wrong axis as the line of symmetry.

Enrichment

- Ask students to perform and describe reflections where the line of symmetry is a diagonal – students tend to find this the most difficult task.
- Students could be asked to produce some shapes that will have reflective symmetry about two lines of symmetry.

Plenary

- Emphasise that students should take care when drawing lines of symmetry (refer to the square and the rectangle again).
- Students can be asked to produce their own shapes that have reflective symmetry. Given some shapes, ask students to describe their symmetry.

reflection line of reflection

Guided practice worksheet

G

1 Draw one line of symmetry on each of the shapes below.

a b c

d e f

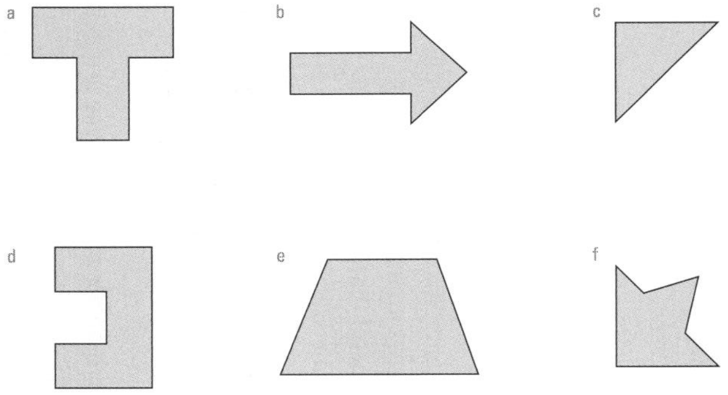

2 Draw all the lines of symmetry on each of the shapes below.

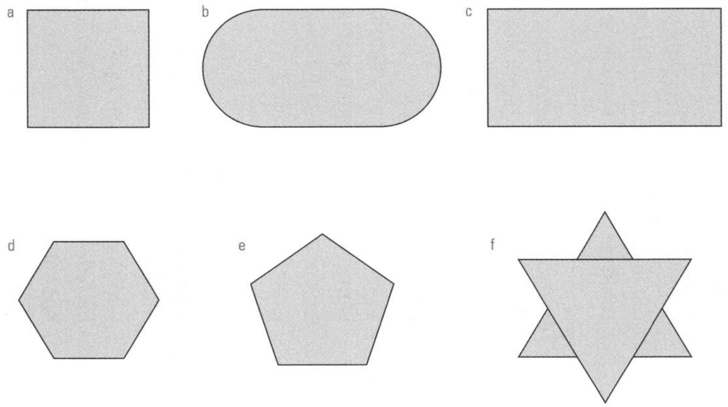

a b c

d e f

Guided practice worksheet

G

3 Draw the reflection in the line of symmetry.

a b c

d e f

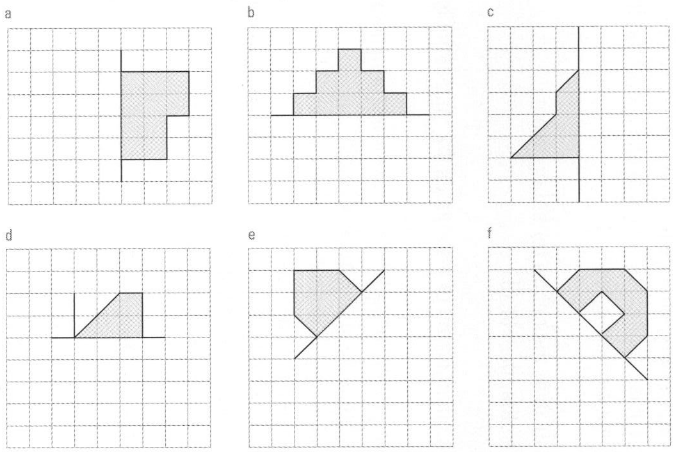

4 Draw the reflection in the line of symmetry.

a b c

d e

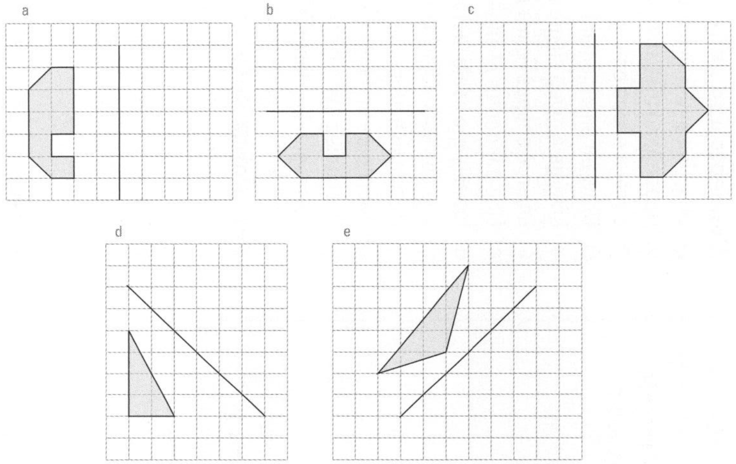

Specification

GCSE 2010

GM l (part) Describe and transform 2D shapes using single... enlargements by a positive scale factor and distinguish properties that are preserved under particular transformations

GM f Understand congruence and similarity

FS Process skills

Use appropriate mathematical procedures

Find results and solutions

FS Performance

Level 1 Apply mathematics in an organised way to find solutions to straightforward practical problems for different purposes

23.5 Enlargement

Concepts and skills

- Describe and transform 2D shapes using enlargements by a positive scale factor.
- Understand that an enlargement is specified by a centre and a scale factor.
- Scale a shape on a grid (without a centre specified).
- Draw an enlargement.
- Enlarge a given shape using (0, 0) as the centre for enlargement.
- Enlarge shapes with a centre other than (0, 0).
- Find the centre of enlargement.
- Identify the scale factor of an enlargement of a shape as the ratio of the lengths of the two corresponding sides.
- Distinguish properties that are preserved under particular transformations.
- Recognise that enlargements preserve angle, but not length.
- Recognise that all corresponding angles in similar shapes are equal in size when the corresponding lengths of sides are not equal in size.

Functional skills

- L1 Construct geometric diagrams, models and shapes.

Prior key knowledge, skills and concepts

- Students need to understand work on coordinate grids, the x- and y-axes, and be able to read and plot coordinates in all four quadrants.

Starter

- Ask students to practise copying pictures and diagrams onto grids that are twice the size.

Main teaching and learning

- Start by producing enlargements of simple shapes on enlarged grids, then move on to grids of the same size (on which enlargements can be produced).
- Explain that enlargements can be of scale factor 2, 3 or 4, but at GCSE we do not deal with enlargements greater than 4; then move to scale factors of $1\frac{1}{2}$, $2\frac{1}{2}$ and so on.
- Explore methods of enlargement from a point (counting squares, using 'ray' lines); students could discuss which method they prefer.
- Explain all the aspects required in a description of an enlargement, and ensure students include these in descriptions of enlargements given.
- Students could discuss effective ways of finding the points of enlargement, and the scale factor of enlargement, for their descriptions.

Common misconceptions

- When using a scale factor students sometimes enlarge some, but not all, of the lines to the required scale factor.
- Sometimes students use the wrong point of enlargement, or ignore the request to use a point of enlargement.
- Lines from the point of enlargement are sometimes drawn incorrectly (for example, the lines fail to go diagonally through all squares on the grid correctly).
- Students sometimes produce an enlargement that is more than that requested, for example if scale factor 2 is requested, some students produce an enlargement of scale factor 3.

Enrichment

- Students could be given more complex shapes.
- Centres of enlargement within a shape are more difficult.
- Include some coordinate work also, where points and/or shapes are described by coordinates.

Plenary

- Ask students to enlarge a given shape by a scale factor. Then include a point of enlargement and ask students to produce another image. Given a shape and its image, can students describe the enlargement?

enlargement scale factor centre of enlargement

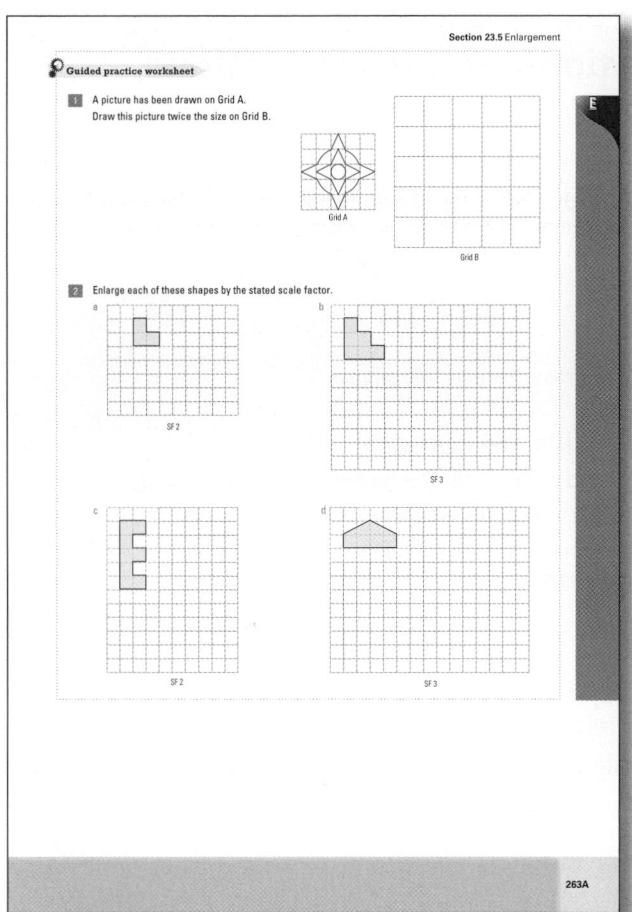
Section 23.5 Enlargement
Guided practice worksheet
1 A picture has been drawn on Grid A.
Draw this picture twice the size on Grid B.
Grid A
Grid B
2 Enlarge each of these shapes by the stated scale factor.
a
SF 2
b
SF 3
c
SF 2
d
SF 3
263A

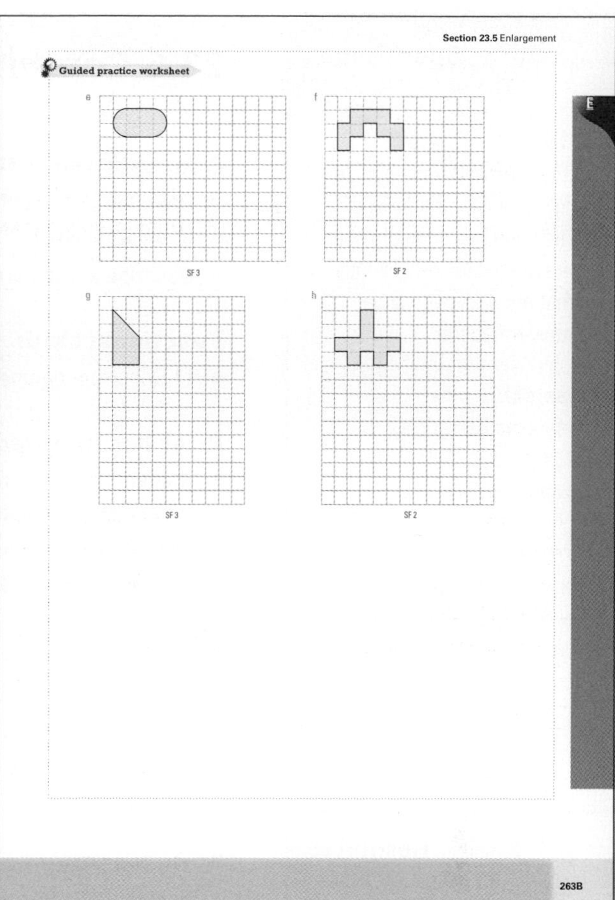
Section 23.5 Enlargement
Guided practice worksheet
e
SF 3
f
SF 2
g
SF 3
h
SF 2
263B

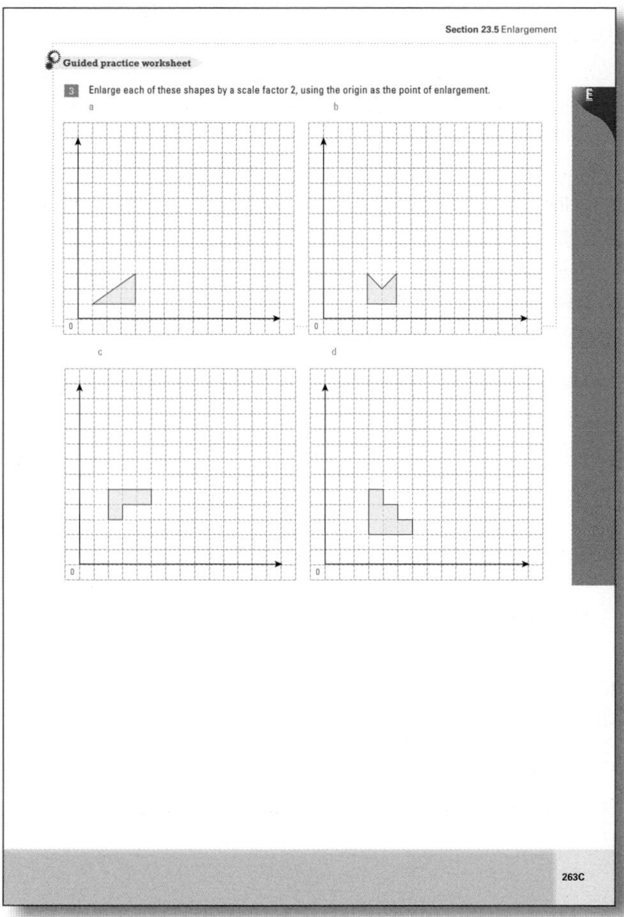
Section 23.5 Enlargement
Guided practice worksheet
3 Enlarge each of these shapes by a scale factor 2, using the origin as the point of enlargement.
a
b
c
d
0
263C

Specification

GCSE 2010
GM I (part) Describe and transform 2D shapes using… combined rotations, reflections, translations, or enlargements by a positive scale factor and distinguish properties that are preserved under particular transformations

FS Process skills
Use appropriate mathematical procedures
Find results and solutions

FS Performance
Level 1 Apply mathematics in an organised way to find solutions to straightforward practical problems for different purposes

Resources

Resources
Tracing paper

ActiveTeach resources
RP KC Transformations knowledge check
RP PS Transformations problem solving

23.6 Combinations of transformations

Concepts and skills

- Describe and transform 2D shapes using combined rotations, reflections, translations or enlargements.
- Describe a transformation.

Functional skills

- L1 Construct geometric diagrams, models and shapes.

Prior key knowledge, skills and concepts

- Students need to understand work on coordinate grids, the x- and y-axes, and be able to read and plot coordinates in all four quadrants.
- They also need to have a working knowledge of the four common transformations covered in Sections 23.2 to 23.5.

Starter

- Do the 'Get ready' exercise given.
- Discuss and summarise all the transformations met so far.
- Students should be aware of the differences between the four common transformations.

Main teaching and learning

- Recap on the four transformations, ensuring students are aware of their features.
- Look for differences between the transformations; ask students how they would identify what type of transformation needs to be described.
- Ensure also that students have a list of the features that need to be described for each transformation.
- Give an example of a multiple transformation, referring to the language used in the question: mapping, image, and the use of letters.
- Emphasise the importance of drawing each transformation clearly, using tracing paper if required, and then identifying the two which should be compared for deriving a description for the single transformation.

Common misconceptions

- Students sometimes select the wrong transformation.
- They might produce incomplete descriptions of features of a chosen transformation.
- Some students might fail to use tracing paper when this would have assisted in drawing the transformations.

Enrichment

- Students can be asked to find combinations of transformations that result in a given single transformation.

Plenary

- Ask students to list the features that need to be included when describing each of the four common transformations.

Guided practice worksheet

1 a

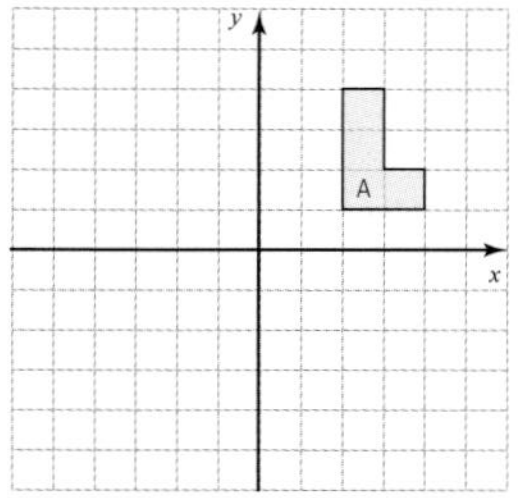

Reflect this shape in the x-axis. Call the answer B.
Then reflect B in the y-axis. Call the answer C.

b

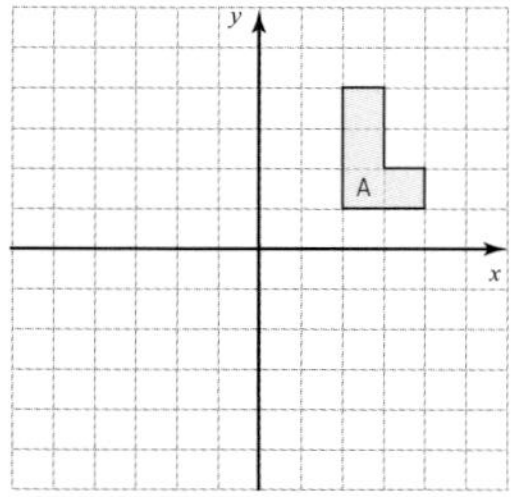

Reflect this shape in the y-axis. Call the answer B.
Then reflect B in the x-axis. Call the answer C.

c Do a and b give you the same result?

....

d What could you do to move directly from A to C in one step?

....

C

Section 23.6 Combinations of transformations

Guided practice worksheet

2 a

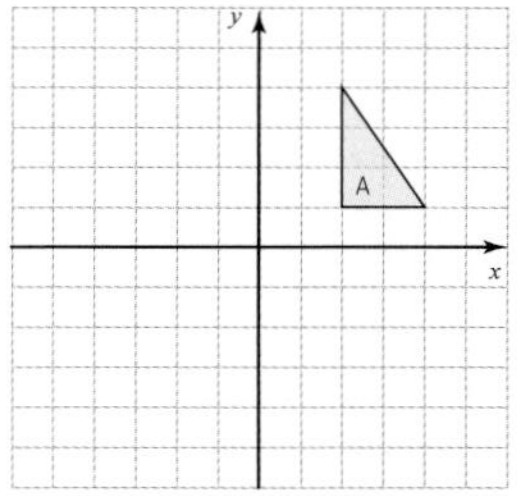

Rotate this shape 90° clockwise. Call the answer B.
Then rotate B 90° clockwise. Call the answer C.

b

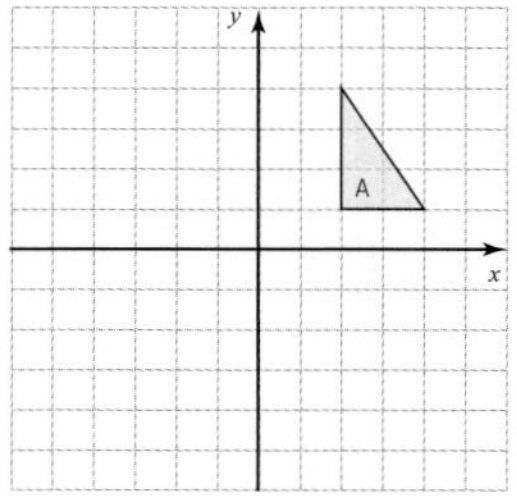

Rotate this shape 90° anticlockwise. Call the answer B.
Then rotate B 90° anticlockwise. Call the answer C.

c Do a and b give you the same result?

....

d What could you do to move directly from A to C in one step?

....

C

Specification

GCSE 2010

N p (part) Use ratio notation, including reduction to its simplest form…

FS Process skills

Recognise that a situation has aspects that can be represented using mathematics
Examine patterns and relationships

FS Performance

Level 2 Apply a range of mathematics to find solutions

Resources

Resources

Card or paper for dominoes, mini whiteboards

Links

http://nrich.maths.org/4793
http://nrich.maths.org/4824

24.1 Introducing ratio

Concepts and skills

- Use ratios.
- Write ratios in their simplest form.

Functional skills

- L2 Understand, use and calculate ratio and proportion, including problems involving scale.

Prior key knowledge, skills and concepts

- Students should be able to multiply and divide by an integer.
- Students should be able to simplify a fraction and find equivalent fractions.
- Students should be able to convert between metric units.

Starter

- Give students various fractions to write in their simplest form. The 'Get ready' questions can be used to provide a further check.

Main teaching and learning

- Tell students that they are going to find out about ratio.
- Discuss students' understanding of the term ratio.
- Display 1 red counter and 2 blue counters. Ask questions such as: '*What is the ratio red : blue?*', '*What is the ratio blue : red?*', '*What fraction of the counters is red?*'
- Discuss how to simplify a ratio, linking to work on simplifying fractions.
- Ask students whether the ratio 2 : 5 can be simplified. Explain that when both sides of the ratio are divided by 2 the ratio is in unitary form.

Common misconceptions

- Emphasise that the order of the numbers in a ratio is important. When asked to write down and simplify a ratio, students should write down the initial ratio before attempting to simplify it.

Enrichment

- Students can work in pairs to make a set of 20 cards, where 10 cards each have a ratio and the other 10 cards have the same ratios in their simplest form. The cards are placed face down in four rows of five and the students take turns to try to turn over a matching pair.
- Problem: *A female fish has 5 stripes and a male fish has 4 stripes. There is a total of 31 stripes in my fish tank. What is the ratio of female fish to male fish?* (3 : 4)

Plenary

- Display several ratios and ask students to write each one in its simplest form and also in the form 1 : n. Mini whiteboards could be used.

ratio unitary

Guided practice worksheet

E

1

Remember: Write the ratio in the correct order.

a What is the ratio of the number of shaded tiles to the number of white tiles?

b What is the ratio of the number of white tiles to the number of shaded tiles?

2

a What is the ratio of the number of circles to the number of squares?

b What is the ratio of the number of squares to the number of circles?

3 The ratio of the number of boys to the number of girls in a class is 2 : 3.
What is the ratio of the number of girls to the number of boys?

4

Hint Use the diagram to help you write the correct fractions.

The ratio of white cubes to shaded cubes is 1 : 2.

a What fraction of these cubes is white? ....

b What fraction of these cubes is shaded? ....

5 A box contains blue pens and black pens in the ratio 3 : 7.
What fraction of these pens is blue?

6 Write these ratios in their simplest form.

Hint Find the highest common factor of the two numbers.

a 2 : 10 .... b 5 : 25 ....

c 12 : 16 .... d 10 : 35 ....

7 In a safari park there are 21 lions and 45 monkeys.
Write down the ratio of the number of lions to the number of monkeys.
Give your ratio in its simplest form.

Guided practice worksheet

E

8 Write each of these ratios in its simplest form.

Hint Make the units the same.

a 20p : £1 .... b 60 cm : 1 m ....

c 6 cm : 4 mm .... d 1 hour : 35 minutes ....

D

9 Write these ratios in the form 1 : n.

a 2 : 6 .... b 3 : 12 ....

c 10 : 45 .... d 5 : 28 ....

10 The length of a model boat is 30 cm. The length of the real boat is 540 cm.
Write down the ratio of the length of the model boat to the length of the real boat.
Give your ratio in the form 1 : n.

Specification

GCSE 2010
N p Use ratio notation, including reduction to its simplest form and its various links to fraction notation
N t Divide a quantity in a given ratio

FS Process skills
Recognise that a situation has aspects that can be represented using mathematics
Examine patterns and relationships

FS Performance
Level 2 Apply a range of mathematics to find solutions

Resources

Links
http://www.bbc.co.uk/schools/gcsebitesize/maths/number/ratiosact.shtml

ActiveTeach resources
Proportion interactive
Cycling 1 video

24.2 Solving ratio problems

Concepts and skills

- Use ratios.
- Solve a ratio problem in context.

Functional skills

- L2 Understand, use and calculate ratio and proportion, including problems involving scale.

Prior key knowledge, skills and concepts

- Students should already be able to find equivalent fractions.

Starter

- Display five fractions $\left(\frac{2}{6}, \frac{5}{15}, \frac{3}{6}, \frac{1}{3}, \frac{4}{12}\right)$. Ask students to identify the odd one out and to justify their answer $\left(\frac{3}{6}\right)$. The 'Get ready' questions can also be used to check understanding of equivalent fractions.

Main teaching and learning

- Tell students that they are going to use ratio to solve problems.
- Introduce an example of mixing paint, e.g. 2 parts red and 5 parts white to make pink. Ask questions such as *How much white would we need if we used 4 parts of red?*
- Use the example of mixing paint to formalise the method shown in Example 6.
- Ask where students might see scales (on maps and scale models). Discuss Example 7.

Common misconceptions

- Encourage students to think about the size of their answers, particularly in scale model questions. Should the answer be smaller or larger than the measurement given in the question?

Enrichment

- Ask students to research the different scales used on maps. Which scale shows an area in the greatest detail?
- Research model cars, recording for each one the scale used and the dimensions. From this information students can work out the dimensions of the real cars.

Plenary

- Display a list of ratios (e.g. 2 : 5, 3 : 2, 6 : 4, 3 : 4, 1 : 2, 6 : 15, 4 : 8) and ask for the odd one out. *Why is it the odd one out?*
- Display a spider diagram with the ratio 24 : 60 in the centre. Ask students to add equivalent ratios to the diagram. *Which one gives the ratio in its simplest form?*
- State that a company is producing model cars using a scale of 1 : 24. Ask how long the real car will be for different lengths of model car.

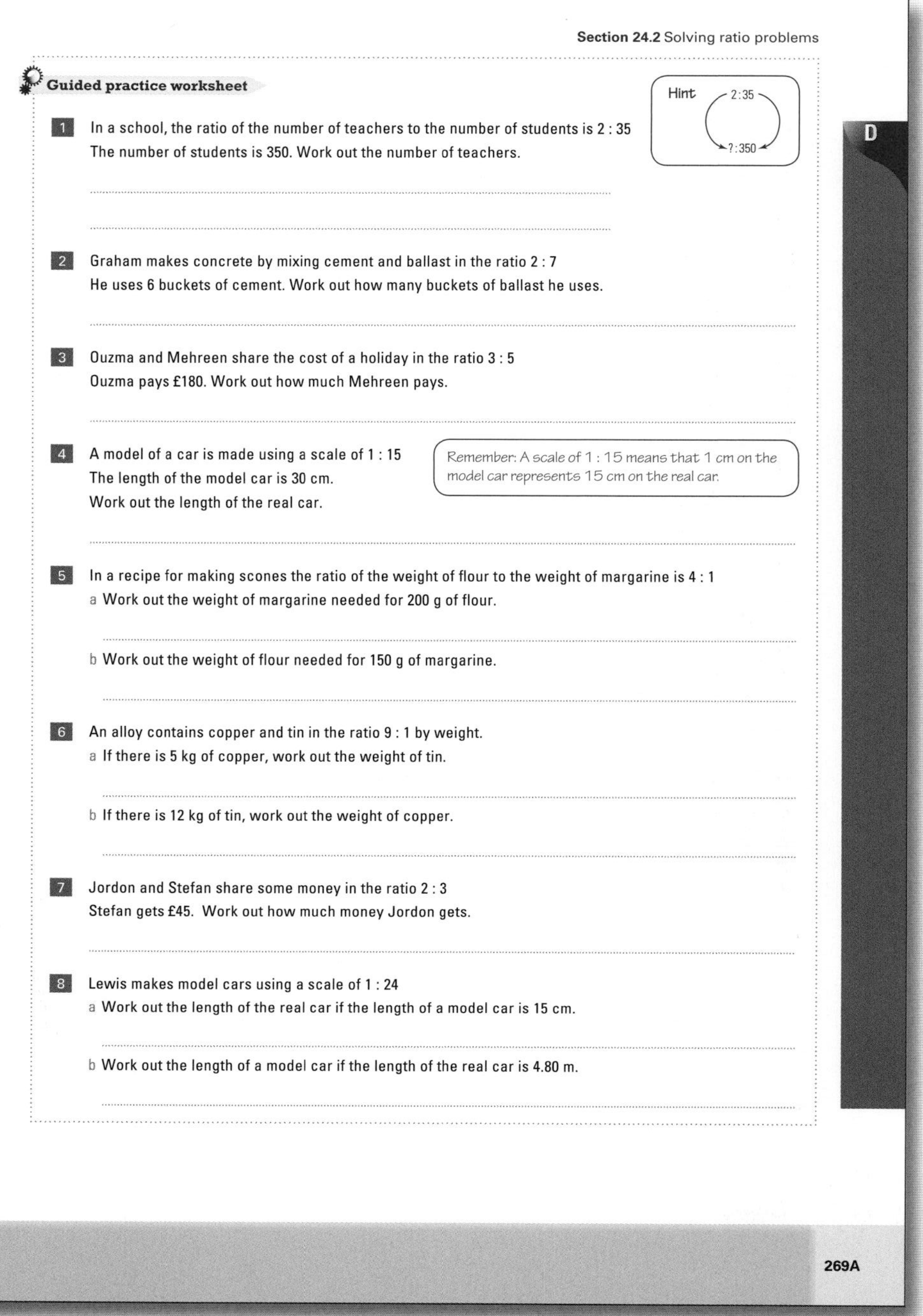

Guided practice worksheet

Hint: 2 : 35 → ? : 350

1. In a school, the ratio of the number of teachers to the number of students is 2 : 35
   The number of students is 350. Work out the number of teachers.

2. Graham makes concrete by mixing cement and ballast in the ratio 2 : 7
   He uses 6 buckets of cement. Work out how many buckets of ballast he uses.

3. Ouzma and Mehreen share the cost of a holiday in the ratio 3 : 5
   Ouzma pays £180. Work out how much Mehreen pays.

4. A model of a car is made using a scale of 1 : 15
   The length of the model car is 30 cm.
   Work out the length of the real car.

   Remember: A scale of 1 : 15 means that 1 cm on the model car represents 15 cm on the real car.

5. In a recipe for making scones the ratio of the weight of flour to the weight of margarine is 4 : 1
   a Work out the weight of margarine needed for 200 g of flour.

   b Work out the weight of flour needed for 150 g of margarine.

6. An alloy contains copper and tin in the ratio 9 : 1 by weight.
   a If there is 5 kg of copper, work out the weight of tin.

   b If there is 12 kg of tin, work out the weight of copper.

7. Jordon and Stefan share some money in the ratio 2 : 3
   Stefan gets £45. Work out how much money Jordon gets.

8. Lewis makes model cars using a scale of 1 : 24
   a Work out the length of the real car if the length of a model car is 15 cm.

   b Work out the length of a model car if the length of the real car is 4.80 m.

D

Section 24.2 Solving ratio problems

Guided practice worksheet

Note: 100 cm = 1 m, 1000 m = 1 km

9. The scale of a map is 1 : 100 000
   On the map the distance between two villages is 7 cm.
   Work out the real distance between the two villages.

10. The scale of a map is 1 : 50 000
    On the map the distance between two churches is 5 cm.
    Work out the real distance between the two churches.

D

Specification

GCSE 2010
N t Divide a quantity in a given ratio

FS Process skills
Recognise that a situation has aspects that can be represented using mathematics
Examine patterns and relationships

FS Performance
Apply mathematics in an organised way to find solutions to straightforward practical problems for different purposes

Resources

Resources
Counters (for starter)

ActiveTeach resources
Ratios interactive
Ink video

24.3 Sharing in a given ratio

Concepts and skills

- Divide a quantity in a given ratio.
- Solve a ratio problem in context.

Functional skills

- L1 Solve simple problems involving ratio, where one number is a multiple of the other.

Prior key knowledge, skills and concepts

- Students should be able to write down a ratio.
- Students should be able to simplify a ratio.

Starter

- Ask students to divide 12 counters in different ratios, e.g. 1 : 1, 1 : 2, 3 : 1, 2 : 3 : 1.

Main teaching and learning

- Tell students that they are going to find out about sharing in a given ratio.
- Choose two students, and say that one will get £3 for every £1 that the other gets. Ask how much each will get when different amounts are shared out.
- Work through Example 8, and remind students that the order of the numbers in a ratio is important.

Common misconceptions

- Emphasise that when sharing in a given ratio students should first work out the total number of shares. A common error is to divide the total amount by each of the numbers in the ratio.

Enrichment

- Ask students to make up some 'sharing in a given ratio' problems for a partner to solve.

Plenary

- Students could produce a spider diagram showing possible ways of sharing £30 between two people. For each way they should give the ratio used and the amount each person gets.
- More able students could share the £30 among three people.

Guided practice worksheet

D

Hint: First, work out the total number of shares.

1 Share £30 in the ratio 2 : 1

2 Share £50 in the ratio 2 : 3

3 Share £40 in the ratio 3 : 5

4 Mr Branch has a wooden post 180 cm long.
He cuts it into two pieces in the ratio 4 : 5
Work out the length of each piece.

5 Neil and Liz share £120 in the ratio 1 : 4
Work out how much each person gets.

6 Faisal tiles a wall. He uses blue tiles and white tiles in the ratio 3 : 4
Altogether he uses 280 tiles. Work out how many blue tiles he uses.

Remember: The order of the numbers in the ratio is important.

7 The ratio of boys to girls in a school is 5 : 7
There are 384 pupils in the school. Work out the number of girls in the school.

8 Ross and Toni share 40 grapes in the ratio 3 : 5
Work out how many more grapes Toni gets than Ross gets.

Section 24.3 Sharing in a given ratio

Guided practice worksheet

C

9 A recipe for cookies uses butter, sugar and flour in the ratio 4 : 3 : 5
Work out how much flour is needed to make 600 g of cookies.

10 Maria, Nikita and Paolo share £400 in the ratio 2 : 3 : 5
Work out how much each person gets.

Specification

GCSE 2010

N t Divide a quantity in a given ratio

FS Process skills

Recognise that a situation has aspects that can be represented using mathematics

Examine patterns and relationships

FS Performance

Level 2 Apply a range of mathematics to find solutions

Resources

Resources

Mini whiteboards, recipe for four people (Example 10), exchange rates, internet access for research

ActiveTeach resources

RP KC Ratio and proportion knowledge check

RP PS Ratio and proportion problem solving

24.4 Solving ratio and proportion problems using the unitary method

Concepts and skills

- Solve a ratio problem in context.

Functional skills

- L2 Understand, use and calculate ratio and proportion, including problems involving scale.

Prior key knowledge, skills and concepts

- Students should already be able to use a calculator to enter numbers and carry out the four operations.

Starter

- Use the 'Get ready' questions and ask a number of similar questions. *If 4 pencils cost £1.20, what does 1 pencil cost?* (30p). *If 5 bottles of water cost £6.25, what does 1 bottle of water cost?* (£1.25).

Main teaching and learning

- Tell students that they are going to find out about direct proportion.
- Work through an example similar to the one at the beginning of the section; 1 pencil costs 20p, 2 pencils cost 40p, 3 pencils cost 60p, etc. Explain that the two quantities are in direct proportion. Show that the ratio between them stays the same. Display the graph and discuss the key features.
- Display a recipe for 4 people (as in Example 10) and ask students how they would adapt it for different numbers of people, e.g. 8 people, 2 people. *What about 7 people?* Discuss how much of each ingredient is needed for one person and why this is useful to know.
- Work through some examples of using the unitary method.

Common misconceptions

- When working on exchange rates (as in Exercise 24M), encourage students to consider whether their answer is reasonable. If, for example, there is more than one euro to each pound then the number of euros should always be greater than the number of pounds.

Enrichment

- Students could find recipes and adapt them for different numbers of people.
- Ask students to find the current exchange rates. They could work out how much they would get in different currencies for £100. The exchange rates could also be used to draw conversion graphs, e.g. pounds to dollars.

Plenary

- Tell students that two bricks weigh 4.6 kg. Ask questions such as: '*What would 4 bricks weigh?*', '*What would 3 bricks weigh?*' Encourage students to justify their answers.
- Display an exchange rate from pounds to euros, e.g. £1 = 1.15 euros. Ask students how many euros they would get for £2, for £5, etc. Answers could be given on mini whiteboards.

direct proportion proportional

Guided practice worksheet

D

1 Elena went on holiday to Poland.
She changed £300 into euros. The exchange was £1 = 1.15 euros.
Work out how many euros Elena got.

Note: For each pound Elena gets 1.15 euros.

2 £1 = $1.45
a Change £450 into dollars.

b Change $464 into pounds.

3 James paid 117 francs for some sunglasses in Switzerland.
The exchange rate was £1 = 1.80 francs.
Work out the cost of the sunglasses in pounds.

4 Four pens cost 96p.
Work out the cost of 7 of these pens.

Hint *First, work out the cost of one item.*

5 2 kg of potatoes cost £1.50.
Work out the cost of 5 kg of potatoes.

6 Five bottles of cola cost £7.50.
Work out the cost of 3 bottles of cola.

7 The cost of 3 metres of material is £5.40.
Work out the cost of 8 metres of material.

8 Eight identical tins of paint cost £26.
Work out the cost of 5 of these tins of paint.

Section 24.4 Solving ratio and proportion problems using the unitary method

Guided practice worksheet

D

9 This is a list of ingredients needed to make date and nut salad for 4 people.

175 g dates
50 g walnut pieces
3 tablespoons lemon juice
150 ml yoghurt

Hint *What must you multiply 4 by to make 12?*

Sally is making date and nut salad for 12 people.
Work out how much of each ingredient she needs.

10 This is a recipe for making 12 oat crunchies.

50 g whole oats
70 g porridge oats
110 g margarine
75 g Demerara sugar

a Work out the amount of porridge oats needed to make 24 oat crunchies.

b Work out the amount of whole oats needed to make 6 oat crunchies.

c Work out the amount of margarine needed to make 18 oat crunchies.

Specification

GCSE 2010

SP g (part) Produce charts and diagrams….

SP i Interpret a wide range of graphs and diagrams and draw conclusions

FS Process skills

Recognise that a situation has aspects that can be represented using mathematics

Interpret results and solutions

FS Performance

Level 2 Identify the situation or problems and identify the mathematical methods needed to solve them

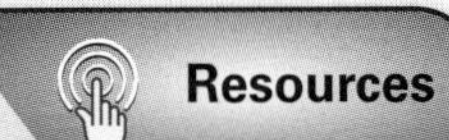

Resources

CD resources

MS PowerPoint presentation 25.1 'Line graphs'

Line graphs edexcel

Weather

		Temperature	Wind	Description
Saturday	00:00	17°C	5 knots	clear sky
	03:00	16°C	5 knots	clear intervals
	06:00	16°C	5 knots	sunny
	09:00	20°C	5 knots	sunny
	12:00	23°C	5 knots	sunny
	15:00	25°C	5 knots	sunny
	18:00	23°C	5 knots	sunny
	21:00	18°C	5 knots	clear intervals
	00:00	16°C	5 knots	clear intervals

Edexcel GCSE Maths Spec A Teacher's Guide © Pearson Education 2010 1

Links

www.visitlondon.com/weather

25.1 Drawing and using line graphs

Concepts and skills

- Produce line graphs.
- Recognise simple patterns, characteristics and relationships in… line graphs….

Functional skills

- L2 Collect and represent discrete and continuous data….

Prior key knowledge, skills and concepts

- Plotting points.

Starter

- *Imagine you are going to London for a couple of days. What sort of weather might you want?* Ask several students what would be ideal weather.

Main teaching and learning

- Tell students that they cannot control the weather, but they can find out what weather to expect. They can get a weather forecast.
- Display PowerPoint 25.1, slide 1 and discuss these points:
  - The weather over two days will vary.
  - The temperature will be different at different times of day.
  - You can plot a graph of temperature against time. This is called a line graph.
  - You can join the points with a straight line. Since you do not know what happens in between given data points, this is a good estimate (PowerPoint 25.1, slide 2).
- Download the next two days' weather from the internet (see links).
  - *Draw a line graph for this data.*
- You can get information from a line graph (PowerPoint 25.1, slide 3). Discuss.
  - *Estimate the temperature at 11.00 on your line graph.*
  - *Find the times when the temperature is at a figure you think most comfortable.*

Common misconceptions

- Students sometimes do not understand that any value found between data points is an estimate.

Enrichment

- Ask the students to draw a line graph for wind speed, and find the times at which it is highest and lowest.

Plenary

- Draw a conversion line graph which plots Sterling against Euros when £1= 1.4 Euros. Use it to give Euro values for:

  (a) 50p (b) £2.00 (c) £10.00 (d) £12.25

Guided practice worksheet

D

1 The line graph shows the diameter of a tree over a period of 60 years.

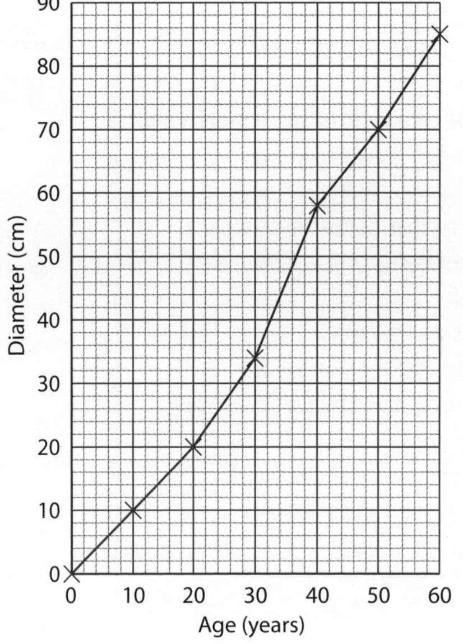

a Estimate the diameter of a trunk of a tree that is 25 years old.

....

b Estimate the age of a tree with a diameter of 80 cm.

....

c Between what ages was the tree growing fastest?

....

d Work out how much the diameter increases between the ages of 20 and 50 years.

....

....

2 Here is a line graph showing the temperature in Carlisle over a 12-hour period in May.

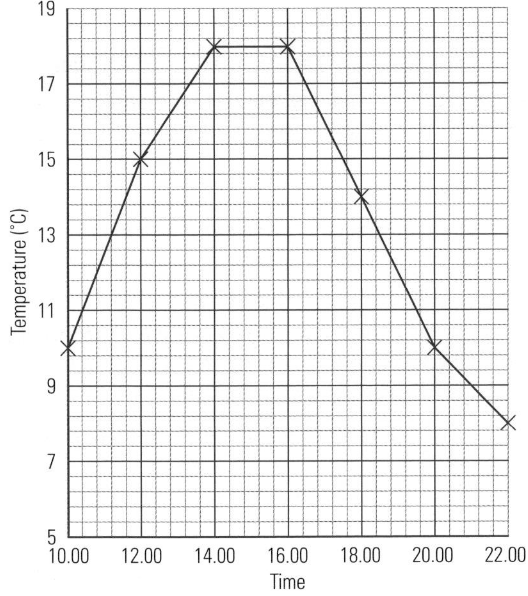

a Estimate the temperature at 13.00.

....

b Between what times is the temperature stable?

....

c Between what times is the temperature falling?

....

d Between what times is the temperature rising fastest?

....

e At what times is the temperature 10°C?

....

 **Specification**

GCSE 2010

SP g (part) Produce charts and diagrams…
SP i Interpret a wide range of graphs and diagrams and draw conclusions
SP k Recognise correlation and draw and/or use lines of best fit by eye, understanding what these represent

FS Process skills

Recognise that a situation has aspects that can be represented using mathematics
Examine patterns and relationships
Interpret results and solutions

FS Performance

Level 2 Identify the situation or problems and identify the mathematical methods needed to solve them

 **Resources**

CD resources

MS PowerPoint presentation 25.2 'Scatter graphs'

Scatter diagrams edexcel

Father's height (cm)	163	164	166	169	171	173
Child's height (cm)	165	163	170	170	167	173

Father's height (cm)	178	182	185	188	190
Child's height (cm)	180	180	186	183	188

Edexcel GCSE Maths Spec A: Teacher's Guide © Pearson Education 2010 1

Links

http://www.teachers.tv/search/list?t=505,2958
http://www.bbc.co.uk/schools/gcsebitesize/maths/data/scatterdiagramsact.shtml
http://experimentsatschool.ntu.ac.uk/resources/teaching/tools/

ActiveTeach resources

RP KC Line diagrams knowledge check
RP PS Line diagrams problem solving

25.2 Drawing and using scatter graphs
25.3 Recognising correlation
25.4 Lines of best fit
25.5 Using lines of best fit to make predictions

Concepts and skills

- Produce scatter graphs.
- Interpret scatter graphs.
- Draw lines of best fit by eye, understanding what these lines represent.
- Distinguish between positive, negative and zero correlation using lines of best fit.
- Use a line of best fit to predict values of one variable given values of the other variable.
- Interpret scatter graphs in terms of the relationship between two variables.
- Interpret correlation in terms of the problem.

Functional skills

- L2 Collect and represent discrete and continuous data….
- L2 Use and interpret statistical measures, tables and diagrams, for discrete and continuous data….

Prior key knowledge, skills and concepts

- Plotting points.

Starter

- *What determines how tall you will be when you grow up?* Ask students to suggest some factors that might affect how tall people are when grown up.

Main teaching and learning

- Tell students that one factor worth investigating is their father. *Do tall fathers have tall children?*
- Display PowerPoint 25.2, slide 1 and discuss these points:
  - It looks from the table as if taller fathers have taller children, but to see better you can plot these pairs of points on a graph. The result is called a scatter diagram (PowerPoint 25.2, slide 2 – each click plots a new point).
  - There seems, from the diagram, to be a general trend for taller fathers to have taller children. The two are **associated**.
- You can draw a line of best fit through the points (PowerPoint 25.2, slide 2 – further click once all points are plotted).
  - This shows a linear (straight line) association.
- You can use the line of best fit to estimate how, given a father of a certain size, you can estimate the child's size.
- Tell students that as the father's height increases, the child's height increases. This is called positive correlation.
  - If the child's height had decreased as the father's increased, this would have been negative correlation.
  - If there was no pattern, there would have been zero correlation.
- You can use the line of best fit to estimate other values (PowerPoint 25.2, slide 3).

Enrichment

- Point out that if the father is above average height, the child is likely to be shorter than him. If below average height the child is likely to be taller than him. This is called regression. Discuss other factors that could affect a child's height, e.g. mother's height.
- Suggest some examples of negative correlation (age of car and value) and no correlation (height and maths mark).

Plenary

- Draw scatter graphs to show positive, negative and zero correlation, with data to demonstrate lines of best fit.

scatter graph correlation no correlation line of best fit positive correlation

Guided practice worksheet

1 The scatter diagram gives some information about lung damage and the number of years of smoking.

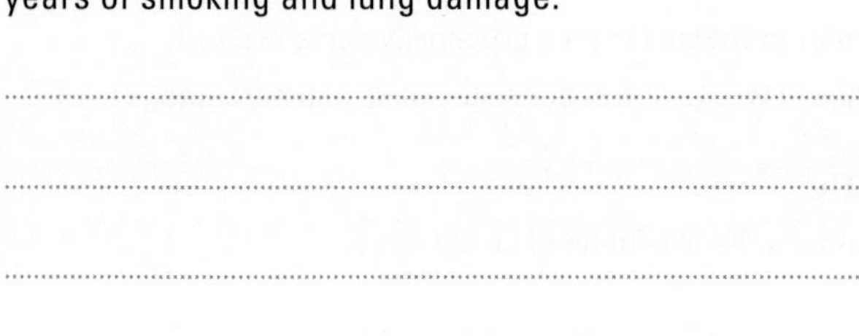

a Describe the relationship between the number of years of smoking and lung damage.

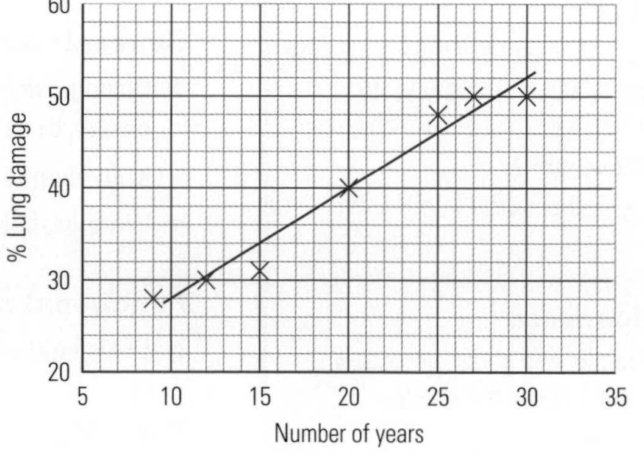

b Describe the correlation.

c Estimate the amount of lung damage after 10 years.

d Estimate the number of years of smoking that is likely to give lung damage of 45%.

2 The scatter graph shows the lengths and widths of some leaves from a tree.

Two more leaves were measured. They measured: 4.5 cm long, 3 cm wide; and 7.5 cm long, 5 cm wide.

a Copy the scatter graph and add these two points.

Hint Line of best fit should be drawn, as near as possible, through the middle of the plotted points.

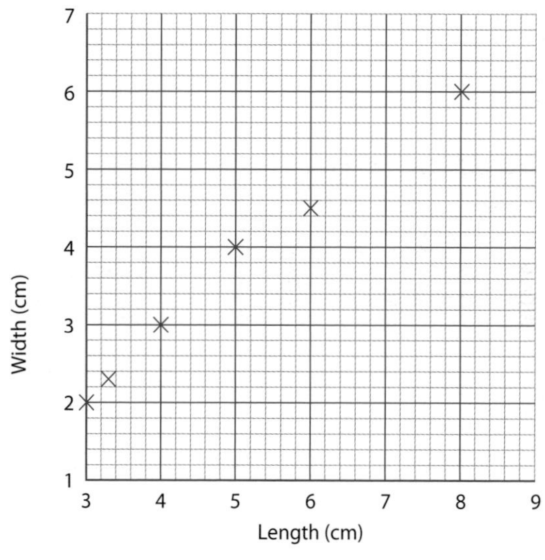

b Add a line of best fit to your scatter graph.

c Describe the correlation.

d Describe the relationship between length and width of these tree leaves.

e Estimate the width of a leaf that is 7 cm long.

Specification

GCSE 2010

SP m Understand and use the vocabulary of probability and probability scale

FS Process skills

Select the mathematical information to use

FS Performance

Level 1 Identify and obtain necessary information to tackle the problem

Resources

Resources

Washing line, drawing pins, cards (approx A5), cards labelled: 'I was born', 'Two heads', 'Rain tomorrow'

CD resources

MS PowerPoint presentation 26.1 'Probability'

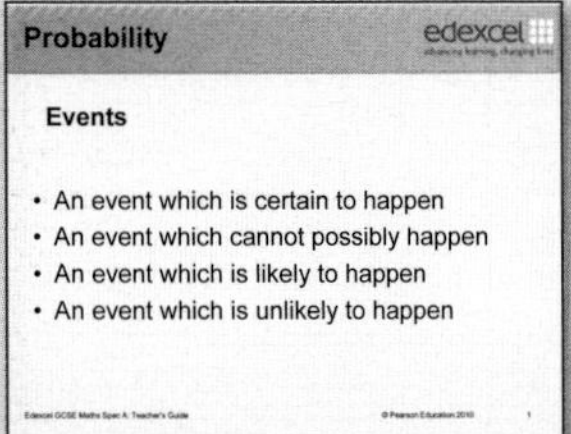

Links

http://www.metoffice.gov.uk/weather/uk/uk_forecast_warnings.html?
http://www.random.org/
http://nrich.maths.org/4335
http://nrich.maths.org/1233
http://www.bbc.co.uk/education/mathsfile/shockwave/games/fish.html

ActiveTeach resources

Probability quiz
Probability scale interactive

26.1 The probability scale

Concepts and skills

- Distinguish between events which are: impossible, unlikely, even chance, likely, and certain to occur.
- Mark events and/or probabilities on a probability scale of 0 to 1.
- Write probabilities in words or fractions, decimals and percentages.

Functional skills

- L1 Use data to assess the likelihood of an outcome.

Prior key knowledge, skills and concepts

- Students should have some recognition that some events are more likely than others.

Starter

- Before students arrive pin a 'washing line' across a notice board. Label one end 'certain' and the other 'impossible'.
- Ask students: '*How likely is it that you were born?*' (certain); '*How likely is it that you will grow a second head?*' (impossible). Ask volunteers to position these on the probability scale.
- Now ask: '*How likely is it that it will rain tomorrow?*' This can lead to a discussion about the use of probability by forecasters.
- Ask a volunteer to position a 'Rain tomorrow' card. Now discuss with the whole class where this should be positioned.

Main teaching and learning

- Working in pairs, ask the students to look at the events detailed on PowerPoint 26.1 slide 1 and suggest examples of each type of event.
- Discuss the students' results and use the washing line to aid discussion of how likely each event is to happen.
- Ask the students to copy the probability scale as shown on PowerPoint 26.1 slide 2 and add their events to the table.
- Now ask students to complete Exercise 26A from the Student Book.

Common misconceptions

- Students sometimes confuse the concept of certainty when they, for example, think their favourite football team is certain to win.

Enrichment

- How likely an event is to happen is something we base decisions on every day:
  - Is rain likely? Shall I take a coat?
  - How likely is my TV to break down? Should I insure it?
  - How likely is the train to run late? Should I catch an earlier one?

Plenary

- Give each student a card, then ask them to write down an event that might happen. The students should remain seated but exchange their cards among the other students seated in the same row in the classroom. The rows compete to be the first to place their cards in order of probability from certain at the front of the row to impossible at the back of the class. The cards should be retained for the next lesson.

probability probability scale certain impossible event

Guided practice worksheet

Hint Decide which is the most likely. Is it sure to happen?

F

1 Decide whether each of the following events is:

certain, very likely, likely, even chance, unlikely, very unlikely, impossible.

a The day after Monday will be Tuesday.

b Someone in your class will eat an apple today.

c A monkey will drive a car past school today.

d You will smile today.

e Tomorrow will be a sunny day.

Place the events in order on the probability scale.

certain — likely — even chance — unlikely — impossible

2 Give an example of each of the following:

a An event which is certain to happen. ....

b An event which is likely to happen. ....

c An event which has about an even chance of happening. ....

d An event which is unlikely but might happen. ....

e An event which could never happen. ....

3 Draw a probability scale and show the probability that:

a You will have maths homework tomorrow night.

b You will not have any homework tomorrow night.

c You will have homework in two different subjects tomorrow night.

4 Tony and Meg toss a coin to begin a game.

Meg says 'I want tails – tails always wins.'

Is she right? Discuss your answer.

....

....

5 Ian is designing a game to raise money for charity at a church fair.

A dart is thrown at the board. He charges 10p a throw and if the dart lands in a black square the player wins 20p.

Do you think his game will raise money for the charity?

Explain your answer.

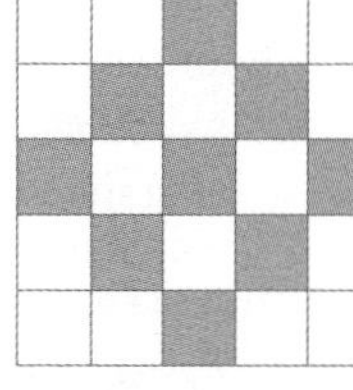

Hint Which colour is the dart most likely to land in? Will players lose enough times to pay the winners?

E

....

....

....

Specification

GCSE 2010

SP m Understand and use the vocabulary of probability and probability scale
SP n (part) Understand and use estimates or measures of probability from theoretical models (including equally likely outcomes)….
SP o (part) List all outcomes for single events…

FS Process skills

Select the mathematical information to use
Find results and solutions

FS Performance

Level 2 Identify the situation or problems and identify the mathematical methods needed to solve them

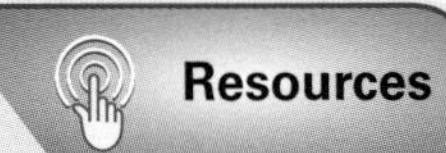

Resources

Resources

Washing line, drawing pins, cards (approx A5), cards from previous lesson
Cards labelled: 0, 1, $\frac{1}{2}$, $\frac{1}{4}$, $\frac{3}{4}$, 50%, 25%, 75%, 100%, 'Severe Weather Warning', 'Severe Weather Alert', 'Wednesday', 'Bike', 'Budgie'

CD resources

MS PowerPoint presentation 26.2 'Writing probabilities as numbers'

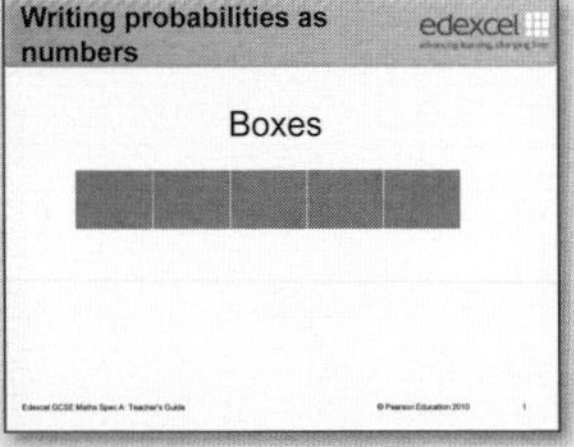

Links

http://www.metoffice.gov.uk/weather/uk/uk_forecast_warnings.html?
http://nrich.maths.org/471

ActiveTeach resources

Qualifying heats 2 video

26.2 Writing probabilities as numbers

Concepts and skills

- Write probabilities in words or fractions, decimals and percentages.
- Find the probability of an event happening using theoretical probability.
- List all outcomes for single events systematically.
- Use theoretical models to include outcomes using dice, spinners, coins.

Functional skills

- L2 Use probability to assess the likelihood of an outcome.

Prior key knowledge, skills and concepts

- Students should be able to order fractions, decimals and percentages on a number line.

Starter

- Before students arrive pin a 'washing line' across a notice board. Label one end 'certain' and the other 'impossible'.
- Explain to the students that the Met Office gives an early warning of severe weather when it is 60% confident, and an alert when it is 80% confident. Ask for volunteers to position these on the washing line.
- Now ask students to position the following on the washing line:
  - the probability of being born on a Wednesday;
  - the probability of owning a bike;
  - the probability of having a pet budgie.
- Ask: '*How can we show that one event is more probable than another?*'
- Discuss with the students the number scale 0–1.
- Place cards 0, 1, $\frac{1}{2}$, $\frac{1}{4}$, $\frac{3}{4}$, on the number line and estimate probabilities for the events already positioned.

Main teaching and learning

- Assign probabilities to the cards from Plenary 25.1.
- Define probability = $\frac{\text{number of successful outcomes}}{\text{total number of outcomes}}$
- Discuss the probability of being born on a Wednesday $\left(\frac{1}{7}\right)$.
- Use the class to find the probability of owning a bike and of having a pet budgie.
- Now ask students to complete Exercise 26B from the Student Book.
- Explain to the students that probabilities may be given as a decimal or a percentage.
- Recap converting between fractions, decimals and percentages, then ask students to convert the answers for Exercise 26B to decimals and percentages.

Common misconceptions

- Students may sometimes give probabilities outside the range 0–1 or may give a probability as a ratio.

Enrichment

- Its is useful to be able to assign a number value to probabilities as this shows more detail of how likely something is to happen. The Met Office always uses a probability and gives out a warning at 60% and an alert at 80%.
- Ask students for other examples where probability is given as numbers. (Trains or aircraft delays, insurance claims, health risks, etc.)

Plenary

- Ask students to draw five boxes as in PowerPoint 26.2 slide 1.
- Now throw a dice and ask the students to write the number thrown in any one of the boxes; once written the number cannot be altered. Throw the dice a further four times, asking the students to write down each number so that all the boxes are filled. The winner is the student with the largest number.
- Discuss strategies and then replay the game.

equally likely mutually exclusive outcome

Guided practice worksheet

1 A fair octagonal dice with sides numbered 1–8 is thrown.

Hint $\text{probability} = \frac{\text{number of successful outcomes}}{\text{total number of outcomes}}$

Write down the probability that each of the numbers described lands on top. Give your answer as a fraction.

a A one ....

b An odd number ....

c A multiple of 4 ....

d A number less than 3 ....

2 Write down the probability of each of the following events as a percentage.

a Getting a head when you toss a coin. ....

b Getting a 5 when you throw a dice. ....

c Getting a number greater than 4 when you throw a dice. ....

d The next baby born will be a girl. ....

e The next person you speak to was born on a Monday. ....

3 The diagram below shows the board for a game.
Write as a decimal the probability of landing on:

Black	White	White	Black
Grey	Black	White	Grey
White	White	White	White
Grey	White	Black	Grey
Black	White	White	Black

a White ....

b Black ....

c Grey ....

d Black or white ....

e Grey or white ....

f Black or grey ....

Hint Count how many squares of each colour there are.

4 A bag contains cards on which are printed the names of 10 students:
Amy, Tom, Andrew, Ann, Sue, Mike, Ahmed, Omar, Owen and Dave.

a Write down the probability of Amy's name being pulled out of the bag.

....

b Write down the probability of a girl's name being pulled out of the bag.

....

c If a girl's name is drawn out first what is the probability of Mike's name being pulled next?

....

d If a boy's name is pulled out first what is the probability of Sue's name being pulled next?

....

5 A token is taken from a bag containing four red counters and three blue counters. Write down the probability that the token will be:

a red..........

b blue..........

c white ....

d red or blue ....

Specification

GCSE 2010

SP p Identify different mutually exclusive outcomes and know that the sum of the probabilities of all these outcomes is 1

FS Process skills

Select the mathematical information to use

Find results and solutions

FS Performance

Level 2 Identify the situation or problems and identify the mathematical methods needed to solve them

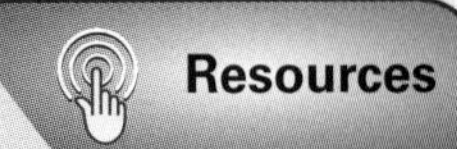

Resources

CD resources

MS PowerPoint presentation 26.3 'The probability that something will NOT happen'

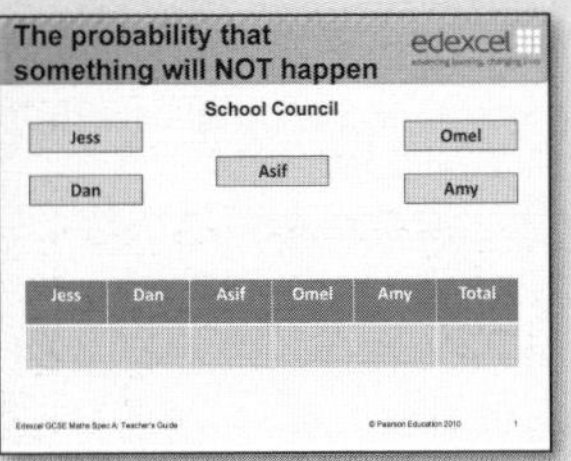

26.3 The probability that something will *not* happen

Concepts and skills

- Addition of simple probabilities.
- Identify different mutually exclusive outcomes and know that the sum of the probabilities of all outcomes is 1.
- Using $1 - p$ as the probability of an event not occurring, where p is the probability of the event occurring.
- Find a missing probability from a list or table.

Functional skills

- L2 Use probability to assess the likelihood of an outcome.

Prior key knowledge, skills and concepts

- Students should already be able to add and subtract fractions, decimals and percentages.

Starter

- Give students the following scenario: A spare place is available for a trip to the theatre. Five people want to go. Their names are put on pieces of card (see PowerPoint 26.3 slide 1). The winning name will be pulled out of the hat.
- Ask students for the probability of each person being pulled out of the hat; complete the table on PowerPoint 26.3 slide 1.
- Ask: '*What is the total of all of the probabilities?*' Show the students PowerPoint 26.3 slide 2.

Main teaching and learning

- Ask students: '*What is the probability that a girl will be chosen?*' $\left(\frac{3}{5}\right)$; '*What is the probability that a boy will be chosen?*' $\left(\frac{2}{5}\right)$
- Now ask students to complete Exercise 26C from the Student Book.
- Ask students to copy the table from PowerPoint 26.3 slide 3 and fill in the probabilities as decimals and percentages.
- Ask: '*What is the probability that Omel will not be chosen?*' $\left(\frac{4}{5}\right)$
- Discuss how the students arrived at this probability: (a) by adding; or (b) $1 - \left(\frac{1}{5}\right)$. Display PowerPoint 26.3 slide 4.
- Now ask students to complete Exercise 26D from the Student Book.

Common misconceptions

- Sometimes students fail to ensure that all of the possible outcomes are represented by probabilities and that the outcomes do not overlap.

Enrichment

- Ask students to provide a strategy for finding a missing probability.
- Give practice in questions where the probabilities are given as relationships, as in the plenary, to encourage the development of problem-solving skills.

Plenary

- Display PowerPoint slide 5, which shows the probability of chickens laying eggs of a certain size. The chickens are twice as likely to lay a small egg as they are to lay a large egg and they are three times as likely to lay a medium egg as a small egg.
- Ask students for an expression for the probability of large, small and medium eggs.
- Ask: '*How can we find the probability of laying each type of egg?*'

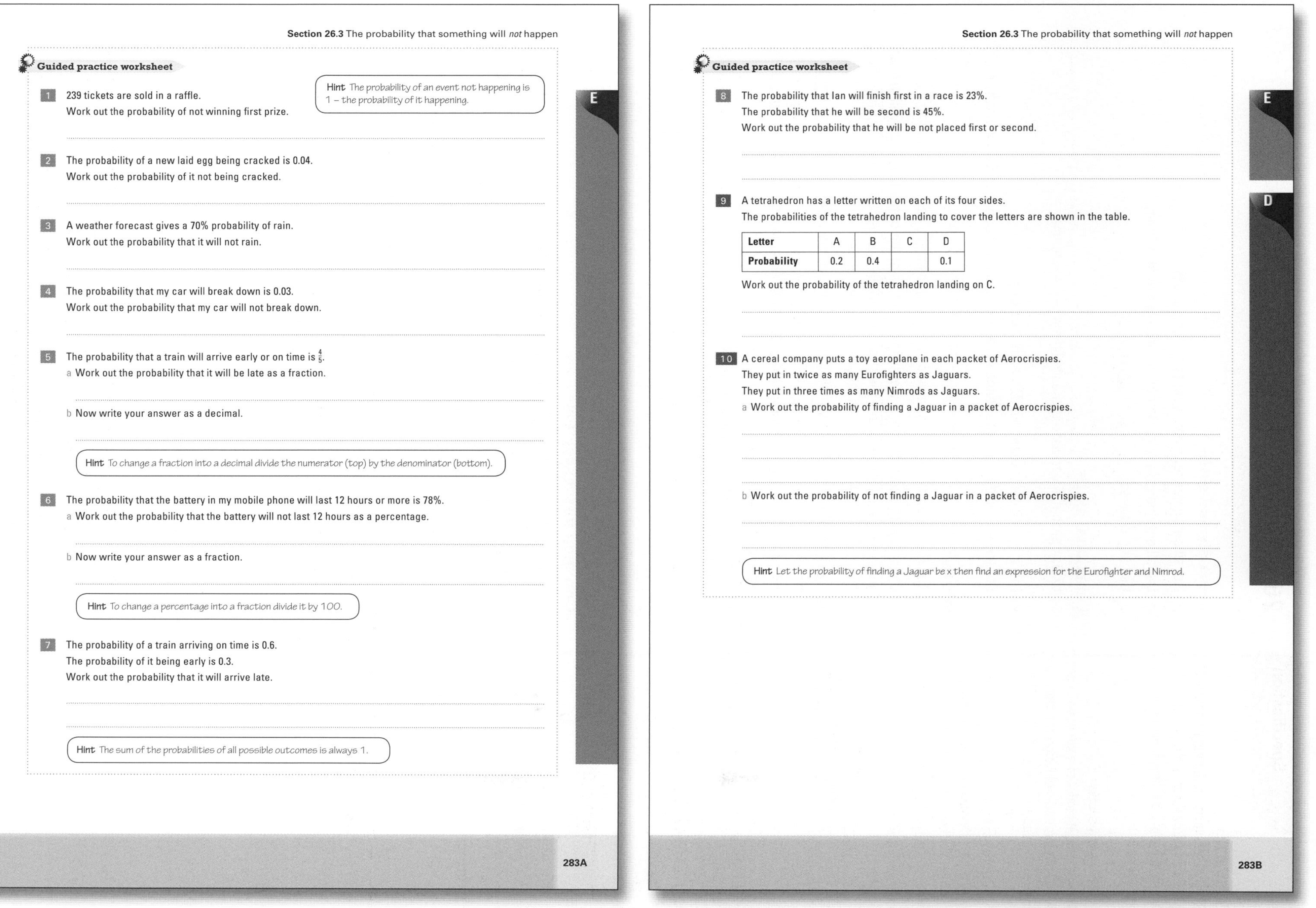

Guided practice worksheet

E

1 239 tickets are sold in a raffle.
Work out the probability of not winning first prize.

Hint The probability of an event not happening is 1 – the probability of it happening.

2 The probability of a new laid egg being cracked is 0.04.
Work out the probability of it not being cracked.

3 A weather forecast gives a 70% probability of rain.
Work out the probability that it will not rain.

4 The probability that my car will break down is 0.03.
Work out the probability that my car will not break down.

5 The probability that a train will arrive early or on time is $\frac{4}{5}$.
a Work out the probability that it will be late as a fraction.

b Now write your answer as a decimal.

Hint To change a fraction into a decimal divide the numerator (top) by the denominator (bottom).

6 The probability that the battery in my mobile phone will last 12 hours or more is 78%.
a Work out the probability that the battery will not last 12 hours as a percentage.

b Now write your answer as a fraction.

Hint To change a percentage into a fraction divide it by 100.

7 The probability of a train arriving on time is 0.6.
The probability of it being early is 0.3.
Work out the probability that it will arrive late.

Hint The sum of the probabilities of all possible outcomes is always 1.

Section 26.3 The probability that something will *not* happen

Guided practice worksheet

E

8 The probability that Ian will finish first in a race is 23%.
The probability that he will be second is 45%.
Work out the probability that he will be not placed first or second.

D

9 A tetrahedron has a letter written on each of its four sides.
The probabilities of the tetrahedron landing to cover the letters are shown in the table.

Letter	A	B	C	D
Probability	0.2	0.4		0.1

Work out the probability of the tetrahedron landing on C.

10 A cereal company puts a toy aeroplane in each packet of Aerocrispies.
They put in twice as many Eurofighters as Jaguars.
They put in three times as many Nimrods as Jaguars.
a Work out the probability of finding a Jaguar in a packet of Aerocrispies.

b Work out the probability of not finding a Jaguar in a packet of Aerocrispies.

Hint Let the probability of finding a Jaguar be x then find an expression for the Eurofighter and Nimrod.

GCSE 2010

SP o List all outcomes for single events, and for two successive events, in a systematic way and derive relative probabilities

FS Process skills

Make an initial model of a situation using suitable forms of representation
Find results and solutions

FS Performance

Level 2 Identify the situation or problems and identify the mathematical methods needed to solve them

Resources

Dice, coin

CD resources

MS PowerPoint presentation 26.4 'Probability'

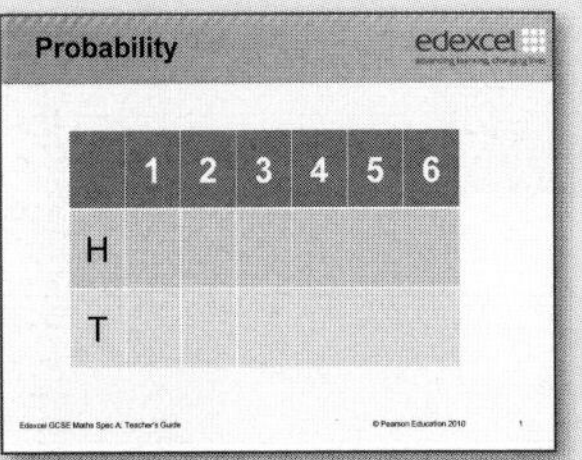

26.4 Sample space diagrams

Concepts and skills

- List all outcomes for single events systematically.
- List all outcomes for two successive events systematically.
- Use and draw sample space diagrams.

Functional skills

- L2 Use probability to assess the likelihood of an outcome.

Prior key knowledge, skills and concepts

- Students should have experience of recording the collection of data in a tally chart.

Starter

- Ask the students for the possible outcomes of tossing a coin and throwing a dice.
- Discuss with students the best way to record all of the outcomes. They will probably begin with a list, but ask how they can be sure they have found them all. Only show PowerPoint 26.4 slide 1 when they have arrived at the correct idea.
- Use PowerPoint 26.4 slide 1 to discuss how we can be sure we have all of the possible outcomes.
- Use the sample space diagram to find the probability of a student throwing a tail and getting an even number. $\left(\frac{3}{12}\right)$

Main teaching and learning

- Consider PowerPoint 26.4 slide 2 and ask students for probabilities from the outcome space. For example, ask: '*What is the probability of a meat burger with chips?*' $\left(\frac{2}{9}\right)$
- Now ask students to complete Exercise 26E from the Student Book for additional practice.

Common misconceptions

- Sometimes students fail to be methodical and consequently miss some of the outcomes.

Enrichment

- Do not give students the outcome table; they should develop it from the list with your help.
- Use the outcome table to solve problems.

Plenary

- Show the students PowerPoint 26.4 slide 3. Ask students to consider the problem and then discuss their answers.

sample space diagram theorectical probability

Guided practice worksheet

D

1 Two fair dice are rolled and the numbers on the top face are added together.

a Write down all of the possible outcomes.

....

b What is the probability of the total being 4?

....

c What is the probability of the total being an even number?

....

d Work out which total is the most likely to be scored.

....

Hint Drawing up the outcome space will help you to answer these questions.

2 I have four coins in my pocket: 1p, 2p, 5p, 10p.
Asif also has four coins in his pocket: 1p, 5p, 10p, 20p.
We each choose a coin at random.

a Write down all of the possible totals.

....

b Write down the probability of the total being 2p.

....

c Write down the probability of the total being 11p.

....

d Write down the probability of the total being 8p.

....

3 My sock drawer contains pairs of blue, red, white and green socks.
My shirt drawer contains blue, red, white and green shirts.
I pull out a pair of socks and a shirt at random.
Find the probability that:

a I pull out red socks and a red shirt.

....

b I do not pull out either red socks or a red shirt.

....

c I pull out red socks and a shirt which does not match.

....

d I pull out socks and shirt which are the same colour.

....

Section 26.4 Sample space diagrams

Guided practice worksheet

D

4 Two fair dice are rolled and the numbers on the top faces are multiplied together to give the product.

a Write down all of the possible outcomes.

b Write down the probability of the product being 36.

....

c Write down the probability of the product being 7.

....

d Write down the probability of the product being 12.

....

e Write down the lowest possible product which can be scored.

....

f Write down which product, or products, are the most likely to be scored.

....

5 The sides of a dice are marked 2, 2, 3, 3, 4, 4.
The dice is rolled twice and the scores are added together.

a Write down the probability of scoring 8.

....

b Write down the probability of scoring 5.

....

c Write down the probability of scoring an even number.

....

d Jess thinks that the most likely total is 6.
Is she correct? Explain your answer.

....

....

Hint Use your outcome table to explain which total is most likely.

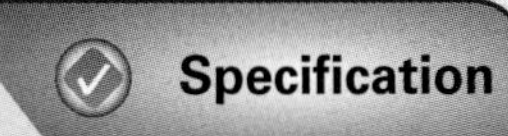

GCSE 2010

SP n Understand and use estimates or measures of probability from theoretical models (including equally likely outcomes), or from relative frequency

SP s Compare experimental data and theoretical probabilities

SP t Understand that if they repeat an experiment, they may – and usually will – get different outcomes, and that increasing sample size generally leads to better estimates of probability and population characteristics

FS Process skills

Make an initial model of a situation using suitable forms of representation

Find results and solutions

Draw conclusions in light of situations

FS Performance

Level 2 Identify the situation or problems and identify the mathematical methods needed to solve them

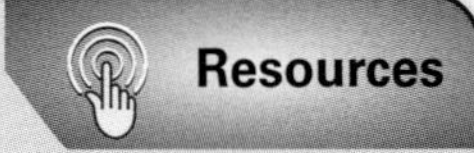

Resources

Dice, coins

CD resources

MS PowerPoint presentation 26.5 'Probability'

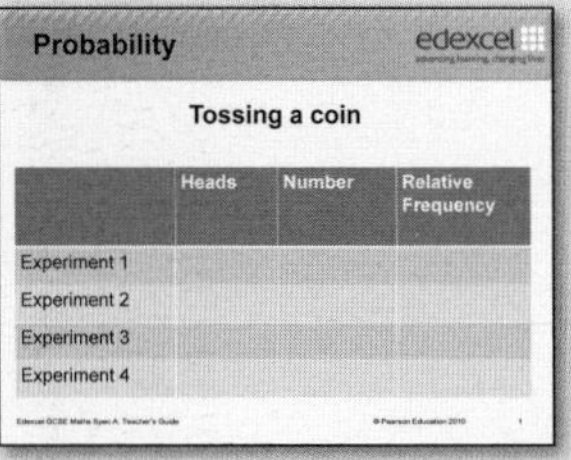

26.5 Relative frequency

Concepts and skills

- Find the probability of an event happening using relative frequency.
- Compare experimental data and theoretical probabilities.
- Compare relative frequencies from samples of different sizes.

Functional skills

- L2 Use probability to assess the likelihood of an outcome.

Prior key knowledge, skills and concepts

- Students should be able to use probability to describe an event and represent probabilities numerically.

Starter

- Tell students you are going to conduct an experiment. Ask a student to toss a coin and ask whether it lands on heads or tails. Ask all students to toss a coin once, then count how many landed on heads. Work out the probability of a coin landing on heads.
- Tell students that this is the experimental probability. It is worked out from the frequency that the coin lands on heads relative to the number of times the coin is tossed and is called the relative frequency.
- Ask students: '*Was the probability found from the relative frequency what we expected?*'
- Explain the theoretical case: probability = $\frac{\text{number of successful outcomes}}{\text{total number of outcomes}}$

Main teaching and learning

- Ask: '*Should we expect the same relative frequency if we repeat the experiment?*'
- Use PowerPoint 26.5 slide 1 to record the results and repeat the experiment three more times.
- Ask: '*Can anyone suggest how we can get a relative frequency closer to the theoretical probability?*' Explain that if we add all the experimental results together we will have more trials; the more trials, the more accurate the result.
- Now ask students to complete Exercise 26F from the Student Book.

Common misconceptions

- Students sometimes confuse experimental probability with theoretical probability.

Enrichment

- Discuss how we can estimate probabilities when it is impracticable or impossible to find the theoretical probability.

Plenary

- Discuss with students scenarios where an exact probability is not known but where relative frequency is used. For example, weather forecasting – where do the probabilities come from?
- Ask students to consider how a light-bulb manufacturer might find the probability of a bulb lasting over 200 hours without testing all his bulbs to destruction.
- Now ask students to suggest how they might estimate the probability of people being left-handed. For example, they might find the frequency of left-handed people in their class.
- Ask: '*How could you improve your estimate? Would your estimate be correct for the whole school? The country? Africa?*'

trial relative frequency

Guided practice worksheet

E

1 Write the numbers 1–5 on small pieces of card or paper and place them in a bag or large envelope. Shuffle the pieces of card.

Pull out a number, record the result on the tally chart then return the number to the bag. Do the experiment 20 times.

Number	Tally	Frequency	Relative frequency	Theoretical probability
1				
2				
3				
4				
5				
Total		20		

a Work out the relative frequencies of each number being chosen. Write the answer in the table.
Josie says that the relative frequencies will be the same as the theoretical probability.
b Work out the theoretical probability for each number being chosen. Write the answer in the table.
c Why is the theoretical probability different to the relative frequency?

....

....

Hint The relative frequency is = $\frac{\text{number of successful experiments}}{\text{total number of experiments}}$

2 Explain how you could find the relative frequency that the next car to pass the school gates is driven by a man.

....

....

....

3 Explain how you could estimate the probability that the number of bags of groceries shoppers carry or push from a supermarket is more than three.

....

....

....

4 Explain how you could estimate the probability of the next person you meet being a vegetarian.

....

....

....

Guided practice worksheet

E

5 Choose a TV channel. Estimate the probability that there will be four adverts between TV programmes. Fill in the table below.

TV Channel			
Adverts	**Tally**	**Frequency**	**Relative Frequency**
More than four			
Exactly four			
Less than four			
Total			

a Work out the relative frequency for more than four adverts.
b Work out the relative frequency for exactly four adverts
c Work out the relative frequency for less than four adverts.
d Do the experiment again using a different TV channel.
e Compare the results for the two channels.

Hint The more experiments you do the closer your relative frequency will be to the probability.

Specification

GCSE 2010
SP p (part) Identify different mutually exclusive outcomes…

FS Process skills
Select the mathematical information to use
Find results and solutions

FS Performance
Level 2 Identify the situation or problems and identify the mathematical methods needed to solve them

Resources

CD resources
MS PowerPoint presentation 26.6 'Two-way tables'

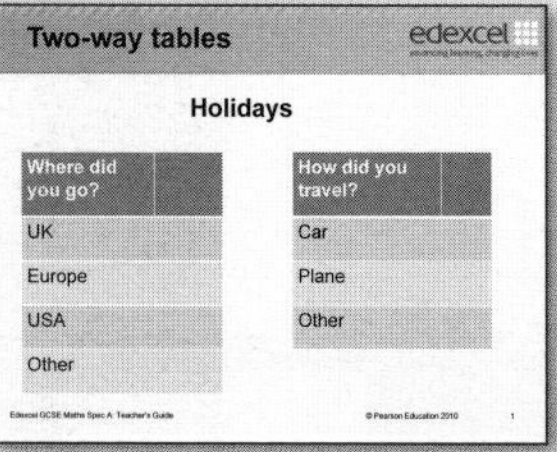

Links
http://www.bbc.co.uk/schools/gcsebitesize/maths/data/representingdata2act.shtml

ActiveTeach resources
Probability questions quiz

26.6 Two-way tables

Concepts and skills

- Find a missing probability from a list or table.

Functional skills

- L2 Use probability to assess the likelihood of an outcome.

Prior key knowledge, skills and concepts

- Students should be able to find totals of rows and columns in a table.

Starter

- Use PowerPoint 26.6 slide 1 to collect information about where students went on holiday and how they travelled to their holiday destination. Using data collected from the class is more motivational than using a pre-prepared table.
- Ask how we could display all this information on one table.
- Display PowerPoint 26.6 slide 2 and point out that the table does not have anywhere to put the information we already have. Ask: *'What else is needed?'* (Totals)
- Fill in the totals you have already then ask: *'How many had a UK holiday by car?'* (PowerPoint 26.6 slide 3)
- Tell students we want to complete the table by asking as few questions as possible and ask them to work in groups to find the least number of questions required.
- Once the groups have finalised their questions, ask the group with the smallest number to ask the class the questions and complete the table. For example, if they have UK by car and plane, they can work out the UK other total. (This can be done with four questions, including the example.)

Main teaching and learning

- Discuss the probability of a student holidaying in the UK by car.
- Explain that this is a good way of summarising their outcomes and finding probabilities when there is more than one variable (in this case destination and mode of travel).
- Ask students to find some more probabilities using their table.
- Now ask students to complete Exercise 26G from the Student Book.

Common misconceptions

- Students do not always look for a row or column with only one piece of missing data as a starting point.

Enrichment

- Students should be aware that two-way tables can help them solve problems even if they are not requested in the question.
- *Dan and Sue worked on Monday and Tuesday questioning 100 people about their holiday. On Monday 45 people were questioned. Sue asked 20 people on Monday and 35 people on Tuesday. How many people did Dan question on Tuesday?* (Answer 20)
  This question is much easier if the information is placed in a table:

	M	T	Total
S	20	35	
D			
Total	45		100

	M	T	Total
S	20	35	(55)
D	(25)	(20)	(45)
Total	45	(55)	100

Plenary

- Display PowerPoint 26.6 slide 4, which shows the number of students from a group of 70 choosing different activities on an adventure holiday.
- Ask students: *'What is the least number of totals needed to complete the table?'*
- Now show PowerPoint 26.6 slide 5 and ask: *'What is the probability of a girl choosing rock climbing?'* $\left(\frac{38}{70}\right)$; *'What is the probability of a student choosing rock climbing?'* $\left(\frac{45}{70}\right)$

Section 26.6 Two-way tables

Guided practice worksheet

D

1 The table below shows the membership of a tennis club. Members are classified by their age group and gender. The club has 56 members.

	Under 18	Over 18	Total
Male		16	
Female	12	14	
Total			

Hint Look for a row or column with just 1 missing result.

a Complete the two-way table.

b Write down the probability that a player chosen at random is over 18.

c Write down the probability that a player chosen at random is female.

d Write down the probability that a player chosen at random is a male aged under 18.

2 100 people were asked what type of accommodation they stayed in for their holidays.
Some of the information is given in this table

	Hotel	Cottage	Camping	Total
Aged over 30		12		48
Aged under 30	6		24	
Total	36			

a Complete the two-way table.

b Write down the probability that a person chosen at random is over 30.

c Write down the probability that a person aged over 30 prefers a hotel.

d Write down the probability that a person chosen at random prefers camping.

Section 26.6 Two-way tables

Guided practice worksheet

D

3 The table shows the size and type of packets of teabags sold by a supermarket in one morning.

	Large	Medium	Small	Total
Breakfast	24	22		74
Earl Grey	13		19	
Herbal		15	24	
Total	69			194

a Complete the two-way table.

b Write down the probability of a person buying breakfast tea.

c Write down the probability of a person buying a large packet of herbal tea.

d Write down the probability of a person buying a medium packet of tea.

4 Debbie has collected some information about the 30 students in her class.
Biology is the favourite subject for 7 members of the class, but only 3 girls enjoy it.
The favourite Science subject for 8 girls is Physics.
6 boys prefer Chemistry. There are 14 boys in the class.

a Use a two-way table to display this data.

Hint Construct a table with the subjects along the top and the boys and girls up the side.

b Write down the probability of a person chosen from the class at random being a girl.

c Write down the probability of a person chosen from the class at random being a girl liking Chemistry best.

d Write down the probability of a person chosen from the class at random being a boy preferring Physics.

Specification

GCSE 2010

SP n Understand and use estimates or measures of probability from theoretical models (including equally likely outcomes), or from relative frequency

FS Process skills

Select the mathematical information to use
Find results and solutions

FS Performance

Level 2 Identify the situation or problems and identify the mathematical methods needed to solve them

Resources

CD resources

MS PowerPoint presentation 26.7 'Predicting outcomes'

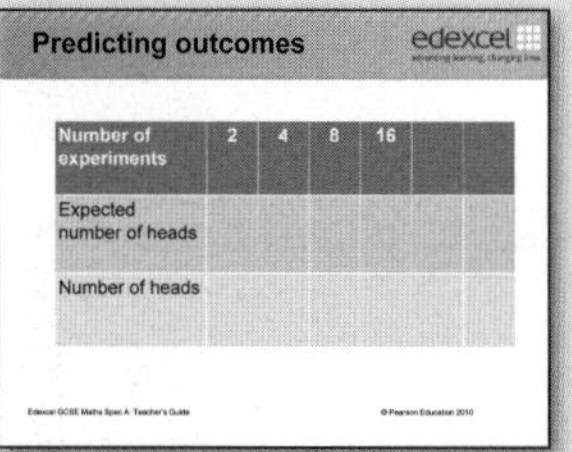

Links

http://www.bbc.co.uk/schools/gcsebitesize/maths/data/probability1act.shtml

ActiveTeach resources

Rings and blocks 1 video
RP KC Probability knowledge check
RP PS Probability problem solving

26.7 Predicting outcomes

Concepts and skills

- Estimate the number of times an event will occur, given the probability and the number of trials.

Functional skills

- L2 Use probability to assess the likelihood of an outcome.

Prior key knowledge, skills and concepts

- Students should be able to estimate probabilities from relative frequencies.
- Students should be able to multiply a whole number by a fraction and round decimals to the nearest whole number.

Starter

- Ask students: *'What is the probability of getting a head or a tail if you toss a coin?'; 'If everyone in the class tosses a coin, how many heads would you expect?'; 'How many tails would you expect?'*
- Now ask how they arrived at this answer $\left(\frac{1}{2} \times \text{number in class}\right)$.

Main teaching and learning

- Ask students: *'If every student in class throws an ordinary dice (1–6)*
  - ☐ *How many would score 6?*
  - ☐ *How many would score 4?*
  - ☐ *How many would score an even number?*
  - ☐ *How many would score a multiple of 3?'*
- Now ask students to complete Exercise 26H.

Common misconceptions

- Students sometimes do not realise that each experiment is independent and does not depend on what has already happened.
- Some students assume that they can predict the next result, e.g. number 6 hasn't appeared on the dice so will definitely appear next time!

Enrichment

- Consider insurance. An insurance company spreads the risk of a breakdown amongst all of the people who take out insurance. They need to estimate how much they will have to pay out.
- If the probability of a washing machine breaking down is 0.01 and a washing machine manufacturer sells 2000 machines, they need to estimate how many repairs they expect to make. (20)

Plenary

- Ask the class what they think will be the outcome if you toss a coin.
- Ask 2 members of the class to toss a coin and ask for a prediction of how many heads or tails.
- Repeat with 4 members of the class, then 8 members, 16 members, and the whole class. Use PowerPoint 26.7 slide 1 to record the results.
- Now ask all members of the class to toss a coin twice and ask for a prediction of how many heads or tails.
- Bring out that the greater the number of experiments, the more accurate the outcome and that probability can only be used for predictions when a large number of events are being considered.

Guided practice worksheet

C

1 The probability of the 8:30 am train arriving on time is 0.95.
How many times can it be expected to arrive on time over the next 6 weeks? (42 days)

2 The probability of a seed from a certain plant germinating is $\frac{43}{50}$.
If 5000 seeds are planted, how many would be expected to germinate?

3 An ordinary dice is thrown 200 times.
Estimate how many times it will land on

a 6

b 7

c a number divisible by 3.

4 The diagram shows a spinner. The spinner is spun 80 times.
Estimate the number of times the spinner will land on

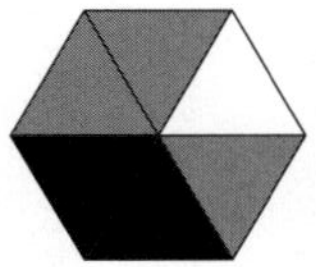

a white

b black

c grey

Hint Consider how many times the dice has been thrown.

5 Alison is testing a dice.
She throws the dice 30 times. 6 appears 6 times.

a Is the dice fair? Explain your answer.

She throws another dice 3000 times. This time 6 appears 600 times.

b Is the dice fair? Explain your answer.

6 Surance Motor Policies estimate that 15% of motorists claim on their car insurance each year. The company has 19 738 policy holders.

a How many claims does the company expect this year?

They received 3000 claims last year.

b Comment on whether this is more or less than expected.

Section 26.7 Predicting outcomes

Guided practice worksheet

C

7 A machine that makes light bulbs is checked for faults.
A sample of 100 bulbs is tested and 6 are found to be faulty.
The machine makes 2000 bulbs per day.

Hint Find the probability of a faulty bulb.

a How many should you expect to be faulty?

George resets the machine the following day and 96 bulbs are found to be faulty.

b Comment on whether George has improved the efficiency of the machine.

8 A school is trying to raise money. They produce their own scratch cards, which they sell for 20p each.
The school pays out £1 for a winning card. The probability that a player wins is $\frac{3}{45}$.
How many cards must they sell to raise £100?

Specification

GCSE 2010
GM g Use Pythagoras' theorem in 2D

FS Process skills
Select the mathematical information to use
Find results and solutions

FS Performance
Level 2 Identify the situation and problems and identify the mathematical methods needed to solve them

Resources

Links
http://nrich.maths.org/public/search.php?search=pythagoras
http://www.bbc.co.uk/schools/gcsebitesize/maths/shapes/pythagorastheoremact.shtml
http://www.mathsnet.net/dynamic/pythagoras/index.html

ActiveTeach resources
Pythagoras' theorem animation

27.1 Finding the length of the hypotenuse of a right-angled triangle

Concepts and skills

- Understand, recall and use Pythagoras' theorem in 2D.

Functional skills

- L2 Understand and use simple formulae and equations involving one- or two-stop operations.

Prior key knowledge, skills and concepts

- Students should already be able to use the square and the square root buttons on a calculator.
- Students should remember the rules of order of operations (BIDMAS).

Starter

- Work through the 'Get ready' section to check understanding of the squaring and square-rooting processes.
- On squared paper draw some right-angled triangles and check whether Pythagoras' theorem works. Start with the 3, 4, 5 family and move onto 5, 12, 13 etc, before trying it out for any right-angled triangle.

Main teaching and learning

- Go through Examples 1 and 2 and work on Exercise 27A.

Common misconceptions

- Students sometimes add the lengths before squaring.
- Students sometimes forget to square root.

Enrichment

- Using the Starter activity as a starting point, investigate Pythagorean triples without using the internet. How many can you find where all the lengths are integers?

Plenary

- Check understanding of the topic by using exercises such as these. *Find the length of the diagonal of a square with side 10 cm.* (14.1 cm) *Find the length of the diagonal of a rectangle with sides 5 cm and 8 cm.* (9.43 cm)

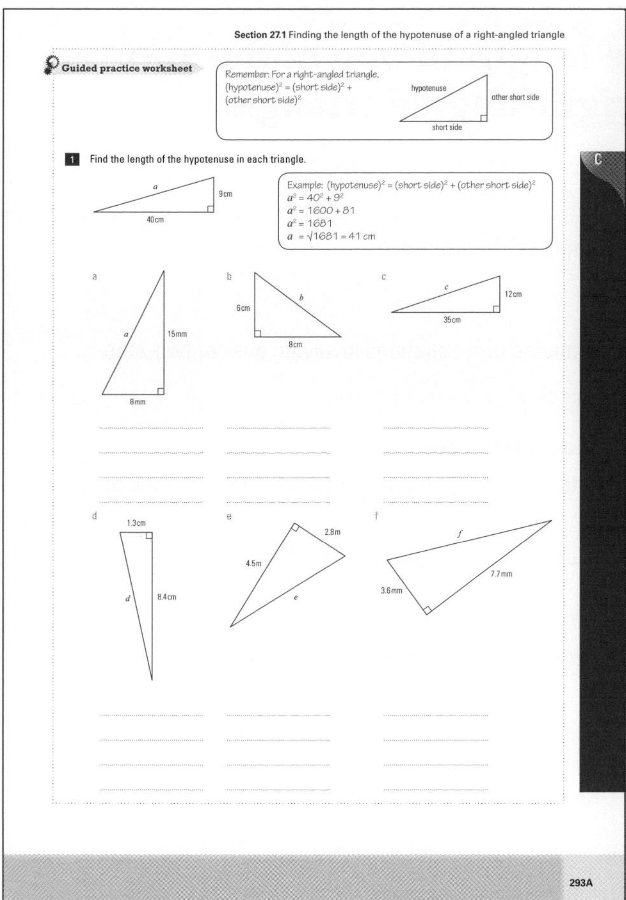

Section 27.1 Finding the length of the hypotenuse of a right-angled triangle

Guided practice worksheet

Remember: For a right-angled triangle, $(\text{hypotenuse})^2 = (\text{short side})^2 + (\text{other short side})^2$

hypotenuse / other short side / short side

1 Find the length of the hypotenuse in each triangle.

Example: $(\text{hypotenuse})^2 = (\text{short side})^2 + (\text{other short side})^2$

$a^2 = 40^2 + 9^2$

$a^2 = 1600 + 81$

$a^2 = 1681$

$a = \sqrt{1681} = 41$ cm

a 15mm, 8mm   b 6cm, 8cm   c 12cm, 35cm

d 1.3cm, 8.4cm   e 2.8m, 4.5m   f 3.6mm, 7.7mm

293A

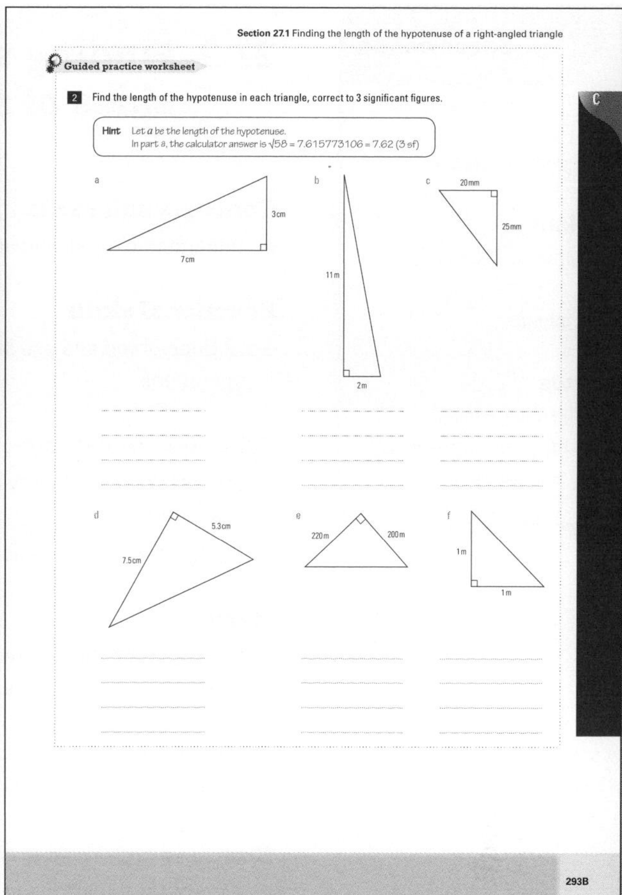

Section 27.1 Finding the length of the hypotenuse of a right-angled triangle

Guided practice worksheet

2 Find the length of the hypotenuse in each triangle, correct to 3 significant figures.

Hint Let a be the length of the hypotenuse. In part a, the calculator answer is $\sqrt{58} = 7.615773106 = 7.62$ (3 sf)

a 3cm, 7cm   b 11m, 2m   c 20mm, 25mm

d 5.3cm, 7.5cm   e 220m, 200m   f 1m, 1m

293B

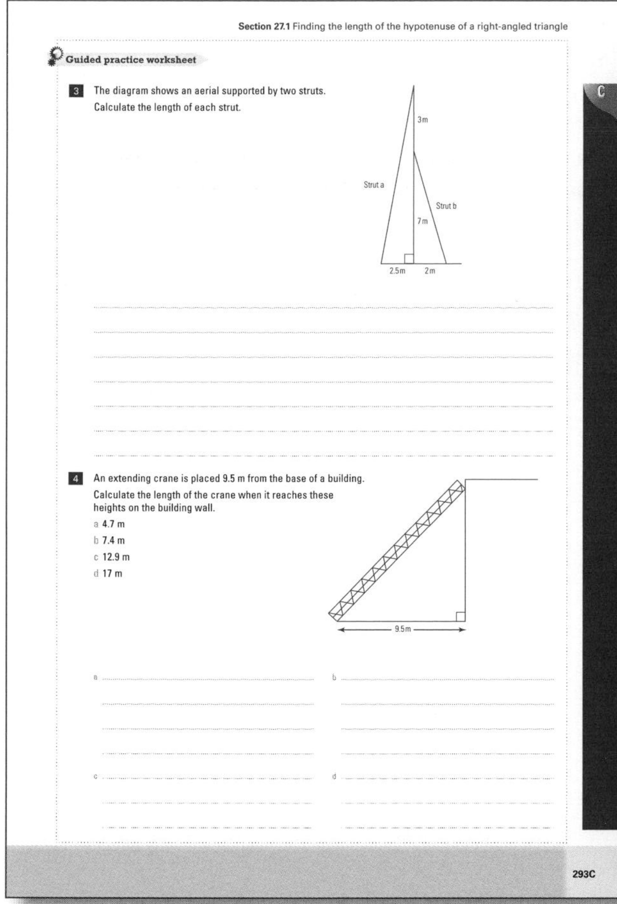

Section 27.1 Finding the length of the hypotenuse of a right-angled triangle

Guided practice worksheet

3 The diagram shows an aerial supported by two struts. Calculate the length of each strut.

3m, 7m, Strut a, Strut b, 2.5m, 2m

4 An extending crane is placed 9.5 m from the base of a building. Calculate the length of the crane when it reaches these heights on the building wall.

a 4.7 m
b 7.4 m
c 12.9 m
d 17 m

9.5m

293C

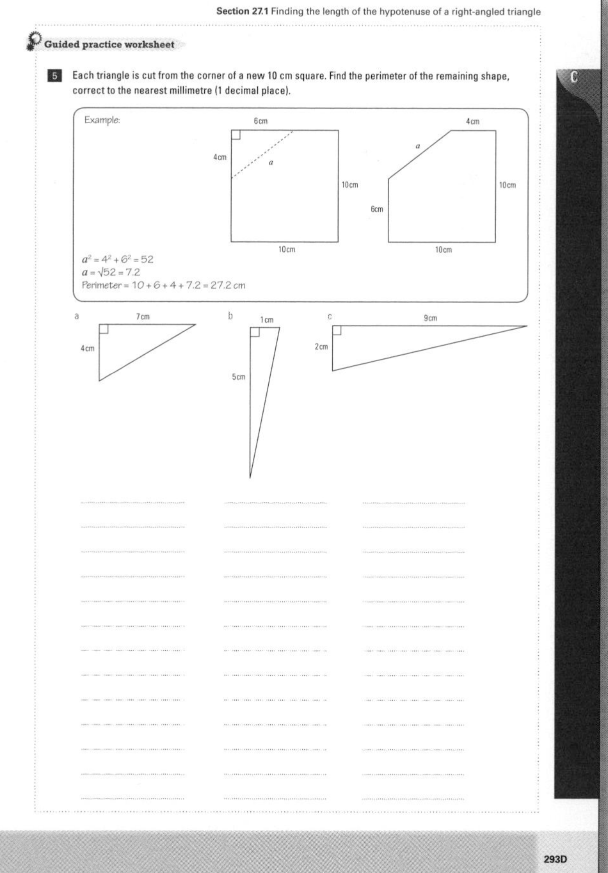

Section 27.1 Finding the length of the hypotenuse of a right-angled triangle

Guided practice worksheet

5 Each triangle is cut from the corner of a new 10 cm square. Find the perimeter of the remaining shape, correct to the nearest millimetre (1 decimal place).

Example: 6cm, 4cm, 10cm, 10cm, 4cm, 6cm, 10cm, 10cm

$a^2 = 4^2 + 6^2 = 52$

$a = \sqrt{52} = 7.2$

Perimeter $= 10 + 6 + 4 + 7.2 = 27.2$ cm

a 7cm, 4cm   b 1cm, 5cm   c 9cm, 2cm

293D

Specification

GCSE 2010
GM g Use Pythagoras' theorem in 2D

FS Process skills
Select the mathematical information to use
Find results and solutions

FS Performance
Level 2 Identify the situation and problems and identify the mathematical methods needed to solve them

27.2 Finding the length of one of the shorter sides of a right-angled triangle

Concepts and skills

- Understand, recall and use Pythagoras' theorem in 2D.

Functional skills

- L2 Understand and use simple formulae and equations involving one- or two-stop operations.

Prior key knowledge, skills and concepts

- Students should already be able to use the square and the square root buttons on a calculator.
- Students should remember the rules of order of operations (BIDMAS).

Starter

- Work through the 'Get ready' section to check understanding of the squaring and square-rooting processes.

Main teaching and learning

- Go through Example 3, then work on Exercise 27B.

Common misconceptions

- Sometimes students add the lengths before squaring.
- Sometimes students forget to square root.
- Sometimes students subtract the lengths before squaring.

Enrichment

- *Ladders are sold in lengths of 1 metre. The smallest ladder you can buy is of length 3 metres. To use a ladder safely, the distance from the wall to the base of the ladder is a quarter of the length of the ladder. Find the minimum length of ladder that will be needed to reach safely to the roof of a house that is 6 metres from the ground.* (7 m)

Plenary

- Check understanding of the topic by using exercises such as these. *Find the length of the side of a square with side diagonal 10 cm long.* (7.07 cm) *Find the length of a rectangle with width 5 cm and diagonal of length 8 cm.* (6.24 cm)

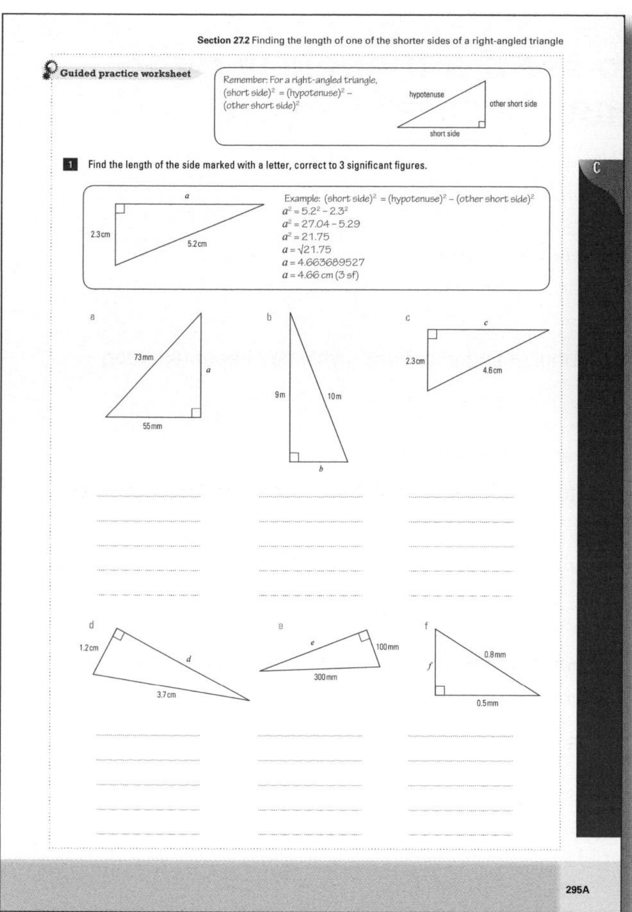

Section 27.2 Finding the length of one of the shorter sides of a right-angled triangle

Guided practice worksheet

Remember: For a right-angled triangle,
(short side)^2 = (hypotenuse)^2 – (other short side)^2

hypotenuse
other short side
short side

1 Find the length of the side marked with a letter, correct to 3 significant figures.

a
2.3 cm
5.2 cm

Example: (short side)^2 = (hypotenuse)^2 – (other short side)^2
$a^2 = 5.2^2 - 2.3^2$
$a^2 = 27.04 - 5.29$
$a^2 = 21.75$
$a = \sqrt{21.75}$
$a = 4.663689527$
$a = 4.66$ cm (3 sf)

a 73 mm, 55 mm, *a*

b 9 m, 10 m, *b*

c 2.3 cm, 4.6 cm, *c*

d 1.2 cm, 3.7 cm, *d*

e 100 mm, 300 mm, *e*

f 0.8 mm, 0.5 mm, *f*

295A

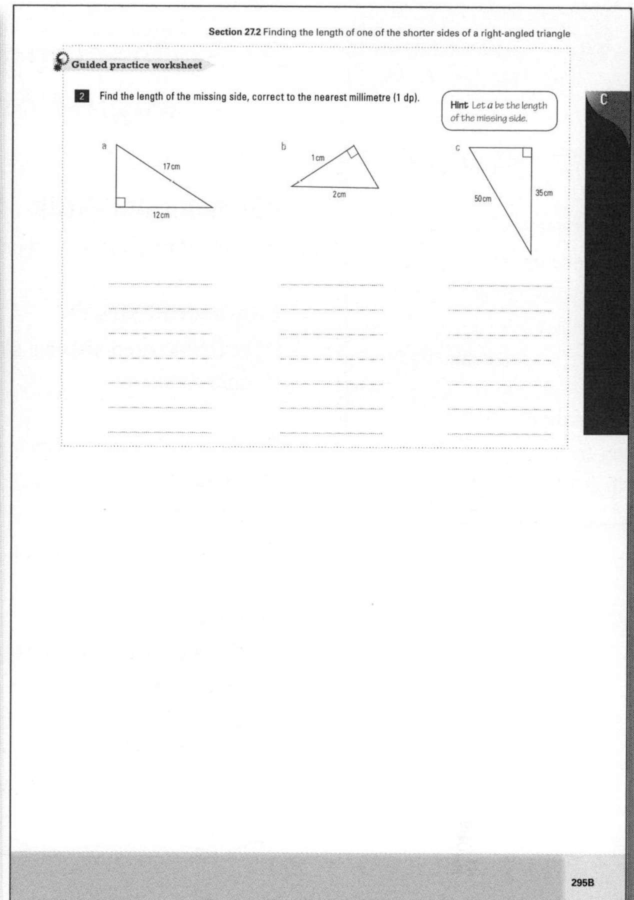

Section 27.2 Finding the length of one of the shorter sides of a right-angled triangle

Guided practice worksheet

2 Find the length of the missing side, correct to the nearest millimetre (1 dp).

Hint: Let *a* be the length of the missing side.

a 17 cm, 12 cm

b 1 cm, 2 cm

c 50 cm, 35 cm

295B

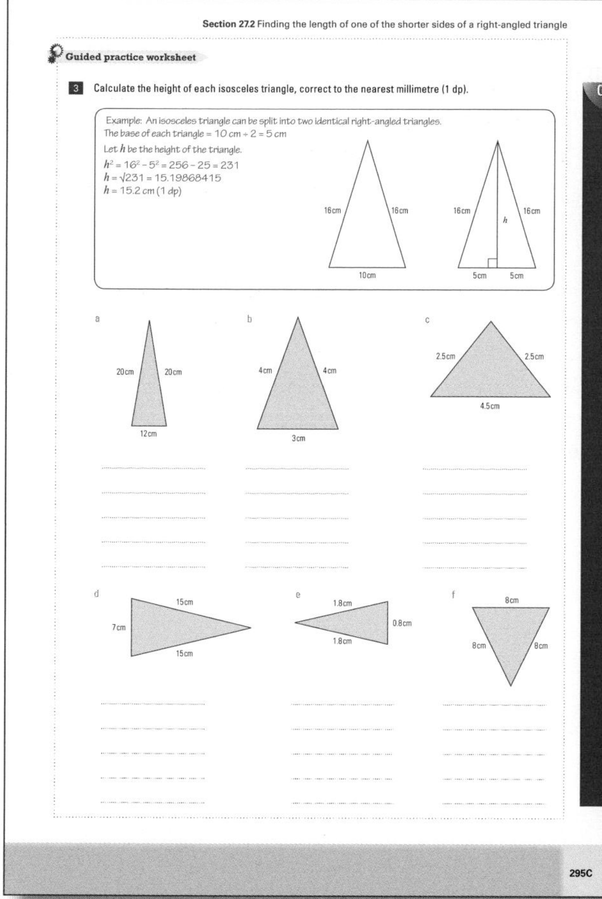

Section 27.2 Finding the length of one of the shorter sides of a right-angled triangle

Guided practice worksheet

3 Calculate the height of each isosceles triangle, correct to the nearest millimetre (1 dp).

Example: An isosceles triangle can be split into two identical right-angled triangles.
The base of each triangle = 10 cm ÷ 2 = 5 cm
Let *h* be the height of the triangle.
$h^2 = 16^2 - 5^2 = 256 - 25 = 231$
$h = \sqrt{231} = 15.19868415$
$h = 15.2$ cm (1 dp)

16 cm, 16 cm, 10 cm
16 cm, 16 cm, *h*, 5 cm, 5 cm

a 20 cm, 20 cm, 12 cm

b 4 cm, 4 cm, 3 cm

c 2.5 cm, 2.5 cm, 4.5 cm

d 15 cm, 15 cm, 7 cm

e 1.8 cm, 1.8 cm, 0.8 cm

f 8 cm, 8 cm, 8 cm

295C

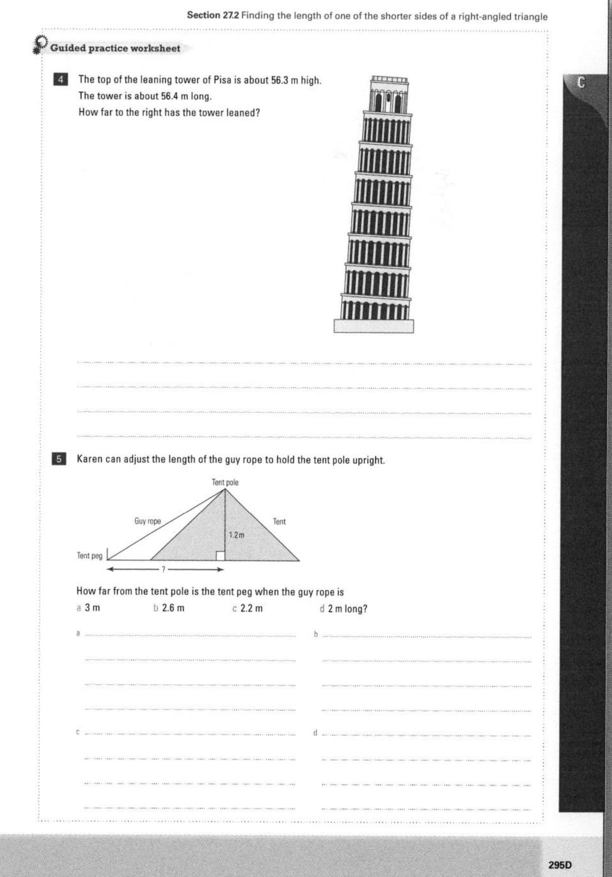

Section 27.2 Finding the length of one of the shorter sides of a right-angled triangle

Guided practice worksheet

4 The top of the leaning tower of Pisa is about 56.3 m high.
The tower is about 56.4 m long.
How far to the right has the tower leaned?

5 Karen can adjust the length of the guy rope to hold the tent pole upright.

Tent pole
Guy rope
Tent
1.2 m
Tent peg
?

How far from the tent pole is the tent peg when the guy rope is
a 3 m b 2.6 m c 2.2 m d 2 m long?

a
b
c
d

295D

Specification

GCSE 2010

GM g Use Pythagoras' theorem in 2D

FS Process skills

Decide on the methods, operations and tools … to use in a situation
Find results and solutions
Draw conclusions in light of situations

FS Performance

Level 2 Draw conclusions and provide mathematical justifications

27.3 Checking to see if a triangle is right-angled or not

Concepts and skills

- Understand, recall and use Pythagoras' theorem in 2D.

Functional skills

- L2 Understand and use simple formulae and equations involving one- or two-stop operations.

Prior key knowledge, skills and concepts

- Students should already be able to use the square and the square root buttons on a calculator.
- Students should remember the rules of order of operations (BIDMAS).

Starter

- *Draw a scalene triangle, a right-angled triangle and an obtuse-angled triangle. Check whether the longest side squared is equal to, smaller than or greater than the sum of the two shorter sides squared.* (In a scalene triangle with three acute angles, the longest side squared is less than the sum of the two shorter sides squared. In a right-angled triangle, the longest side squared is equal to the sum of the two shorter sides squared. In an obtuse-angled triangle, the longest side squared is greater than the sum of the two shorter sides squared.)

Main teaching and learning

- Go through Examples 4 and 5, then work on Exercise 27C.

Common misconceptions

- Sometimes students add the lengths before squaring.
- Sometimes students forget to square root.
- Sometimes students subtract the lengths before squaring.

Enrichment

- *Find a rule, involving Pythagoras' theorem, to see if a triangle is scalene, right-angled or obtuse-angled.*

Plenary

- Check understanding of the topic by using pair work and getting students to make up three triangles; one scalene, one right-angled and one obtuse-angled. They then pass them to their partner and check which triangle is which.

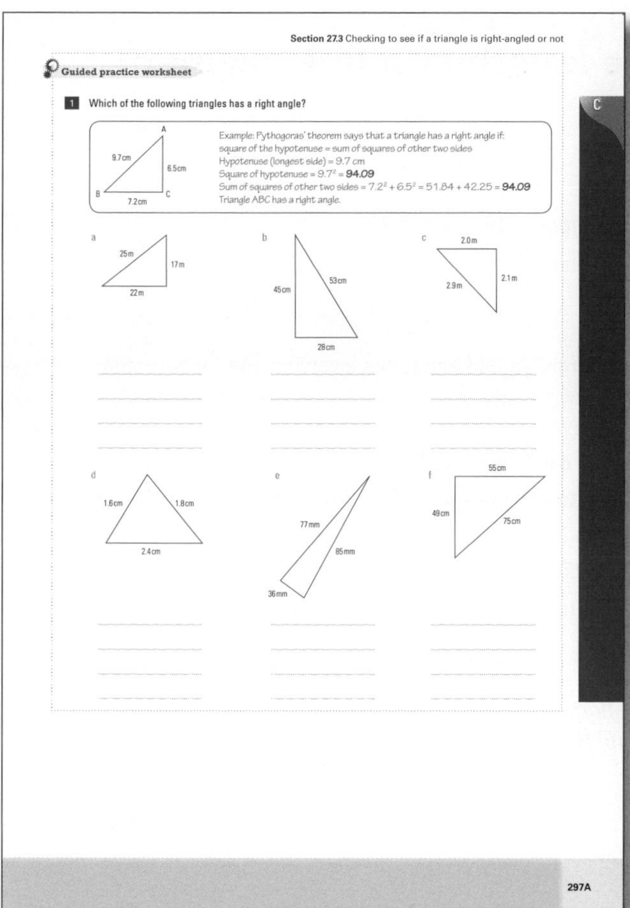

Guided practice worksheet

1 Which of the following triangles has a right angle?

Example: Pythagoras' theorem says that a triangle has a right angle if: square of the hypotenuse = sum of squares of other two sides
Hypotenuse (longest side) = 9.7 cm
Square of hypotenuse = 9.7^2 = **94.09**
Sum of squares of other two sides = $7.2^2 + 6.5^2$ = 51.84 + 42.25 = **94.09**
Triangle ABC has a right angle.

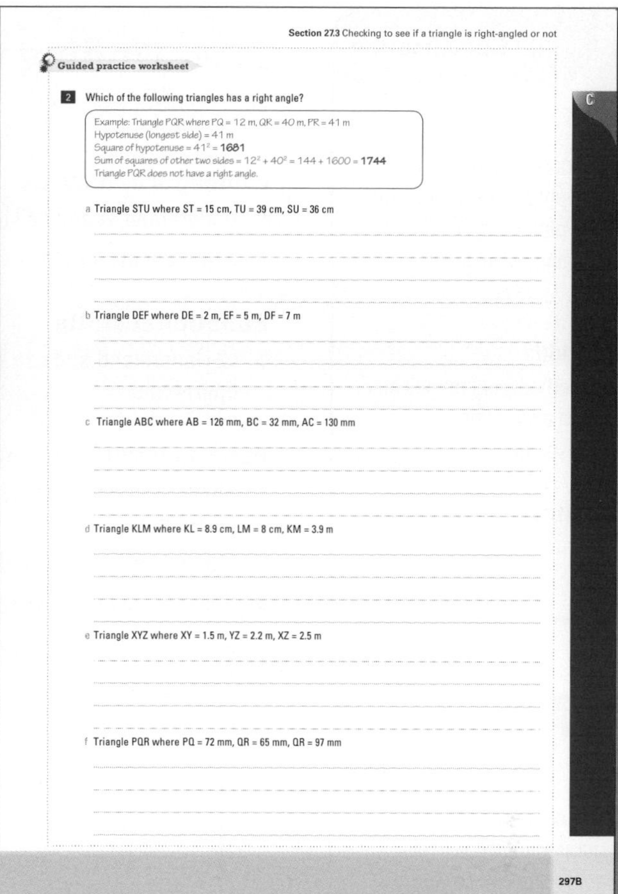

Guided practice worksheet

2 Which of the following triangles has a right angle?

Example: Triangle PQR where PQ = 12 m, QR = 40 m, PR = 41 m
Hypotenuse (longest side) = 41 m
Square of hypotenuse = 41^2 = **1681**
Sum of squares of other two sides = $12^2 + 40^2$ = 144 + 1600 = **1744**
Triangle PQR does not have a right angle.

a Triangle STU where ST = 15 cm, TU = 39 cm, SU = 36 cm

b Triangle DEF where DE = 2 m, EF = 5 m, DF = 7 m

c Triangle ABC where AB = 126 mm, BC = 32 mm, AC = 130 mm

d Triangle KLM where KL = 8.9 cm, LM = 8 cm, KM = 3.9 m

e Triangle XYZ where XY = 1.5 m, YZ = 2.2 m, XZ = 2.5 m

f Triangle PQR where PQ = 72 mm, QR = 65 mm, QR = 97 mm

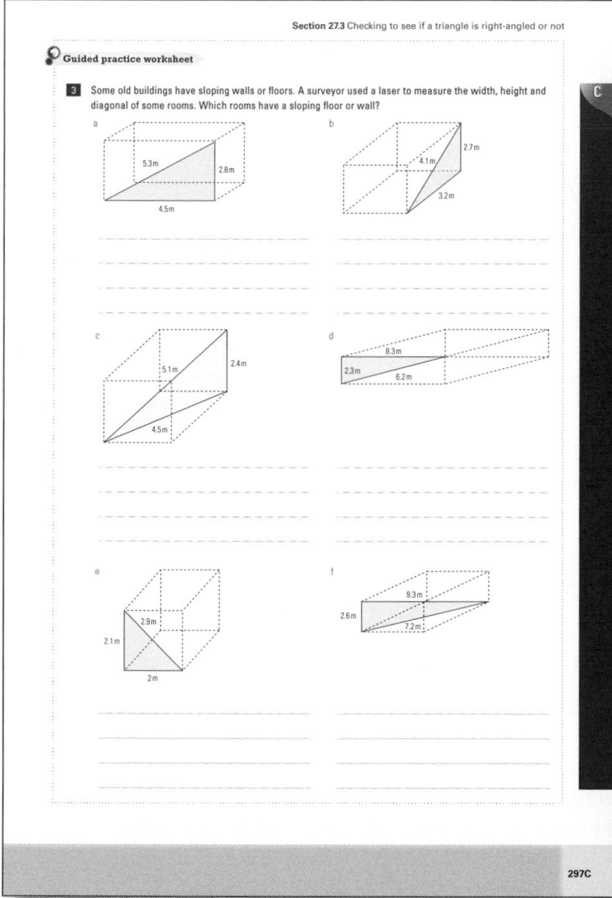

Guided practice worksheet

3 Some old buildings have sloping walls or floors. A surveyor used a laser to measure the width, height and diagonal of some rooms. Which rooms have a sloping floor or wall?

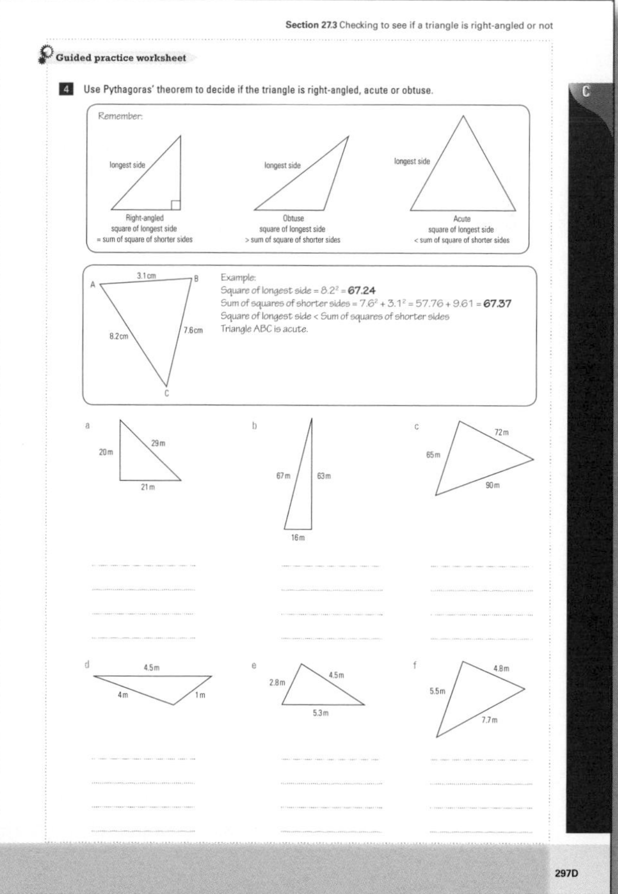

Guided practice worksheet

4 Use Pythagoras' theorem to decide if the triangle is right-angled, acute or obtuse.

Remember:

Example:
Square of longest side = 8.2^2 = **67.24**
Sum of squares of shorter sides = $7.6^2 + 3.1^2$ = 57.76 + 9.61 = **67.37**
Square of longest side < Sum of squares of shorter sides
Triangle ABC is acute.

Specification

GCSE 2010
GM g Use Pythagoras' theorem in 2D
A k Use the conventions for coordinates in the plane and plot points in all four quadrants, including using geometric information

FS Process skills
Decide on the methods, operations and tools ... to use in a situation
Find results and solutions

FS Performance
Level 2 Apply a range of mathematics to find solutions

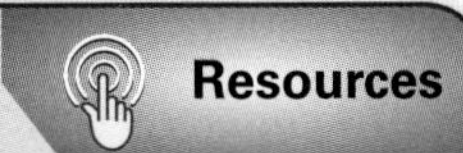

Resources

ActiveTeach resources
RP KC Pythagoras knowledge check
RP PS Pythagoras problem solving

27.4 Finding the length of a line segment

Concepts and skills

- Understand, recall and use Pythagoras' theorem in 2D.
- Calculate the length of a line segment.

Functional skills

- L2 Understand and use simple formulae and equations involving one- or two-stop operations.

Prior key knowledge, skills and concepts

- Students should already be able to use the square and the square root buttons on a calculator.
- Students should remember the rules of order of operations (BIDMAS).
- Students should already be able to add and subtract negative numbers.

Starter

- *Work out the lengths of the shorter sides of the right-angled triangles where the hypotenuse is: (a) OA* (4, 6) *(b) BC* (2, 4) *(c) DE* (2, 3) *(d) FG* (3, 3) *(e) HJ.* (5, 2)

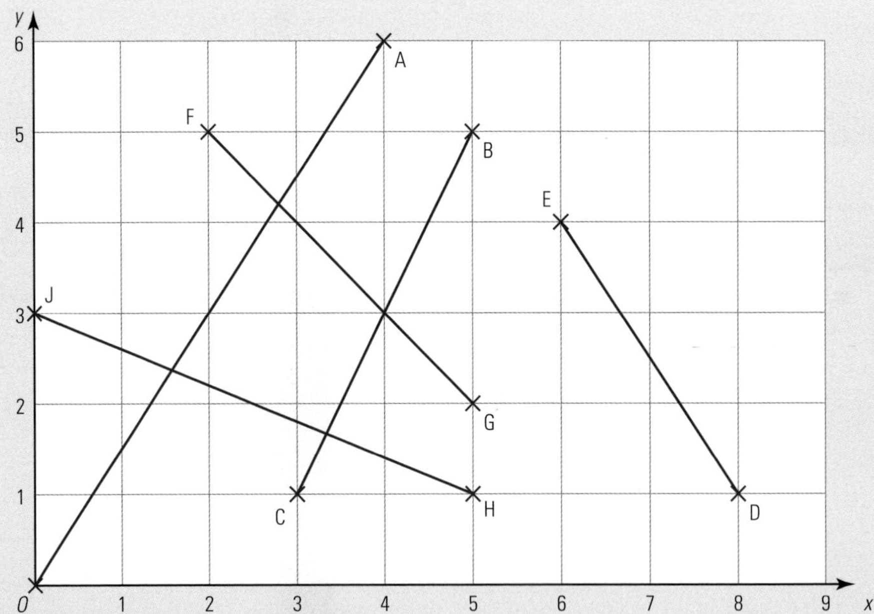

Main teaching and learning

- Go through Examples 6 and 7, then work on Exercise 27D.

Common misconceptions

- Sometimes students add the lengths before squaring.
- Sometimes students forget to square root.
- Sometimes students subtract the lengths before squaring.

Enrichment

- *What happens if you use the areas of semi-circles rather than squares on the sides of a right-angled triangle?* (The rule is the same: the area of the semi-circle on the longest side is equal to the areas of the semi-circles of the shorter sides added together.)

Plenary

- *Find the distance between the points with coordinates (–3, 4) and (4, –3).* (9.9 units)

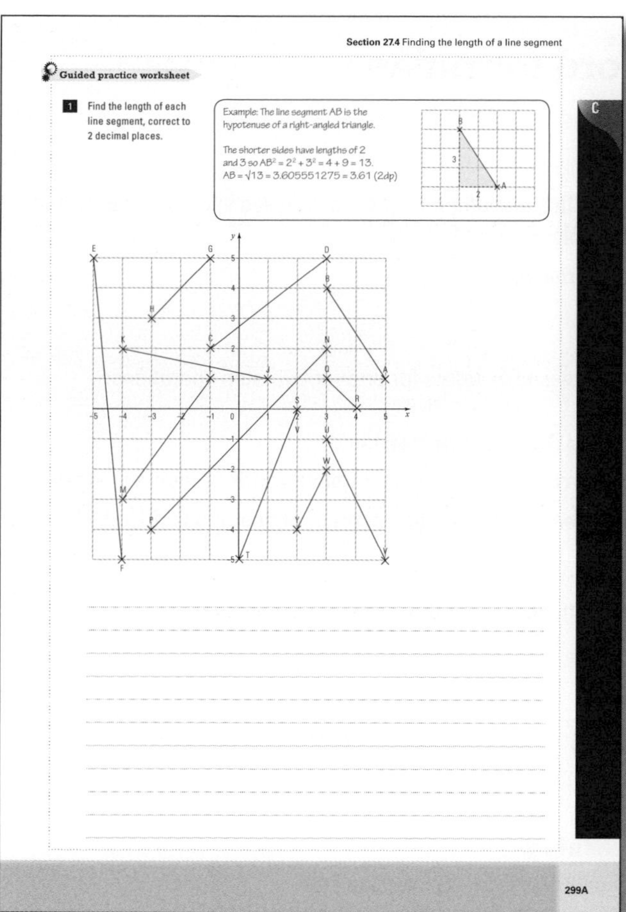

Guided practice worksheet

1 Find the length of each line segment, correct to 2 decimal places.

Example: The line segment AB is the hypotenuse of a right-angled triangle.

The shorter sides have lengths of 2 and 3 so $AB^2 = 2^2 + 3^2 = 4 + 9 = 13$.
$AB = \sqrt{13} = 3.605551275 = 3.61$ (2dp)

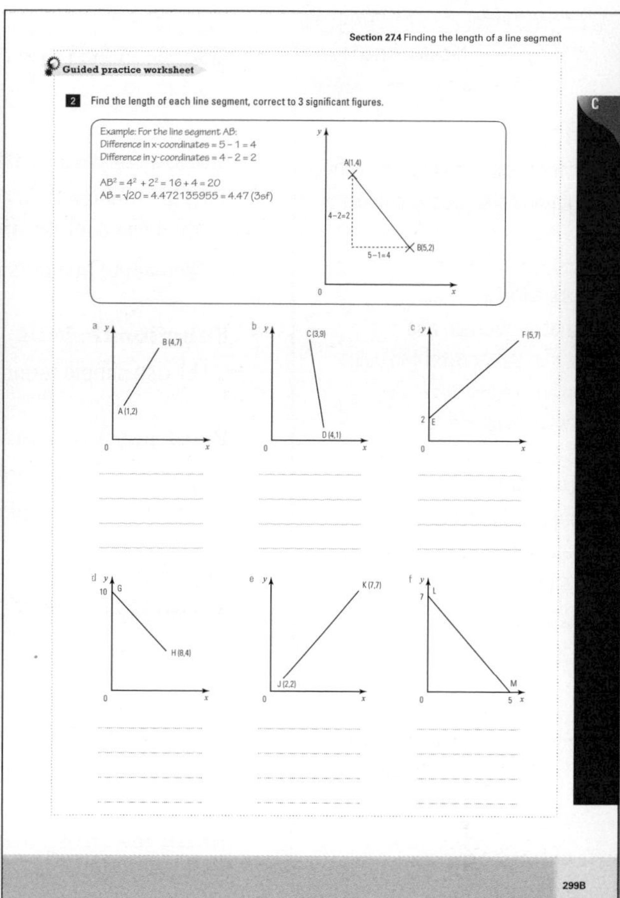

Guided practice worksheet

2 Find the length of each line segment, correct to 3 significant figures.

Example: For the line segment AB:
Difference in x-coordinates = 5 − 1 = 4
Difference in y-coordinates = 4 − 2 = 2

$AB^2 = 4^2 + 2^2 = 16 + 4 = 20$
$AB = \sqrt{20} = 4.472135955 = 4.47$ (3sf)

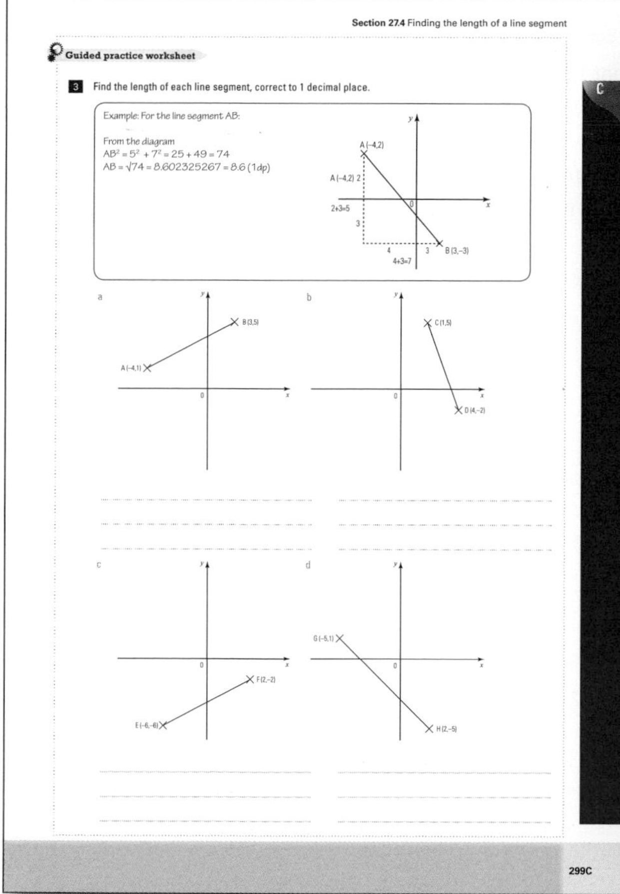

Guided practice worksheet

3 Find the length of each line segment, correct to 1 decimal place.

Example: For the line segment AB:

From the diagram
$AB^2 = 5^2 + 7^2 = 25 + 49 = 74$
$AB = \sqrt{74} = 8.602325267 = 8.6$ (1dp)

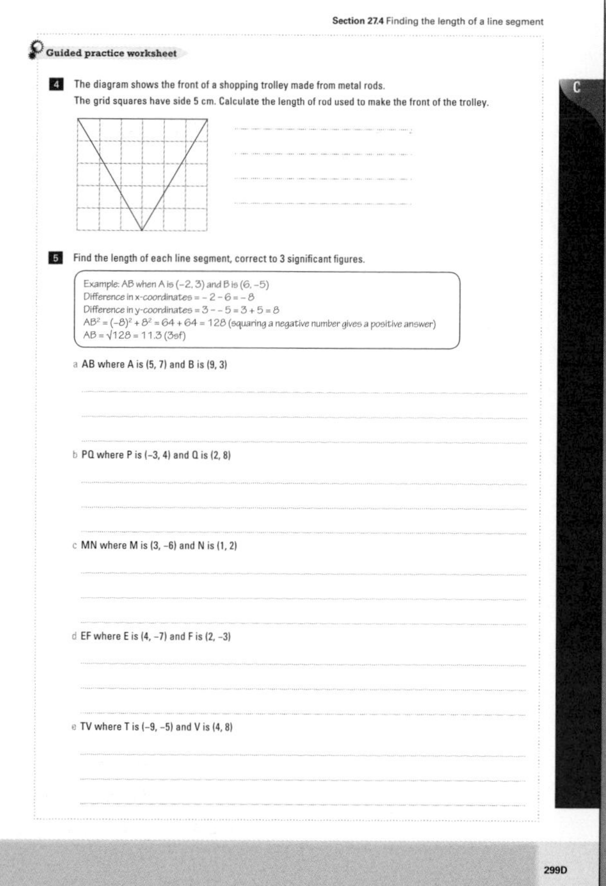

Guided practice worksheet

4 The diagram shows the front of a shopping trolley made from metal rods.
The grid squares have side 5 cm. Calculate the length of rod used to make the front of the trolley.

5 Find the length of each line segment, correct to 3 significant figures.

Example: AB when A is (−2, 3) and B is (6, −5)
Difference in x-coordinates = −2 − 6 = −8
Difference in y-coordinates = 3 − −5 = 3 + 5 = 8
$AB^2 = (-8)^2 + 8^2 = 64 + 64 = 128$ (squaring a negative number gives a positive answer)
$AB = \sqrt{128} = 11.3$ (3sf)

a AB where A is (5, 7) and B is (9, 3)

b PQ where P is (−3, 4) and Q is (2, 8)

c MN where M is (3, −6) and N is (1, 2)

d EF where E is (4, −7) and F is (2, −3)

e TV where T is (−9, −5) and V is (4, 8)

Specification

GCSE 2010

A f Derive a formula, substitute numbers into a formula and change the subject of a formula

FS Process skills

Recognise that a situation has aspects that can be represented using mathematics

Find results and solutions

FS Performance

Level 1 Understand practical problems in familiar and unfamiliar contexts and situations, some of which are non-routine

Resources

ActiveTeach resources

Word formulae interactive

28.1 Using word formulae

Concepts and skills

- Use formulae from mathematics and other subjects expressed initially in words and then using letters and symbols.
- Substitute numbers into a formula.

Functional skills

- L1 Use simple formulae expressed in words for one- or two-step operations.

Prior key knowledge, skills and concepts

- Students should already know that numbers can replace words or letters in algebra.
- Students should be able to remember the rules of order of operations (BIDMAS).

Starter

- *Work out:*

  (a) *3 × 5* (15)

  (b) *4 × 2.5* (10)

  (c) *2 × 3 + 4* (10)

  (d) *2 + 3 × 4* (14)

  (e) *12 ÷ 4* (3)

  (f) *20 ÷ 8* (2.5)

  (g) *4 × £3.65 + £12* (£26.60)

Main teaching and learning

- Go through Examples 1 and 2 and work on Exercise 28A.

Common misconceptions

- Some students might not realise that the letters stand for numbers.
- Some students do not realise that $2x$ is $x + x$ or $2 \times x$.
- If $x = 3$, then $2x = 6$ and not 23.

Plenary

- Check understanding of the topic by using pair work and getting students to make up three questions like those in Exercise 28A to give their partner and see who gets more correct.

Guided practice worksheet

F

1 This word formula can be used to find the unknown angle of a right-angle triangle:

Unknown angle = 90 – Known angle

Use the formula to find the unknown angle, when the known angle is 72°.

2 Delia uses this formula to calculate her hourly rate of pay:

$$\text{Hourly rate} = \frac{\text{Weekly wage}}{\text{Hours worked}}$$

Use the formula to calculate her hourly rate if she earned £430 in a 36 hour working week.

3 This word formula can be used to work out the perimeter of a semi-circle:

perimeter = $(\pi + 2) \times$ radius

Use the formula to find the perimeter of a semi-circle of radius 7.2 cm, to the nearest centimetre.

4 Shania walks 80 metres every minute.

a Write a word formula to work out how far she walks in a certain number of minutes.

b Use your formula to work out how far she walks in 15 minutes.

5 Bok Lum stores a computer file on a DVD of capacity 4.6 GigaBytes.

a Write a word formula to find the space remaining on the DVD.

b The computer file is 2.2 GigaBytes. Use your formula to work out the space remaining on the DVD.

Guided practice worksheet

F

6 a Write a word formula for the number of Snak bars that can be bought using a £5 note. Work in pence.

b If Snak bars cost 65p, use your formula to find the number of Snak bars that can be bought using a £5 note.

E

7 Archie sells printed badges in an online auction and posts them in a Jiffy bag. He uses this word formula to work out the total weight of a pack of badges:

Total weight = Number of Badges × Weight of a Badge + Weight of Jiffy Bag

Use the formula to find the total weight of a pack of 7 badges if each badge weighs 25 grams and a Jiffy bag weighs 20 grams.

8 An object was dropped and its speed (metres per second) measured after a certain amount of time (seconds). This word formula can be used to estimate its speed:

Speed = 5 × Time × Time

Use the formula to estimate the speed of the object 1.5 seconds after it was dropped.

9 A gardener plants 2 rows of beans plus an extra 5 beans in case some of the others don't grow.

a Write a word formula for the total number of beans planted.

b Use your formula to find the total number of beans if there are 18 beans in a row.

10 A scoop of ice cream holds 80 grams.

a Write a word formula to find the ice cream remaining in a tub after a number of scoops have been eaten.

b Use your formula to find the ice cream remaining from a 1 kg tub after eating 12 scoops.

Specification

GCSE 2010

A f Derive a formula, substitute numbers into a formula and change the subject of a formula

FS Process skills

Find results and solutions

FS Performance

Level 2 Use appropriate checking procedures and evaluate their effectiveness at each stage

28.2 Substituting numbers into expressions

Concepts and skills

- Substitute positive and negative numbers into expressions such as $3x^2 + 4$ and $2x^3$.

Functional skills

- L2 Understand and use simple formulae and equations involving one- or two-step operations.

Prior key knowledge, skills and concepts

- Students should already know that numbers can replace letters in algebra.
- Students should be able to remember the rules of order of operations (BIDMAS).

Starter

- *Work out:*

  (a) $3 \times 5 + 4$ (19)
  (b) $4 + 2.5 \times 5$ (16.5)
  (c) 2×3^2 (18)
  (d) 3×2^3 (24)
  (e) $2 \times (7 - 3)$ (8)
  (f) $5(2 + 3)^2$ (125)
  (g) $4^2 + 5^2$ (41)
  (h) $5^3 - 10^2$ (25)
  (i) $2 \times -3 + 5$ (−1)
  (j) $3 \times (-2)^2$ (12)
  (k) $-5 \times (-2)^3$ (1)
  (l) $-5 - 3 \times -2$ (−11)

Main teaching and learning

- Go through Example 3 on positive number replacement, then work on Exercise 28B.
- Go through Example 4 on negative number replacement, then work on Exercise 28C.

Common misconceptions

- $3 + 2 \times 5 = 13$ and not 25.
- When $a = 2$ and $b = 3$, then $ab = 2 \times 3 = 6$ and not 23.
- $-3 - 2 = -5$ and not $+5$ or even $+6$.
- $-5 + 8 = +3$ and not -3.

Plenary

- Check understanding with the following exercises.

  1 *Substitute $a = 2$ and $b = 3$ into:*
  (a) $a + b$ (5) (b) $a - b$ (−1) (c) ab (6) (d) $b \div a$ (1.5)

  2 *Substitute $a = -2$ and $b = 3$ into:*
  (a) $a + b$ (1) (b) $a - b$ (−5) (c) ab (−6) (d) $b \div a$ (−1.5)

  3 *Substitute $a = 2$ and $b = -3$ into:*
  (a) $a + b$ (−1) (b) $a - b$ (5) (c) ab (−6) (d) $b \div a$ (−1.5)

  4 *Substitute $a = -2$ and $b = -3$ into:*
  (a) $a + b$ (−5) (b) $a - b$ (1) (c) ab (6) (d) $b \div a$ (1.5)

Section 28.2 Substituting numbers into expressions

Guided practice worksheet

Remember: Use BIDMAS when calculating

1 Given that $a = 4$, $b = 2$, $c = 5$, find the value of each expression.

Example: $5abc = 5 \times 4 \times 2 \times 5$
$= 200$

Example: $3c - b^2 = 3 \times 5 - 2^2$ (use BIDMAS)
$= 3 \times 5 - 4$ (indices before × and −)
$= 15 - 4$ (× before −)
$= 11$

a $2ac$ b $a - b + c$

c $3c - ab$ d $a^2 + b^2$

e $\frac{a}{b}$ f $5(c - b)$

g $3ab - 2ac$ h $3a^2$

i $4b + a(c - 2)$

Hint: the 3 is not squared; only *a* is squared

j $\frac{2c - a}{b}$ k $(a + b)^2$

E D

303A

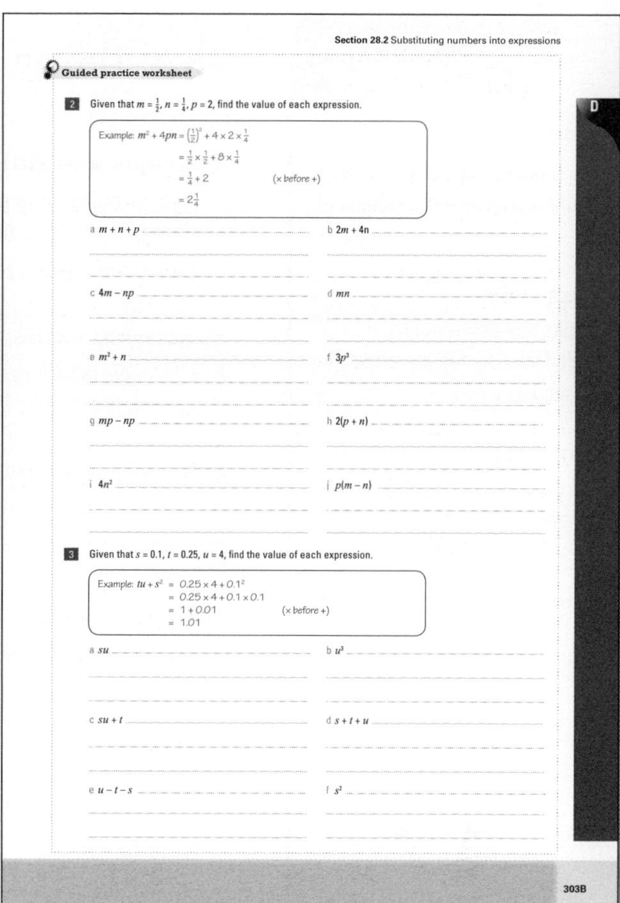

Section 28.2 Substituting numbers into expressions

Guided practice worksheet

2 Given that $m = \frac{1}{2}$, $n = \frac{1}{4}$, $p = 2$, find the value of each expression.

Example: $m^2 + 4pn = \left(\frac{1}{2}\right)^2 + 4 \times 2 \times \frac{1}{4}$
$= \frac{1}{2} \times \frac{1}{2} + 8 \times \frac{1}{4}$
$= \frac{1}{4} + 2$ (× before +)
$= 2\frac{1}{4}$

a $m + n + p$ b $2m + 4n$

c $4m - np$ d mn

e $m^2 + n$ f $3p^2$

g $mp - np$ h $2(p + n)$

i $4n^2$ j $p(m - n)$

3 Given that $s = 0.1$, $t = 0.25$, $u = 4$, find the value of each expression.

Example: $tu + s^2 = 0.25 \times 4 + 0.1^2$
$= 0.25 \times 4 + 0.1 \times 0.1$
$= 1 + 0.01$ (× before +)
$= 1.01$

a su b u^2

c $su + t$ d $s + t + u$

e $u - t - s$ f s^2

D

303B

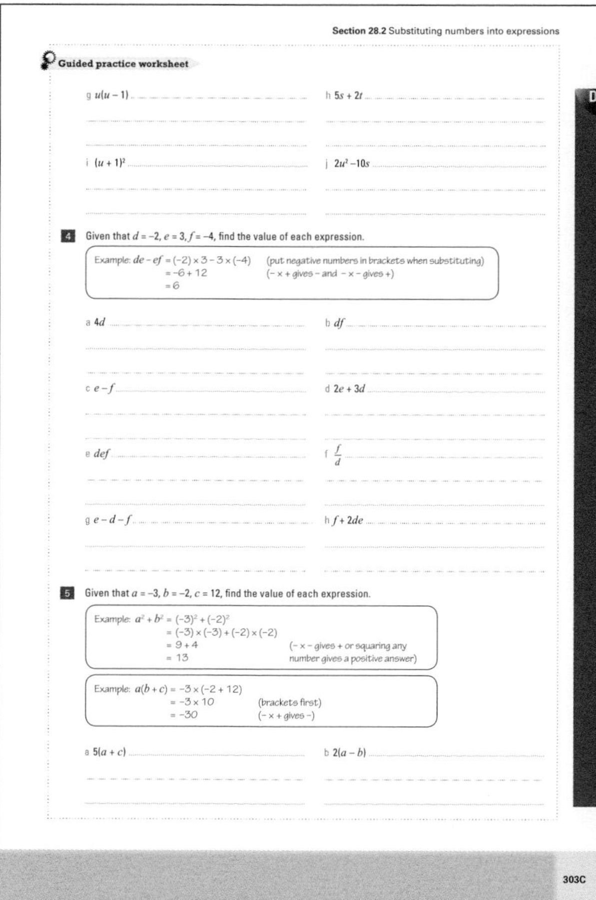

Section 28.2 Substituting numbers into expressions

Guided practice worksheet

g $u(u - 1)$ h $5s + 2t$

i $(u + 1)^2$ j $2u^2 - 10s$

4 Given that $d = -2$, $e = 3$, $f = -4$, find the value of each expression.

Example: $de - ef = (-2) \times 3 - 3 \times (-4)$ (put negative numbers in brackets when substituting)
$= -6 + 12$ (− × + gives − and − × − gives +)
$= 6$

a $4d$ b df

c $e - f$ d $2e + 3d$

e def f $\frac{f}{d}$

g $e - d - f$ h $f + 2de$

5 Given that $a = -3$, $b = -2$, $c = 12$, find the value of each expression.

Example: $a^2 + b^2 = (-3)^2 + (-2)^2$
$= (-3) \times (-3) + (-2) \times (-2)$
$= 9 + 4$ (− × − gives + or squaring any number gives a positive answer)
$= 13$

Example: $a(b + c) = -3 \times (-2 + 12)$
$= -3 \times 10$ (brackets first)
$= -30$ (− × + gives −)

a $5(a + c)$ b $2(a - b)$

D

303C

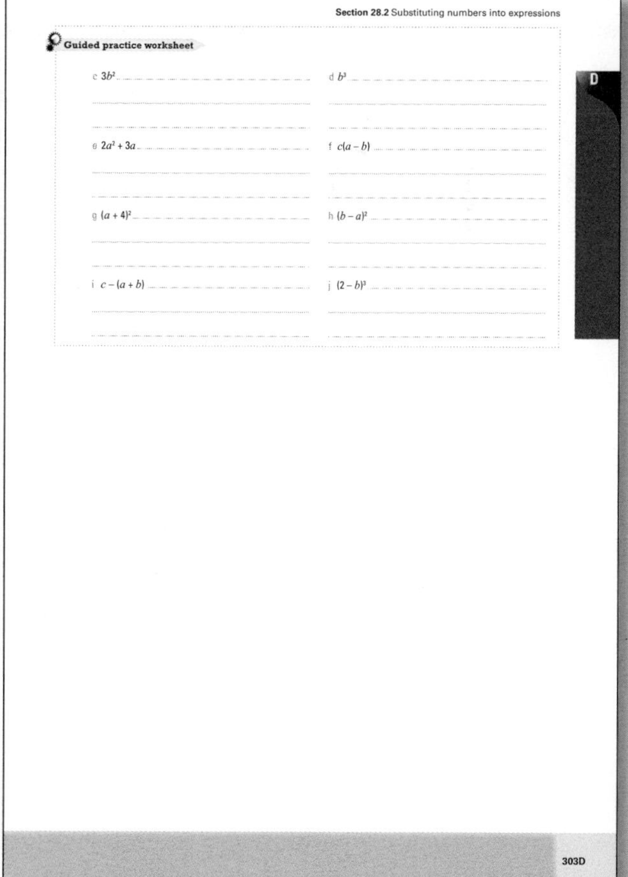

Section 28.2 Substituting numbers into expressions

Guided practice worksheet

c $3b^2$ d b^3

e $2a^2 + 3a$ f $c(a - b)$

g $(a + 4)^2$ h $(b - a)^2$

i $c - (a + b)$ j $(2 - b)^3$

D

303D

Specification

GCSE 2010

A f Derive a formula, substitute numbers into a formula and change the subject of a formula

FS Process skills

Change values and assumptions or adjust relationships to see the effects on answers in models

FS Performance

Level 2 Use appropriate checking procedures and evaluate their effectiveness at each stage

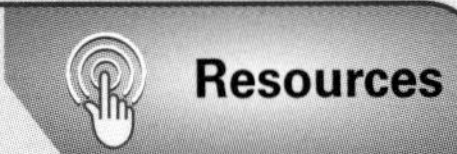

Resources

Links

http://www.bbc.co.uk/education/mathsfile/shockwave/games/equationmatch.html

ActiveTeach resources

Substitution interactive

28.3 Using algebraic formulae

Concepts and skills

- Use formulae from mathematics and other subjects expressed initially in words and then using letters and symbols
- Substitute numbers into a formula.

Functional skills

- L2 Understand and use simple formulae and equations involving one- or two-step operations.

Prior key knowledge, skills and concepts

- Students should already know that numbers can replace letters in algebra.
- Students should remember the rules of order of operations (BIDMAS).

Starter

- *1 Find the value of these expressions when $a = 3$ and $b = 4$.*
  (a) $a + b$ (7) (b) $a - b$ (–1) (c) ab (12) (d) $b \div a$ $\left(1\frac{1}{3}\right)$ (e) $b - a$ (1)
- *2 Find the value of these expressions when $a = -3$ and $b = 4$.*
  (a) $a + b$ (1) (b) $a - b$ (–7) (c) ab (–12) (d) $b \div a$ $\left(-1\frac{1}{3}\right)$ (e) $b - a$ (7)
- *3 Find the value of these expressions when $a = 3$ and $b = -4$.*
  (a) $a + b$ (–1) (b) $a - b$ (7) (c) ab (–12) (d) $b \div a$ $\left(-1\frac{1}{3}\right)$ (e) $b - a$ (–7)
- *4 Find the value of these expressions when $a = -3$ and $b = -4$.*
  (a) $a + b$ (–7) (b) $a - b$ (–1) (c) ab (12) (d) $b \div a$ $\left(1\frac{1}{3}\right)$ (e) $b - a$ (–1)

Main teaching and learning

- Go through Examples 5 and 6 then work on Exercise 28D.

Common misconceptions

- Errors frequently occur in the order of operations.

Plenary

- Check understanding of the topic by using pair work and getting students to make up five formulae such as those in Exercise 28D to give to their partner and seeing who gets more correct.

algebraic formula subject

Guided practice worksheet

E

1 The area of a square of side d is given by the formula $A = d^2$.
Find the value of A when

a $d = 7$ cm

b $d = 1.5$ cm

c $d = 30$ *mm*

d $d = 100$ *m*

2 The force F needed to give an object of mass m an acceleration a is given by the formula $F = ma$
Find the value of F when

a $m = 3$ and $a = 7$

b $m = 4.6$ and $a = 10$

c $m = 20$ and $a = 12$

d $m = 0.3$ and $a = 8$

D

3 Bike*R* calculate their hire charge H for a scooter using the formula $H = nr + C$ where
n is the number of hours
r is the rate per hour
C is the additional fixed charge.
Calculate the hire charge £H when

a $n = 4$ hours, $r = £2$, $C = £10$

b $n = 6$ hours, $r = £2.50$, $C = £8$

c $n = 2.5$ hours, $r = £3$, $C = £5$

d $n = 8$ hours, $r = £1.80$, $C = £13.50$

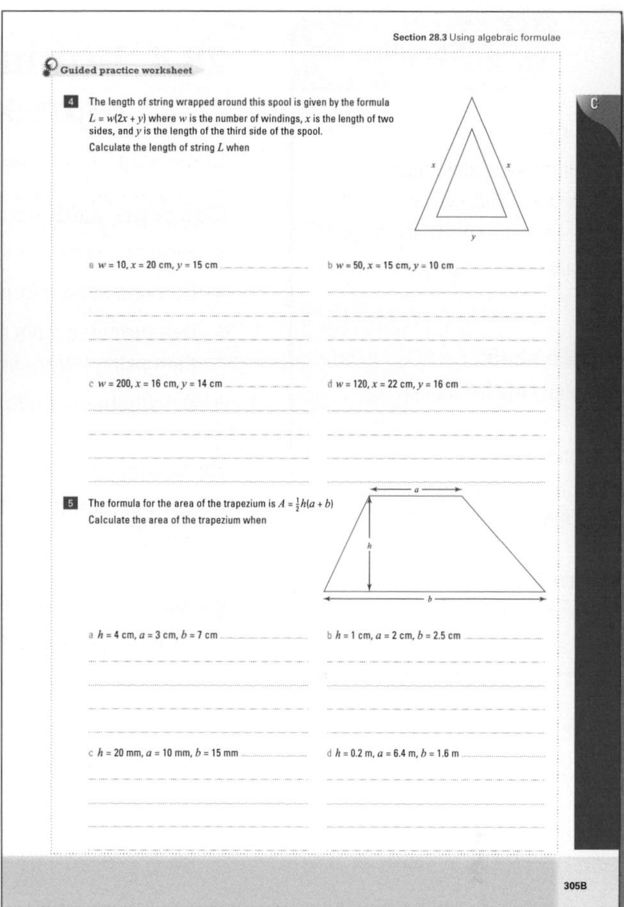

Section 28.3 Using algebraic formulae

Guided practice worksheet

C

4 The length of string wrapped around this spool is given by the formula $L = w(2x + y)$ where w is the number of windings, x is the length of two sides, and y is the length of the third side of the spool.
Calculate the length of string L when

a $w = 10$, $x = 20$ cm, $y = 15$ cm

b $w = 50$, $x = 15$ cm, $y = 10$ cm

c $w = 200$, $x = 16$ cm, $y = 14$ cm

d $w = 120$, $x = 22$ cm, $y = 16$ cm

5 The formula for the area of the trapezium is $A = \frac{1}{2}h(a + b)$
Calculate the area of the trapezium when

a $h = 4$ cm, $a = 3$ cm, $b = 7$ cm

b $h = 1$ cm, $a = 2$ cm, $b = 2.5$ cm

c $h = 20$ mm, $a = 10$ mm, $b = 15$ mm

d $h = 0.2$ m, $a = 6.4$ m, $b = 1.6$ m

305B

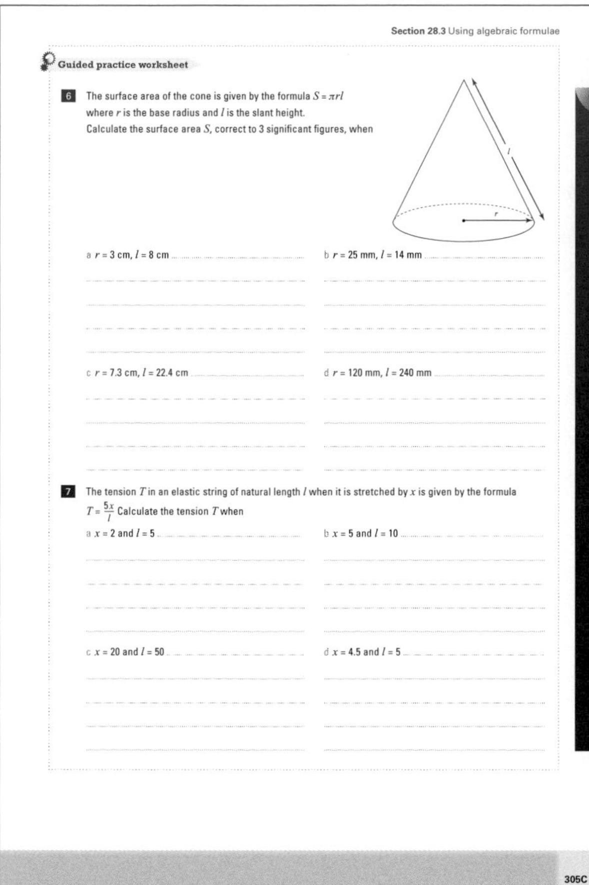

Section 28.3 Using algebraic formulae

Guided practice worksheet

C

6 The surface area of the cone is given by the formula $S = \pi rl$
where r is the base radius and l is the slant height.
Calculate the surface area S, correct to 3 significant figures, when

a $r = 3$ cm, $l = 8$ cm

b $r = 25$ mm, $l = 14$ mm

c $r = 7.3$ cm, $l = 22.4$ cm

d $r = 120$ mm, $l = 240$ mm

7 The tension T in an elastic string of natural length l when it is stretched by x is given by the formula
$T = \frac{5x}{l}$ Calculate the tension T when

a $x = 2$ and $l = 5$

b $x = 5$ and $l = 10$

c $x = 20$ and $l = 50$

d $x = 4.5$ and $l = 5$

305C

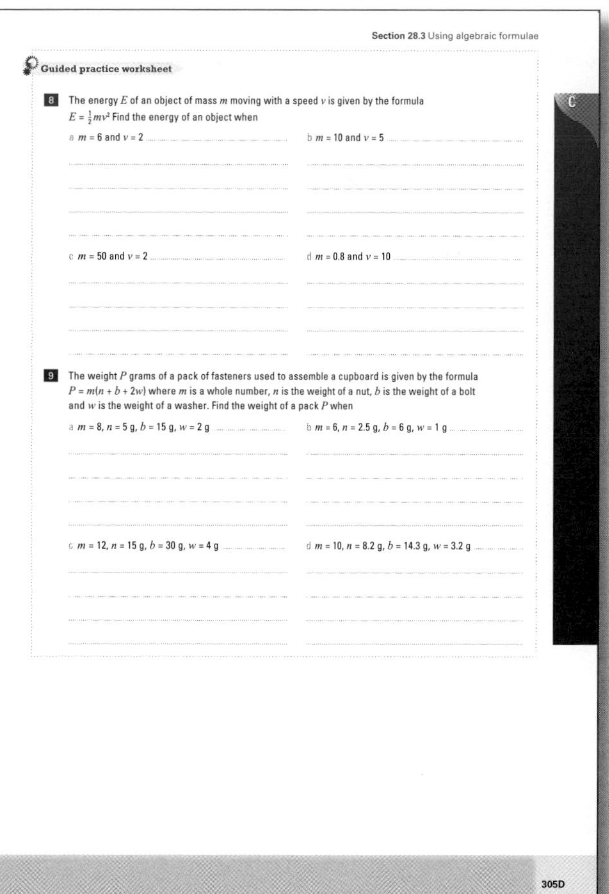

Section 28.3 Using algebraic formulae

Guided practice worksheet

C

8 The energy E of an object of mass m moving with a speed v is given by the formula
$E = \frac{1}{2}mv^2$ Find the energy of an object when

a $m = 6$ and $v = 2$

b $m = 10$ and $v = 5$

c $m = 50$ and $v = 2$

d $m = 0.8$ and $v = 10$

9 The weight P grams of a pack of fasteners used to assemble a cupboard is given by the formula
$P = m(n + b + 2w)$ where m is a whole number, n is the weight of a nut, b is the weight of a bolt and w is the weight of a washer. Find the weight of a pack P when

a $m = 8$, $n = 5$ g, $b = 15$ g, $w = 2$ g

b $m = 6$, $n = 2.5$ g, $b = 6$ g, $w = 1$ g

c $m = 12$, $n = 15$ g, $b = 30$ g, $w = 4$ g

d $m = 10$, $n = 8.2$ g, $b = 14.3$ g, $w = 3.2$ g

305D

Specification

GCSE 2010

A c (part) Manipulate algebraic expressions …

A f Derive a formula, substitute numbers into a formula and change the subject of a formula

FS Process skills

Use appropriate mathematical procedures

Change values and assumptions or adjust relationships to see the effects on answers in models

FS Performance

Level 2 Use appropriate checking procedures and evaluate their effectiveness at each stage

28.4 Writing an algebraic formula to represent a problem

Concepts and skills

- Write expressions to solve problems.
- Derive a simple formula, including those with squares, cubes and roots.
- Use formulae from mathematics and other subjects expressed initially in words and then using letters and symbols.
- Substitute numbers into a formula.

Functional skills

- L2 Understand and use simple formulae and equations involving one- or two-step operations.

Prior key knowledge, skills and concepts

- Students should already know that numbers can replace letters in algebra.
- Students should remember the rules of order of operations (BIDMAS).

Starter

- *Find the value of P in the following formulae when $a = 2$, $b = -3$, $c = 5$*

  (a) $P = a + b - c$ (–6) (b) $P = ab - c$ (–11) (c) $P = a(b + c)$ (4)

  (d) $P = a^2 + b^2$(13) (e) $P = a^2 - b^2$ (–5) (f) $P = \sqrt{a^2 + b^2}$ (3.61)

Main teaching and learning

- Go through Example 7, then work on Exercise 28E.

Common misconceptions

- Errors frequently occur in the order of operations.

Enrichment

- *Use the internet to find formulae for finding areas of shapes.* (By inspection.)
- *Find the formula for changing from Kelvin to degrees Celsius.* (Temperature in degrees Celsius = temperature in Kelvin – 273)

Plenary

- *Write a formula for working out someone's pay P when their hourly rate is R and they work for H hours, but have to pay deductions D.* ($P = RH - D$)
- Use your formula to find P when $H = 40$, $T = 4$ and $D = 20$. ($P = 140$)

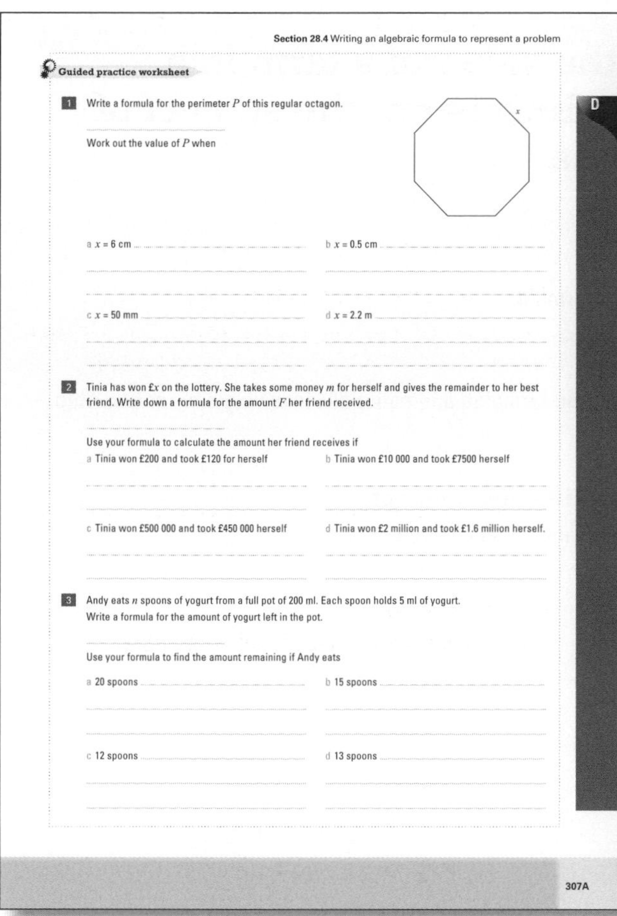

Section 28.4 Writing an algebraic formula to represent a problem

Guided practice worksheet

D

1 Write a formula for the perimeter P of this regular octagon.

Work out the value of P when

a $x = 6$ cm

b $x = 0.5$ cm

c $x = 50$ mm

d $x = 2.2$ m

2 Tinia has won £x on the lottery. She takes some money m for herself and gives the remainder to her best friend. Write down a formula for the amount F her friend received.

Use your formula to calculate the amount her friend receives if

a Tinia won £200 and took £120 for herself

b Tinia won £10 000 and took £7500 herself

c Tinia won £500 000 and took £450 000 herself

d Tinia won £2 million and took £1.6 million herself.

3 Andy eats n spoons of yogurt from a full pot of 200 ml. Each spoon holds 5 ml of yogurt. Write a formula for the amount of yogurt left in the pot.

Use your formula to find the amount remaining if Andy eats

a 20 spoons

b 15 spoons

c 12 spoons

d 13 spoons

307A

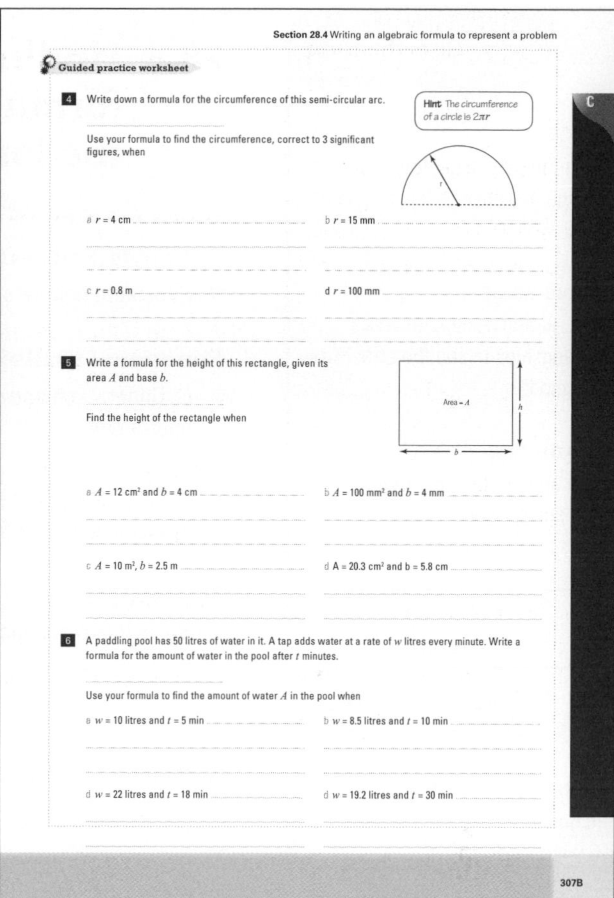

Section 28.4 Writing an algebraic formula to represent a problem

Guided practice worksheet

C

4 Write down a formula for the circumference of this semi-circular arc.

Hint: The circumference of a circle is $2\pi r$

Use your formula to find the circumference, correct to 3 significant figures, when

a $r = 4$ cm

b $r = 15$ mm

c $r = 0.8$ m

d $r = 100$ mm

5 Write a formula for the height of this rectangle, given its area A and base b.

Find the height of the rectangle when

a $A = 12$ cm² and $b = 4$ cm

b $A = 100$ mm² and $b = 4$ mm

c $A = 10$ m², $b = 2.5$ m

d A = 20.3 cm² and b = 5.8 cm

6 A paddling pool has 50 litres of water in it. A tap adds water at a rate of w litres every minute. Write a formula for the amount of water in the pool after t minutes.

Use your formula to find the amount of water A in the pool when

a $w = 10$ litres and $t = 5$ min

b $w = 8.5$ litres and $t = 10$ min

d $w = 22$ litres and $t = 18$ min

d $w = 19.2$ litres and $t = 30$ min

307B

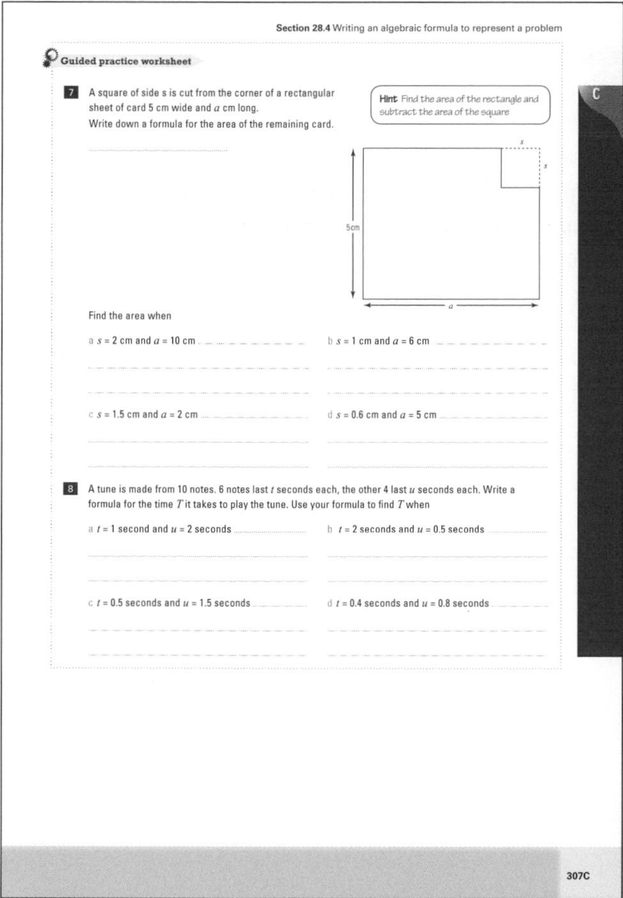

Section 28.4 Writing an algebraic formula to represent a problem

Guided practice worksheet

C

7 A square of side s is cut from the corner of a rectangular sheet of card 5 cm wide and a cm long. Write down a formula for the area of the remaining card.

Hint: Find the area of the rectangle and subtract the area of the square

Find the area when

a $s = 2$ cm and $a = 10$ cm

b $s = 1$ cm and $a = 6$ cm

c $s = 1.5$ cm and $a = 2$ cm

d $s = 0.6$ cm and $a = 5$ cm

8 A tune is made from 10 notes. 6 notes last t seconds each, the other 4 last u seconds each. Write a formula for the time T it takes to play the tune. Use your formula to find T when

a $t = 1$ second and $u = 2$ seconds

b $t = 2$ seconds and $u = 0.5$ seconds

c $t = 0.5$ seconds and $u = 1.5$ seconds

d $t = 0.4$ seconds and $u = 0.8$ seconds

307C

Specification

GCSE 2010

A f Derive a formula, substitute numbers into a formula and change the subject of a formula

FS Process skills

Change values and assumptions or adjust relationships to see the effects on answers in models

FS Performance

Level 2 Use appropriate checking procedures and evaluate their effectiveness at each stage

Resources

ActiveTeach resources

Formulae quiz

28.5 Finding the value of a term in a formula which is not the subject of the formula

Concepts and skills

- Substitute numbers into a formula.

Functional skills

- L2 Understand and use simple formulae and equations involving one- or two-step operations.

Prior key knowledge, skills and concepts

- Students should already be able to solve equations.

Starter

- *Solve these equations.*

(a) $a + 3 = 7$ ($a = 4$)

(b) $b - 5 = 2$ ($b = 7$)

(c) $3c = 18$ ($c = 6$)

(d) $\frac{x}{6} = 2$ ($x = 12$)

(e) $2b + 5 = 11$ ($b = 3$)

(f) $3c - 4 = 2$ ($c = 2$)

(g) $3(x + 4) = 12$ ($x = 0$)

(h) $5(2p - 3) = 10$ ($p = 2.5$)

(i) $3t + 2 = t - 7$ ($t = -4.5$)

(j) $4p + 5 = 8 - 2p$ ($p = 0.5$)

Main teaching and learning

- Go through Example 8 and then work on Exercise 28F.

Common misconceptions

- Errors frequently occur in the order of operations.

Plenary

- Check understanding of the topic by using pair work and getting students to make up 3 questions of their own like those in Exercise 28F and give them to their partner and seeing who gets most correct.

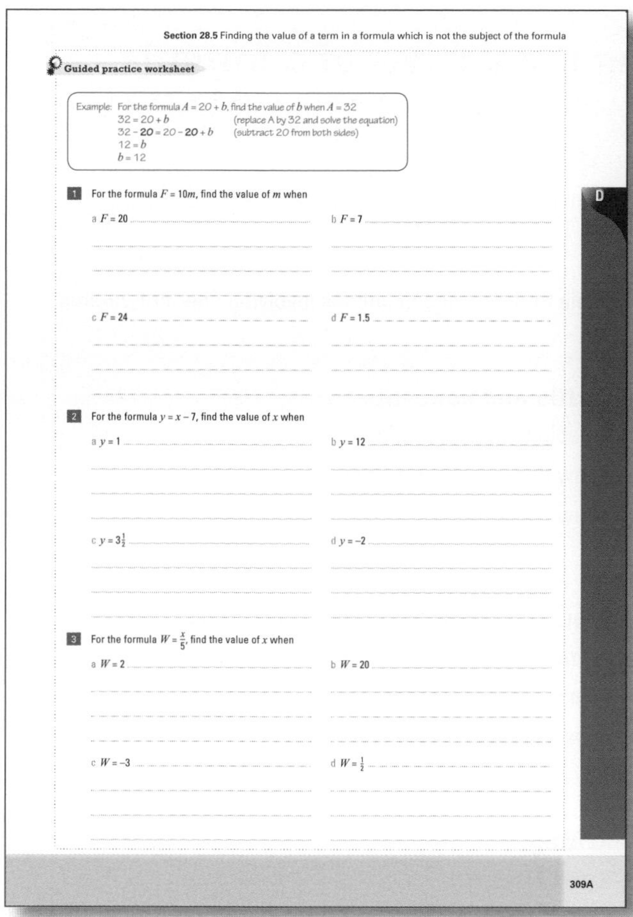

Section 28.5 Finding the value of a term in a formula which is not the subject of the formula

Guided practice worksheet

Example: For the formula $A = 20 + b$, find the value of b when $A = 32$
$32 = 20 + b$ (replace A by 32 and solve the equation)
$32 - \mathbf{20} = 20 - \mathbf{20} + b$ (subtract 20 from both sides)
$12 = b$
$b = 12$

1 For the formula $F = 10m$, find the value of m when

a $F = 20$ b $F = 7$

c $F = 24$ d $F = 1.5$

2 For the formula $y = x - 7$, find the value of x when

a $y = 1$ b $y = 12$

c $y = 3\frac{1}{2}$ d $y = -2$

3 For the formula $W = \frac{x}{5}$, find the value of x when

a $W = 2$ b $W = 20$

c $W = -3$ d $W = \frac{1}{2}$

D

309A

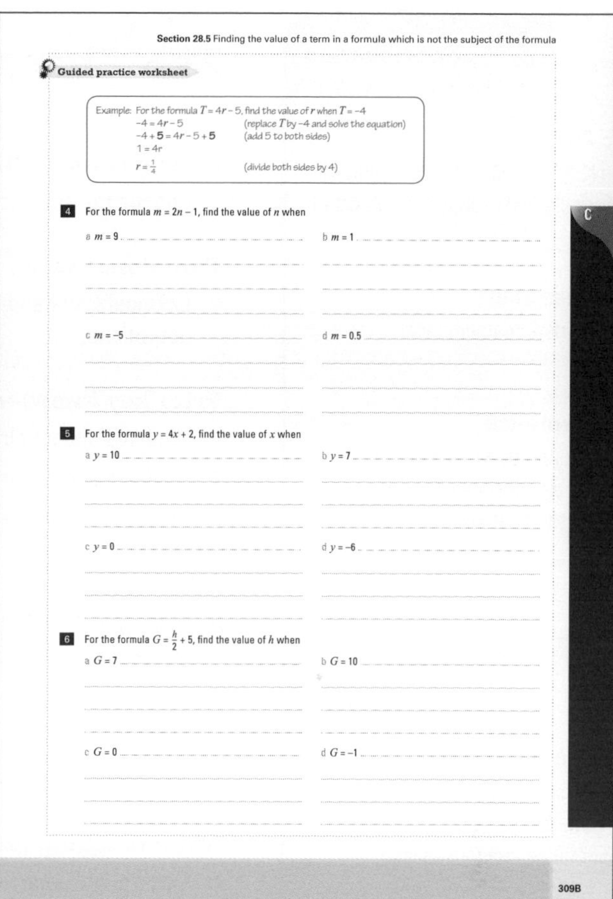

Section 28.5 Finding the value of a term in a formula which is not the subject of the formula

Guided practice worksheet

Example: For the formula $T = 4r - 5$, find the value of r when $T = -4$
$-4 = 4r - 5$ (replace T by -4 and solve the equation)
$-4 + \mathbf{5} = 4r - 5 + \mathbf{5}$ (add 5 to both sides)
$1 = 4r$
$r = \frac{1}{4}$ (divide both sides by 4)

4 For the formula $m = 2n - 1$, find the value of n when

a $m = 9$ b $m = 1$

c $m = -5$ d $m = 0.5$

5 For the formula $y = 4x + 2$, find the value of x when

a $y = 10$ b $y = 7$

c $y = 0$ d $y = -6$

6 For the formula $G = \frac{h}{2} + 5$, find the value of h when

a $G = 7$ b $G = 10$

c $G = 0$ d $G = -1$

C

309B

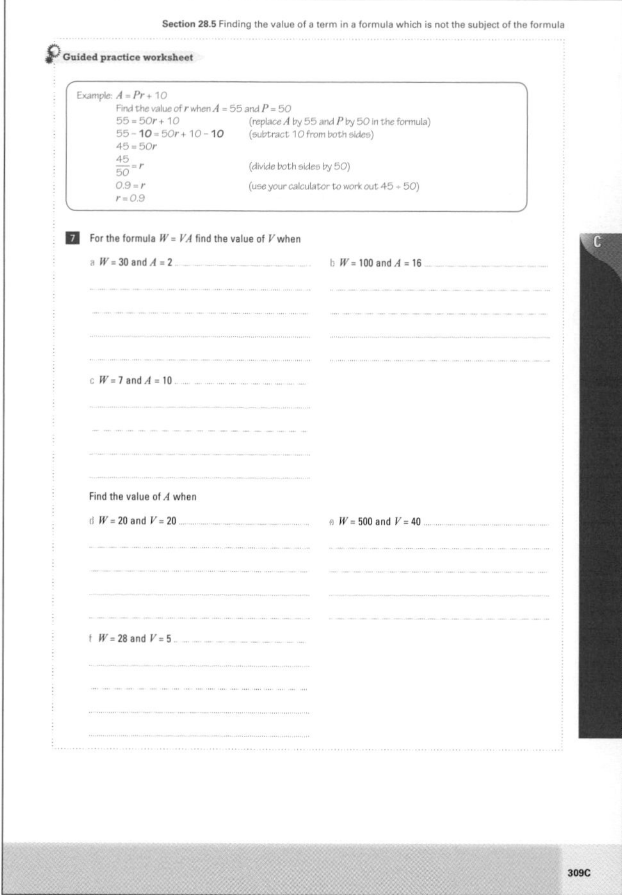

Section 28.5 Finding the value of a term in a formula which is not the subject of the formula

Guided practice worksheet

Example: $A = Pr + 10$
Find the value of r when $A = 55$ and $P = 50$
$55 = 50r + 10$ (replace A by 55 and P by 50 in the formula)
$55 - \mathbf{10} = 50r + 10 - \mathbf{10}$ (subtract 10 from both sides)
$45 = 50r$
$\frac{45}{50} = r$ (divide both sides by 50)
$0.9 = r$ (use your calculator to work out $45 \div 50$)
$r = 0.9$

7 For the formula $W = VA$ find the value of V when

a $W = 30$ and $A = 2$ b $W = 100$ and $A = 16$

c $W = 7$ and $A = 10$

Find the value of A when

d $W = 20$ and $V = 20$ e $W = 500$ and $V = 40$

f $W = 28$ and $V = 5$

C

309C

Section 28.5 Finding the value of a term in a formula which is not the subject of the formula

Guided practice worksheet

8 For the formula $S = 4a + c$ find the value of c when

a $S = 10$ and $a = 2$ b $S = 25$ and $a = 6$

c $S = 12$ and $a = 5$

Find the value of a when

d $S = 5$ and $c = 1$ e $S = 15$ and $c = 2$

f $S = 8$ and $c = -4$

9 For the formula $A = \pi rl$, find the value of r, correct to 3 significant figures, when $\pi = 3.14$ and

a $A = 20$ and $l = 4$ b $A = 2.5$ and $l = 10$

c $A = 1000$ and $l = 25$

C

309D

Specification

GCSE 2010
A f Derive a formula, substitute numbers into a formula and change the subject of a formula

FS Process skills
Use appropriate mathematical procedures

FS Performance
Level 2 Use appropriate checking procedures and evaluate their effectiveness at each stage

Resources

ActiveTeach resources
Inverse formulae quiz
RP KC Formulae knowledge check
RP PS Formulae problem solving

28.6 Changing the subject of a formula

Concepts and skills

- Change the subject of a formula.

Functional skills

- L2 Understand and use simple formulae and equations involving one- or two-step operations.

Prior key knowledge, skills and concepts

- Students should already be able to solve equations.
- Students should already know that + and – are inverse operations.
- Students should already know that × and ÷ are inverse operations.

Starter

- Check understanding of inverses by asking questions such as these.
  What do you add to 5 to get to zero? (–5)
  What do you take away from 6 to get to zero? (6)
  What do you divide 8 by to get to 1? (8)
  What do you multiply 3 by to get to 1? $\left(\frac{1}{3}\right)$

Main teaching and learning

- Go through Examples 9, 10 and 11.
- Get students to work on Exercise 28G.
- Use the Review exercise to practise skills from the whole chapter.

Common misconceptions

- Students sometimes get the syntax incorrect.

Enrichment

- By substituting the value of u in $v = u + at$ into $v^2 = u^2 + 2aS$, find another formula connecting v, a and S. $\left(S = vt - \frac{1}{2}at^2\right)$

Plenary

- Pick one of the questions from the exercises and do it as a worked example, showing the full method.

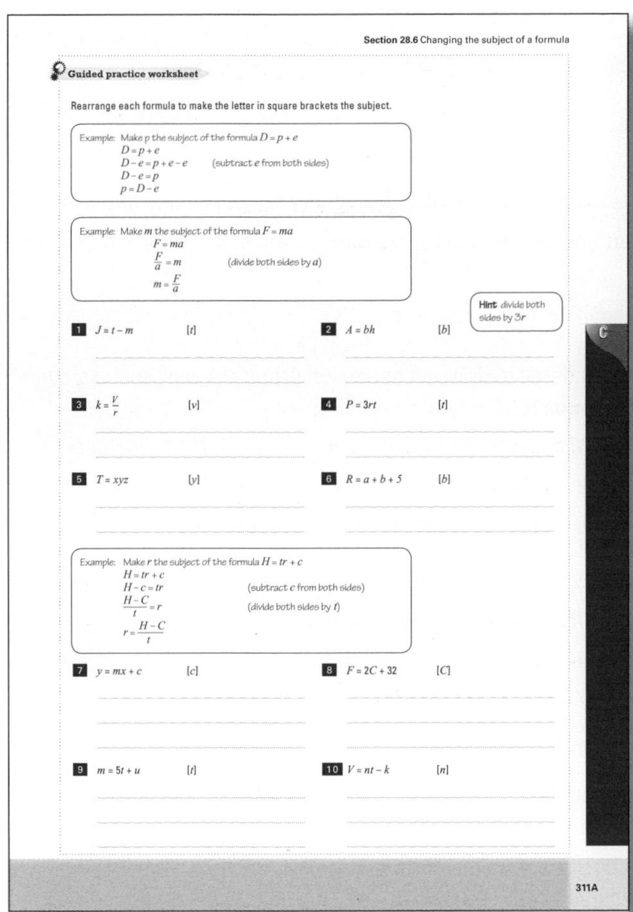

Section 28.6 Changing the subject of a formula

Guided practice worksheet

Rearrange each formula to make the letter in square brackets the subject.

Example: Make p the subject of the formula $D = p + e$

$D = p + e$
$D - e = p + e - e$ (subtract e from both sides)
$D - e = p$
$p = D - e$

Example: Make m the subject of the formula $F = ma$

$F = ma$
$\frac{F}{a} = m$ (divide both sides by a)
$m = \frac{F}{a}$

Hint: divide both sides by $3r$

1 $J = t - m$ [t]

2 $A = bh$ [b]

3 $k = \frac{V}{r}$ [v]

4 $P = 3rt$ [t]

5 $T = xyz$ [y]

6 $R = a + b + 5$ [b]

Example: Make r the subject of the formula $H = tr + c$

$H = tr + c$
$H - c = tr$ (subtract c from both sides)
$\frac{H - C}{t} = r$ (divide both sides by t)
$r = \frac{H - C}{t}$

7 $y = mx + c$ [c]

8 $F = 2C + 32$ [C]

9 $m = 5t + u$ [t]

10 $V = nt - k$ [n]

311A

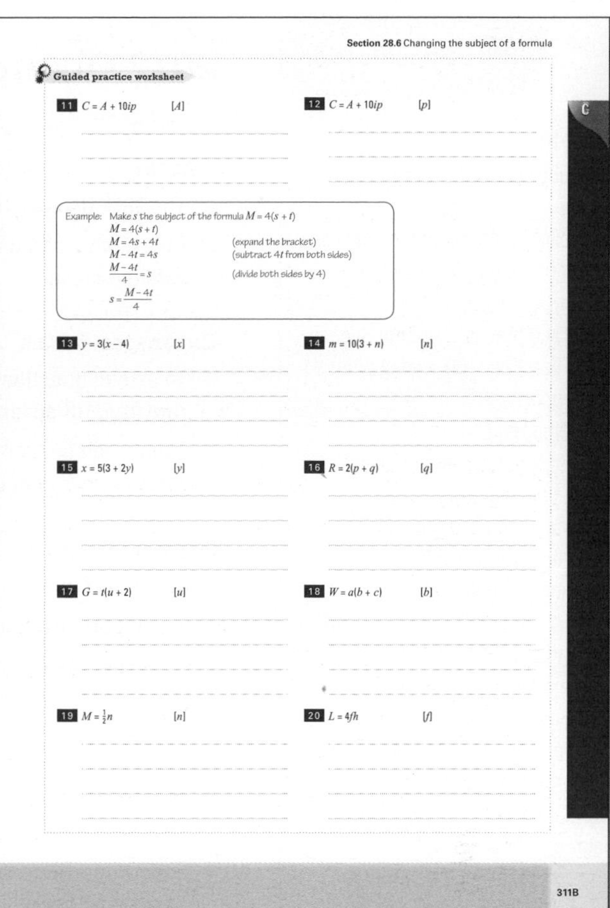

Section 28.6 Changing the subject of a formula

Guided practice worksheet

11 $C = A + 10ip$ [A]

12 $C = A + 10ip$ [p]

Example: Make s the subject of the formula $M = 4(s + t)$

$M = 4(s + t)$
$M = 4s + 4t$ (expand the bracket)
$M - 4t = 4s$ (subtract $4t$ from both sides)
$\frac{M - 4t}{4} = s$ (divide both sides by 4)
$s = \frac{M - 4t}{4}$

13 $y = 3(x - 4)$ [x]

14 $m = 10(3 + n)$ [n]

15 $x = 5(3 + 2y)$ [y]

16 $R = 2(p + q)$ [q]

17 $G = t(u + 2)$ [u]

18 $W = a(b + c)$ [b]

19 $M = \frac{1}{2}n$ [n]

20 $L = 4fh$ [f]

311B

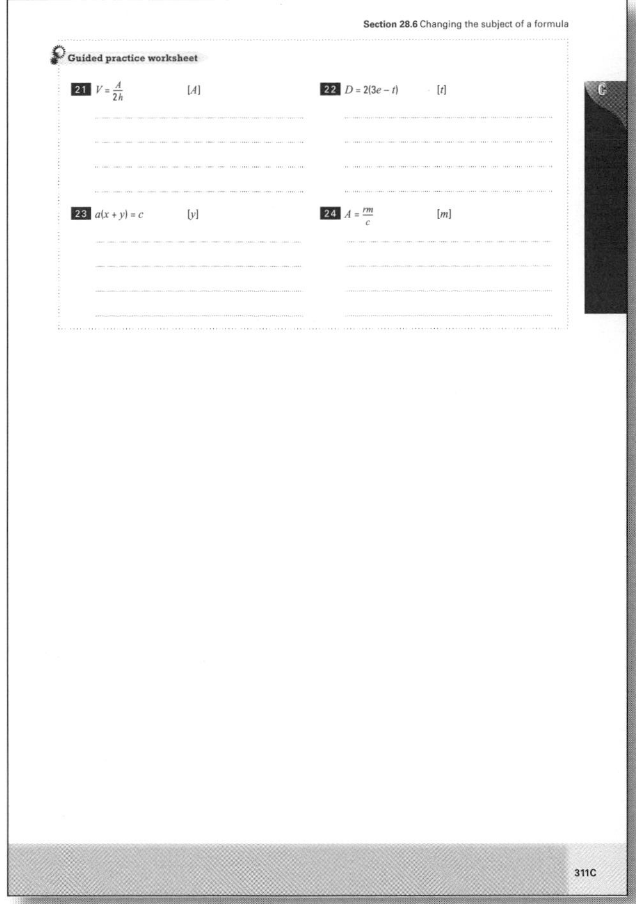

Section 28.6 Changing the subject of a formula

Guided practice worksheet

21 $V = \frac{A}{2h}$ [A]

22 $D = 2(3e - t)$ [t]

23 $a(x + y) = c$ [y]

24 $A = \frac{rm}{c}$ [m]

311C

Specification

GCSE 2010

N a Add, subtract, multiply and divide any number
N j Use decimal notation and recognise that each terminating decimal is a fraction
N l Understand that 'percentage' means 'number of parts per 100' and use this to compare proportions
N m Use percentage
N o Interpret fractions, decimals and percentages as operators
N q Understand and use number operations and the relationships between them, including inverse operations and hierarchy of operations
N u Approximate to specified or appropriate degrees of accuracy including a given power of ten, number of decimal places and significant figures
A f Derive a formula, substitute numbers into a formula and change the subject of a formula
GM o Interpret scales on a range of measuring instruments and recognise the inaccuracy of measurements
GM q Make sensible estimates of a range of measures

2012 Olympics

Starter

- The 2012 Olympic Games open on 27 July 2012. Ask students: '*How many days are left?*'
- Give each student a sport and get them to list the maths used in that sport, then share with the class.

Extension tasks

- To extend question 2, ask students to draw a conversion graph showing the exchange rate from US dollars ($) to euros (€).
- To extend question 3, ask: '*20 contestants compete against each other. Calculate the total number of bouts.*'

Support tasks

- To support question 1, ask: '*What time is it in London when the team leave?*'
- To support question 2, ask: '*If a T-shirt costs £8.99, how much is that in dollars?*'
- To support question 3, ask: '*If athletes completed the swimming and running back to back, what order would they finish in?*'

Plenary

- Discuss the reasons why people often make mistakes when converting between seconds, minutes and hours.
- Encourage students to consider why time differences exist and how a country's position on the globe decides its time relative to GMT, e.g. longitude or latitude.

 **Specification**

CSE 2010

a Add, subtract, multiply and divide
ny number

l Understand that 'percentage' means
umber of parts per 100' and use this to
ompare proportions

m Use percentage

o Interpret fractions, decimals and
ercentages as operators

u Approximate to specified or
ppropriate degrees of accuracy
cluding a given power of ten, number
f decimal places and significant figures

v Use calculators effectively and
fficiently including statistical functions

M q Make sensible estimates of a
nge of measures

P a Understand and use statistical
roblem solving process/handling data
ycle

P e Extract data from printed tables
nd lists

P f Design and use two-way tables for
screte and grouped data

P i Interpret a wide range of graphs and
agrams and draw conclusions

Learning to drive

Starter

- Ask students to estimate the cost of learning to drive.
- Ask students to estimate the distances between pairs of cities.
- Ask students to consider what maths is required when learning to drive.

Extension tasks

- To extend question 1, tell students that when it's raining you double the stopping distance and when it's freezing you multiply by 10. Ask: *'If you drive at 20 mph when it's freezing, what speed would you have to be travelling at to need the equivalent stopping distance when it's raining?'*
  Ask students to estimate the total stopping distance at 100 mph. Explain how stopping distances change as speed increases.
- To extend question 2, ask: *'How many one hour and fifteen minute lessons have the same total cost as 30 one hour lessons?'* Remember the first lesson is free.
- To extend question 3, ask students to work out what percentage of the cost of a car you could save by buying privately rather than from a dealer.
  Explain why expensive cars depreciate more for every 1000 miles they are driven.

Support tasks

- To support question 1, ask students to only calculate total stopping distances.
- To support question 3, tell students not to adjust the price for mileage.

Plenary

- How could you show the changing value of a car over a period of time?
- Encourage students to explain their approach to question 3.

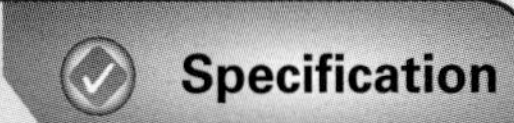

GCSE 2010

N a Add, subtract, multiply and divide any number

N j Use decimal notation and recognise that each terminating decimal is a fraction

N l Understand that 'percentage' means 'number of parts per 100' and use this to compare proportions

N o Interpret fractions, decimals and percentages as operators

N u Approximate to specified or appropriate degrees of accuracy including a given power of ten, number of decimal places and significant figures

GM o Interpret scales on a range of measuring instruments and recognise the inaccuracy of measurements

GM q Make sensible estimates of a range of measures

SP a Understand and use statistical problem solving process/handling data cycle

SP e Extract data from printed tables and lists

SP i Interpret a wide range of graphs and diagrams and draw conclusions

Healthy living

Starter

- Complete a percentage spider diagram for a variety of different starting values.
- Asks students to estimate the quantities of carbohydrate, protein, fat etc. in different types of food.
- Ask questions on converting units, e.g. '*How many ml in a pint of milk?*'
- Ask students to match percentage and fraction pairs.

Extension tasks

- To extend question 1, ask: '*A pizza weighs 365 g. A chicken nugget weighs 16.4 g. How many chicken nuggets contain the same amount of fibre as one pizza?*'
- To extend question 2, ask students to describe the difference in weight/BMI between Reception and Year 6 children.
- To extend question 3, ask students to write a 3-hour exercise schedule for Rochelle. To extend further, use harder percentages for the pie chart.

Support tasks

- To support question 1, ask: '*How much fat is there in one pizza? How many calories are there in one chicken nugget?*'
- To support question 2, ask students to write down the percentage of obese Year 6 children. Ask: '*How many reception children are underweight?*'
- To support question 3, divide the pie chart into ten slices.

Plenary

- Discuss different ways of representing the data in question 2.
- Discuss the different methods used in question 3.
- List the different types of graph you can use to represent data and summarise what they show.

Specification

GCSE 2010

a Add, subtract, multiply and divide any number

m Use percentage

o Interpret fractions, decimals and percentages as operators

v Use calculators effectively and efficiently, including statistical functions

f Derive a formula, substitute numbers into a formula and change the subject of a formula

Money management

Starter

- Discuss different forms of taxation with the class.
- Complete a percentage spider diagram for a variety of different starting values.

Extension tasks

- To extend question 2, ask: *How much NIC would you pay on a £22000 annual salary? How much does your annual salary need to be before you pay NIC?*
- To extend question 3, ask: *If a 10% tax on earnings over £3500 was introduced, who would it have the greatest affect on?*

Support tasks

- To support question 1, ask: *How much EMA could someone earn in a year?*
- To support question 2, ask: *How much would you pay in NIC if you earned £200 in a week?*
- To support question 3, ask: *How much income tax would you pay on a salary of £10000?*

Plenary

- Discuss different methods for calculating percentages with and without a calculator.
- Discuss the different amounts of income tax and NIC paid by someone with a salary of £10000 and someone with a salary of £100000. Encourage students to consider tax as a proportion of total income.

Specification

GCSE 2010

N a Add, subtract, multiply and divide any number
N v Use calculators effectively and efficiently, including statistical functions
GM k Use 2D representations of 3D shapes
GM m Use and interpret maps and scale drawings
GM n Understand the effect of enlargement for perimeter, area and volume of shapes and solids
GM p Convert measurements from one unit to another
GM u Draw triangles and other 2D shapes using ruler and protractor
GM v Use straight edge and a pair of compasses to do constructions

Kitchen design

Starter

- Match up different metric measurements.
- Ask students to estimate the dimensions of the classroom.
- Ask students to consider what maths a kitchen fitter might use.
- Ask students: '*When designing a kitchen, what factors should be taken into account?*'

Extension tasks

- To extend question 1, ask students to construct the side and front elevations for their designs. Ask: '*What proportion of the kitchen's area is open floor space?*'
- To extend question 2, ask: '*How much money could be saved by not tiling under the units?*'
- To extend question 3, ask students, using the same conditions as before, to create a design that has rotational symmetry of order 4.

Support tasks

- To support question 1, provide a centimetre square grid.
- To support question 2, ask students to calculate for 30 cm × 30 cm tiles that cost £10 per pack of 10.
- To support question 3, tell students to ignore the ratio given.

Plenary

- Discuss the approach taken in question 2.
- Peer assess question 3.

ɜCSE 2010

a Add, subtract, multiply and divide ny number

h Understand equivalent fractions, implifying a fraction by cancelling all ommon factors

l Understand that 'percentage' means umber of parts per 100' and use this to ompare proportions

m Use percentage

o Interpret fractions, decimals and ercentages as operators

p Use ratio notation, including duction to its simplest form and its arious links to fraction notation

t Divide a quantity in a given ratio

u Approximate to specified or ppropriate degrees of accuracy ncluding a given power of ten, number f decimal places and significant figures

M k Use 2D representations of 3D hapes

M p Convert measurements from one nit to another

m q Make sensible estimates of a nge of measures

M x Calculate perimeters and areas f shapes made from triangles and ectangles

University

Starter

- Ask students to estimate the cost of living for 1 year at university.
- Ask students to estimate the area of floor in their own houses.

Extension tasks

- To extend question 1, tell students that the ground floor ceiling is 2 m high and the first floor ceiling is 2.4m high. Ask: '*How much would Elaine and her friends pay if the rent for each room was calculated as a proportion of the volume of the house?*'
- To extend question 2, ask: '*If a tin of tomatoes has a capacity of 0.4 litres and a mass of 1 lb, what is the density in g/cm*^{3}.'
- To extend question 3, ask: '*If Elaine was allowed to drop her worst unit, what mark would she require in Unit 6?*'

Support tasks

- To support question 1, ask students to work out the area of each room. Ask: '*Who has the biggest room? Write the rooms in order of size.*'
- To support question 2, tell students to work just in imperial units.
  Ask students to calculate for 9 people.
  Ask students to calculate per person.
  Provide a lb to kg conversion.
- To support question 3, ask: '*In which unit did Elaine achieve the highest percentage?' Is she on track to achieve 40%? What is the maximum overall percentage that Elaine could achieve?*'

Plenary

- Discuss whether it is easier to calculate compound areas in question 1 by adding rectangles or by subtracting them.
- Encourage students to look at how they have set out their method in question 3.
- Write a step-by-step guide for calculating the amount of each ingredient needed when adjusting a recipe for x people to the amount required for y people.

COVERAGE AND RANGE	2012 Olympics	Learn to drive	Healthy living	Money	Kitchen design	University
Level 1						
• Understand and use whole numbers and recognise negative numbers in practical contexts.	✓				✓	✓
• Add, subtract, multiply and divide whole numbers using a range of mental methods.	✓	✓	✓	✓	✓	✓
• Multiply and divide whole numbers by 10 and 100 using mental arithmetic.	✓			✓	✓	✓
• Understand and use equivalencies between common fractions, decimals and percentages.		✓	✓	✓		✓
• Add and subtract decimals up to two decimal places.	✓	✓		✓	✓	✓
• Solve simple problems involving ratio, where one number is a multiple of the other.	✓		✓		✓	✓
• Use simple formulae expressed in words for one- or two-step operations.	✓	✓		✓		
• Solve problems requiring calculation, with common measures including money, time, length, weight, capacity and temperature.	✓	✓	✓	✓	✓	✓
• Convert units of measure in the same system.	✓		✓		✓	
• Work out areas, perimeters and volumes.						✓
• Extract and interpret information from lists, tables, diagrams, charts and graphs.		✓	✓			
• Collect and record discrete data and organise and represent information in different ways.						
• Construct models and draw shapes, measuring and drawing angles and identifying line symmetry.					✓	
• Understand outcomes, check calculations and explain results.	✓	✓	✓	✓	✓	✓

Level 2	2012 Olympics	Learn to drive	Healthy living	Money	Kitchen design	University
• Understand and use positive and negative numbers of any size in practical contexts.	✓			✓	✓	✓
• Carry out calculations with numbers of any size in practical contexts.	✓	✓	✓	✓	✓	✓
• Understand, use and calculate ratio and proportion, including problems involving scale.	✓	✓	✓		✓	✓
• Understand and use simple equations and simple formulae involving one- or two-step operations.	✓					
• Recognise and use 2D representations of 3D objects.					✓	✓

• Find the area, perimeter and volume of common shapes.						✓
• Use, convert and calculate using metric and, where appropriate, imperial measures.	✓		✓		✓	✓
• Add and subtract fractions; add, subtract, multiply and divide decimals and percentages.				✓	✓	✓
• Understand and use equivalencies between fractions, decimals and percentages.		✓	✓	✓		✓
• Understand and use simple equations and simple formulae involving one- or two-step operations.		✓				
• Extract and interpret information from lists, tables, diagrams, charts and graphs.		✓				
• Understand outcomes, check calculations and explain results.		✓				
• Collect and represent discrete and continuous data, using ICT where appropriate.			✓			

PERFORMANCE						
Level 1						
• Understand practical problems in familiar and unfamiliar contexts and situations, some of which are non-routine.	✓	✓	✓	✓	✓	✓
• Identify and obtain necessary information to tackle the problem.	✓	✓	✓	✓	✓	✓
• Select and apply mathematics in an organised way to find solutions to practical problems for different purposes.	✓	✓	✓	✓	✓	✓
• Use appropriate checking procedures at each stage.	✓	✓	✓	✓	✓	✓
• Interpret and communicate solutions to practical problems, drawing simple conclusions and giving explanations.	✓	✓	✓	✓	✓	✓

Level 2						
• Understand routine and non-routine problems in a wide range of familiar and unfamiliar contexts and situations.	✓	✓	✓	✓	✓	✓
• Identify the situation or problem and the mathematical methods needed to tackle it.	✓	✓	✓	✓	✓	✓
• Select and apply a range of mathematics to find solutions.	✓	✓	✓	✓	✓	✓
• Use appropriate checking procedures and evaluate their effectiveness at each stage.	✓	✓	✓	✓	✓	✓
• Interpret and communicate solutions to practical problems in familiar and unfamiliar routine contexts and situations.	✓	✓	✓	✓	✓	✓
• Draw conclusions and provide mathematical justifications.	✓	✓	✓	✓	✓	✓

Answers

Worksheet 1.1–1.3

1 Two thousands, three hundreds, seven tens and six units
2 a Three hundred and twenty-six
b Four thousand, one hundred and fifty-two
c Fifteen thousand, three hundred and seventy
d Two thousand and six
3 a 837 b 9325 c 22 053 d 3605
4 6452, 6524, 6542, 9781, 15 361
5 20 317, 8711, 2731, 2371, 2317
6 98 431, 13 489

Worksheet 1.4

1 a 64 b 416 c 121 d 218
e 100 f 432
2 a 25 b 212 c 32 d 327
e 4813
3 142 km
4 Through Q by 7 km
5 30 people

Worksheet 1.5

1 a 46 b 111 c 910 d 2232
e 1530
2 a 730 b 1460 c 7300 d 146 000
3 a 1820 b 4150 c 1640 d 5740
e 42 900
4 a 567 b 1062 c 896 d 1455
e 874
5 a 71 b 63 c 96 d 175
6 a 423 b 182 c 39 d 22
e 237
7 a 49 b 35 c 7
8 a 160 b 244 c 121 d 128
9 732
10 a 21 b 283 c 75 d 324
e 73
11 21
12 £6912

Worksheet 1.6

1 a 60 b 20 c 80 d 40
e 10 f 230 g 360 h 760
i 290 j 310 k 1000 l 3200
m 3000 n 560
2 a 200 b 400 c 100 d 5400
e 400 f 600 g 12 400 h 53 800
i 100 100 j 231 000 k 0
3 a 6000 b 1000 c 3000 d 6000
e 10 000 f 24 000
4 4100

Worksheet 1.7–1.9

1 –12, –7, –4, –2, 3, 5
2 a –4°C b 7°C c 2°C
3 a –2°C b 12°C
4 a –1 b 2 c –10 d –7
e –2
5 a –6 b 7 c 2 d 11
e –8
6 a –12 b 15 c 12 d –21
7 a –5 b –4 c 16 d –5
8 a –4 b –2 c 3 d 8
e –8 f –5

Worksheet 1.10

1 1742, 1472, 4172, 4712, 7142, 7412, 1274, 1724, 2174, 2714, 7124, 7214
2 Assuming she starts at the low numbers end: 6, 14, 20, 22, 28, 34, 31, 17, 9, 3
3 a 1, 2, 4, 8, 16, 32
b 1, 2, 3, 6, 9, 18, 27, 54
c 1, 3, 9, 27
d 1, 2, 3, 4, 6, 9, 12, 18, 36
4 a For example, 12, 24, 36
b For example, 6, 12, 18
c For example, 20, 40, 60
d For example, 29, 58, 87
5 a 3, 8 b 105 c 3, 13, 11, 59
6 The last digit must be odd, but 4, 2, 0, 8 are all even.
7 For example, 23

Worksheet 1.11

1 a 1 and 2 b 2
2 a i 1, 2, 3, 6 ii 1, 2, 3, 6 iii 1, 2, 3, 4, 6, 12
b The factors are also factors of the difference.
3 a Every 6 steps.
b Every 12 steps.
4 168 m
5 a 120 is a common multiple of 4, 5, 6.
b Yes, on the 60th turn.

Worksheet 1.12

1 1 squared $= 1^2 = 1 \times 1 = 1$
2 squared $= 2^2 = 2 \times 2 = 4$
3 squared $= 3^2 = 3 \times 3 = 9$
4 squared $= 4^2 = 4 \times 4 = 16$
5 squared $= 5^2 = 5 \times 5 = 25$
6 squared $= 6^2 = 6 \times 6 = 36$
7 squared $= 7^2 = 7 \times 7 = 49$
8 squared $= 8^2 = 8 \times 8 = 64$
9 squared $= 9^2 = 9 \times 9 = 81$
10 squared $= 10^2 = 10 \times 10 = 100$
11 squared $= 11^2 = 11 \times 11 = 121$
12 squared $= 12^2 = 12 \times 12 = 144$
13 squared $= 13^2 = 13 \times 13 = 169$
14 squared $= 14^2 = 14 \times 14 = 196$
15 squared $= 15^2 = 15 \times 15 = 225$
2 a $5 = 1 + 4$ b $8 = 4 + 4$ or $9 - 1$
c $13 = 4 + 9$ or $49 - 36$ d $58 = 9 + 49$
e $20 = 4 + 16$ f $29 = 4 + 25$ or $225 - 196$
g $61 = 25 + 36$ h $80 = 16 + 64$
i $90 = 9 + 81$
3 1 cubed $= 1^3 = 1 \times 1 \times 1 = 1$
2 cubed $= 2^3 = 2 \times 2 \times 2 = 8$
3 cubed $= 3^3 = 3 \times 3 \times 3 = 27$
4 cubed $= 4^3 = 4 \times 4 \times 4 = 64$
5 cubed $= 5^3 = 5 \times 5 \times 5 = 125$
6 cubed $= 6^3 = 6 \times 6 \times 6 = 216$
4 225
5 8

Worksheet 2.1–2.3

1 Angle ABC is an obtuse angle, angle DEF is a right angle, angle GHI is an acute angle, angle JKL is a reflex angle.

2 **a** Drawing of an acute angle

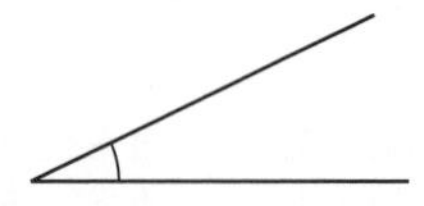

b Drawing of a reflex angle

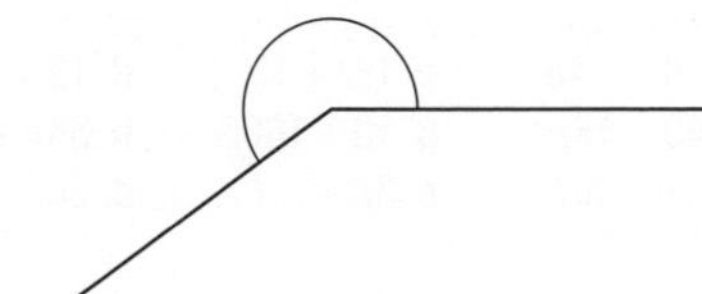

c Drawing of a right angle

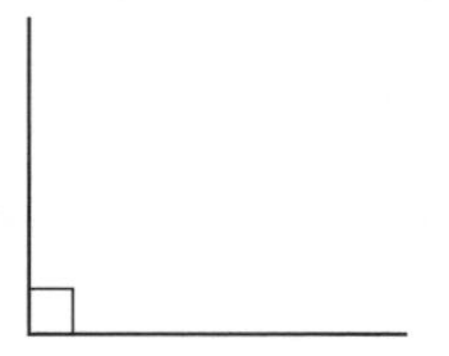

d Drawing of an obtuse angle

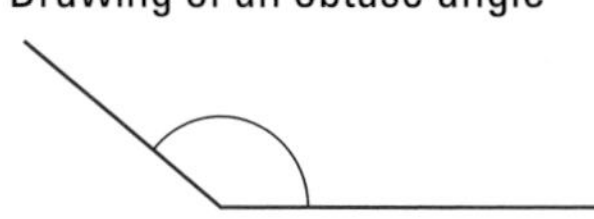

3 Students' own answers.

4 **a** EAB is a right angle.
b ABC is an obtuse angle.
c Angle BCD is an acute angle.

Worksheet 2.4–2.5

1 **a** ABC, DEF, JKL **b** GHI

2 Students' estimates.

3 ABC = 347° DEF = 124° GHI = 25° JKL = 148°

4 225°

Worksheet 2.6

1 **a** Sketch of 45°. **b** Sketch of 110°.
c Sketch of 75°. **d** Sketch of 165°.

2 Students' measurements of angles in question 1.

3 Students' accurate drawings of angles of 30°, 105°, 77° and 142°.

4 **a** 6.1 cm **b** 52°

Worksheet 2.7

Equilateral triangles have three equal sides and three equal angles.
Isosceles triangles have two equal sides and two equal angles.
All right angled triangles have three sides and a right angle.

Worksheet 2.8

1 **a** 200° **b** 150° **c** 273° **d** 117°

2 **a** 150° **b** 40° **c** 127° **d** 68°

3 **a** 123° **b** 117° **c** 15°

4 A = 162° B = 82° C = 77° D = 103° E = 43° F = 137° G = 137°

Worksheet 3.1

1 Meal type and price.

2 **a i** Height, number of pets
ii Eye colour, breed
b i Number of pets
ii Height

3 **a** Discrete **b** Continuous **c** Continuous **d** Discrete

4 **a** Engine size **b** Make **c** Miles **d** Year

Worksheet 3.2

1

Make	Frequency
Ford	𝍸 I
Skoda	𝍸 I
BMW	II
Vauxhall	𝍸
Jaguar	III
Volvo	III

2

Number of different birds	Frequency
5	5
6	12
7	7
8	7

3

Height	Tally	Frequency
90–99	𝍸	5
100–109	𝍸 I	6
110–119	𝍸	5
120–129	𝍸 𝍸	10
130–139	𝍸	5
Total	31	31

4 Data logging

Worksheet 3.3

1 Leading question, no option for no.

2 A = c, B = b, C = b, D = a, E = c

3 It isn't clear what 'sports fan' covers. Unlikely to throw much light on whether people want a free gym.

4 Which age group do you belong to?
0–18, 19–35, 36–50, 51–65, over 65

5 A, C and D are leading questions.

Worksheet 3.4

1 Asking everyone would take too long.

2 More accurate data.

3 Ask only people who have telephones and only in 10 cities.

4 People at the swimming pool may not be representative of the population.

5 One hour on a Saturday may not be representative of the traffic the rest of the time.

Worksheet 3.5

1 **a** 122 **b** 52 **c** 64
d Drink and crisps

2 **a** Australia **b** Scotland **c** England **d** 154
e 1625

3

	France	Spain	Total
Self-catering	34	24	58
Full board	16	48	64
Total	50	72	122

Worksheet 4.1

1 a $2b$ b $5c$ c $5a$ d $4a$
e $5c$ f $3p$ g $8t$ h $9m$
i $10K$
2 a $t+5$ b $e-7$ c $x+1$ d $s-5$
e $y+2$ f $g-3$ g $d+40$ h $m-5$
i $P+99$
3 a $s-10$ b $y+2$ c $k-1$ d $m+4$
e $m+n$ f $t-c$
4 a $3n$ b $8m$ c $5f$
d $18d+5n$ pence
e $5b+10a$ f $5m+6e$ g $5x+20y$

Worksheet 4.2

1 a p, r b b c s, t d a, b, c
e d, p f m, n, t g p, k h d, g
2 a $4m, 2y$ b $7p, 4$ c a, b d $9, 3t$
e $4, 2d, 4e$ f $3W, 2X, 3C$
3 a $4a, -2b$ b $w, -3s$ c $12m, -10$ d $4, -4j$
e $2a, 2b, -2c$ f $8f, -2k, 3d$ g $2a, 2b, -10$
h $8g, -h, -2i$ i $3q, -6, 5k$ j $2n, 2, -3n$
4 a $a+k, k-a$ [for all answers in **4**, more answers are valid with students' choices of + or –]
b $2f-3t, 3t+2f$
c $2e-4, 4-2e$
d $a+b-c, b-c-a$
e $5t+3u+8v, 3u-5t-8v$
f $3r+s+9, 9-s+3r$
g $3y-5y+y, y-3y+5y$
5 a $ab, 2d$ b $2pq, 4tf$ c $5m, 3mn$ d $2d, -5ef$
e x^2, y^2 f $3c^2, -2d$ g $4rs, t^3$
h $k^2, 4k, -2ks$
6 Students' own answers.

Worksheet 4.3

1 a $3d$ b $6s$
2 a $8k$ b $3a$ c $7r$ d w
e $9h$
3 a $7v$ b $8d$ c $6q$
4 a $6t+9y$ b $3a+6g$ c $8u+3b$ d $4h+3i$
e $8m+5t$ f $y+4x$
5 a $7m+9j$ b $5i+3h$ c $4s+6t$ d $2u+3g$
e $8t+7$ f $2f+k+6$
6 a $-3x$ c $-4y$ c $-4t$ d $-6m+5x$
e $3g-4f$ f $-4d-4e$
7 a $-3ab$ b $7x^2+2mn$ c $7pq+3ef$ d $7x^2+5y^2$
e $6u^2+2u$ f $mn-2m^2$ g $5x^2+3x+5$

Worksheet 4.4–4.5

1 a pq b mnp c $5r$ d $2de$
e $2fg$ f $3dpr$
2 a e^2 b t^5 c q^2t^2 d j^3k^2
e $8c^5$ f $6m^3$ g $9e^3f^2$ h $5v^4w^2$
3 a $fghp$ b d^2ef c $8e^2g$ d $4ab^2c$
e $2gmy^2$ f $21cf$ g $12v^2$ h $6k^3$
i $8fg^2$ j $36d^2e^2$
4 a $2t$ b $2k$ c $2pq$ d $4x^2$
e $3f$ f $2e$ g $3tu$ h $5mn$

5 a $8h$ b $4m$ c $10d$ d $2c$
e 9 f 6 g $16s$ h $9r$
6 a $2t$ b $5d$ c $3c$ d $3p$
e 3 f 4 g w h $3u$

Worksheet 4.6

1 a $2a+10$ b $4p+8$ c $8e+32$ d $63+7g$
e $10x+100$ f $15+3k$ g $8h+8$ h $81+9R$
2 a $6d-12$ b $2t-6$ c $3q+15$ d $10-5f$
e $8b+16$ f $7h-28$
3 a $8s+4$ b $18d-48$ c $15t+15$ d $12+6r$
e $10d-10$ f $40-16m$ g $10+100j$ h $36y+36$
4 a $sw+2w$ b $dq-5d$ c $3c+cd$ d $2ab+3a$
e $3et-2t$ f $k-fk$
5 a a^2+3a b j^2-5j c $3y+y^2$ d $2e^2+e$
e $5rt-4r$ f $3k-2k^2$ g $10h^2+10h$ h $4B+2B^2$
6 a $12f^2-8f$ b $6t^2+9t$ c $3d-2d^2$
d $20W^2+8W$ e $3r-9r^2$ f $12u^2-36u$
7 a $5a+11$ b $7p+18$ c $12k+3$ d $10s$
e $17d+10$ f $19f+16$ g $20y+1$ h $34-2u$
i $19t-12$ j $-5-6e$

Worksheet 4.7

1 a $2(f+4)$ b $5(t+2)$ c $3(k+4)$ d $7(d-2)$
e $6(h+4)$ f $4(g-4)$ g $11(w-2)$ h $3(4+m)$
2 a $s(s+4)$ b $f(f+3)$ c $k(k-6)$ d $d(d+10)$
e $a(4+a)$ f $p(3-p)$ g $r(r+20)$ h $R(R-8)$
3 a $j(j+1)$ b $m(m+1)$ c $h(h-1)$ d $k(1+k)$
e $r(r-1)$ f $w(1-w)$
4 a $3u(u+2)$ b $2p(p+4)$ c $5k(k-2)$ d $3d(d+1)$
e $4n(n-1)$ f $3v(3+v)$ g $5s(3-s)$ h $7c(c+4)$
5 a $3a^2(a+3)$ b $2d^2(d-4)$ c $5h^2(h+2)$ d $7d^2(d-3)$
e $d^2(d+2)$ f $f(f^2-5)$ g $e^2(e+1)$ h $4w^2(2+w)$
6 a $2g(g^2+2)$ b $5h(1-3h)$ c $e^2(e+3)$ d $10v^2(v+5)$
e $2(3k+1)$ f $5i(2-i^2)$ g $6(2-p^2)$ h $2d(2d+1)$

Worksheet 4.8

1 **a**, **c**, **d**, **f**, **h** are expressions
2 a Expression b Identity c Identity
d Expression e Identity f Identity
g Expression
3 a Formula b Identity c Expression d Identity
e Formula f Identity g Expression h Formula
4 a Identity b Equation c Equation d Identity
e Identity f Equation g Equation h Identity
5 a Formula b Equation c Expression d Identity
e Equation f Formula g Identity
h Expression i Formula j Equation

Worksheet 4.9

1 a 8 b 12 c –3 d 14
e 1 f –2
2 a 9 b 8 c 14 d 6
e 36 f –5
3 a 6 b 10 c 20 d –1
e 22 f 1
4 a 16 b 16 c 26 d 25
e –18 f –12
5 a 48 b 20 c –10 d 24
e 12 f –40
6 a 32 b –28 c 18 d –7
e –6 f 2 g –3 h 10

Worksheet 5.1–5.2

1 a i 5 ii 1
b i 9 ii 7

c i 2 ii 7
d i 6 ii 0
e i 4 ii 9

2 a hundredths b tenths
c thousandths d tenths
e hundredths

3 0.093, 0.317, 0.32, 0.326, 0.4

4 0.76, 0.714, 0.71, 0.703, 0.6993

Worksheet 5.3

1 a 0.7 b 1.2 c 3.2 d 7.08
e 2.691

2 a 0.5 b 0.9 c 1.5 d 0.218
e 0.089

3 a 1.681 b 5.1051 c 0.1238 d 7.62
e 8.04 f 4.303

4 a 1.1 b 0.8 c 0.14 d 1.36
e 0.053 f 1.503 g 0.0678 h 0.344

5 £2.86

Worksheet 5.4–5.6

1 a 0.8 b 1.5 c 2.8 d 5.6
e 3 f 7.8

2 a 1.5 b 1.5 c 0.15 d 0.4
e 15.6

3 £26.01

4 a 529 b 5.29 c 52 900

5 a 12.285 b 18.522 c 26.04 d 0.1216

6 a 18.25 b 8.64

7 a £10.75 b £60.55 c £1.55

8 a 1331 b 1.331 c 1 331 000

9 a 0.36 b 0.216

10 0.0009

11 a 0.3 b 0.5 c 9 d 0.42
e 4.2

12 a 1.2 b 120 c 1.2 d 0.12

Worksheet 5.7

1 a 4 kg b 4 cm c 10 s d 910 m
e 3 cm f 10 s g 1503 km h 8 g

2 a 1500 m b 300 g c 100 s d 100 cm

3 a 3.5 b 12.1 c 0.7 d 0.1
e 10.0

4 81 minutes

5 a 7.78 b 13.93 c 0.35 d 0.05
e 6.01

6 a 0.09 b 0.0 c 0.667 d 1.1

7 880 cm

Worksheet 5.8–5.9

1 £50 000 should be used in headline.

2 a 3 b 0.3 c 200 d 1
e 4000 f 20

3 a 750 b 2.7 c 0.099 d 4400
e 400 f 0.081

4 a 900 b 1000 c 1100 d 3.08
e 0.00564

5 a 2 b 4 c 3 d 5
e 2 f 2

Worksheet 5.10

1 a 180 b 20 000 000 c 2 d 6 or 7
e 0.2 f 30

2 a 6 b 5 c 3 d 4

3 £100

4 1200 matches

5 £3

6 900 mm

7 1400

8 a 400 b 5 c 20

9 a 10 b 3 c 1

Worksheet 5.11

1 a 19.32 b 193.2 c 193.2 d 1932

2 a 33.11 b 33.11 c 331.1 d 331.1

3 a 812 b 8.12 c 81.2 d 8.12

4 a 6.6 b 66 c 0.66 d 660

5 a 16 b 16 c 16 d 160

6 a 24 b 2400 c 2.4 d 2.4

7 a 105 b 10.5 c 1.05 d 10.5

8 a 234 b 2.34 c 234 d 2340

Worksheet 6.1

1 a Equilateral triangle + Acute-angled triangle
b Obtuse-angled triangle + Scalene triangle
c Isosceles triangle + Acute-angled triangle
d Right-angled triangle + Isosceles triangle
e Right-angled triangle + Scalene triangle
f Acute-angled triangle + Isosceles triangle

2 a B + F b B + E c A + C d F
e D + E

3 a b

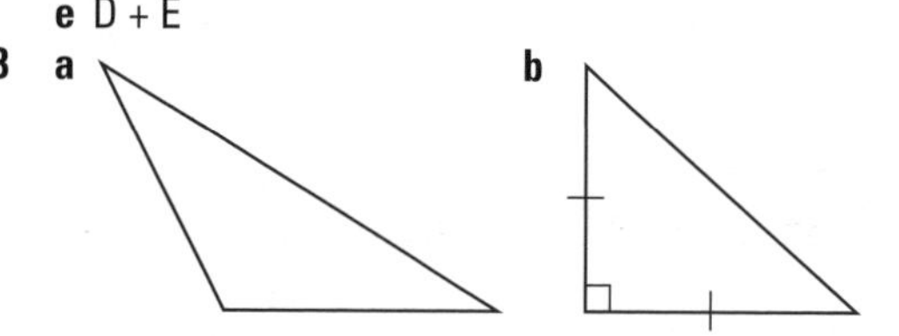

4 a Isosceles triangle
b Obtuse-angled triangle
c Equilateral triangle

5 An equilateral triangle has all its angles equal to 60° so one angle cannot be 90°.

Worksheet 6.2

1 a Parallelogram b Trapezium
c Rhombus

2 a Trapezium b Square
c Rectangle d Kite
e Rectangle f Parallelogram
g Parallelogram h Parallelogram
i Trapezium j Trapezium

3 a Kite b Trapezium
c Rectangle

4 a Rectangle b Rhombus
c Kite

Worksheet 6.3

1 a A and D b B and C c D d A and B

2 a Yes b Yes c No d No

3 One equilateral triangle could be bigger than another, e.g.
and

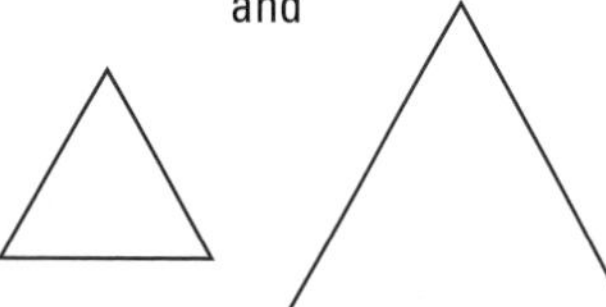

Worksheet 6.4

Students' drawings.

Worksheet 6.5–6.6

1 a Join the centre dot to any of the dots on the circumference.
 b Join any two dots on the circumference except the two dots in the answer to **c**.
 c
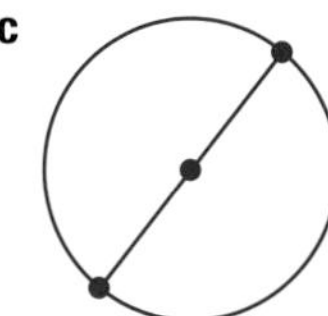
 d Join any two dots on the circumference that make a curve on the circumference.

2 a Sector b Diameter c Chord d Tangent
 e Centre f Segment g Radius
 h Semi-circle

3 a Students' drawings.
 b Students' drawings.
 c Students' drawings.

Worksheet 6.7

1

2 a b c
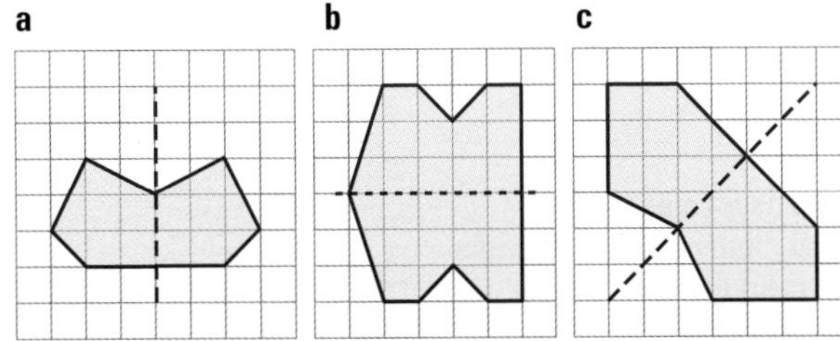

3 a b c
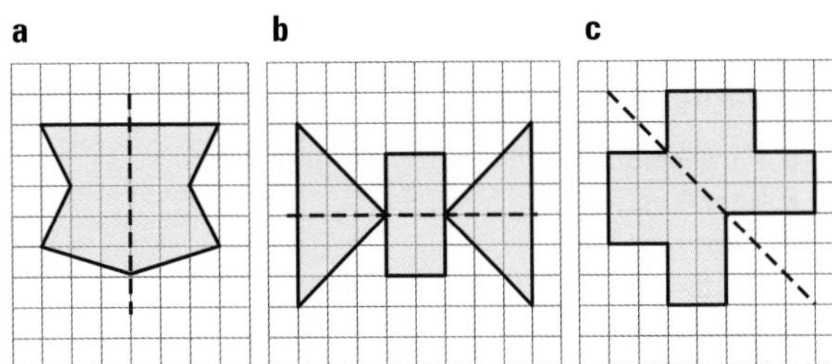

4 a b c
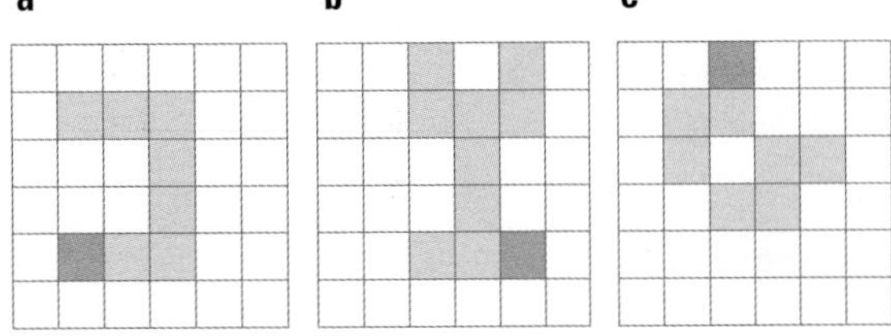

Worksheet 6.8

1 a 2 b 6 c 4 d 3

2 a b c
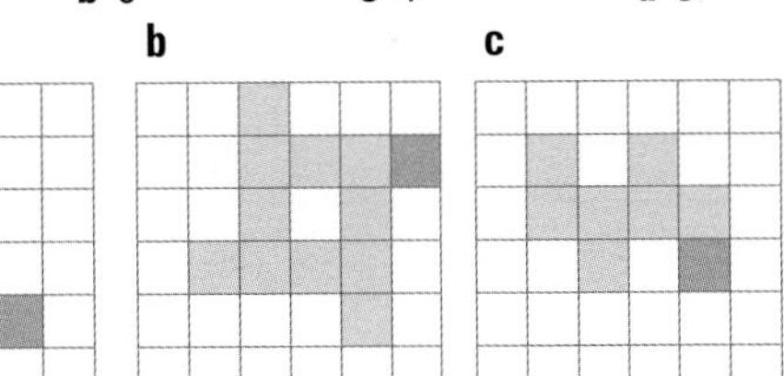

3 a Yes, order 2 b No
 c Yes, order 4 d Yes, order 6
 e Yes, order 2 f Yes, order 4

Worksheet 7.1

1 $73° + 101° + 67° + 120° = 360°$

2 a 105° b 112° c 123° d 120°

Worksheet 7.2

1

	Name of shape	Sum of interior angle
1	Triangle	180°
2	Quadrilateral	360°
3	Pentagon	540°
4	Hexagon	720°
5	Heptagon	900°
6	Octagon	1080°

2 180°

3 1440°

4 3240°

5 $(n - 2) \times 180°$

Worksheet 7.3

1 a 108° b 72°, angles on a straight line
 c 360°

2 Depends on the polygon drawn

3 110°

4 a 24° b 156°

5 a 144° b 10

Worksheet 7.4

1 By inspection

2 The hexagon and square tessellate. Their internal angles are factors of 360°

3 Square

Worksheet 7.5–7.6

1 a BE and CD, DE and BC
 b BE and DE, BE and BC, CD and DE, CD and BC

2 a alternate b corresponding
 c alternate d corresponding
 e equal f equal

3 $a = 67°$, $b = 113°$, $c = 113°$, $d = 67°$

4 $a = 50°$, $b = 78°$, $c = 52°$

Worksheet 7.7

1 $a + b = 180°$ because they are on a straight line
 $b + c = 180°$ because they are on a straight line

2 $a + b + c = 180°$ because they are the angles in a triangle
 $a + b + d = 180°$ because they are the angles in a triangle
 $c + d = 180°$ because they are on a straight line
 $c = 90°$ because substituting $c = d$ in $c + d = 180°$ shows this

3 $b = c$ because they are angles in an isosceles triangle
 $b + c = 90°$ because the angles in a triangle total 180°, the other angle is a right angle
 $c = 45°$ because substituting $b = c$ in $b + c = 90°$ shows this
 $a = e$ because they are angles in an isosceles triangle
 $a + e = 90°$ because the angles in a triangle total 180°, the other angle is a right angle
 $a = 45°$ because substituting $a = e$ in $a + e = 90°$ shows this
 $d = 90°$ because $a + d + c = 180°$ and $a = c = 45°$

4 $a + p + r = 180°$ because they are the angles in a triangle
 $c + q + s = 180°$ because they are the angles in a triangle
 So $a + p + r + c + q + s = 360°$
 $a + b + c + d = 360°$ because $b = p + q$ and $d = r + s$

Worksheet 7.8

1 **a** 138° **b** 331° **c** 036° **d** 236°
e 068° **f** 305° **g** 235°

2 **a** **b** **c**

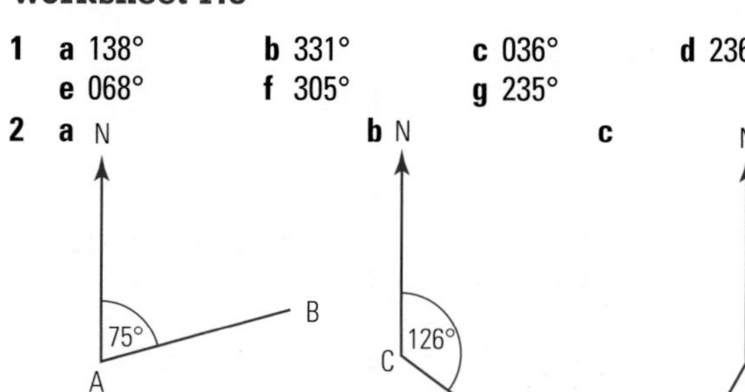

d **e** **f**

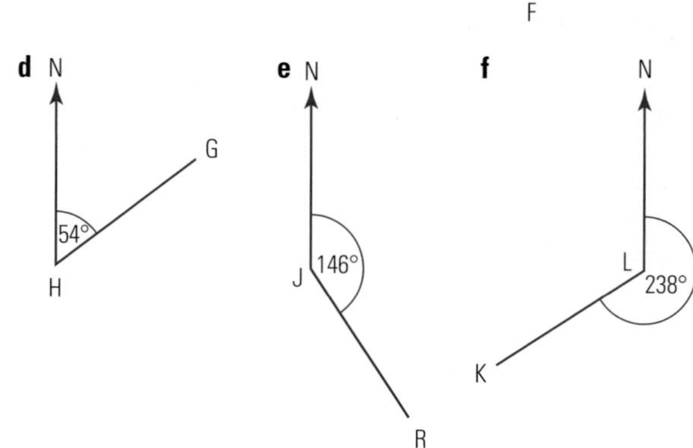

3 247°
4 057°
5 269°
6

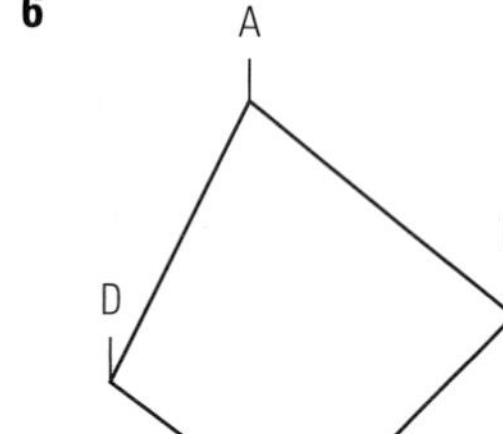

Worksheet 7.9

1 **a** 4.5 km **b** 1.25 km **c** 14.5 km **d** 8.6 km
e 11 km **f** 850 m

2 **a** 16.5 cm **b** 18 cm **c** 25.2 cm **d** 16 cm
e 4.5 cm **f** 6 cm

3

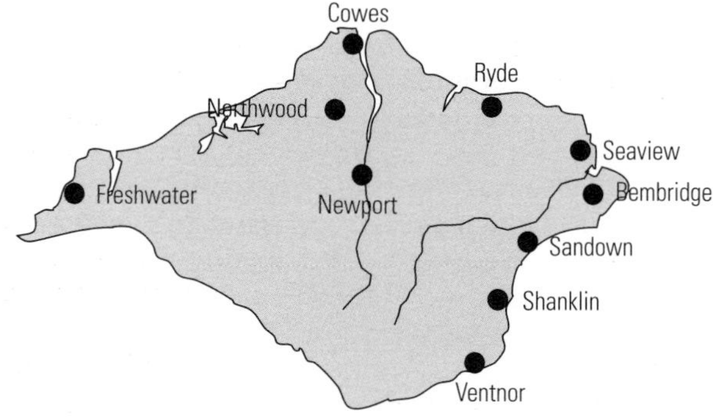

a i 1.7 cm **ii** 8.5 km **b i** 1.5 cm **ii** 7.5 km
c i 0.7 cm **ii** 3.5 km **d i** 3.3 cm **ii** 16.5 km
e i 4.9 cm **ii** 24.5 km **f i** 3.8 cm **ii** 19 km
g i 5.8 cm **ii** 29 km **h i** 1.5 cm **ii** 7.5 km

4 By inspection.
5 By inspection.
6

7 **a**

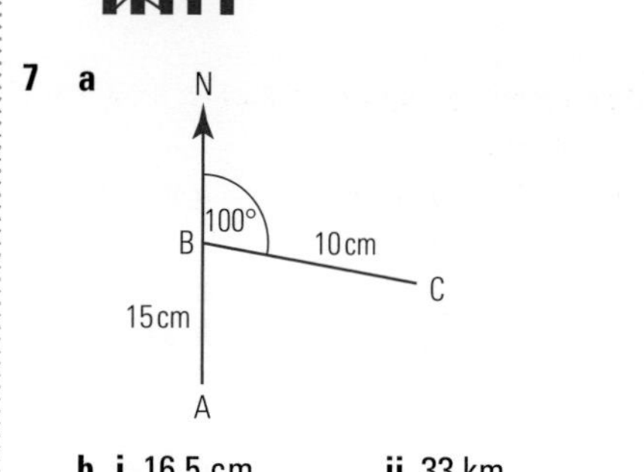

b i 16.5 cm **ii** 33 km
c 215°

Worksheet 8.1–8.3

1 **a** $\frac{1}{4}$ **b** $\frac{2}{5}$ **c** $\frac{3}{8}$

2 $\frac{4}{25}$

3 $\frac{16}{48}, \frac{8}{24}, \frac{4}{12}, \frac{2}{6}$

4 $\frac{6}{10}, \frac{18}{30}, \frac{24}{40}, \frac{27}{45}, \frac{21}{35}, \frac{72}{120}, \frac{90}{150}$

5 **a** $\frac{4}{9}$ **b** $\frac{3}{4}$ **c** $\frac{3}{10}$ **d** $\frac{5}{8}$
e $\frac{1}{4}$ **f** $\frac{4}{5}$

Worksheet 8.4

1 **a** $1\frac{1}{5}$ **b** $1\frac{7}{10}$ **c** $4\frac{4}{5}$ **d** $6\frac{1}{6}$
e $2\frac{5}{7}$ **f** $5\frac{3}{8}$

2 **a** $\frac{13}{4}$ **b** $\frac{12}{5}$ **c** $\frac{25}{16}$ **d** $\frac{35}{8}$
e $\frac{53}{10}$ **f** $\frac{65}{12}$

Worksheet 8.5–8.6

1 **a** $\frac{2}{15}$ **b** $\frac{2}{15}$ **c** $\frac{9}{40}$ **d** $\frac{35}{72}$

2 **a** $\frac{1}{21}$ **b** $\frac{1}{12}$ **c** $\frac{1}{2}$ **d** $\frac{1}{9}$

3 **a** $1\frac{1}{3}$ **b** $1\frac{1}{2}$ **c** $1\frac{2}{3}$ **d** $\frac{4}{5}$

4 **a** $\frac{1}{4}$ **b** $\frac{1}{5}$ **c** $\frac{2}{9}$ **d** $\frac{5}{32}$

5 **a** $\frac{5}{6}$ **b** $\frac{7}{9}$ **c** $\frac{9}{10}$ **d** $\frac{4}{7}$

6 **a** $3\frac{3}{8}$ **b** $8\frac{1}{2}$ **c** $5\frac{2}{15}$ **d** $9\frac{3}{5}$
e 18

7 **a** $1\frac{1}{3}$ **b** $1\frac{1}{4}$ **c** $\frac{1}{6}$ **d** $\frac{5}{6}$

Worksheet 8.7

1 $\frac{2}{5}$

2 **a** $\frac{3}{8}$ **b** $\frac{3}{5}$ **c** $\frac{5}{7}$ **d** $\frac{7}{9}$

3 **a** $\frac{1}{5}$ **b** $\frac{2}{7}$ **c** $\frac{1}{2}$ **d** $\frac{2}{11}$

4 **a** $1\frac{1}{2}$ **b** $\frac{11}{15}$ **c** $\frac{17}{20}$ **d** $\frac{37}{45}$

5 **a** $\frac{1}{2}$ **b** $\frac{7}{20}$ **c** $\frac{4}{15}$ **d** $\frac{1}{12}$

6 **a** $1\frac{3}{20}$ **b** $\frac{29}{36}$ **c** $\frac{24}{35}$ **d** $\frac{41}{60}$

7 a $\frac{5}{12}$ b $\frac{7}{20}$ c $\frac{13}{35}$ d $\frac{11}{40}$

8 a $3\frac{4}{5}$ b $3\frac{2}{3}$ c $6\frac{5}{12}$ d $6\frac{17}{40}$

9 a $1\frac{1}{3}$ b $1\frac{9}{14}$ c $3\frac{1}{8}$ d $\frac{1}{2}$ e $1\frac{33}{40}$

Worksheet 8.8

1 a $\frac{8}{25}$ b $\frac{1}{20}$ c $\frac{7}{40}$ d $\frac{1}{40}$

2 $\frac{4}{7}, \frac{3}{5}, \frac{5}{8}, \frac{7}{11}, \frac{2}{3}$

Worksheet 9.1

1 a 3^2 b 4^5 c 10^3 d 8^7 e 10^8 f $1^3 = 1$ g 2^{16}

2 a 32 b 64 c 25 d 1 000 000 e 216 f 1 g 16 h 243

3 a 48 b 32 c 10 000 000 d 160 e 32 f 270

4 a 144 b 32 c 200 d 2700 e 10 000 000 f 162 g 729 h 10 000 000 000

5

Power of 2	Index	Value
2^1	1	2
2^5	5	32
2^6	6	64
2^7	7	128
2^3	3	8
2^8	8	256
2^2	2	4
2^4	4	16
2^9	9	512

6 a 4 b 3 c 2 d 6 e 3 f 7 g 9 h 12

7 a 3^2 b 2^5 c Equal d 4^1 e 3^3 f 2^6 g 2^{10}

Worksheet 9.2

1 a 3^6 b 2^8 c 10^5 d 8^6 e 5^4 f 3^5 g 7^4 h 10^{20}

2 a 2^{12} b 5^{10} c 10^{12} d 4^6 e 6^7 f 8^6 g 10^7 h 9^5

3 a 5^2 b 2^5 c 8^2 d 10^4 e 4^3 f 7^3 g 10^9 h 3^4

4 a 2^{12} b 5^6 c 10^8 d 2^{100}

5 a 4^7 b 6^2 c 10^6 d 1 e 3^9 f 12^2 g 4^6 h 3^4

Worksheet 9.3

1 a r^8 b p^9 c e^{20} d w^4 e m^7 f h^8

2 a d^4 b s^6 c k^4 d b e 1 f d^5 g b h V^4

3 a $2c^7$ b $4g^7$ c $7r^5$ d $6m^5$ e $24G^8$ f $8h^4$

4 a $4u^3$ b $2h^2$ c $5y^4$ d $5p^3$ e $2t^3$ f $4p^4$ g a^7 h m^6

Worksheet 9.4

1 a 7 b 0 c 6 d 2

2 a 13 b 2 c 16 d 22 e 4 f 5 g −2

3 a 14 b 18 c 11 d 30 e 20 f −1

4 a 2 b 20 c 36 d 25 e 1 f 10 g 12

5 a 2 b 2 c 4 d 2 e 4 f 2 g 3

6 a 26 b 16 c 4 d 2 e 3 f 8

Worksheet 9.5

1 a $3e + 9$ b $30 + 10b$ c $6s + 9t$ d $10m - 4n$

2 a $6u + 10$ b $8x + 1$ c $5g - 16$ d $2d + 11$

3 a $9y + 5x$ b $5e - 5f$ c $14w - 5c$ d $9t - 16k$

4 a $-2a - 8$ b $-4d + 12$ c $-6m - 4n$ d $-6t + 18p$ e $-6x + 2$ f $5d + 10e$

5 a $3d + 11$ b $3c + 30$ c $3w + 3g$ d $9a - 4b$

6 a $d^2 - da$ b $5t^2 + 10t$ c $6m^2 + 3mn$ d $-3s^2 + 6st$

7 a $5a^2 + 12a$ b $8t^2 - 12t$ c $4c^2 + 6c$ d $5h^2 + 2hg - 6h$ e $8p^2 + 2pq + 9p$ f $-2m^2 - 2mn + 15m$

Worksheet 9.6

1 a $2(u + 4)$ b $3(g - 3)$ c $7(t - 3)$ d $2(m + 1)$ e $2(3 - h)$ f $3(ab + 2)$

2 a $2(2d + 3)$ b $3(3s - 2)$ c $4(2w + 3)$ d $10(v - 2)$ e $8(2k - 1)$ f $6(2m + 3)$

3 a $t(5u + 3)$ b $b(8s - 3)$ c $a(b + c)$ d $m(3n - 1)$ e $h(8i + 5j)$ f $y(1 + 7f)$

4 a $3m(n + 2)$ b $5h(1 - 3k)$ c $2p(q - 4)$ d $3c(2v + 3)$ e $4h(2g - 1)$ f $4d(4e - 5f)$

5 a $a(a + 3)$ b $q(q - 2)$ c $b(b + 1)$ d $d(d - 1)$ e $s(6 + s)$ f $T(10 - T)$

6 a $b(3b + 2)$ b $k(2k - 5)$ c $m(4m + 1)$ d $w(2 + 5w)$ e $c(8c - 1)$ f $f(8 - 9f)$

7 a $2u(u + 3)$ b $3k(k - 3)$ c $2p(4p + 1)$ d $5f(2f - 3)$ e $3t(3t + 1)$ f $5h(2h + 1)$

Worksheet 10.1

1 0.25

2 0.625

3 a 0.875 b 0.3125 c 0.35 d 0.72

4 a 0.325 b 0.4625 c 0.4375 d 0.46

5 $0.\dot{3}$

6 $0.\dot{1}$

7 a True b True c False d True

8 a $0.\dot{2}\dot{7}$ b $0.58\dot{3}$ c $0.8\dot{6}\dot{3}$ d $0.\dot{4}\dot{6}$

Worksheet 10.2

1 0.2

2 0.05

3 $0.\dot{3}$

4 5

5 The reciprocal of 4.

6 $1.\dot{3}$

7 2.5

8 32
9 0.125 and 8, $\frac{2}{3}$ and $1\frac{1}{2}$, $1\frac{1}{4}$ and $\frac{4}{5}$, 4 and 0.25

Worksheet 10.3

1 £14.60
2 £5.70
3 £11.60
4 £2.93
5 14 packets
6 44 boxes
7 85 calculators
8 9 coaches
9 £31.70
10 13 tanks

Worksheet 10.4

1 **a** 324 **b** 7.29 **c** 1024
2 **a** 1.728 **b** 343 **c** 17.576
3 2.1^3
4 **a** 128 **b** 625 **c** 7776
5 2^8
6 **a** 3.2 **b** 6.1 **c** 1.3
7 **a** 11.8 **b** 6.7 **c** 9.2
8 10
9 $\sqrt{70}$
10 **a** 5 **b** 8 **c** 13

Worksheet 10.5

1 **a** 50.41 **b** 18.49
2 **a** 512 **b** 288
3 **a** 0.9539 **b** 17
4 **a** 1.704347826 **b** 9.938128384
5 **a** 7.39100346 **b** 0.3228169014

Worksheet 11.1

1 **a** 2 **b** 3 **c** 6 **d** 1.3
e 2.7 **f** 5.4 **g** 6.7 **h** 4.7
i 4.8
2 **a** 6 cm **b** 8 cm **c** 3 cm **d** 5.5 cm
e 7.5 cm **f** 4.8 cm **g** 3.7cm **h** 6.4 cm
3 **a** 60 mm **b** 80 mm **c** 35 mm **d** 55 mm
e 75 mm **f** 43 mm **g** 33 mm **h** 66 mm
4 **a** 1.6 **b** 2.3 **c** 3.4
5 **a** 0.2 **b** 2.6 **c** 0.7

Worksheet 11.2

1 **a** **i** 9.00 am **ii** 0900 hours
b **i** 3.00 am **ii** 0300 hours
c **i** 7.30 am **ii** 0730 hours
d **i** 1.30 am **ii** 0130 hours
e **i** 2.15 am **ii** 0215 hours
f **i** 7.15 am **ii** 0715 hours
g **i** 5.20 am **ii** 0520 hours
h **i** 9.50 am **ii** 0950 hours
2 **a** **i** 4.00 pm **ii** 1600 hours
b **i** 8.00 pm **ii** 2000 hours
c **i** 10.30 pm **ii** 2230 hours
d **i** 4.30 pm **ii** 1630 hours
e **i** 3.15 pm **ii** 1515 hours
f **i** 8.45 pm **ii** 2045 hours
g **i** 4.40 pm **ii** 1640 hours
h **i** 10.20 pm **ii** 2220 hours
3 **i** 6 hours **ii** 6 hours **iii** 5 hours
iv 4 hours 30 minutes
4 **i** 4 hours **ii** 6 hours **iii** 5 hours 30 minutes
iv 5 hours 40 minutes
5 **a** 1 hours 10 minutes **b** 3 hours 20 minutes
c 2 hours 15 minutes **d** 2 hours 20 minutes
e 3 hours 50 minutes **f** 2 hours 10 minutes
g 8 hours 20 minutes **h** 3 hours 10 minutes

Worksheet 11.3

1 **a** ml **b** mm or cm **c** grams **d** litres
e metres **f** kg **g** km **h** tonnes
2 **a** 200 cm **b** 300 cm **c** 550 cm **d** 4 cm
3 **a** 70 mm **b** 45 mm **c** 800 mm **d** 240 mm
4 **a** 4000 m **b** 7 m **c** 30 000 m **d** 0.2 m
5 **a** 6000 g **b** 40 000 g **c** 2500 g **d** 35 000 g
6 **a** 8 *l* **b** 30 *l* **c** 0.05 *l* **d** 0.9 *l*
7 **a** 4000 m*l* **b** 70 000 m*l* **c** 2500 m*l* **d** 500 m*l*
8 **a** 4 km **b** 20 km **c** 0.5 km **d** 2.5 km

Worksheet 11.4

1 **a** 1 inch **b** $4\frac{1}{4}$ inches **c** $1\frac{1}{2}$ inches **d** $4\frac{3}{4}$ inches
e $3\frac{1}{4}$ inches **f** $7\frac{1}{4}$ inches
2 **a** **i** 10 stone **ii** 11 stone 7 pounds
iii 14 stone 4 pounds **iv** 11 stone 6 pounds
v 13 stone 11 pounds **vi** 10 stone 4 pounds
b **i** 140 pounds **ii** 161 pounds **iii** 200 pounds
iv 160 pounds **v** 193 pounds **vi** 144 pounds
3 **a** 24 inches **b** 9 feet **c** 2 gallons **d** 4 yards
e 4 feet **f** 42 pounds **g** 24 pints **h** 10 stone
i 32 ounces
4 **a** 2 feet **b** 2 gallons **c** 4 inches **d** 11 pounds
e 250 g **f** 90 cm **g** 20 cm **h** 16 km
i 22.5 litres

Worksheet 11.5

1 **a** 50 miles **b** 100 miles **c** 150 miles **d** 200 miles
e 250 miles
2 **a** **i** 5 miles **ii** 10 miles **iii** 30 miles
iv 60 miles **v** 120 miles
b 60 mph
3 **a** 100 km **b** 200 km **c** 400 km **d** 500 km
e 1400 km
4 30 mph
5 3 mph
6 40 mph
7 135 mph
8 225 miles
9 $1\frac{1}{2}$ hours
10 $4\frac{1}{2}$ hours

Worksheet 11.6

1 **a** 11.5 kg **b** 25.5 kg
2 minimum 28.5°, maximum 29.5°
3 **a** 10.5 ml
b 9.7 ml is between 9.5 ml and 10.5 ml, so you should not complain.
4 **a** 8.5 m^2
b Tariq cannot be sure that a tin would cover 7.6 m^2 as the minimum coverage could be 7.5 m^2.
5 19.45 cm
6 2.735 m × 1.515 m, 2.745 m × 1.525 m
7 2.655 litres
8 All batteries that last for 11.5 hours or more would be within Better Batteries' claim. The claim is correct in this case.
9 1 foot is between 304.5 mm and 305.5 mm in length

10 **a** min 35 g, max 45 g **b** min 95 g, max 105 g
c min 195 g, max 205 g **d** min 5 g, max 15 g

11 **a** min 4.15 km, max 4.25 km **b** min 1.55 km, max 1.65 km
c min 0.65 km, max 0.75 km

Worksheet 12.1

1 **a** Size 37 **b** Size 35 **c** 6 people **d** 24 people

2 **a** 7 students

b

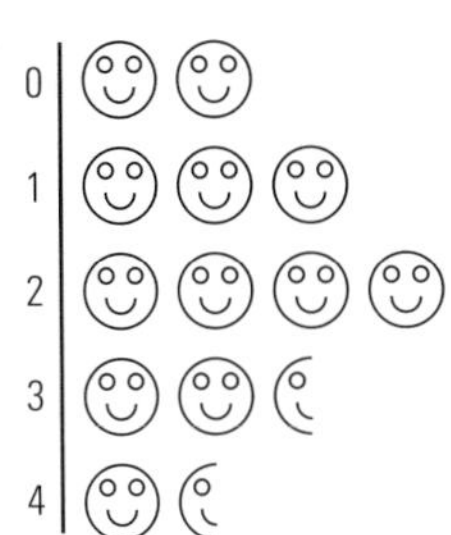

3

Worksheet 12.2

1 **a** England **b** Wales

2 **a** 18 days **b** 2 days

3 **a**

Age	Frequency	Angle of pie chart
Over 10 years	48	144°
7 to 10 years	24	72°
3 to 6 years	30	90°
Less than 3 years	18	54°

b

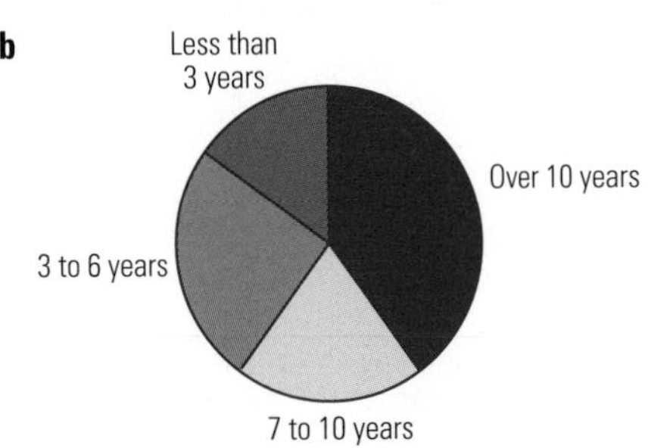

Worksheet 12.3

1 **a** 7 cars **b** 1 occupant **c** 53

2 **a**

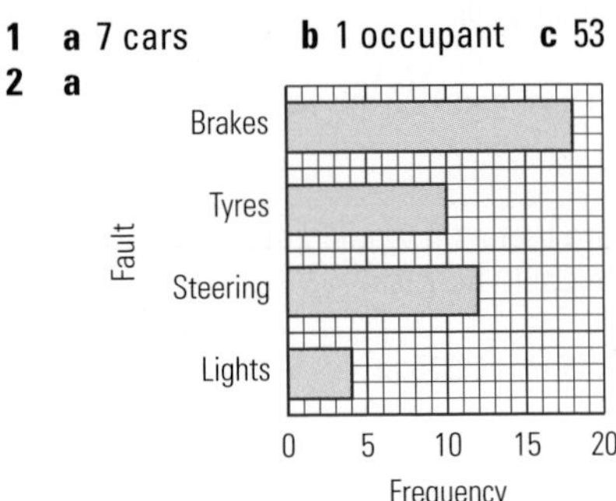

b Brakes

3

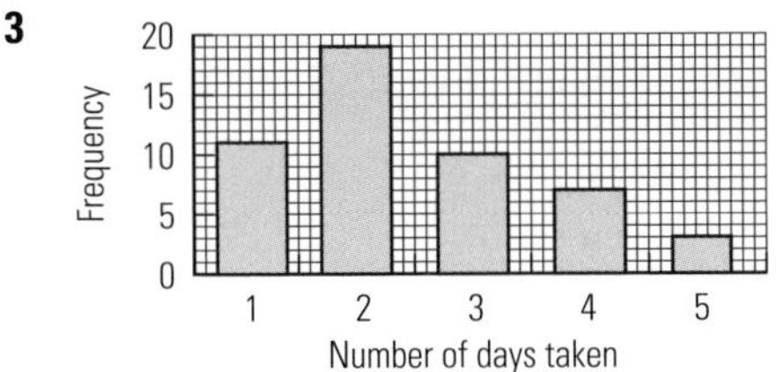

Worksheet 12.4

1 **a** Size 25 **b** 5
c The boys take a larger shoe size on average (boys mode 25, girls mode 23). However, the range of shoe sizes is the same for boys and girls.

2 **a** Type O **b** Type A **c** 10

Worksheet 12.5–6

1

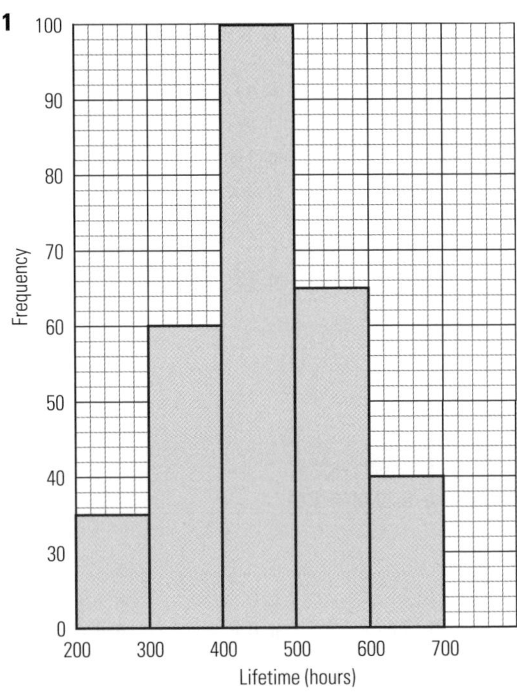

2 **a**

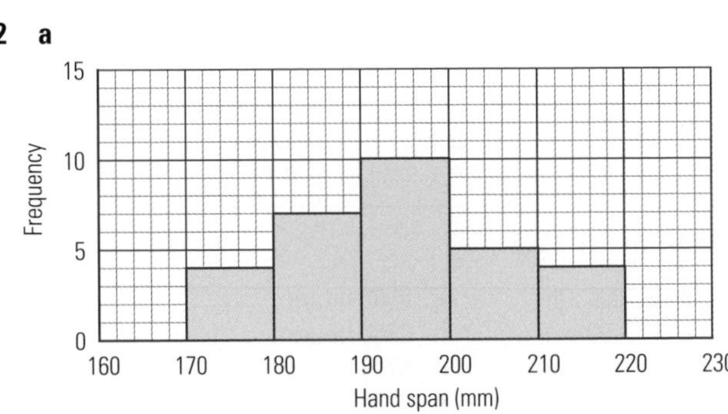

b > 190 mm but $\leqslant 200$ mm

3 The most common waist size is 85–90 cm. The waist sizes are between 65 cm and 105 cm, giving a range of 40 cm.

Worksheet 13.1

1 **a** 3, 7, 11, 15, 19 **b** 17, 15, 13, 11, 9
c 4, 40, 400, 4000, 40 000 **d** 16, 8, 4, 2, 1

2 **a** **i** Add 2 **ii** 13, 15
b **i** Add 4 **ii** 18, 22
c **i** Add 8 **ii** 41, 49
d **i** Add 25 **ii** 90, 115
e **i** Add 40 **ii** 330, 370

3 **a** **i** Subtract 2 **ii** 14, 12
b **i** Subtract 5 **ii** 30, 25
c **i** Subtract 11 **ii** 76, 65
d **i** Subtract 70 **ii** 1720, 1650
e **i** Subtract 3 **ii** −6, −9

4 **a** **i** Multiply by 2 **ii** 32, 64
b **i** Multiply by 5 **ii** 125, 625
c **i** Multiply by 10 **ii** 10 000, 100 000
d **i** Multiply by 20 **ii** 8000, 160 000
e **i** Multiply by 5 **ii** 375, 1875

5 **a** **i** Divide by 2 **ii** 48, 24
b **i** Divide by 2 **ii** 64, 32
c **i** Divide by 10 **ii** 4500, 450
d **i** Divide by 4 **ii** 64, 16
e **i** Divide by 2 **ii** 60, 30

6 **a** 22, 14, 12 **b** 18, 23 **c** 3, 81, 729 **d** 24, 6
e 10, 1250, 6250 **f** 48, 42
g 19, 26, 33 **h** 4000, 4, 0.4

7 **a** Students' own answers.
b

Savings at beginning of week	1	2	3	4	5	6	7	8	9
Dan	£10	£15	£20	£25	£30	£35	£40	£45	£50
Jane	25p	50p	£1	£2	£4	£8	£16	£32	£64

8 **a** **i**
ii 16
b **i**

ii 22
c **i**
ii 50

Worksheet 13.2

1 **a** 4 **b** 7 **c** 1 **d** 6

2 **a**

Term number	1	2	3	4	5
Term	8	9	10	11	12

b

Term number	1	2	3	4	5
Term	9	18	27	36	45

c

Term number	1	2	3	4	5	6	7	8
Term	11	12	13	14	15	16	17	18

d

Term number	1	2	3	4	5	6	7	8
Term	20	40	60	80	100	120	140	160

e

Term number	1	2	3	4	5	6	7	8
Term	−1	0	1	2	3	4	5	6

f

Term number	1	2	3	...	8	9	...	15
Term	6	12	18	...	48	54	...	90

g

Term number	1	2	3	...	8	9	...	30
Term	11	22	33	...	88	99	...	330

3 **a** Add 7 to the term number.
b Multiply the term number by 9.
c Add 10 to the term number.
d Multiply the term number by 20.
e Subtract 2 from the term number.
f Multiply the term number by 6.
g Multiply the term number by 11.

4 **a** +1 **b** +9 **c** +1 **d** +20
e +1 **f** +6 **g** +11

5 **a** 27 **b** 180 **c** 30 **d** 400
e 18 **f** 120 **g** 220

6 **a**

Term number	1	2	3	4	5	6	7	8
Term	7	9	11	13	15	17	19	21

b

Term number	1	2	3	4	5	6	7	8
Term	7	10	13	16	19	22	25	28

c

Term number	1	2	3	4	5	6	7	8
Term	15	25	35	45	55	65	75	85

d

Term number	1	2	3	4	5	6	7	8
Term	3	7	11	15	19	23	27	31

e

Term number	1	2	3	4	5	6	7	8
Term	5	11	17	23	29	35	41	47

f

Term number	1	2	3	...	8	9	10	11
Term	11	19	27	...	67	75	83	91

g

Term number	1	2	3	...	10	11	...	25
Term	11	13	15	...	29	31	...	59

h

Term number	1	2	3	...	7	8	...	11
Term	13	23	33	...	73	83	...	113

7 **a** Multiply the term number by 2 then add 5.
b Multiply the term number by 3 then add 4.
c Multiply the term number by 10 then add 5.
d Multiply the term number by 4 then subtract 1.
e Multiply the term number by 6 then subtract 1.
f Multiply the term number by 8 then add 3.
g Multiply the term number by 2 then add 9.
h Multiply the term number by 10 then add 3.

8 **a** Add 2 **b** Add 3 **c** Add 10 **d** Add 4
e Add 6 **f** Add 8 **g** Add 2 **h** Add 10

9 **a** 35 **b** 49 **c** 155 **d** 59
e 89 **f** 123 **g** 39 **h** 153

Worksheet 13.3

1 **a** **i** 3, 6, 9, 12, 15 **ii** 60
b **i** 8, 11, 14, 17, 20 **ii** 65
c **i** 5, 10, 15, 20, 25 **ii** 100
d **i** 7, 12, 17, 22, 27 **ii** 102
e **i** 4, 8, 12, 16, 20 **ii** 80
f **i** 1, 5, 9, 13, 17 **ii** 77
g **i** 3, 8, 13, 18, 23 **ii** 98
h **i** 7, 13, 19, 25, 31 **ii** 121
i **i** 3, 13, 23, 33, 43 **ii** 193
j **i** 13, 21, 29, 37, 45 **ii** 165

2 **a** **i** $4n + 3$ **ii** 83
b **i** $5n + 2$ **ii** 102
c **i** $4n + 10$ **ii** 90
d **i** $5n - 4$ **ii** 96
e **i** $10n + 3$ **ii** 203
f **i** $6n - 4$ **ii** 116
g **i** $2n + 9$ **ii** 49
h **i** $20n - 10$ **ii** 390

3 **a** **i** $27 - 2n$ **ii** 7
b **i** $105 - 5n$ **ii** 55
c **i** $35 - 3n$ **ii** 5
d **i** $54 - 4n$ **ii** 14
e **i** $100 - 2n$ **ii** 80
f **i** $320 - 20n$ **ii** 120
g **i** $100 - 10n$ **ii** 0
h **i** $16 - n$ **ii** 6

4 **a** **i** • • • • / • • • • •
ii 3, 5, 7, 9, 11, 13
iii $2n + 1$
iv 15

b **i** •
ii 5, 9, 13, 17, 21, 25
iii $4n + 1$
iv 29

c **i** • • • • • / • / • • • • •
ii 17, 15, 13, 11, 9, 7
iii $19 - 2n$
iv 5

Worksheet 13.4

1 **a** 76 **b** 120, 95 **c** 52 **d** 103
e 63, 73 **f** 200 **g** 7 **h** 24
i 88

2 **a** 13 **b** 6 **c** 75 **d** 28
e 41 **f** 60 **g** 66 **h** 44

Worksheet 14.1

1 **a** A: 5cm, 2cm; B: 6 cm, 3 cm; C: 9 cm, 1 cm
b A: 14 cm, B: 18 cm, C: 20 cm

2 3 cm × 2 cm, 3.5 cm × 2.8 cm, 3.6 cm × 2.3 cm

3 **a** 2.1 **b** 4.9 **c** 5; perimeter 12.5 cm

4 **a** 12 cm **b** 3cm × 3cm square

5 A: 30 cm; B: 120 cm; C: 60 cm

6 26 cm

7 **a** 8 cm **b** 5 cm **c** 26 cm

8 150 m

Worksheet 14.2

1 **a** 5 cm² **b** 20 cm² **c** 16 cm² **d** 8 cm²
e 12 cm² **f** 13.5 cm²

2 **a** 13 cm² **b** 5.5 cm² **c** 11 cm²

Worksheet 14.3

1 35 cm² **2** 81 cm² **3** 75 cm² **4** 24 cm²
5 42 cm² **6** 30 cm² **7** 110 cm² **8** 15 m²
9 87.5 cm² **10** 250 cm²

Worksheet 14.4

1 **a** 31 m² **b** 120 cm² **c** 99 cm² **d** 2500 cm²

2 **a** 20 **b** £189

3 **a** 300 cm² **b** 21.5 cm² **c** 48 cm²

Worksheet 15.1

1 **a** **i** (1, 2) **ii** (10, 5) **iii** (0, 6)
iv (8, 0) **v** (6, 9) **vi** (3, 4)
b **i** Hotel **ii** Police station
iii Museum **iv** Toilets **v** Railway station
vi Bus station

2 **a** **i** (4, 8) **ii** (8, 8) **iii** (8, 4)
b **i** F **ii** N **iii** E
c **ii** (4, 4)
d **ii** (0 , 1)

3 **a** (2, 0), (2, 4), (0, 4), (0, 5), (5, 5), (5, 4), (3, 4), (3, 0)
b (8, 2), (9, 2), (8, 3), (9, 3)
c

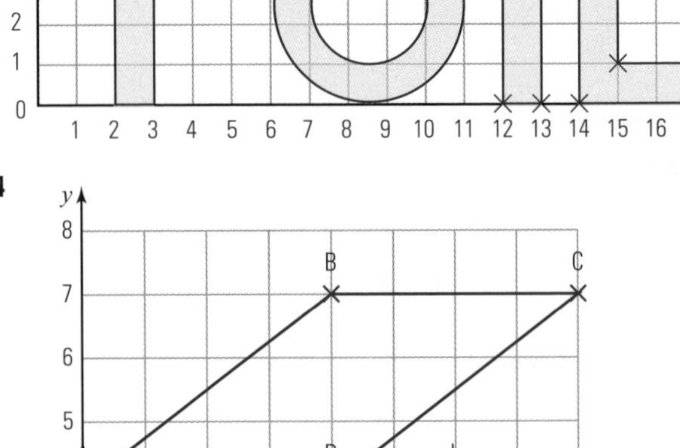

4

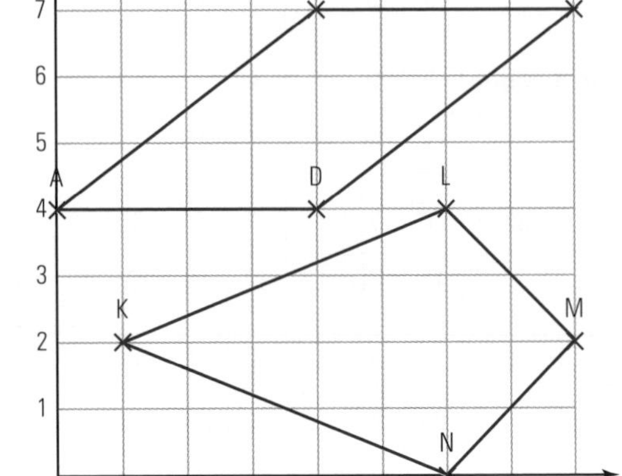

a Parallelogram
b **ii** (6, 0)

5 a i (1, 3), (4, 3), (5, 4), (6, 5), (6, 6), (5, 7)
ii (1, 0), (2, 1), (1, 2), (0, 3), (1, 4), (5, 6)

b

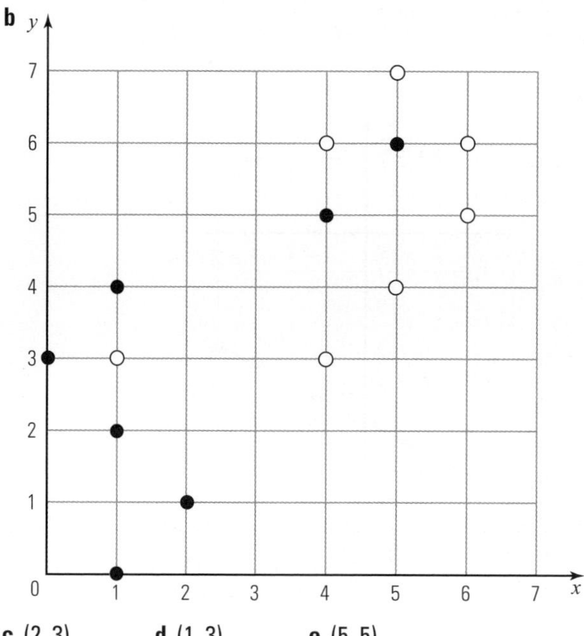

c (2, 3) **d** (1, 3) **e** (5, 5)

Worksheet 15.2

1 A(3, 4), B(1, −2), C(−4, 1), D(−3, −5), E(3, −4), F(−3, 0), G(0, −4), H(−2, 3), I(−5, −5)

2

3 a

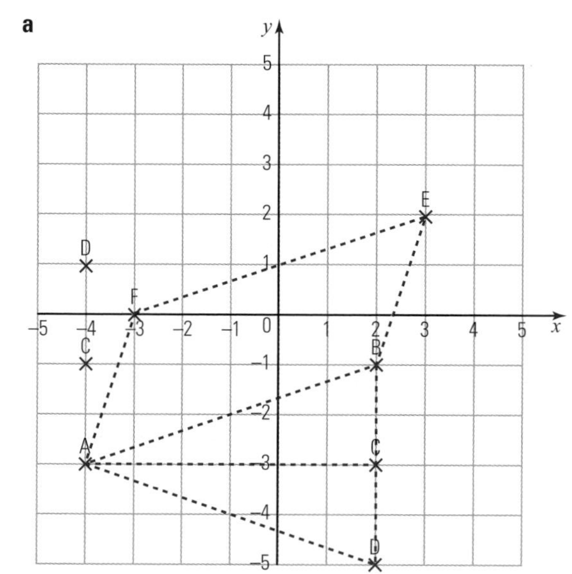

b ii C(2, −3) or C(−4, −1)
c ii D(2, −5) or D(−4, 1)
d i, ii Answers will vary

Worksheet 15.3

1 a A(1, 10) to B(10, 8); C(2, 9) to D(0, 5); E(2, 7) to F(8, 7); G(10, 7) to H(10, 3); J(1, 4) to K(2, 0); L(4, 6) to M(3, 1); N(6, 5) to P(10, 0)

b Midpoint of AB is (5.5, 9); midpoint of CD is (1, 7); midpoint of EF is (5, 7); midpoint of GH is (10, 5); midpoint of JK is (1.5, 2); midpoint of LM is (3.5, 3.5); midpoint of NP is (8, 2.5)

2

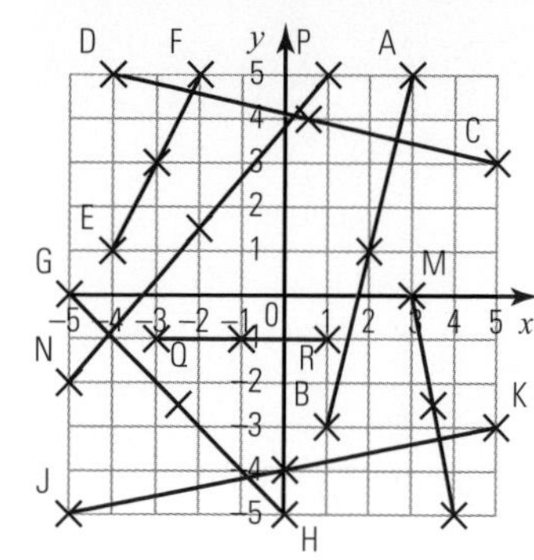

b i AB (2, 1) **ii** CD $\left(\frac{1}{2}, 4\right)$
iii EF (−3, 3) **iv** GH $\left(-2\frac{1}{2}, -2\frac{1}{2}\right)$
v JK (0, −4) **vi** LM $\left(3\frac{1}{2}, -2\frac{1}{2}\right)$
vii NP $\left(-2, 1\frac{1}{2}\right)$ **viii** QR (−1, −1)

3 a Bunny (3, 5), Rushcliffe (−2, 4), West Leake (−4, 1), East Leake (−1, 1), Costock (2, 1), Thorpe (5, 1), Rempstone (1.5, −1), South Bonnington (−6, −2), Hoton (1, −3), Zourch (−6, −4), Stanford (−2.5, −4), Prestworld (1, −4), Hathern (−6, −5), Burton (5, −5)

d East Leake, Costock, Rempstone, and Stanford all lie midway between villages.

Worksheet 15.4

1 a $y = 4$ **b** $y = 2$ **c** $y = 0.5$ **d** $y = -1$
e $y = -3$

2 a $x = 3.5$ **b** $x = 1$ **c** $x = -2$ **d** $x = -4$

3

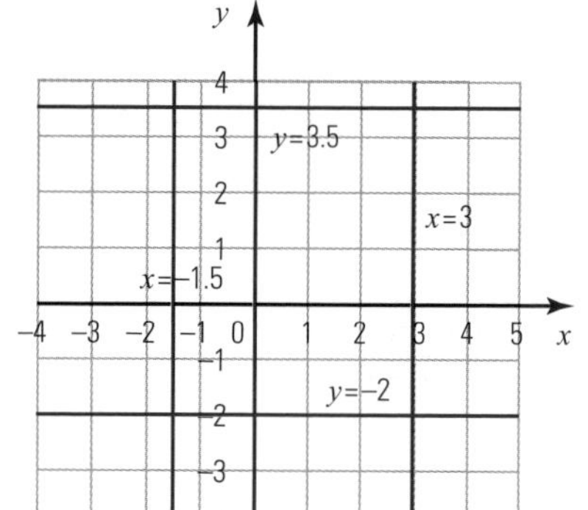

4 a $x = 1, y = 3$ **b** (1, 3)

5 a i $x = 4$ **ii** $y = 5$
b i $x = -7$ **ii** $y = 1$
c i $x = 0$ **ii** $y = 5$
d i $x = -10$ **ii** $y = 0$

6 i $y = 0$ **ii** $x = 0$

Worksheet 15.5

1 a

x	0	1	2	3	4
$y = x + 5$	5	6	7	8	9

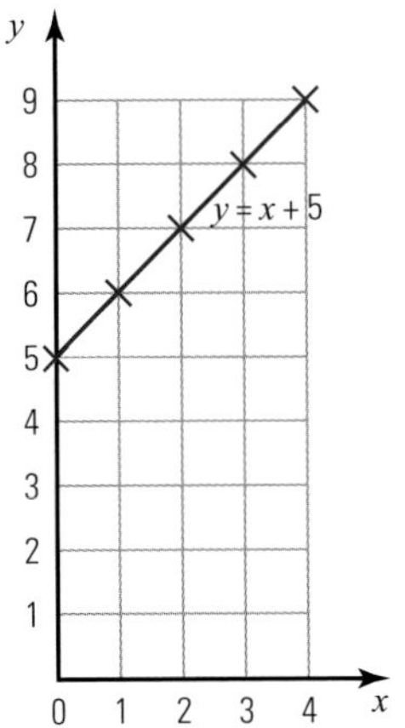

b

x	0	5	10
$y = x - 5$	−5	0	5

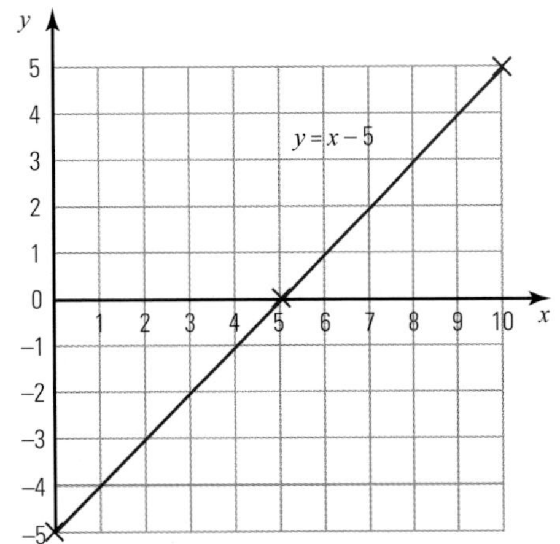

c

x	−3	−2	−1	0	1
$y = 2x + 5$	−1	1	3	5	7

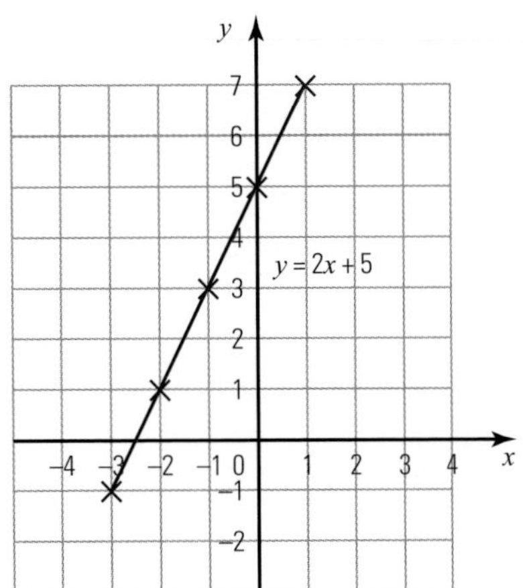

d

x	−4	0	4
$y = \frac{1}{2}x - 5$	−7	−5	−3

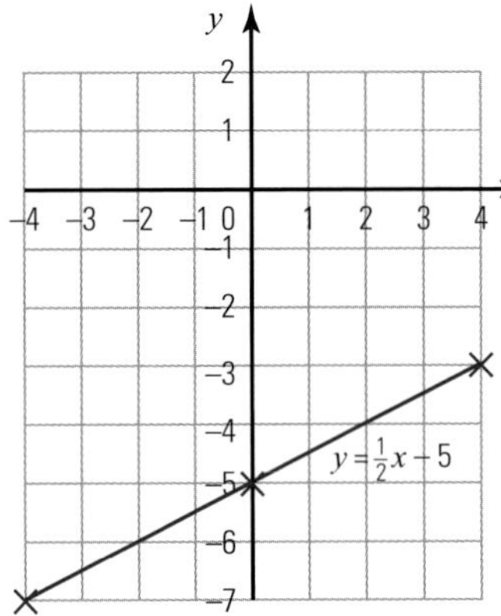

e

x	0	5	10
$y = -x + 5$	5	0	−5

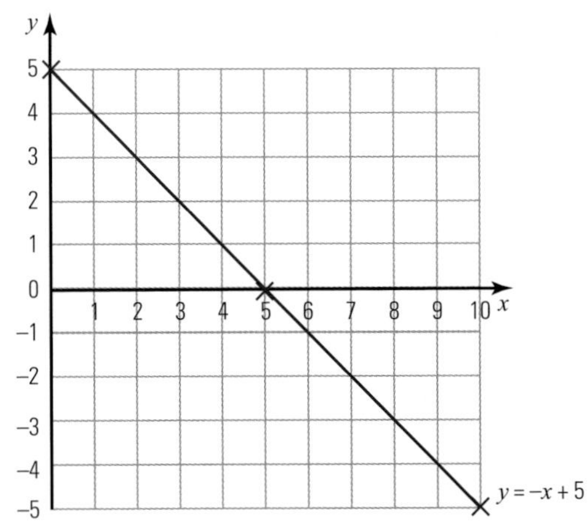

f

x	0	1	2	3	4
$y = -2x + 5$	5	3	1	−1	−3

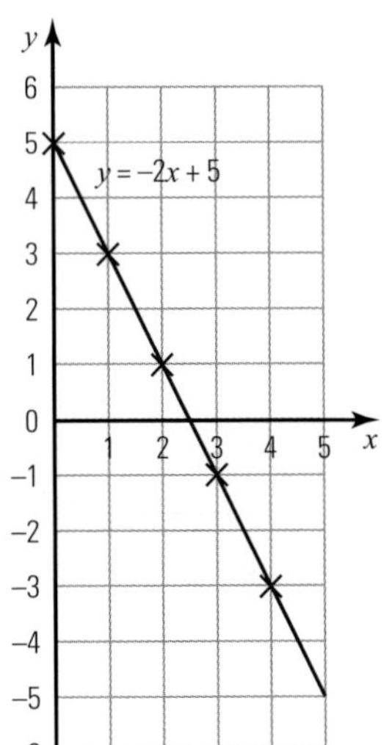

2 a

x	–3	0	3
$y = x - 7$	–10	–7	–4

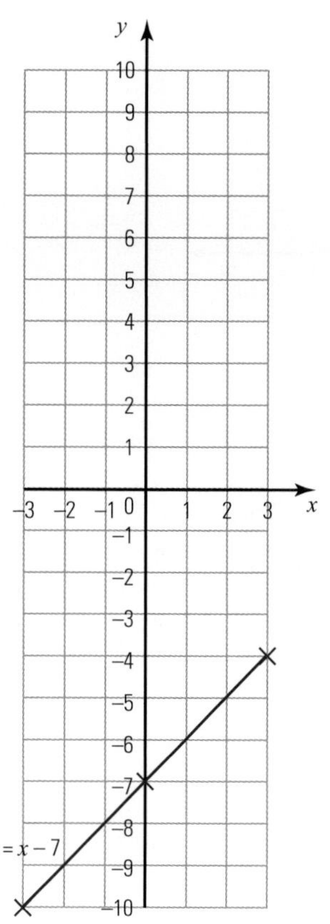

b

x	–3	0	3
$y = 2x + 4$	–2	4	10

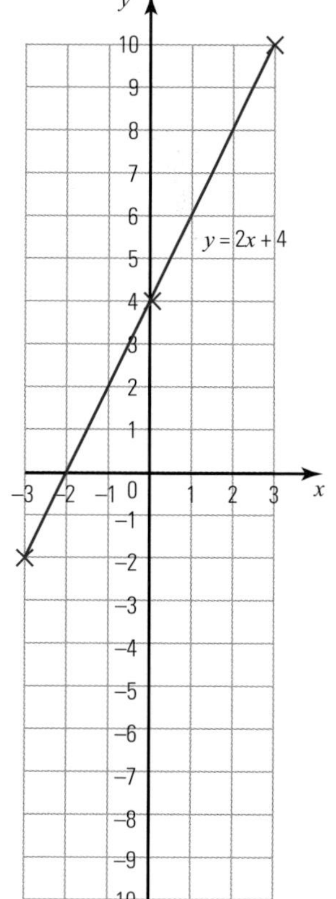

c

x	–2	0	2
$y = \frac{1}{2}x + 8$	7	8	9

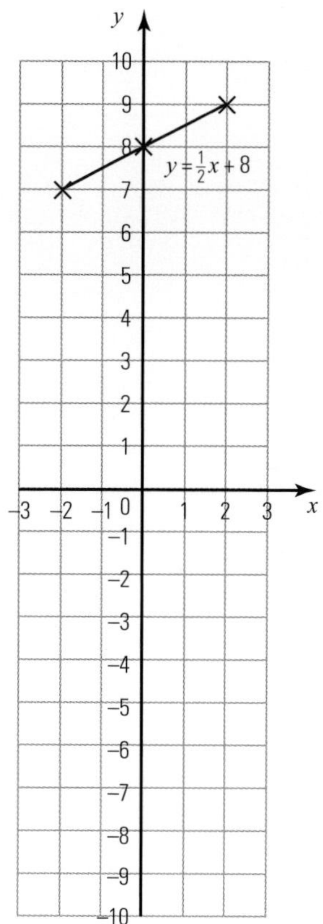

d

x	–1	0	3
$y = 3x - 5$	–8	–5	4

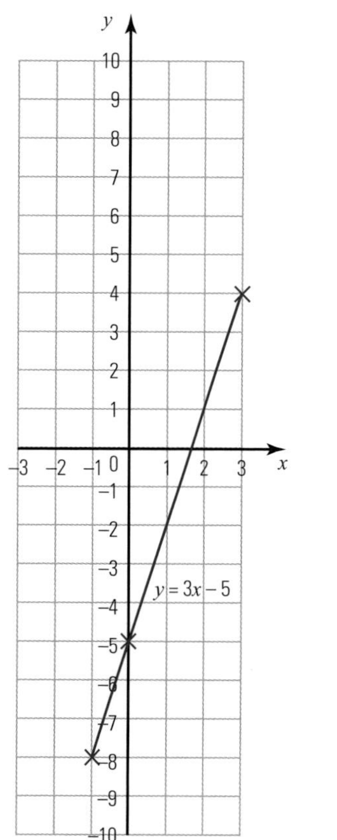

Guided practice worksheet answers

e

x	−3	0	1
$y = 4x + 4$	−8	4	8

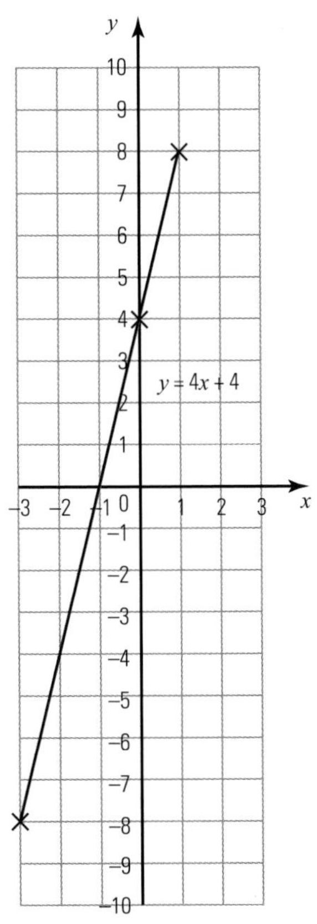

Worksheet 15.6

1

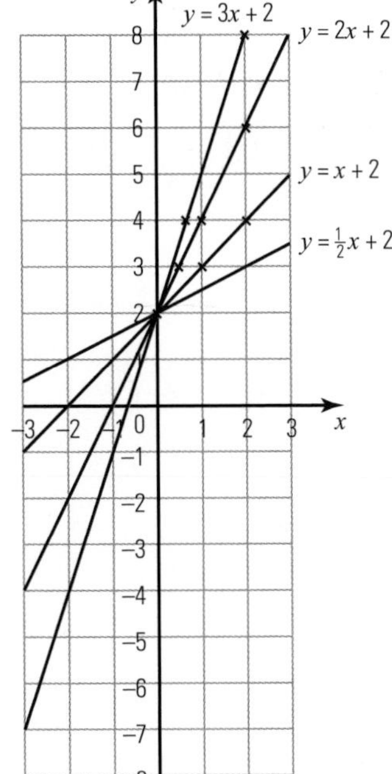

2

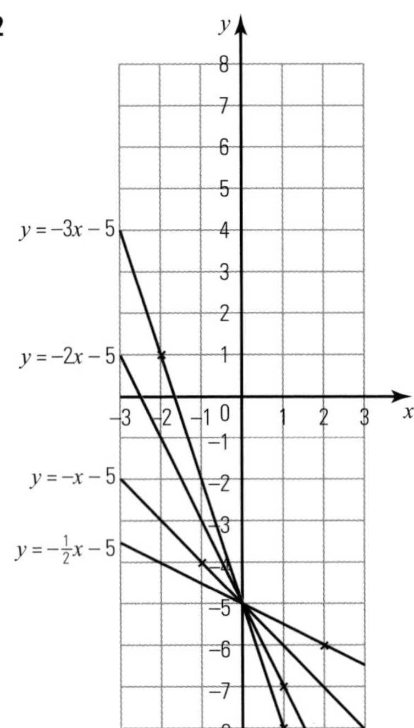

3

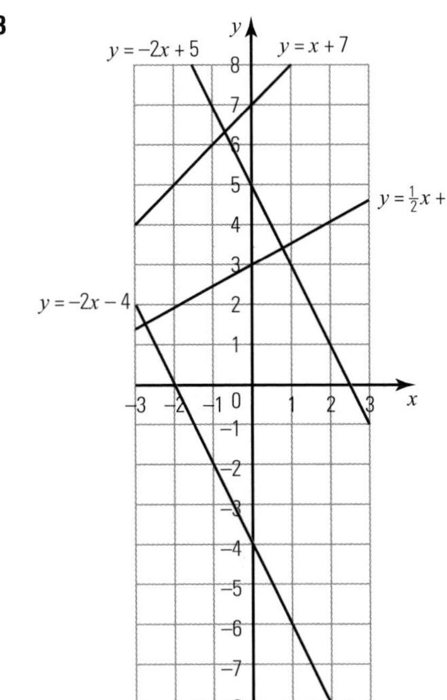

4

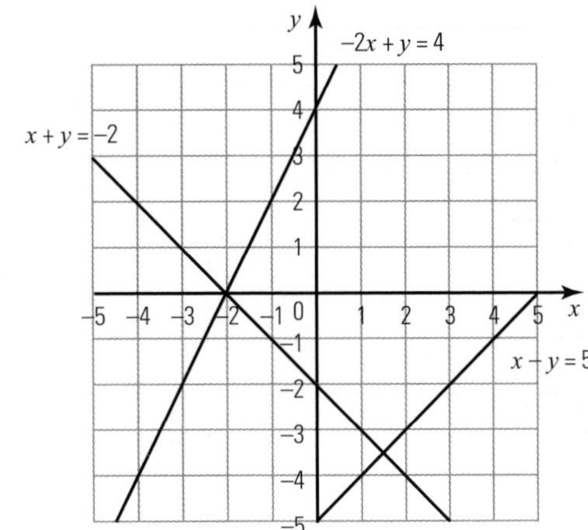

Worksheet 15.7

1 a 3 b 4 c 1 d −3
2 a 2 b −1 c $\frac{1}{2}$ d $-\frac{1}{2}$
3 a $y = 2x + 3$ b $y = -x + 4$ or $y = 4 - x$
c $y = \frac{1}{2}x + 1$ d $y = -\frac{1}{2}x - 3$
4 a $y = -\frac{1}{2}x + 5$ or $y = 5 - \frac{1}{2}x$ b $y = x - 4$
c $y = 2x$ d $y = 3x + 5$ e $y = -x - 2$

Worksheet 16.1–16.3

1 a 1 b 9 c 8 d 6
2 a 7 b 9 c 6
3 a 10 b 9 c 8 d 8
4 When you want to know the value that occurs most often.
5 When extreme values distort the mean.
6 Mode
7 a £100 b £156 c £194
d The median is best here. The mode is the lowest value and the mean is distorted by one high value.

Worksheet 16.4

1 a 33 minutes b 26 minutes c 28 minutes
2 a 43 minutes b 28 minutes c 38 minutes
3 a

1	2 3 6 8 9
2	2 3 4 6 8 9
3	0 0 0 2 3 4
4	0

b i 30 lessons ii 27 lessons iii 28 lessons

Worksheet 16.5

1 a

Number of letters x	Frequency f	fx
0	0	0
1	8	8
2	7	14
3	4	12
4	2	8
Total	21	42

b 1 letter
c 2 letters
d 2 letters

2 a

Number of goals scored x	0	1	2	3	4	5
Frequency f	4	8	9	6	8	2
fx	0	8	18	18	32	10

b 2 goals
c 2 goals
d 2.32 goals
3 a 3 items b 2 items c 2.2 items

Worksheet 16.6–16.7

1 a

Number of books	Frequency f	Mid-point of class x	fx
1–3	4	2	8
4–6	6	5	30
7–9	6	8	48
10–12	2	11	22
Total	18		108

b 4–6 and 7–9 books
c 4–6 books
d 6 books
2 a 6–8 chargers
b 3–5 chargers
c 5 chargers
3 a 5–9 flowers b 5–9 flowers c 8.5 flowers

Worksheet 17.1

1 a 16 cm b 8.8 cm c 5.2 cm
2 a 5 cm b 3.2 cm c 1.9 cm
3 a 50.27 cm b 62.83 m c 31.42 cm d 43.98 cm
e 8.17 m f 314.16 cm g 69.12 cm h 12.57 m
i 188.50 cm j 50.27 cm k 70.37 m l 314.16 cm
4 a 7.6 m b 2.5 cm c 3.2 cm d 20.1 mm
e 15.9 cm
5 a 2.4 cm b 8.9 mm c 4.3 cm d 8.1 cm
e 11.8 m

Worksheet 17.2–17.3

1 a 28.27 b 102.07 c 72.38 d 260.16
2 a 50.3 b 8.04 c 0.882 d 26.4
3 a 78.5 cm^2 b 216 cm^2 c 314 cm^2 d 1.54 cm^2
e 63.6 m^2 f 21.2 cm^2
4 a 113.10 cm^2 b 490.87 m^2 c 0.28 cm^2 d 47.78 cm^2
e 66.48 m^2 f 1963.50 cm^2
5 a 101 cm^2 b 51.0 cm^2 c 353 cm^2

Worksheet 18.1

1 a By inspection.
b By inspection.
2 By inspection.

Worksheet 18.2

1 By inspection.
2 a

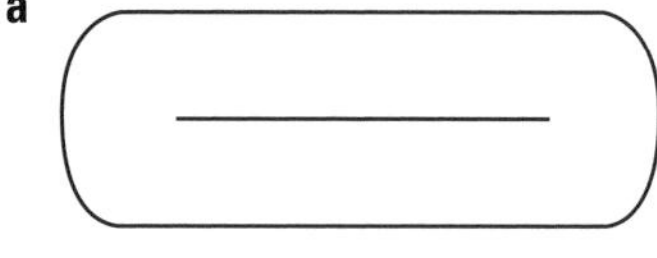

b

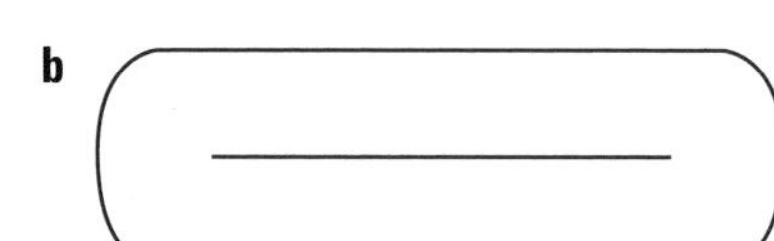

c

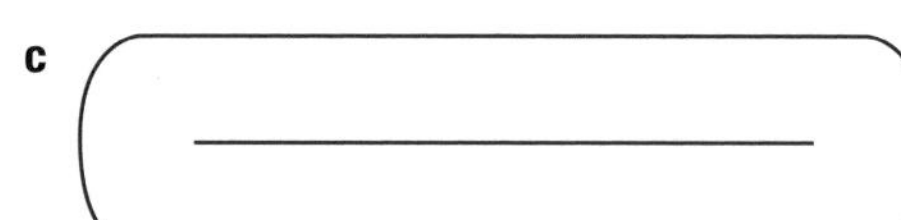

3 a **b**

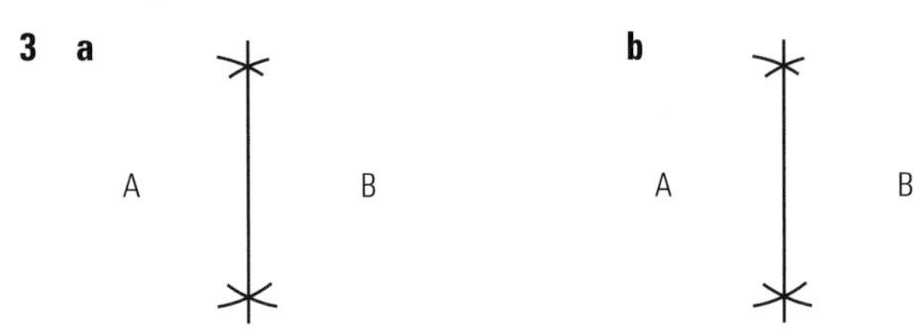

c **d**

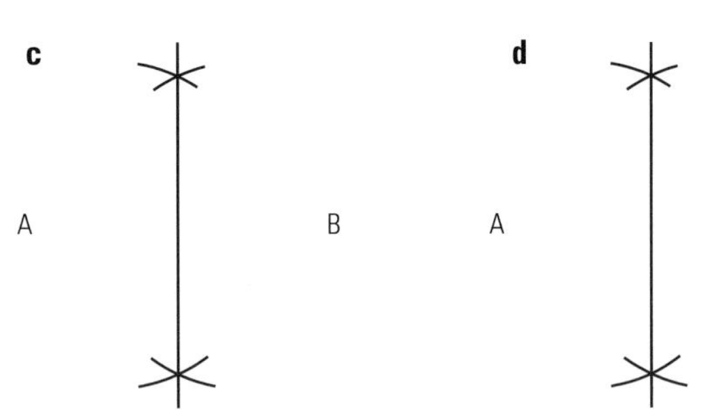

Worksheet 18.3

1 a

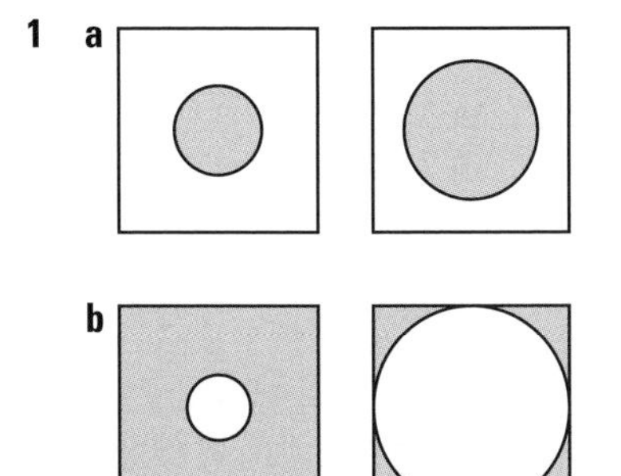

b

2 Accurate circles, which are shaded on the inside, with radii:
a 2 cm **b** 2.5 cm **c** 3 cm **d** 3.5 cm

3 a **b** **c**

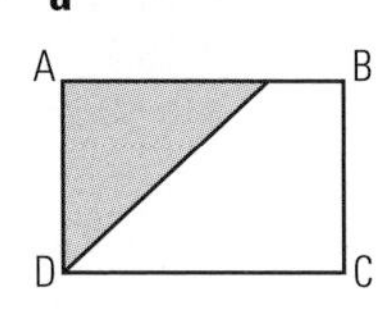

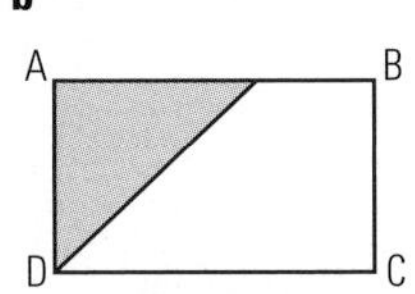

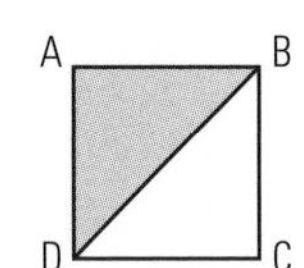

4 a **b** **c**

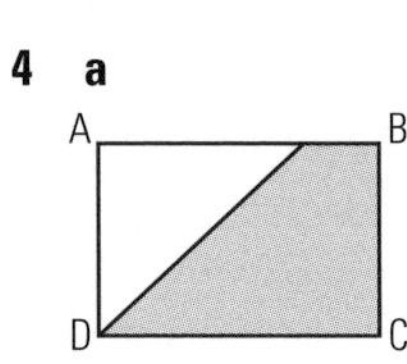

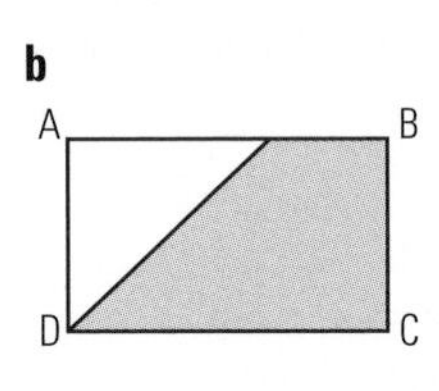

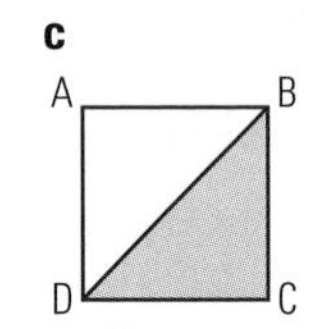

5 a **b** **c**

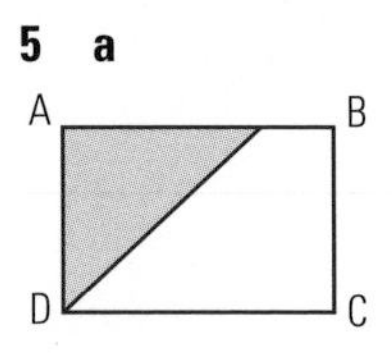

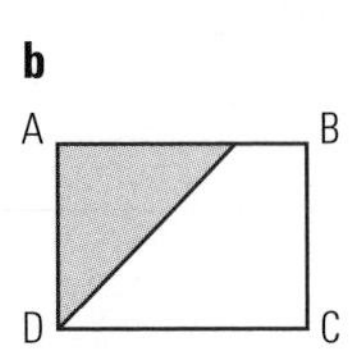

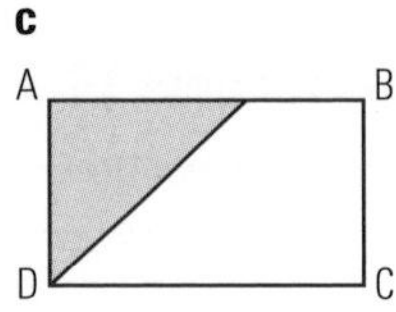

Worksheet 19.1

1 a 60% **b** 85% **c** 25%
2 70%
3 25%
4 a 0.6 **b** 0.35 **c** 0.27 **d** 0.8
e 0.08
5 0.175
6 a $\frac{1}{2}$ **b** $\frac{1}{4}$ **c** $\frac{3}{4}$ **d** $\frac{1}{10}$
e $\frac{3}{10}$
7 a $\frac{7}{10}$ **b** $\frac{1}{5}$ **c** $\frac{3}{5}$ **d** $\frac{9}{20}$
e $\frac{16}{25}$
8 $\frac{9}{25}$
9 $\frac{3}{4}$
10 a $\frac{1}{4}$, 27%, 0.3 **b** $\frac{2}{5}$, 0.42, 45% **c** 60%, $\frac{5}{8}$, 0.64, $\frac{2}{3}$

Worksheet 19.2

1 a £20 **b** 12 cm **c** £5 **d** 12 km
2 a 30 kg **b** £12 **c** 18 g **d** £45
3 a 3 kg **b** £5 **c** £8 **d** £6.50
4 a 1 cm **b** £12 **c** 60 m **d** £6
5 13 students
6 95 new cars
7 153 semi-detached houses
8 a £7.40 **b** 9.2 km **c** £44.80 **d** 22.4 kg
e 15.2 kg **f** £266.40 **g** 103.2 m **h** £539.50
9 £54
10 8 biscuits
11 77 litres
12 £20 400

Worksheet 19.3

1 a £3 **b** £27
2 a 24p **b** £2.64
3 £530
4 a £261 **b** £340 **c** £132
5 £663
6 £1934.40
7 £423

Worksheet 19.4

1 40%
2 35%
3 85%
4 75%
5 37.5%
6 66.7%
7 Maths
8 a 46% **b** 30% **c** 90% **d** 60%
e 56%
9 a 60% **b** 40% **c** 62.5% **d** 35%
e 80%

Worksheet 20.1

Name	Faces	Edges	Vertices
Cuboid	6	12	8
Cylinder	3	2	0
Pentagonal prism	7	15	10
Sphere	1	0	0
Cone	2	1	1
Tetrahedron	4	6	4
Pyramid	5	8	5

For the polyhedra (solids with flat faces and straight edges):
Faces – Edges + Vertices = 2

Worksheet 20.2

1

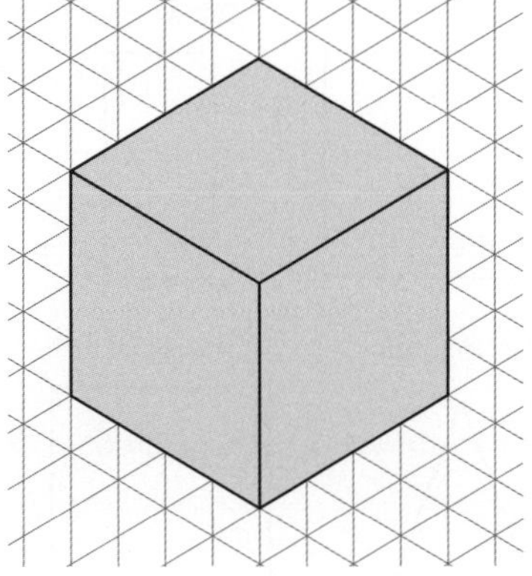

2 a

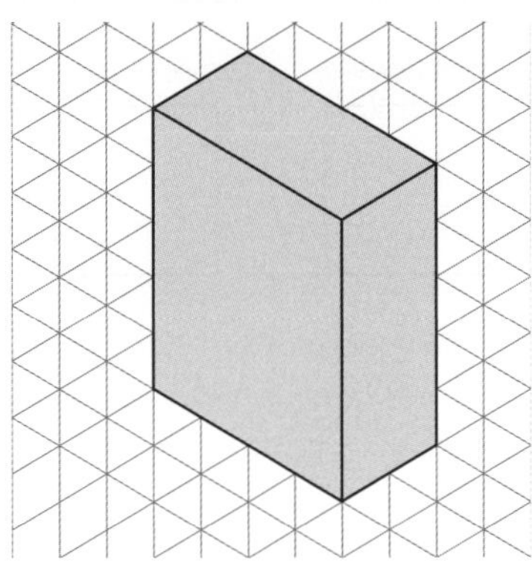

b

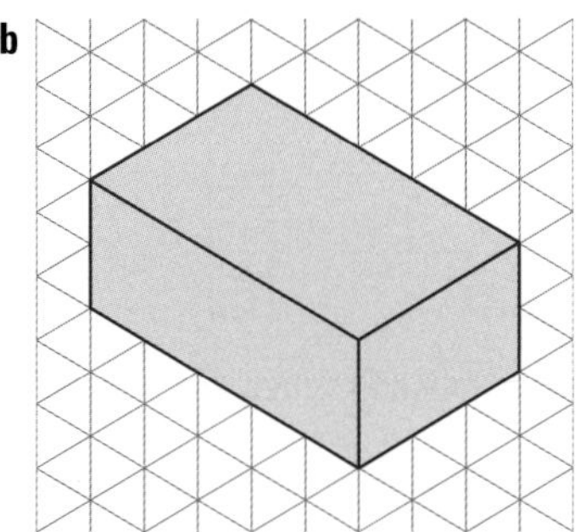

c

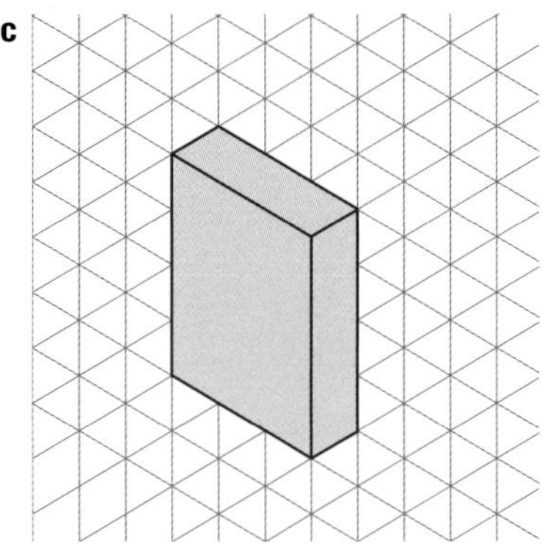

d

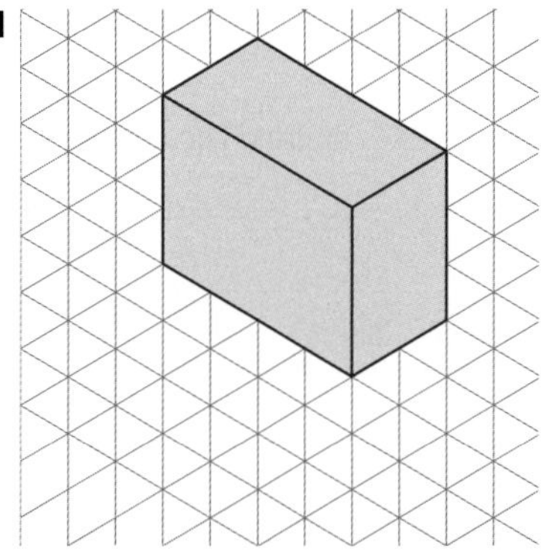

3 e.g.

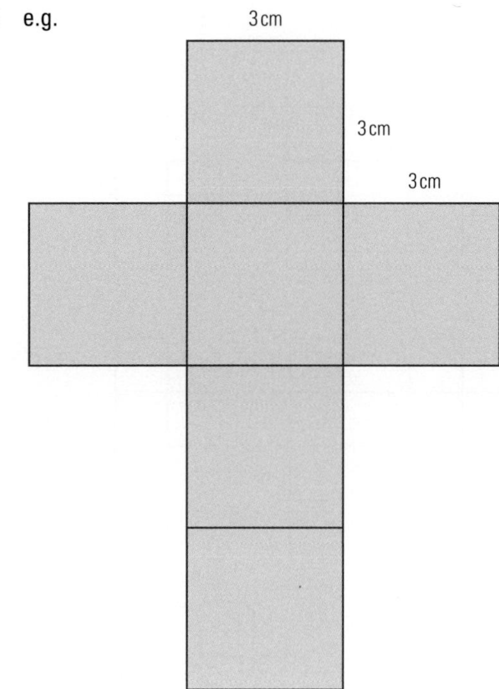

4 e.g.

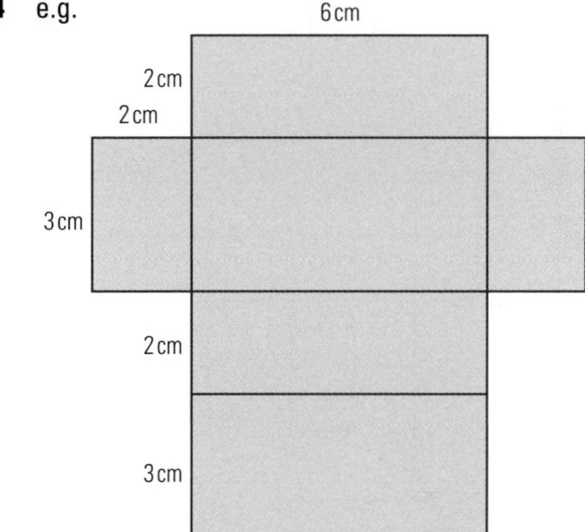

5

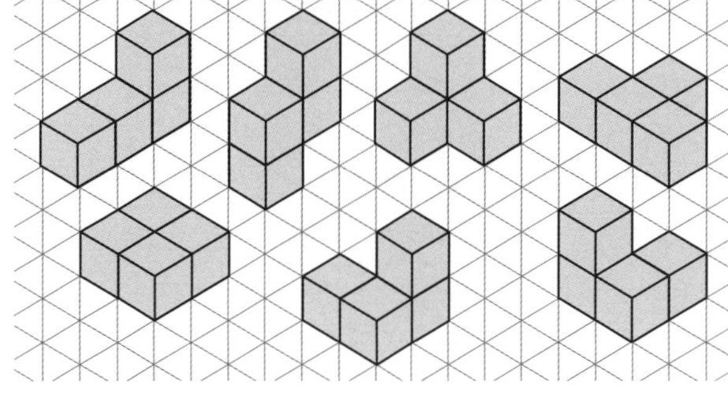

6

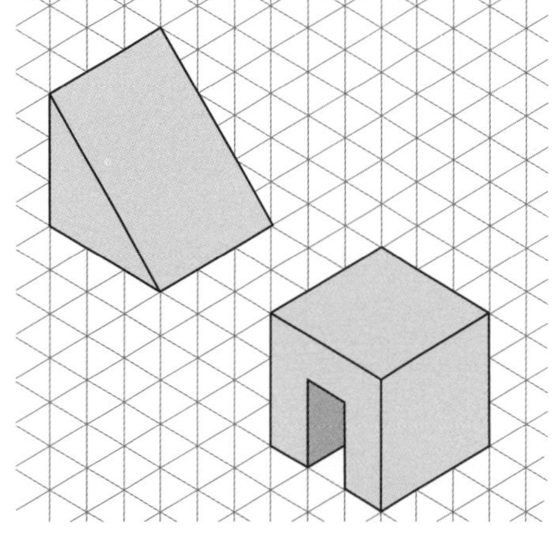

7 Any two out of:

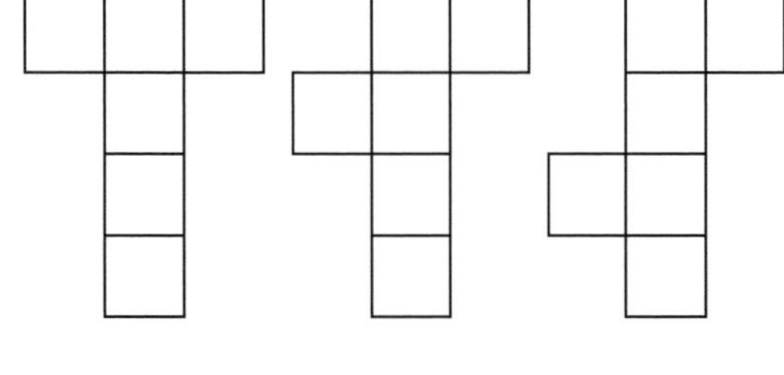

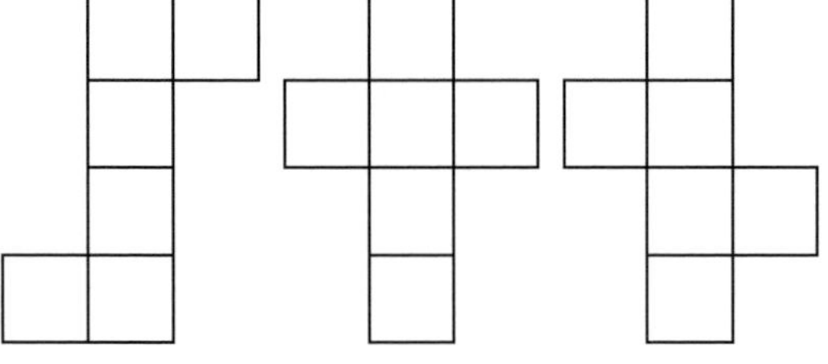

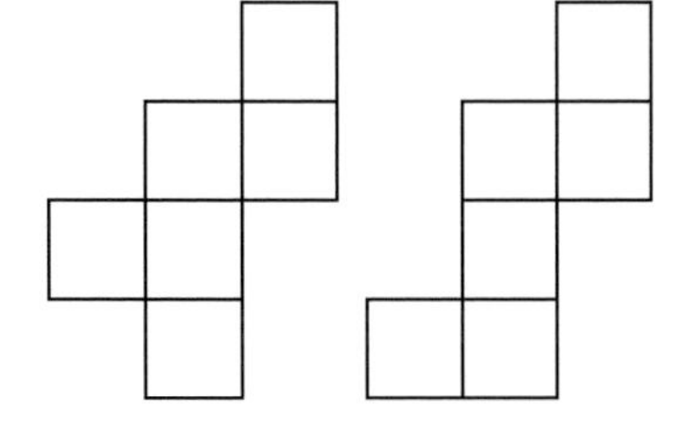

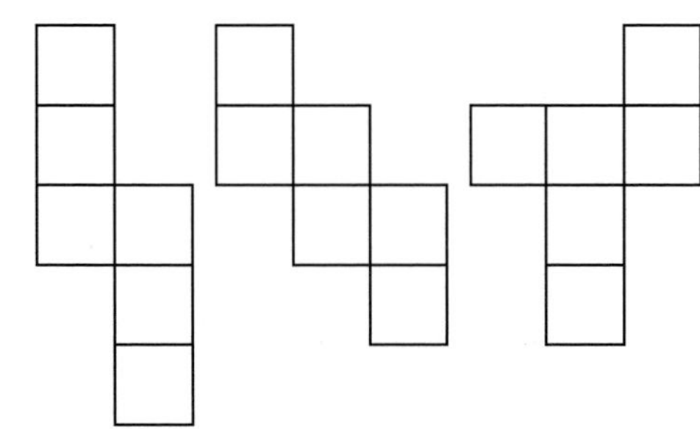

8

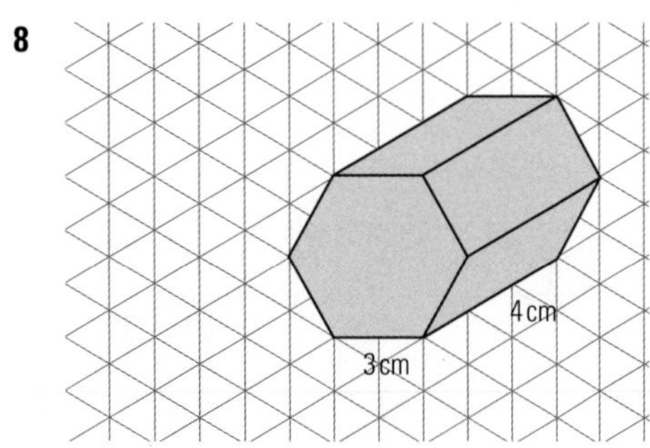

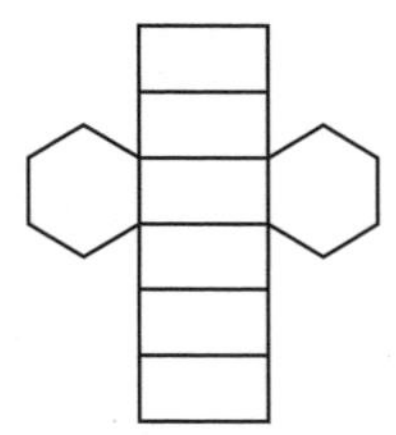

Worksheet 20.3

1 Plan Front elevation Side elevation

2 **a** Plan Front elevation Side elevation

b Plan Front elevation Side elevation

c Plan Front elevation Side elevation

d Plan Front elevation Side elevation

3 Students' solid made with multilink cubes.

4 Plan Front elevation Side elevation

Worksheet 20.4

1 **a** 26.91 cm^3 **b** 39.732 cm^3
2 **a** 17.544 cm^3 **b** 30 m^3 **c** 1.2 m^3
3 242.516 cm^3
4 **a** 94.5 cm^3 **b** 54 cm^3 **c** 135 cm^3
5 441.8 cm^3
6 6.25 cm
7 48 cans will fit. The volume of beans in each can is 397.6 cm^3. The volume of space in the carton which is not filled with beans is 15 915 cm^3.
8 180 packets
9 Two of the lengths are given in metres. The correct volume is 9 m^3 or 9 000 000 cm^3.

Worksheet 20.5

1 **a** 260 cm^2, 240 cm^2, 100 cm^2, 30 cm^2
b 660 cm^2

2 **a**

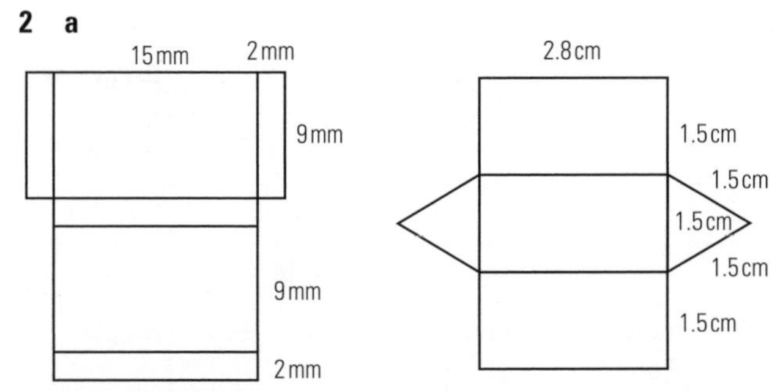

b **i** 366 mm²
ii 14.55 cm²

3 **a** 88 m² **b** 264.5 cm² **c** 238 cm² **d** 166 mm²

4 **a** 101 m² **b** 292 cm² **c** 8.8 m²

Worksheet 20.6

1 **a** **i** 12 cm **ii** 9 **iii** 63 cm²
b **i** 10 cm **ii** 4 **iii** 200 cm²
c **i** 15 mm **ii** 2.25 **iii** 81 mm²

2 **a** **i** 3 **ii** 21 mm **iii** 9 **iv** 18 mm²
b **i** 2.5 **ii** 75 cm **iii** 6.25 **iv** 87.5 cm²
c **i** 1.75 **ii** 22.75 mm **iii** 3.0625 **iv** 16.2 mm²

3 **a** 9 **b** 81 cm²

4 **a** 1.5 **b** 2.25 **c** 30.4 cm²

5 58.8 cm²

6 231.5 cm³

7 135 000 cm³

8 204.8 cm³

Worksheet 20.7

1 **a** 250 000 mm² **b** 14 000 cm² **c** 340 mm² **d** 240 cm²
e 30 000 mm² **f** 70 mm² **g** 400 mm² **h** 6600 mm²

2 **a** 0.45 m² **b** 3.4 m² **c** 3.2 cm² **d** 40 cm²
e 0.034 m² **f** 0.5 m² **g** 4 m² **h** 26.5 cm²

3 **a** 42 mm² **b** 0.062 m² **c** 2.37 cm² **d** 0.52 m²
e 44 cm² **f** 24 mm² **g** 3.5 cm² **h** 0.42 m²

4 3440 postcards

5 **a** 640 mm³ **b** 4000 cm³ **c** 500 000 mm³ **d** 2300 mm³
e 2 mm³ **f** 2000 mm³ **g** 5200 cm³ **h** 10 mm³

6 **a** 0.64 m³ **b** 4 cm³ **c** 0.3 cm³ **d** 0.0495 m³
e 22.326 cm³ **f** 0.25 m³ **g** 0.01 m³ **h** 0.776 m³

7 **a** 7.2 cm³ **b** 400 cm³ **c** 30 mm³ **d** 200 cm³
e 2000 mm³ **f** 0.45 m³ **g** 2600 mm³
h 50 000 000 000 mm³

8 9000 bottles

9 **a** 2.7 cm³ **b** 2700 mm³

10 **a** 450 cm³ **b** 1555 slabs

Worksheet 21.1

1 **a** 4 **b** 5 **c** 9 **d** 4
e 10 **f** 4 **g** 4 **h** 9

2 Using letter x:
a $5 + x = 9, x = 4$ **b** $x - 3 = 2, x = 5$
c $10 - x = 1, x = 9$ **d** $2x = 8, x = 4$
e $\frac{x}{2} = 5, x = 10$ **f** $\frac{12}{x} = 3, x = 4$
g $5x = 20, x = 4$ **h** $-x = -9, x = 9$

3 **a** $p + 3 = 11, p = 8$ **b** $\frac{p}{2} = 8, p = 16$
c $p - 10 = 12, p = 22$ **d** $7p = 28, p = 4$
e $p + 50 = 65, p = 15$ **f** $\frac{p}{10} = 7, p = 70$
g $\frac{12}{p} = 4, p = 3$

4 **a** 3 **b** 2 **c** 3 **d** 6
e 3 **f** 2 **g** 2 **h** 1
i 2

5 Using letter x:
a $2x + 1 = 7, x = 3$ **b** $4x - 3 = 5, x = 2$
c $10 - 2x = 4, x = 3$ **d** $\frac{x}{2} + 5 = 8, x = 6$
e $3x + 2 = 11, x = 3$ **f** $\frac{12}{x} + 1 = 7, x = 2$
g $30 - 5x = 20, x = 2$ **h** $5 + 2x = 7, x = 1$
i $4(x + 1) = 12, x = 2$

6 **a** $2d + 3 = 7, d = 2$ **b** $\frac{d}{2} + 4 = 9, d = 10$
c $4d - 1 = 11, d = 3$ **d** $3d - 2 = 19, d = 7$
e $\frac{d}{5} + 3 = 6, d = 15$ **f** $10d - 30 = 40, d = 7$
g $3(d + 1) = 15, d = 4$ **h** $4(d - 2) = 12, d = 5$

Worksheet 21.2

1 **a** $m = 7$ **b** $k = 11$ **c** $h = 3$ **d** $w = 4$
e $h = 6$ **f** $a = 9$

2 **a** $y = 7$ **b** $e = 30$ **c** $n = 8$ **d** $f = 35$
e $y = 13$ **f** $b = 35$

3 **a** $s = 4$ **b** $t = 12$ **c** $r = 21$ **d** $d = 6$
e $e = 12$ **f** $p = 12$

4 **a** $m = 3$ **b** $w = 5$ **c** $k = 9$ **d** $y = 3$
e $j = 10$ **f** $u = 18$

5 **a** $u = 6$ **b** $y = 15$ **c** $p = 16$ **d** $c = 12$
e $k = 99$ **f** $x = 100$

6 **a** $w = 4$ **b** $t = 3$ **c** $u = 45$ **d** $h = 21$
e $f = 20$ **f** $q = 3$ **g** $n = 4$ **h** $t = 30$
i $g = 0$ **j** $p = 5$

Worksheet 21.3

1 **a** $p = 3$ **b** $w = 7$ **c** $t = 4$ **d** $x = 2$
e $n = 2$ **f** $g = 5$

2 **a** $p = 8$ **b** $h = 15$ **c** $u = 15$ **d** $d = 24$
e $m = 20$ **f** $v = 35$

3 **a** $m = 1\frac{2}{3}$ **b** $w = 1\frac{1}{5}$ **c** $w = 1\frac{1}{3}$ **d** $t = 4\frac{1}{2}$
e $k = \frac{3}{4}$ **f** $f = \frac{5}{9}$ **g** $e = 2\frac{2}{3}$ **h** $x = 3\frac{1}{2}$

4 **a** $p = -2$ **b** $j = -4$ **c** $w = -2$ **d** $r = -12$
e $d = -5$ **f** $g = -25$

5 **a** $t = 3\frac{2}{3}$ **b** $r = -12$ **c** $y = -\frac{4}{5}$ **d** $h = -12$
e $s = -1\frac{1}{4}$ **f** $c = -\frac{1}{3}$ **g** $e = -10$ **h** $y = 0$

Worksheet 21.4

1 **a** $2f + 10$ **b** $3p - 6$ **c** $8y + 4$ **d** $7g - 28$
e $15r - 30$ **f** $8w + 28$

2 **a** $x = 3$ **b** $a = 5$ **c** $d = 8$ **d** $f = 3$
e $m = 2$ **f** $r = 5$ **g** $s = 3$ **h** $t = 4$

3 **a** $r = 3\frac{3}{4}$ **b** $s = 8\frac{1}{2}$ **c** $p = -2$ **d** $n = 1\frac{5}{8}$
e $n = -3$ **f** $k = 1\frac{4}{5}$ **g** $t = -3\frac{2}{3}$ **h** $y = -1\frac{1}{6}$

4 **a** $s = 10$ **b** $h = 14$ **c** $k = 11$ **d** $e = 8$
e $y = 7$ **f** $m = -3$ **g** $m = 3\frac{1}{3}$ **h** $d = -\frac{1}{5}$

5 **a** $b = 4$ **b** $e = 7\frac{2}{3}$ **c** $p = -2\frac{1}{5}$ **d** $w = -2$
e $j = 19$ **f** $k = 2\frac{5}{8}$ **g** $m = 3\frac{1}{3}$ **h** $u = 1\frac{4}{5}$

Worksheet 21.5

1 **a** $u = 2$ **b** $e = 3$ **c** $s = 4$ **d** $c = 4$
e $f = 2$ **f** $g = 2\frac{1}{2}$ **g** $w = -4$ **h** $h = 2\frac{1}{5}$

2 **a** $d = 3$ **b** $v = 2$ **c** $k = 2$ **d** $p = 5$
e $t = 2$ **f** $f = 2$ **g** $w = -11$ **h** $t = 2\frac{1}{2}$
3 **a** $t = 4$ **b** $e = 2$ **c** $u = 3$ **d** $r = 2$
e $h = -5$ **f** $f = 4$ **g** $d = 1$ **h** $k = 3$
4 **a** $p = 3\frac{3}{4}$ **b** $r = 2\frac{1}{4}$ **c** $e = -3$ **d** $m = 3\frac{1}{2}$
e $a = \frac{2}{3}$ **f** $b = -\frac{1}{3}$
5 **a** $m = \frac{2}{3}$ **b** $w = 3$ **c** $v = 2$ **d** $e = 15$

Worksheet 21.6

1 **a** $f = 5$ **b** $g = 4$ **c** $e = 2$ **d** $m = -3$
e $y = -1$ **f** $f = -8$
2 **a** $e = 2$ **b** $b = 3$ **c** $k = 4$ **d** $t = 2$
e $y = 2$ **f** $x = 5$
3 **a** $t = 3$ **b** $f = 3$ **c** $d = 3$ **d** $k = 2$
e $v = -3$ **f** $c = 8$
4 **a** $h = 3$ **b** $f = -3$ **c** $t = 1$ **d** $r = 1$
e $d = -2$ **f** $m = -4$
5 **a** $g = \frac{3}{5}$ **b** $f = 3\frac{2}{3}$ **c** $a = -7\frac{1}{2}$ **d** $h = 1\frac{1}{3}$
e $s = 2\frac{2}{3}$ **f** $b = 0$ **g** $j = -2\frac{3}{5}$ **h** $f = -1\frac{3}{7}$

Worksheet 21.7

1 **a** **i** $6x + 10 = 40, x = 5$ **ii** 15 cm, 15 cm
b **i** $3x + 9 = 24, x = 5$ **ii** 5 m, 9 m, 10 m
c **i** $6x + 8 = 26, x = 3$
ii 8 mm, 5 mm, 8 mm, 5 mm
d **i** $9x + 1 = 37, x = 4$
ii 8 cm, 10 cm, 8 cm, 11 cm
2 **a** **i** 20° **ii** 80°
b **i** 15° **ii** 25°, 65°
c **i** 40° **ii** 40°, 120°, 200°
d **i** 37.5° **ii** 57.5°, 47.5°, 75°
3 **a** $t + 3 = 3t$ **b** $t = 1.5$
c Terry walked 1.5 miles. Caroline walked 4.5 miles.
4 **a** $d + 16 = 2d$ **b** $d = 16$
c Daljit is 16 years old. Gavin is 32 years old.
5 23°
6 **a** 17 cm **b** $16\frac{2}{3}$ **c** 12 mm, 13 mm
7 10 years
8 20°, 80°, 80°
9 $3\frac{1}{2}$

Worksheet 21.8

1

x		$x^2 + 3x$	**Bigger or smaller than 12**
2		$2^2 + 3 \times 2 = 10$	Smaller
3	try a bigger value	$3^2 + 3 \times 3 = 18$	Bigger
2.5	halfway between 2 and 3	$2.5^2 + 3 \times 2.5 = 13.75$	Bigger
2.3	try a smaller value	$2.3^2 + 3 \times 2.3 = 12.19$	Bigger
2.2	try a smaller value	$2.2^2 + 3 \times 2.2 = 11.44$	Smaller
2.25	halfway between 2.2 and 2.3	$2.25^2 + 3 \times 2.25 = 11.8125$	Smaller

x must lie between 2.25 and 2.3.
So $x = 2.3$ to 1 d.p.

2

x		$x^2 - 5x$	**Bigger or smaller than 8**
6		$6^2 - 5 \times 6 = 6$	Smaller
7		$7^2 - 5 \times 7 = 14$	Bigger
6.5	halfway between 6 and 7	$6.5^2 - 5 \times 6.5 = 9.75$	Bigger
6.4	try a smaller value	$6.4^2 - 5 \times 6.4 = 8.96$	Bigger
6.3	try a smaller value	$6.3^2 - 5 \times 6.3 = 8.19$	Bigger
6.2	try a smaller value	$6.2^2 - 5 \times 6.2 = 7.44$	Smaller
6.25	halfway between 6.2 and 6.3	$6.25^2 - 5 \times 6.25 = 7.8125$	Smaller

x must lie between 6.25 and 6.3.
So $x = 6.3$ to 1 d.p.

3

x		$x^3 + 5x$	**Bigger or smaller than 20**
1		$1^3 + 5 \times 1 = 1 + 5 = 6$	Smaller
2	try a bigger value	$2^3 + 5 \times 2 = 8 + 10 = 18$	Smaller
3	try a bigger value	$3^3 + 5 \times 3 = 27 + 15 = 42$	Bigger
2.5	halfway between 2 and 3	$2.5^3 + 5 \times 2.5 = 28.125$	Bigger
2.3	try a smaller value	$2.3^3 + 5 \times 2.3 = 23.667$	Bigger
2.2	try a smaller value	$2.2^3 + 5 \times 2.2 = 21.648$	Bigger
2.1	try a smaller value	$2.1^3 + 5 \times 2.1 = 19.761$	Smaller
2.15	halfway between 2.1 and 2.2	$2.15^3 + 5 \times 2.15 = 20.688375$	Bigger

x must lie between 2.1 and 2.15.
So $x = 2.1$ to 1 d.p.

4

x		$\frac{x^2}{1+x}$	**Bigger or smaller than 4**
3		$\frac{3^2}{1+3} = \frac{9}{4} = 2.25$	Smaller
4	try a bigger value	$\frac{4^2}{(1+4)} = \frac{16}{5} = 3.2$	Smaller
5	try a bigger value	$\frac{5^2}{(1+5)} = \frac{25}{6} = 4.1666$	Bigger
4.5	halfway between 4 and 5	$\frac{4.5^2}{(1+4.5)} = 3.68$	Smaller
4.8	try a bigger value	$\frac{4.8^2}{(1+4.8)} = 3.97$	Smaller
4.9	try a bigger value	$\frac{4.9^2}{(1+4.9)} = 4.069$	Bigger
4.85	halfway between 4.8 and 4.9	$\frac{4.85^2}{(1+4.85)} = 4.02$	Bigger

x must lie between 4.8 and 4.85.
So $x = 4.8$ to 1 d.p.

5

x		$\frac{x^2+1}{x}$	**Bigger or smaller than 5**
4		$\frac{4^2+1}{4} = \frac{16+1}{4}$ $= 17 \div 4 = 4.25$	Smaller
5	try a bigger value	$\frac{5^2+1}{5} = 5.2$	Bigger
4.5	halfway between 4 and 5	$\frac{4.5^2+1}{4.5} = 4.72$	Smaller
4.7	try a bigger value	$\frac{4.7^2+1}{4.7} = 4.91$	Smaller
4.8	try a bigger value	$\frac{4.8^2+1}{4.8} = 5.008$	Bigger
4.75	halfway between 4.7 and 4.8	$\frac{4.75^2+1}{4.75} = 4.96$	Smaller
4.78	try a bigger value	$\frac{4.78^2+1}{4.78} = 4.989$	Smaller
4.79	try a bigger value	$\frac{4.79^2+1}{4.79} = 4.998$	Smaller
4.795	halfway between 4.79 and 4.80	$\frac{4.795^2+1}{4.795} = 5.003$	Bigger

x must lie between 4.79 and 4.795.
So $x = 4.79$ to 2 d.p.

6

x		$x^2 - 4x$	**Bigger or smaller than 7**
5		$5^2 - 4 \times 5 = 5$	Smaller
6	try a bigger value	$6^2 - 4 \times 6 = 12$	Bigger
5.5	halfway between 5 and 6	$5.5^2 - 4 \times 5.5 = 8.25$	Bigger
5.3	try a smaller value	$5.3^2 - 4 \times 5.3 = 6.89$	Smaller
5.4	try a bigger value	$5.4^2 - 4 \times 5.4 = 7.56$	Bigger
5.35	halfway between 5.3 and 5.4	$5.35^2 - 4 \times 5.35 = 7.2225$	Bigger
5.32	try a smaller value	$5.32^2 - 4 \times 5.32 = 7.0224$	Bigger
5.31	try a smaller value	$5.31^2 - 4 \times 5.31 = 6.9561$	Smaller
5.315	halfway between 5.31 and 5.32	$5.315^2 - 4 \times 5.315 = 6.989225$	Smaller

x must lie between 5.315 and 5.32.
So $x = 5.32$ to 2 d.p.

Worksheet 21.9

1 **a** $5 < 8$ **b** $10 > 1$ **c** $4 = 4$ **d** $9 > 2$
e $0.7 < 1$ **f** $\frac{1}{3} < \frac{2}{3}$ **g** $8.3 > 8.03$ **h** $\frac{1}{2} = 0.5$

2 Maria is correct.

3 **a** False, $5 = 5$ **b** True
c True **d** False, $-3 < -2$
e True **f** False, $-9 < 8$
g False, $1.5 < \frac{5}{2}$ **h** False, $-3 < 0$

4 **a** Any three numbers less than 7.
b Any three numbers greater than −3, e.g. −2, 0, 5.
c Any three negative numbers.
d Any three numbers less than 0.5, e.g. −20, 0, 0.2.
e Any three numbers greater than 1 000 000.
f Any three numbers less than −200, e.g. −500, −700, −1000.

5 **a** 4, 5, 6 **b** 7, 8, 9 **c** −2, −1, 0 **d** −2, −1, 0
e 999, 1000, 1001 **f** −10, −9, −8
g −1, 0, 1 **h** −3, −2, −1

6 **a** 1, 2, 3, 4 **b** 5, 6, 7, 8, 9 **c** 6, 7, 8 **d** 1, 2, 3, 4, 5
e −3, −2, −1, 0 **f** 100 **g** 0, 1, 2 **h** −7, −6, −5
i 1, 2, 3, 4, 5, 6 **j** −3, −2, −1, 0

7 **a** Any one of:
$1 < x < 6$ $2 \leqslant x < 6$ $1 < x \leqslant 5$ $2 \leqslant x \leqslant 5$
b $x > 3$ or $x \geqslant 4$
c $x < 10$ or $x \leqslant 9$
d $x > -1$ or $x \geqslant 0$
e Any one of:
$-3 < x < 1$ $-2 \leqslant x < 1$ $-3 < x \leqslant 0$ $-2 \leqslant x \leqslant 0$
f $x > -4$ or $x \geqslant -3$
g Any one of:
$-1 < x < 8$ $0 \leqslant x < 8$ $-1 < x \geqslant 7$ $0 \leqslant x \leqslant 7$
h $x < -4$ or $x \leqslant -3$

Guided practice worksheet answers

Worksheet 21.10

1 a

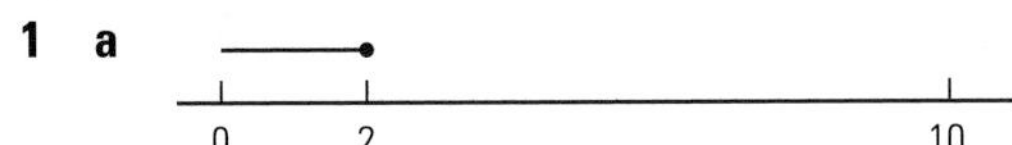

b

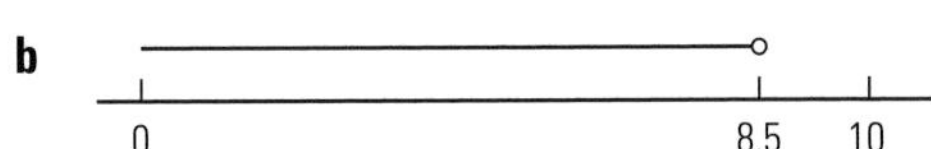

c −5 0 5

d −5 −3 0 5

e 0 10

f −5 −1.5 0 5

2 **a** $x > 1$ **b** $x \leqslant -2$ **c** $x \geqslant 3.5$ **d** $x < -0.5$
e $x > 16$ **f** $x \leqslant -30$

3 a 0 4 8 10

b −5 −1 0 5

c 0 4.5 10

d 0 6 10

e −5 −4 0 5

f −5 −3 2 5

4 **a** $1 < x \leqslant 5$ **b** $-3 \leqslant x < 1$ **c** $0 \leqslant x \leqslant 2.5$
d $-1 < x < 3$ **e** $-20 < x \leqslant 1$ **f** $0 \leqslant x \leqslant 150$

5 a 0 7 10

b −5 −3 0 5

c 0 18 20

d −5 10

e 100 200 300

f 1 1.5 2

g

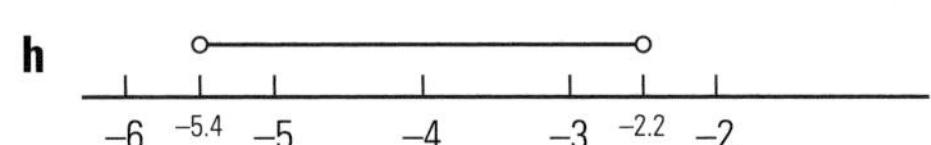

h −6 −5.4 −5 −4 −3 −2.2 −2

Worksheet 21.11

1 a $x \geqslant 6$

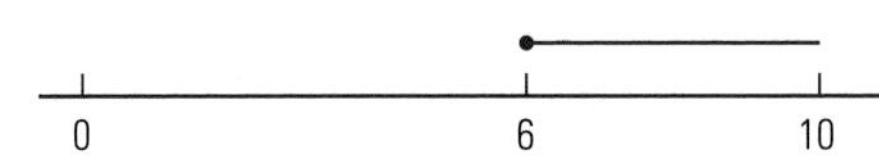

b $x < 9$

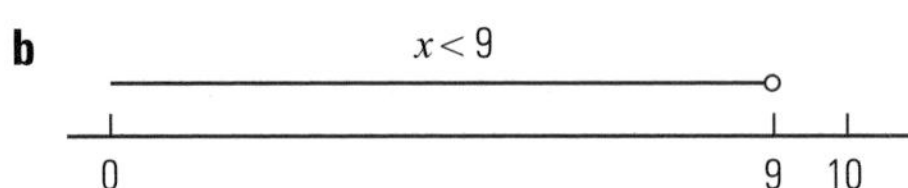

c $x \geqslant -2$

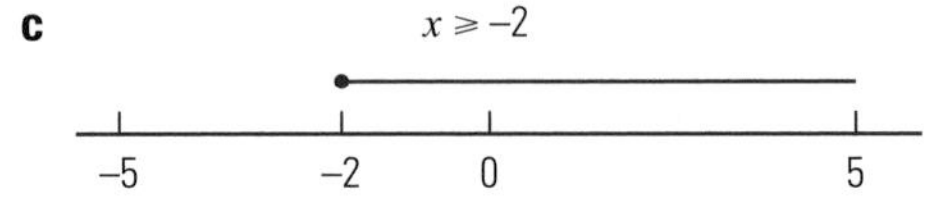

d $x < 8$

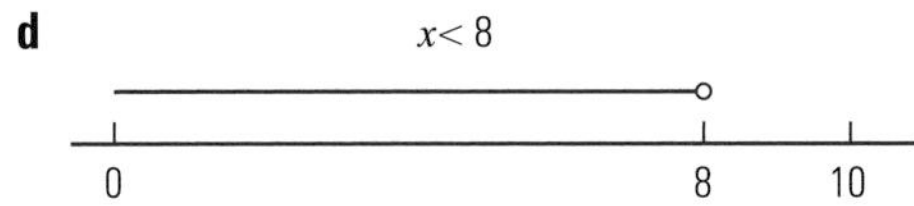

e $x > \frac{2}{3}$

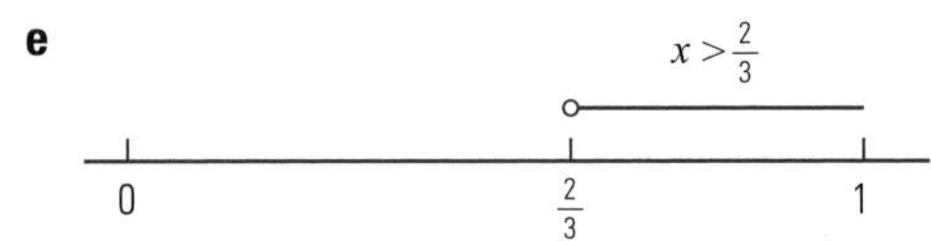

f $x < 4$

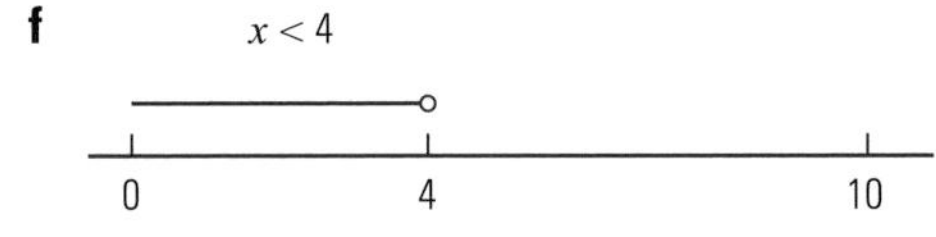

g $x < 60$

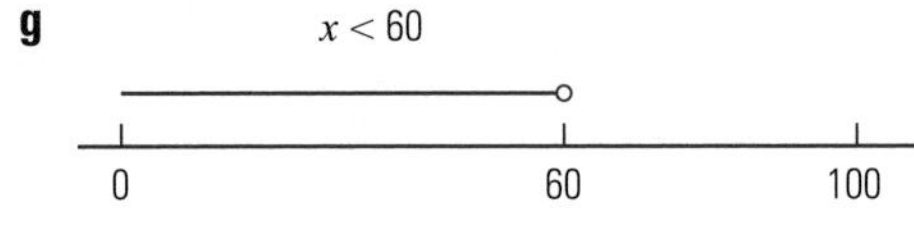

h $x \leqslant 0.8$

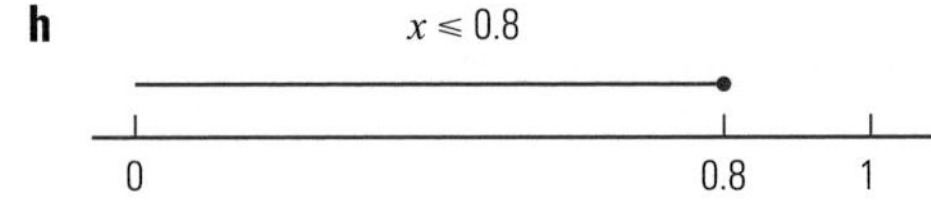

2 a $2 \leqslant x < 4$

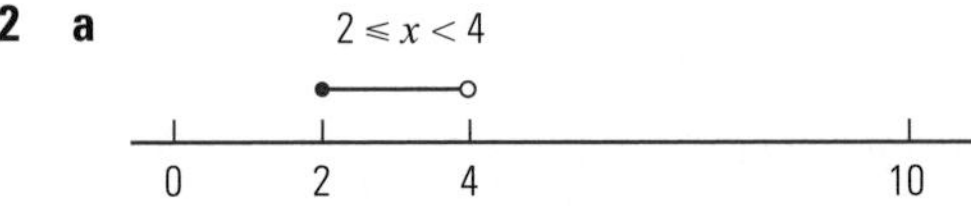

b $2 < x < 4$

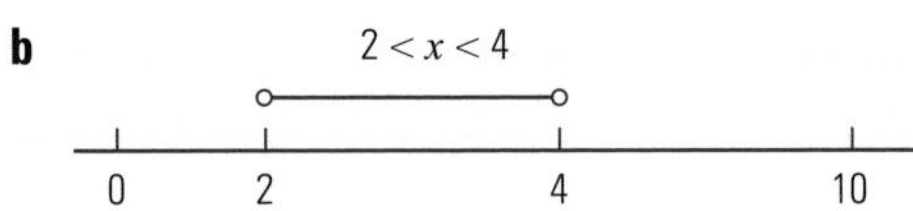

c $-2 \leqslant x \leqslant 1$

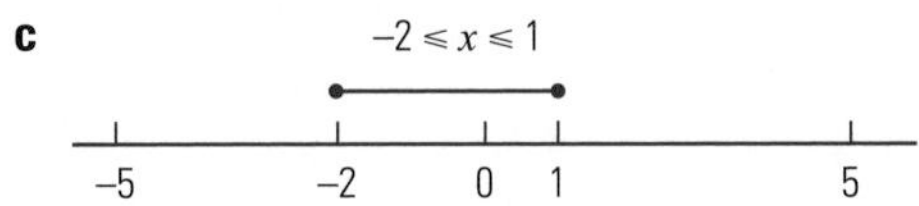

d $0 < x \leqslant 5.5$

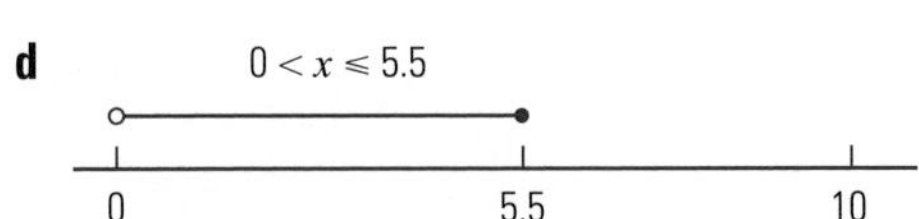

e $-1.5 \leqslant x < 1.5$

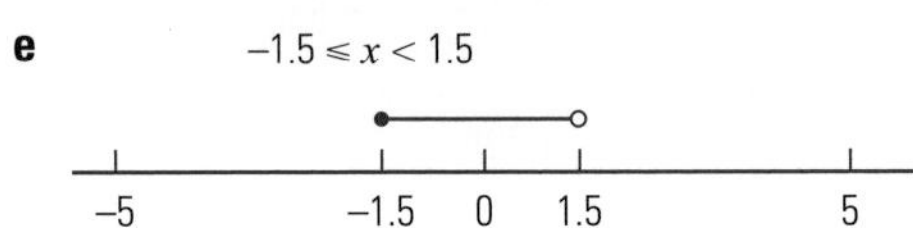

f $-3.5 \leq x \leq 3$

g 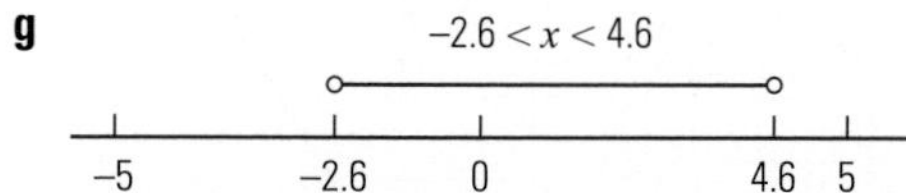

h $-200 \leq x < 200$

3 **a** 5, 6 **b** 2, 3
c −1, 0, 1, 2, 3, 4 **d** −3, −2, −1, 0, 1, 2, 3
e 1, 2, 3, 4, 5, 6, 7 **f** −4, −3, −2, −1, 0, 1
g 1, 2, 3, 4, 5 **h** −4

4 **a** 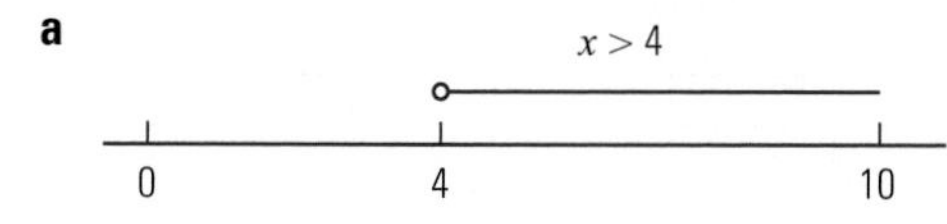

b $x < -2$

c 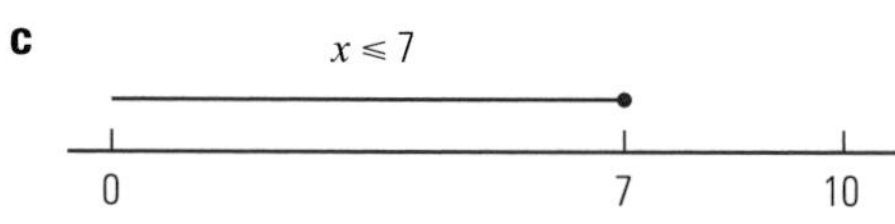

d 

e 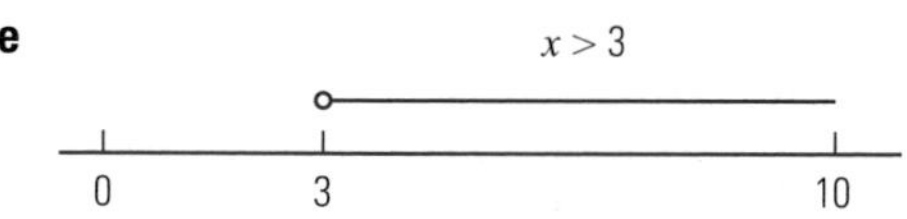

f 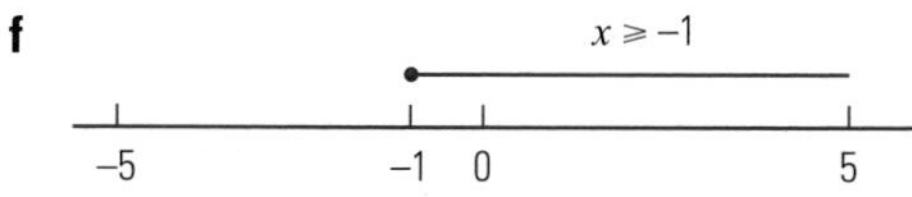

g 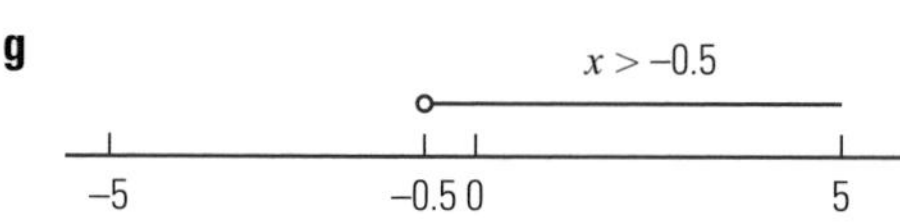

h 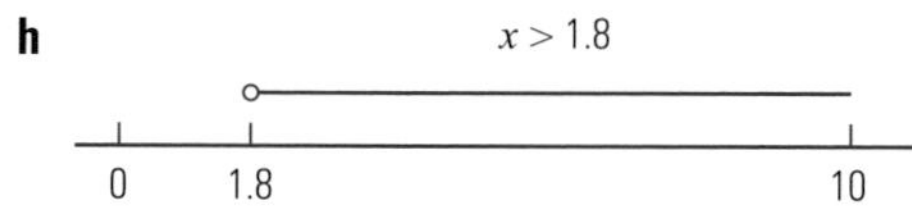

5 2
6 3

Worksheet 22.1

1 **a**

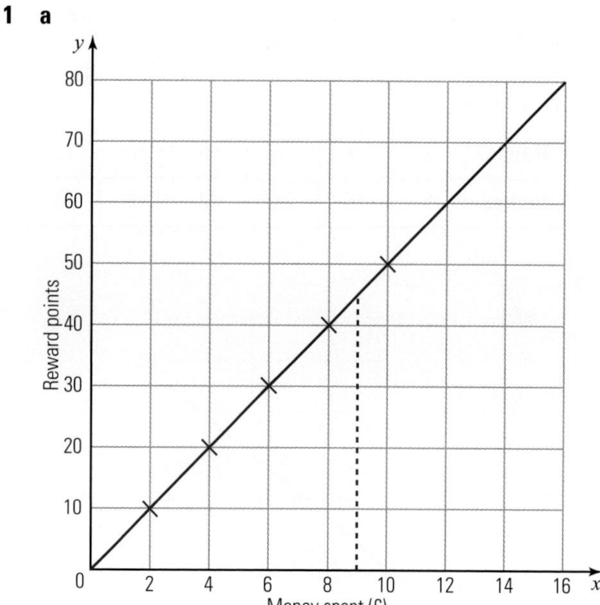

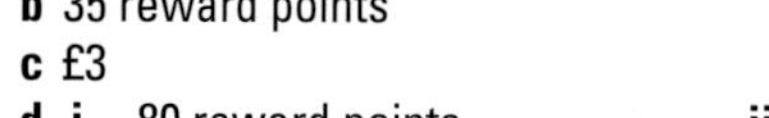

b 35 reward points
c £3

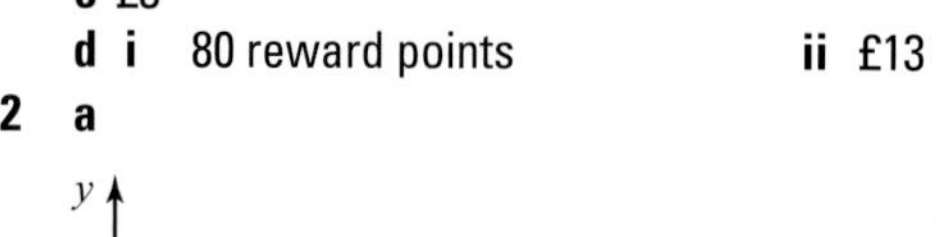

d **i** 80 reward points **ii** £13

2 **a**

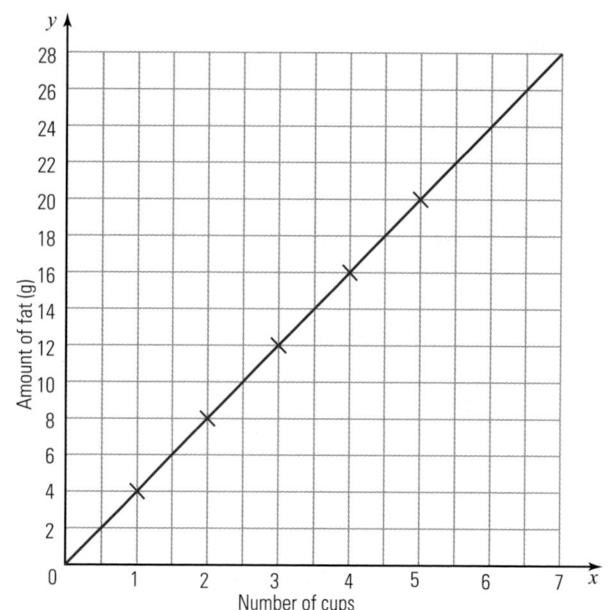

b **i** 10 g
ii 4.5 cups, so can fill 4 cups
c 28 g

3 **a** A: Ski2
B: SnowBiz
C: Tracks
b Tracks
c SnowBiz
d Ski2, because it is never cheaper than the others.

Worksheet 22.2

1 **a** **i** 16 inches **ii** 40 inches **iii** 28 inches
iv 4 inches **v** 18 inches
b **i** 9 hands **ii** 5 hands **iii** 12 hands
iv 8 hands
c

Hands	2	4	6	8	10	12
Inches	8	16	24	32	40	48

2 a
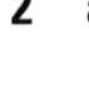
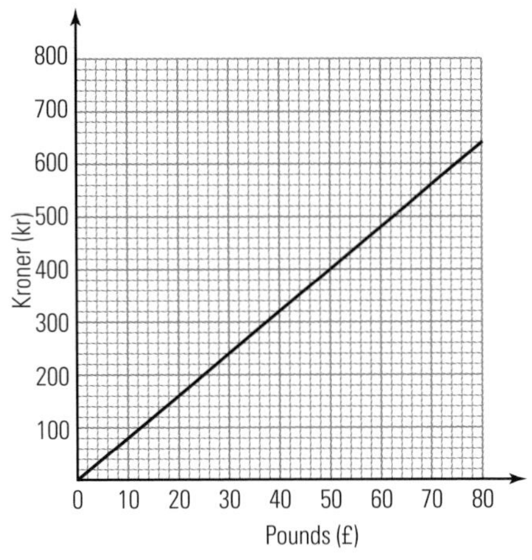

b

Pounds (£)	10	20	30	40	50	60	70	80
Kroner (kr)	80	160	240	320	400	480	560	640

c £65
d **i** kr520 **ii** £27.50

3 **a**
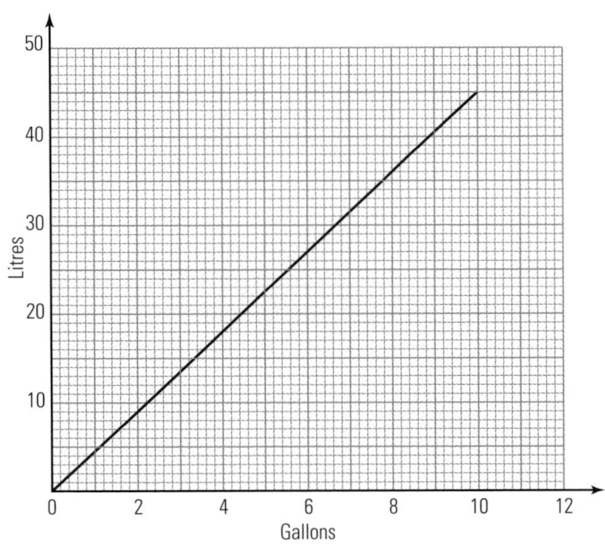

b

Gallons	0	2	4	6	8	10
Litres	0	9	18	27	36	45

c 3.3 gallons
d 58.5 litres

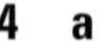
4 **a**
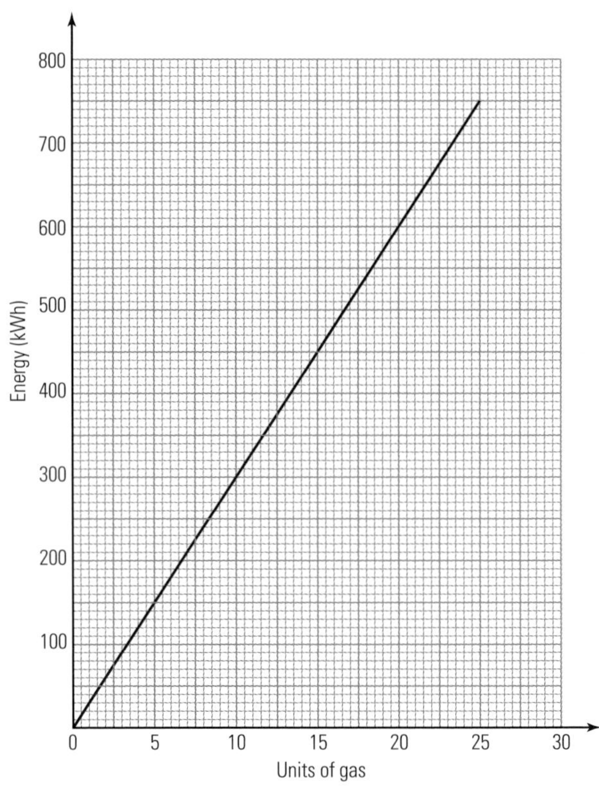

b

Units of gas	0	5	10	15	20	25
Energy (kWh)	0	150	300	450	600	750

c 390 kWh
d 21.5 units

Worksheet 22.3

1 **a** 30 miles **b** 1.5 hours **c** 20 miles per hour
d 1.5 hours **e** 1 hour **f** 30 miles per hour
2 **a** 800 m **b** 16 minutes
c **i** 50 metres per minute
ii 3 kilometres per hour
d 14 minutes **e** 400 m **f** 6 minutes
g **i** 66.7 metres per minute
ii 4 kilometres per hour
3 **a**
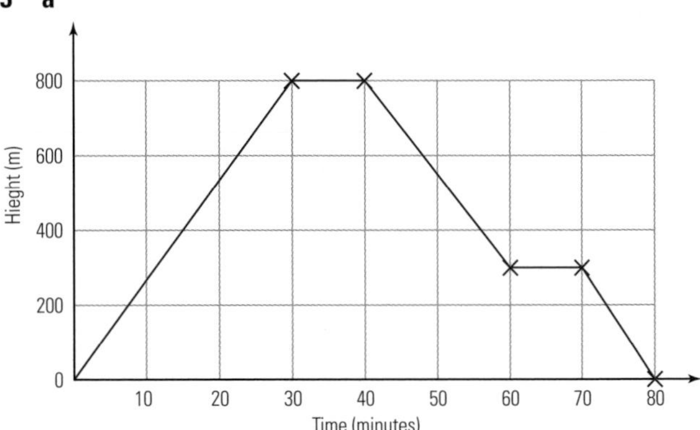

b **i** 30 metres per minute **ii** 1.8 km per hour
4 **a** **i** 30 miles **ii** 10 miles
b 2.18 pm

c Fiona left London Bridge at 2.18pm and arrived in Croydon at 3.30pm.
Jaleel left Brighton at 2pm and arrived in Croydon at 2.48pm. He waited 42 minutes for Fiona to arrive. They spent 72 minutes together. Jaleel caught the 4.42pm train to Brighton, arriving at 5.42pm. Fiona caught the 5pm train to London Bridge, arriving at 6pm.

d 37.5 miles per hour

e 10 miles per hour

Worksheet 22.4

1 a i

x	−3	−2	−1	0	1	2	3
$y = 2x^2$	18	8	2	0	2	8	18

ii

x	−3	−2	−1	0	1	2	3
$y = 2x^2 + 10$	28	18	12	10	12	18	28

iii

x	−2	−1	0	1	2
$y = 2x^2 + 20$	28	22	20	22	28

iv

x	−3	−2	−1	0	1	2	3
$y = 2x^2 - 10$	8	−2	−8	−10	−8	−2	8

b

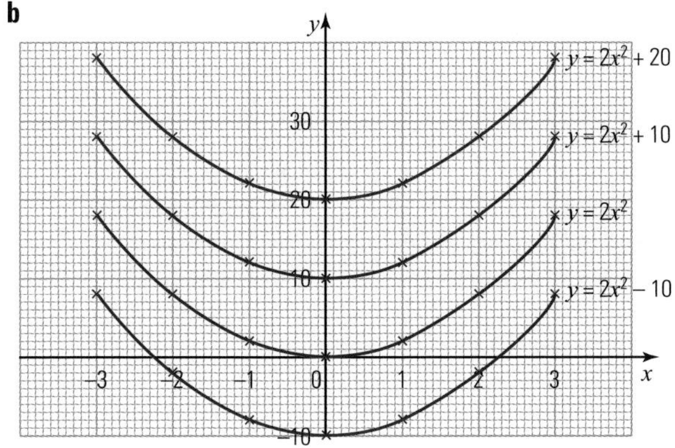

2 a

x	−3	−2	−1	0	1	2
x^2	9	4	1	0	1	4
$+4x$	−12	−8	−4	0	+4	+8
$+6$	+6	+6	+6	+6	+6	+6
$y = x^2 + 4x + 6$	3	2	3	6	11	18

b

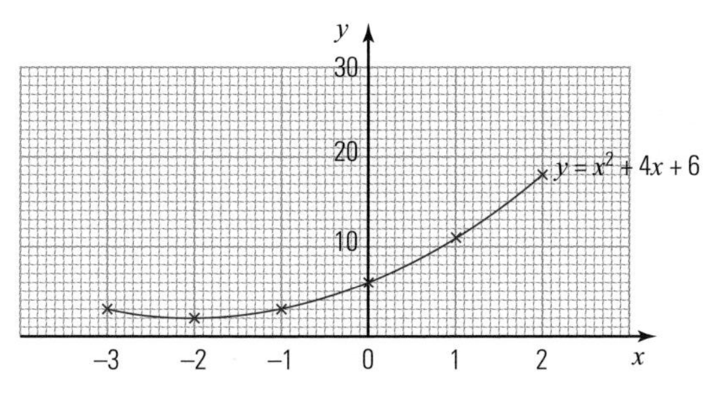

3 a i

x	−3	−2	−1	0	1	2	3
$y = x^2 + 2$	11	6	3	2	3	6	11

ii

x	−3	−2	−1	0	1	2	3
$y = 2x^2 + 2$	20	10	4	2	4	10	20

iii

x	−3	−2	−1	0	1	2	3
$y = -x^2 + 2$	−7	−2	1	2	1	−2	−7

iv

x	−3	−2	−1	0	1	2	3
$y = -2x^2 + 2$	−16	−6	0	2	0	−6	−16

b

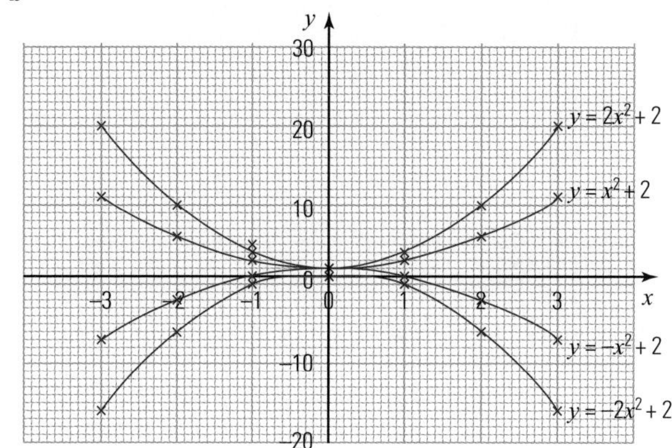

Worksheet 22.5

1 a

x	−3	−2	−1	0	1	2
x^2	9	4	1	0	1	4
x	−3	−2	−1	0	1	2
$y = x^2 + x$	6	2	0	0	2	6

b

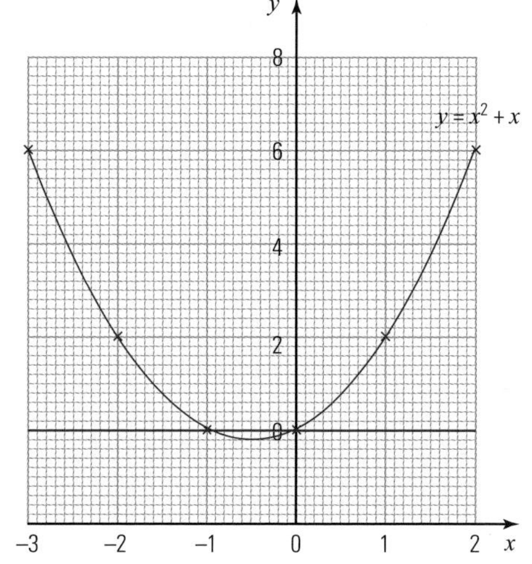

c i $x = 0, -1$

2 a

x	0	1	2	3	4	5
x^2	0	1	4	9	16	25
$-4x$	0	−4	−8	−12	−16	−20
+2	2	2	2	2	2	2
$y = x^2 - 4x + 2$	2	−1	−2	−1	2	7

b

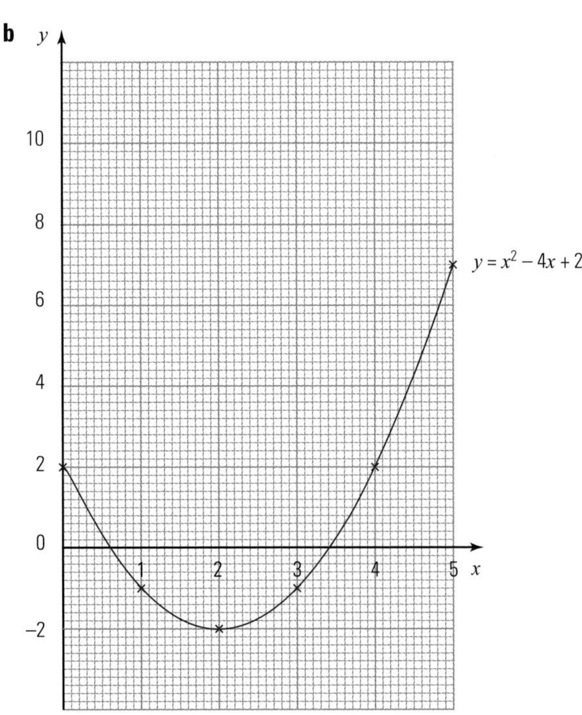

c i $x = 0.6$ or 3.4 **ii** $x = 1$ or 3

3 a

x	−3	−2	−1	0	1	2
$2x^2$	18	8	2	0	2	8
$+3x$	−9	−6	−3	0	3	6
−2	−2	−2	−2	−2	−2	−2
$y = 2x^2 + 3x - 2$	7	0	−3	−2	3	12

b

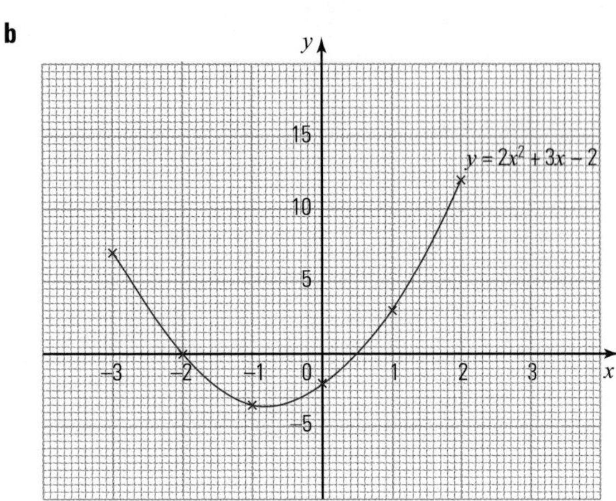

c $x = -2, 0.5$

Worksheet 23.1

1 **a** rotation **b** enlargement **c** reflection **d** translation

2 **a** rotation **b** enlargement **c** translation **d** reflection **e** translation **f** enlargement **g** rotation **h** reflection

Worksheet 23.2

1

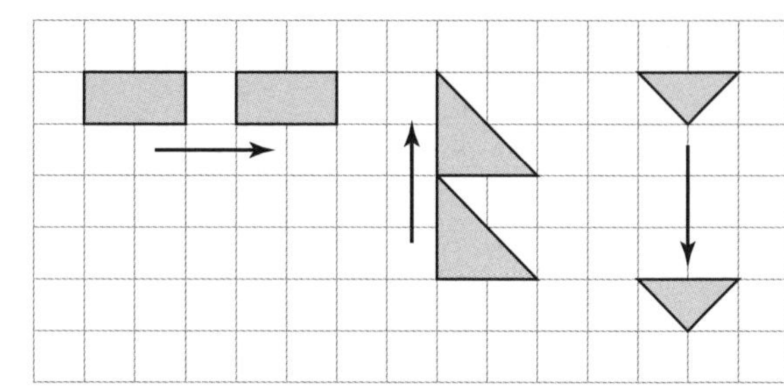

2

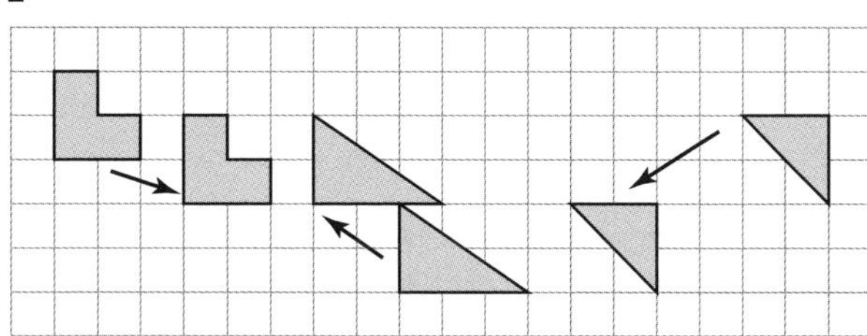

3 **a** 5 right 2 down or $\begin{pmatrix} 5 \\ -2 \end{pmatrix}$ **b** 4 left 2 down or $\begin{pmatrix} -4 \\ -2 \end{pmatrix}$

c 4 right 2 down or $\begin{pmatrix} 4 \\ -2 \end{pmatrix}$ **d** 5 left 2 up or $\begin{pmatrix} -5 \\ 2 \end{pmatrix}$

e 4 left 2 down or $\begin{pmatrix} -4 \\ -2 \end{pmatrix}$ **f** 3 left 2 up or $\begin{pmatrix} -3 \\ 2 \end{pmatrix}$

4 **a** 1 right 3 up **b** 4 right 5 up **c** 2 left 1 up **d** 3 right 2 down **e** 4 left 5 up **f** 1 left 4 down **g** 3 right 2 down **h** 2 right 1 up

Worksheet 23.3

1 A, D, E, G, I, J

2 **a** 2 **b** 3 **c** 2 **d** 4 **e** 5 **f** 5 **g** 3 **h** 4 **i** 2

3 **a** **b**

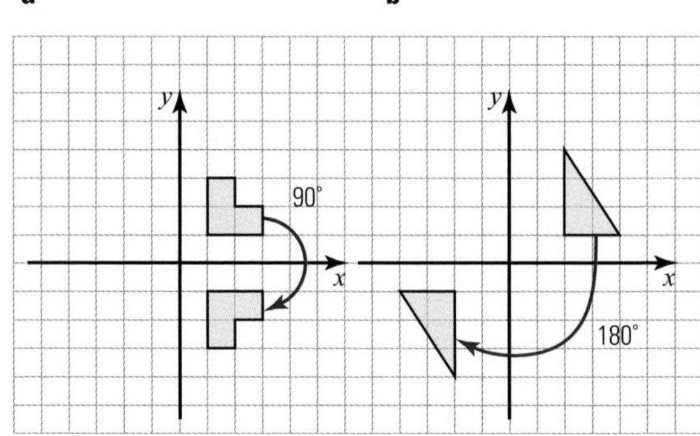

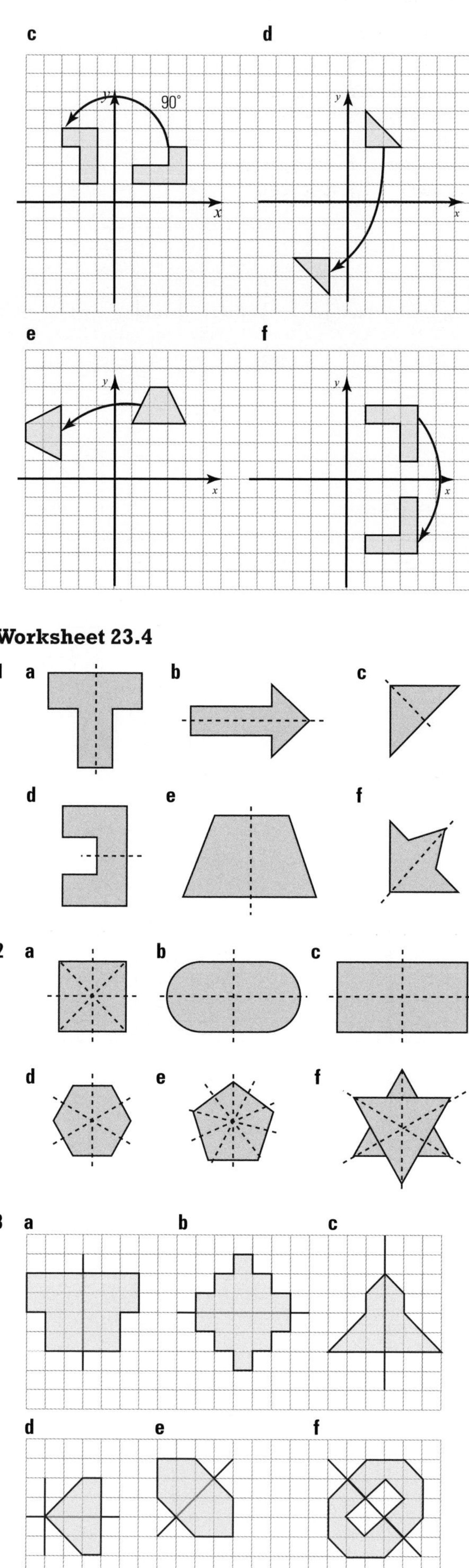
c
d
90°
y
x
e
f
Worksheet 23.4
1 a
b
c
d
e
f
2 a
b
c
d
e
f
3 a
b
c
d
e
f

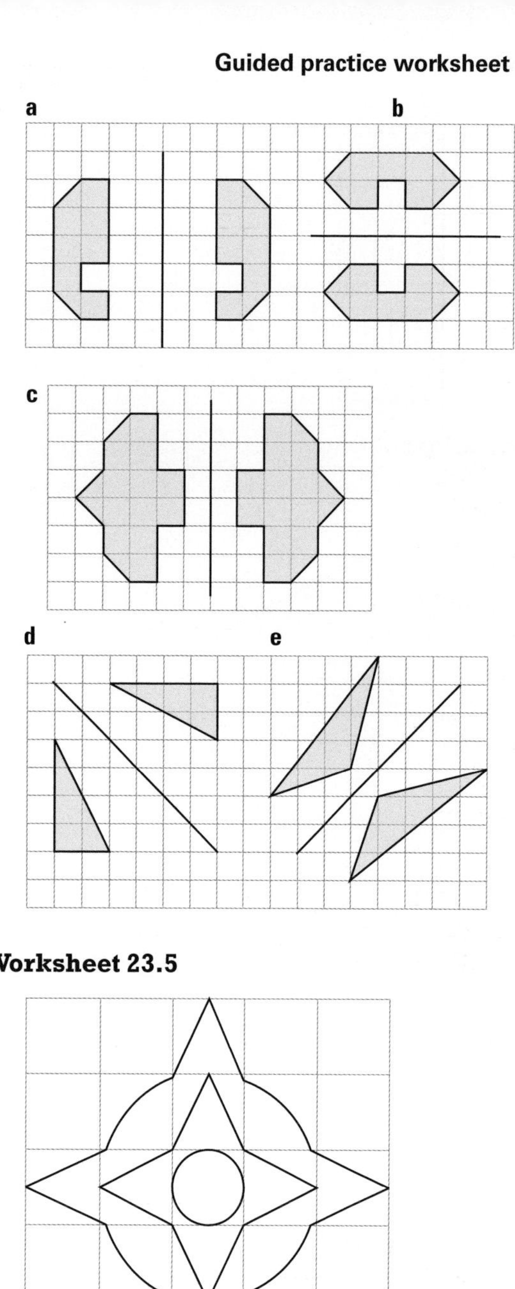
4 a
b
c
d
e

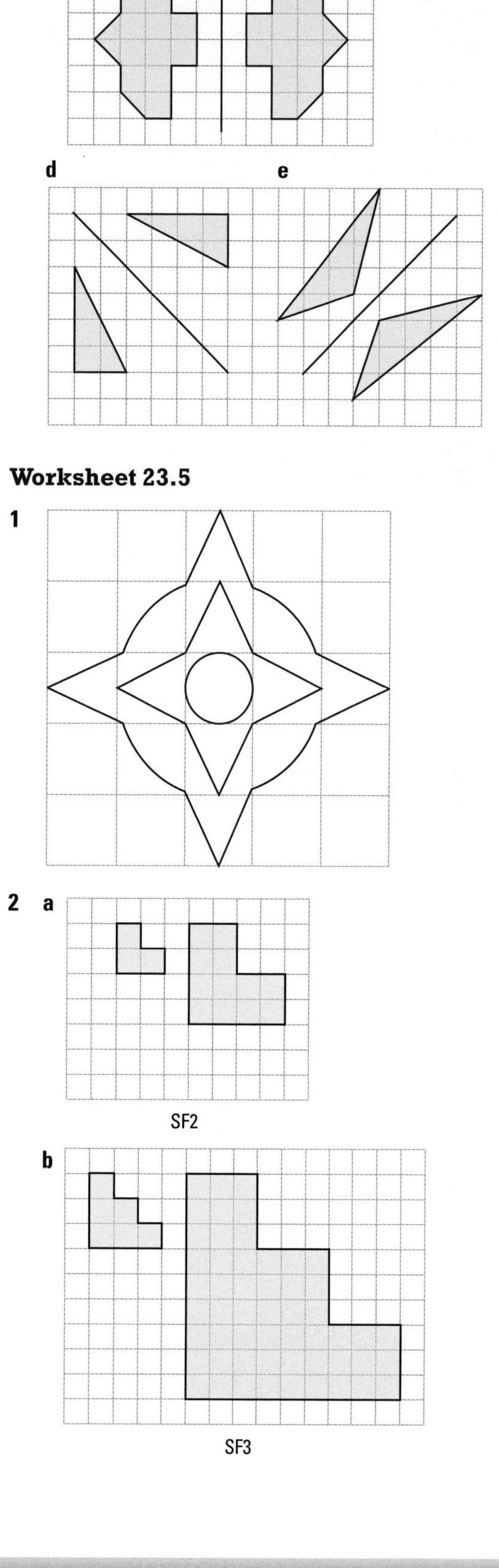
Worksheet 23.5
1
2 a
SF2
b
SF3

c

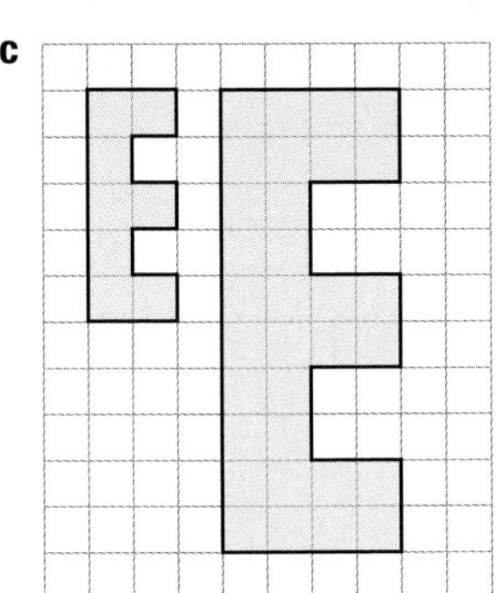

SF2

d

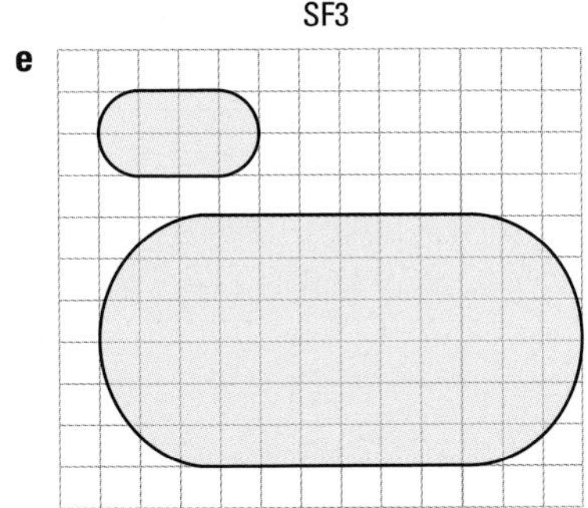

SF3

e

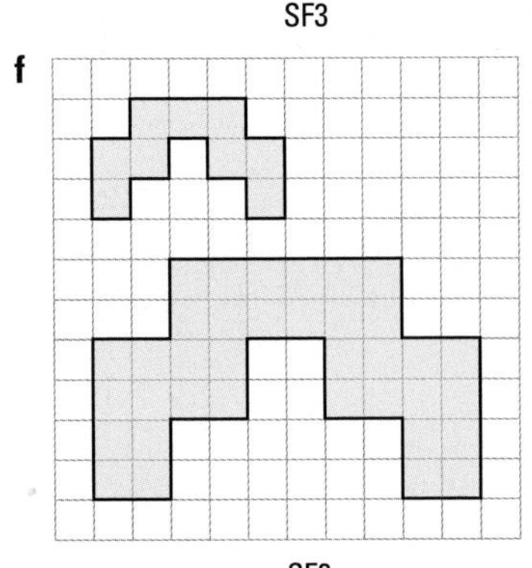

SF3

f

SF2

g

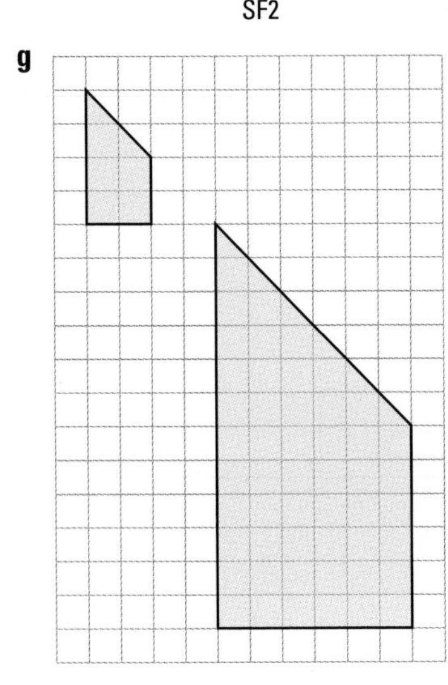

SF3

h

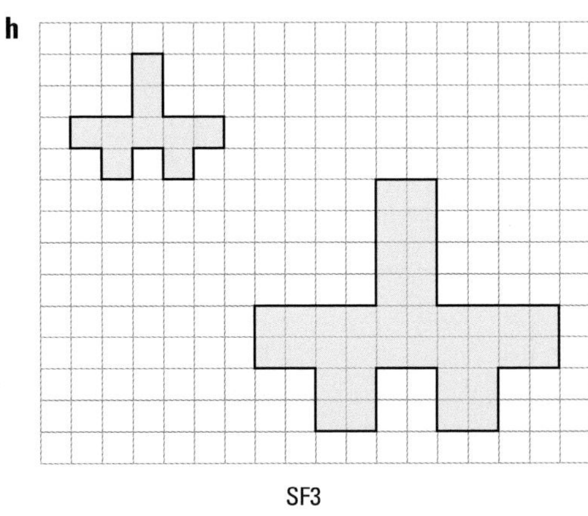

SF3

3 a

b

c

d

Worksheet 23.6

1 a

b

c Yes **d** Rotate 180° around the origin

2 a

b

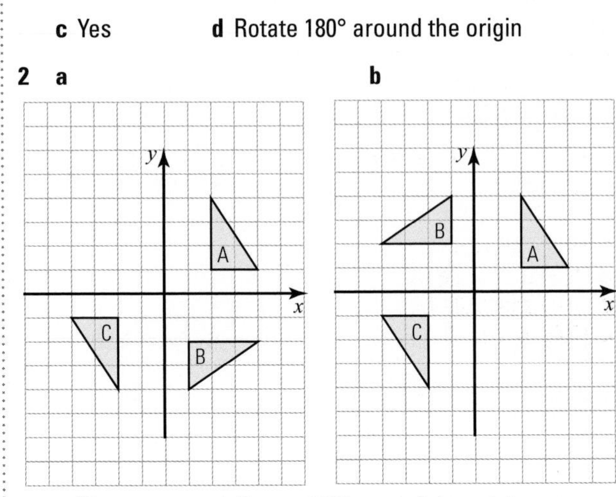

c Yes **d** Rotate 180° around the origin

Worksheet 24.1

1 **a** 3 : 7 **b** 7 : 3
2 **a** 2 : 5 **b** 5 : 2
3 3 : 2
4 **a** $\frac{1}{3}$ **b** $\frac{2}{3}$
5 $\frac{3}{10}$
6 **a** 1 : 5 **b** 1 : 5 **c** 3 : 4 **d** 2 : 7
7 7 : 15
8 **a** 1 : 5 **b** 3 : 5 **c** 15 : 1 **d** 12 : 7
9 **a** 1 : 3 **b** 1 : 4 **c** 1 : 4.5 **d** 1 : 5.6
10 1 : 18

Worksheet 24.2

1 20 teachers
2 21 buckets
3 £300
4 4.5 m
5 **a** 50 g **b** 600 g
6 **a** 556 g **b** 108 kg
7 £30
8 **a** 3.6 m **b** 20 cm
9 7 km
10 2.5 km

Worksheet 24.3

1 £20 : £10
2 £20 : £30
3 £15 : £25
4 80 cm : 100 cm
5 Neil £24, Liz £96
6 120 blue tiles
7 224 girls
8 10 more grapes
9 250 g
10 Maria £80, Nikita £120, Paolo £200

Worksheet 24.4

1 345 euros
2 **a** \$652.50 **b** £320
3 £65
4 £1.68
5 £3.75
6 £4.50
7 £14.40
8 £16.25
9 525 g dates, 150 g walnut pieces, 9 tablespoons lemon juice, 450 ml yoghurt
10 **a** 140 g **b** 25 g **c** 165 g

Worksheet 25.1

1 **a** 27 cm **b** 56 years **c** 30 and 40 years
d 50 cm
2 **a** 16.6°C
b 14.00 and 16.00
c 16.00 and 22.00
d 10.00 and 12.00
e 10.00 and 20.00

Worksheet 25.2–25.5

1 **a** The greater the number of years, the greater the lung damage.
b Positive correlation
c 28%
d 24 years

2 **a, b**

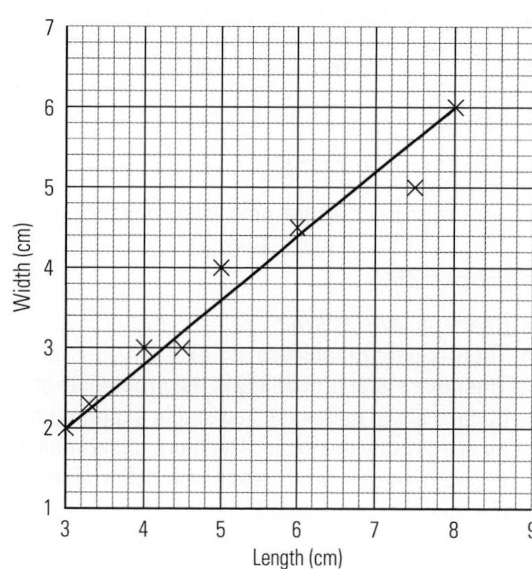

c Positive correlation
d The longer the leaf, the wider it is.
e About 5 cm

Worksheet 26.1

1 **a** Certain **b** Likely **c** Impossible
d Very likely **e** Even chance
2 Students' own answers.
3 Students' own answers.
4 No. If it is a fair coin, heads and tails are equally likely.
5 Yes. The probability of landing on black is $\frac{9}{25}$. So the average winnings are $\frac{9}{25} \times 20\text{p} = 7.2\text{p}$ per person, which is less than 10p.

Worksheet 26.2

1 **a** $\frac{1}{8}$ **b** $\frac{1}{2}$ or $\frac{4}{8}$ **c** $\frac{1}{4}$ or $\frac{2}{8}$ **d** $\frac{1}{4}$ or $\frac{2}{8}$
2 **a** 50% **b** 17% **c** 33% **d** 50%
e 14%
3 **a** 0.5 **b** 0.3 **c** 0.2 **d** 0.8
e 0.7 **f** 0.5
4 **a** $\frac{1}{10}$ **b** $\frac{3}{10}$ **c** $\frac{1}{9}$ **d** $\frac{1}{9}$
5 **a** $\frac{4}{7}$ **b** $\frac{3}{7}$ **c** 0 **d** 1

Worksheet 26.3

1 $\frac{238}{239}$
2 0.96
3 30%
4 0.97
5 **a** $\frac{1}{5}$ **b** 0.2
6 **a** 22% **b** $\frac{22}{100}$ or $\frac{11}{50}$
7 0.1
8 32%
9 0.3
10 **a** $\frac{1}{6}$ **b** $\frac{5}{6}$

Worksheet 26.4

1 **a** 2, 3, 4, 5, 6, 7, 8, 9, 10, 11, 12
b $\frac{3}{36}$ or $\frac{1}{12}$ **c** $\frac{18}{36}$ or $\frac{1}{2}$ **d** 7
2 **a** 2, 3, 4, 6, 7, 10, 11, 12, 15, 20
b $\frac{1}{16}$ **c** $\frac{2}{16}$ or $\frac{1}{8}$ **d** 0
3 **a** $\frac{1}{16}$ **b** $\frac{9}{16}$ **c** $\frac{3}{16}$ **d** $\frac{4}{16}$ or $\frac{1}{4}$

4 **a** 1, 2, 3, 4, 5, 6, 8, 9, 10, 12, 15, 16, 18, 20, 24, 25, 30, 36
b $\frac{1}{36}$ **c** 0 **d** $\frac{4}{36}$ or $\frac{1}{9}$ **e** 1
f 6 or 12

5 **a** $\frac{4}{36}$ or $\frac{1}{9}$ **b** $\frac{8}{36}$ or $\frac{2}{9}$ **c** $\frac{20}{36}$ or $\frac{5}{9}$
d Jess is correct, as the probability of scoring 6 is $\frac{12}{36}$ or $\frac{1}{3}$.

Worksheet 26.5

1 **a** Students' own answer.
b Theoretical probabilities are all $\frac{1}{5}$.
c The theoretical probability is the probability of any piece of card being pulled out in a single experiment provided all are exactly the same. The more experiments you conduct, the closer the experimental probability will be to the theoretical probability.

2 Count the number of cars driven by men passing the school gates and the total number of cars passing the school gates on a large number of occasions. Divide the number of cars driven by men by the total number of cars.

3 Count the number of shoppers carrying more than three bags and the total number of shoppers on a large number of occasions. Divide the number with more than three bags by the total number of shoppers.

4 Ask the people you meet if they are vegetarians and count how many are. Divide the number who are vegetarian by the total number.

5 This will depend upon choice of channel. Comparison should discuss more and less than.

Worksheet 26.6

1 **a**

	Under-18	Over-18	Total
Male	**14**	16	**30**
Female	12	14	**26**
Total	**26**	**30**	**56**

b $\frac{30}{56}$ or $\frac{15}{28}$ **c** $\frac{26}{56}$ or $\frac{13}{28}$ **d** $\frac{14}{56}$ or $\frac{1}{4}$

2 **a**

	Hotel	Cottage	Camping	Total
Aged over 30	**30**	12	**6**	48
Aged under 30	6	**22**	24	**52**
Total	36	**34**	**30**	**100**

b $\frac{48}{100}$ or $\frac{12}{25}$ **c** $\frac{30}{48}$ or $\frac{5}{8}$ **d** $\frac{30}{100}$ or $\frac{3}{10}$

3 **a**

	Large	Medium	Small	Total
Breakfast	24	22	**28**	74
Earl Grey	13	**17**	19	**49**
Herbal	**32**	15	24	**71**
Total	69	**54**	**71**	194

b $\frac{74}{194}$ or $\frac{37}{97}$ **c** $\frac{32}{194}$ or $\frac{16}{97}$ **d** $\frac{54}{194}$ or $\frac{27}{97}$

4 **a**

	Biology	Chemistry	Physics	Total
Boys	4	6	4	14
Girls	3	5	8	16
Total	7	11	12	30

b $\frac{16}{30}$ or $\frac{8}{15}$ **c** $\frac{5}{30}$ or $\frac{1}{6}$ **d** $\frac{4}{30}$ or $\frac{2}{15}$

Worksheet 26.7

1 40
2 4300
3 **a** 33 times **b** Never **c** 67 times
4 **a** 13 **b** 27 **c** 40
5 **a** You would expect 6 to appear about 5 times in 30 throws, so the dice appears to be fair. However, Alison hasn't carried out enough trials to be sure.
b No. You would expect the 6 to appear about 500 times.
6 **a** 2961 claims
b 3000 is about the number expected as it is 15%, to the nearest whole number.
7 **a** 120
b George has improved the efficiency of the machine as this is less than would be expected.
8 750

Worksheet 27.1

1 **a** 17 mm **b** 10 cm **c** 37 cm **d** 8.5 cm **e** 5.1 m **f** 8.5 mm
2 **a** 7.62 cm **b** 11.2 m **c** 32.0 mm **d** 9.18 cm **e** 297 m **f** 1.41 m
3 **a** 10.31 m **b** 7.28 m
4 **a** 10.6 m **b** 12.0 m **c** 16.0 m **d** 19.5 m
5 **a** 37.1 cm **b** 39.1 cm **c** 38.2 cm

Worksheet 27.2

1 **a** 48 mm **b** 4.36 m **c** 3.98 cm **d** 3.5 cm **e** 283 mm **f** 0.624 m
2 **a** 12.0 cm **b** 1.7 cm **c** 35.7 cm
3 **a** 19.1 cm **b** 3.7 cm **c** 1.1 cm **d** 14.6 cm **e** 1.8 cm **f** 6.9 cm
4 3.36 m
5 **a** 2.75 m **b** 2.31 m **c** 1.84 m **d** 1.6 m

Worksheet 27.3

1 **a** Not right-angled **b** Right-angled
c Right-angled **d** Not right-angled
e Right-angled **f** Not right-angled
2 **a** Right-angled **b** Not right-angled
c Right-angled **d** Right-angled
e Not right-angled **f** Right-angled
3 **a** Not sloping **b** Sloping
c Not sloping **d** Sloping
e Not sloping **f** Sloping
4 **a** Right-angled **b** Obtuse
c Acute **d** Obtuse
e Right-angled **f** Obtuse

Worksheet 27.4

1 AB = 3.61, CD = 5.00, EF = 10.05
GH = 2.83, JK = 5.10, LM = 5.00
NP = 8.49, QR = 1.41, ST = 5.39
UV = 4.47, WY = 2.24

2 a 5.83 b 8.06 c 7.07 d 10
e 7.07 f 8.60
3 a 8.1 b 7.6 c 8.9 d 9.2
4 366.7 cm
5 a 5.66 b 6.40 c 8.25 d 4.47
e 18.4

Worksheet 28.1

1 18°
2 £11.94
3 37 cm
4 a How far walked = 80 × amount of minutes
b 1200 m
5 a Space remaining = 4.6 – Size of file
b 2.4 Gigabytes
6 a Number of bars = 500 / price of bar [round answer down]
b 7 bars
7 195 g
8 11.25 ms^{-1}
9 a Number of beans = 2 × number in each row + 5
b 41 beans
10 a Ice cream left = size of tub – 80 × number of scoops taken
b 40 g

Worksheet 28.2

1 a 40 b 7 c 7 d 20
e 2 f 15 g –16 h 48
i 20 j 3 k 36
2 a $2\frac{3}{4}$ b 2 c $1\frac{1}{2}$ d $\frac{1}{8}$
e $\frac{1}{2}$ f 24 g $\frac{1}{2}$ h $4\frac{1}{2}$
i $\frac{1}{4}$ j $\frac{1}{2}$
3 a 0.4 b 64 c 0.65 d 4.35
e 3.65 f 0.01 g 12 h 1
i 25 j 31
4 a –8 b 8 c 7 d 0
e 24 f 2 g 9 h –16
5 a 45 b –2 c 12 d –8
e 9 f –12 g 1 h 1
i 17 j 64

Worksheet 28.3

1 a 49 cm^2 b 2.25 cm^2 c 900 mm^2 d 10 000 m^2
2 a 21 b 46 c 240 d 2.4
3 a £18 b £23 c £12.50 d £27.90
4 a 550 cm, 5.5 m b 2000 cm, 20 m
c 9200 cm, 92 m d 7200 cm, 72 m
5 a 20 cm^2 b 2.25 cm^2 c 250 mm^2 d 0.8 m^2
6 a 75.4 cm^2 b 1100 mm^2 c 514 cm^2 d 90 500 mm^2
7 a 2 b 2.5 c 2 d 4.5
8 a 12 b 125 c 100 d 40
9 a 192 g b 63 g c 636 g d 289 g

Worksheet 28.4

1 $P = 8x$
a 48 cm b 4 cm c 400 mm d 17.6 m
2 $F = x - m$
a £80 b £2500 c £50 000
d £400 000 or £0.4 million
3 $R = 200 - 5n$
a 100 ml b 125 ml c 140 ml d 135 ml
4 $C = \pi r$
a 12.6 cm b 47.1 mm c 2.51 m d 314 mm
5 $h = \frac{A}{b}$
a 3 cm b 25 mm c 4 m d 3.5 cm
6 $A = 50 + tw$
a 100 litres b 135 litres c 446 litres d 626 litres
7 $R = 5a - s^2$
a 46 cm^2 b 29 cm^2 c 7.75 cm^2 d 24.64 cm^2
8 $T = 6t + 4u$
a 14 seconds b 14 seconds c 9 seconds
d 5.6 seconds

Worksheet 28.5

1 a 2 b 0.7 c 2.4 d 0.15
2 a 8 b 19 c 10.5 d 5
3 a 10 b 100 c –15 d 2.5
4 a 5 b 1 c –2 d 0.75
5 a 2 b 1.25 c –0.5 d –2
6 a 4 b 10 c –10 d –12
7 a 15 b 6.25 c 0.7 d 1
e 12.5 f 5.6
8 a 2 b 1 c –8 d 1
e 3.25 f 3
9 a 1.59 b 0.0796 c 12.7

Worksheet 28.6

1 $t = J + m$ 2 $b = \frac{A}{h}$
3 $v = kr$ 4 $t = \frac{P}{3r}$
5 $y = \frac{T}{xz}$ 6 $b = R - a - 5$
7 $c = y - mx$ 8 $C = \frac{F - 32}{2}$
9 $t = \frac{m - u}{5}$ 10 $n = \frac{V + k}{t}$
11 $A = C - 10ip$ 12 $p = \frac{C - A}{10i}$
13 $x = \frac{y + 12}{3}$ 14 $n = \frac{m - 30}{10}$
15 $y = \frac{x - 15}{10}$ 16 $q = \frac{R - 2p}{2}$
17 $u = \frac{G - 2t}{t}$ 18 $b = \frac{W - ac}{a}$
19 $n = 2M$ 20 $f = \frac{L}{4h}$
21 $A = 2Vh$ 22 $t = \frac{6e - D}{2}$
23 $y = \frac{c - ax}{a}$ 24 $m = \frac{AC}{r}$

Licence Agreement: Edexcel GCSE Maths Specification A Linear Foundation Teacher Guide CD-ROM (978-1-846-90087-7)

Disclaimer

This material has been published on behalf of Edexcel and offers high-quality support for the delivery of Edexcel qualifications.

This does not mean that the material is essential to achieve any Edexcel qualification, nor does it mean that it is the only suitable material available to support any Edexcel qualification. Edexcel material will not be used verbatim in setting any Edexcel examination or assessment. Any resource lists produced by Edexcel shall include this and other appropriate resources.

Copies of official specifications for all Edexcel qualifications may be found on the Edexcel website: www.edexcel.com

Warning:

This is a legally binding agreement between You (the user or purchasing institution) and Pearson Education Limited of Edinburgh Gate, Harlow, Essex, CM20 2JE, United Kingdom ('PEL').

By retaining this Licence, any software media or accompanying written materials or carrying out any of the permitted activities You are agreeing to be bound by the terms and conditions of this Licence. If You do not agree to the terms and conditions of this Licence, do not continue to use the Edexcel GCSE Maths Specification A Linear Foundation Teacher Guide CD-ROM and promptly return the entire publication (this Licence and all software, written materials, packaging and any other component received with it) with Your sales receipt to Your supplier for a full refund.

Intellectual Property Rights:

This Edexcel GCSE Maths Specification A Linear Foundation Teacher Guide CD-ROM consists of copyright software and data. All intellectual property rights, including the copyright is owned by PEL or its licensors and shall remain vested in them at all times. You only own the disk on which the software is supplied. If You do not continue to do only what You are allowed to do as contained in this Licence you will be in breach of the Licence and PEL shall have the right to terminate this Licence by written notice and take action to recover from you any damages suffered by PEL as a result of your breach.

The PEL name, PEL logo, Edexcel name, Edexcel logo and all other trademarks appearing on the software and Edexcel GCSE Maths Specification A Linear Foundation Teacher Guide CD-ROM are trademarks of PEL and/or its Licensors. You shall not utilise any such trademarks for any purpose whatsoever other than as they appear on the software and Edexcel GCSE Maths Specification A Linear Foundation Teacher Guide CD-ROM.

Yes, You can:

1. use this Edexcel GCSE Maths Specification A Linear Foundation Teacher Guide CD-ROM on Your own personal computer as a single individual user;
2. use or install this Edexcel GCSE Maths Specification A Linear Foundation Teacher Guide CD-ROM on a network, server or on more than one personal computer within your school; (VLE version downloadable online, subject to its own end user licence agreement).

No, You cannot:

1. copy this Edexcel GCSE Maths Specification A Linear Foundation Teacher Guide CD-ROM (other than making one copy for back-up purposes);
2. alter, disassemble, or modify this Edexcel GCSE Maths Specification A Linear Foundation Teacher Guide CD-ROM, or in any way reverse engineer, decompile or create a derivative product from the contents of the database or any software included in it:
3. include any materials or software data from the Edexcel GCSE Maths Specification A Linear Foundation Teacher Guide CD-ROM in any other product or software materials;
4. rent, hire, lend, sub-licence or sell the Edexcel GCSE Maths Specification A Linear Foundation Teacher Guide CD-ROM;
5. copy or edit any part of the documentation except where specifically indicated otherwise;
6. use the software in any way not specified above without the prior written consent of PEL;
7. subject the software, Edexcel GCSE Maths Specification A Linear Foundation Teacher Guide CD-ROM or any PEL content to any derogatory treatment or use them in such a way that would bring PEL into disrepute or cause PEL to incur liability to any third party.

Grant of Licence:

PEL grants You, provided You only do what is allowed under the 'Yes, You can' table above, and do nothing under the 'No, You cannot' table above, a non-exclusive, non-transferable Licence to use this Edexcel GCSE Maths Specification A Linear Foundation Teacher Guide CD-ROM.

The terms and conditions of this Licence become operative when using this Edexcel GCSE Maths Specification A Linear Foundation Teacher Guide CD-ROM.

Limited Warranty:

PEL warrants that the disk or CD-ROM on which the software is supplied is free from defects in material and workmanship in normal use for ninety (90) days from the date You receive it. This warranty is limited to You and is not transferable.

This limited warranty is void if any damage has resulted from accident, abuse, misapplication, service or modification by someone other than PEL. In no event shall PEL be liable for any damages whatsoever arising out of installation of the software, even if advised of the possibility of such damages. PEL will not be liable for any loss or damage of any nature suffered by any party as a result of reliance upon or reproduction of any errors in the content of the publication.

PEL does not warrant that the functions of the software meet Your requirements or that the media is compatible with any computer system on which it is used or that the operation of the software will be unlimited or error free. You assume responsibility for selecting the software to achieve Your intended results and for the installation of, the use of and the results obtained from the software.

PEL shall not be liable for any loss or damage of any kind (except for personal injury or death) arising from the use of this Edexcel GCSE Maths Specification A Linear Foundation Teacher Guide CD-ROM or from errors, deficiencies or faults therein, whether such loss or damage is caused by negligence or otherwise.

The entire liability of PEL and your only remedy shall be replacement free of charge of the components that do not meet this warranty.

No information or advice (oral, written or otherwise) given by PEL or PEL's agents shall create a warranty or in any way increase the scope of this warranty.

To the extent the law permits, PEL disclaims all other warranties, either express or implied, including by way of example and not limitation, warranties of merchantability and fitness for a particular purpose in respect of this Edexcel GCSE Maths Specification A Linear Foundation Teacher Guide CD-ROM.

Termination:

This Licence shall automatically terminate without notice from PEL if you fail to comply with any of its provisions. PEL may also terminate this Licence by notice in writing. Upon termination for whatever reason You agree to destroy the Edexcel GCSE Maths Specification A Linear Foundation Teacher Guide CD-ROM and any back-up copies and delete any part of the Edexcel GCSE Maths Specification A Linear Foundation Teacher Guide CD-ROM stored on the purchasing institution's servers, secure network or any computer or storage device under the purchasing institution's control.

Governing Law:

This Licence will be governed by and construed in accordance with English law.

Important notice

This product is suitable for use on a Windows® PC only. It will not run on Macintosh OS X.

System requirements

- OS: Windows XP* sp2. RAM: 512MB (1GB for Vista) 1GHz processor (2GHz for Vista)
- Microsoft Office 2003*, Adobe Flash Player 9*, Adobe Reader 8*, Internet Explorer 7*/Firefox 3
- Screen display minimum 1024x768 at 32bpp

  *or later versions

Playing the product / Standalone installation

This product may be installed to your computer.

When you insert the disc into your CD/DVD drive, the launcher should start automatically, giving you the option to play or install the product.

If it does not, please follow these steps:

- Double-click 'My computer'
- Right-click the CD/DVD drive
- Select 'Launcher.exe' and follow the on-screen instructions

Network installation

For network installation and RM Networks deployments, please review the relevant section of the Readme.txt file located on the disc.

Note that server-based installations of software powered by ActiveTeach must reside on a mapped network drive.

VLE hosting

The VLE pack(s) that support this product are available for download from:
http://vlepacks.pearson.com

Please review the 'Readme.txt' within the VLE folder on the disc for additional information.